US · AVEBURY · ALES STENAR · SONNENOBS̶ ... ̶LES · RING O'BRODGAR · MEGALITHIC TEMPLES
ES DE NÎMES · HERCULANEUM · AKROTIRI ... · LALIBELA · ROCK DWELLINGS OF MESA VERDE
SOL · CIUDAD PERDIDA · TIWANAKU · HU ... THAYA · ANURADHAPURA · HAMPI · NARA · PAK
ARIS CASTLE · KARAK CASTLE, KARAK · BE ... HARA BUDDHAS · AIT BENHADDOU · MAIDEN
ENQUE · POTALA PALACE · LEPTIS MAGNA · ... NTAR OBSERVATORY · METEORAS MONASTERIES
MPLE · THE ARK · YONGHEGONG · OSTIA A ... ASTERY · LUGO'S ROMAN WALLS · EL CARACOL
ICHAEL · PLAIN OF JARS · STARI MOST · PA ... · SALVADOR CARNIVAL · MAZATLÁN CARNIVAL
ESERT · RAJASTHAN INTERNATIONAL FOLK MUSIC F ... USIC FESTIVAL · FESTIVAL OF WORLD SACRED MUSIC
RTS FESTIVAL · AVIGNON FESTIVAL · HAY FESTIVAL CARTAGENA · W ... IVAL · INTERNATIONAL FESTIVAL OF ARTS & IDEAS
GAY PRIDE, AMSTERDAM · MONTREAL JAZZ FESTIVAL · COPENHAGEN JAZZ FESTIVAL · CAPE TOWN INTERNATIONAL JAZZ FESTIVAL · ST
BERSHOOT · BESTIVAL · BONNAROO MUSIC AND ARTS FESTIVAL · ROSKILDE · SEATTLE FOLKLIFE FESTIVAL · BONFIRE NIGHT · PUSHKAR
A ORANGE FESTIVAL · CADIZ CARNIVAL · ORURO CARNIVAL · FÊTES DE MASQUES · PARO TSECHU · BOI-BUMBA · TOONIK TYMEA · ONAM
AD RAT BALL · TET FESTIVAL · CROP OVER · LIMOUX CARNIVAL · FESTIVAL OF THE DHOW COUNTRIES · WIFE CARRYING CHAMPIONSHIPS
CITRUS FESTIVAL · GION MATSURI · EID, DAMASCUS · CARNIVAL, BASEL, SWITZERLAND · MUD FESTIVAL · CARNIVAL, GUALEGUAYCHÚ, AR-
EVARA TRAIL · SALAR DE UYUNI · COR ... A BL ... AINE · COA ... ROU ... 5 · EVANGELINE TRAIL · KAROO NATION-
CONCORDIA, KARAKORAM RANGE · CO ... R ... OUT ... · CHOMOLHARI TREK · THE PALACE ON WHEELS
O ROME · CANTERBURY · LOURDES ... ASER · RIVER SEINE · SYDNEY HARBOUR
HOU · LESS-TRAVELLED INDIA · KOLKATA · KAZIRANGA NATIONAL PARK · GANGOTRI · SHEKHAWATI · ORCHHA · MADURAI · CORSICA'S
REK · WAINWRIGHT'S COAST-TO-COAST WALK · FRANKINCENSE TRAIL · BEIJING/SHANGHAI-LHASA TRAIN · MILFORD TRACK · HA LONG
S PARKWAY DRIVE · LLAMA TREK · MEKONG RIVER · SAHARA CAMEL CARAVAN · E&O EXPRESS · KAYAKING IN BAY OF CORTEZ · THE GREAT
· HORSEBACK CATTLE DRIVE · THE GHAN · SOUTH DOWNS WAY · DOURO VALLEY WINE CRUISE · CASCADE LOOP DRIVE · VANUATU AR-
IGRATION · DRÂA VALLEY DRIVE · SAN JUAN SKYWAY DRIVE · THE VIKING TRAIL · MONGOLIA ON HORSEBACK · WALKING MONT BLANC'S
N COAST DRIVE · MARLBOROUGH WINE TOUR · CAMINO REAL TREK · HAGHIA SOPHIA · ST CATHERINE'S MONASTERY · MOUNT ATHOS,
DUOMO, FLORENCE · DOME OF THE ROCK · GREAT STUPA OF SANCHI · SAN GIMIGNANO · HUQIU TOWER · LEANING TOWER OF TELUK
DAFO TEMPLE · LAMA TEMPLE · JOKHANG TEMPLE · MENCIUS TEMPLE · WALT DISNEY CONCERT HALL · ROYAL ONTARIO MUSEUM · NEUE
ICT · PONTCYSYLLTE AQUEDUCT · CAESAREA MARITIMA · AGUAS LIVRES AQUEDUCT · AQUEDUCTO DE LOS MILAGROS · AQUEDUC ST-CLÉ-
ADE – THEATRES ON THE BAY · MARINA BAY · PANAMA CANAL · PUENTE DE LA MUJER · THE GOMATESHWARA STATUE · HEDDAL STAVKIRKE
GER BUILDING · THE ATOMIUM · HOLOCAUST MEMORIAL · SHIBAM · ENNIS HOUSE · MADRASSAH MIR-I-ARAB · CASA BATLLO · SHUKHOV
OSHIMA PEACE CENTER · TAIPEI 101 · THE WORLD'S FAIR · THE OMAYYAD MOSQUE · CRYSTAL CATHEDRAL · KREMLIN · THE RYUGYONG
EMEYER · THE MELNIKOV HOUSE · SALINE ROYALE · SEA RANCH CHAPEL · TWA BUILDING · VILLA MAJORELLE · SAADIAN TOMBS · DEVILS
PARAGUAY · HUANG HO · ALLAGASH RIVER · NIGER RIVER · THE CHILEAN LAKES · THE GLACIAL LAKES OF SLOVENIA · THE PLITVICE LAKES
DE CHELLY · THE PATAGONIAN FJORDS · FERNANDO DE NORONHA · WESTERN UGANDA RESERVES · HLUHLUWE-IMFOLOZI GAME RESERVE
IN JAPAN · THE WILD FLOWERS OF THE DRAKENSBERG MOUNTAINS · SPRING FLOWERS · WILD RHODODENDRONS IN THE HIMALAYAS
OLIAN ISLANDS · STOCKHOLM ARCHIPELAGO · AZORES, PORTUGAL · FIJI · IGUAÇU FALLS · ANGEL FALLS · JOG FALLS · DETTIFOSS FALLS ·
A ATLÀNTICA · BORNEO JUNGLE · JIUZHAI GOU LAKES · AGGTELEK CAVES · ARCHES NATIONAL PARK · BAKO NATIONAL PARK · BEARA PEN-
AL PARK · FISH RIVER CANYON · GLACIER NATIONAL PARK · ALDABRA ATOLL · LAKE BAIKAL · GLOW-WORM DISPLAYS · SAN JUAN ISLANDS
· PANTANAL · MONUMENT VALLEY · MANDAI ORCHID GARDEN · RIO GRANDE GORGES · SAMARIA GORGE · WADI EL-HITÁN · PLAYA OS-
TURE RESERVE · PHOSPHORESCENT BAY · PAINTED CANYON · TEIDE NATIONAL PARK · SOSSUSVLEI, NAMIB DESERT · KYUSHU AZALEAS ·
S · COTTESLOE BEACH · AL-MAMZAR BEACH · AMAGER BEACH PARK · NON NUOC BEACH · CHELTENHAM BEACH · MUIZENBERG BEACH
ISO WETLAND PARK · SHELA BEACH · EAST COAST OF ZANZIBAR · SAADANI NATIONAL PARK · SABRATHA · MANZANILLO BEACH · IHURU
· SOPOT BEACH · DOG'S BAY · PUNTA DEL ESTE · PUERTO ESCONDIDO · SOUTH BEACH · COZUMEL · SALINAS · AITUTAKI · ANSE SOURCE
E · WHITE BEACH · BIG BUDDHA BEACH · HOLY ISLAND · LLANDUDNO BEACH · MAJAHUITAS · LOPES MENDEZ · MONKEY BAY · INGONISH
PE MAY · MATIRA BEACH · DON DAENG ISLAND · EMERALD BAY · ESSAOUIRA · GRAYTON BEACH · MORNE ROUGE · SARAKINIKO BEACH ·
KA · LAS ISLAS CIES · OFU BEACH · OXWICH BAY · KICKING HORSE · VOSS · RED MOUNTAIN · SAINTE FOY · KAMCHATKA · ÅRE · THE PARIS
BAHIA · THE LEVANT & ISTANBUL · MOUNT STANLEY · MOUNT WILHELM · MAUNA LOA · COPA · MOUNT KINABALU · COTOPAXI · REYKJA-
AQABA · LIGHTHOUSE REEF · BANDA ISLANDS · PEMBA · BLUE CORNER · CAPPADOCIA · TRAIL 401 · APOLOBAMBA ROAD · FREEDOM TRAIL
· SKERRIES · THE MACAU GRAND PRIX · SCARBOROUGH · LANDSHAAG · THE SOUP BOWL · JEFFREYS BAY · CHICAMA · G-LAND · THURSO
M SOUND, ALASKA · PLANICA SKI JUMP, SLOVENIA · FISHING, DENMARK · KLOOFING, SOUTH AFRICA · WRESTLING, MEXICO CITY · BUSH-
AIR BALLOONING, TURKEY · CAVING, PUERTO RICO · MOUNTAINBOARDING, ITALIAN DOLOMITES · HORSE SAFARIS IN THE MASAI MARA,
NGHU ISLANDS, TAIWAN · KITESURFING, PREÁ, BRAZIL · TOUR SKATING, SWEDEN · CAPOEIRA, BRAZIL · LUMBERJACK WORLD CHAMPION-
NEA · PLAYING CARAMBOLE POOL, THE NETHERLANDS · SKIING IN YONGPYEONG, KOREA · KAYAKING IN GWAII HAANAS NATIONAL PARK,
EP SEA FISHING, CAPE TOWN, SOUTH AFRICA · CAMEL-TREKKING, MOROCCO · DIVING AT NINGALOO, AUSTRALIA · HIKING IN WYOMING,
D · A DAY AT THE RACES, IRELAND · GOLF IN EDINBURGH, SCOTLAND · ALTERNATIVE PARIS ART · MUSÉE NATIONAL DU MOYEN AGE · IN-
NE DELACROIX · WINE-TASTING IN MENDOZA · COLUMBIA GORGE · CAPE WINELANDS · MARLBOROUGH · TOKAJ WINE REGION · CRAZY
· MURUJUGA · FONT-DE-GAUME · LYONNAISE CUISINE · CAPE TOWN · ALEPPO · MONTREAL · MELBOURNE · CAPITOLINE MUSEUMS · GAL-
O · OSTIA ANTICA · SAN SEBASTIAN · BERLINALE · VENICE FILM FESTIVAL · FILM FESTIVAL LOCARNO · MOTOVUN FILM FESTIVAL · UMBRIA
IX-EN-PROVENCE FESTIVAL · TANGLEWOOD MUSIC FESTIVAL · EDINBURGH INTERNATIONAL FESTIVAL · NEW YORK'S INDEPENDENT GAL-
ROYAUX DES BEAUX-ARTS DE BELGIQUE · GIOTTO FRESCOES · SCROVEGNI · GARMA FESTIVAL · VILLA MAJORELLE · THE BOATHOUSE · BAU-
HOTOGRAPHERS' GALLERY · AMAZON THEATRE · NATIONAL MUSEUM OF MALI · MUSEUM OF ISLAMIC ART · AMBER ROOM · BERLIN FILM-
JLOUSE-LAUTREC MUSEUM · LAS POZAS · KEATS-SHELLEY HOUSE · WINE FESTIVAL, BURGUNDY · STRATFORD SHAKESPEARE FESTIVAL · MIHO
DENNIS SEVERS' HOUSE · SIR JOHN SOANE'S MUSEUM · FONDATION MARGUERITE ET AIMÉ MAEGHT · CENTRE BELGE DE LA BANDE DESSI-
AMERICAN ART · FADO MUSEUM · PRECITA EYES MURAL ARTS CENTER · CAVE OF THE SWIMMERS · ISLAMIC ART MUSEUM MALAYSIA · DELFT
UM · SHERLOCK HOLMES MUSEUM · KING'S HEAD THEATRE · OLD RED LION THEATRE · FINBOROUGH THEATRE · LANDOR THEATRE · RE-
N MARKET · WALTHAMSTOW MARKET · COLUMBIA ROAD FLOWER MARKET · GREENWICH MARKET · BRICK LANE · STOKE NEWINGTON ·
ROADWAY · SOHO · NOHO · NOLITA · KIRNA ZABETE · COCO & DELILAH · SIGERSON AND MORRISON · BETSEY JOHNSON · KENNETH COLE
· CAKESHOP · CORNELIA STREET CAFÉ · MORNINGSIDE HEIGHTS · CMJ MUSIC MARATHON · PUBLIC THEATER · ASTOR PLACE · ST MARKS
RIGHTON BEACH · QUEENS · RENO · GYEONGJU · LESS-EXPLORED HONG KONG · VICTORIA HARBOUR · KOWLOON · VICTORIA PEAK · NA-
E · TSIM SHA TSUI · HONG KONG MUSEUM OF ART · UNIVERSITY MUSEUM & ART GALLERY · THE HONG KONG PLANNING & INFRASTRUC-
ORIES · KADOORIE FARM & BOTANIC GARDEN · SHEK O COUNTRY PARK · DRAGON'S BACK PEAK TRAIL · BIG WAVE BAY · LAMMA ISLAND ·
ICT · FEZ · SANA'A, YEMEN · TUNIS, TUNISIA · ALEPPO, SYRIA · LESS-EXPLORED VENICE · PIAZZA SAN MARCO · GRAND CANAL · MURANO ·
ZO QUERINI STAMPALIA MUSEUM · THE NAVAL HISTORY MUSEUM · MUSEO DEL MERLETTO · GLASS MUSEUM · VENICE LAGOON · SAN SER-
RIGA · ČESKY KRUMLOV · BOLOGNA · BRATISLAVA · CARCASSONNE · GDAŃSK · BRUGES · LESS-EXPLORED SAN FRANSICO · NORTH BEACH
THE MISSION DISTRICT · HAYES VALLEY · RICHMOND · JAPANESE TEA GARDEN · GOLDEN GATE NATIONAL RECREATION AREA · LINCOLN
NOB HILL'S GRACE CATHEDRAL · KONG CHOW TEMPLE · SAINTS PETER AND PAUL CATHOLIC CHURCH · GOLDEN GATE FORTUNE COOKIE
CATECAS · LESS-EXPLORED PARIS · BELLEVILLE · MARAIS MANSIONS · MUSEUM OF HUNTING AND NATURE · HÔTEL GUÉNÉGAUD · HÔTEL
ARTHE · MUSÉE DE L'EVENTAIL · PASSAGES COUVERTS · GALÉRIE VIVIENNE · PASSAGE DU GRAND CERF · PASSAGE DES PANORAMAS · THÉÂTRE
WOLLOMBI · ST ALBANS · CAVES HOUSE · JENOLAN CAVES · KUR-RING-GAI CHASE NATIONAL PARK · AKUNA BAY · MILK BEACH · NIELSON
IAL PARK · MEMORIAL WALK · BOTANY BAY NATIONAL PARK · PORT HACKING · CRONULLA BEACH · BUNDEENA · PITTWATER HARBOUR ·
WHARF · THE COAST GOLF CLUB · MILSONS POINT · LUZERN, SWITZERLAND · HELSINKI, FINLAND · CORK, IRELAND · LIJIANG, CHINA ·
CUBA · HUE, VIETNAM · COCHIN, INDIA · SOZOPOL, BULGARIA · LUANG PRABANG, LAOS · LECCE, ITALY · DARWIN, AUSTRALIA · ALEPPO,
AL · ADDIS ABABA, ETHIOPIA · SIENA, ITALY · SAVANNAH, GEORGIA, USA · HEIDELBERG, GERMANY · ODESSA, UKRAINE · TOURS, FRANCE ·
TEVIDEO, URUGUAY · ISFAHAN, IRAN · KANAZAWA, JAPAN · SALVADOR, BRAZIL · NANCY, FRANCE · TAOS, NEW MEXICO, USA · VIENTIANE

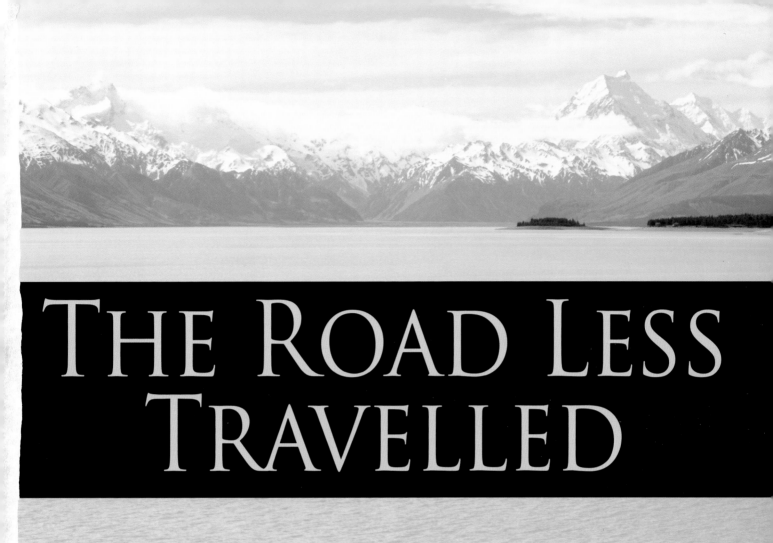

THE ROAD LESS TRAVELLED

THE ROAD LESS
TRAVELLED

1,000 AMAZING PLACES OFF THE TOURIST TRAIL

FOREWORD BY BILL BRYSON

LONDON, NEW YORK, MELBOURNE, MUNICH AND DELHI

LIST MANAGER Christine Stroyan
SENIOR EDITOR Sadie Smith
PROJECT EDITOR Alexandra Whittleton
EDITORS Fay Franklin, Michael Fullalove,
Justine Montgomery, Ros Walford

DESIGN MANAGER Sunita Gahir
DESIGNERS Nicola Erdpresser, Paul Jackson
DTP DESIGNER Jason Little

PICTURE RESEARCHER Ellen Root
PHOTOGRAPHERS Stuart James, Casper Morris
PRODUCTION CONTROLLER Liz Cherry

PUBLISHER Douglas Amrine

QUADRUM SOLUTIONS PVT. LTD
www.quadrumltd.com

First Published in Great Britain in 2009
by Dorling Kindersley Limited
80 Strand, London WC2R 0RL

This edition published in 2011

Every effort has been made to ensure that this book is as up-to-date as possible at the time of going to press. Some details, however, such as phone numbers, opening hours, prices, and travel information are liable to change. The publishers cannot accept responsibility for any consequences arising from the use of this book, nor for any material on third-party websites, and cannot guarantee that any website address in this book will be a suitable source of travel information. We value the views and suggestions of our readers very highly. Please write to: Publisher, DK Travel Guides, Dorling Kindersley, 80 Strand, London, WC2R 0RL, Great Britain or email travelguides@uk.dk.com.

www.traveldk.com

Cover image Stupas and Buddhas of Borobudur, Java, Indonesia
Half title page image Lake Pukaki, New Zealand
Title page image Barges on Canal du Midi, Toulouse, France

CONTENTS

Apadana Staircase, Persepolis, Iran *(p44)*

FOREWORD *by* BILL BRYSON

There are even more eye-popping, life-enhancing sights and experiences out there than I had ever dreamed existed

I have just finished reading this gorgeous and remarkable book, and I have good news and bad news to report. The bad news is that there are more fantastic things in the world to see than you can ever possibly hope to get to. You are just not going to live long enough. Sorry.

The good news, however, is that there are more fantastic things in the world to see than you can ever possibly hope to get to.

I am sure you take my point. It is always slightly appalling to be reminded that you are never going to get to do all the things you want to do in life. I feel even worse about this now (you will too shortly) because, thanks to this estimable tome, I have discovered that there are even more eye-popping, life-enhancing sights and experiences out there than I had ever dreamed existed, and I thought I was fairly worldly.

I had never heard of the Cordillera Blanca, a 112-mile walk through the mountains of Peru, but it looks fantastic and I really, really want to be with the people pictured on page 85. I want even more

to go to the Great Stupa of Sanchi – with a name like that, who could not? – and the mighty Pyramid of Cholula and Punta del Este and Zacatecas and – well, just all of it. And mostly I never will, which is kind of discouraging.

On the other hand – and this really is the crucial point – it is tremendously exciting to be part of a planet that is so packed with wonders that you have to choose which fraction of them you will visit. How dreary it would be, after all, if you actually could go everywhere and do everything. There would be nothing left to dream about, and dreaming, in my view, is often the best part of travel (and certainly the cheapest).

I don't suppose many people would think of now as being a golden age of travel – people hardly ever think of the present as being a golden age of anything, in my experience – but in fact I believe it is. Oh, I know airports are hopelessly thronged and a lot of popular destinations like Machu Picchu and the pyramids of Giza and many others are vastly more crowded than they were a generation ago, but that's because a generation ago most people couldn't afford to go to them.

We are the first generation that can pretty much afford to go wherever we want – and so of course that is what we do. If you don't wish to holiday with millions of others, you simply have to take a little more care choosing where you go.

And that is why this book – so trustworthy, so engaging, so endlessly perusable – is more valuable to the serious traveller than any book I have seen in a long time. It has been put together with authority and care by experts who have been everywhere and genuinely want you to have the best possible experience when you travel.

So why are you just sitting there? Turn the page, for goodness sake, and start planning.

Bill Bryson

ANCIENT AND HISTORICAL SIGHTS

Monk in front of one of the enormous Gal Vihara Buddha statues at Polonnaruwa, Sri Lanka *(p44)*

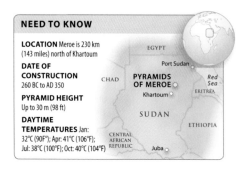

PYRAMIDS OF MEROE
VS PYRAMIDS OF GIZA

*So often overlooked in favour of Giza's better-known monuments,
the pyramids of Meroe are among Africa's forgotten treasures*

NEED TO KNOW

LOCATION Meroe is 230 km
(143 miles) north of Khartoum

**DATE OF
CONSTRUCTION**
260 BC to AD 350

PYRAMID HEIGHT
Up to 30 m (98 ft)

**DAYTIME
TEMPERATURES** Jan:
32°C (90°F); Apr: 41°C (106°F);
Jul: 38°C (100°F); Oct: 40°C (104°F)

Some ideas are too good to be forgotten. When Egypt's pyramid boom burned out in 2500 BC, the country's signature tomb design found its way up the Nile to northern Sudan, where it was embraced more than 2,000 years later by the Kushite Kingdom. Evidence of this architectural revival can be found at the great royal cemeteries of Bagrawiya, better known as the pyramids of Meroe, where dozens of steep-sided, chocolate-coloured pyramids litter the desert. This may be Sudan's most iconic sight, but visitors are likely to have the tombs all to themselves, with little more accompaniment than the sound of the desert wind in their ears.

The Kushite rulers had seen themselves as the true inheritors of Egyptian religion and culture long before they built the pyramids at Meroe, and even invaded their northern neighbour in the 8th century BC to establish an empire stretching as far as Libya and Palestine. Although Egypt later came under

Roman control, it continued to influence the cultural life of the Kushite Kingdom. The pyramids of Meroe are all that remain of a once-magnificent Kushite city, and bear witness to an empire once powerful enough to hold its own against Rome.

Not all of the pyramids at Meroe are intact. In fact, many look as if they have been bitten off at the top, one after the other, like a row of quickly sampled Easter eggs. This vandalism was the work of a 19th-century Italian treasure-hunter who dismantled the monuments as part of his largely unsuccessful search for gold. The decapitated pyramids reveal rubble cores covered in brick – an ancient, quick-fix building technique that allowed Sudanese rulers to erect huge numbers of the structures with ease. Each pyramid sits above a simple tomb chamber, which is dug into the rock below. The porch-like structures on the eastern sides of the pyramids house funeral chapels decorated with carvings and hieroglyphs, designed to ease the dead into the next world.

A small town now stands slightly away from the pyramids on the banks of the Nile. Excavation here is ongoing, in the hope that more clues to the mysterious Kushite Kingdom will be unearthed. Any visitors to Meroe who want to know more about the ancient Kushite people will relish a trip to the excellently preserved temples of Naqa and Musawwarat to the south, where beautiful carvings show the mix of Egyptian, African and Roman influences that fed into Kushite art.

ABOVE Tour buses lined up beside the Great Pyramid of Giza

FORGET THE PYRAMIDS OF GIZA?

THE BUILD-UP The Pyramids of Giza have a good claim to be the world's oldest tourist sight, having had a constant stream of visitors ever since the Greek historian Herodotus wrote about them in the 5th century BC. The awe-inspiring pyramids remain among the largest man-made structures in existence: the Great Pyramid of Giza stands at 145 m (476 ft) high and has a base area of 52,900 sq m (63,270 sq yards).

THE LETDOWN Cairo's urban sprawl has seen houses and fast-food chains expand to the very edge of the ancient site, where an unbroken procession of tour buses spill out their charges. The Egyptians have had thousands of years to perfect the tourist hard sell, and relentlessly offer camel and donkey rides to visitors.

GOING ANYWAY? The Egyptian authorities plan improved fencing around the pyramids to reduce the hassle from touts. In the meantime, visiting as early in the morning as possible gets you away from the big groups, as will riding in by horse from the desert side of the site.

PRACTICAL INFORMATION

Getting There and Around
Khartoum International Airport, on the outskirts of the capital, is the main point of entry into Sudan. Tourist visas are readily available, and the peaceful north is a long way from the troubled Darfur region. From Khartoum, the pyramids are easily accessible for day trips on public transport. Naqa and Musawwarat lie off road, halfway between Meroe and Khartoum, and a trip to either town will require 4WD hire.

Where to Eat
Khartoum has a virtually non-existent restaurant scene, and alcohol is banned. Breakfast, which is the most important meal of the day, is served in the late morning in nameless canteen-type eateries on every street. It

consists of *ful* (mashed beans), salad, cheese and bread. Meat and fish are also popular.

Where to Stay
Most visitors choose to visit from Khartoum, but if you want the site to yourself, the Meroe Tented Camp (www.italtoursudan.com), 2 km (1 mile) to the north, has plush tents overlooking the pyramids.

When to Go
The coolest time to visit is from October to March; summer is ferociously hot and best avoided.

Budget per Day for Two
£200 if you stay at the Meroe Tented Camp and hire a 4WD. Entry to the pyramids costs £6.

Website
www.sudan-tourism.gov.sd

MAIN IMAGE The topless brown Pyramids of Meroe
BELOW (left to right) Roman-style temple at Naqa; nomads riding camels near Meroe; Temple of Amun, Naqa

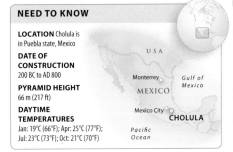

Iglesia de Mercedes atop the Great Pyramid of Cholula, Mexico

GREAT PYRAMID OF CHOLULA

NEED TO KNOW

LOCATION Cholula is in Puebla state, Mexico

DATE OF CONSTRUCTION 200 BC to AD 800

PYRAMID HEIGHT 66 m (217 ft)

DAYTIME TEMPERATURES Jan: 19°C (66°F); Apr: 25°C (77°F); Jul: 23°C (73°F); Oct: 21°C (70°F)

Cholula's pyramid is so enormous and overgrown that first-time visitors regularly mistake it for a hill. Although it is not as high as the Great Pyramid of Giza, it is actually larger, measuring a staggering 160,000 sq m (191,360 sq yards) at the base. Built over a period of 1,000 years, the monument is made up of several pyramids built one over the other like Russian dolls. The giant structure was once topped with a temple dedicated to the Aztec god Quetzalcoatl, but this was later replaced with a church built by the conquistadors. Visitors can relive Indiana Jones fantasies by exploring some of the 8 km (5 miles) of tunnels that burrow into the heart of the massive structure.

Practical Information

Getting There Cholula is on the outskirts of Puebla, the capital city of Puebla state, and is 3 hours southeast of Mexico City by road.

When to Go Any time of year is pleasant, although July to September is a particularly rainy period.

Website www.mexonline.com/cholula-pyramid.htm

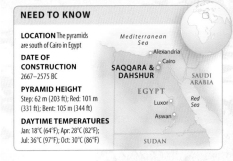

The Step Pyramid of Zoser in the evening sun, Saqqara, Egypt

PYRAMIDS OF SAQQARA & DAHSHUR

NEED TO KNOW

LOCATION The pyramids are south of Cairo in Egypt

DATE OF CONSTRUCTION 2667–2575 BC

PYRAMID HEIGHT Step: 62 m (203 ft); Red: 101 m (331 ft); Bent: 105 m (344 ft)

DAYTIME TEMPERATURES Jan: 18°C (64°F); Apr: 28°C (82°F); Jul: 36°C (97°F); Oct: 30°C (86°F)

The pyramids at Giza didn't arrive fully formed – it took the ancient Egyptians around 400 years to perfect their building art. Evidence of this architectural experimentation lies a short drive south of Giza at the older sites of Saqqara and Dahshur, where several pyramids, including one stepped, one bent and one red, form the necropolis for the old royal city of Memphis.

The idea of using pyramids as mausoleums arose during the Third Dynasty of ancient Egypt, and the funerary complex at Saqqara contains five of the original structures, along with a cluster of smaller mastaba (mudbrick) tombs that provided an early model for the pyramids. Dominating the site is the Step Pyramid of Zoser – the first Egyptian pyramid and the tomb of Pharaoh Zoser. The royal sarcophagus was sunk into the bedrock of the desert, then surrounded by a granite platform that was gradually expanded into a four- and then six-step pyramid according to very precise calculations. The pharaoh's engineer, Imhotep, oversaw the design and construction of this pyramid so well that he was later raised into the pantheon of the gods – an honour only bestowed on a handful of people in ancient Egypt. Although smaller pyramids surround Zoser's resting place, the tomb of Imhotep – the world's first-named architect – has never been found.

The pharaohs of the Sixth Dynasty chose Dahshur, to the south of Saqqara, as the site for their cemetery. Leading the way was the ruler, Snefru, who ordered the building of Dahshur's two most iconic pyramids, the Red Pyramid and the Bent Pyramid, and kick-started the golden age of Egyptian pyramids in the process. The Red Pyramid, named after the colour of its limestone blocks, is thought to be the first true pyramid, with sloping slides rather than steps and descending passages through the blockwork to a series of tomb chambers. The construction techniques obviously

Architectural detail at Brihadishwara Temple, Thanjavur, India

The white-marble Pyramid of Cestius, Rome

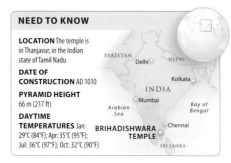

ABOVE The Bent Pyramid of Dahshur, Egypt, with its uneven side

took time to hone, though, since the nearby Bent Pyramid displays a noticeable – and unexplained – change in angle halfway up one side. It also strangely has two separate entrances. Snefru's son Cheops, inspired by his father's architectural efforts at Dahshur, went on to build the Great Pyramid of Giza, which was completed in around 2560 BC.

Practical Information

Getting There Saqqara and Dahshur are respectively 25 km (16 miles) and 35 km (22 miles) south of Cairo. This accessible location makes the pyramid sites ideal for a day trip from the city.

When to Go The best time to visit Egypt is from October through to April, when the weather is at its coolest.

Website www.egypt.travel

BRIHADISHWARA TEMPLE

NEED TO KNOW

LOCATION The temple is in Thanjavur, in the Indian state of Tamil Nadu

DATE OF CONSTRUCTION AD 1010

PYRAMID HEIGHT 66 m (217 ft)

DAYTIME TEMPERATURES Jan: 29°C (84°F); Apr: 35°C (95°F); Jul: 36°C (97°F); Oct: 32°C (90°F)

This magnificent temple, known colloquially as the "Big Temple", represents the architectural pinnacle of the Tamil Chola Empire, which once dominated Southern India. The huge complex, now a UNESCO World Heritage Site, is dedicated to the Hindu god Shiva, and is decorated with statues and images representing the many elements of Hindu cosmology. The pyramidal temple at the building's heart stands 13 storeys high, and is gloriously decorated with carvings of the gods. The temple's inner sanctum contains a huge stone, which worshippers walk around as part of their dedication to Shiva. This is one of the largest temples in India, and at its height over 600 attendants would have served its needs.

Practical Information

Getting There Thanjavur is a 9-hour bus or train ride south of Chennai (Madras). Brihadishwara Temple is only a short walk from the train station in Thanjavur.

When to Go Aim to visit between November and March, so that you avoid the hot summer and monsoon season.

Website www.kumbakonam.info

PYRAMID OF CESTIUS

NEED TO KNOW

LOCATION The Pyramid of Cestius is in Rome, Italy

DATE OF CONSTRUCTION 12 BC

PYRAMID HEIGHT 27 m (89 ft)

DAYTIME TEMPERATURES Jan: 11°C (52°F); Apr: 19°C (66°F); Jul: 30°C (86°F); Oct: 22°C (72°F)

The impact of ancient Egyptian culture spread far and wide. In the years after the Roman conquest of Egypt in 30 BC, scores of administrators and soldiers moved to the North African country, where they developed a taste for all things pharaonic. The Roman magistrate Caius Cestius was so impressed by the pyramids that he decided to be buried in one. His handsome tomb was faced in bright white marble, and forms part of Rome's city walls. However, Cestius proved less immortal than the pharaohs, and by the Middle Ages locals believed the pyramid was the tomb of Remus, one of Rome's legendary founders.

Practical Information

Getting There The pyramid is in south-central Rome, a stone's throw from the Porta San Paolo train station and the appropriately named Piramide metro station.

When to Go Any time of year. The interior of the pyramid is open on alternate Saturdays.

Website www.romaturismo.it

AVEBURY
VS STONEHENGE

Stonehenge is one of the world's great megalithic sights – but nearby Avebury is much larger and has a more accessible stone circle

NEED TO KNOW

LOCATION Avebury lies between Marlborough and Calne in Wiltshire, 142 km (85 miles) west of London, England

ACCESS Circle site open all year round, free entry

DAYTIME TEMPERATURES
Jan: 7°C (45°F); Apr: 14°C (57°F); Jul: 21°C (70°F); Oct: 12°C (54°F)

Crowning the skyline on treeless Salisbury Plain, the spectacle of Stonehenge reduces the passing traffic to a perpetual crawl. A line of coaches disgorge load after load of snap-happy visitors. In fact, it is so popular that the site has to be fenced off for fear of damage, putting the magnificent stones out of bounds. To really get hands-on with mysterious ancient stones, and to see the world from a 5,000-year-old perspective, try Avebury, located 33 km (20 miles) to the north. This mystic circle of stones, or henge, was erected around the same time and occupies what appears to be a

ABOVE The stone circle standing within the boundaries of a ditch

village green. Avebury's stones are not as huge as those at Stonehenge, but the site is four times the size, making it the world's largest henge.

Within a ditch which measures nearly a mile in circumference, the remaining giant gnarled thumbs of sandstone are complemented by concrete blocks showing how the circle and its outer and inner rings once stood. It is possible that some stones are still underground, and some beneath the village which, over the centuries, has unfortunately quarried the henge for building materials. In fact, the entire modern history of Avebury is mixed up with the stones, and can be explored in the local museum set up by the marmalade millionaire and amateur archaeologist Alexander Keiller.

The great attraction of Avebury, however, is that, like the resident sheep, you can wander freely among the stones, touching them and seeing if some of their mystery will rub off on you. Nobody really knows the purpose of the stones but, like most great constructions of early civilizations, they must have been involved in a culture that combined religion with the heavens and afterlife. This ritual centre was connected to another stone circle, the Sanctuary, just over 2 km (1 mile) away at the end of the West Kennet Avenue, a path flanked with stones. As big as Stonehenge, the Sanctuary has no standing stones. Less than a mile away are the West Kennet Long Barrow burial chambers, so it is possible that the avenue and the second circle had to do with journeys into the afterlife. Between the henges, less than a mile to the west is Silbury Hill, a 40-m- (130-ft-) high conical mound made at about the same time as the henges, the purpose of which has not been fully ascertained. To the north lies Windmill Hill, which shows signs of a Neolithic settlement and was probably where Avebury's architects and builders lived.

FORGET STONEHENGE?

THE BUILD-UP Stonehenge is famous, its stones astonishingly huge and its setting dramatic. The summer solstice ceremony held by druids and New Agers confirms it as a cathedral to mystical paganism. Even when seen from the road in a car, it is a magnificent sight.

THE LETDOWN During normal visiting hours you can't touch it, you can't wander about its space and you have to pay an entrance fee to see it. Located in a bleak spot, the henge has no sense of intimacy, and offers little shelter in bad weather. There is no museum that explores the significance of Stonehenge, and visitor facilities are limited.

GOING ANYWAY? Stonehenge is worth seeing, under any circumstances. Take advantage of the audio tour, which is included in the entrance fee. It is possible to gain access to the stone circle on pre-paid private tours, which take place outside visiting hours (www.english-heritage.org.uk).

ABOVE Visitors at Stonehenge standing behind fencing, admiring the ruins from a distance

PRACTICAL INFORMATION

Getting There and Around
From London, Avebury is easily accessible by public transport. It is a 1-hour train ride from Paddington to Swindon. From there, bus no. 49 leaves every hour for Avebury. However, if you hire a car, you can also take in Stonehenge by driving via the M4.

Where to Eat
You can stop for a meal at the 400-year-old thatched Red Lion, which is Avebury's village pub. The food is served from an extensive menu and includes snacks, sandwiches and wraps, and jacket potatoes (tel. +44 1672 539 266).

Where to Stay
The pub also has four cottage-style rooms available, but tales of the rooms being inhabited by ghosts may be a deterrent. The Castle and Ball (www.castleandball.com), located in nearby Marlborough, is a good alternative, and also has a great restaurant.

When to Go
Visit any time from Easter to the end of October, for a chance of better weather.

Budget per Day for Two
£280 including car hire.

Website
www.avebury-web.co.uk

MAIN IMAGE Visitors and sheep among the Avebury stones
BELOW (left to right) Silbury Hill's conical peak; standing stones at West Kennet Long Barrow; burial chamber, West Kennet Long Barrow

6 MORE ANCIENT SITES TO RIVAL STONEHENGE

Concentric circles of the Sonnenobservatorium, built by one of Europe's oldest civilizations

Stones of Ales Stenar, on a picturesque grassy headland looking out to sea, near Kåseberga

Ancient megalithic standing stones in a sea of verdant greenery at Carnac

ALES STENAR, SWEDEN

NEED TO KNOW

LOCATION Ales Stenar is located near the fishing village of Kåseberga in southern Sweden

ACCESS Free

DAYTIME TEMPERATURES
Jan: 2°C (36°F);
Apr: 17°C (63°F);
Jul: 18°C (64°F);
Oct: 9°C (48°F)

At first sight, Ales Stenar might look like a henge, but it is in fact oval, not circular, the stones at each end markedly larger than the rest. Floating on a wave of green in an ocean of grassy headland lapped by the Baltic Sea, this is the most significant of Sweden's thousand or more "ship settings" – rings of standing stones in the shape of a boat, with the large stone acting as the prow, and another as the stern with a small "rudder" behind. The stones probably date from the Viking period – a clay pot and a few burnt human bones found on the site have been traced back to AD 600.

Practical Information

Getting There and Around The nearest town is Ystad, which is 18 km (11 miles) away and has bus services. There are frequent trains from Malmö in Sweden, which is 45 minutes away by car. Copenhagen in Denmark also offers train services, or you can make the 1-hour journey by road. From Kåseberga, it is a short walk through fields up to the site.

When to Go May to October.

Websites www.skane.com; www.zwoje-scrolls.com/as/aleseng

SONNEN-OBSERVATORIUM, GERMANY

NEED TO KNOW

LOCATION The site is beside the town of Goseck in Germany

ACCESS Open Apr–Oct: 10am–6pm; Nov–Mar: 11am–4pm

DAYTIME TEMPERATURES
Jan: 3°C (37°F);
Apr: 7°C (45°F);
Jul: 20°C (68°F);
Oct: 9°C (48°F)

Four concentric circles spotted in a wheatfield at Goseck in 1991 led two archaeologists to start investigating 11 years later. They found the mound, ditch and the remains of two palisades of a Neolithic wooden henge, like many seen across Europe, except this one was 7,000 years old. Research has revealed that it may have been a kind of solar observatory – the earliest known in Europe. The henge was rebuilt using more than 2,000 hand-hewn wooden posts to create two rows of palisades and three gates. The southeast and southwest gates catch the sun at midday on the winter solstice, which is why this day was chosen to open the site to the public in 2005.

Practical Information

Getting There and Around From Berlin, it's just over a 2-hour drive to Goseck. Alternatively, the regional Leipzig-Halle Airport has direct flights from Paris and Vienna. Goseck is 60 km (36 miles) away by road.

When to Go You can visit the site in summer, but the winter solstice has special significance.

Website www.himmelswege.de/101/

CARNAC, FRANCE

NEED TO KNOW

LOCATION On the Atlantic Coast of southern Brittany, Carnac is 140 km (88 miles) from Nantes and 500 km (300 miles) west of Paris

ACCESS Restricted in summer to reduce site erosion

DAYTIME TEMPERATURES Jan: 9°C (48°F); Apr: 13°C (55°F); Jul: 20°C (68°F); Oct: 16°C (61°F)

The mossy-green landscape around the town of Carnac, scattered with thousands of ancient stones, makes this the very picture of the Celtic twilight, although the Neolithic culture that created it predates the Celts. Made from local stone, these mysterious rough-shaped rocks were erected around 4500 BC. The standing stones (menhirs) are up to 6.5 m (21 ft) tall and some are in rows, such as the Ménec and Kermario alignments. There are also groups of stone slabs known as dolmens, and mounds of earth called tumuli – both burial sites. The stones were clearly central to the culture and may have had some astrological significance. The Musée de Préhistoire de Carnac tells visitors all there is to know about these enigmatic stones.

Practical Information

Getting There and Around The nearest airports are at Rennes and Nantes. Alternatively, you can take a train from Paris to Auray or Vannes. The stones can be seen along the D196 outside Carnac. There is a car park at Kermario.

When to Go In summer, access to the stones is only possible by a guided tour; in winter, the sites are more accessible (but subject to variation).

Websites www.megalithia.com/brittany/carnac; www.ot-carnac.fr

Tapering Ring o'Brodgar stones surrounded by a floral landscape, Orkney Island

A Wassu Stone Circle resembling people gathered for a square dance, on the banks of the Gambia river

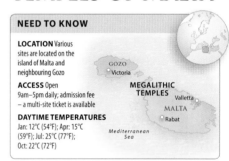

Ancient complex of extraordinary Maltese megalithic temples of Mnajdra

WASSU STONE CIRCLES, GAMBIA

NEED TO KNOW

LOCATION The stone circles are near the island and town of Janjangbureh (formerly Georgetown), Gambia

ACCESS Open daily; admission fee

DAYTIME TEMPERATURES
Jan: 23°C (73°F); Apr: 32°C (90°F); Jul: 28°C (82°F); Oct: 29°C (84°F)

At Wassu, ancient stones of similar shape have been arranged in circles, like people getting together for a square dance. This site has 11 such circles, and is one of the largest stone-circle complexes among hundreds spread over 333 km (200 miles) on the Gambia river's north bank. It is said to be the world's greatest concentration of stone circles. Most were made between 1300 BC and AD 750 from a local sandstone, laterite, and the largest can weigh up to 10 tons. They form part of a burial ritual and superstition about their powers has kept them from being plundered. A museum in Wassu explains their mysteries.

Practical Information

Getting There and Around The town of Janjangbureh on a river island is the nearest base, and is a 5-hour drive from the capital, Banjul. From there, you can hire taxis from the ferry terminal on the north bank 10 km (6 miles) from Wassu.

When to Go The weather is good year-round. To avoid rain, visit Nov–Jun.

Website www.gambia.dk/stones/html

RING O'BRODGAR, ORKNEY ISLANDS

NEED TO KNOW

LOCATION The Ring o'Brodgar stands in the West Mainland parish Stenness, in the Orkney Islands, which lie off the northern tip of Scotland

ACCESS Free

DAYTIME TEMPERATURES
Jan: 4°C (39°F); Apr: 6°C (43°F); Jul: 12°C (54°F); Oct: 8°C (47°F)

On summer evenings, the tall, thin standing stones of Brodgar cast long shadows, like fingers pointing towards some far-off mystery. This hauntingly beautiful place is on a narrow isthmus between two lochs, where the wind blows freely and light plays dramatic tricks throughout the day. A perfect circle exactly the same size as Avebury's two inner rings, this henge is much younger, erected around 2000 BC, on the eve of the Bronze Age. It is surrounded by a wide ditch cut into the bedrock, and crossed by two narrow causeways, one in the southeast and a wider one in the northwest. As well as the Ring o'Brodgar, which was clearly an important ritual centre for the Neolithic people, other sites here include burial mounds, earthworks and the Stones o' Stenness, an earlier henge less than a mile away.

Practical Information

Getting There and Around Brodgar is located 20 km (12 miles) to the west of Kirkwall, which is Orkney's main town and airport. You can also take a ferry from Scrabster on the mainland to Stromness, which is 7 km (4 miles) from Brodgar.

When to Go Mid-Jun–Oct, when it never gets dark, is ideal.

Websites www.orkney.org; www.orkneyjar.com

MEGALITHIC TEMPLES OF MALTA

NEED TO KNOW

LOCATION Various sites are located on the island of Malta and neighbouring Gozo

ACCESS Open 9am–5pm daily; admission fee – a multi-site ticket is available

DAYTIME TEMPERATURES
Jan: 12°C (54°F); Apr: 15°C (59°F); Jul: 25°C (77°F); Oct: 22°C (72°F)

Dawn, either during equinox or solstice, is the time to visit the Mnajdra megalithic temples on Malta's southern coast. The site opens early to catch the sun as it creeps over the massive, decorated slabs of the temples and warms their weathered surfaces. Mnajdra is perhaps the most appealing of the half-dozen extraordinary temple complexes on the island and on neighbouring Gozo, although each has its plus point, such as the animal carvings at Tarxien. Older than Stonehenge, these magnificent temples date from 5000 BC and were at their peak between 3600 and 3200 BC, a time known as the Ggantija, or Giant, period – for who else but giants could have made them?

Practical Information

Getting There and Around Malta's main airport is 8 km (5 miles) from the capital, Valletta. Either hire a car or go on a tour. The shortest crossing to Gozo is from Cirkewwa and takes 20 minutes.

When to Go High summer can be uncomfortably hot – the best time to visit is in Apr–May.

Website www.heritagemalta.org

AGRIGENTO AND SELINUNTE, SICILY
VS THE ACROPOLIS, ATHENS

The Acropolis in Athens is a potent symbol of the classical world, but the temples of Sicily, set in beautiful landscapes, can be more evocative of the power and majesty of Ancient Greece

ABOVE Tourists on the steps of the Propylaea, the magnificent gateway to the Acropolis, Athens, Greece

NEED TO KNOW

LOCATION Agrigento and Selinunte are 100 km (62 miles) apart in southern Sicily, Italy

NUMBER OF TEMPLES
Agrigento: 8; Selinunte: 7

DAYTIME TEMPERATURES
Jan: 14°C (57°F); Apr: 15°C (59°F); Jul: 24°C (75°F); Oct: 20°C (68°F)

The Acropolis in Athens, built during the Greek Golden Age (500–300 BC), is today such a dominant icon that many other fine Hellenic sites are often overlooked in its favour. More than 100 years before the Acropolis was built, the cities of Sicily were the richest and greatest in all of Magna Graecia (Greater Greece). It was here that the first large-scale temples were erected and they can still be seen on the southwest coast in Agrigento's glorious Valle dei Templi (Valley of the Temples) and at Selinunte.

The acropolis at Agrigento, which is known as Akrakas in Greek, is now lost beneath the modern town, but a series of stunning Doric temples remain on a ridge on the southern side of the town, bringing the classical world to life. These ancient monuments, which rise above picturesque, Arcadian fields of olive and almond trees on one side and the Mediterranean coastline on the other, are a spectacular sight, especially at night, when they are atmospherically illuminated.

Of the eight monumental temples built here in the 6th and 5th centuries BC, the Tempio della Concordia is considered to be the best preserved in the world after the Theseion in Athens, and its harmony with nature is emphasized by its warm earthy colours, which change with the moving sun and shadows of the day. The Tempio de Hera is the most romantic of the ruins at Agrigento, while the uncompleted Tempio di Zeus Olimpico, which is the size of a football pitch, was the largest Doric temple ever built. Its columns included 38 giant human figures, one of which lies in repose on the

site. It requires the best part of a day to visit the Valley of Temples and its other treasures, which include the agora (market place), shrines, sanctuaries, catacombs, sacrificial altars, a villa, museums and a church.

Selinunte, the furthest west of Magna Graecia's colonies, is as sun-bleached as nearby North Africa. This vast archaeological site was the largest in Greece and lies between two rivers, Belice and Modione, by the sea on the edge of a fertile plain far enough from the nearest resort, Marinella, to have remained unspoilt. The site takes its name from *selinon*, the Greek word for "wild parsley", which still grows in the fields of wild flowers surrounding the monuments. Selinunte had a short life that lasted from 650 BC until its destruction by the Carthaginians in 409 BC, but it flourished long enough for an acropolis and seven temples to be constructed. The largest of these is actually longer than Agrigento's Tempio di Zeus Olimpico, but not as wide. Although the ruins at Selinunte are not as well preserved as those at Agrigento, these silent sentinels, by a dazzling blue sea, invite contemplation, study and wonder.

PRACTICAL INFORMATION

Getting There and Around
The airport in Palermo, Sicily's capital city, receives international flights at regular intervals. It is 210 km (130 miles) from the airport to Agrigento and 200 km (125 miles) to Selinunte. If you are travelling by car from Messina, the port for ferries across to mainland Italy, it is a 420-km (260-mile) trip to Agrigento and a further 100 km (60 miles) on to Selinunte.

Where to Eat
Pretty Via Panoramica dei Templi near Agrigento has several good restaurants. Trattoria dei Templi (tel. +39 0922 403110) is one of the best. In Marinella de Selinunte, which is near the Selinunte ruins, have a fresh fish dish at the charming, authentic Ristorante

La Pineta (www.ristorantelapinetaselinunte.it).

Where to Stay
The stylish 18th-century Villa Athena (www.athenahotels.com) is actually in the Valle dei Templi at Agrigento. Hotel Garzia (www.hotelgarzia.com) in Marinella de Selinunte has great sea views and a good restaurant.

When to Go
High summer can be ferociously hot, so visit in Mar–Jun or Sep–Oct.

Budget per Day for Two
£260 including car hire, food, accommodation and entrance fees.

Websites
Agrigento: www.valleyofthetemples.com; Selinunte: www.selinunte.net

FORGET THE ATHENS ACROPOLIS?

THE BUILD-UP The word "acropolis" means "high city" in Greek, and most ancient Greek cities had a dominant, defendable upper town. But the monument in Athens, which sits on a rock that towers 150 m (490 ft) above sea level, is so well known that it is simply referred to as the Acropolis. Its main buildings, including the Parthenon – a temple to the goddess Athena – were built in the 5th century BC when Athens was at the height of its power.

THE LETDOWN Like many famous landmarks, the Acropolis suffers from the danger of over-anticipation, and romantic Hellenophiles may imagine it without tourist buses and crowds or the surrounding chaotic city, but this is simply not the case. And what you see when you get there isn't all real. The sculptured figures on the Erechtheum (a temple just north of the Acropolis) are copies, and of course the fascinating Parthenon frieze is nowhere to be seen – it has long been housed in the British Museum.

GOING ANYWAY? The importance of the Acropolis cannot be ignored. If you do go, be sure to visit the nearby Acropolis Museum. The avenues beneath the monument are a fine way to approach it, but avoid them in the heat of day.

MAIN IMAGE The dramatically lit Tempio de Hera at dusk, Agrigento
BELOW (left to right) The huge acropolis at Selinunte from above; Temple E at Selinunte

4 MORE GREEK RUINS TO RIVAL THE ACROPOLIS

THE ACROPOLIS, RHODES CITY, RHODES This 2nd- to 3rd-century-BC acropolis has an excellent location in the city centre and comprises a temple, stadium and small theatre.

EMPÚRIES, CATALONIA, SPAIN A Greek sea wall in the middle of the Gulf of Roses flags this ancient trading settlement, which was founded in 575 BC and later occupied by the Romans.

ASSOS, BEHRAMKALE, TURKEY On moonlit nights romantics head for the Tempio de Athena, overlooking the sea, at this former Greek colony founded by the islanders of nearby Lesbos.

CYRENE, CYRENAICA, LIBYA One of the most important classical cities in North Africa, Cyrene, which gave the eastern part of Libya its name, lies away from the coast in a fertile valley.

PULA ARENA, CROATIA
VS THE COLOSSEUM, ROME

Rome's Colosseum, an ancient circus of death and glory, is a symbol of the city, but across the Adriatic Sea is an equally imposing and magnificent arena in Pula

NEED TO KNOW

LOCATION The Arena is located in the port city of Pula, on Croatia's Adriatic Coast

CAPACITY 23,000

DAYTIME TEMPERATURES Jan: 6°C (43°F); Apr: 12°C (54°F); Jul: 26°C (79°F); Oct: 14°C (58°F)

Map showing SLOVENIA, Zagreb, CROATIA, PULA, BOSNIA & HERZEGOVINA, Split, Adriatic Sea, Dubrovnik

It is generally acknowledged that the Colosseum is one of the greatest engineering feats of the Romans – it was certainly the largest amphitheatre they ever built. Standing inside, seeing the tunnels where wild animals would be prodded into deadly games, and climbing the precipitous tiers of the arena, it is easy to imagine an enormous crowd – shielded by awnings from the heat of the day – roaring with excitement and disapproval.

Visiting the Arena in Pula will evoke much the same feeling, except that here the space is more intimate. Chances are that you may well be among a more orderly crowd here, listening to music or watching opera or dance because, unlike the Colosseum, Croatia's best-preserved classical monument remains a place of entertainment. As host to the annual Pula Film Festival that hands out the Golden Arena Awards, this amphitheatre has been described as the most beautiful cinema in the world. When music echoes around the limestone escarpments of its walls on a balmy summer evening, it is hard to imagine the games of death and gore that were once held here.

Pula was – and still is – an important port, but the Romans sited the amphitheatre just outside the city walls on the Via Flavia, which ran up the coast to the ancient Roman city of Aquileia. Today, it sits in an idyllic location overlooking the harbour.

Arena is the Latin word for sand, which covered the central area – it was useful for soaking up the blood. Built at the same time as the Colosseum in the 1st century AD, Pula's Arena is the sixth largest of the 200 or so amphitheatres that the Romans erected in their centres of power. A particular feature of this amphitheatre is the gutter running around the top of its walls that collected rainwater in tanks in four still-standing towers. Perfume was added to the water, which was then sprayed over what must have sometimes been a less-than-fragrant audience. Of a similar elliptical design to the Colosseum, but one tier shorter and lacking its heavy grandeur, Pula Arena has a much freer, friendlier appeal. Its original banks of seats have long since been removed – some taken to Venice to build *palazzi* – but a newer semi-circle of seats rises to grassy banks. As you wander around, the audio-tour clamped to your ears, the centuries slip away and you're transported back in time, but you only become fully aware that this was once an extremely violent place when you reach the dark cells beneath, where martyrs and animals were confined until their final performance.

FORGET ROME'S COLOSSEUM?

THE BUILD-UP American composer Cole Porter said it all when he said, "You're the top! You're the Colosseum." Tourists have been enthusing about the Colosseum since the 18th-century Grand Tour of Europe, which the English elite had popularized. Even as a partial ruin, it can still take your breath away.

THE LETDOWN Italy's most-visited sight is often crowded and usually has long queues. The entire building is a traffic roundabout and the interior is too precious to host concerts. Your visit will be even more memorable if you fall victim to a pickpocket.

GOING ANYWAY? The Colosseum really is an extraordinary achievement. It's best to visit early in the morning or late in the afternoon when it's less crowded. For a good overview, climb to the gallery tier. To avoid queues for tickets, go to the Palatine first – a ticket there covers both sights, so afterwards you can walk straight in.

ABOVE Heavy traffic on what must be the most spectacular roundabout in the world, the Colosseum

PRACTICAL INFORMATION

Getting There and Around
Pula has an international airport 6 km (4 miles) from the city centre. The city is not large and buses are efficient means of transport. Taxis are available and inexpensive. There is a regular boat from Venice in summer.

Where to Eat
For cutting-edge dishes in a beautiful setting, it's hard to beat the award-winning Valsabbion, part of a hotel and spa (tel. +385 52 218 033; www.valsabbion.hr; closed Jan). Near the Arena, the Pizzeria Jupiter (tel. +385 52 214 333) is known for its pasta and pizza.

Where to Stay
Most accommodation is on the Verudela Peninsula, Pula's playground to the south of the city. A short walk from the Arena is the small family-owned Scaletta Hotel (tel. +385 52 541 599; www.hotel-scaletta. com) with a good restaurant. The Hotel Riviera is also close by (tel. +385 52 211 166).

When to Go
Being a tourist centre, Pula is more crowded in summer. Warm weather makes it pleasant during Mar–Oct. Check in advance for details about the events held in the Arena.

Budget per Day for Two
£125 including a visit to the Arena, food and accommodation.

Website
www.istra.hr

MAIN IMAGE Rows of seats at the Pula amphitheatre **BELOW (left to right)** Roman amphorae on display at a subterranean gallery; aerial view of Pula Arena; a performance in the amphitheatre

6 MORE DRAMATIC AMPHITHEATRES TO RIVAL THE COLOSSEUM

Tiers of seating hewn into the rock at Leptis Magna's amphitheatre

Grand-scale colonnades at the great amphitheatre in El Djem

Grassy slopes distinguish Trier's unusual earthen amphitheatre

LEPTIS MAGNA, LIBYA

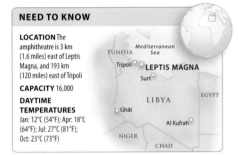

NEED TO KNOW

LOCATION The amphitheatre is 3 km (1.6 miles) east of Leptis Magna, and 193 km (120 miles) east of Tripoli

CAPACITY 16,000

DAYTIME TEMPERATURES
Jan: 12°C (54°F); Apr: 18°C (64°F); Jul: 27°C (81°F); Oct: 23°C (73°F)

The site of Leptis Magna, on the coast of Libya, has some of the most impressive Roman remains in Africa (see p45). Three kilometres (1.6 miles) east of the main site, by a beach where Greek and Roman columns lie stranded like driftwood, stands a magnificent amphitheatre, its honey-coloured stone blending into its sandy surrounds in sharp contrast to the blue of the sea beyond. Created in the bowl of a former quarry that supplied much of the stone for the ancient city's buildings, it lies below ground level, with tunnels and holding cells for animals carved out of the rock. Its surrounding colonnade is long gone, leaving a beautifully harmonious saucer of seats.

Practical Information

Getting There British Airways and Lufthansa are among the airlines that fly to Tripoli. Leptis Magna is 3 km (1.6 miles) from the town of Al-Khums. Domestic transfers must be arranged through a Libyan tour operator.

When to Go Between October and June, to avoid the summer heat. Look out for concerts staged in the Roman theatre at Leptis Magna's main site.

Website www.libyaonline.com/tourism

EL DJEM, TUNISIA

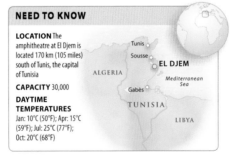

NEED TO KNOW

LOCATION The amphitheatre at El Djem is located 170 km (105 miles) south of Tunis, the capital of Tunisia

CAPACITY 30,000

DAYTIME TEMPERATURES
Jan: 10°C (50°F); Apr: 15°C (59°F); Jul: 25°C (77°F); Oct: 20°C (68°F)

The amphitheatre in El Djem (Roman Thysdrus) dominates the town, visible for miles from the surrounding desert. Rising three storeys high, it seems more like a fortress than a palace of entertainment – and indeed it has been used as one. It is the largest amphitheatre outside Italy, and was probably the last to be built, in the late 3rd century AD. It is also wonderfully preserved, revealing clearly how the animals, gladiators and actors entered the arena, via passages that slope down from outside to the underground galleries. Two lift shafts show where the stars of the show were carried to their deadly moment of glory.

Practical Information

Getting There Fly to Tunis, then travel to El Djem by train (3 hours) or taxi (2 hours). It makes an easy day trip from Tunisia's Mediterranean resorts.

When to Go Winter (Oct–Apr) is a good time to visit, though it can be wet. Alternatively, catch the International Festival of Symphonic Music (www.istc.org), which is held here each summer.

Website www.tourismtunisia.com

TRIER, GERMANY

NEED TO KNOW

LOCATION Trier is located in the west German state of Rhineland-Palatinate, near the Luxembourg border

CAPACITY 25,000

DAYTIME TEMPERATURES
Jan: 2°C (36°F); Apr: 9°C (48°F); Jul: 19°C (66°F); Oct: 10°C (50°F)

The Romans did not build all their amphitheatres out of stone. In Trier, the most important Roman city north of the Alps and once briefly capital of the Western Roman Empire, they dug up a hill – using the slope itself to create one side, and heaping up the earth dug out of the arena to create the other. The great basement beneath the arena has been fully excavated and is open to visitors. To descend into its dank, stygian gloom is to feel the chill that must have come over the animals, contestants and martyrs who awaited their fate here. The arena's acoustics remain impeccable and the space is now used for concerts and an annual re-enactment of gladiatorial contests.

Practical Information

Getting There Trier is easily accessible by train or by car via Germany's A1 motorway. The closest international airport is Luxembourg, 40 km (25 miles) away; Frankfurt am Main airport is 150 km (95 miles) away. The arena itself is just outside the old city walls, and can be reached on foot or by bus.

When to Go Any time, though November to March will be cold. Check the tourist office (see website below) for events in the amphitheatre.

Websites www.arena-trier.de; www.trier.de

Spectacular opera staging inside Verona's stunning oval arena

Aerial view of Mérida's Roman amphitheatre, with the theatre beyond

ANFITEATRO DI MÉRIDA, SPAIN

NEED TO KNOW

LOCATION The city of Mérida lies in western Spain's Extremadura region, 280 km (175 miles) from the capital, Madrid

CAPACITY 15,000

DAYTIME TEMPERATURES Jan: 6°C (43°F); Apr: 24°C (75°F); Jul: 37°C (99°F); Oct: 26°C (79°F)

On the hot, dusty plains of Spain's high Meseta lies the lovely ruined *municipium* of Mérida. This was the provincial capital of Lusitania, and its ensemble of stunningly preserved ruins makes it one of the finest Roman sites in Europe. Its amphitheatre, entered through brick arches, is an arid bowl, open to the skies and unshielded by the high walls of later surviving examples. It is complemented by an adjoining circus and 5,000-seat theatre, connected to the amphitheatre by underground tunnels. The Roman museum has the finest collection of such artifacts outside Italy.

Practical Information

Getting There Mérida lies on the N-V motorway between Madrid and Lisbon, and is served by regular trains and buses from Badajoz (1 hour), Seville (3 hours) and Madrid (5–6 hours). The nearest international airport is Badajoz, 45 km (28 miles) west, near the border with Portugal.

When to Go Spring (Apr–Jun) and autumn (Sep–Oct) are most pleasant. The Mérida Festival runs July–August, with concerts in the Roman ruins.

Websites www.merida.es; www.festivaldemerida.es

ARENA DI VERONA, ITALY

NEED TO KNOW

LOCATION The city of Verona is in the Veneto region of northern Italy, 255 km (160 miles) from Milan and 195 km (120 miles) from Venice

CAPACITY 25,000

DAYTIME TEMPERATURES Jan: 2°C (36°F); Apr: 14°C (57°F); Jul: 25°C (77°F); Oct: 15°C (59°F)

Although you don't have to see a performance to appreciate the harmonious structure of Verona's amphitheatre, a summer night watching the opera here is unforgettable. For these incomparable events, the building is transformed into a theatre, with a wide stage at one end and additional seating arranged across the arena floor, creating an auditorium for 15,000. Although it looks complete, it was once encased in three-storey outer walls, faced in pink and white limestone, which provided the access galleries to the 42 rows of stone seating. The amphitheatre's museum shows how its hydraulic system worked.

Practical Information

Getting There Verona is linked by shuttle bus to its own airport (10 km/ 6 miles from the city centre) and Brescia airport (52 km/30 miles away). It lies on the A4 Milan–Venice motorway and has direct train services to the main northern Italian cities, including Venice (1.5 hours), Milan (2 hours) and Rome (5 hours). Verona's historic centre is easily explored on foot.

When to Go Between Easter and November. The annual Opera Festival takes place between June and August.

Website www.arena.it

ARÈNES DE NÎMES, FRANCE

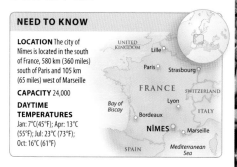

Monument to the bull-fighting tradition at the Arènes de Nîmes

NEED TO KNOW

LOCATION The city of Nîmes is located in the south of France, 580 km (360 miles) south of Paris and 105 km (65 miles) west of Marseille

CAPACITY 24,000

DAYTIME TEMPERATURES Jan: 7°C (45°F); Apr: 13°C (55°F); Jul: 23°C (73°F); Oct: 16°C (61°F)

This is the most complete surviving Roman amphitheatre in the world. It still entertains the crowds today, regarded as one of the country's best music venues as well as playing host to a season of bullfights. It is easy, on a balmy night, in this incredible atmosphere, to forget that the building is 2,000 years old. Its 34 rows of seats are arranged in three tiers, originally socially graded – from the front seats reserved for dignitaries to the distant, high rows allocated to slaves. It's no surprise that every sporting stadium built since then has been modelled on this ideal design.

Practical Information

Getting There Nîmes lies on France's A4 motorway. Its own airport is only served by UK budget airlines, but larger airports exist in Marseille and Montpellier. By rail, there are high-speed TGV links to Paris (3–4 hours), and frequent services to Marseille (1 hour) and other cities in the region.

When to Go The mild climate here makes it pleasant most of the year. Try to catch the Feria de Pentecôte, a 5-day event centred on the Arena in May.

Website www.arenes-nimes.com

HERCULANEUM
VS POMPEII

Herculaneum, with its beautifully preserved Roman ruins, offers an atmospheric and uncrowded alternative to its better-known rival, Pompeii

NEED TO KNOW

LOCATION Herculaneum is in the Bay of Naples, 8 km (5 miles) south of Naples and 16 km (10 miles) north of Pompeii

DATE OF CONSTRUCTION 6th century BC

DAYTIME TEMPERATURES Jan: 12°C (54°F); Apr: 18°C (65°F); Jul: 29°C (85°F); Oct: 23°C (71°F)

ITALY
Milan • Venice
• Rome
Adriatic Sea
HERCULANEUM
Tyrrhenian Sea
Ionian Sea

The small Roman town of Herculaneum was obliterated by the same fateful explosion of Mount Vesuvius that wiped out Pompeii in AD 79. And for many people, it is Herculaneum that offers the more concise and moving monument to the great Vesuvian eruption. Its ruins might be less extensive than those at Pompeii, but they are far better preserved. Many of the buildings have weathered the centuries so well that they look virtually the same as they would have done millennia ago. A remarkable wealth of decorative detail and everyday objects have also survived, including superb mosaics and murals, wooden benches and even fragments of glass, creating a touchingly vivid and immediate sense of the lives of the people who lived here.

Herculaneum initially escaped the volcanic inferno that enveloped Pompeii, and it was not until much later in the eruption that mud and lava flows from Vesuvius swamped the town, followed by a devastating flow of scalding gas and pumice, which killed all those who had not already fled. But a fortuitous combination of natural phenomena during the eruption gave rise to Herculaneum's remarkable state of preservation. The deluge of mud from the volcano filled the buildings, which prevented them from collapsing, and the intense heat of other volcanic debris left all exposed wood in a slightly charred condition, much of which has survived intact. Finally, a 25-m (82-ft) layer of tufa rock was formed from solidified mud – compared to a mere 4 m (13 ft) of tufa at Pompeii – and this solid blanket created an airtight seal over the city

for 1,700 years, until the remains of the town were accidentally discovered in the early 18th century by labourers digging a well.

As you wander around the ancient city's dusty streets, in and out of the haunting, echoey ruins of fine Roman villas and courtyards, it is easy to imagine Herculaneum as it once must have been – a flourishing residential centre. The town was much smaller and wealthier than Pompeii, and although it lacks the large public spaces and imposing civic architecture of its bigger neighbour, the architecture generally exhibits far higher standards of craftsmanship. The town's two lavish public baths, for example, date from 10 BC and boast original doors, detailed stuccowork, and wooden benches and shelves. Incredibly, there are even shards of glass in some of the window frames. Other notable sights include the grand House of the Mosaic Atrium, with its dazzling geometric tiled floor and superbly decorated courtyard. There is also an eerily well-preserved line of shops, including a baker's, a weaver's and a dyer's.

PRACTICAL INFORMATION

Getting There and Around
The nearest airport is at Naples, and there are regular buses from here to the site. Herculaneum is also easily reached by train on the Circumvesuviana line. Head to Ercolano station, which is 25 minutes from Naples and 40 minutes from Sorrento.

Where to Eat
Unsurprisingly, as the city that claims to have invented pizza, Naples has an excellent range of places to eat. Try the legendary Da Michele at Via Cesare Sersale 1, one of the city's most famous pizzerias, founded in 1870. Only two types of pizza are on offer here – margherita and marinara. You cannot book and there's almost always a queue, so make sure you leave plenty of time.

Where to Stay
Most visitors stay in Naples or Sorrento. In Naples, the unusual Hotel San Francisco al Monte (tel. +39 81 251 2461) occupies a converted 16th-century monastery in a superb location overlooking the bay. The former monks' cells have been beautifully transformed into luxury rooms. Facilities include an open-air bar in the cloisters and a swimming pool.

When to Go
Herculaneum is a year-round destination, although July and August can be unpleasantly hot.

Budget per Day for Two
£175 including transport, food, accommodation and admission.

Website
www.herculaneum.org

ABOVE Tourists crowding around a body cast at Pompeii, Italy

FORGET POMPEII?

THE BUILD-UP The remarkably intact ruins of Pompeii make up one of Europe's most compelling archaeological sites, offering a fantastic insight into life at the height of the Roman Empire, as well as a chilling parable of a flourishing civilization suddenly extinguished by unforeseen natural catastrophe.

THE LETDOWN With around 2.5 million visitors a year, Pompeii is now the most popular tourist site in Italy, and at busy times the crowds can be oppressive. The site is also very spread out, and can be tiring to explore, especially in the hot summer months. Some of Pompeii's ruins have also been severely compromised by badly executed 20th-century restorations that aimed to recreate the "atmosphere" of the ancient city by rebuilding walls and roofs, often using unsightly concrete and steel.

GOING ANYWAY? Don't try to rush Pompeii: it's a big site, so devote a whole day to exploring the place, aiming to be at the most popular sights at the beginning and end of the day. Be selective, too, rather than trying to charge around seeing absolutely everything, and have a look at the site map before you set off in order to check which parts of the city are currently closed for restoration.

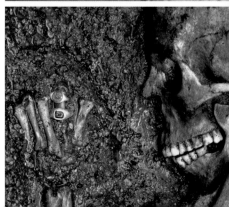

MAIN IMAGE Interior of the magnificent Roman baths at Herculaneum
BELOW (left to right) Fossilized human skeleton with two gold rings on its fingers; mosaic depicting Neptune and Amphitrite; ruins at Herculaneum

ANCIENT AND HISTORICAL SIGHTS

AKROTIRI

NEED TO KNOW

LOCATION Akrotiri is on Santorini in the Cyclades island group, Greece

DATE OF CONSTRUCTION 20th–17th centuries BC

DAYTIME TEMPERATURES Jan: 12°C (54°F); Apr: 16°C (61°F); Jul: 25°C (77°F); Oct: 19°C (66°F)

The Bronze Age settlement of Akrotiri, once the largest Minoan city outside Crete, suffered a Pompeii-like end when it was buried in ash following the explosion of the volcanic island of Thera (modern-day Santorini) around 1500 BC. This eruption was one of the most devastating in recorded history, and is thought to have inspired Plato's legend of Atlantis, which told of an island that vanished without trace. The ash preserved much of Akrotiri in a near-perfect condition, and today you'll find three-storey houses replete with pottery and furniture as well as a remarkable array of frescoes. Most of these artifacts are now in Athens, though excellent replicas are displayed at the Thíra Foundation in the island's capital, Firá.

Practical Information

Getting There International flights go in and out of Athens regularly. You can then take a local flight or a ferry to Santorini.

When to Go May, June and September are pleasantly warm but not too hot. Avoid the summer crowds and *meltémi* (winds) of July and August.

Website www.santorini.net/123

Ceramic vases found at the ancient site of Akrotiri, Santorini, Greece

KOURION

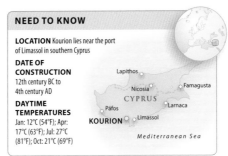

NEED TO KNOW

LOCATION Kourion lies near the port of Limassol in southern Cyprus

DATE OF CONSTRUCTION 12th century BC to 4th century AD

DAYTIME TEMPERATURES Jan: 12°C (54°F); Apr: 17°C (63°F); Jul: 27°C (81°F); Oct: 21°C (69°F)

Ancient Kourion, which is perched on a cliff overlooking the Mediterranean, emerged as a major Mycenaean settlement in around 1200 BC. The city remained a flourishing centre until the Middle Ages, when a massive earthquake destroyed many of its buildings and drove away its inhabitants. Despite this catastrophe, a remarkable array of Hellenistic, Roman and early-Christian monuments still stand here. There's a stunning theatre, which is still in use, beautiful floor mosaics, a basilica, public baths and an enormous amphitheatre, which boasts fantastic views. Nearby is a shrine to the Hellenistic deity Apollo dating from the 7th century BC.

Practical Information

Getting There There are plenty of international flights into Larnaca airport, and from there you can drive or catch a bus to Limassol.

When to Go The island's beautiful Mediterranean climate makes a visit possible at any time of year, although you might want to avoid the peak summer months (Jun–Aug), when temperatures are high, accommodation is pricey and the city is at its most touristy.

Website www.limassolmunicipal.com.cy/kourion

The ruined city of Kourion, Cyprus, with a well-preserved mosaic floor in the foreground

TIMGAD

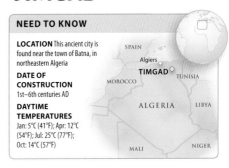

NEED TO KNOW

LOCATION This ancient city is found near the town of Batna, in northeastern Algeria

DATE OF CONSTRUCTION 1st–6th centuries AD

DAYTIME TEMPERATURES Jan: 5°C (41°F); Apr: 12°C (54°F); Jul: 25°C (77°F); Oct: 14°C (57°F)

Timgad was established in AD 100 by the Roman Emperor Trajan, and for six centuries was one of North Africa's most prosperous Roman settlements. But in 430 it was sacked by the Vandals – the same group that went on to plunder Rome in 455 – and the town was abandoned and gradually swallowed up by the encroaching Sahara. Now dug out of the sand and restored, Timgad presents the haunting sight of a Roman town miraculously preserved in the middle of nowhere. Sights include a 12-m (39-ft) high Trajan's Arch, a 3,500-seat theatre and a large Christian basilica, as well as a fine on-site museum.

Practical Information

Getting There Fly to Batna, 40 km (25 miles) from Timgad, and hire a taxi or arrange a tour with a local guide to reach the site.

When to Go This is one of the coolest parts of Algeria, although it's still best to avoid the climatic extremes of winter and summer and stick to the more temperate seasons of autumn and spring.

Website http://whc.unesco.org/en/list/194

Mosaic depicting the Goddess Diana bathing, Timgad, Algeria

PALMYRA

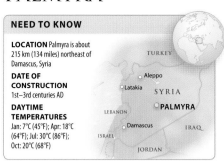

ABOVE Candle-lit sarcophagi in an underground tomb, Palmyra

Palmyra, also known by its Arabic name of Tadmor, is one of the oldest cities in the Middle East. It is thought to date back to Babylonian times, but most of the surviving buildings date from the 1st to 3rd centuries, when the city was incorporated into the Roman Empire. Palmyra served as an important meeting point between the Persian Empire to the east and the Greco-Roman world to the west. Its fabled oasis, a symbol of fertility in a barren landscape, is thought to have inspired the nickname "the Bride of the Desert", and made Palmyra a popular stop on the caravan route between Persia and the Mediterranean on the old trans-Asian Silk Road. The city's heyday lasted until 273, when Queen Zenobia, who claimed to be a descendant of Cleopatra and was famed for her beauty, learning and courage, led a rebellion against the Romans. The city's fortunes gradually declined following this rebellion until, by the 6th century, it was nothing more than a fortified outpost at the edge of the Roman Empire.

Majestic Palmyra, Syria, in the early morning sun

An extraordinary collection of uncannily well-preserved remains, most of which date from the city's early Roman period and have turned pink with age, lie scattered across the desert here. The original city's comprehensive outlines can still clearly be seen, from the main street to the agora (marketplace). Highlights include the enormous, striking Temple of Ba'al (or Bel), the smaller Temple of Nebo and a beautifully restored theatre, with its nine rows of seating. Bisecting the ancient city is the magnificent Great Colonnade – the remains of what was once the city's principal street – which is lined with dozens of columns standing in incongruous, antique splendour amid the endless barren desert.

Practical Information

Getting There Fly to Damascus, and then hire a car or jump on the bus from the airport to Palmyra.

When to Go Spring and autumn are the best times to visit – this way you avoid the scorching extremes of summer and the chilly winter nights.

Website www.syriagate.com/Syria/about/cities/Homs/palmyra.htm

SKARA BRAE

In a beautifully windswept location on the west coast of Orkney lies Skara Brae, Europe's most complete Neolithic village. The site comprises a group of ten dwellings that were occupied from 3100 to 2500 BC and remained undiscovered until 1850, when a violent storm tore away the mound of grass and soil that had grown over them. The houses, which were originally sunk into the ground and covered with turf, remain excellently preserved, and even retain some of their original "furniture" – beds, shelves, boxes and seats made out of stone slabs. The village even had its own elaborate drainage system, complete with primitive stone toilets in every dwelling, which can still be seen today.

Practical Information

Getting There Fly from the Scottish mainland to Kirkwall or catch a ferry to Stromness. The site is only a short trip from either of these towns by car, taxi or bicycle.

When to Go May or September. The weather is likely to be just as good as in the summer, but with far fewer visitors around.

Website www.orkneyjar.com/history/skarabrae

The Bronze Age village at Skara Brae, Orkney, Scotland

ABOVE Dozens of sightseers outside the Treasury (Al Khazneh) at Petra, Jordan

FORGET PETRA?

THE BUILD-UP Rising out of rose-red sandstone in a hidden valley is the city of Petra, Jordan's top attraction. The impressive site was built in the 3rd century BC by the Nabataeans, Arab traders who created an empire based on the control of the highly lucrative trade in frankincense. The city comprises tombs, temples, storerooms and stables cut out of the rock.

THE LETDOWN Firmly featuring on the itinerary of every traveller to the Middle East since the days of the Grand Tour, Petra is one of the most visited sites in the Middle East. The tourism village that has grown up around Petra now threatens to outsize the ancient city itself.

GOING ANYWAY? Though a trip to Petra is worthwhile at any time, try to visit in the off-season (outside the main European holidays), and avoid weekends and local school holidays above all. Arriving at the site early in the morning will also give you a head start on the coach parties.

LALIBELA
VS PETRA

Lalibela's extraordinary rock-hewn monuments challenge Jordan's Petra in number, artistic accomplishment and, above all, atmosphere

NEED TO KNOW

LOCATION Lalibela is 644 km (400 miles) north of Addis Ababa, in the Lasta Mountains

DATE OF CONSTRUCTION 12th and 13th centuries, according to locals

DAYTIME TERMPERATURES Jan: 14°C (57°F); Apr: 17°C (63°F); Jul: 15°C (59°F); Oct: 15°C (59°F)

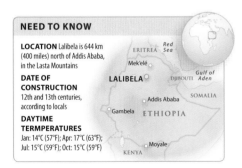

For over 500 years, travellers have raved about the rock-hewn churches of Lalibela. Francisco Alvares, a 16th-century Portuguese explorer and writer, described them as "edifices, the like of which – and so many – cannot be found anywhere else in the world". Petra's rock-carved monuments may be far better known, but Lalibela's are unusual in a number of ways, not least because so many are found in such a small area, with several seemingly freestanding and all unusually refined architecturally. Lalibela's masons, benefiting from 1,000 years of architectural know-how passed down through the generations since the days of the ancient Ethiopian Kingdom of Aksum, certainly knew what they were doing.

Lalibela was the capital of the Zagwe Dynasty during the 12th and 13th centuries, and was named after the king credited with the construction of the churches. One local legend has it that King Lalibela was exiled to Jerusalem by his usurping half-brother, and was inspired by the churches he saw there. Upon returning to claim his kingdom, he vowed to build a new holy city accessible to all Ethiopian people.

Unlike Petra, Lalibela remains a flourishing religious centre. Pilgrims flock from miles around to visit its dozen or so churches – and countless others in the surrounding area – or to attend one of its vibrant religious festivals. Hermits, clutching old rosaries and studying ancient parchment, continue to inhabit tiny holes in the rock, and robed priests, deacons and monks float down the dimly lit passageways that connect the churches, as they have done for centuries. From hidden crypts and grottoes drifts the sound of chanting, and in the deep, cool recesses of the interiors, the smell of incense and beeswax candles still pervades.

Much mystery still surrounds the rock-carved churches of Lalibela. Exactly how, when and by whom they were built remains unknown, though scholars believe it would have taken a workforce of some 40,000 to build them. Many Ethiopians believe that angels were partly responsible.

PRACTICAL INFORMATION

Getting There and Around
Flights go from Addis Ababa to Lalibela's airport, which is 23 km (14 miles) from the town and site. Local hotels and travel agencies offer airport transfer services. Buses link Lalibela with Woldia, the nearest large town, which is 120 km (75 miles) to the east.

Where to Eat
Little-developed Lalibela may not boast the richest of dining scenes, but there are a handful of restaurants here offering wholesome home cooking at affordable prices. Try Helen Hotel (tel +251 39 00 98), which also brews its own *tej* (the famous Lalibela honey mead). *Azmaris* – or Ethiopian minstrels – perform here regularly in the evenings.

Where to Stay
The Jerusalem Guest House (tel. +251 36 00 47), set in pleasant grounds, offers simple but comfortable rooms with balconies. The restaurant is designed like a *tukul* (traditional Ethiopian hut).

When to Go
It's worth timing your visit to coincide with one of Ethiopia's colourful religious festivals, the most famous of which – Timkat (Ethiopian Christmas) and Leddet (Epiphany) – occur in January. Otherwise, September boasts good weather and green scenery.

Budget per Day for Two
£30–50 depending on where you stay.

Website
http://whc.unesco.org/en/list/18

MAIN IMAGE A colourful Christian procession during Timkat (Ethiopian Christmas), Lalibela **BELOW (left to right)** Inside one of Lalibela's rock-hewn buildings; robed priest; aerial view of Lalibela's Church of Saint George

Sandstone houses, Mesa Verde National Park, USA

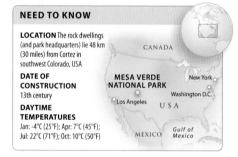

Lycian tombs in the cliffs above the Dalyan river, Turkey

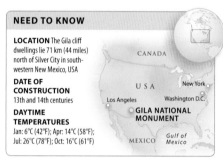

Inside one of the cliff dwellings at Gila National Monument, USA

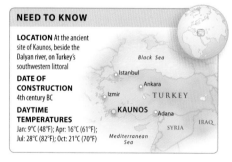

ROCK DWELLINGS OF MESA VERDE

NEED TO KNOW

LOCATION The rock dwellings (and park headquarters) lie 48 km (30 miles) from Cortez in southwest Colorado, USA

DATE OF CONSTRUCTION 13th century

DAYTIME TEMPERATURES Jan: -4°C (25°F); Apr: 7°C (45°F); Jul: 22°C (71°F); Oct: 10°C (50°F)

The well-preserved cliff dwellings of Mesa Verde National Park provide a precious and fascinating insight into the life and times of the "lost civilization" of the Ancient Puebloans (formerly known as the "Anasazi"), ancestors of modern-day Native American peoples in the southwest. The park and its natural cliff alcoves were inhabited from as early as AD 500, but it is thought that the 600 cliff homes here were not built until the 13th century. Though these remarkable stone villages must have been a mighty building project for the community, they were inhabited for less than 100 years. The people and rock dwellings of Mesa Verde remain shrouded in mystery.

Practical Information

Getting There and Around Cortez is linked to the rest of the USA by air and road. The area also offers car-rental companies, taxis and intercity bus services.

When to Go June and September are probably the best months to visit. July and August can be hot and thundery, and snow storms can occur from as early as October to as late as May.

Website www.nps.gov/meve/planyourvisit/visitcliffdwelling.htm

LYCIAN ROCK-CUT TOMBS, KAUNOS

NEED TO KNOW

LOCATION At the ancient site of Kaunos, beside the Dalyan river, on Turkey's southwestern littoral

DATE OF CONSTRUCTION 4th century BC

DAYTIME TEMPERATURES Jan: 9°C (48°F); Apr: 16°C (61°F); Jul: 28°C (82°F); Oct: 21°C (70°F)

Ancient Kaunos was founded in the 9th century BC by the Carians, who inhabited the Caria region of Anatolia. The city later formed part of the Kingdom of Lycia, which stretched between the bays of Antalya and Fethiye in modern-day Turkey. Famous for their form of government, which was the first example of democratic federalism in the world, the Lycians are today also known for the dozen or so distinctive and beautiful tombs they carved into the cliffs at Kaunos as part of their ancient tradition of ancestral worship.

Practical Information

Getting There and Around Dalyan, the closest town to the ruins, lies 25 km (16 miles) from Dalaman's international airport, and can be reached by taxi. The ruins are accessible either by foot or by boat from Dalyan.

When to Go Spring (Apr–May) and autumn (Sep–Oct) are the most pleasant times to visit, weather-wise.

Website www.lycianturkey.com/lycian_tombs.htm

GILA CLIFF DWELLINGS

NEED TO KNOW

LOCATION The Gila cliff dwellings lie 71 km (44 miles) north of Silver City in south-western New Mexico, USA

DATE OF CONSTRUCTION 13th and 14th centuries

DAYTIME TEMPERATURES Jan: 6°C (42°F); Apr: 14°C (58°F); Jul: 26°C (78°F); Oct: 16°C (61°F)

In the heart of the Gila wilderness of New Mexico is Gila National Monument, established in 1907 to preserve dozens of ancient cliff dwellings. The homes, which were built into caves in a narrow canyon, shed some light on the mysterious Mogollon people, whose distinct and important Native-American culture was endemic to southwestern New Mexico, western Texas, southeastern Arizona and northern Mexico. More than 103 historic buildings are located here, including an enormous dwelling with around 200 rooms. Other monolithic buildings to explore at the site include rock shelters and pit houses.

Practical Information

Getting There and Around There is no public transport to the ruins. The nearest major airports are found at Albuquerque, El Paso, Tucson and Phoenix, all of which are around 4 to 6 hours' drive away. Car rental is also available.

When to Go Spring (Apr–May) and autumn (Sep–Oct) are the most pleasant times to visit, weather-wise.

Website www.nps.gov/gicl

Close-up of a Buddha statue inside the Longmen Caves, China

Longmen Caves, Henan Province

NEED TO KNOW

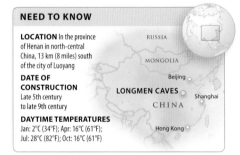

LOCATION In the province of Henan in north-central China, 13 km (8 miles) south of the city of Luoyang

DATE OF CONSTRUCTION Late 5th century to late 9th century

DAYTIME TEMPERATURES Jan: 2°C (34°F); Apr: 16°C (61°F); Jul: 28°C (82°F); Oct: 16°C (61°F)

Construction first began on the Longmen caves in AD 495, under the Northern Wei Dynasty, and spanned four Chinese dynasties and over 400 years. The site consists of over 1,300 grottoes and 400 pagodas, and spreads for a kilometre (half-a-mile) on both sides of the Yi river. Inside the caves are nearly 100,000 Buddhist statues of all shapes, styles and sizes. The smallest of these measures less than an inch and the largest, carved for the Empress Wu Zetian of the Tang Dynasty, is nearly 18 m (60 ft) high. The caves are considered an icon of Buddhist art, and one of the greatest religious, historical and cultural masterpieces of China.

Practical Information
Getting There and Around Luoyang is linked to some of China's major cities, including Beijing and Shanghai, by air, train and road. Taxis can transport you from Luoyang to the caves.

When to Go Spring (Apr–May) and autumn (Sep–Oct) have the best weather.

Website www.travelchinaguide.com/attraction/henan/luoyang /longmen.htm

Ladder at the entrance to a rock-hewn kiva, Bandelier National Monument, USA

Bandelier's Rock-cut Pueblos

NEED TO KNOW

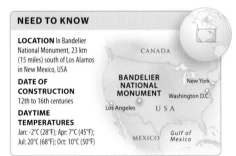

LOCATION In Bandelier National Monument, 23 km (15 miles) south of Los Alamos in New Mexico, USA

DATE OF CONSTRUCTION 12th to 16th centuries

DAYTIME TEMPERATURES Jan: -2°C (28°F); Apr: 7°C (45°F); Jul: 20°C (68°F); Oct: 10°C (50°F)

Set above the Pajarito Plateau amid mesas, canyons and chasms, Bandelier National Monument boasts a spectacular setting. The park comprises rock dwellings, kivas (circular ceremonial structures), rock paintings and carvings, and provides a rare glimpse into the lives of the Ancient Puebloan people of the southwest. Though the Puebloans mysteriously abandoned the site – probably due to changing climatic conditions – the ruins are very well preserved and many of them have been fully excavated. A well-signed, 1.6-km (1-mile) circular trail leads visitors past cliff houses, cave dwellings and communal stone structures.

Practical Information
Getting There and Around There are no bus or train services to Bandelier National Monument, but cars can be hired from Los Alamos, Albuquerque and Santa Fe. Albuquerque is the nearest commercial airport.

When to Go Spring (Apr–May) and autumn (Sep–Oct) are the most pleasant times to visit, weather-wise.

Website www.nps.gov/band

Kailasa Temple, Carpenter's Caves, India

Carpenter's Caves, Ellora

NEED TO KNOW

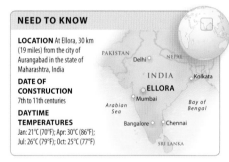

LOCATION At Ellora, 30 km (19 miles) from the city of Aurangabad in the state of Maharashtra, India

DATE OF CONSTRUCTION 7th to 11th centuries

DAYTIME TEMPERATURES Jan: 21°C (70°F); Apr: 30°C (86°F); Jul: 26°C (79°F); Oct: 25°C (77°F)

Ellora's famous "caves", which are actually a series of temples and monasteries carved into the side of the Charanadari Hills, represent the apogee of Indian rock-cut architecture. They are unique for their large size, architectural mastery, and above all, for representing, side by side, three of India's major religions: Hinduism, Buddhism and Jainism. Sited on an ancient trade route, the 34 monuments saw merchants, priests and pilgrims refresh themselves both physically and spiritually on their way to the ports of India's western littoral.

Practical Information
Getting There and Around Aurangabad is connected to some of India's major cities, including Delhi and Mumbai, by air, rail and road. Taxis to the site are available from nearby towns.

When to Go Plan your visit for the winter (Oct–Feb), when temperatures and humidity are lower.

Website www.indiaforvisitors.com/states/maharashtra/ellora.htm

ISLA DEL SOL
VS MACHU PICCHU

Where to go to see the birthplace of the fabled Inca? Not Machu Picchu, that's for sure.
Head instead for Bolivia's Isla del Sol, where this civilization first rose to greatness

NEED TO KNOW

LOCATION Isla del Sol is located on Lake Titicaca, which lies on the border of Bolivia and Peru in South America

VISITORS PER YEAR Fewer than 8,000

DAYTIME TEMPERATURES
Jan: 16°C (61°F); Apr: 12°C (54°F); Jul: 11°C (52°F); Oct: 15°C (59°F)

If you thought you needed to go to Machu Picchu to see the Inca civilization on its own terms, you're off by a few hundred miles and some centuries to boot! The birthplace of one of the world's most fabled societies is actually further southeast, on Isla del Sol (Island of the Sun) – the largest of the 41 islands located on what may be the world's most stunning body of water, Lake Titicaca. This lake was considered sacred by the Inca, and after one look at its indescribably blue waters, it's easy to

see why. Situated at nearly 3,200 m (10,500 ft) above sea level, the lake is so clear it is said that the original inhabitants believed that they could see the entrance to another world at the bottom. Small wonder most travellers don't make it to the island when the scenery around is this beautiful.

The tiny island itself is littered with remnants of the Inca. Nearly 200 ruins, most in pristine condition, attest to the presence of this mighty people. This is a harsh place and little has changed over the centuries. There are no roads, and the 5,000 or so inhabitants – many of them descendants of the first Inca – still cling to their centuries-old lifestyle. Anthropologists have suggested that many of the tiny fishing hamlets that dot the shore have remained virtually unchanged for over a thousand years.

According to legend, the Inca creator god, Viracocha, willed his two children, Manco Kapac and Mama Oclio, to come to life on the shores of the island. Titi Kharka (Puma Rock), on the northern end near the ancient town of Cha'llapampa,

commemorates their birthplace. The mysterious Chinkana labyrinth, possibly a training ground for Inca priests, is also nearby. Three sacred springs on the south coast still issue the same fresh water the earliest Inca used in their ceremonies, and are now regarded by the locals as youth-restoring founts. Exactly 206 steps from this triad of waters, the island's largest town, Yumani, descends directly into the lake. In the distance sits Pilcocaina, a stone sentinel whose purpose is shrouded in mystery.

Nearby, Isla de la Luna also looms large in Inca legend. Once the home of the goddess Mama Quila, it is also home to what may have been the first order of nuns on the continent. Here the Virgins of the Sun lived in seclusion, weaving tunics of alpaca and ministering to the Sun God.

Beneath the depths of the lake lie more mysteries: a recently discovered and still-unexplored temple (the natives don't want to disturb the lake) and, some say, the remnants of the lost Atlantis civilization. The full story of these people may never be known, but no other place on earth provides such a vivid insight into the origins of the great Inca as the atmospheric Isla del Sol.

FORGET MACHU PICCHU?

THE BUILD-UP There's no doubt that Machu Picchu holds its own as a premier tourist stop. Possibly South America's most-promoted destination, it has held the top spot for travellers eager to see the majesty of the Inca for several years.

THE LETDOWN The journey to Machu Picchu is not pleasant, and the entrance fee has risen to more than £25. Add to this the round-trip train fare to the village at the foot of the mountain (the most common means of transport from Cusco), the bus fare from here to the site, plus the food and water you'll need during the day, and you're well above £100 before you've even set foot in Machu Picchu...that is if you fall within the number of people allowed in daily.

GOING ANYWAY? The flood of tourists making this pilgrimage has made it essential that you book your stay months ahead. December through to March has fewer visitors, so your wait will be shorter in these months. Regardless, mornings always see fewer tourists at any time of the year.

ABOVE Crowds waiting to get onto the train from Cusco to Machu Picchu

PRACTICAL INFORMATION

Getting There and Around
The ideal way to reach Isla del Sol is to drive on the paved road from the capital, La Paz, to Copacabana, on Lake Titicaca's shores, and complete the trip by ferry. It's better to rent a car than take a bus, as there are many side trips worth taking.

Where to Eat
La Orilla (tel. +591 862 2267) in Copacabana serves both local and international food, along with the country's best trout.

Where to Stay
There are no formal overnight facilities on Isla de Sol. Instead, stay at the ecologically sensitive

Hotel Rosario del Lago (www.hotelrosario.com/lago) in Copacabana. The hotel can arrange visits to the island.

When to Go
The best time to visit is during the southern hemisphere's winter, Jun–Aug, when there is maximum sun and minimal rain.

Budget per Day for Two
Isla del Sol and its surroundings are fairly inexpensive. £100 is more than enough to cover costs and leave change.

Website
www.sacred-destinations.com/bolivia/lake-titicaca.htm

MAIN IMAGE Inca temple ruins on Isla del Sol, Lake Titicaca **BELOW (left to right)** Ruin of a sacrificial table; indigenous island family; stunning view of the deep crystalline waters of Lake Titicaca

ANCIENT AND HISTORICAL SIGHTS

Stone steps leading into the heart of the jungle at Ciudad Perdida in Colombia's Sierra Nevada

CIUDAD PERDIDA

NEED TO KNOW

LOCATION Ciudad Perdida is hidden in the Sierra Nevada inland from Santa Marta, northern Colombia

VISITORS PER YEAR Fewer than 3,000

DAYTIME TEMPERATURES Jan: 26°C (79°F); Apr: 28°C (82°F); Jul: 26°C (79°F); Oct: 23°C (73°F)

Older by centuries than Machu Picchu, South America's northernmost archaeological site has only recently reopened to the public after intermittent warfare in the region between the government and guerrilla fighters. Ciudad Perdida, whose origins are unknown, is made up of 169 intricate terraces carved into a mountain, a baffling maze of interconnecting roads and circular plazas with an entrance that can be reached only after climbing over 1,200 stone steps in the heart of the jungle. The gruelling but infinitely rewarding journey averages five days, and is one of the last of its kind in South America.

Practical Information

Getting There and Around Ciudad Perdida is a 20-km (12-mile) trek from a trail leading from the region of Mamey in Santa Marta. There are no roads or any other means of transport.

When to Go The best time to visit the Sierra Nevada region is Dec–Feb, when there is very little rainfall and less humidity.

Website www.hosteltrail.com/turcol

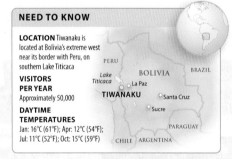

A cluster of visitors standing before the architectural ruins of a temple at Tiwanaku, Bolivia

TIWANAKU

NEED TO KNOW

LOCATION Tiwanaku is located at Bolivia's extreme west near its border with Peru, on southern Lake Titicaca

VISITORS PER YEAR Approximately 50,000

DAYTIME TEMPERATURES Jan: 16°C (61°F); Apr: 12°C (54°F); Jul: 11°C (52°F); Oct: 15°C (59°F)

Tiwanaku (often spelt Tiahuanaco or Tiahuanacu) is one of South America's most important archaeological sites and is the former home of a remarkable civilization by the same name. Many scholars think the remnants of this people later formed the mighty Inca empire. But to this day no one knows why the city – which, at its height 1,500 years ago, may have held as many as a million inhabitants – disappeared around AD 1000. Legends of powerful emperor-gods (also priests, for good measure), astronomers whose knowledge of the universe astounds scientists today and masters of long-vanished crafts abound. Their descendants, the Aymara, still live in the region, in villages scarcely changed over two millennia.

The ruins of Tiwanaku visible now are impressive reminders that it was indeed once the most powerful civilization in the western hemisphere. Giant stone reminders are everywhere: the Kalasasaya (standing stones) statues and temple with their still largely undeciphered motifs; the vestiges of the Akapana pyramid, possibly the second-largest ever built; the famous Puerta del Sol (Gate of the Sun), whose artistic form influenced a continent for centuries; the Templo Semisubterráneo (Sunken Temple) with its rows of enigmatic faces along its walls; and mysterious Pumapunku (The Door of the Puma), with its thousands of 200-ton blocks that this pre-Inca society somehow moved to a height of 4,000 m (13,120 ft) without leaving any trace of how they managed this feat. All these wonders are spread out over an area less than 5 km (3 miles) across, where your only companion will be intense silence, sometimes broken by the mournful winds of the Altiplano.

While the number of visitors arriving at Tiwanaku is steadily increasing, it is still a remote place. Many come for the spring equinox, to watch the sun rise exactly through the centre of the archway of the Gate of the Sun on the first day of spring. Tiwanaku is filled with astronomical and mathematical legacies, leading some to believe it is linked with ancient Egypt and Babylon, two other civilizations with advanced astronomical calendars. While no one knows for

Spectacular Inca ruins in the hills behind the market town of Pisac, Peru

Visitors descending the steep stairway leading from the top of Huayna Picchu mountain, Peru

ABOVE The intricately carved Puerta del Sol, or the Gate of the Sun, located in the Kalasasaya, Tiwanaku

sure, there is no doubt that the people who inhabited Tiwanaku were among the most scientifically advanced of any age.

Whether its many legends are true or not, Tiwanaku is as mysterious a place as it gets. Its evocative ruins, vanished civilization, incredible feats of engineering and astronomy, and surrounding stillness make it one of the most charmed places on the continent.

Practical Information

Getting There and Around A rental car is the best way to visit Tiwanaku and its environs, although there are several daily buses from La Paz that make the trip.

When to Go The ideal time for seeing the ruins and the surrounding region is Jun–Aug.

Website http://whc.unesco.org/en/list/567

HUAYNA PICCHU

NEED TO KNOW

LOCATION Huayna Picchu is situated in southeast Peru, northwest of Cusco, within the Machu Picchu site

VISITORS PER YEAR Fewer than 50,000

DAYTIME TEMPERATURES Jan: 10°C (50°F); Apr: 14°C (57°F); Jul: 14°C (57°F); Oct: 15°C (59°F)

At 2,720 m (8,920 ft), the cone-shaped pinnacle of Huayna Picchu is 360 m (1,180 ft) higher than Machu Picchu below, but receives far fewer visitors. The view of Machu Picchu is vastly superior from this summit, a village of Inca royalty and priests centuries ago. The climb is quite challenging and definitely not for the faint of heart. Steep stone steps suddenly turn into narrow passages overlooking ravines far below, and twist their way along slippery, narrow paths before abruptly ending at a wonderfully preserved Inca storehouse. Only 400 visitors a day are permitted; if you're one of the lucky few, you'll see why many claim Huayna Picchu as the highlight of their visit to Machu Picchu.

Practical Information

Getting There and Around The trail ascending Huayna Picchu begins near the Sacred Rock at the north side of the Machu Picchu site.

When to Go The best time to visit is Dec–Mar. You must sign in at Huayna Picchu by 1pm on the day of your visit to Machu Picchu.

Website www.incatrail-peru.com

PISAC

NEED TO KNOW

LOCATION Pisac lies on Peru's Urubamba river, just north of Cusco

VISITORS PER YEAR Fewer than 9,000

DAYTIME TEMPERATURES Jan: 10°C (50°F); Apr: 14°C (57°F); Jul: 14°C (57°F); Oct: 15°C (59°F)

The tranquil market town of Pisac takes little notice of the magnificent ruins in the hills behind it. For that matter, you'd be hard-pressed to recognize its historic link to the Inca Trail. Which is probably just as well for travellers who want to see near-intact remnants of a glorious Inca civilization. To this day, the hillside is lined with terraces constructed by the Inca and still in use. The ruins themselves are divided into four areas, of which Q'allaqasa (the citadel) and Intihuatana (the Temple of the Sun) are the best preserved. The views from Intihuatana of the Sacred Valley below are nothing short of amazing. Pisac is also something of a trekker's delight, with the area around ideal for spring and autumn hikes. Visitors arriving here look to combine low-impact trekking with cultural tourism – a niche the town fills perfectly.

Practical Information

Getting There and Around Pisac can be visited as part of a trek on the Inca Trail, only it is north of Cusco and can be easily reached by road. If you have a private vehicle, you're better off as there are other nearby sites worth exploring.

When to Go Dec–Mar, when there is little rain and lots of sunshine.

Website www.andeantravelweb.com/peru/destinations/cusco/pisac.html

BOROBUDUR
VS ANGKOR

Escape the crowded temples of Angkor and head to the equally spectacular, but far less touristy, Borobudur – one of the true wonders of the ancient Buddhist world

ABOVE Tourists climbing the stairs to the upper level of Angkor Wat, Cambodia

NEED TO KNOW

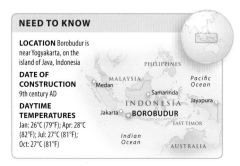

LOCATION Borobudur is near Yogyakarta, on the island of Java, Indonesia

DATE OF CONSTRUCTION
9th century AD

DAYTIME TEMPERATURES
Jan: 26°C (79°F); Apr: 28°C (82°F); Jul: 27°C (81°F); Oct: 27°C (81°F)

In the second half of the 20th century, the majestic Buddhist temples at Angkor in Cambodia formed one of Asia's most legendary – and most inaccessible – attractions. No longer. Angkor has established itself firmly in the mainstream of international tourism and draws hundreds of thousands of visitors every year. Those in search of unspoilt Buddhist monuments must now look elsewhere: to Burma, Sri Lanka or, for the greatest rewards, to the impressive stupa of Borobudur in central Java.

Borobudur was built in the form of a gigantic mandala – an architectural representation of the cosmos – and is one of the most spectacular religious monuments in Asia. It was modelled on Mount Meru, a legendary mountain in Buddhist, Jain and Hindu mythology, which is thought to be the centre of both the physical and spiritual universes. The building's statistics alone are staggering. An estimated 56,630 cubic metres (2 million cubic feet) of stone were used to build the ancient structure, which comprises nine levels holding 504 Buddha statues and with 2,672 bas-relief carvings. Unsurprisingly, Borobudur is often claimed to be the world's largest stupa and the biggest ancient monument in the southern hemisphere – only the great stupas of Sri Lanka, built at around the same time, come close.

For Buddhist pilgrims and non-Buddhist tourists alike, a visit here remains a powerfully uplifting experience. As you climb to the top of the monument, you'll pass through successively diminishing levels and along endless corridors embellished with wonderfully detailed scenes from Buddhist legend and cosmology. This upward journey, which leads you through three areas of Buddhist cosmology, mirrors the Buddhist journey towards enlightenment. You'll pass through *Kamadhat*, "the world of desire", where vivid carvings depicting human greed and passion line the walls. Next comes *Rupadhatu*, "the world of forms", which is decorated with scenes from the Buddha's life. And on the monument's sparsely decorated circular terraces, you'll find *Arupadhatu*, "the world of formlessness". As you emerge on Borobudur's uppermost level, which boasts 72 Buddha statues each encased in a miniature stupa, an unforgettable view across the tranquil rural heartlands of central Java and out towards a distant ring of hazy volcanoes will open up before your eyes. This is every bit as unforgettable a setting as Angkor's verdant jungles.

PRACTICAL INFORMATION

Getting There and Around
There are a limited number of direct international flights to Yogyakarta airport, so it's likely you'll have to fly into the city on a domestic service from the Indonesian capital, Jakarta, or Denpasar on Bali. Borobudur is about 40 km (25 miles) from Yogyakarta, from where you can hire a car, join a tour or catch a local bus to the ancient site.

Where to Eat
Yogyakarta is one of the best places in the country to eat top-notch Indonesian cuisine. Try the popular Omah Dhuwur restaurant (tel +62 274 374 952), which is a little way out of town, but worth the trek for its excellent array of local dishes and other international and Asian-fusion offerings.

Where to Stay
The romantic Dusun Jogja Village Inn (www.jvidusun.co.id) bills itself as Yogyakarta's first boutique hotel. Despite its central location, the hotel has a pleasantly rustic atmosphere and boasts accommodation in Javanese-style cottages. It also has a large pool in palm-filled grounds.

When to Go
Temperatures in Java are fairly constant all year round, though travel is generally more pleasant during the dry season, which is from May to September.

Budget per Day for Two
£50 a day will give you a decent hotel and private car hire with driver to the site.

Website
www.borobudurpark.com

FORGET ANGKOR?

THE BUILD-UP Angkor boasts some of the most jaw-dropping Buddhist monuments in Southeast Asia. The dozens of spectacular temples here are crowned by the peerless Angkor Wat – the site's largest monument – in a memorably atmospheric setting among gnarled jungles and glass-like paddy fields.

THE LETDOWN Unfortunately, there's no escaping the crowds here. The days when Angkor was a remote and challenging destination are sadly long gone. The temples are now firmly on the international sightseeing circuit, making it hard to appreciate their majestic architecture and profound religious significance in anything approaching peace and quiet.

GOING ANYWAY? Sunrise and sunset are the most magical hours at Angkor: not only do the monuments look their best at these times, but also the crowds are at their thinnest. Don't try to rush your trip here – the temples cover a vast area, so set aside three days or so for exploring the site. Make sure you visit some of the less-touristed outlying temples too.

MAIN IMAGE A misty dawn scene at Borobudur, Java
BELOW (left to right) Stone carvings at Borobudur; aerial view of the stupa; monks at Borobudur during the festival of Vesak (Buddha Day)

ANCIENT AND HISTORICAL SIGHTS

AYUTTHAYA

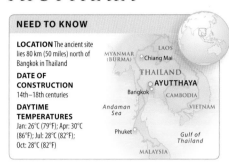

NEED TO KNOW

LOCATION The ancient site lies 80 km (50 miles) north of Bangkok in Thailand

DATE OF CONSTRUCTION
14th–18th centuries

DAYTIME TEMPERATURES
Jan: 26°C (79°F); Apr: 30°C (86°F); Jul: 28°C (82°F); Oct: 28°C (82°F)

The great city of Ayutthaya was founded in 1351 by King Ramathibodi I, who came here from the disease-ravaged city of Lopburi. It served as the Thai capital for over 400 years and boasted three royal palaces, hundreds of temples, 140 km (87 miles) of canals and a cosmopolitan population of a million people, including merchants from Portugal and samurai bodyguards from Japan. Ayutthaya's glory days ended abruptly in 1767, when it was sacked and destroyed by the Burmese, who left the ruins that we see today. These include several needle-sharp stupas, innumerable statues of Buddhas staring soulfully into space and many crumbling Buddhist temples, including Wat Phra Mahathat, known for its eerie stone Buddha's head smothered with overgrown tree roots.

Practical Information

Getting There Fly into Bangkok, from which point it's a short journey by train, bus, car or boat to Ayutthaya.

When to Go Visit from November to February, the coolest, driest months.

Website www.tourismthailand.org

Buddha's head encased in tangled tree roots at Wat Phra Mahathat, Ayutthaya, Thailand

ANURADHAPURA

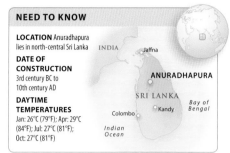

NEED TO KNOW

LOCATION Anuradhapura lies in north-central Sri Lanka

DATE OF CONSTRUCTION
3rd century BC to 10th century AD

DAYTIME TEMPERATURES
Jan: 26°C (79°F); Apr: 29°C (84°F); Jul: 27°C (81°F); Oct: 27°C (81°F)

The capital of ancient Sri Lanka for over 1,000 years, Anuradhapura was one of the greatest monastic cities the world has ever seen. In its heyday, it was the archetypal Buddhist theocracy; a miniature kingdom where divinely ordained kings ruled alongside a powerful Buddhist clergy, and where the boundaries between the secular and the religious remained hazy at best. The city had a population of some 10,000 monks and its monasteries were a powerhouse of Buddhist learning and theology, the influence of which spread to India, Burma, Thailand and beyond.

Anuradhapura fell into terminal decline following an Indian invasion in AD 993, but its ruins still paint a memorable picture of the large and sophisticated society that once flourished here. Pride of place goes to the city's succession of gargantuan stupas, including the Thuparama Dagoba, which is surrounded by narrow stone pillars, and the mighty Jetavanaramaya Dagoba,

Reclining Buddha statue in a temple at Anuradhapura, Sri Lanka

ABOVE Thuparama Dagoba and its pillars, Anuradhapura, Sri Lanka

which is almost 100 m (328 ft) high and was built using an estimated 90 million bricks. This is the second-largest man-made structure in the ancient world, surpassed only by the pyramids at Giza in Egypt. Be sure to follow the crowds of sarong-clad locals to the Sri Maha Bodhi, a 2,000-year-old sacred fig tree that was allegedly grown from a cutting of the tree in India where the Buddha himself gained enlightenment. This is thought to be the world's oldest human-planted tree, and attracts thousands of Buddhist pilgrims every year. Finally, take a trip to the ancient reservoirs and irrigation works that pepper the countryside near Anuradhapura and serve as an enduring reminder of the city's once-thriving agrarian society.

Practical Information

Getting There Take a flight straight to Colombo, and then travel by train, bus or car to Anuradhapura, which is 206 km (128 miles) away. The site is quite spread out and is most easily and enjoyably tackled on a bicycle.

When to Go The best time to visit Sri Lanka is from November to April, outside the main monsoon months, although Anuradhapura itself remains fairly dry all year round.

Website www.tourslanka.com/Anuradhapura.htm

HAMPI

NEED TO KNOW

LOCATION The ancient city of Hampi lies near Hospet in the Indian state of Karnataka

DATE OF CONSTRUCTION 14th–16th centuries

DAYTIME TEMPERATURES Jan: 21°C (70°F); Apr: 28°C (82°F); Jul: 24°C (75°F); Oct: 24°C (75°F)

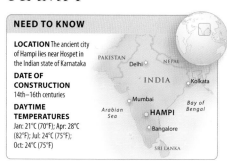

The great ruined city of Vijayanagar, more commonly known as Hampi, is all that survives of the capital of what was once the most powerful kingdom in central India, the Vijayanagara Empire. The city was largely destroyed in a siege in 1565, and today its ruins lie scattered over more than 20 km (12 miles) of countryside. The monuments range from the intricately carved Achyutharaya, Vitthala and Virupaksha temples to the former royal quarters, complete with its famous set of elephant stables – a lavish stone palace fit for a prince, let alone elephants. Surrounding the city is a surreal, beautiful landscape bisected by the meandering Tungabhadra river and studded with rocky hills and gigantic boulders said to have been tossed down by the armies of the Hindu god Hanuman in a superhuman show of strength.

Practical Information

Getting There The nearest major airport is at Bangalore, which receives both domestic and international flights. From here, there are regular trains to the city of Hospet, which is close to the ancient site.

When to Go The best time to visit is in the dry season (Oct–Mar).

Website www.karnataka.com/tourism/hampi

Stone chariot at Vitthala Temple, Hampi, India

NARA

NEED TO KNOW

LOCATION Nara lies 35 km (22 miles) south of Kyoto and 30 km (19 miles) east of Osaka, in Japan's Kansai region

DATE OF CONSTRUCTION 7th–8th centuries

DAYTIME TEMPERATURES Jan: 3°C (38°F); Apr: 13°C (56°F); Jul: 25°C (78°F); Oct: 16°C (61°F)

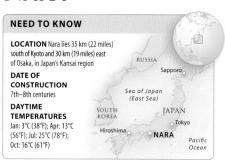

The capital of Japan from AD 710 to 794, when it was succeeded by Kyoto, the small city of Nara is located at the very centre of the country and is regarded as the birthplace of Japanese culture. It was during Nara's era of prosperity in the 7th and 8th centuries that Buddhism became firmly established in Japan, prompting the construction of a number of superb temples that survive to this day. Pre-eminent among these shrines is Tōdai-ji, with its spectacular, revered 15-m- (49-ft-) high bronze Buddha statue, and Hōryū-ji, which is the country's oldest Buddhist temple. Hōryū-ji also boasts a fascinating collection of religious statues and ancient artifacts, as well as the world's oldest surviving wooden building.

Practical Information

Getting There Fly into the international airport at either Kyoto or Osaka, from which points you can take a train, car or bus to Nara.

When to Go Visit during the pleasantly temperate spring and autumn months (Mar–May and Sep–Oct), in order to avoid the tropical heat of summer and the freezing temperatures of winter.

Website www.pref.nara.jp/english

Statue guarding the temple of Tōdai-ji, Nara, Japan

PAK OU CAVES

NEED TO KNOW

LOCATION Near the city of Luang Prabang, Laos

DATE OF CONSTRUCTION The caves have housed the statues for around 600 years

DAYTIME TEMPERATURES Jan: 19°C (66°F); Apr: 27°C (81°F); Jul: 27°C (81°F); Oct: 25°C (77°F)

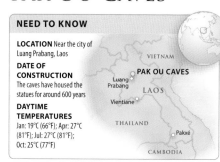

Honeycombing the limestone cliffs above the confluence of the Mekong and Nam Ou rivers, the atmospheric caves of Pak Ou are one of Southeast Asia's more unusual historic sights. The caves have been used for centuries as storehouses for damaged or outdated Buddha statues that have outlasted their practical use and can no longer be venerated in a working temple. Around 4,000 such statues now jostle for elbow room in Pak Ou's two main caves, combining spooky tourist appeal with an enduring religious pull that continues to draw Buddhist pilgrims from across Laos and further afield.

Practical Information

Getting There The caves are 25 km (15 miles) north of Luang Prabang. The best way to get to the Pak Ou Caves is on an hour-long boat trip from Luang Prabang, although they are also accessible by road.

When to Go Aim to visit in the cool months, from November to March.

Website www.laostravel.info/Cave/index.htm

Buddha statues assembled in the Pak Ou Caves, Laos

TIKAL
vs Chichén Itzá

If you like your Mayan sites tame and manageable, Mexico's Chichén Itzá fits the bill, but if you prefer your ruins living, breathing and vertigo-inducing, it has to be Tikal

ABOVE Tourists crowding around El Castillo, the largest pyramid at Chichén Itzá, Mexico

NEED TO KNOW

LOCATION Tikal National Park is northeast of Flores in the Petén region of northern Guatemala

VISITORS PER YEAR Around 215,000

DAYTIME TEMPERATURES
Jan: 28°C (82°F); Apr: 31°C (88°F); Jul: 30°C (86°F); Oct: 29°C (84°F)

(map showing TIKAL, Flores, BELIZE, MEXICO, GUATEMALA, Guatemala City, HONDURAS, EL SALVADOR, Pacific Ocean)

If Tikal were a volcano, it would be on perpetual amber alert. You tell yourself that nothing's going to happen while you're there, but then again, once *in situ* suddenly you aren't so sure. Perhaps it's the incessant chattering, rustling wildlife or the feeling that the on-site archaeologists are on the verge of unearthing something spectacular, but this ancient site has the air of a place about to rumble into action at any moment. Whereas better-known Chichén Itzá can feel a little like a historical theme park, Tikal's winding jungle pathways and remote location combine with its sheer scale to devastating hairs-on-the-back-of-your-neck effect.

At one time the epicentre of the Mayan civilization, the city of Tikal dominated Mesoamerica in the 6th century AD, during the region's late Classic period. The most impressive of Tikal's structures are its six huge step pyramids, known as Temples I–VI, some of which tower over 61 m (200 ft) above the humble tourist. Yet the majesty of Tikal is apparent wherever you are, whether you're craning your neck upwards, peering giddily downwards, or

ABOVE Temple I and the Plaza Mayor, Tikal

gazing across the Plaza Mayor at the temple tops rising above the rainforest canopy.

Much of Tikal remains unexcavated, unlike Chichén Itzá, which was fully cleared in the 1930s and is all there, catalogued and on a plate. Tikal leaves much more to the imagination – its ancient ruins are always keeping something back, whether shrouded in dawn mist or covered in tropical foliage. And when you've found yourself a spot in which to sit and take it all in, Tikal allows you to believe that if you closed your eyes and drifted into a daydream, you might open them again to find yourself in the midst of a Mayan ceremony; an ancient ball game, perhaps, or a shamanic ritual. It's almost as though the Maya had downed tools and left this, their largest city, hours before your arrival.

While Chichén Itzá provides the stage for Plácido Domingo concerts, Tikal has played host since the 1990s to sacred rituals and traditional festivals. During modern Mayan ceremonies, such as the anti-Columbus Day gathering in October, huge fires are lit in Plaza Mayor, and the spirits are recalled to this once-powerful citadel, which to this day, although ruined, is a very long way from being spoilt.

PRACTICAL INFORMATION

Getting There and Around
Visiting Tikal entails a 7-hour bus journey or a 45-minute flight from Guatemala City to Flores, which is in the steamy Petén area of northern Guatemala. Tikal is an hour's road journey from Flores.

Where to Eat
There is plenty of choice in Flores itself, where the cuisine tends to be international and more Tex-Mex than gourmet. Café Yaxha (www.cafeyaxha.com) has a decent menu as well as books and photos on Mayan culture.

Where to Stay
There are three hotels at Tikal itself, all of which are pricey and often booked out by groups. Avoid these and head to the picturesque island city of Flores,

from where it's a 20-minute boat trip across Lake Petén Itzá to the four-cabin Ni'tun Lodge (www.nitun.com), a charming, peaceful eco-retreat.

When to Go
Visit between December and February, when mornings and nights are cool. Avoid Easter and Christmas, which can get busy, and May to September, the peak time for rain and mosquitoes.

Budget per Day for Two
£150 including accommodation at Ni'tun Lodge, food and travel to and from Flores. Prices for Tikal tours vary considerably and are best booked locally.

Website
www.visitguatemala.com

FORGET CHICHÉN ITZÁ?

THE BUILD-UP Iconic Chichén Itzá was crowned one of the New Seven Wonders of the World in 2007 (Tikal didn't even make the final) and is undoubtedly one of the essential Mayan must-sees. The main temple of Kukulkán is particularly spectacular at the Equinox ceremonies of light and shadow.

THE LETDOWN Chichén Itzá is just too accessible from Cancún to maintain any sort of mystery. The site is on the receiving end of a long line of coaches morning and evening, so don't expect a "real deal" experience – even climbing the pyramids is now forbidden.

GOING ANYWAY? Make sure you stay overnight at one of the nearby hotels and arrive at the site at first light or in the late afternoon to beat the coachloads of tourists. As well as being crowded, it will be seriously hot around midday, so visiting at this time is best avoided.

MAIN IMAGE Visitors scaling the steps of Temple II, Tikal
BELOW (left to right) Tree roots growing around a ruin, Tikal; scarlet macaw in the nearby jungle; re-enactment of a Mayan ceremony, Tikal

4 MORE MAYAN SITES TO RIVAL CHICHÉN ITZÁ

BONAMPAK, CHIAPAS, MEXICO Size isn't everything and Bonampak doesn't win prizes for scale. It is, however, famous for its fine murals and frescoes, which offer fascinating and unique insights into the lives of the ancient Maya.

LAMANAI, ORANGE WALK DISTRICT, BELIZE A remote and only partly uncovered site, Lamanai isn't easy to get to, but that only adds to its romance. That and the fact that its name means "submerged crocodile" in Maya.

COPÁN, COPÁN DEPARTMENT, HONDURAS Experts love Copán for its remarkably well-preserved hieroglyphic stairway, elaborate sculptures and fine *stelae* (inscribed stone columns), as well as its wide plazas, underground tunnels and ball court.

EDZNÁ, YUCATÁN, MEXICO The ruins of Edzná are located deep in the rainforest, an hour south of Campeche. This relative newcomer was only rediscovered in the mid-20th century, so you might just have its five-floored pyramid to yourself.

KRAK DES CHEVALIERS
VS THE TOWER OF LONDON

The superb design and dramatic location of Syria's Krak des Chevaliers, the finest Crusader castle ever built, puts the Tower of London in the shade

NEED TO KNOW

LOCATION Krak des Chevaliers is in western Syria, about 180 km (112 miles) north of the capital, Damascus

ALTITUDE 750 m (2,500 ft) above sea level

DAYTIME TEMPERATURES
Jan: 12°C (54°F); Apr: 24°C (75°F); Jul: 36°C (97°F); Oct: 27°C (81°F)

"**It is the Camelot of your dreams** – the castle of every fairy tale." So said the 20th-century British travel writer H V Morton of the mighty Krak des Chevaliers, which sits majestically high above the rolling plains of western Syria. This monumental castle, built by Crusaders in the 12th century, has often been likened to a ship, its prow nosing out high above a fertile expanse of vineyards, olive groves, farms and villages. Think of a medieval castle in Europe and you might picture a showpiece fortress, carefully preserved and protected, with pristine stonework and neatly mowed lawns. And if that fortress is at the heart of a city – as the once-prominent Tower of London is – it is likely to be dwarfed by glass-and-steel office blocks. The cities these strongholds once dominated have now overpowered them. Yet in Syria, Krak des Chevaliers retains its rough-edged authenticity. Here, little

ABOVE Terrain around Krak des Chevaliers, Syria

quarter has been given to modern ideas of commercialization, and the impressive structure still stands aloof – a bleak, brooding presence redolent with the ghosts of past battles.

The castle was expertly positioned atop a rocky spur that dominates the Homs Gap, the only break in the long chain of mountains that runs parallel to the coast from southern Turkey into northern Israel. It thus dominated access routes between the Mediterranean coast and the Syrian interior, as well as the north-south passage between Damascus and Aleppo – lending it a strategic importance that remains as clear today as it did 900 years ago, unlike the Tower of London's once-imposing Thames-side location.

The name Krak des Chevaliers, a mixture of Arabic and French, means "Fortress of the Knights". In 1144, the local Crusader lord, Raymond II, Count of Tripoli, handed control of what was then a small, simple fortress to the Knights Hospitallers – a religious order that took on military duties in the Crusader realms (as did its contemporary, the Knights Templar). The knights expanded the castle and added a 3-m (9-ft) thick encircling outer wall studded with towers to create a virtually impregnable ring of defences, making it the Holy Land's largest and most sophisticated stronghold.

Today, you cross the moat and climb a dark, twisting passage through to the inner courtyard, which contains a beautiful Gothic cloister and grand hall, complete with its original vaulting. Explore the Crusader kitchens and storerooms, the austere 12th-century chapel, the ramparts and the Grand Master's apartments in the highest tower, which have elegant Gothic windows offering commanding views. You're likely to have the castle all to yourself.

Krak des Chevaliers was eventually taken in 1271 by the Mamluk Sultan Baybars. Around this time, Prince Edward of England was in the Holy Land as part of the Ninth Crusade and visited the castle. He returned home in 1272 and, as King Edward I, set about conquering Wales: the castles he built at Beaumaris, Caernarfon, Harlech and elsewhere – with their concentric rings of defences – were all modelled on the Syrian original.

FORGET THE TOWER OF LONDON?

THE BUILD-UP The Tower of London, which overlooks the River Thames in the centre of the city, is a spectacular example of medieval military architecture. It embodies many of London's most iconic images, from its resident ravens and famous "Beefeater" guards to the Crown Jewels.

THE LETDOWN This is one of the most popular attractions in Britain – more than two million people visit each year – so you can be sure you won't be alone when you go. Adding insult to injury, there's a hefty admission cost for both adults and children. Then there's the lack of historical context: in 2006, UNESCO warned that it might add the Tower to its "at risk" list, because of the encroachment of unsightly modern office blocks on all sides.

GOING ANYWAY? Avoid the summer peak season (Jun–Aug), when the crowds can be stifling. If you can, visit on weekdays and plan to arrive at 9am, when the Tower opens – but nonetheless be prepared to find yourself at the centre of a tourist maelstrom.

ABOVE The Tower of London surrounded by the high-rise office blocks of the city's financial district, UK

PRACTICAL INFORMATION

Getting There and Around
The nearest international airport to Krak des Chevaliers is at Damascus, the Syrian capital, from where buses and trains run north to the city of Homs. From here, "microbuses" (vans) run frequently to the castle.

Where to Eat
The popular Al-Kalaa restaurant (tel. +963 31 740 493) stands on the next hilltop along from Krak des Chevaliers. It's a simple place serving standard Syrian cuisine, including salads and grilled-meat kebabs, and has spectacular views of the castle.

Where to Stay
Within walking distance of the castle is the fine Al-Wadi Hotel (www.alwadihotel.com). Its attractive, Oriental-style guest rooms have a touch of class, and many have balconies with fabulous views of the castle silhouetted against the sky.

When to Go
The best seasons to visit Syria are spring (Mar–May) and autumn (Sep–Nov), when you'll find the surrounding hills carpeted with wild flowers and lush vegetation. Summer temperatures are scorching and winters can be chilly, with rain and often snow.

Budget per Day for Two
You could get by on as little as £40–50, though £100 is more realistic.

Website
www.syriatourism.org

MAIN IMAGE Magnificent Krak des Chevaliers, with wild flowers in the foreground **BELOW (left to right)** Ruined walls and archways inside the castle; interior of the vaulted Gothic cloister at Krak des Chevaliers

4 MORE MEDIEVAL FORTRESSES TO RIVAL THE TOWER OF LONDON

BEAUMARIS CASTLE, ANGLESEY, WALES Acclaimed as the finest concentric castle in Europe, this impressive fortress was built by King Edward I in 1295 on the island of Anglesey, off the Welsh coast, as part of his campaign to subdue the principality.

KARAK CASTLE, KARAK, JORDAN This splendid Crusader castle stands at a strategic crossroads in southern Jordan and occupies the highest point of a prominent hill. Extraordinarily, the modern town of Karak, which has grown up alongside the castle, is enclosed by the medieval walls that encircle the hilltop.

BEAUFORT CASTLE, NABATIEH, LEBANON Lebanon's finest Crusader castle dates from 1139. The stronghold has also played a part in modern warfare, with control of the ruins in recent decades passing between local militias and the Israeli army.

CHATEAU GAILLARD, EURE, FRANCE Built in 1197 under the orders of King Richard I (the Lionheart) – who was also duke of Normandy – this ruined hulk stands near Rouen, its mighty round tower dominating a curve in the Seine.

ABOVE Monumental figures of Buddha at Gal Vihara, carved from the rock cliff at Polonnaruwa, Sri Lanka
RIGHT Evocative walled town of Ait Benhaddou, Morocco, on the fringe of the Sahara

GAL VIHARA BUDDHAS, POLONNARUWA, SRI LANKA These four huge, exquisite figures of Buddha near the beautiful ancient city of Polonnaruwa were cut from a single granite cliff. They include a standing figure more than three times life-size and, twice bigger still, a Buddha in the reclining "lion posture" (*simhasana*) in which he attained his final nirvana. The two other Buddhas are seated. The figures, which remain unsurpassed in Sinhalese art, were commissioned by the rich and devout 12th-century King Parakramabahu, but nobody knows who it was that carved them.

AIT BENHADDOU, MOROCCO Looking like something out of a living bible, it is no surprise that Aït Benhaddou has featured as the backdrop in numerous historical films. This beautiful walled collection of ancient fortresses or kasbahs, which make up the *ksar*, seems to rise out of the red earth from another era. The town dates from the 16th century and it thrived on trade, being in a prime location on the caravan route between the Sahara and Marrakech. Today, with its earthen houses and decorative crenellated towers gradually eroded by the rain, it is inhabited by fewer than ten families.

MAIDEN CASTLE, DORSET, UK Just south of Dorchester lie the remains of the largest iron-age hill fort in Britain, a series of towering earthworks some 6 m (20 ft) high. Among the finds made here are skeletons of the men who fought in vain to defend it against Roman invasion in AD 43.

TEMPLE OF SETI I, ABYDOS, EGYPT Abydos was dedicated to the ruler of the Underworld and this temple, built under Seti I in the 13th century BC, was the burial site for all the pharaohs of the first dynasty. Its List of Kings – 76 cartouches carved into the walls – is especially fascinating.

CITADELLE LAFERRIERE, HAITI This dramatic fortress is perched like some deity's ship on top of a high mountain, with a sheer drop on three sides. Built for Henri Christophe, leader of the slave rebellion, it is said to be the largest citadel in the western hemisphere, its walls reaching 40 m (130 ft) high and 4 m (13 ft) thick. Some 20,000 workers are said to have died during its construction. It was designed to support the island community for up to a year, in case the country should ever come under siege by the French. The expected attack never came, however, and it remains a symbol of Haiti's independence.

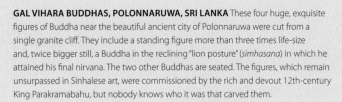

SERGIYEV POSAD, RUSSIA Sergiyev Posad is home to the Troitse-Sergiyeva Lavra monastery – spiritual centre of the Russian Orthodox Church and an artistic treasurehouse. This magical enclave of onion domes and churches was founded by St Sergius, Russia's patron saint, in the 14th century. Among its cathedrals is one added by Ivan the Terrible, and another decorated by icon painter Andrei Rublev.

PERSEPOLIS, IRAN This, the glory of ancient Persia, is the city of kings Darius and Xerxes, a metropolis which buzzed with traders from the 5th century BC. Set on an immense terrace, it was approached from the plains up shallow steps, leading to the monumental Gate of All Nations. The portal, carved with bulls' heads, has inscriptions in three languages urging travellers to respect each other's cultures.

MOUNTAIN RESORT, CHENGDE, CHINA This walled estate is the final flourish of imperial China, built by the emperors of the Qing Dynasty between 1703 and 1792 as an escape from the heat and intrigue of court life in Beijing. Inside, a replica of the Forbidden City stands among new palaces, temples and other buildings, all beautifully landscaped to mirror different facets of the country.

CUEVAS DE POMIER, SAN CRISTÓBAL, DOMINICAN REPUBLIC A collection of more than 50 interconnecting caves, the Cuevas de Pomier contain several thousand spectacular drawings, carvings and pictographs portraying human figures, birds, reptiles and religious rites. They were created some 2,000 years ago using charcoal and animal fat, and are principally the work of the Taíno people.

ERUM, OMAN Though little is visible but its foundations, to look on the remains of Erum is to look on a legend. The "City of 1,000 Pillars", which flourished between 3,000 BC and the 1st century AD, was discovered in the 1980s using satellite technology to track its whereabouts in the Rub' al-Khali Desert. Until then, it was thought to exist only in folk tales and ancient records, including the Qur'an.

PALENQUE, MEXICO Visitors who come upon this majestic Mayan city, emerging from the jungle canopy and watched over by toucans and howler monkeys, feel as if they are the first to set eyes on it. Though not the largest of its kind, the site has some impressive buildings. Of the few excavated, most notable are the Temple of Inscriptions, a palace with intriguing carvings, and an observatory.

ABOVE Imposing palatial structure of Potala Palace, historic home of the Dalai Lamas, situated high up on an outcrop above the Lhasa Valley, Tibet

POTALA PALACE, LHASA, TIBET A match for the dramatic mountains that surround it, the great Red Palace sits on top of the great White Palace, which in turn sits on top of Red Hill, 300 m (985 ft) above Lhasa. At 3,700 m (12,140 ft) above sea level, the whole rich, historic complex is also way above most of the rest of the world. Potala Palace was the home of the Dalai Lamas from 1649 to 1959, and it is a place of immensities, with 200,000 statues, 10,000 shrines and 1,000 rooms. The opening of the Qingzang railway from China in 2006 has brought many visitors, keen for an insight into this remote and spiritual place.

LEPTIS MAGNA, LIBYA On the Mediterranean coast, east of Tripoli, stand the most wonderful Roman remains in Africa. The city began life under the Phoenicians in the 10th century BC. It was incorporated into the Roman Empire in AD 43, and went on to flourish as a trading post, particularly after a native son, Septimius Severus, became emperor. Excavations have revealed large marbled baths, a beautiful theatre (see p22), a market place and a basilica as well as some of the finest figurative mosaic floors ever discovered. There are also some strikingly modern details, such as dado rails and skirting boards.

JERASH, JORDAN All the power and brilliance of Rome can be seen in these stupendous ruins. With beautifully preserved city walls, temples, baths and theatres, and a main street flanked with imposing pillars, some consider this to be the best Roman site outside Italy.

GLENDALOUGH, IRELAND In the heart of the Wicklow Mountains lies a glacial valley with two lakes, famous for its beauty and its "city of seven churches". Founded as a monastery in the 6th century, the site is noted for its distinctive tower, decorated crosses and 11th–12th-century churches.

TRÔO, LOIR-ET-CHER, FRANCE Carved into the white cliff above the Loir river, the pretty troglodyte village of Trôo (from *trou* – "hole") has provided safe lodging for centuries; its oldest dwellings date from the 12th century. They are still in demand as second homes for stylish Parisians.

JANTAR MANTAR OBSERVATORY, JAIPUR, INDIA From the pyramids of Egypt to the standing stones of Stonehenge and the Bighorn Medicine Wheel, man has always studied the heavens. This astronomical observatory in west central India, however, is a real curiosity. Jantar Mantar is the largest and best preserved of five similar ensembles built by Maharajah Jai Singh II between 1727 and 1734. It consists of a series of 16 stone and marble structures which act as instruments for measuring time and the movement of celestial bodies. They were designed on a large scale for greater accuracy, and its Great Sundial, the world's largest, can tell the time to within 2 seconds. Some of the instruments are still used to forecast how hot the summer months will be, as well as the expected duration and intensity of the monsoon.

METEORAS MONASTERIES, GREECE Fittingly named after *meteora*, Greek for "suspended in air", this collection of 16 monasteries hovers atop astonishing pillars of rock. Ropes and pulleys were used for supplies, and ladders could be pulled up in case of attack. Remote and unbreachable, they helped to keep alive the traditions of the Orthodox Church during the 500 years of Ottoman rule.

SACSAYHUAMAN, PERU Just outside the city of Cusco stands an Inca complex of huge walls and vast boulders, which fit as if nature had fashioned them. It consists of three tiered walls zigzagging towards a tower, interrupted by great doorways. Built in the 15th century over 70 years, with a labour force of 20,000, it is a masterly feat of Inca construction. Pizarro's forces took the fort in 1536 after weeks of seige.

TRE CASTELLI, BELLINZONA, SWITZERLAND Though small, Bellinzona is of strategic importance as a gateway to Italy, guarding the St Gotthard Pass and the Ticino valley. Fortified since the 1st century BC, it was the focus of a power struggle between its Italian occupants and Swiss neighbours in the 13th–15th centuries, resulting in an ensemble of three castles, joined by lofty city walls.

PAESTUM, CAMPAGNA, ITALY This is the most important ancient Greek site south of Naples. Paestum has three massive Doric temples in an excellent state of repair: the Basilica, or Temple of Hera (mid-6th century BC); the Temple of Neptune (5th century BC); and the Temple of Ceres, thought to date between its two neighbours. One of its finest treasures is the Tomb of the Diver.

PANCHA RATHAS, MAMALLAPURAM, INDIA The Pancha Rathas are five lovely 7th-century rock temples cut from single pink granite outcrops. Being attached to the earth they could not be consecrated, so they were never used for worship. With beams, lintels and "thatched" roofs in imitation of earlier, wooden examples, they influenced the design of Hindu temples over the following 1,000 years.

ABOVE Stunning mosaic decoration inside the Galla Placidia Mausoleum, Ravenna
RIGHT Stately Hatshepsut Temple rising out of the red Egyptian desert

GALLA PLACIDIA MAUSOLEUM, RAVENNA, ITALY Most visitors go to Ravenna to see the beautiful mosaics of the Basilica di San Vitale, unaware that just a few footsteps away, within the grounds of the church, lies a splendid cruciform mausoleum. The Mausoleum of Galla Placidia (AD 425–30) is decorated with some of the earliest and most fabulous mosaics in Western art. Heavenly blue covers the ceiling, and the Apostles are all represented, while over the door a Christ-figure sits in a country setting guarding his flock. The window panes are made of stone panels so thin that light seeps through them.

HATSHEPSUT TEMPLE, EGYPT Called "the sublime of sublimes" by the ancient Egyptians, the mortuary temple of Queen Hatshepsut (1479–58 BC) was the grandest in the whole of Thebes. Designed by Hatshepsut's architect, Senenmut, during the 18th Dynasty, the partly rock-hewn building rises theatrically from the valley of Deir el-Bahri in a series of colonnaded terraces, beneath the golden limestone curtain of rocks that separates the area from the Valley of the Kings. The temple contains exquisite decorative reliefs and murals, including scenes portraying the divine birth of the queen.

THE ARK, BUKHARA, UZBEKISTAN The fortress that lies at the heart of Bukhara dates back 2,000 years. It was the home of the emirs who ruled over this great city on the Silk Road. Inside its mud-brick walls lie beautiful mosques, former ceremonial rooms and the remains of the harem.

YONGHEGONG, BEIJING This beautiful 17th-century Buddhist temple, also known as the Lama Temple, comprises five main halls, elegant courtyards and stunning statuary. In the Pavilion of Ten Thousand Happinesses is a 25-m (80-ft) wooden Buddha carved from a single tree.

AXUM, ETHIOPIA Hidden in the remote mountains of northern Ethiopia lies Axum, a gem of the ancient world that was founded in the 1st century BC as the capital of the Axumite Empire. One of Ethiopia's holiest sites and the supposed home of the Queen of Sheba, Axum houses many different Islamic and Christian archaeological treasures, including giant 4th-century obelisks thought to be memorials of Abyssinian kings, and the alleged remains of the mystical Ark of the Covenant, in the church of St Mary of Zion. Despite intensive research, surprisingly little is known about this once-powerful commercial centre.

EPHESUS, TURKEY More than any other classical site, the ruined city of Ephesus shows the harmonious way in which Greek architecture segued into Roman. Paved marble streets lead to the Library of Celsus (AD 114–17) and the Hellenistic 25,000-seat amphitheatre, which was renovated by the Romans. Pause to imagine the ancient rattle of trade echoing around this enormous port.

NURAGHI, SARDINIA, ITALY Thousands of circular forts dating from 1500 BC are scattered around Sardinia, although this is probably a quarter of the number originally built. These unusual, truncated cones were renovated in Roman times, but little else is known about them. The largest is Su Nuraxi in Barùmini, which rises to three storeys. The structures have come to represent the mystical spirit of the island.

LABRANG MONASTERY, XIAHE, CHINA This extensive monastery is in a beautiful mountain setting by the Daxia river, high on the Tibetan plateau. Outside Tibet, it is the most important centre of the Yellow Hat Sect (Gelugpa), of which the Dalai Lama is leader. Inside are halls, learning institutes and sutras. Closed during the Cultural Revolution, it reopened in 1980, and is now home to around 2,000 monks.

LUGO'S ROMAN WALLS, SPAIN Western Europe's finest surviving Roman walls completely surround the town of Lugo. Set beside the Minho river in Galicia, northwest Spain, Lugo was important to the Romans because of its thermal waters and the vast deposits of gold that were found nearby. Walk around the top of the walls, which are 10-m (32-ft) high, passing its many gateways and towers on the way.

EL CARACOL, BELIZE The Sky Palace, soaring 42 m (140 ft) above the jungle floor, is just one of thousands of buildings identified in this ancient Mayan city. At its peak in the 7th century, El Caracol was twice the size of Belize City, which is today the capital. Its power was felt for miles around, and it frequently fought against, and defeated, its neighbouring city-states, including Tikal in Guatamala *(see pp40–41)*.

NEMRUT DAGI, TURKEY This tumble of temples and statuary on a tawny peak in the Anti-Taurus mountain range is the burial ground of King Antiochus I Theos, who ruled the Commagene kingdom between 64 and 38 BC. Antiochus built two temples and what is assumed to be his burial tumulus. To glorify his rule, he had three terraces carved into the hillside and adorned with statues of himself.

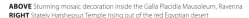

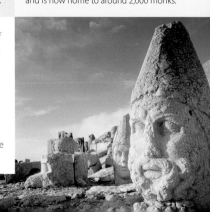

ABOVE Locals harvesting below Thikse Monastery, Leh
LEFT The majestic wooden Church of the Transfiguration, Kizhi

CHURCH OF THE TRANSFIGURATION, KIZHI, RUSSIA Kizhi, an island in Lake Onega in northwest Russia, is known for its extraordinary collection of wooden buildings, several of which are 18th-century, multi-domed churches. The ensemble has come together over a 250-year period, with many new additions since the 1950s. The highlight is the Church of the Transfiguration, built in 1714 out of pine wood. It has a string of onion domes and four apses, each of which faces a cardinal point. Wood is definitely the word here, and fishermen and museum staff live in the island's log-cabin villages.

THIKSE MONASTERY, LEH, INDIA Spectacular both from a distance and at close quarters, the 15th-century Thikse Monastery perches on top of a hillock high in the Himalayas. This is a *gompa*, a fortified monastery and education centre for followers of the Dalai Lama's Yellow Hat Sect (Gelugpa). The complex is a dozen storeys high, comprises many temples and is considered an architectural highlight of Ladakh – this region of India, which is sometimes called "little Tibet" after its neighbour. Inside the monastery is a fine collection of paintings and a huge golden Buddha. Monks and nuns still live here.

CHÂTEAU D'AZAY-LE-RIDEAU, LOIRE, FRANCE One of the earliest Renaissance châteaux, Azay, with its fairytale turrets and spires, displays the transition from the Gothic to the Renaissance style. It was built by Philippa Lesbahy, wife of Francois I's corrupt advisor Gilles Berthelot.

VISBY, SWEDEN Once a Viking trading post and later a member of the Hanseatic League of trading cities, Visby is a fascinating place to visit. Set against the rugged coastline and picturesque countryside of the island of Gotland, this once-thriving port retains the feel of a flourishing community. With the remains of several medieval churches, a harbour, a towered boundary wall and beautiful botanical gardens, this charming town – now a UNESCO World Heritage Site – certainly deserves the nickname "City of Roses and Ruins". Its lively Medieval Week celebrations in summer draw costumed revellers from far and wide.

PERGAMUM, TURKEY The acropolis in the great Hellenistic city of Pergamum sits atop a 300-m (985-ft) hill, and is one of the most dramatic sights in Turkey. Explore the 3rd-century-BC amphitheatre, the few pillars of the white-marble Trajan's Temple, and the remains of the library, which once housed 200,000 parchment scrolls. Much of the city's treasure is now in Berlin's Pergamonmuseum.

SKELLIG MICHAEL, KERRY, IRELAND A brutal asceticism accompanied the lives of early monks, who clung to life in remote and inhospitable places. The island of Skellig Michael, off the west coast of Ireland, is one such place. Here, near the island's craggy summit, early Christians built beehive-shaped stone huts that were inhabited by up to a dozen monks for some 600 years.

PLAIN OF JARS, XIENG KHOUANG, LAOS Legend has it that a race of giants lived on the Xieng Khouang plain of the Laos Highlands, which is no surprise given the huge stone pots that lie scattered across the landscape here. Nobody knows exactly how they were made, but it's believed the Mon-Khmer people made them in the 1st to 5th centuries AD, either for storage or as funerary urns.

STARI MOST, MOSTAR, BOSNIA AND HERZEGOVINA This handsome bridge over the Neretva river is one of the most potent symbols of the 1990s Balkan War. Stari Most (Old Bridge) was built in the 16th century to replace its Roman predecessor, and is an important example of Ottoman architecture. It was destroyed, along with much of the Old Town, in 1993, but was rebuilt in 2004.

PALAZZO DUCALE, URBINO, ITALY Though a little out of the way, this palace is a highlight on the Italian Renaissance trail. Built for the enlightened Duke Federico da Montefeltro, it displays the full power and splendour of 15th-century Italy. Its 250 rooms include a vast library. Today the building houses the Galleria Nazionale delle Marche, which has one of Italy's greatest collections of Renaissance art.

SALAMIS, CYPRUS Salamis was the main port and capital of Cyprus for 1,000 years, and although most of the excavated ruins are Roman, it was shaped by many empires. In the Middle Ages, it was largely covered by sand, which saved much of it from plunder and decay. The site includes a gymnasium, theatre and baths. Enjoy its spectacular shoreline location among mimosa and pines.

BASILICA CISTERN, ISTANBUL, TURKEY Built beneath the city's main square during the reign of Justinian in the 6th century AD, this sumptuous Byzantine water cistern contains marble columns and two giant heads of Medusa, one on its side and the other mysteriously, turned upside down. Visitors tread walkways to the mixed sounds of classical music and dripping water.

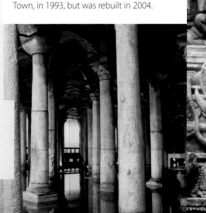

FESTIVALS AND PARTIES

Dazzling street parade in Port of Spain during Trinidad Carnival *(p53)*

SALVADOR CARNIVAL
VS RIO CARNIVAL

Officially the biggest street party on the planet, Salvador's awesome carnival offers greater participation and much more fun than its more famous counterpart in Rio

NEED TO KNOW

LOCATION The coastal city of Salvador is the capital of Brazil's Bahia province and the gateway to the beaches of the north

WHEN Salvador Carnival takes place in the week before Ash Wednesday

ORIGINS First held in the 16th century when the Portuguese came to Brazil

POPULATION Salvador: 6 million

Rio Carnival may have the edge when it comes to glitzy befeathered costumes, but Salvador is where the real party is. According to the *Guinness Book of World Records*, Salvador hosts the biggest street party on the planet, with more than two million revellers turning out each year for the festivities. During this anarchic week, almost 30 km (19 miles) of the city's streets are claimed by wild party-goers, costumed dancers and live bands playing every kind of music.

There are two procession circuits in the city for floats and *trio eléctricos* – trucks stacked high with massive sound systems and stages where live bands perform. Three more routes accommodate scores of vibrant *blocos* (parades). Campo Grande, the oldest of these, runs through the narrow streets of downtown Salvador, while the Ondina route keeps mainly to the beach areas. Pelourinho, Salvador Carnival's newest circuit, attracts highly rhythmic bands and performers dressed in lavish costumes. Countless parades and processions weave tirelessly along these routes during carnival, turning the city into a spectacular mosaic of colour and motion.

There are three ways to experience carnival as the locals do. You can pay to join a *bloco* or for access to a *camarote* (balcony) overlooking the processions, where there is usually entertainment, food and a busy bar. If you choose either of these options, you'll be given a free *abadá* (branded T-shirt), which gives you access to other exclusive areas. Alternatively, you can simply be out there on the streets with the partying masses, dancing, eating, drinking and generally soaking up the atmosphere.

Though Rio Carnival focuses on the admittedly splendid *samba* parade, Salvador offers much more

ABOVE Revellers partying around a *trio eléctrico*, Ondina circuit, Salvador

variety. A staggering 10,000 street parties blast their individual sounds across the city at all hours of the day and night, from beside amply stocked bars. And while most carnival celebrations around the world finish late on Shrove Tuesday, Salvador's knees-up continues well into Ash Wednesday, with the legendary *arrastão* (round-up), a parade that winds its way from Farol da Barra to Ondina for one final fling – a no-holds-barred party on the beach.

FORGET RIO CARNIVAL?

THE BUILD-UP Rio Carnival, which was so riotous it had to be banned in the 19th century, is today the most famous party on the planet. Performers charge the atmosphere with their outrageous costumes – mainly erotic variations on fancy dress – and the *samba* bands energize the crowded streets throughout the night.

THE LETDOWN Not only are prices in Rio extortionate during carnival, but worse still, if you're a visitor to the city it can be quite hard to participate in the action. It's one thing to be on the sidelines watching everyone parading, but quite another to be (as in Salvador) part of a full-on street party.

GOING ANYWAY? You'll have a great time if you choose to go to Rio Carnival, but do remember to leave your valuables in the hotel safe. Apart from that, talk to as many merrymakers as you can and enjoy the brilliant *samba*.

ABOVE Rows of spectators watching a magnificent *samba* school parade during Rio Carnival, Brazil

PRACTICAL INFORMATION

Getting There and Around
It's a 40-minute drive from Salvador International Airport to the city centre. Moving around within Salvador can be problematic once carnival is underway, because buses and taxis no longer run on most roads. The city centre, old port and Pelourinho neighbourhood are all within walking distance of each other. Barra neighbourhood, another popular place to stay, is slightly further away, but offers the added attractions of a lovely beach and trendy bars and cafés.

Where to Eat
In Pelhourinho, the Jardim das Delicias (tel. +55 71 322 1449) offers respite from the hectic carnival streets on its pleasant garden patio, where fine Brazilian and international cuisine is served, often to the soothing sounds of jazz bands and ballad singers.

Where to Stay
A good hotel, close to the carnival action in Salvador, is the Pousada Azul (www.pousadaazul.com.br), which boasts comfortable, spacious rooms and friendly service.

Daytime Temperature
30°C (86°F) during carnival.

Budget per Day for Two
From £140 for accommodation and food. Entering a *bloco* for the whole of carnival costs £120–50 per person, and a day's access to a *camarote* is £60 per person.

Website
www.salvadorcarnival.com

MAIN IMAGE Vibrantly clad participants in front of the Igreja e Convento de São Francisco, Salvador Carnival **BELOW (left to right)** Revellers in imaginative fancy dress; parade dancers; drummers in a procession

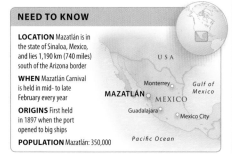

Reveller throwing confetti at Mazatlán Carnival, Mexico

MAZATLÁN CARNIVAL

NEED TO KNOW

LOCATION Mazatlán is in the state of Sinaloa, Mexico, and lies 1,190 km (740 miles) south of the Arizona border

WHEN Mazatlán Carnival is held in mid- to late February every year

ORIGINS First held in 1897 when the port opened to big ships

POPULATION Mazatlán: 350,000

Mazatlán's exuberant carnival celebrations, which run for five days before Ash Wednesday, draw up to 400,000 participants every year. The festivities take place on a 10-km (6-mile) stretch of the city's long ocean-side street, the Malecón. Seafood and cold beer fuel the party, where infectious rhythms from roving mariachi bands and *pachanga* (a type of Latin American music) ensembles mingle in the confetti-filled air. Mazatlán Carnival is less hectic than many other celebrations around the world, and is particularly popular with families. There are several idyllic beaches nearby, which offer party-goers a welcome break from the city's bustling streets.

Practical Information

Getting There and Around International flights go from Miami and Los Angeles to Mazatlán, and there are regional flights from Mexico City. Taxis are the best way to get around the city, which is spread out along 24 km (15 miles) of coastline.

Daytime Temperature 25°C (77°F) during carnival.

Website www.carnavalmazatlan.net/index-en.php

A line of dancers wearing extraordinary tasselled costumes during Ati-Atihan, the Philippines

ATI-ATIHAN

NEED TO KNOW

LOCATION The feast is held in Kalibo town on Panay Island, the Visayas island group, the Philippines

WHEN Ati-Atihan takes place in mid-January

ORIGINS First held in the 13th century as an indigenous festival and later influenced by the Spanish

POPULATION Kalibo: 62,000

Ati-Atihan, with its vibrant costumes and parades, is like carnival elsewhere in the world, only it's much wilder. Here, the frenzied masses take to the streets in such an unruly free-for-all that the world's best-known carnival celebrations seem quiet by comparison. The fortnight-long shindig has non-Christian roots, but these days it is held in honour of the Christ Child, Santo Niño, who was introduced to the islanders by the Spanish in the 19th century.

Ati-Atihan's distinguishing feature is that the revellers all paint their faces black. The story goes that in the 13th century, a band of roaming Malay tribesmen came to the island of Panay to escape from trouble in Borneo. Here they met the islanders, the Ati people, who gave them some land on which to live. Every year since then, the settlers have celebrated this act of generosity with an enormous feast, and by painting their faces black to look like the Ati people. The very name "Ati-Atihan" means "to be like an Ati". Many indigenous Ati people still live on the island and join in the festivities every year.

Although Ati-Atihan takes place over two weeks in January, it isn't until the last few days of the second week that the real party gets going. Before then, the focus is on religious processions, art fairs and theatre performances, although significant ritual and ceremony is also evident during the three final days of mayhem. On the first of these days, locals worship Santo Niño in the cathedral in a formal and spiritual build-up to the partying, which is accompanied by deafening tribal drumming. Parades of Catholic and indigenous pagan iconography and dancers in stunning tribal costumes fill the streets, where percussion from road-side bands forms an endless, mesmeric soundtrack to events. It's impossible not to want to join the dance.

At dawn the next day, a rosary procession and Mass are held before the cavorting on the streets gets under way again. And on the final day, the party reaches fever pitch when different

Thousands of carnival-goers crowd a bridge in Recife, Brazil

Girls in exotic fancy dress walking on stilts, Trinidad Carnival

ABOVE Tribal group covered in black paint, Ati-Atihan

tribal groups in lavish feather and leaf costumes take part in the parading competition. By this point in the proceedings, the party is so riotous that the impassioned revellers dance freely in and out of Kalibo Church. A torch-lit procession then leads everyone to Ati-Atihan's grand finale – an elaborate masquerade ball. It's easy to see why this colourful event has the motto *Hala Bira, Puera Pasma*, which means "Keep on going, no tiring".

Practical Information

Getting There and Around Getting to the Philippines is easy enough by international flight to either Manila or Cebu airports. From Cebu it's an easy ferry-boat ride to Kalibo and the festival island. Getting around Kalibo town during the festival will be mostly on foot (probably dancing!).

Daytime Temperature 28°C (82°F) during Ati-Atihan.

Website http://tourism-philippines.com/ati-atihan-experience/

OLINDA AND RECIFE CARNIVALS

NEED TO KNOW

LOCATION This double carnival extravaganza is based in Recife and nearby Olinda, on the northeast coast of Brazil

WHEN Both carnivals take place in mid- to late February, but sometimes run into March

ORIGINS First held by the Portuguese in the 16th century

POPULATION Olinda: 380,000; Recife 1.5 million

People come from far and wide to attend these two neighbouring carnivals, which each have their own distinctive character. Olinda Carnival, which is the third-largest in Brazil after Rio and Salvador, attracts scores of local artists who spend all year preparing for a procession of 560 unusually creative *blocos* (parades), including colourful transvestite dancing groups. Carnival in Recife, which is just 30 minutes away by bus, is a much smaller affair. At this event, once the Carnival King and Queen are crowned, the focus is on parades of *trio eléctricos* (trucks with stereos and stages for live bands). Both events boast constant music, flowing beer, fabulous costumes and atmospheric, thronging crowds.

Practical Information

Getting There and Around Unless you're already in northeast Brazil, it's best to fly directly to Recife International Airport. From here, Olinda is 30 minutes by taxi or bus, and Recife city centre is only a few minutes' drive.

Daytime Temperature 30°C (86°F) during carnival.

Website www.recifeguide.com/olinda/carnival.html

TRINIDAD CARNIVAL

NEED TO KNOW

LOCATION The best carnival events take place in the island's majestic colonial capital, Port of Spain

WHEN Carnival gets fully underway during the weekend before Ash Wednesday

ORIGINS First held in the late 18th century

POPULATION Port of Spain: 310,000

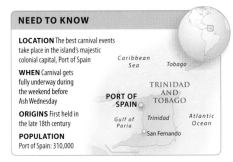

The island of Trinidad comes alive on the Friday prior to Lent as thousands of people gather on the streets and beaches to dance to calypso, watch glitzy parades and drink rum. In Port of Spain, the island's capital, traditional contests for the Carnival King and Queen get under way. Locals certainly live up to the city's motto – "Together we inspire, together we achieve" – as endless parades of trucks carrying bands and DJs blast steel and electric sounds across the city and out to sea. While the roots of the island's carnival celebrations are clearly West African, the "playing mas" (or masquerading processions) of the festival are also strongly influenced by the island's immigrant European, South American and Asian populations.

Practical Information

Getting There and Around Most visitors arrive in Trinidad by air to Piarco International Airport in Port of Spain. Buses are a reliable way of getting around the island, and taxis are cheap and abundant.

Daytime Temperature 24°C (75°F) during carnival.

Website www.tntisland.com

MAMAIA
VS IBIZA

With its prices up and new laws laid down, the erstwhile queen of clubs, Ibiza, is seeing its fans move on to Mamaia, the new party paradise on the Black Sea coast

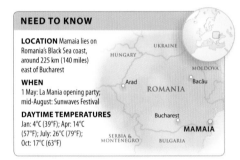

NEED TO KNOW

LOCATION Mamaia lies on Romania's Black Sea coast, around 225 km (140 miles) east of Bucharest

WHEN
1 May: La Mania opening party; mid-August: Sunwaves Festival

DAYTIME TEMPERATURES
Jan: 4°C (39°F); Apr: 14°C (57°F); July: 26°C (79°F); Oct: 17°C (63°F)

Once upon a time Ibiza was an island Aphrodite emerging from the cobalt wash of the Mediterranean, heaven sent to welcome young, wild, beautiful dancers from the world over. Unfortunately, not even goddesses are immune to the ravages of excessive late nights and vodka lemonade. Roofs crept over the open-air pleasure palaces; rules silenced the bongo pulse of full-moon parties and – worst of all – package holidays transformed an enchanted hideaway into an overpriced stop on the 18–30 tourist trail. A new generation of hedonists, craving the freedom and spontaneity that made Ibiza legendary, is increasingly heading east, to the Black Sea.

Sun-soaked, carefree clubbing may have been born in Ibiza, but Mamaia, in Romania, is where it has come to evolve. Set on the west coast of the Black Sea, Mamaia's striking beaches provide a dazzling backdrop to the throbbing beats of its super-clubs, La Mania and Kristal. Sea, sun and stunning bodies are obvious charms, but it is the heady mix of liberality, low prices and a ravenous appetite for cutting-edge electronic music that has the dance cognoscenti bobbing with glee.

Just 8 km (5 miles) long, Mamaia cleans up in the hedonism-per-square-metre stakes. In striking contrast to Ibiza, where the club scene is largely tourist-fuelled (the locals tend to prefer rock), Romania buzzes with passionate home-grown clubbers. Dance music is still fresh and exciting, and there is a real sense of freedom after years of dreary Communism. Every weekend, tailbacks

unfurl on the highway leading from Bucharest as thousands of workers flee the capital for a weekend of seaside debauchery.

DJs who are bored of Ibiza's chilly attitude towards partying are flocking to Mamaia. La Mania and Kristal attract A-listers such as M.A.N.D.Y., Loco Dice and Booka Shade, who can't get enough of its giddy atmosphere. Unlike the blasé clubbers in Ibiza, who linger around the bars before breaking any shapes, the fans here get on the dancefloor early and stay there till the last record plays.

Mamaia even has its own festival, Sunwaves, held in August. Headliners have included Danny Tenaglia, John Digweed, Ricardo Villalobos, Troy Pierce and local boys Rhadoo, Raresh and Pedro, all for the ticket price of £15. In most Ibiza clubs, you'd be lucky to get a drink for that. Even DJs such as Luciano, who made his name at Ibiza's famous after-hours club DC10, can't stop raving about Romania. Finally, the next generation of dance fans has found its own island in the sun.

PRACTICAL INFORMATION

Getting There and Around
Fly to Bucharest and travel by train (3–4 hrs), car or coach to Mamaia. Alternatively, fly to Budapest, in Hungary, from where you can catch a flight to Constanta Mihail Kogălniceanu International Airport, which is about 25 km (15 miles) from Mamaia and served by taxis and buses. Local bus routes 23E, 41 and 301 also run from Constanta to Mamaia.

Where to Eat
Romanian fare is rich in meat, fish and dairy – think cheese and cold cuts to start, followed by meat or fish stew. For a slap-up meal with a choice of local and international cuisine try the restaurant at the 4-star Iaki Hotel (www.iaki.ro).

Alternatively, for something budget-friendly but equally delicious, opt for one of the traditional eateries along the seafront, specializing in hearty grilled meats to refuel you for the night's adventures.

Where to Stay
The bright, cheerful beachfront Hotel Ambasador (www.hotel-ambasador.ro/index_eng.html) is a perfect place to recharge.

When to Go
July and August is peak season. Devoted clubbers arrive early for La Mania's 1 May opening party.

Budget per Day for Two
£120

Websites
www.romaniatourism.com/constanta.html

FORGET IBIZA?

THE BUILD-UP Centuries ago, the Phoenician inhabitants of Ibiza worshipped Bes, the god of dance. In the 1980s, sun-starved Brits caught on and flocked to the island, turning it into ground zero for electronic culture. Loyal fans claim Ibiza has the best clubs, the coolest DJs and the most gorgeous beaches in the world.

THE LETDOWN Package tourism and over-development have blighted Ibiza's rustic charm. San An's West End strip is a haven of tacky strip clubs and British theme pubs. Strict licensing laws have put an end to its famous after-party scene and open-air events have largely died out due to noise restrictions. The major clubs are eye-wateringly expensive.

GOING ANYWAY? Stay out of the main resorts, San An and Playa d'en Bossa. A villa or, at a push, an apartment in Ibiza Town makes a good base. Car-hire is cheap and wheels are vital for exploring the island's numerous beautiful beaches. Plan your club nights in advance to take advantage of cheaper pre-sale tickets. Visit in June or September; avoid August.

ABOVE Party-goers thronging a street in San Antonio, Ibiza

MAIN IMAGE La Mania, featuring many of the world's top DJs, is a hot spot for keen clubbers **BELOW (left to right)** Soaking up the sun at Mamaia beach; DJ Troy Pierce playing his set; Sunwaves Festival pulls in the crowds

4 MORE MUSICAL NIRVANAS TO RIVAL IBIZA

KAZANTIP FESTIVAL, POPOVKA, UKRAINE The ultimate hardcore, open-air dance festival. More than 100,000 revellers flock to the Crimean coast during the course of its six-week run from mid-July to August.

CAVO PARADISO, MYKONOS, GREECE This stunning club, with a capacity of 4,000, is built into a cliff high above the Mediterranean. The dancefloor is arranged around a swimming pool; sunrise from the terrace is the crowning glory.

CLUB AQUARIUS, ZAGREB, CROATIA Drawing the spotlight to the Adriatic coast, Club Aquarius is the sort of place where, according to the promoters, people don't bother booking hotels, they just stay to dance all day and night.

BENICASSIM, SPAIN Attracting artists as diverse as Justice, Gnarls Barkley, Tricky and Hot Chip, this awesomely eclectic four-day music festival is followed by Electrosplash – a free, week-long dance fest that keeps the beach party rocking.

MAIN IMAGE Festival musicians performing in vibrant costumes
BELOW (left to right) Musicians beating a rhythm in Essaouira; fishing boats in Essaouira harbour beside the ramparts of the medina

4 MORE WORLD MUSIC FESTIVALS TO RIVAL WOMAD

FESTIVAL IN THE DESERT, MALI Three days of Malian music, Touareg culture and sounds from around the world. This remote, hip and sandy concert takes place in Essakane each January.

RAJASTHAN INTERNATIONAL FOLK MUSIC FESTIVAL, INDIA This colourful celebration of regional roots music, dance and the performing arts is held every October at Jodphur's spectacular Meherangarh Fort.

RAINFOREST WORLD MUSIC FESTIVAL, SARAWAK, MALAYSIA Venues don't get more exotic than this. At this festival in the heart of Borneo, local artists perform surrounded by verdant jungle and exotic flowers, alongside internationally recognized names.

FESTIVAL OF WORLD SACRED MUSIC, MOROCCO Held amid the palaces and courtyards of the ancient city of Fez in June each year, this Sufi-oriented festival celebrates spiritual values, pluralism and cultural diversity.

GNAWA AND WORLD MUSIC FESTIVAL
VS WOMAD

Essaouira's atmospheric festival will immerse you in the music of an ancient African culture, while WOMAD just skims the surface

Since 1998, the music of Africa's funkiest, most mystical religious brotherhoods has been celebrated at the Gnawa and World Music Festival. Unlike Britain's WOMAD festival, where the range of music can seem overwhelming, this progressive event champions just one culture. Morocco's Gnawa people are descendants of sub-Saharan slaves who celebrate spirit possession through ritual music and dance. Today, the Gnawa are fêted by many for their spectacular religious performances that mix Islamic Sufism with African traditions.

The pentatonic (five-note) sounds of Gnawa music underpinning the festival in Essaouira have been adopted by many Western rock, blues and jazz musicians, including Jimi Hendrix and Cat Stevens who both stayed in the town in the 1960s. According to the Gnawa's *Maalem* elders, their music cannot survive without stretching its boundaries, so each year international musicians are invited to jam with them. The mix doesn't always work, but at what's been dubbed "the biggest jam session on the planet" the element of risk is all part of the excitement.

A typical jam might see Gnawa superstar *Maalem* Mahmoud Guinea strutting the stage in cowrie-shell-bedecked robes and wielding chords on his *guimbri* bass. Behind him a line of male musicians in colourful leather slippers dance like Cossacks and clack huge metal castanets shaped like egg poachers. A packed crowd – young men with girlfriends on their shoulders, children and parents, the odd tourist – cheer them on. The riffs loop over each other, echoing the singers' repeated chants to Allah in Arabic and the occasional word in West African Bambara.

ABOVE Crowds in the main square at the Gnawa Festival

Essaouira's neat size means that the nine festival stages are within easy walking distance of each other. Crowds of around 450,000 pack out the town's indoor acoustic concert venues and swarm around its large outdoor stages. Mainly Moroccan youths convulse to its late-night *lila* rituals – healing ceremonies in which spirits are invoked and trances entered into.

The Gnawa *Maalems* say that music frees the soul. And nowhere is that better exemplified than in Essaouira each June.

FORGET WOMAD?

THE BUILD-UP Pioneered by the musician Peter Gabriel and various others back in 1982, the UK's annual WOMAD Festival has become a byword for quality live music from all corners of the planet. World Music's mainstream acceptance is largely due to this family-friendly festival, treasured by many as an institution on the alternative festival scene and held in July at Wiltshire's Charlton Park.

THE LETDOWN WOMAD's wide-ranging programme can mean the choice of who to see is overwhelming. The feeling that you might be missing the next big thing is palpable; the phrase "you should have been there" widespread.

GOING ANYWAY? Don't just stand there watching, join in: WOMAD has an extensive programme of dance and percussion workshops that get you closer to the cultures concerned. Then unwind: there are yoga sessions, cookery classes and even a WOMAD spa. Can't put up a tent? There are tipis, yurts and people to do it for you.

ABOVE Festival-goers milling around among fluttering silk flags at WOMAD

ABOVE Colourful lanterns in Chinatown during Chinese New Year, Singapore

NEW YEAR, SINGAPORE VS NEW YEAR, HONG KONG

Chinese New Year in exotic, cosmopolitan Singapore outstrips the Hong Kong party

NEED TO KNOW

LOCATION Singapore is an island city-state situated 96 km (60 miles) north of the equator, at the tip of the Malaysian peninsula in Southeast Asia

WHEN Chinese New Year is in the first month of the Chinese lunar calendar (Jan–Feb)

VISITORS PER YEAR Around 1 million people – foreign and local – attend the event

MALAYSIA

Changi International Airport

SINGAPORE

CHINATOWN

Strait of Singapore

The most important event of the Chinese calendar is a breath of fresh air in Singapore, where revellers can join in the celebrations without being swallowed up by crowds, overwhelmed by long queues and hindered by city-wide restaurant and shop closings typical of the holiday in Hong Kong.

Leading up to the event, Singapore's Chinatown is a bustling hive of shoppers. The neighbourhood's picturesque narrow streets, lined with charming pre-war shophouses, are draped with red lanterns, twinkling lights and banners. Hawkers sell traditional Chinese goodies, such as Mandarin orange shrubs, peach blossoms, potted bamboo stalks, *bak kwa* (barbecued pork), pineapple tarts and decorations for the home. Late into the evening, visitors can watch lion dances and other music, dance and theatre performances in the streets.

Locals and tourists alike flock to Marina Bay to see in the New Year, which is welcomed with eye-popping fireworks over the water, set spectacularly against the city skyline. In Chinatown, a countdown party kicks off an all-night street rave that throbs with music from international DJs and live bands. All over the city, parties carry on until the wee hours.

A festival feel continues throughout the city well into the New Year with the 15-day Singapore River Hongbao, held in Esplanade Park. At this event, which is unique to Singapore, visitors are sprinkled with gold dust and confetti bearing lucky numbers, towering displays depict mythological figures from Chinese lore, and nightly performances feature acrobatics, traditional music and martial arts. Carnival rides run along the waterfront and nightly firework displays illuminate the city skyline. At the same time, the iconic riverside complex known as Esplanade – Theatres on the Bay hosts the Huayi Chinese Festival of the Arts, which stages visual arts performances that embody the spirit of Chinese culture.

The climax of Singapore's Chinese New Year, the Chingay Parade of DreamS is a night-time spectacle of enormous floats, 4,000 performers in glittering costumes and performances by guest troupes. The parade winds through historic downtown and is followed by an all-night dance party under the stars.

ABOVE Street dancers rehearsing for the Chingay Parade of DreamS

FORGET NEW YEAR IN HONG KONG?

THE BUILD-UP Hong Kong's festivities are the model for Chinese New Year celebrations in every Chinatown around the world. The Cathay Pacific International Chinese New Year Night Parade is undoubtedly the world's largest Chinese New Year parade, and Hong Kong's computer-controlled fireworks display over Victoria Harbour is certainly a stunner.

THE LETDOWN Hong Kong swells with visitors during this time, the majority of whom come from mainland China. The choke on services, hotel rooms and public transport is frustrating, and in recent years visitors have complained about unscrupulous touts seeking money for admission at events that are supposed to be free of charge. The party's famous parade has also been moved from its traditional downtown Hong Kong route to Tsim Sha Tsui in nearby Kowloon. While there's more breathing space for spectators here, many people complain that the spectacle has lost its authentic flavour.

GOING ANYWAY? Book early. Reserve your flights, hotel rooms and even meals well in advance, and be prepared for delays, queues and surcharges everywhere you go.

ABOVE Partying masses on the street during Hong Kong's Chinese New Year celebrations, China

PRACTICAL INFORMATION

Getting There and Around
Singapore's Changi International Airport is a 25-minute drive from the city centre. Taxis are the best way to travel to the city, and within the city they are a reliable option. Buses and a train system called the MRT are also easy to use.

Where to Eat
Singapore's dining scene is very diverse. During the festival, some restaurants close and others get fully booked, but there will always be something tempting open. Try Doc Cheng's at the Raffles Hotel (www.raffleshotel.com) for a taste of East meets West, Singapore-style.

Where to Stay
Request a room facing Marina Bay at the Ritz-Carlton, Millennia Singapore (www.ritzcarlton.com).

Daytime Temperature
30°C (86°F) at the time of Chinese New Year.

Budget per Day for Two
£320, including food, transport, accommodation and entrance fees.

Website
www.yoursingapore.com

ABOVE A jubilant, wine-drenched crowd after the Haro Wine Battle, Spain

HARO WINE BATTLE
VS LA TOMATINA

If you liked La Tomatina, you'll love the messy, vino-fuelled fiesta that is the Haro Wine Battle

> **NEED TO KNOW**
>
> **LOCATION** Haro Wine Battle takes place in the village of Riscos de Bilibio, which is 6 km (4 miles) north of Haro, in La Rioja in northern Spain
>
> **WHEN**
> The fun takes place on 29 June each year
>
> **VISITORS PER YEAR** 5,000

The **tomato-throwing festival** of La Tomatina seems to offer an unparalleled opportunity for a chaotic, bizarre adrenalin release – until you hear about Haro's Wine Battle, that is. This equally anarchic, lesser-known event, which takes place in northern Spain earlier in the summer and involves throwing red wine, not tomatoes, all over the place, certainly gives the over-hyped food fight a run for its money.

Unlike the Tomatina, which is a relatively recent invention with no tradition behind it, the Haro Wine Battle has a long and interesting history. According to a royal proclamation of 1290, the small wine-producing town of Haro had to reassert, annually, its right of possession over the vineyards where the battle now takes place, against a claim by the nearby town of Miranda del Ebro. The event began as a low-key bounds-beating ceremony that involved hoisting a flag and holding Mass, but in 1906, participants decided to liven proceedings up

by "baptizing" each other with wine. It wasn't long before this ritual became a messy wine battle that overshadowed the event's more sober formalities.

Today, the pattern of the battle is well established. It begins with a procession of some 5,000 people, wearing white T-shirts and clutching pieces of religious paraphernalia, including crucifixes and bibles, from Haro to the site of an isolated chapel, where a flag is hoisted and a Mass said. Then battle commences, and pristine T-shirts soon turn a deep shade of purple as over 20,000 litres of wine are thrown around. Anyone within range is a fair target – including photographers and television camera crews, whose equipment is covered in protective plastic – and any delivery system is permitted. Water pistols, *botas* (leather drinking bottles), plastic bottles and buckets are the common weapons of war, but experienced participants who really mean business come equipped with ultra-modern industrial crop-sprayers fed by tanks on their backs.

When supplies of ammunition have been exhausted, the berry-coloured crowd troops down the hill to breakfast on snails and red wine. They then return in procession to Haro, drying off in the sunshine on the way, where they continue the festivities with singing, dancing, fireworks, bullfights and, of course, more drinking.

ABOVE Locals harvesting grapes, Haro, Spain

FORGET LA TOMATINA?

THE BUILD-UP La Tomatina, the tomato-throwing free-for-all that is held in Buñol, near Valencia, every August, has become a magnet for revellers, who come dressed in disposable clothes and spend an exhilarating hour pelting each other with overripe fruit.

THE LETDOWN La Tomatina may have started as a local affair, but thanks to media hype it has become swamped by outsiders, including many foreigners. There is only so much room in the narrow streets of town, and not everyone gets their hands on the tomatoes before they've been reduced to pulp by repeated throwing. Surprisingly, tomatoes can be very painful projectiles and some people in the throng can get vicious.

GOING ANYWAY? The event takes place on the morning of the last Wednesday in August. Before you turn up, make sure you have memorized the rules: don't take bottles or other potentially dangerous objects with you; don't tear anyone else's T-shirt; squash every tomato before you throw it, so it isn't too hard; don't get in the way of the tomato-bearing lorries; and stop throwing when you hear the signal to end the fight.

ABOVE Revellers in a vat of squashed tomatoes, La Tomatina, Buñol, Spain

> **PRACTICAL INFORMATION**
>
> **Getting There and Around**
> The nearest international airports to Haro are at Vitoria, 44 km (27 miles) to the northeast, and Bilbao, 91 km (57 miles) to the north. Logroño, 42 km (26 miles) to the southeast, has a domestic airport. Haro is just off the A68 motorway, and has bus and rail connections with Bilbao, Zaragoza and Barcelona.
>
> **Where to Eat**
> Riojan cuisine is very varied and makes great use of fresh fruit and vegetables. A good place to eat is La Cueva de Doña Isabela
>
> (www.lacuevadedonaisabela.com), which is in a restored 17th-century building.
>
> **Where to Stay**
> Stay at the charming Los Agustinos in Haro (www.hotellosagustinos.es).
>
> **Daytime Temperature**
> 27°C (81°F) in late June.
>
> **Budget per Day for Two**
> £200 including food, transport and accommodation.
>
> **Website**
> www.haro.org/ingles/turismo1.htm

ESALA PERAHERA, SRI LANKA
VS ST PATRICK'S DAY, NYC

New York's St Patrick's Day parade is one of the biggest, but for a memorable procession, head to Sri Lanka's Esala Perahera, a showpiece of dancing, drumming and elephants

NEED TO KNOW

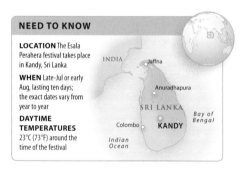

LOCATION The Esala Perahera festival takes place in Kandy, Sri Lanka

WHEN Late-Jul or early Aug, lasting ten days; the exact dates vary from year to year

DAYTIME TEMPERATURES 23°C (73°F) around the time of the festival

Religious processions of one kind or another are a worldwide phenomenon, celebrated by Christians, Muslims, Hindus and Buddhists alike in countries spanning continents, from Japan to Brazil. St Patrick's Day in New York City is one of the biggest and most popular, first celebrated in 1762 and now attracting vast crowds, who come to ogle the marching bagpipers, firemen, policemen and members of assorted Hibernian societies. Everyone puts on green for the day and drinks a bit too much Guinness. But although it's a great party, its religious origins have got lost over the years, and as a spectacle it has become relatively forgettable.

For a truly memorable religious procession, head for the flamboyant Esala Perahera festival at

ABOVE Dalada Maligawa, the Temple of the Tooth at Kandy

Kandy in Sri Lanka instead. Dating back to the 4th century AD, the festival celebrates the Tooth Relic, one of Buddhism's most venerated objects. Said to be a tooth from the mouth of the Buddha himself, it was rescued from his funeral pyre in north India and eventually brought to Sri Lanka in the 4th century AD. The Tooth Relic now resides in the Temple of the Tooth in Kandy. Once a year, for ten days during the lunar month of Esala (late July/ early August), the tooth (in recent years, a replica) is taken in a procession from various starting points around the streets of Kandy, while thousands of spectators congregate from across Sri Lanka and many foreign lands to watch.

The parade is one of Asia's great visual spectacles and starts at night. Soon after darkness falls, a deafening cannon shot announces its start. First, torch-bearers walk slowly through the streets, cracking whips to ensure silence and chase away evil spirits. Then the procession hoves into view. Hundreds of drummers appear, pounding away at their instruments and filling the streets with deafening rhythms, while acrobatic dancers dressed in elaborate traditional costumes turn and spin around them. They are followed by the elephants, brightly caparisoned and decorated with miniature lights, accompanied by flag-waving retainers, stilt-walking acrobats and bigwigs dressed up as kings and nobles in 18th-century Kandyan attire. The biggest cheer is reserved for the mighty Maligawa Tusker. The biggest and most brilliantly dressed of the 100-plus elephants on view, this splendid male elephant is entrusted with carrying the replica of the Tooth itself. The enormous procession continues for around 2 hours, parading three times around the streets, while dancers, drummers and acrobats work themselves up to ever greater levels of virtuosity. A second cannon shot signals the end – at least until the entire spectacle resumes again after darkness the following night.

DAY IN NEW YORK?

THE BUILD-UP New York's St Patrick's Day is one of the world's most famous saint's day festivals, first celebrated in 1762 by Irish soldiers in the British Army and held every year since. The festival attracts huge crowds of enthusiastic participants and spectators, after which seemingly the entire city retires to the nearest pub to celebrate the festivities in an atmosphere of cheerful bonhomie.

THE LETDOWN St Patrick's Day in New York is the expression of everything Irish – at least if by "Irish" you mean green beer, fake leprechauns and giant styrofoam shamrocks. For many, the saint's day in New York is now less a genuine celebration of Celtic culture and the Catholic faith than a send-up of Irishry and its stereotypes, accompanied by rampant commercialism and vast crowds of tanked-up revellers.

GOING ANYWAY? The best places to watch the parade are towards the north end of the route, away from the crowds that gather on the sidewalks below 59th Street. Try sitting at the top of the steps outside the Metropolitan Museum of Art for a great view, or catching a close-up glimpse of the marchers as the parade turns east along 86th Street.

ABOVE Revellers garbed in green, cheering from the sidelines as the St Patrick's Day parade marches up Fifth Avenue

PRACTICAL INFORMATION

Getting There and Around
The nearest airport is at Colombo, around 3 hours by road or rail from Kandy.

Where to Eat
There is a dearth of great places to dine in Kandy. However, Devon's and The Pub, in the city centre on Dalada Vidiya are both passable options. Alternatively, try Sri Rams on Colombo Street for cheap South Indian food.

Where to Stay
Helga's Folly (www.helgasfolly. com) is one of Sri Lanka's quirkiest and most colourful places to stay. The atmospheric hotel is set high above the town in a wackily decorated house, complete with weird and wonderful décor and artworks – from period photographs and fashion magazine cut-outs to wax-encrusted candelabras.

Budget per Day for Two
Around £100, including accommodation and dining at the hotels and restaurants recommended.

Websites
www.daladamaligawa.org

MAIN IMAGE A resplendent elephant decked out in lights parading through the streets BELOW (left to right) Drummers followed by the Maligawa Tusker; costumed children; performers at Esala Perahera

3 MORE FESTIVALS TO RIVAL ST PATRICK'S DAY, NYC

ROMERIA DEL ROCIO, ANDALUCIA, SPAIN Throughout Pentecost weekend, people from all over Spain converge on the shrine of Nuestra Señora del Rocío (the "Virgin of the Dew") on the edge of the Doñana National Park. It is a pilgrimage of colourful celebration well worth seeing.

RATH YATRA (CHARIOT FESTIVAL), PURI, INDIA Puri, in the Indian state of Orissa, is home to one of the most extraordinary religious processions every June or July, when the huge chariot of Lord Jagannath is dragged around the streets through impassioned crowds. To be crushed to death beneath Jagannath's chariot is considered particularly auspicious.

CIRIO DE NAZARÉ, BELÉM, BRAZIL Brazil's second-largest street party after Rio Carnival, Cirio de Nazaré honours the city of Belém's Virgin – Nossa Senhora de Nazaré. After a very solemn procession, the merriment begins, with much drinking and dancing to be had. Held on the second Sunday in October.

MAIN IMAGE Façade of The Famous Spiegeltent **BELOW (left to right)**
Opening night celebrations on Federation Square; indigenous musician
Ruby Hunter; Lucy Guerin Dance Company in performance

MELBOURNE ARTS FESTIVAL
VS THE EDINBURGH FRINGE FESTIVAL

The Melbourne International Arts Festival can rival the artistic quality and cultural variety of the Edinburgh Fringe Festival – but without the crowds or the struggle for top tickets

NEED TO KNOW

LOCATION Melbourne is on Australia's southeast coast, 1,040 km (650 miles) from the national capital, Canberra

WHEN The festival runs for 17 days every October

VISITORS PER YEAR Around 475,000

DAYTIME TEMPERATURE 19°C (67°F) in October

The Melbourne International Arts Festival is Australia's foremost celebration of global performing and visual arts. Established in 1986 as a sister festival to the Festival dei Due Mondi in Spoleto, Italy *(see pp268–9)*, and the Spoleto Festival USA, in Charleston, South Carolina (whose "two worlds" are those of European and American culture), the festival was first known as the Spoleto Festival Melbourne but took on its current name in 2003. Today, it is renowned for premiering and promoting some of the best national and international artistes and

companies. Unlike the sprawling, all-embracing Edinburgh Fringe, with its hit-and-miss aesthetic, everything here – no matter how avant-garde or experimental – is staged on the merit of its quality.

The Melbourne Festival offers its visitors a multicultural smorgasbord of dance, theatre, opera, music, visual arts, multimedia and outdoor events. Each year boasts around 60 to 80 events held in a host of inner-city venues, including the flagship Arts Centre, home to the Playhouse and State Theatres, nestled next to the Yarra River and topped by Melbourne's now-iconic spire; The Famous Spiegeltent, a European Mirror Tent billed as "the ultimate cabaret and music salon", which is pitched in the Arts Centre forecourt for the duration; and the National Gallery of Victoria, with its striking "water wall" and stained-glass ceiling.

Federation Square acts as the central point of the festivities, and the opening and closing parties are held in this colourful open-plan space. Both events celebrate the artists, the audiences and the multicultural city of Melbourne itself. Melburnians have long prided themselves on being Australia's

cultural ambassadors: the accent is considered more refined; the main thoroughfare, Collins Street, has a leafy "Paris End"; and a plethora of theatres and galleries ensures a healthy arts diet all year. The Melbourne Festival boosts this much-vaunted reputation with 17 days of ticketed and free events, most of them programmed by a high-profile artistic director on a three- or four-year contract.

Previous programmes have included recitals from the classical Schönberg Ensemble collective; performances by the Merce Cunningham Dance Company; a photography exhibition and concert by the "Godmother of Punk", artist and musician Patti Smith, as well as a collaborative event with the composer Philip Glass; and a performance by the all-star indigenous Australian collective, the Black Arm Band. As a background to the live shows, an *In Conversation* discussion series offers insights into the thoughts of many extraordinary artistes. There are also workshops in dance, theatre and music, lectures and school and family events. With entertainment for night owls at the Beck's Bar, Artist Bar and The Famous Spiegeltent, the Melbourne Festival is as inclusive as it is inspiring.

FORGET "THE FRINGE"?

THE BUILD-UP The Edinburgh Fringe Festival is officially the largest arts festival in the world. For three hectic weeks each August, "The Fringe", as it is known, encompasses over 30,000 performances by hundreds of groups, spanning theatre, stand-up, music, dance and children's entertainment in around 250 venues.

THE LETDOWN Huge crowds mill along Edinburgh's Royal Mile to watch street performers, buy tickets from the Fringe Shop and amass flyers for shows. Well-reviewed shows sell out very early, leaving a choice of less-than-satisfactory alternatives: with no selection and approval process, quality varies widely.

GOING ANYWAY? Take time out to relax on a café terrace, stroll along the Water of Leith Walkway or visit the city's spectacular castle. On the second Sunday in August, head to the large green expanse of the Meadows for the carnivalesque Fringe Sunday, a free showcase of events.

ABOVE Crowds thronging the streets of Edinburgh city centre during The Fringe Festival

PRACTICAL INFORMATION

Getting There and Around
Most major international airlines fly to Melbourne's Tullamarine Airport, 22 km (14 miles) from the city centre. Take a taxi or the 24-hour Skybus into Melbourne. The city centre is a neat grid on the Yarra River, compact enough to be covered on foot, but with good public transport too.

Where to Eat
For exceptional tapas visit MoVida (www.movida.com.au); revisit the French classics at Bistro Guillaume (www.bistroguillaume.com.au); or indulge in some spectacular haute cuisine at Vue de Monde (www.vuedemonde.com.au).

For modern Australian food, Rockpool Bar & Grill is hard to beat (www.rockpool.com.au).

Where to Stay
The Grand Hyatt is on stylish Collins St (www.melbourne.grand.hyatt.com); the central, boutique-style Hotel Lindrum has a club-like ambience (www.hotellindrum.com.au); Crown Promenade on lively Southbank is smart and affordable (www.crownpromenade.com.au).

Budget per Day for Two
£180, including accommodation, meals and public transport.

Website
www.melbournefestival.com.au

Dancers performing at Palais des Papes during the Avignon Festival

AVIGNON FESTIVAL

NEED TO KNOW

LOCATION Avignon is 90 km (55 miles) northwest of Marseille and 600 km (370 miles) southeast of Paris

WHEN The festival takes place over three weeks in July

VISITORS PER YEAR Around 100,000

DAYTIME TEMPERATURE 25°C (77°F) in July

Founded in 1947 by respected theatre director Jean Vilar, the Festival d'Avignon is an enormous celebration of the arts and the oldest extant festival in France. With its handsome medieval architecture and massive ramparts, the pretty town of Avignon provides a unique setting for the event, which represents all aspects of culture, from theatre and ballet to the latest in dance, music, cinema and opera. The floodlit inner courtyard of the historic Palais des Papes, one of the most important Gothic buildings in Europe, plays host to many productions during the three-week period, though there are plenty of other venues around town, including the charming cobbled streets.

Practical Information

Getting There and Around There are regular flights from Paris to Aéroport Avignon-Caumont, located 8 km (5 miles) southeast of Avignon. Taxis and buses run regularly from here to the centre. There are also TGV trains to Avignon from Paris, Marseille and Arles. Avignon itself has an extensive bus network, with reduced-price tickets on some lines during the festival.

Website www.festival-avignon.com

Literary discussion taking place inside the Teatro Heredia, Cartagena

HAY FESTIVAL CARTAGENA

NEED TO KNOW

LOCATION Cartagena is a large seaport on the northern coast of Colombia, 660 km (410 miles) northwest of the capital, Bogotá

WHEN The four-day festival takes place over last weekend in January

VISITORS PER YEAR Around 28,000

DAYTIME TEMPERATURE 21°C (70°F) in January

An offshoot of the famous literary event held in the Welsh town of Hay-on-Wye, the colourful Hay Festival Cartagena takes place in a colonial walled city in Colombia overlooking the Caribbean. Poets, authors, journalists and screenwriters from all over the world meet with stars of Hispanic-American literature in this UNESCO-protected city to take part in talks and debates and give readings. Venues range from theatres to bars and street corners. Don't miss the excellent creative-writing workshops or the daily official festival newspaper. A side festival, Hay Festivalito, is aimed at children and teenagers.

Practical Information

Getting There and Around All major Colombian carriers fly to Rafael Núñez Airport, 3 km (2 miles) from the city centre. A bus, taxi or *colectivo* (shared taxi) will take you into and around Cartagena, which is best explored on foot.

Website www.hayfestival.com

Magnificent interior of the Mariinskiy Theatre, St Petersburg

WHITE NIGHTS FESTIVAL

NEED TO KNOW

LOCATION St Petersburg lies on the Gulf of Finland, 380 km (235 miles) from Helsinki in Finland and 700 km (300 miles) from the capital, Moscow

WHEN The festival runs from May to July

VISITORS PER YEAR Around 1 million

DAYTIME TEMPERATURES 15–20°C (59–68°F), May–July

A three-month international cultural event, the White Nights Festival is a series of classical ballet, opera and music performances staged during a season when the sun hardly sets. The festival draws high-profile Russian performers and international guest stars: expect renowned conductors and soloists at The Stars of the White Nights Festival, the event's opening celebration, held at the famous Mariinskiy Theatre and new Mariinskiy Concert Hall. Watch out for other star appearances at Palace Square, where Paul McCartney and the Rolling Stones have done turns, and the spectacular fireworks at the popular closing Scarlet Sails party.

Practical Information

Getting There and Around Most major airlines fly direct from European cities to St Petersburg's Pulkovo Airport; travellers from elsewhere may have to change planes in Moscow. The airport is 17 km (11 miles) south of the city centre, and buses and taxis make the journey regularly. Once in the city, you can get around by bus, trolleybus or tram.

Website www.mariinsky.ru/en

Open-air concert at the International Festival of Arts & Ideas, New Haven, Connecticut

Choir competition during the Eisteddfod, Wales

INTERNATIONAL FESTIVAL OF ARTS & IDEAS

NEED TO KNOW

LOCATION New Haven is located in south-central Connecticut, on the north shore of Long Island Sound, 130 km (80 miles) from New York

WHEN The festival takes place in the last 16 days in June

VISITORS PER YEAR Around 17,000

DAYTIME TEMPERATURE 25°C (77°F) during June

Established in New Haven in 1996 with the aim of highlighting and developing the city's strong cultural and educational traditions, the International Festival of Arts & Ideas is today one of the most noteworthy arts festivals in the world. World-class performers, pre-eminent thinkers and inspirational leaders descend on the pretty harbourside city for the 16-day celebration, which stands out from other international arts festivals by virtue of its innovative focus – the fusion of arts and ideas.

Performers from more than 20 countries put on hundreds of shows and events. New Haven sparkles with activity at this time, and an upbeat summer vibe prevails, not least because 85 per cent of the events are free. Visitors flock to see concerts and art installations in venues all over the city, including the Long Wharf Theatre, the renowned Shubert Theater and the famed Yale University. There are also many open-air shows.

ABOVE Nottingham Playhouse Theatre Company, from the UK

The festival's heartbeat is New Haven Green, a recreation area named as one of America's ten most beautiful spaces. Past highlights at the event have included the Metropolitan Opera's stunning rendition of Puccini's *La Bohème;* a concert by blues singer and civil-rights activist Mavis Staples; and a closing-night performance by choreographer and political philosopher Liz Lerman and hundreds of "citizen dancers".

Designed to inspire new ways of thinking, this unusual and fascinating series of events embraces the traditional and experimental, the well-known and new. It is socially cohesive, occasionally controversial and – as those who return year after year will testify – a lot of fun.

Practical Information

Getting There and Around New York's La Guardia and JFK airports are located 2 hours' drive from downtown New Haven; taxis and shuttle buses make the trip regularly. Interstate trains and buses run between the two cities, and a ferry service operates from Long Island in New York to Bridgeport in Connecticut, 30 km (20 miles) from New Haven. Downtown New Haven has an efficient bus system and is compact enough to be explored on foot or by bicycle.

Website www.artidea.org

THE EISTEDDFOD

NEED TO KNOW

LOCATION The Eisteddfod moves to different locations in Wales, returning every four years to the capital, Cardiff, in the southeast of the country

WHEN Eisteddfod takes place in the first week of August

VISITORS PER YEAR Around 160,000

DAYTIME TEMPERATURE 16°C (60°F) in August

Taking its name from the Welsh word *eistedd* ("sit"), this vibrant eight-day festival is an out-and-out celebration of Welsh culture and heritage, staged entirely in the Welsh language. First held in 1176 and revived in its present form in 1860, the Eisteddfod is today the most famous festival in Wales. More than 6,000 people take part in drama, music, poetry and prose competitions, held in a different Welsh location each year. The Eisteddfod Pavilion, an enormous tent set up in the host town, is the focal point of the event (portable hand-sets providing English translations are on offer here). A wealth of performances, exhibitions and concerts take place in other nearby venues.

Practical Information

Getting There and Around There are regular flights to Cardiff from the neighbouring English cities of Birmingham, Bristol and Manchester. Long-distance bus services run between many English and Welsh towns. Check timetables for train times.

Website www.eisteddfod.org.uk

Sydney Gay & Lesbian Mardi Gras

vs the Parada do Orgulho GLBT

Sydney's Gay & Lesbian Mardi Gras might be smaller than its São Paolo counterpart but it's big, and sequinned, where it counts

ABOVE Jam-packed crowds battle for space during the Parada do Orgulho, São Paolo

NEED TO KNOW

LOCATION Sydney lies on the east coast of Australia and is the capital of the state of New South Wales

WHEN From mid-February for three weeks

VISITORS PER YEAR Mardi Gras parade: 10,000 participants and 500,000 spectators; final party: 20,000

Sydney Gay & Lesbian Mardi Gras trumps São Paolo when it comes to choice, so much choice. The same-sex season kicks off in mid-February with a series of art exhibitions, film viewings, theatre performances and live concerts that take place three weeks before the main Mardi Gras events – an infamous parade along Oxford Street in Sydney's Darlinghurst neighbourhood and a raucous, glitzy final party.

This global gay event, which began more than 30 years ago when a handful of pioneers took to the streets demanding their rights, has both a political and a playful message – acceptance, tolerance and diversity go hand in manicured hand with tinsel, tulle and toned bodies. Events in Sydney include the Sol y Luna Harbour Party, known for its cool cocktails and live sounds, the family-friendly Fair Day, and a pooch parade par excellence known as Doggywood. But for most

people, the highlight of the three-week period is the main parade and its notorious after-party, which has hosted everyone from Chaka Khan to Rupert Everett under its pulsing lights. One airline even stages a special "pink flight" to carry muscled merrymakers from San Francisco to Sydney for the big day.

Leading the parade is the Dykes on Bikes motorcycle group, which is followed by 150 floats manned by every kind of costumed dancer under the sun. Some 10,000 partygoers strap on soaring stilettos, technicolour outfits, diabolical wigs, infinitesimal shorts, codpieces and lashings of leather for this wild event, leaving a 4-km (2-mile) trail of glitter behind them. Police officers and military personnel keep step with dancing drag queens in flying-saucer-shaped dresses in what has been hailed as one of the world's top ten costume parties. Some 500,000 onlookers line the streets to take in the spectacle, cheering and waving rainbow-patterned flags as the parade sashays towards the Royal Hall of Industries in Moore Park. Here, a star-studded line-up of live performers and DJs get the party started at 10pm and keep it pumping until 8am for the more enthusiastic revellers.

PRACTICAL INFORMATION

Getting There and Around
Sydney's Kingsford Smith Airport is 8 km (5 miles) from the city centre. The Airport Link train takes you directly from the airport into the city, where taxis are plentiful. The best way to get around Sydney is on foot.

Where to Eat
Sydney has a fantastic dining scene, as multicultural and distinctive as the city itself. Try Icebergs Dining Room and Bar (www.idrb.com), with its fresh seafood and Italian-influenced

dishes and fantastic views of Bondi Beach.

Where to Stay
Try the elegant and contemporary Kirketon Hotel (www.kirketon.com.au), located just moments from Oxford Street.

Daytime Temperature
22°C (72°F) during Mardi Gras.

Budget per Day for Two
Around £130 including food, accommodation and transport.

Website
www.mardigras.org.au

ABOVE Rupert Everett with a costumed reveller, Sydney Mardi Gras

FORGET THE PARADA DO ORGULHO?

THE BUILD-UP The Parada do Orgulho GLBT (gays, lesbians, bisexuals, transvestites) de São Paulo first kicked off in 1997 with just 2,000 participants. It now draws more than 3 million, making it the biggest gay pride celebration in the world. Brazilians are famed for their easy going attitude and street party prowess and the Paulistanos are no slouches when it comes to having fun. Costumed carousers, floats booming out a beat, cheering onlookers, activists and rainbow flags turn the city's business hub into pink-party central.

THE LETDOWN Streets are crammed and feeling like a crushed grape is the norm. Pickpockets love the jostling crowds – wallets, cameras, phones and watches are frequent targets. Because of the hordes, the parade moves at a snail's pace, taking up to eight hours to pass. There has been a little anti-gay violence post-parade, including a homemade bomb attack in 2009 in a GLBT haunt, as well as assaults and robberies.

GOING ANYWAY? Book flights and hotels early. There's no avoiding the crowds, so just go with the flow and be prepared for delays. Outside of the official agenda, there are lots of independent gay parties in clubs, bars and private venues.

MAIN IMAGE Costumed dancers at Sydney Mardi Gras
BELOW (left to right) Members of the Dykes on Bikes parade group;
the Gaydar Float making its way along Oxford Street, Sydney Mardi Gras

4 MORE PARTIES TO RIVAL
THE PARADA DO ORGHULHO

HALLOWEEN PARADE, NEW YORK CITY, USA The world's
largest Halloween party (31 October) boasts more than 50,000
participants and 2 million spectators dressed as giant ghosts,
goblins, dinosaurs, skeletons and all manner of monsters.

FANTASY FEST, KEY WEST, USA This huge Caribbean-style
fancy-dress party stretches over ten party-filled days at the end
of October and culminates in the Captain Morgan Fantasy Fest
Parade, where camp costumes and buckets of body paint rule.

GAY PRIDE, SÃO PAULO, BRAZIL With an annual attendance
of millions, this event, held in June, is one of the largest of its kind.
Brazil knows how to throw a great party and this one, with its
techno beats, carnival floats and wild costumes, is no exception.

GAY PRIDE, AMSTERDAM, THE NETHERLANDS A week of
street parties in the Dutch capital culminates in the Gay Pride
Canal Parade on the first Saturday in August. Spectators line the
Prinsengracht to watch a procession of 100 decorated boats.

MAIN IMAGE Performers in front of the Montreal Jazz Festival's logo
BELOW (left to right) The legendary Ray Charles at the 2003 festival;
panoramic view of a concert in one of the open-air venues

3 MORE JAZZ FESTIVALS
TO RIVAL MONTREUX

COPENHAGEN JAZZ FESTIVAL Since it was established in
1979, the Copenhagen Jazz Festival has wowed crowds each
July with a week-long celebration that sets the Danish capital
buzzing. Choose from numerous outdoor concerts in public
squares, parks and along the waterfront, or check out the city's
bars, clubs and concert halls for gigs by Scandinavian and
global music stars.

CAPE TOWN INTERNATIONAL JAZZ FESTIVAL Dubbed
"Africa's Grandest Gathering" by toe-tapping musical aficionados,
Cape Town's two-day event in April each year attracts around
40 acts and is one of Africa's most prestigious musical events.

ST LUCIA JAZZ What started as a simple marketing ploy to
boost tourism during the May low season is now a bona fide
St Lucian tradition that includes everything from jamming
sessions to concerts of flamboyant straight-ahead jazz. The
late-night, alfresco picnic-style events are particularly intimate.

MONTREAL JAZZ FESTIVAL
VS MONTREUX JAZZ FESTIVAL

With over 750 concerts by 3,000 artists from more than 30 countries, Montreal's show-stopping, multi-genre music festival dwarfs the one in Montreux, and whips millions of festival-goers into a frenzy each year

NEED TO KNOW

LOCATION Montreal is in the province of Quebec, in eastern Canada

WHEN The festival takes place at the end of June/ beginning of July in a four-block site at the heart of downtown Montreal

VISITORS PER YEAR More than 2.5 million people descend on the city for the festival

Switzerland's Montreux Jazz Festival claims to be the biggest in the world – an assertion that doesn't quite stand up to scrutiny when you compare it with the jazz festival in Montreal. Quebec's full-on musical jamboree sends pulsating rhythms coursing through downtown Montreal's arterials. Rapturous melodies permeate every bar, café, basement joint and city square – from syncopated staccato trumpet solos and soul serenades to big-band jazz, R&B classics and percussive bossa nova beats. This is the jazz festival that Guinness World Records logs as the largest on the planet. And it's

an intoxicating musical cocktail, a kaleidoscope of intermingling energies and styles set against a vibrant urban backdrop.

The Festival International de Jazz de Montréal – to give the event its full name – lasts 11 days and 11 nights. Around 750 concerts take place in that time. Over half are outdoors and free. But there are also countless impromptu gigs, so you can soak up the carnival atmosphere of Latin jazz, take in some smouldering salsa, or follow the gentle strains of acoustic folk in an underground bar.

Arrive at the festival in time for the morning sound-checks to claim your place for the supporting acts at noon, then party on into the wee small hours to an eclectic musical repertoire. The summer celebrations and the city's funky mix of cafés, galleries, bistros and green spaces draw crowds of every age, every musical taste and from every corner of the globe, and unite them in a heady celebration of melody and rhythm.

Founder Alain Simard demonstrates an unshakable belief in Montreal's musical pedigree. He's the man responsible for bringing such big-name acts as Miles Davis, Ella Fitzgerald,

John Lee Hooker, Dave Brubeck, Dizzy Gillespie, Muddy Waters and Ray Charles to an event he felt sure would wow the international stage. And from the very first festival in 1980, his magical laid-back formula has worked. The easy-going atmosphere he creates encourages both musical discovery and revelry. It's an environment in which global stars are content to rub shoulders with up-and-coming local talent hoping for a springboard break.

The festival brings Montreal's traffic to a standstill as downtown becomes one huge musical extravaganza. Midway through the festivities comes the "Special Big Event" – now a Montreal tradition. It's a show of epic proportions – perhaps a gig by Urban Sax, stellar guitarist Pat Metheny or South African musician Johnny Clegg – and usually draws an audience of around 200,000.

Away from the music, a popular art exhibition presents exclusive works by some of the artists who have performed here – Miles Davis, Diana Krall, Norah Jones and Tony Bennett, to name but a few.

Surpassing the wildest dreams of even its founder, the Montreal Jazz Festival is the world's ultimate jazz rendezvous.

FORGET THE MONTREUX JAZZ FESTIVAL?

THE BUILD-UP Switzerland's ground-breaking festival is an annual showcase of every imaginable style of music. It has placed the quaint village of Montreux on the map since 1967, and is a popular musical getaway for European festival-lovers.

THE LETDOWN It takes Swiss precision to organize one of the world's largest music festivals and this super-slick operation is oiled so perfectly it lacks the spontaneity that's synonymous with raw jazz. A decade ago, the festival expanded to become a three-week extravaganza including music from all continents, to the disapproval of some festival-goers who feel it has lost its focus.

GOING ANYWAY? For an up-close-and-personal Montreux experience, give the two main stages a miss in favour of the smaller Montreux Jazz Café and the cluster of tiny open-air venues. Even better, attend the intimate performances that take place on cruise-boats on the lake.

ABOVE A turn-off for many hardcore jazz fans – the Montreux festival's recent focus on world music

PRACTICAL INFORMATION

Getting There and Around
Trudeau International Airport is around 30 minutes by cab from downtown Montreal. Many of the city's streets become traffic-free for the festival. Getting from A to B is a breeze – simply hop aboard the Métro or make your journey by foot.

Where to Eat
In terms of the number of restaurants per capita, Canada's gastronomic capital is second only to New York City in North America. Gallic flourishes abound – a culinary legacy of the country's French colonial past. Thousands of high-caliber cafés, bistros and restaurants make good use of a huge variety of fresh, top-quality produce. Food

is inexpensive – even at high-end joints – compared to other global cities. Check out Le Piment Rouge (www.lepimentrouge.com) for a flavour-packed gourmet thrill.

Where to Stay
For excellent links to buses, the Métro, bars, restaurants and venues, check in to Hotel Jazz (www.hoteljazzmontreal.com), in the heart of the downtown Latin Quarter (Quartier Latin).

Budget per Day for Two
Around £100.

Daytime Temperature
A rather warm and sticky 30°C (86°F) at festival time.

Website
www.montrealjazzfest.com

ABOVE Goa, a party hotspot with travellers since the 1960s

GOA'S FULL MOON PARTIES VS KO PHA NGAN

For the ultimate old-school raves, dedicated party-lovers make for India not Thailand

NEED TO KNOW

LOCATION Goa is on the Malabar Coast of India, south of Mumbai

WHEN Parties take place regularly on full moons from October to March, and at Christmas and New Year things go into overdrive

VISITORS PER YEAR About 2 million, but most people go to Goa for the beaches, not the beach parties

You can't announce a party on a billboard and expect it to be a real party. The best ones take place at secret locations. Invitations go out by word of mouth, and everybody in the place has to be united in pursuit of the same bacchanalian goal. So it is with Goa's famous full moon parties. You won't find listings for them in the entertainment section of the *Goan Herald*. These are proper raves, in the old-school tradition. If your only experience of full moon parties is the touristy ones of Thailand's Ko Pha Ngan, prepare for the real deal.

The venues for these hedonistic dance extravaganzas are kept secret until the last second. News of the next party filters along the Malabar Coast, from Anjuna to Arambol, by phone, email and text message, moving from guest house to Internet café to beach bar. Then, come nightfall, a convoy of mopeds and motorcycles sets out into the steamy Indian night, to gather at a secluded

beach, a clearing in the mangroves or a cluster of beach huts. The music starts up, dancers begin to swirl and the sound systems are set to throb till dawn. Fortunately, the beach is to hand for you to relax on the next day.

The DJs at Goa's full moon parties are masters of Goa trance, one of India's greatest contributions to the world of dance music. The genre can trace its origins back to the early 1990s, when the trippy sounds of local DJs reached the ears of their big-name counterparts in Britain. But the trance movement was simply building on the groundwork of the hippies who'd dropped in and blissed out in Goa in the 1960s. Along the coast you'll still see veterans from the original "Summer of Love" raving with the crowds of young European, Israeli, Russian, Japanese and Indian partygoers.

Finding a full moon party is largely a process of trial and error. The day is easy enough to predict, of course, but you'll have to talk to likely-looking people on the beach to discover the actual location. Nine times out of ten, though, you'll end up immersed in a sea of pumping bass, somewhere around Anjuna or Chapora. The secrecy is partly out of necessity – the local police periodically make raids on the parties in search of drug-dealers and drug-takers. But for many of Goa's partygoers, being underground is part of the appeal. After all, how much fun is a beach party that has its own website?

ABOVE Hippies selling trinkets at the market in Anjuna, India

FORGET KO PHA NGAN?

THE BUILD-UP In the early 1980s, travellers started to arrive on the shores of Ko Pha Ngan island, following a whispered rumour of all-night raves on the silver sands. The rumour turned into a scene, which went on to become a phenomenon. Two decades later Ko Pha Ngan's full moon parties are up there with Ibiza on the international party circuit.

THE LETDOWN Hat Rin may have been the epicentre of the beach-party scene in 1995, but these days Ko Pha Ngan is as mainstream as Starbucks coffee in Bangkok's Siam Square. By becoming an established tourist attraction, the full moon parties have lost part of their mystery and – some would say – their soul.

GOING ANYWAY? Accommodation around Hat Rin fills up days before each full moon party, so aim to arrive a few days early, or rent a moped and stay at one of the nicer, more secluded beaches on the north coast of the island. Hat Khuat and Hat Khom are two of the old favourites.

ABOVE Crammed on to the beach, hundreds of ravers at an all-night full moon party on Ko Pha Ngan, Thailand

PRACTICAL INFORMATION

Getting There and Around
Getting to Goa by air involves a charter flight to Dabolim airport or a 1-hour flight from Mumbai. By train the journey from Mumbai takes 6–12 hours or 14 hours by bus. Local buses and taxis run to Anjuna and other resorts along the Malabar Coast.

Where to Eat
Vendors selling *chai* (spiced tea), omelettes, samosas and water set up camp on party nights. The resorts are packed with restaurants serving global traveller food, as well as Goa's signature curry: vindaloo made with pork, wine vinegar and plenty of chilli. New York-trained chef Saleem Agha cooks up a treat at Sublime (tel. +91 982 248 4051), near the flea market in Anjuna.

Where to Stay
Anjuna is the centre of the trance scene and the best place to get information about upcoming parties. Ravers also head for Vagator, Chapora and Arambol. One well-kept secret is Siolim House (www.siolimhouse.com), near Chapora, a glorious 300-year-old Portuguese mansion with a secluded pool. It's well worth the splurge.

Daytime Temperatures
Oct: 31°C (88°F); Jan: 31°C (88°F); Mar: 32°C (90°F)

Budget per Day for Two
Bank on £150, including accommodation at Siolim House, food and moped hire.

Website
www.goaindiatourism.org/

ABOVE The colourful procession of the Christ figure during Semana Santa in Cusco, Peru

SEMANA SANTA, CUSCO VS SEMANA SANTA, SEVILLE

The ancient Inca capital's atmospheric Easter celebrations rival Seville's robed cavalcade

NEED TO KNOW

LOCATION Cusco is located 1,100 km (685 miles) southeast of the Peruvian capital, Lima, and 3,400 m (11,000 ft) above sea level

WHEN Cusco's Semana Santa celebrations take place in the week before Easter

VISITORS PER YEAR Around 700,000

Forget the gigantic floats and hooded penitents for which Seville's Semana Santa is famous. Picture instead the streets of Cusco, filled with hundreds of diminutive Andean devotees dressed in vibrant fabrics, the women with long black plaits cascading from saucer-like red hats, hailing the city's protector, a black Christ. It's a colourful, charming scene.

Unlike Seville, where Good Friday is the focus of the festival, Holy Monday is the highlight in Cusco. At dawn in the city's cathedral, *servidores* (servants) prepare a figure of Christ on the cross for the main procession. They replace his crown of thorns with a garland of *ñucchu* flowers, comb his hair, anoint him with perfume and dress him up in jewels, while small choirs, known as *chaynas* or *jilgueras*, sing out in Quechua, the language of the Inca.

At 3pm, church bells announce Christ's departure from the cathedral, the city's colonial shrine, which is built on top of Inca foundations. The enormous effigy is then paraded through the streets, just as the mummies of Inca rulers were centuries ago. Legend has it that in 1650, when the sacred relic was first borne through the town, it brought to an end a devastating earthquake, and ever since then the figure has been known as El Señor de los Temblores (Lord of the Earthquakes).

Cusco is unshakably Andean in its devotion, with a liberal dash of Catholicism. Crimson *ñucchu* flowers, once an offering to the Inca gods but now symbolizing the blood of a Christian divinity, rain down on the procession from balconies, and fiery garlands flank the dark Christ on his swaying silver dais. Tapestries of coloured petals depicting sacred icons pave the streets, and firecrackers herald the Christ figure's approach. At 7pm the bells ring out again and devotees fall to their knees in the Plaza de Armas, the city's main square, as El Señor returns to the cathedral, gracefully bowing three times before retreating and closing the door on another year.

Thousands of pilgrims from remote mountain villages flock to Cusco for this vibrant, stirring event, which continues for the rest of Holy Week with smaller religious processions, ceremonies and re-enactments from the Bible. Local food looms large at this time. Stalls dispensing sweet *empanadas* and corn bread invade the Plaza de Armas, and on Holy Thursday, families traditionally gather to share 12 dishes – representing the 12 apostles – of potatoes, seafood, *tarwi* (Andean lupin) and *llullucha* (algae).

FORGET SEVILLE?

THE BUILD-UP With its melding of Christianity, paganism and pleasure, Semana Santa in Seville is both a solemn and cheerily raucous spectacle. Penitents in long robes and conical hoods trail behind hefty floats that are held aloft by the faithful, while brass bands sound a mournful lament. Spectators pray and push and pull for the best position as the effigies pass by. Later, they gather in bars and restaurants to tuck into tapas and bull's-tail stew.

THE LETDOWN An estimated one million people visit Seville during Semana Santa, and as a result price-gouging in the city is rampant. The narrow streets get incredibly crowded, and spending 10–12 hours at a time on your feet, caught up in processions, isn't unusual. It's noisy, busy and tiring, and everyone is forcibly vying for the best view.

GOING ANYWAY? Pick up a leaflet specifying the departure times and the routes of the *pasos* (processions), and then stake out your vantage point early. Navigating the streets at this time can be painfully slow, so be patient and not pushy. Book your hotel well ahead of your trip. Be sure to wear comfortable shoes.

ABOVE A packed street in Seville, Spain, during a Semana Santa procession

PRACTICAL INFORMATION

Getting There and Around
Aeropuerto Alejandro Velasco Astete is 5 km (3 miles) from the centre of Cusco. Only use official taxis to travel from here to the city (drivers have identification badges). Walking is the best way to get around Cusco.

Where to Eat
Cusco has an excellent range of places to eat, from casual cafés to upmarket restaurants and cosy pubs. La Cicciolina (tel. +51 84 239 510) has a laid-back tapas bar, an upscale dining room and an eat-in bakery downstairs.

Where to Stay
Try the cosy and traditional Casa Andina Private Collection (www.casa-andina.com).

Daytime Temperature
21°C (70°F) during Semana Santa.

Budget per Day for Two
£80 including accommodation, food and transport.

Website
www.peru.info

Asti Palio
vs Siena Palio

They've been racing thoroughbreds in Asti's old town since 1275 – years before the smaller palio *of Siena was established*

ABOVE A crush of spectators watching the race from behind fences at the Siena *palio*

FORGET SIENA PALIO?

THE BUILD-UP Everyone has heard of Siena's *palio*, and Tuscany is a long-established tourist destination. The Italian hill town is a medieval jewel and famous for its fine wines and excellent cuisine. With its central location, Siena is also an ideal starting point for visits to the rest of Tuscany – Pisa and Florence are both just an hour away and many of the nearby villages, such as San Gimignano and Monteriggione, are well worth exploring.

THE LETDOWN Unless you've been invited into one of the exclusive homes that overlook the square where the race takes place, there is no seating at the *palio*. Most spectators have to stand for hours in excruciating heat during the two races, which take place in July and August.

GOING ANYWAY? Prepare for the midday summer heat with sunscreen, a hat and water. Make the most of the festive atmosphere after the race by joining in the raucous street parties.

NEED TO KNOW

LOCATION Asti is one of the major towns in the Piedmont region of northwestern Italy

WHEN The *palio* takes place each year on the third weekend in September

VISITORS PER YEAR 100,000 come on the day for the street party, though only 10,000 can fit into the piazza, so it's advisable to book ahead

Siena's *palio* is the most celebrated festival in Italy and takes place each July and August. But why not wait until September, when the tourist high season is over, and enjoy the *palio* in Asti? With more races and more horses, it offers a more sumptuous and full day for spectators. It also has a dramatic and colourful procession of over 1,000 flag-throwers and characters in medieval dress.

Both *palios* take place in large squares in the medieval town centres, but the piazza in Asti is more challenging, owing to the tight curves of the near-triangular track (the route in Siena is circular). Jockeys race bareback, with neither saddles nor stirrups, but only in Asti do they ride thoroughbreds, making the race even more nerve-racking – less sturdy and more difficult to handle, the thoroughbred horses struggle to keep their footing on the cobblestones of the piazza and the jockeys must employ greater skill in a race that's faster.

Siena runs its *palio* twice every summer, with ten horses participating at a time. At Asti, there's much more to see – each of the 21 neighbourhoods and villages in and around Asti enters a horse dressed in its own colours, and all 21 of them run in four races during a single day, thundering round the tight corners of the track again and again. The three qualifying rounds lead up to the eagerly anticipated final, in which the top seven compete. The winner's prize is the coveted *palio* (victory banner). The loser receives a meagre anchovy as a consolation prize.

Asti offers 5,000 standing places free, but if you want to watch the race in style, book numbered seats in one of the stalls that are specially erected for the event. These are reasonably priced and are easy to reserve online up to a year in advance. With so much going on at Asti, you'll be glad of the comfort the stalls afford. The day is much busier than in Siena, with more racing and more pageantry. And as night falls, the fun really hots up. Join in the exuberant street parties or enjoy the celebrations in one of the local trattorias. After a long day at the races, you'll be ready to try some of the excellent local Barbera d'Asti, which connoisseurs believe to be one of Italy's best red wines.

ABOVE Asti wine cellar full of robust red wines, among them Barbera d'Asti

PRACTICAL INFORMATION

Getting There
The nearest airport is Turin, about an hour by car or train from Asti.

Where to Eat
Piedmont is foodie paradise. Try some of the local truffles washed down with one of the region's fine wines. The area is better known for risotto than pasta. Tacabanda (tel. +39 0141 530 999) is great for local specialities.

Where to Stay
There are hotels of all categories in Asti, the most famous of which is Hotel Reale (www.

hotelristorantereale.it) in the piazza where the *palio* takes place. Accommodation is hard to find on the weekend of the *palio*, so book months in advance.

Budget per Day for Two
Around £180 if you stay in a double at the Hotel Reale. For those on a budget, try one of the local *agriturismos* (farm stays).

Daytime Temperature
23°C (73°F) in September.

Website
www.comune.asti.it

MAIN IMAGE Townsfolk in medieval costume displaying their flag-throwing skills before the *palio* in Asti **BELOW (left to right)** Rooftop view of the town of Asti; the Asti *palio* in full swing

4 MORE HORSE RACES TO RIVAL SIENA'S PALIO

NAADAM, MONGOLIA This ancient festival, held each July, is a celebration of equestrian events, archery and wrestling. Its roots lie in the nomad wedding assemblies and hunting extravaganzas of the Mongolian army.

WHITE TURF, SWITZERLAND The White Turf international horse races on St Moritz's frozen lake are one of the most spectacular winter events in Europe. They take place in February.

SA SARTIGLIA, SARDINIA, ITALY In the build-up to Lent in the town of Oristano, horsemen compete with one another in an ancient tournament to select the masked rider who will conquer the ring and the symbolic star.

BIRDSVILLE RACES, AUSTRALIA This popular outback racing derby is held in Queensland in September to raise money for charity. Picnickers and campers arrive from all over Australia to participate in the fun in this remote location. When the races are on, the local population increases from 100 to over 6,000.

MAIN IMAGE The Space Needle and a Ferris wheel reflected in windows at the EMP **BELOW (left to right)** Costumed performer at Bumbershoot; Zimbabwean musician Oliver Mtukudzi playing at Bumbershoot

4 MORE MUSIC FESTIVALS TO RIVAL LOLLAPALOOZA

BESTIVAL, ISLE OF WIGHT, UK This off-the-wall festival is a relative newcomer. The three-day event, held in the late summer, boasts weird and wonderful attractions, such as a Victorian insect circus, as well as big-name performers.

BONNAROO MUSIC AND ARTS FESTIVAL, TENNESSEE, USA At Bonnaroo, which takes place every June on a huge plot in rural Tennessee, camping is the done thing. Bands affiliated with the "jam" subcategory of rock perform for fans of all ages.

ROSKILDE, DENMARK Scandinavia has its own glorious rock festival, with a history stretching back more than 30 years. Attendance at the four-day festival, which begins on the last Sunday in June, grows nearly every year.

SEATTLE FOLKLIFE FESTIVAL, WASHINGTON, USA Held on the same grounds as Bumbershoot on May's Memorial Day weekend, this free festival features ethnic and authentic folk music from all corners of the globe. More music, less amplitude.

BUMBERSHOOT
VS LOLLAPALOOZA

The crush of Lollapalooza's 166,000 sweaty rock fans, coupled with the smell of teen spirit, could well be your thing; otherwise, consider Bumbershoot for a far wider range of audience and artistry

Seattle lives on the edge, and not only because of its Pacific Rim location in northwestern Washington State. The city's youthful population continually shakes things up, whether it's technology and coffee drinks or arts and entertainment. The latter reaches its apex every year at Bumbershoot, an enormous three-day festival with a colourful history dating back nearly 40 years, and with performances that leave Lollapalooza in the dust.

The festivities are held during the Labor Day holiday, as summer's heat abates and the region's autumn weather begins to descend on Puget Sound. The Bumbershoot experience is unparalleled, partly due to the memorable setting of the Seattle Center (the once-futuristic grounds built for the 1962 World's Fair). This impeccably landscaped site, located close to downtown, is anchored by the Space Needle, the city's most recognized landmark. More than 20 deluxe indoor and outdoor concert venues, originally built for everything from children's theatre to the Seattle Opera, host performances of music, dance, film and spoken word. It's a remarkable spectrum of creative expression.

Audiences of all ages and backgrounds come to the events to bask in the kaleidoscopic range of performers. First-name acts in every denomination of rock, jazz and folk join a carousel of local bands just back from their first tours. Even outfits with more promise than experience can have their time under the lights if they pass the application process.

Of course the festival gets crowded, but unlike Lollapalooza, where nearly the entire concert population heads for the main stage, Bumbershoot has many venues scattered over a 30-ha (74-acre)

ABOVE The strangely shaped façade of the Experience Music Project

site that was designed with crowd-control in mind. You can always find areas where foot traffic subsides.

The Seattle Center also tempts the concert-weary to explore other pursuits without leaving the grounds. You can visit the Experience Music Project (EMP), the high-tech rock music museum designed by Frank Gehry; ride the monorail that runs through the EMP between downtown and the Space Needle; or ride up the Space Needle's external elevators to see the to-die-for view of city, mountains and sea.

FORGET LOLLAPALOOZA?

THE BUILD-UP Perry Farrell, lead singer of the rock band Jane's Addiction, launched Lollapalooza in 1991 to celebrate his band's last tour and to carry the flag of alternative rock music. The festival hailed a new rebellion against mainstream music and galvanized the burgeoning under-30 subculture. It toured the USA until 1997, had a revival in 2003 and, since 2005, has taken place every year in Chicago's Grant Park.

THE LETDOWN Now that Lollapalooza no longer tours, fans have only one shot to attend, which means denser, more desperate crowds – the mosh pit will turn heads. Be prepared for the often-scorching summer heat – temperatures during the festival have been known to soar to 40°C (104°F). Remember that Chicago is an expensive city, so finding affordable accommodation will be tough.

GOING ANYWAY? Get an early start and consult the festival map of Grant Park assiduously – not only for stage information, but also for details on public transport and suitable areas for down time and refreshments. Chicago is one of America's gastronomic hotspots, so leave enough time to explore the city and its diverse food culture.

ABOVE Crowds of festival-goers trying to get close to the main stage at Lollapalooza

44 MORE INTOXICATING FESTIVALS AND PARTIES

ABOVE Burning crosses setting the streets ablaze during the annual Bonfire Night parade in Lewes, UK
RIGHT Led by Hindu devotees, a train of camels on the way to the Camel Fair in Pushkar, India

BONFIRE NIGHT, LEWES, UK A walk down the steep, cobbled streets of Lewes on 5 November is not for the fainthearted: the atmosphere of this costumed torchlit parade is raucous, and the air thick with smoke. The procession is accompanied by deafening bangers, and burning barrels and crosses are tossed into the River Ouse. The festival commemorates the Gunpowder Plot of 1605, when Guy Fawkes failed in his attempt to blow up the Parliament in London. Elaborate effigies, known as "Guys", are thrown onto a vast bonfire, and the evening culminates in an impressive firework display.

PUSHKAR CAMEL FAIR, RAJASTHAN, INDIA Boasting over 400 temples, Pushkar is a sacred place for Hindus, who believe that over the course of this five-day festival the gods pay a visit to the region and bless the devout. Each **November**, the still waters of the Pushkar Lake are disturbed by thousands of devotees who converge upon the spot, submerging themselves and filling the air with the sound of their prayers. Their religious fervour is accompanied by a grand-scale camel fair, at which hundreds of animals are raced, bought and sold, and paraded in fine jewellery, bells and bangles.

LA FOLLE JOURNÉE DE NANTES, FRANCE For five days in January, the city of Nantes becomes classical music's Woodstock. Drawing buffs and beginners alike, each concert lasts 45 minutes, tickets are reasonable, and different composers and genres are featured each year.

SPLASHY FEN, SOUTH AFRICA What began as a ramshackle folk festival is now one of the country's foremost musical events, attracting over 10,000 people over five days every **Easter**. It features a wide range of national bands as well as family-friendly sports and activities.

CARNIVAL, BINCHE, BELGIUM Dressed in the Belgian national colours of red, yellow and black, the character of Gille de Binche dominates this carnival. Wearing masks with spectacles and moustaches, and hats laden with ostrich feathers, festival-goers known as "Gilles" stomp away the winter gloom in wooden clogs at the town's Grand Place, and toss Seville oranges into an excitable crowd. This three-day festival, which takes place at the **end of February**, dates back to the 16th century and attracts thousands of revellers, who dance in the streets beneath a firework-filled sky to the sound of local brass bands.

CHRISTMAS MARKET, PRAGUE, CZECH REPUBLIC A tall tree draped in lights, against a Gothic backdrop, sets the scene for this most atmospheric of Christmas festivals. Each **December** the sound of carols fills the air, and the Old Town Square and Wenceslas Square fill with visitors, who stroll amid bright wooden huts browsing traditional crafts, trailing steam from cups of mulled wine.

RUSTLER'S VALLEY FESTIVAL, SOUTH AFRICA Set in the foothills of the Maluti Mountains, amid verdant pasture, this four-day **Easter** festival is a holistic, New Age experience. Here you'll find bands, drumming and world music on the main stage, trance and dance tents, a picturesque campsite and some delicious vegetarian food. The New Year's Eve celebrations also draw crowds.

IVREA ORANGE FESTIVAL, ITALY On Shrove Tuesday (**Feb–Mar**) Ivrea's quiet streets fill with costumed revellers pelting each other with sweet-smelling oranges. This four-day carnival commemorates the townsfolk's 12th-century struggle against a local tyrant. Those on foot represent the peasants; those on chariots the aristocracy. Traditional *fagioli grassi* (beans and pork) is served to the participants.

CADIZ CARNIVAL, SPAIN At carnival time (**end Feb–Mar**), the narrow, twisting streets of this tranquil Moorish city are transformed for 10 days. Among the most popular musical performers are *chirigotas*, whose lyrics offer a satirical take on current events; *comparsas*, who show off more serious classical talent; and solo *romanceros*, who serenade passers-by from stairwells.

ORURO CARNIVAL, BOLIVIA For three days in **February**, the thin, cold air of the high-altitude mining town of Oruro comes alive to the sound of hundreds of marching bands, while dancers in elaborate costumes enact tales of their Andean past. The festival culminates outside the cathedral with a performance of the *diablada* – a dance representing the struggle between Good and Evil.

FÊTES DE MASQUES, PAYS DOGON, MALI On a vast, arid escarpment in central Mali, six men in dramatic hand-painted masks dance vigorously before an enthusiastic crowd. These enactments are said to symbolize Dogon cosmology and to help ward off evil spirits. Two big festivals, Sigui and Dama, take place every 60 and 12 years respectively, but dances are performed **throughout the year**.

ABOVE Buddhist monks carrying offerings in honour of Guru Padmasambhava during Paro Tsechu, Bhutan
RIGHT An extravagantly costumed dancer at the spirited samba celebrations of Boi-Bumbá, Brazil

PARO TSECHU, BHUTAN Every **March**, monks in bright and often fearsome costumes perform a series of dances over five days to the sound of flutes, cymbals and trumpets, cheered on by Bhutanese families dressed in their finest traditional clothing. The festival honours Guru Padmasambhava, a Buddhist teacher and guide, and the dances tell stories from his life, depicting a host of gods and demons and the triumph of joy and religion over evil. It all culminates on the final day with the unrolling, at dawn, of the elaborate silk Thangka, a vast religious scroll from which worshippers seek a blessing.

BOI-BUMBA, PARINTINS, BRAZIL Even by Brazil's ecstatic standards, the Boi-Bumbá of northeastern Brazil, held over three days in **June**, is a frenzied celebration. Retelling a local legend about the death and resurrection of an ox, the festival pits two rival samba schools against one another in Parintins' vast arena, the *Bumbódromo*, which holds nearly 40,000 people. Every night the schools, divided into their rival colours of blue and red, try to outdance, outplay and outdress each other in a spectacular 3-hour display complete with extravagant costumes, elaborate floats and a steamy, joyful atmosphere.

TOONIK TYME, IQALIT, CANADA As the Arctic winter recedes, this week-long festival in **March** celebrates the coming of spring. The community gathers to fish, hunt and compete in snowmobile and dog-team races, and evenings are spent eating and drinking to the sound of local music.

ONAM, KERALA, INDIA Kerala is at its loveliest during the ten-day festival of Onam (**Aug–Sep**), its trees brimming with fruit under warm sunshine. This is an inclusive, secular event that honours King Mahabali who, it is said, ruled over a period of happiness and prosperity in the region. It brings out all the spectacle of Keralan culture: courtyards are dressed with floral carpets, there are costumed dances and sports, and chanting oarsmen steer a popular Snake Boat Race along the Pampa river. *Onasadya*, a nine-course feast served on banana leaves, showcases the region's delicate and varied cuisine.

FIESTA DE SANTO TOMAS, CHICHICASTENANGO, GUATEMALA Come **December**, the blazing colours of Chichicastenango market reach their zenith. Villagers from the highlands pour into town, all in distinct traditional dress. Clouds of incense and deafening bangers accompany a parade in honour of the patron saint, and plenty of drinking, dancing and falling over is enjoyed by all.

WINTER FESTIVAL, QUEENSTOWN, NEW ZEALAND Far from hibernating, Queenstown greets its winter (**Jun–Jul**) with a ten-day jamboree attracting 60,000 party-goers. It combines eccentricities such as the Birdman and Dog Derby with Mardi Gras parades, fireworks, live music and comedy. The party continues on the slopes with snow mountain-biking and night skiing.

ST. PAUL WINTER CARNIVAL, MINNESOTA, USA St. Paul's carnival was born in **January** 1886, in defiance of an allegation made by a New York reporter that the city in winter was "unfit for human habitation". An intricate ice castle is built, and each year a king and queen are crowned and parade through the city. There are skiing and bobsledding contests, toboggan slides and snow sculptures.

EASTER, KALYMNOS, GREECE Easter celebrations here are varied and elaborate, starting on **Holy Friday** with a candlelit procession that follows flower-decked "epitaphs", symbolizing Christ's tomb, to the cathedral for a celebratory Mass. On Saturday a feast of lamb stuffed with rice and liver is prepared and, at midnight, the church bells ring out and dynamite is lit on the mountains behind the port.

CALLE OCHO LATINO FESTIVAL, MIAMI, USA Every year in **mid-March**, Miami's "Little Havana" district is given over to a huge street party celebrating Latino culture, music and dance. Stages on the streets showcase salsa, merengue, reggaeton and jazz, and tempting smells of *tamales* and *arepas* waft from sizzling stalls. There are cook-offs, sporting events, and a popular domino tournament.

DEAD RAT BALL, OSTEND, BELGIUM Headdresses, 4-inch heels, feathers and sequins: an unexpected find in a 1950s red-brick casino in Ostend. This burlesque festival was established by local artist James Ensor in the late 19th century after a visit to the Rat Mort Cabaret in Paris, France. Some 2,500 visitors of all ages converge each **March** to dress up around an annual theme.

TET FESTIVAL, VIETNAM Tet celebrates Chinese New Year (**late Jan**), and is a time for Vietnamese families to get together and feast. The streets glow pink with flowering peach trees – a symbol of new life and good fortune – and stalls sell sweets, kumquat bushes, fruit and flowers, turning the city into a riot of colour. There are fireworks and parades, and firecrackers are thrown to ward off evil forces.

ABOVE Spectacular costumes add sparkle to Bridgetown's streets at the annual Crop Over festival, Barbados
RIGHT Masked Pierrots, clad in satin, are a distinctive feature of the Carnival at Limoux, France

CROP OVER, BARBADOS Crop Over was originally a celebration of the successful completion of the sugar harvest. Today, for almost two months each **summer**, the capital, Bridgetown, pulsates with the rhythm of calypso, folk music and dance. On the spectacular East Coast Road, sweaty calypso practitioners compete with rival groups against a backdrop of crashing Atlantic surf, while spectators gather on the surrounding hillsides with picnics, beer and rum. The festival culminates with the Grand Kadooment, a joyful street carnival parade flaunting magnificent costumes and energetic dances.

LIMOUX CARNIVAL, FRANCE The dance of the Pierrot is graceful and slow. A masked figure, dressed in baggy clothes and satin tights, he marches through the cold streets of Limoux, bantering with spectators and scattering confetti, a band of musicians in his wake. This unusual festival, thought to date back to the Middle Ages, takes places over a two-month period beginning in **January**, with the marching bands and costumed characters taking over the town each weekend. On the final evening a straw dummy, known as the "King of the Carnival", is burned on a pyre in the main square.

FESTIVAL OF THE DHOW COUNTRIES, STONE TOWN, ZANZIBAR In late June, the evocative, spice-scented island of Zanzibar is the scene of a week-long celebration of all things cultural, drawing film, music and theatre from countries strung along dhow trading routes of old.

WIFE CARRYING CHAMPIONSHIPS, FINLAND Every **July**, some 8,000 visitors descend on Sonkajärvi, eastern Finland, to watch the town's husbands navigate an obstacle-course relay with their better half wrapped around them. Sensibly, the men down plenty of beer throughout.

BUN BANG FAI, YASOTHON, THAILAND With an ear-splitting explosion, a rocket 4 m (13 ft) long, packing several kilos of gunpowder, shoots from a bamboo launch into the clear blue sky. The sound is greeted by cheering and murmurs of approval from an appreciative crowd. The "rocket festival", held each **May**, has its origins in local mythology: the rural community believed that their far-flung offerings would be rewarded by the rain god, who would bless them with plenty of water for the upcoming rice harvest. The celebrations span three days and are accompanied by music, dancing and drinking.

CHEYENNE FRONTIER DAYS, WYOMING, USA Cheyenne's ten-day rodeo festival each **July** regards itself as "the daddy of 'em all". A celebration of the Old West, it sees Stetsons fly as young men battle to stay on bucking bulls for a full 8 seconds, for prize money of over a million dollars. The town's streets bustle with visitors taking in the Grand Parade and nightly musical performances.

LATITUDE, SOUTHWOLD, UK Once described as "the festival for people who don't like festivals", Latitude, held in **July**, is environmentally conscious and attracts a rather well-heeled crowd. You're as likely to find yourself listening to a poetry reading as to a band. It features literature and comedy as well as music, and the small, scenic site makes it pleasant simply to wander and lap up the atmosphere.

BURNING MAN, NEVADA, USA Black Rock Desert, with its cracked earth and searing heat, emphasizes the spirituality of the Burning Man experience. An air of inclusion and self-reliance pervades it, and festival-goers are not so much spectators as participants, encouraged to come together for a week (in **Aug–Sep**) to devise art installations, costumes and performances around a central theme.

GOLDEN SHEARS, MASTERTON, NEW ZEALAND The town of Masterton, host to what it claims is the "world's greatest shearing competition", greets visitors with a giant pair of golden shears. Each **February** it draws hundreds of entrants from North and South Island to take part in sheep-shearing and wool-handling contests. Dating back to 1961, competition is fierce and winners become local heroes.

MIMOSA FESTIVAL, HERCEG NOVI, MONTENEGRO The gentle fragrance of mimosa wafts over Herceg Novi's sunny streets during this annual festival every **February**. Floral floats fill the promenade and local horticulturists strive to outdo one another with imaginative displays. There is local theatre, music and dance, and the chance to go mimosa-picking along the lush banks of the riviera.

PUNAKHA DOMCHOE, BHUTAN Featuring war cries and fireworks, silk skirts and resplendent swords, this three-day military festival takes place during the first month of Bhutan's lunar year (Feb–Mar). A recreation of Bhutan's 17th-century victory over Tibet, the final battle is re-enacted with costumed *pazaps* (warriors), who perform in the courtyard of the majestic *dzong* (fortress).

ABOVE Kimono-clad musicians are borne along on a float in a parade during the Gion Matsuri festival, Kyoto, Japan
LEFT A Taj Mahal made of oranges and lemons: one of the feats of fruity virtuosity at Menton's citrus festival, France

CITRUS FESTIVAL, MENTON, FRANCE In late February each year this small town on the French Riviera celebrates all things citrus. Floats bearing immense constructions made from oranges and lemons are paraded through the streets on Sundays, and elaborate fruity sculptures are assembled for all to see at the Biovès Gardens. During the evenings carnival bursts into action at the Moonlit Parade, with acrobats, costumed musicians and dancing filling the seafront promenade. The tradition dates back to the 1920s, when the town was Europe's leading supplier of lemons.

GION MATSURI, KYOTO, JAPAN The highlight of the ancient, month-long Gion festival is Yamahoko-yoko, in which vast floats – some weighing more than 9 tonnes – are paraded through the streets, adorned with 15th-century tapestries. Throughout **July** the streets throng with festival-goers dressed in traditional summer kimonos and wooden shoes; delicious smells of *yakitori* (skewered chicken) and traditional battered octopus waft from vendors' stalls. The parade dates back to the year 869 when Kyoto fell victim to a terrible plague, and a procession was initiated to appease the gods.

EID, DAMASCUS, SYRIA To celebrate the end of Ramadan, the city's maze-like medieval streets are strewn with ribbons, and locals dress in their finest clothes. Visits to family take up most of the day but, gradually, the streets fill with stalls and music, and fireworks light up the sky.

CARNIVAL, BASEL, SWITZERLAND It's 4am on the Monday after Ash Wednesday (Feb–Mar), the city's lights are switched off, and the party begins with a procession illuminated by huge, colourful lanterns. This is Fasnacht, an elaborate three-day festival dating back to the 14th century. Basel's old town resonates with the sound of drums and piccolos, as musical troupes wend their way through the winding streets, their faces obscured by elaborate papier-mâché masks. It's very much a local affair, with participants drawing on topical stories to poke fun at local personalities and politicians with their satirical verse.

MUD FESTIVAL, BORYEONG, SOUTH KOREA Each July, Daecheon Beach and the figures partying along its sands are daubed black with mud. An atmosphere of abandon pervades as tourists hurl themselves gleefully down a mud slide and take each other on in mud-wrestling contests. The festival attracts over a million visitors, and has buoyed a local economy traditionally reliant on agriculture.

CARNIVAL, GUALEGUAYCHÚ, ARGENTINA Everybody's heard of Rio, but few are familiar with the annual street party in Gualeguaychú, held over ten successive Saturdays in **January and February**. An undiscovered joy, the town's festivities are authenticity incarnate, with lithe footwork, skimpy costumes and pulsating music aplenty, but no hordes of camera-wielding visitors.

OUD FESTIVAL, JERUSALEM, ISRAEL Named after the short-necked lute traditionally played across the Middle East, Oud, held in **November**, uses music to reach beyond religious and political divisions to showcase the rich ethnic and social traditions that inspire music, poetry and literature in Jerusalem today. Concerts feature modern and traditional music with Bedouin, Flamenco and Sufi influences.

PUSHCART DERBY, DISCOVERY BAY, JAMAICA The humble pushcart, used for transporting fruit and other wares, is ubiquitous in Jamaica. It comes into its own each **August**, when pushcart owners compete in a frenetic derby, watched by tens of thousands of spectators and accompanied by live music and marching bands. They are said to have inspired the creation of the national bobsleigh team.

VEGETARIAN FESTIVAL, PHUKET, THAILAND Over this nine-day festival (in **Sept–Oct**), you might spot entranced men walking over hot coals, or a woman with her cheeks pierced by a long skewer. Such acts, along with abstinence from meat and alcohol, are believed to offer protection from evil. Stalls of vegetarian food share the street with processions and fireworks in this colourful celebration.

TENERIFE CARNIVAL, SANTA CRUZ, CANARY ISLANDS Tenerife's **February** carnival is among the hardest to beat for noise and sheer enthusiasm. The parade route is an exuberant river of shimmying costumes, bands and dancers; the Carnival Queen's dress so heavy and elaborate that it is affixed with wheels. The event closes with fireworks and the burning of a vast papier-mâché sardine.

PARRANDA, REMEDIOS, CUBA On Christmas Eve, little colonial Remedios explodes with pyrotechnics and a cacophony of cowbells, trumpets and drums, while dancing and floats crowd its streets. The festival began when a local priest, dismayed by poor attendance at Midnight Mass, sent children out with whistles and tin cans to wake everyone up and force them to church.

GREAT JOURNEYS

Donkeys crossing a suspension bridge above the Kali Gandaki river, Annapurna region, Nepal *(pp90–1)*

THE APOLOBAMBA TREK
VS THE INCA TRAIL

The masterwork of the Inca Empire is an enormous 22,530-km (14,000-mile) network of roads built eight centuries ago. Trekkers have thoroughly tramped the 40-km (25-mile) section leading to Machu Picchu – it's time to discover the rest of the route

NEED TO KNOW

LOCATION The Cordillera Apolobamba is in western Bolivia, north of Lake Titicaca and near the Peruvian border

VISITORS PER YEAR Even the most popular trek in the area is undertaken by fewer than 500 people every year

CLIMATE You're in the tropics, but at this elevation it's chilly all year, with sub-arctic conditions higher up

Once the largest nation on earth, the Inca Empire stretched for 4,000 km (2,500 miles) along South America's Andean backbone. Its ancient highways, many of which cross mountain passes over 5,000 m (16,000 ft) high, were superbly successful in nurturing trade and communications throughout the far-flung empire. If you long to explore this ancient road network without the crowds of the Inca Trail, then head to Bolivia's Cordillera Apolobamba, which will lead you across high terrain and into the remarkably unchanged world of today's Inca descendants.

The Cordillera Apolobamba is a national protected area of Bolivia, established to conserve the natural resources and biodiversity of the region. Of the various trekking routes that traverse the range, the most popular is a 5-day trek connecting the villages of Curva and Pelechuco, through Andean highlands where the Kallawayas, a group of traditional healers who performed brain surgery 1,000 years ago and were the first in the world to use penicillin and quinine, still practise their healing craft and rituals.

After leaving the picturesque hilltop village of Curva, views of Akamani, the sacred mountain of the Kallawayas, loom large. From here the elevation of the trek stays almost entirely above 4,000 m (13,125 ft) and the stunning mountain views are accompanied by beautiful waterfalls and glacial lakes. Domesticated alpacas and llamas graze the high grasslands and sightings of wild vicuñas, viscachas and condors are expected. Elusive pumas and spectacled bears still roam the most remote regions of the Apolobamba range. The settlement at Jatunpampa, inhabited by three families and their sheep, alpacas and horses, is a convenient

stopover where trekkers can catch trout for their supper barehanded in the Atumpampa river.

Although this 115-km (71-mile) trek can be tackled in either direction, the south-to-north option offers great views that improve daily and passes that increase in elevation, with the Sunchuli pass, the highest of the whole trek at 5,060 m (16,600 ft), coming near the end of the journey. Soon after this you'll come to the village of Pelechuco, which was founded in 1560 by Jesuit missionaries and still relies on small-scale gold-mining as its economic base. While most guides treat Pelechuco as the end of the trek, another hour on to Agua Blanca will take you to the ruins of Huatara and a comfortable hostel for the final night. Although the trek covers wild and remote terrain, the route is well marked and promoted in sufficient detail that it can be done independently. But for a small additional cost, you can arrange to have a well-informed local guide and an *arriero* (muleteer) to tend to the pack animals. Using these local guides, who operate under the auspices of the park, also provides needed employment and economic benefit to the isolated communities of the Cordillera Apolobamba.

FORGET THE INCA TRAIL?

THE BUILD-UP Peru's legendary Inca Trail starts in the Sacred Valley of the Urubamba river and culminates with the descent into the magnificent ruins of Machu Picchu. There is some outstanding Andean scenery and mountainous jungle trekking along the way, but the major draw is Machu Picchu.

THE LETDOWN Now so heavily travelled that you need a reservation months in advance just to get your foot on the path, the trail is overrun with as many tour guides and operators as hikers, and its camp sites are crowded and dirty – hardly a wilderness experience. The constant influx has led the government to impose a limit of 400 visitors per day and hefty entrance fees.

GOING ANYWAY? Consider a day-long trek to Machu Picchu beginning at Kilometre 104 on the railway line. You'll pass the breathtaking ruins at Wiñay Wayna and the dramatic Sun Gate along the way, and still have a day or more to explore Machu Picchu. If you opt for this route, you won't have to stay at any of the trail's crowded camp sites.

ABOVE A tour group arriving at Machu Picchu on the Inca Trail, Peru

PRACTICAL INFORMATION

Getting There and Around
From La Paz, a bus runs three times a week on a 12-hour trip to the Curva starting point and returns daily from Pelechuco. A private 4WD vehicle and driver can also be arranged in La Paz at a significantly higher cost.

Where to Stay
Community-run hostels in Lagunilla (10 minutes on foot from Curva) and Agua Blanca (an hour on foot from Pelechuco) offer simple, comfortable dormitory accommodation, hot showers and meals. Neither hostel has a website or requires a reservation, so just pitch up if you need a bed for the night.

Where to Eat
Your most rewarding meal will come at the end of a trek in front of the fireplace at the Agua Blanca hostel. The menu depends on what arrives by bus, but generally includes llama or lamb.

When to Go
Trekking is great here at any time of year, but the mildest, driest weather is from January to April and in October and November.

Budget per Day for Two
Less than £40 including a guide, pack burros, accommodation and transport to and from La Paz.

Website
www.trekapolobamba.com

MAIN IMAGE The snowcapped peaks of the Cordillera Apolobamba
BELOW (left to right) The village of Curva shrouded in mist; indigenous Kallawaya woman; vicuñas on a mountain slope, Cordillera Apolobamba

Inca ruin at Samaipata, at the start of the Che Guevara Trail, Bolivia

CHE GUEVARA TRAIL

NEED TO KNOW

LOCATION The trail runs through several towns in the south of Bolivia's Santa Cruz province

VISITORS PER YEAR An estimated 1,000–4,000 travellers pass through parts of this trail every year

CLIMATE The area is generally hot and humid, with sub-tropical temperatures between 20°C (68°F) and 30°C (86°F) for most of the year

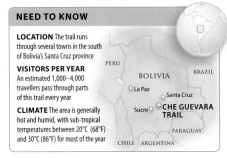

A challenging trekking route with a political twist, the Che Guevara Trail cuts through subtropical valleys and rocky hills while retracing the footsteps of the revolutionary leader Che Guevara during his final days. The route is generally considered to start in the beautiful highland village of Samaipata, the site of an important Inca ruin, and ends in the equally picturesque town of Vallegrande. The long trail measures 150 km (93 miles), and most visitors opt for a 4WD to cover the more difficult stretches. To make the most of your trip, you should allow at least a week to complete the route and book into one of the rustic campsites along the way.

Practical Information

Getting There The trailhead at Samaipata is reached by road from the city of Santa Cruz, in Bolivia's Santa Cruz province. All but a few experienced trekkers require a 4WD to cover parts of this long trail.

When to Go The best time to visit the normally humid and hot central valleys is between April and September, when the temperatures are cooler and the rains are still a month or two away.

Website www.boliviabella.com/ruta-del-che.html

The expansive, pristine salt plains of the Salar de Uyuni, Bolivia, drenched in evening sunlight

SALAR DE UYUNI

NEED TO KNOW

LOCATION In Bolivia's southwestern Potosí province, about 80 km (50 miles) east of the border with Chile

VISITORS PER YEAR 10,000; this is Bolivia's fastest-growing tourism destination

CLIMATE Temperatures range from 20°C (68°F) on a dry day in summer to a bitterly cold low of -25°C (-13°F) on winter nights

Bolivia's Salar de Uyuni defies adequate description, although calling it a blinding, surreal expanse of endless pure-white flatness that must be seen to be believed comes very close. This eerily silent and awe-inspiring *salar* (salt flat) is one of the most otherworldly environments on earth, and all that remains of an enormous inland sea that evaporated thousands of years ago. Covering an area of about 11,000 sq km (4,250 sq miles), these sun-baked plains hold enormous quantities of salt – 9 billion tonnes, in fact – and are home to some of the most fantastic wildlife in South America. And for those intrepid travellers who want the full experience, there's even a hotel here built entirely from blocks of salt.

This extraordinary wilderness draws trekkers who are in search of solitude and adventure. Most require a 4WD to complete the journey across the flats, which measure 150 km (93 miles), but which often seem ten times that distance because of the daunting emptiness of the place. Sunlight reflects so brightly off the salt that you're likely to be dazzled for much of the journey. This bright and pristine landscape is interrupted only by one or two rocky "islands" full of cacti, the occasional blood-red flamingo or long-tailed chinchilla, a haunting antique train graveyard, and weird and wonderful mirages that come and go in the distance. You might also see the odd miner panning the flats for salt, a centuries-old tradition that is still going strong today. The atmosphere here is considered by many scientists to be the purest on the planet, and the air is so dry and free from variation that the Salar de Uyuni is used as a calibration point for satellites far above the earth.

Although the traditional end-to-end trekking route can be covered in one day by 4WD, the majority of visitors prefer to span it out over three or four days to make the most of the region's wonders on their own two feet and at their own pace. Most drive to one of the several trail heads, walk as much of the distance as they wish, and arrange for a pick-up a few miles from the other end. Watching the sun rise and set, tinting the

Hikers in Peru's Cordillera Blanca, with a snowcapped mountain peak in the background

The bright blue Nordenskjöld Lake in Torres del Paine National Park, Patagonia, Chile

ABOVE View of Salar de Uyuni from Isla de los Pescadores, a rocky outcrop covered in cacti in the middle of the salt flats

clouds every colour of the rainbow above this immense sheet of white oblivion, is a truly unforgettable experience. While neither the longest nor most arduous trek on the continent, tackling the magnificent Salar de Uyuni, one of the world's most harsh and arid environments, surely ranks as the strangest of all.

Practical Information

Getting There Almost all visitors arrive by train from Oruro. There are also buses from La Paz that run daily, although these are not recommended – some of the roads approaching the flats are incredibly steep and unsafe. 4WD tours across the flats are increasingly popular.

When to Go The dry season in these parts is from April to October, although February and March usually mean warmer temperatures.

Website www.gonomad.com/destinations/0409/salar_de_uyuni_bolivia.html

CORDILLERA BLANCA

NEED TO KNOW

LOCATION The Cordillera Blanca is located in central Peru, between Trujillo and Lima and less than 100 km (62 miles) inland from the Pacific Ocean

VISITORS PER YEAR Around 5,500

CLIMATE Coastal winds keep temperatures between 15°C (59°F) and 27°C (81°F) for most of the year

This little-explored mountain range not far inland from Peru's humid central coast is becoming increasing popular with adventurous travellers. The route is less than 180 km (112 miles) long, yet the range comprises more than 60 peaks above 5,000 m (16,400 ft), making it a mountaineer's delight. And when you consider that the weather here is not as harsh as it is in Peru's windswept Altiplano (Andean plateau) further east, that there are plenty of trekking outfitters along the way who can provide equipment and guides, and that the landscape boasts some of the most awesome mountains in the world, you'll have more than enough reasons to make this unforgettable trip.

Practical Information

Getting There Fly north from Lima to the town of Huaraz. One access route leads from here, although a more popular option starts in the Llanganuco valley 40 km (25 miles) to the north.

When to Go The best weather is between May and September. The earlier part of the season tends to be the most popular with climbers.

Website www.cordillerablancaclimbing.com

TORRES DEL PAINE

NEED TO KNOW

LOCATION The Torres del Paine lie in Chile's southernmost region of Patagonia, 400 km (250 miles) northwest of Punta Arenas

VISITORS PER YEAR Almost 25,000

CLIMATE The temperature at this southern extremity of South America rarely rises above 20°C (68°F), and winters are often well below freezing

The harsh and beautiful wilderness region of Patagonia, which is shared by Argentina and Chile, does not give up its secrets easily, but rewards the few people who make it this far south with some truly breathtaking scenery. Home to mountains, fjords, glaciers, unbelievably blue lakes and perhaps the best fishing and big-game hunting to be found on the continent, Torres del Paine National Park (see also p150) is the epicentre of all that is untamed and unspoilt in the area. A trek through its many spectacular peaks – most of which can be scaled by mid-level climbers – is guaranteed to send you back for more. In fact, most of its visitors are returning trekkers.

Practical Information

Getting There Torres del Paine National Park isn't a cheap destination. Most visitors fly the 2,200-km (1,350-mile) journey from Santiago to Punta Arenas, and then travel by road on to the park. Some people arrive by ship or bus at Puerto Natales, which is 115 km (70 miles) south of the park.

When to Go Between October and April, when days have up to 16 hours of direct sunlight, is the best time to visit, although the park is open all year.

Website www.torresdelpaine.com/ingles/index.asp

COASTAL ROUTE 15
VS ROUTE 66

Think the fabled US Route 66 is the ultimate road trip? Think again: sun, sand and endless stretches of coastal beauty make Mexico's Coastal Route 15 a better choice

NEED TO KNOW

LOCATION Stretching from the border town of Nogales to Tepic, Route 15 runs halfway down Mexico's Pacific coast

VISITORS PER YEAR Tens of thousands, but few drive the entire 1,000-km (600-mile) distance

DAYTIME TEMPERATURES Hot (26°C/79°F) and humid, but moderated on the coast by the ocean

Nogales · USA · COASTAL ROUTE 15 · Gulf of Mexico · MEXICO · Tepic · Mexico City · Acupulco · Pacific Ocean

There are few places in the world where you can drive for hours on end with the open expanse of the ocean on one side and everything from desert landscapes to tropical forests on the other. Of the handful of such routes that still remain, the little-known coastal portion of Mexico's Route 15 is one of the best anywhere. It's a journey you can make in as little as five days, or take six months to savour. Along the way, you'll see what's left of old Mexico – sadly, soon to be lost forever – and some memorable landscapes. The views are punctuated by tiny seaside *pueblos* (houses) and colonial villages, endless fields of blue agave, prehistoric landscapes, Toltec ruins and, further south, several of the world's most famous ocean resorts.

Heading south, the approach favoured by most, Route 15 begins in the interior border town of Nogales and plunges towards the Sea of Cortez, taking in the wild Sonora Desert scenery and

passing through the city of Hermosillo before reaching the brilliant blue coast in Guaymas. Making it this far is an adventure in itself, as you cross paths with venomous Gila monsters, roadrunners and the occasional vulture circling overhead. This is the Wild West of legend, brought to life in front of your eyes, before it gives way to the cooling sight of the Pacific Ocean glinting ahead.

From here onwards, it's mostly a coastal road, the likes of which you will never forget. A hundred or more kilometres brings you to the city of Mazatlán, the "Pearl of the Pacific", with more than 20 km (12 miles) of uninterrupted beaches, one of the longest stretches of sand in the world. Quaint little fishing villages and plenty of classic Mexican scenery lie ahead before Route 15 veers inward again to the east and heads toward Tepic. But you can continue south along the coast on Route 200 and reach the resorts collectively known as the Big Five. Live it up at Puerto Vallarta, Manzanillo, Ixtapa, Acapulco and Puerto Escondido – before finally driving onto the border with Guatemala.

PRACTICAL INFORMATION

Getting There and Around
You can either start this road trip in Nogales and head south, or you can pick up Route 200 from the border with Guatemala and head north along the Pacific Coast, joining Route 15 at Tepic. Parts of the route run parallel to rail lines, but you definitely need your own set of wheels for this epic journey.

Where to Eat
There are thousands of spots along Route 15 where you can stop for a bite, from the tiniest taco stands to enormous five-star restaurants. By the time you reach Guaymas, you deserve something special. Stop at Los Barcos (corner of the Malecón Malpica and Calle 22; tel. +52 622 222 7650) and treat yourself to what may be the first of many seafood meals to come.

Where to Stay
There are many places to stay along the route, but the best pick is Villa Bella (www.villabella-lacruz.com) in La Cruz de Huancaxtle. It isn't the cheapest stop, but it has everything a seaside villa should have and nothing it shouldn't.

When to Go
The Pacific stretch of Mexico tends to be hot and humid through the year, but many travellers prefer to make the pilgrimage in the high season, from late November to early May.

Budget per Day for Two
Allow at least £50, with occasional splurges of up to £110, especially if you opt to continue south from Tepic.

Website
www.visitmexico.com

ABOVE Traffic on Chicago's Michigan Avenue, part of the erstwhile Route 66

FORGET ROUTE 66?

THE BUILD-UP Up until a few decades ago, the famous Route 66, or "Main Street America" as it was then known, cut across the mid-western and southwestern United States in a wide arc, starting in Chicago and ending in Santa Monica, California. An entire popular culture grew up around this legendary route, and to this day, it continues to be the best-known road in the country.

THE LETDOWN There's just one problem, and it's a big one – Route 66 no longer exists. It hasn't for more than two decades. Parts of it are still around as state roads (not interstate highways), but the iconic cross-country route has been renamed and chopped up into unrecognizable bits. In theory, yes, you can follow the original trail, but it would not be the same thing.

GOING ANYWAY? At least the memory of this old route survives, and it's online to boot. Check out the wonderful "The Mother Road: Historic Route 66" website (www.historic66.com), which even has step-by-step directions for retracing the former asphalt glory.

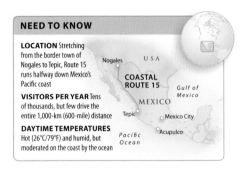
ABOVE A view of the capital city of Sonora, Hermosillo

MAIN IMAGE Rocky outcrop jutting out into the ocean, Mazatlán
BELOW (left to right) Moonrise at sunset, near San Carlos Sonora Desert; magnificent sweeping beach at Guaymas; cliff diver in Acapulco

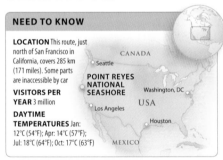

Visitors along the bridge leading to the Point Reyes Lighthouse at the Point Reyes National Seashore, USA

Ostriches walking freely through the shrubland at the Karoo National Park, South Africa

View of the rolling fields of the Annapolis Valley on the Evangeline Trail near Kentville, Canada

EVANGELINE TRAIL

NEED TO KNOW

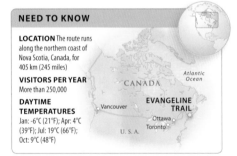

LOCATION The route runs along the northern coast of Nova Scotia, Canada, for 405 km (245 miles)

VISITORS PER YEAR More than 250,000

DAYTIME TEMPERATURES Jan: -6°C (21°F); Apr: 4°C (39°F); Jul: 19°C (66°F); Oct: 9°C (48°F)

Anyone who has travelled even a small portion of Nova Scotia's Evangeline Trail knows why it is one of Canada's premier destinations. Widely considered to be the most beautiful coastal trail in North America, the trip can be made in two days. However, because of its incredible scenery, most visitors allow at least five days. The road runs parallel to the Fundy Coast and passes through the delightful villages and orchards of the Annapolis Valley. It is the quintessential journey for those who enjoy quiet seaside towns, historic sites and breathtaking natural beauty in a pristine marine environment.

Practical Information

Getting There and Around A ferry to Yarmouth (the trail's traditional starting point) from the US state of Maine is the preferred option for this route, but then you can drive or cycle (cars and bikes are permitted on the ferry).

When to Go May–Oct is prime season here. Autumn has fewer visitors and the scenery is picture perfect.

Website www.novascotia.com/en/home/planatrip

KAROO NATIONAL PARK

NEED TO KNOW

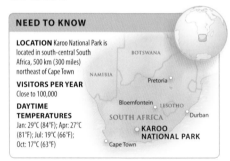

LOCATION Karoo National Park is located in south-central South Africa, 500 km (300 miles) northeast of Cape Town

VISITORS PER YEAR Close to 100,000

DAYTIME TEMPERATURES Jan: 29°C (84°F); Apr: 27°C (81°F); Jul: 19°C (66°F); Oct: 17°C (63°F)

Where should one go in South Africa to see as much of its famed flora and fauna as possible, up close and personal? Just head to Karoo National Park – which has it all, and in abundance. The park is embedded within the wild and unforgiving area known as the Great Karoo, the country's largest – and most diverse – ecosystem. Much of the park's wildlife is specially adapted to the harsh environment, and thanks to conservation programmes, many species of endangered game have returned to call it home. You can see these from the relative comfort and safety of your 4WD.

Practical Information

Getting There and Around You'll need a 4WD to make the most of this rugged national park. While trekking is allowed in a few spots, for the most part, visitors must stay with their vehicles.

When to Go The best time for a visit is any time between August and February.

Website www.sanparks.org/parks/karoo

POINT REYES NATIONAL SEASHORE

NEED TO KNOW

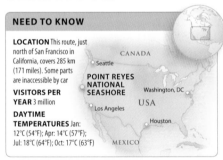

LOCATION This route, just north of San Francisco in California, covers 285 km (171 miles). Some parts are inaccessible by car

VISITORS PER YEAR 3 million

DAYTIME TEMPERATURES Jan: 12°C (54°F); Apr: 14°C (57°F); Jul: 18°C (64°F); Oct: 17°C (63°F)

It's hard to deny that California has a lock on natural scenic beauty, especially if you're lucky enough to travel through Point Reyes National Seashore. Set in one of the world's most famous regions, Marin County's coast between Napa Valley wine country and the cosmopolitan city of San Francisco, the region seems to exist in another century. Herds of endangered tule elk roam through the grasslands, bald eagles circle overhead and rare breeds of seals frolic in its coastal waters. Add to that the fact that much of the protected seashore can be explored on bicycle, by boat or on foot, and you have the makings of a perfect excursion.

Practical Information

Getting There and Around You'll need a car to visit much of Point Reyes – now designated a National Seashore. Once inside, several areas are closed to vehicles, to protect the ecosystem. However, there are designated walking and hiking trails.

When to Go Apr–Oct, to enjoy California's superb temperatures.

Website www.nps.gov/pore

Pan-American Highway meandering through quilted wheat fields, near Quetzaltenango, Guatemala

A dramatic stretch of the Great Ocean Road winding between Victoria's mountain range and the stunning Great Australian Bight

GREAT OCEAN ROAD

NEED TO KNOW

LOCATION This road stretches almost 300 km (180 miles) along the coast of Victoria, Australia

VISITORS PER YEAR 250,000

DAYTIME TEMPERATURES
Jan: 23°C (73°F); Apr: 19°C (66°F); Jul: 14°C (57°F); Oct: 18°C (64°F)

Australia's Great Ocean Road is acclaimed by Aussies and others alike as the continent's most stunning coastal route, and with good reason. One of the first highways in the country built specifically for tourism, it follows the southern coast of Victoria for roughly 300 km (180 miles), winding its way through some astounding ocean scenery. The loosely defined Great Ocean Road region includes well-known sites such as the 12 Apostles, the protected Otways rainforest, and for those with an appetite for the sea, Bells Beach, the continent's only coastal mountain range. And, of course, there's the Great Ocean Road itself.

Practical Information
Getting There and Around The Great Ocean Road was built expressly for touring vehicles, although there are several day-hikes possible. Cycling is not an option in most parts.

When to Go Aug–Nov and Mar–May, when the weather is cool. The mountainous regions have chilly evenings any time of the year.

Website www.greatoceanrd.org.au

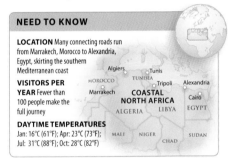

The monumental Roman ruins at Leptis Magna on the North African coastal route in Libya

COASTAL NORTH AFRICA

NEED TO KNOW

LOCATION Many connecting roads run from Marrakech, Morocco to Alexandria, Egypt, skirting the southern Mediterranean coast

VISITORS PER YEAR Fewer than 100 people make the full journey

DAYTIME TEMPERATURES
Jan: 16°C (61°F); Apr: 23°C (73°F); Jul: 31°C (88°F); Oct: 28°C (82°F)

A journey along coastal North Africa is not for the faint of heart. On the other hand, this is one of the last great stretches of coastal highway that, outside of the major cities, is relatively free from commercialization and the less attractive side of 21st-century life. Surprisingly, considering the dry terrain, some of the world's finest desert flora and fauna is to be found here too. Along this route stretching for more than 3,000 km (1,800 miles) – only partly paved – you'll see a variety of sights, from an occasional nomadic Bedouin caravan to grand French and Italian colonial villas to Roman ruins, such as the impressive Leptis Magna *(see p45)*.

Practical Information
Getting There and Around You can fly into the major cities, several of which are connected by rail.

When to Go The winter months between Nov–Feb afford a little bit of protection against the sun, which can be relentlessly oppressive. If you visit during this period, you are likely to encounter some cooling rain as well.

Website www.wildernesstravel.com/itins/medcoast.html

PAN-AMERICAN HIGHWAY

NEED TO KNOW

LOCATION The world's longest highway runs from Alaska to Patagonia for almost 48,000 km (28,800 miles)

VISITORS PER YEAR Millions travel sections of the route, very few do the whole trip

DAYTIME TEMPERATURES Arctic lows of -30°C (-22°F) to tropical highs of over 40°C (104°F)

Trying to describe the world's longest highway is like trying to describe the entire Western American Hemisphere, as that's exactly what the Pan-American Highway is – a link that travels from the Arctic to the Antarctic. Apart from the notorious Darien Gap, a tantalizing 150-km (90-mile) strip in Panama, you can travel from Alaska's Prudhoe Bay to the southernmost town in Tierra del Fuego and never leave this mega-highway. Literally almost every ecosystem and habitat on earth is encountered along the way, making this truly the world's "ultimate road trip". It is estimated that fewer than 500 people have ever completed the entire gruelling journey.

Practical Information
Getting There and Around The Pan-American Highway is so vast that the only way it can be taken in is by a reliable vehicle over a period of several months (some say years).

When to Go Given the vast expanse of the highway, you're almost guaranteed to encounter climatic extremes – and everything in between – no matter when you go. However, leaving from Alaska anytime between Nov and Mar is never a good idea.

Website www.go-panamerican.com

ANNAPURNA
VS EVEREST BASE CAMP

An incomparable Himalayan journey leads trekkers to the base camp of the world's most demanding mountain, crowned with icy eddies of swirling clouds – and it's not Everest

NEED TO KNOW

LOCATION The Himalaya mountain range, Nepal

VISITORS PER YEAR Approximately 8,000

DAYTIME TEMPERATURES Kathmandu – Jan: 10°C (50°F); Apr: 19°C (67°F); Jul: 23°C (75°F); Oct: 19°C (67°F). The air can be much cooler in the mountains

CHINA
Tibet · Lhasa
ANNAPURNA
· NEPAL
Pokhara · Kathmandu
BHUTAN
INDIA

Among the world's highest peaks – that exclusive club of 14 summits rising over 8,000 m (26,240 ft) – no mountain is more feared by climbers and as rarely climbed as Annapurna I. It is also the most deadly mountain in the world, with a horrific fatality rate of around 40 per cent, so just trekking to the Annapurna Sanctuary, the lofty glacial bowl that serves as base camp for climbing expeditions, is sufficiently thrilling for most people in search of high elevations and stunning mountain views.

Pokhara, Nepal's second-largest city, makes a great base for trekking in the surrounding area, which is easily accessible and filled with diverse scenery. The route to the Annapurna Sanctuary, 40 km (25 miles) north of the verdant Pokhara Valley, offers a more picturesque and intimate experience than the trek to Everest Base Camp.

Leaving the valley, the trail climbs steeply through forests of rhododendron laced with orchids, bamboo, terraced rice fields, and into alpine meadows. Along the way, you will pass several villages, traverse canyons and cross streams on

rickety suspension footbridges. Leaving woodlands behind and entering a rugged realm of ice and snow, a night at the first base camp gives a taste of what's to come as you rest beneath the shimmering "fish-tail" summit of Macchapuchare, one of the most dramatically beautiful of all Himalayan peaks.

The following day, after ascending a narrow pass that was first penetrated by Westerners in 1956, you'll arrive at the Annapurna Sanctuary, a mountain amphitheatre at an elevation of 4,100 m (13,450 ft) ringed by eight peaks over 7,000 m (22,965 ft), including Annapurna I. Here the surrounding mountains rise up so sharply and so high that the Sanctuary receives only 7 hours of sunlight a day, even in midsummer. Sacred to the local villagers who consider it to be the home of the gods, the Sanctuary was off-limits to Dalits (the "untouchable" caste) and women until recently.

The Annapurna Sanctuary trek has not been affected by road-building schemes that have already impacted on other classic treks in the region. However, modernization is expected to increase, so dedicated trekkers are advised to follow this incredible route sooner rather than later.

PRACTICAL INFORMATION

Getting There and Around
From Kathmandu, the capital of Nepal, take a short flight to Pokhara. When the weather is clear, the flight offers stupendous views of the entire Himalaya range.

Where to Eat
The lakeside Bistro Caroline (tel. +977 61 531341) in Pokhara caters to upscale tastes with an excellent menu of Indian, Nepali and European cuisine. It's pricey for locals, but affordable by Western standards.

Where to Stay
In the area around Pokhara, guesthouses for budget-bound trekkers are plentiful. But for a post-trek splurge, consider the Fulbari Resort & Spa

(tel. +977 61 432451, www. fulbari.com), a five-star hotel built in the architectural style of Nepal's golden age, offering panoramic mountain and valley views, with doubles from £115 per night.

When to Go
March–April and October–November usually offer decent weather and avoid the June–September monsoons.

Budget per Day for Two
Guided trekking with accommodation in teahouses and tents, including meals, can range from £50 to £100 per night per couple.

Website
www.asian-trekking.com/home

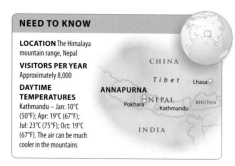
ABOVE The "fish-tail" peak of Macchapuchare

FORGET THE TREK TO EVEREST BASE CAMP?

THE BUILD-UP This is the world's highest peak – Mount Everest, *Sagarmatha*, the roof of the world – where mountaineering legends are born. The base camp is the closest you can get to the summit without full mountaineering gear and there are dramatic views of the Khumbu Glacier and the treacherous icefall.

THE LETDOWN The trail from Lukla to the Everest Base Camp is one of the most crowded in Nepal and sadly littered with beer bottles and rubbish. For most, the highlight of the trek is not the base camp, but the ascent to Kala Pattar at 5,545 m (18,192 ft) for views of Everest.

GOING ANYWAY? To avoid the crowds, opt for the March–May season. Rather than starting from Lukla, consider starting from Jiri, on the old access route used by early Everest climbers on the successful first ascent. It is a longer trek, but less crowded, and the terrain abounds with colourful villages and ancient monasteries.

ABOVE Trekkers pitching their tents at Everest Base Camp

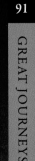

MAIN IMAGE A stupa, or Buddhist shrine, in the Annapurna Sanctuary
BELOW (left to right) Terraced rice fields; children at Ghandruk village; a hiker on a bamboo bridge crossing the Marsygandi river

4 MORE GREAT TREKS TO RIVAL EVEREST BASE CAMP

CONCORDIA, KARAKORAM RANGE, PAKISTAN A trek into the heart of the Karakorams leads through the earth's highest concentration of glaciers. The camp at Concordia is located below four of only 14 peaks in the world that are over 8,000 m (26,246 ft), including K2 – the world's second-highest peak.

CORDILLERA HUAYHUASH, PERU Circle a range of 6,000 m (19,685 ft) peaks almost unknown to international trekkers. The route crosses the South American continental divide.

HAUTE ROUTE, THE ALPS, FRANCE AND SWITZERLAND On this classic route from Mont Blanc to the Matterhorn, trekkers pass by ten of the 12 highest peaks in the Alps and enjoy comfortable lodging and hearty meals in mountain huts.

CHOMOLHARI TREK, BHUTAN Tourists are a rare commodity in Bhutan. This trek leads through rhododendron-canopied forests to high-alpine meadows where there are more yaks than people. The destination is the 7,314-m (23,996 ft) Chomolhari.

MAIN IMAGE Interior of the Palace on Wheels **BELOW (left to right)** Hawa Mahal or Palace of the Winds, Jaipur; a tiger strolling in front of visitors to Ranthambhore Wildlife Park; the Palace on Wheels locomotive

THE PALACE ON WHEELS
VS THE ORIENT EXPRESS

The fabled Orient Express is now oriental in name only – book a berth on the Palace on Wheels instead, and travel across the Indian desert state of Rajasthan on one of the world's most inspirational train journeys

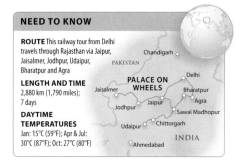

NEED TO KNOW

ROUTE This railway tour from Delhi travels through Rajasthan via Jaipur, Jaisalmer, Jodhpur, Udaipur, Bharatpur and Agra

LENGTH AND TIME
2,880 km (1,790 miles);
7 days

DAYTIME TEMPERATURES
Jan: 15°C (59°F); Apr & Jul: 30°C (87°F); Oct: 27°C (80°F)

Railways are an integral part of the fabric of Indian life – from chuntering third-class local services with daredevil commuters hanging off every available space, to the fast and efficient modern expresses which connect the major cities. There's no better way to enjoy the slowly unwinding landscapes of the subcontinent than from a window seat aboard one of the country's thousands of trains.

None of the trains, however, can surpass the legendary Palace on Wheels. It offers a memorable taste of the style and opulence of the Raj era, and of the sumptuous lifestyles enjoyed by Indian maharajas and British colonial bigwigs alike. The Palace on Wheels first entered service in 1982, using the lavishly decorated coaches once owned by Indian and colonial notables, including the former rulers of the princely states of Gujarat and Rajputana, the Nizam of Hyderabad and the British Viceroy of India. The old train was subsequently replaced with new, fully modernized and air-conditioned carriages in 1991, but much of the ambience of the original remains, with luxurious private cabins, a well-stocked bar, two dining cars and devoted personal service from a group of highly trained retainers.

Starting from Delhi, the Palace on Wheels makes a seven-day tour of one of India's most magical regions, travelling through the state of Rajasthan, with its iconic desert landscapes dotted with magnificent forts, palaces and cities. The tour begins with visits to three of the state's finest cities: Jaipur, the famous Pink City; the fabulous desert citadel of Jaisalmer; and Jodhpur, home to the

ABOVE One of the most iconic buildings in the world, the Taj Mahal in Agra, set on the banks of the Yamuna river

majestic Meherangarh Fort, one of the mightiest in India. The train then proceeds to Sawai Madhopur and the Ranthambhore National Park – one of the best places on the planet to spot tigers in the wild – and then to Chittorgarh, the site of another iconic Indian fort. Then it's on to the romantic lakeside city of Udaipur, before heading back north to the village of Bharatpur, site of the Keoladeo Ghana National Park, one of the world's finest bird sanctuaries. The best, however, is saved for the end of the tour, with the last stop being the famous city of Agra, home of the unforgettable Taj Mahal, Agra Fort and nearby Fatehpur Sikri, all UNESCO World Heritage Sites.

FORGET THE ORIENT EXPRESS?

THE BUILD-UP The most famous train in Europe, if not the world, the Orient Express has become synonymous with luxury, romance and intrigue, immortalized in books and on film.

THE LETDOWN The original Paris–Istanbul route was steadily cut back over the years, and much-changed Orient Express made its final journey from Strasbourg to Vienna on 12 December 2009. To recreate the original route, you'll either have to put together a route combining four trains, or shell out a staggering £6,560 per person to travel on the privately run Venice-Simplon Orient Express (which doesn't, strictly speaking, have anything to do with the original at all).

ABOVE Tourists boarding the original Orient Express in Salzburg, Austria

GOING ANYWAY? Plan a journey on one of the Venice-Simplon Orient Express trains. It still offers one of the most comfortable ways of travelling around Europe and provides services to eight major European destinations between March and November.

PRACTICAL INFORMATION

Getting There and Around
From New Delhi airport, it's a short taxi ride to Safdarjung railway station, from where the train departs.

Where to Eat
The Palace on Wheels has two dining cars which serve international and Indian food.

Where to Stay
There are 14 fully equipped deluxe rooms in the train.

When to Go
Oct–Mar is the best time, as it is outside the monsoon period and before the weather gets too hot.

Budget for Two
The 7-day tour starts at around £3,700 based on two sharing and includes accommodation and food on the train as well as entrance fees specified in the itinerary.

Website
www.palaceonwheels.net

The sumptuous interior of the Observation Car on Rovos Rail's luxurious Pride of Africa train

The Canadian passing by a lake and lush greenery on its Toronto–Vancouver route

The Glacier Special Express travelling through the frozen winter landscape of Blitzingen village, Switzerland

THE GLACIER EXPRESS

NEED TO KNOW

ROUTE This train journey takes you from Zermatt to St Moritz, Switzerland

LENGTH AND TIME 290 km (180 miles); 7 hours, 30 minutes

DAYTIME TEMPERATURES
Jan: 1°C (31°F);
Apr: 8°C (46°F);
Jul: 18°C (64°F);
Oct: 9°C (48°F)

The most jaw-dropping train ride in Europe, the Glacier Express travels across some of the continent's wildest and most beautiful mountain terrain. Billed as "the world's slowest express", the journey is an extraordinary feat of engineering – with 91 tunnels, 291 bridges and the highest point being 2,033 m (6,668 ft) above sea level at the crest of the Oberalp Pass. You are afforded a memorable spectacle as the tracks switchback between mountain passes and Alpine valleys, before ascending to Zermatt, beneath the outline of the majestic Matterhorn.

Practical Information

Train Schedule Departs four times daily in summer, once daily in winter.

When to Go The best time to visit is during the pleasantly temperate months between May and October, although tourist attractions become very busy during the peak summer season in July and August.

Website www.glacierexpress.ch

THE CANADIAN

NEED TO KNOW

ROUTE This journey takes you from Toronto to Vancouver

LENGTH AND TIME
4,400 km (2,740 miles);
3 days

DAYTIME TEMPERATURES
Jan: 3°C (37°F);
Apr: 9°C (48°F);
Jul: 17°C (63°F);
Oct: 10°C (50°F)

The longest railway journey in North America, the Canadian journeys three times a week between Toronto and Vancouver via Sudbury Junction, Winnipeg, Saskatoon, Edmonton, Jasper and Kamloops. The railway traverses the windswept lake lands of northern Ontario as well as the rolling western plains of the prairies before the most magnificent section of the route – the climb up into the craggy heights of the Canadian Rockies – wrapping up its journey on British Columbia's Pacific Coast. Between Sudbury Junction and Winnipeg, travellers wishing to get totally off the beaten track can request a special stop at any point along the line which offers unrivalled access to some of the most stunning Canadian wilderness.

Practical Information

Train Schedule Three departures every week in each direction.

When to Go The pleasantly warm summer months from June to September are a good time to travel.

Website www.viarail.ca

ROVOS RAIL

NEED TO KNOW

ROUTE Routes run across Southern Africa

LENGTH AND TIME The train does not have a fixed route; 1–14 days along various routes

DAYTIME TEMPERATURES
Jan: 26°C (79°F);
Apr: 23°C (73°F);
Jul: 17°C (63°F);
Oct: 21°C (70°F)

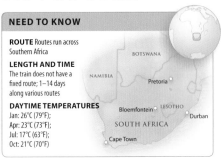

Billed as the world's most luxurious railway, Rovos Rail offers unforgettable trips through southern Africa from its base near Pretoria. The company operates two beautifully rebuilt classic trains, featuring wood-panelled coaches and Edwardian period decor. Facilities include sumptuous dining cars and observation carriages, while the spacious suites come with a private bathroom and lounge, and 24-hour room service. Most itineraries feature journeys around South Africa from Pretoria to Durban or Cape Town, with stops at tourist attractions and safari parks. The train's route passes through magnificent landscapes, including the starkly beautiful Great Karoo. There are also longer excursions to Namibia, taking in some amazing sights such as the Fish River Canyon, Botswana, Zimbabwe and Tanzania.

Practical Information

Train Schedule No fixed schedule for departures.

When to Go October to May; it gets very busy during the peak holiday months of December and January.

Website www.rovos.com

One of the world's longest train journeys, the Indian Pacific Railway, crossing the scenic Blue Mountains

The Sunset Limited Amtrak train passing through wild and barren American terrain

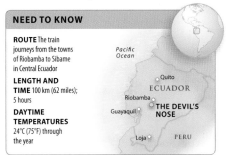

Passengers enjoying the dizzying panorama from the roof of El Nariz del Diablo

INDIAN PACIFIC RAILWAY

NEED TO KNOW

ROUTE The route runs between Sydney and Perth, Australia

LENGTH AND TIME
4,352 km (2,704 miles);
3 days

DAYTIME TEMPERATURES
Jan: 28°C (82°F);
Apr: 22°C (72°F);
Jul: 14°C (57°F);
Oct: 21°C (70°F)

One of the world's longest train journeys, the Indian Pacific straddles Australia, running from Sydney on the east coast to Perth on the west via Broken Hill, Adelaide, Kalgoorlie and the remote desert settlement of Cook. Starting from Sydney, the journey begins by crossing the eucalyptus-clad heights of the Blue Mountains *(see p178)* before descending into the great open spaces of the Australian Outback. The journey is best known for its fabled crossing of the treeless plains of the Nullabor Desert, between Kalgoorlie and Perth, which includes the world's longest stretch of absolutely straight railway track: a staggering 478 km (297 miles) without a single bend or twist in the rails.

Practical Information

Train Schedule Departs twice in a week in both directions.

When to Go December to March, during the southern hemisphere summer.

Website www.gsr.com.au

SUNSET LIMITED

NEED TO KNOW

ROUTE The train runs from New Orleans to Los Angeles, USA

LENGTH AND TIME
3,211 km (1,995 miles);
2 days

DAYTIME TEMPERATURES
Jan: 14°C (57°F);
Apr: 21°C (70°F);
Jul: 29°C (84°F);
Oct: 23°C (73°F)

Sunset Limited is the nearest thing to a transcontinental railway in the USA, currently running from New Orleans to Los Angeles. Until 2005, the train ran from Orlando to Los Angeles, and may do so again in the future. The journey offers a fascinating snapshot of the continent's contrasting landscapes, from the swampy landscape of Lousiana to the vast expanses of Texan plains and the towering mountains of California. Students of engineering will enjoy the crossing, just outside New Orleans, of the fittingly named Huey P. Long Bridge – the longest railroad bridge in the USA, 8 km (5 miles) in length – which carries the train 41 m (135 ft) above the great Mississippi River.

Practical Information

Train Schedule Departs three times a week in each direction.

When to Go Early spring or late fall (roughly Feb to May & Oct), avoiding the worst of the summer heat, and hurricane season in the south.

Website www.amtrak.com

THE DEVIL'S NOSE (EL NARIZ DEL DIABLO)

NEED TO KNOW

ROUTE The train journeys from the towns of Riobamba to Sibame in Central Ecuador

LENGTH AND TIME 100 km (62 miles);
5 hours

DAYTIME TEMPERATURES
24°C (75°F) through the year

The dramatic railway line between Riobamba and Sibame is all that survives of the route which formerly connected Quito, in the Ecuadorian highlands, with Guayaquil on the coast. Dubbed "the world's most difficult railway", construction of the line across the high Andean massif presented almost insuperable challenges, particularly the near-vertical section of rock known as The Devil's Nose (El Nariz del Diablo). Engineers conquered the problem by using an ingenious system of zig-zagging lines, with trains alternately travelling backwards and forwards in order to negotiate the switchback tracks. The line is now a popular attraction and visitors sit on the roof to enjoy the stupendous Andean vistas.

Practical Information

Train Schedule Departs three times a week in each direction.

When to Go The dry months, from June to August, although temperatures are pretty much constant all year round.

Website www.ecuadorexplorer.com/html/train.html

MAIN IMAGE Field of sunflowers with San Gimignano in the distance, Tuscany **BELOW (left to right)** Monastery of Saint Bernard; the view from the Pass; thousands of pilgrims gathered in St Peter's Square, Rome

PILGRIMAGE TO ROME
VS CAMINO DE SANTIAGO

The annual scramble across Europe to the shrine of Santiago in Spain has become so hectic that it's surely time to turn your boots toward the older charms of the Via Francigena, the ancient road to Rome

With over 100,000 pilgrims flowing in an endless stream to Santiago de Compostela every year, each one fighting for the best beds and the best stories, it can be hard not to feel like a spiritual commuter on a conveyor belt to salvation. The Via Francigena (the great pilgrim route from Canterbury in England to Rome), on the other hand, is not only emptier, but, even on a "short" section, offers a fascinatingly diverse succession of landscapes and civilizations, the likes of which could hardly be imagined on the parched plains of the Spanish *meseta*.

Pilgrims have been heading to Rome since the early days of the Christian church, following the Roman roads used by St Augustine in AD 596–7. They come to touch the relics of Saint Peter and Saint Paul, and to marvel at the many wonders of the Eternal City. It is still possible to walk in their footsteps for all or part of the journey, to feel history flowing in through the soles of your feet.

You can march with the ghosts of Roman Legions along stretches of elegantly paved road, the great basalt slabs as solid today as when those soldiers first laid them. You'll pass Etruscan amphitheatres that were already ancient when the first pilgrims passed this way, and pause at the Roman temples and baths that sprang up alongside them.

Ancient tracks hewn into the Alps guide you to the Col du Grand St-Bernard and the shelter of the monastery where trusty Saint Bernard dogs are still bred. Later, you will follow paths through the Apennines that bend beneath quarries of the dazzling white marble once worked by Michelangelo. From the Apennines you descend to the bucolic, cypress-topped hills of Tuscany, where the road

leads you straight along the main streets of turreted San Gimignano *(see pp124–5)* and honey-hued Siena. Then come the sun-kissed villages and volcanic lakes of Rome's own region, Lazio.

Where Spanish Santiago announces its stolid granite presence in the rains that roll in from the Atlantic, Rome proclaims itself on the warm breath of the Mediterranean. Yet, as it draws ever closer, so it seems increasingly ethereal, dissolving into the sea of its own mythology. And, as the vision of Rome melts away, so does the flotsam of everyday existence. You are left simply to lace up your boots, walk, eat and find somewhere to sleep at night.

However, when you finally reach Rome, its marvellous, marbled reality easily bears the weight of hundreds of miles of expectation. All the aches and pains of the route vanish within the embrace of Bernini's extraordinary elliptical colonnade, gathering pilgrims within its porticoed arms before the vast Basilica of Saint Peter.

In Santiago, every second person seems to be a pilgrim. In Rome, though, everyone else is a tourist, and the sweetness of this knowledge gives wings to each airy step through the Eternal City.

FORGET THE CAMINO DE SANTIAGO?

THE BUILD-UP Since the miraculous discovery, in the 9th century, of the relics of Saint James, millions of pilgrims have made their way to his shrine at Santiago de Compostela. Countless churches, monasteries and refuges line the Camino, and people have dedicated their lives to the welfare of pilgrims, providing food and shelter, building bridges and hospitals.

THE LETDOWN Along with fame come the freeloaders, ready to take advantage of cheap (or free) hospitality en route. Increasing numbers of cyclists whizz past, and you'll find them settled into the best beds by the time you hobble into your hostel.

GOING ANYWAY? For any long walking route you should travel as lightly as possible, and stock up on things like blister relief and good socks. On the Camino, avoid the hot holiday months, especially around the Fiestas de Santiago (25 Jul).

ABOVE Pilgrims arrive in front of the imposing Cathedral in Santiago de Compostela

Medieval pilgrims, shown travelling on foot and horseback, in one of Canterbury Cathedral's beautiful stained-glass windows

Spectacular nave of the Cathedral of Nidaros in Trondheim

CANTERBURY

NEED TO KNOW

LOCATION The Pilgrims' Way crosses southern England from Hampshire to Kent

WEATHER Daytime temperatures in summer are 14–23°C (57–73°F), in spring and autumn 8–14°C (46–57°F). Rain is possible at any time

DISTANCE The walk from Winchester to Canterbury is 195 km (120 miles)

For most of its course, the Pilgrims' Way follows the crest of the North Downs. The route was already ancient when, in the 12th century, pilgrims first set out from Winchester, England's ancient capital, to visit the shrine of Thomas à Beckett in Canterbury Cathedral. It was established three millennia ago, to transport tin and iron from the West Country to Kent, and thence to mainland Europe. It offers some glorious views, although it occasionally dips into a valley to pass through fine market towns such as Farnham and Dorking. From Canterbury, you can continue south on the Via Francigena (see pp96–7), or head north to London on the route used by Chaucer's pilgrims.

Practical Information

Getting There and Around Winchester is 1 hr by train from London Waterloo. Canterbury is 1½ hrs from London (Victoria or Charing Cross) by train, and 20 minutes from the port of Dover and the Channel Tunnel.

When to Go Due to southern England's temperate climate, the pilgrimage can be undertaken anytime between March and October. In July and August you may need to book your accommodation well in advance.

Website www.nationaltrail.co.uk

Candles lit by visitors to the Shrine of St Bernadette in Lourdes

LOURDES

NEED TO KNOW

LOCATION Lourdes is in southwest France, in the foothills of the Pyrenees

WEATHER Spring is mild and sunny. May–Oct highs average 20–25°C (68–77°F) with most rain in autumn. Winter can be very cold

DISTANCE St-Jean-Pied-de-Port to Lourdes is a walk of 150 km (95 miles)

In 1858, the Virgin Mary appeared to a young peasant girl, Bernadette Soubirous, above the town of Lourdes. The place of this visitation is now among the great pilgrimage sites of the world, and the nightly candlelit procession to the Basilica of the Rosary is one of the most moving events in Christendom. Though most pilgrims wouldn't dream of walking here, one of the principal branches of the Camino de Santiago goes straight through the town. In fact, the route from St-Jean-Pied-de-Port to Lourdes, passing beneath the dramatic heights of the Pyrenees, is perhaps the loveliest stretch of the Camino.

Practical Information

Getting There and Around St-Jean-Pied-de-Port is a delightful hour by train from Bayonne, which has an international airport. There are charter flights to Lourdes–Tarbes–Pyrénées airport from Apr to Nov.

When to Go The most important Marian Feast Days in Lourdes are 11 Feb, 31 May and 7 Oct. Late spring and early autumn are best for the walk.

Website www.epyrenees.com

TRONDHEIM

NEED TO KNOW

LOCATION Trondheim is situated just 480 km (300 miles) south of the Arctic Circle

WEATHER The Gulf Stream spares Trondheim from the worst Arctic weather. April and May are the driest months, and summer daytime temperatures range from 10 to 18°C (50 to 64°F)

DISTANCE Trondheim is a 645-km (400-mile) walk from Oslo

In the 11th century, Trondheim was known as "the Jerusalem of the North", completing the pilgrimage compass points of Santiago in the west, Rome to the south and Jerusalem in the east. The great Cathedral of Nidaros, the finest in all Scandinavia, was built over the tomb of Saint Olav, the Norwegian king who evangelized the lands of the Vikings in 1024. Pilgrims came in their thousands to be blessed at his tomb. The route disappeared after the 16th-century Reformation but, in the 1970s, Saint Olav's Way, from Oslo to Trondheim, was rediscovered. Ancient chapels and burial mounds that dotted the landscape were renovated, and great granite stones hauled into place to guide pilgrims northwards.

Practical Information

Getting There and Around Both Trondheim and Oslo have international airports. There are excellent rail and air links between them, and with other Scandinavian cities such as Copenhagen and Stockholm.

When to Go In May, the flowers en route are particularly lovely. Summer temperatures are perfect for walking, and the sun hardly sets at all.

Website www.trondheim.com

Devout pilgrims entering the Great Temple of Badrinath

Glorious frescoes in the Upper Basilica of San Francesco, Assisi

BADRINATH

NEED TO KNOW

LOCATION Badrinath lies in the foothills of the Indian Himalayas, close to the Tibetan border

WEATHER The high altitude means that, even during summer, days can be rainy and nights cold

DISTANCE Badrinath is around 300 km (180 miles) from both Rishikesh and Haridwar

CHINA
Tibet
BADRINATH
PAKISTAN   NEPAL
Delhi
   Kolkata
INDIA
Arabian
Sea   Mumbai   *Bay of*
Bengal
   Bangalore

Town and temple complex of Badrinath, on the Alaknanda river

On the right bank of the Holy River of Alaknanda, hemmed in by the sacred mountains of Nar and Narayan, stands the 9th-century temple of the Hindu god Vishnu. For a thousand years, pilgrims have trekked here to seek the blessing of "Lord Badrinath". These days most people, aside from the occasional Sadhu armed with water pot and umbrella, drive or are driven to Badrinath.

The spectacular route follows the winding course of the Ganges from the plains below Rishikesh, through Srinagar and Rudraprayag, and onwards and upwards through the tortuous curves and cliffs of the Himalayas. Just beyond Joshimath lies the greatest surprise of the journey, the near-mythical Valley of Flowers. This national park, in a range of relatively gentle hills squeezed between the Zanskar Mountains and the Great Himalaya, has breathtakingly beautiful meadows of alpine flowers, myriad butterflies and rare wildlife such as the snow leopard and the Himalayan golden eagle. Beyond the park, the road climbs again towards Badrinath, where plumes of steam from the hot springs of Tapt

Kund announce that you are nearing the Great Temple. After bathing in the warm, curative waters you may go and pay homage to Vishnu. Later, explore the area to see the stone-bound impression left by the serpent Shesh Nag, and the footprints of Vishnu himself, embedded in a massive boulder called Charanpaduka.

Those pilgrims reinvigorated by the healing springs can make the short trek on foot to Mana, the last Indian village before Tibet, and to the spectacular waterfalls and glaciers of Vasudhara and Alkapuri, passing the cave where the epic *Mahabharata* is said to have been composed.

Practical Information

Getting There and Around The nearest airport is at Dehradun (320 km/ 198 miles). Regular bus services run from Rishikesh and Haridwar. There is a complicated system of road closures on the narrow roads to Badrinath, so allow two days' travelling time.

When to Go The best time to visit is from May to September. The temple closes in September, and Badrinath is almost unreachable outside these months anyway, due to inclement weather and landslides. The Valley of Flowers is at its finest in July and August.

Website www.garhwaltourism.com

ASSISI

NEED TO KNOW

LOCATION Assisi is just south of Perugia, 175 km (110 miles) north of Rome

WEATHER Temperatures in summer can exceed 30°C (84°F)

DISTANCE It is 210 km (130 miles) from Camaldoli to Assisi. A shorter pilgrimage up Monte Subasio from Spello (12 km/7.5 miles) traces the (bare) footsteps of St Francis

Milan   Venice
Camaldoli
ITALY   ASSISI
Rome   *Adriatic*
   Naples   *Sea*
Tyrrhenian
Sea   *Ionian*
   Palermo   *Sea*

Saint Francis of Assisi spent his life walking but in recent years, few people have actually trekked on foot to the spectacular medieval basilica built in his name. However, a new pilgrimage, the Cammino di Assisi, links together several shorter routes connected with the saint's life, and takes pilgrims through some of the most unspoilt landscapes in Italy. Starting at the Benedictine monastery in Camaldoli, set in forested mountains, it descends into the Tiber valley and passes through several great medieval towns, such as Città di Castello and San Sepolcro. The entry on foot into Assisi must rank among the most thrilling arrivals anywhere.

Practical Information

Getting There and Around Camaldoli is 12 km (8 miles) from the train station at Poppi. Spello is 30 mins by train from Perugia. Assisi is linked by bus and rail to international airports at Perugia, Florence and Rome.

When to Go Spring and autumn are ideal. Christmas is also a magical time in Assisi, though much of the route may be hidden under snow.

Website www.camminodiassisi.it

CRUISING LAKE NASSER
VS CRUISING THE NILE

Starkly beautiful Lake Nasser is a far more tranquil place than the Nile to see some of Egypt's astonishing ancient monuments from the water

NEED TO KNOW

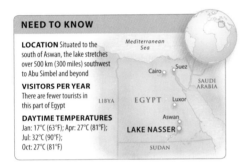

LOCATION Situated to the south of Aswan, the lake stretches over 500 km (300 miles) southwest to Abu Simbel and beyond

VISITORS PER YEAR There are fewer tourists in this part of Egypt

DAYTIME TEMPERATURES Jan: 17°C (63°F); Apr: 27°C (81°F); Jul: 32°C (90°F); Oct: 27°C (81°F)

When you are gliding over the waters of Lake Nasser, sitting on the deck of a luxurious cruise ship or sailing on a traditional wooden felucca with its tall white sail catching the breeze, you feel as though you're in the middle of the ocean. One of the world's largest artificial lakes, Lake Nasser was created when the Aswan Dam was built to regulate the waters of the Nile, and is in one of the most remote regions of Egypt – only a handful of fishermen and the occasional small tourist cruise ship or felucca can be seen on its waters.

As you drift towards the shore, you can see the honey-coloured sand dunes that stretch for miles into the wilderness, to the Western Desert in one direction and Sudan to the south, inaccessible to all but the most adventurous. Nearer the river, you may catch sight of local Bedouins tending the land or their animals. You will see clusters of date palms with lush growth beneath them, and mud-brick houses where rural Egyptians still live. And you'll see a sight that nothing can prepare you for – the magnificent golden temples of Abu Simbel.

The Great Temple of Abu Simbel was built to honour the pharaoh Ramses II, while the smaller of the two was for his wife, Nefertari. Dating back to the 13th century BC, these astonishing temples were once carved into the cliffs along the Nile. They were of such significance that when the Aswan Dam was to be constructed, UNESCO stepped in to cut the temples from the cliffside

and move them in their entirety up to higher ground, to save them from being covered by the rising waters of Lake Nasser.

While cruising flotilla-like with many other boats on the Nile, you will glimpse temples among the houses, shops and hotels of Luxor, and disembark to travel by coach to see Luxor's other sights. But nothing beats a quiet cruise on the open waters of Lake Nasser past temples looking much the same as they did when they were built.

The water of Lake Nasser has an attractive blue hue that the Nile fails to achieve. While the Nile is iconic, it is also home to some dangerous parasites and has become heavily silted over the years. Lake Nasser, however, reaches depths of around 183 m (600 ft) in some places and is clear. Monuments from ancient civilizations that could not be moved when the lake was created still lie beneath. It is a pleasure to gaze over the lake and imagine what treasures are submerged in its depths.

PRACTICAL INFORMATION

Getting There and Around
You can fly into Aswan with local carrier EgyptAir, or board an express train from Cairo or Luxor. Then, hire a felucca or take a cruise boat from the waterside. The other option is to fly from Cairo or Aswan to Abu Simbel's small airfield, from where you can rent a boat.

Where to Eat
The cuisine of southern Egypt depends heavily on fruit and vegetables from the land and fish from the lake. With Middle Eastern and Mediterranean influences, the food is delicious, wholesome and healthy. There are many restaurants in Aswan, but if you want to get a feel of stepping back in time, head to the restaurant of the Old Cataract

Hotel, a favourite of novelist Agatha Christie (www.sofitel. com; tel. +20 97 231 6000).

Where to Stay
Overlooking Lake Nasser, the Nefertari Hotel is among the best of the few hotels in Abu Simbel and within walking distance of the temples (tel. +20 97 340 0509).

When to Go
Visit Nov–May, but avoid mid-Feb–mid-Apr, when the Khamsin, a strong desert wind, can make your trip uncomfortable.

Budget per Day for Two
Around £200 should be enough to cover all expenses.

Website
www.egypt.travel

FORGET THE NILE?

THE BUILD-UP The Nile has been a source of inspiration for generations. English novelist Agatha Christie captured the air of whimsical days and romantic nights under the stars onboard a fabulous old steamer in her famous work *Death on the Nile*.

THE LETDOWN The Nile is busy with commercial barges, cruise ships and motorized ferries darting back and forth. As you board or disembark a vessel, you will be surrounded by people wanting to sell you goods or take you sightseeing for a fee – what is known as *baksheesh*. The water is dangerous and swimming should be avoided.

GOING ANYWAY? The most memorable way to experience the Nile is on cruise ships which travel from Luxor to Aswan and back. Some of these also offer five-star luxury – select the best according to your budget. You could take a felucca, but it's not as tranquil as on Lake Nasser.

ABOVE A clutch of crowded boats moored close to each other along the Nile

MAIN IMAGE Abu Simbel Temple on the shore of Lake Nasser
BELOW (left to right) The elegant Kertassi kiosk in the Kalabsha Temple; Nubian jewellery vendors; feluccas on Lake Nasser

4 MORE BOAT TRIPS TO RIVAL A NILE CRUISE

THE SEINE, PARIS, FRANCE Looking across the Paris skyline from the Seine, the city appears wonderfully romantic. Take a cruise past Notre-Dame and the Louvre, or spend a few days on board and continue to the Normandy coast.

SYDNEY HARBOUR, AUSTRALIA One of the busiest harbours in the world, Sydney Harbour offers an exciting glimpse of the city from an altogether different perspective. The highlight is sailing past the landmark Sydney Opera House.

CANAL CRUISING, AMSTERDAM Hop aboard a cruise boat for a trip around Amsterdam's canals. Whether on a candlelit dinner cruise or a day's sightseeing, the city's great architecture and street scenes can be enjoyed from a wonderful new angle.

NORFOLK BROADS, ENGLAND Meandering gently along the waters of the Norfolk Broads, one of Britain's largest inland waterways and a protected wetland area, offers the chance to see exceptionally beautiful countryside and rare wildlife.

LESS-TRAVELLED CHINA

After a period of isolation, China's vast lands and myriad ethnicities are opening up for exploration, revealing attractions beyond its big-name imperial monuments

NEED TO KNOW

LOCATION The world's fourth-largest country, China stretches from the Siberian border to tropical Hainan Island, and from the East China Sea to Central Asia. The capital city is Beijing

POPULATION Around 1.3 billion

LANGUAGES Mandarin, Cantonese in the provinces of the south, and numerous dialects

Over a period of 30 years, China has undergone a remarkable transformation: from isolated Communist state at the death of Chairman Mao in 1976, to Olympic host nation and impending global superpower today. Its appeal as a tourist destination is growing, as is the list of sites accessible to visitors. Regions little known to anyone but the locals are following the lead of Beijing and Shanghai, and beginning to let foreign travellers into their secrets.

Known locally as Zhongguo, or Middle Kingdom, China is so vast and geographically diverse that it appears more like a continent than a country. First-time visitors face a standard conundrum: "Where do I begin?" Most travellers arrive through one of three gateways: Hong Kong in the south; Shanghai in the east; or the capital, Beijing, in the north. Each city is multi-layered, with its own distinctive culture, cuisine and nightlife as well as plentiful sights through which the China of the past, present and future comes alive. Nevertheless, these cities represent only a part of this vast country's multifaceted appeal.

Planning a more extensive trip will involve travelling large distances. Fortunately, China's transport system is improving almost daily. Massive investment in air and rail travel is speeding up journey times and improving levels of comfort and service. Japanese-style "bullet" trains already serve certain shorter inter-city routes, and are due to be rolled out on longer trips over the next few years.

The standard China tourist route traditionally encompasses the imperial palaces of Beijing and Emperor Qin Shi Huang's terracotta warriors in the former capital, Xi'an. From there, it's customary to head south for a boat journey along the Yangtze river, or to visit the town of Lijiang, a UNESCO World Heritage Site in the alpine terrain of Yunnan province. A popular "last stop" is China's capital of hedonism: Shanghai, where the legacy of early 20th-century foreign domination clashes spectacularly with the country's self-confident sense of futurism.

In recent years, getting off the established tourist trail in China has become much easier. Two of its largest and most historically significant cities, Guangzhou and Chongqing, are investing heavily to attract more visitors. The ancient gardens and canals of Suzhou are being restored and improved to entice day-trippers from Shanghai. And a visit to the remote province of Guizhou, in southwest China, is particularly rewarding, affording a fascinating insight into the culture and traditions of the ethnic Miao people, whose picturesque villages dot the lower reaches of the fertile alpine countryside.

PRACTICAL INFORMATION

Entry Requirements
Visitors to China must obtain a visa in their home country in advance of their trip. It is not possible to get a visa on arrival.

When to Go
Spring and autumn usually offer the most pleasant temperatures.

Air Travel
China's gateway cities (Beijing, Hong Kong and Shanghai) are served by international airlines. The country also has a good network of domestic flights, with frequent daily flights to and from all the major cities. The website www.ctrip.com is a useful resource for bookings.

Train Travel
Chinese train travel is being revolutionized by ongoing investment in new tracks and the gradual introduction of high-speed inter-city "bullet" trains. See www.travelchina guide.com/china-trains

Road Travel
China has an extensive network of inter-city coaches, but the distances are vast, journeys long and levels of comfort low. Visitors who wish to drive themselves must obtain a Chinese licence – but be warned, the rules of the road applied in many countries are largely absent in China.

Climate
Temperatures vary considerably, from tropical areas in the south to desert in the west, and long frozen winters in the north. Most areas experience hot, rainy summers and cold, dry winters.

Website
www.travelchinaguide.com

ABOVE Sculptures carved from the hillside at Dazu, west of Chongqing

ABOVE Tourists stream along the Great Wall of China

FORGET CHINA'S TOURIST TRAIL?

THE BUILD-UP China claims several millennia of civilization and, while its rapidly expanding cities hold some attractions, it's the historic landmarks that draw visitors. Built to prevent Mongol raids on Beijing, the Great Wall of China tops the "must see" list. The capital's clutch of stellar sights includes the Forbidden City, Temple of Heaven, Summer Palace and Tiananmen Square. Beyond Beijing, the famed Terracotta Warriors of Xi'an, the Three Gorges section of the Yangtze river, and the buzzy brashness of Shanghai all provide an insight into the country's fascinating culture, history and landscape.

THE LETDOWN Tours in China are usually led in large groups led by a guide wearing a microphone. As a result, the major stops on the tourist trail are frequently crowded and unnecessarily noisy. The Chinese state also has very defined views about how China is portrayed to foreigners, and "information control" is most evident at major attractions.

DOING IT ANYWAY? While the guides are expert at reeling off official dates and figures, they rarely volunteer much in the way of context. Don't be afraid to ask polite questions. Doing some research yourself can also help to ensure you're in a position to form an objective opinion.

ABOVE The Gothic-style Catholic Church of the Sacred Heart, Guangzhou
LEFT Traditional boats on the narrow, ancient waterways in Suzhou

GUANGZHOU

Formerly known as Canton, the capital of China's southern manufacturing heartland attracts plenty of business travellers, but is largely overlooked by tourists. While less dramatic than Beijing and Shanghai in an aesthetic sense, Guangzhou is nonetheless an intriguing city. Conscious of its forthcoming star turn as host of the Asian Games in 2010, it is undergoing a massive urban facelift. New structures include China's tallest building, the 610-m (2,000-ft) Guangzhou New Television Tower; a futuristic opera house designed by Zaha Hadid; and a Beijing Olympics-style "Water Cube" aquatics arena. Located on China's strategic southern coast and spliced by the Pearl River, Guangzhou was for a long time China's sole maritime connection with the outside world. In the late 19th century, it became a foreign treaty port. Shamian Island, in the city's Liwan district, boasts a rich architectural legacy from that period. Neo-Classical banks, mansions, consulates and churches were constructed amid the tropical greenery, and fine granite buildings line the old waterfront Bund, which is reminiscent of its namesake in Shanghai. The impressive Gothic-style Catholic Church of the Sacred Heart, completed in 1888 under the Emperor Guangxu, was modelled on the cathedral of Notre Dame in Paris. Guangzhou's other significant draw-card is its sublime Cantonese cuisine, China's most cherished culinary genre. According to proud locals, this is the place to feast on the Middle Kingdom's finest dim sum and seafood.

PRACTICAL INFORMATION

Getting There and Around Domestic and some international airlines serve Guangzhou airport (www.guangzhouairportonline.com), which is 28 km (17 miles) from the city centre. Public transport within the city is good, with a subway, buses, trams and water buses.

Where to Eat Experience authentic Cantonese cuisine at Panxi Restaurant (151 Longjin Xi Lu, Tianhe District; tel. +86 20 8181 5718), which serves fine seafood in a classical garden setting.

Where to Stay The Grand Palace Hotel Guangzhou (www.grandpalace-hotel.com), in the heart of the financial district, has smartly furnished rooms, and more character than many of the city's business-focused hotels.

When to Go April–May and October are the most pleasant periods to visit, being less hot and sticky than the summer months.

Budget per Day for Two £80–100

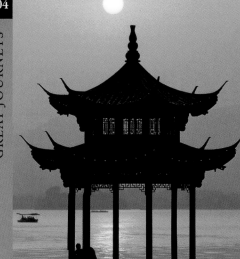

Elegant pagoda adding to the mystical beauty of West Lake, Hangzhou

HANGZHOU

The calm waters and sublime sunsets of West Lake (Xihu in Chinese), surrounded by meandering hills, have made Hangzhou a cherished retreat for emperors, artists and writers throughout history. Today, this fast-growing city has become a popular destination for those wishing to enjoy its shaded parks, ancient temples and refined pace of life. Though weekend crowds threaten the becalming ambience, Hangzhou easily merits a couple of days respite from the relentless pace of modern China. A little outside town, the new Liangzhu Culture Museum offers an insight into one of the country's earliest and most significant civilizations. Designed by British architect David Chipperfield, the museum is built on the site where archaeologists uncovered the treasures of the Liangzhu people, who lived on a fertile plain of the Yangtze river delta around the time of the Egyptian Pharaohs. One of the first cultures to use plough agriculture and irrigation systems, the Liangzhu were skilled craftsmen who created black-burnished pottery, lacquerware and jade implements, cooking vessels and burial disks. Comprising a series of courtyards radiating inwards from a man-made lake, the museum showcases the unearthed treasures of this Neolithic "Jade Culture", dating back 5,000 years.

PRACTICAL INFORMATION

Getting There and Around Hangzhou has a large airport, well served by international and domestic airlines. It is also easily accessible by rail and road from Shanghai, 180 km (112 miles) away. The Liangzhu Culture Museum (Liangzhu town; tel. +86 571 8877 0700; open 8:30am–4pm Tue–Sun), is a 45-minute drive from the city centre by taxi or bus number 513.

Where to Eat Fei Le (7 Baifu Road; tel. +86 571 8706 0766) serves sumptuous Hangzhounese seafood in private dining rooms.

Where to Stay The exquisitely landscaped gardens of Xihu State Guest House (www.xihusgh.com), situated on West Lake, make for an idyllic stay.

When to Go Catch the spring blossom (Apr–Jun), or autumn mists (Sep–Oct).

Budget per Day for Two £80–100

Suzhou Museum, a striking blend of modern and traditional design

SUZHOU

Located on Lake Tai, Suzhou was once the Yangtze river delta region's wealthiest, most culturally diverse city. Eulogized as a "paradise on earth" by an old Chinese proverb, it is best known for its UNESCO-listed Chinese gardens, ancient temples and historic silk industry. Weekdays are the quietest time to visit, offering the chance to explore this characterful city in relative tranquillity. Most striking architecturally are its whitewashed "scholar houses", with grey slate roofs, upturned eaves and carved gateposts. In various states of disrepair and restoration, the finest old examples line the city's canals, remnants of a once-extensive network of waterways that criss-crossed Suzhou. Its finest new building is the Suzhou Museum, designed by Guangzhou-born architect I M Pei, who spent time here as a child. Though often bypassed by visitors in favour of the city's classical gardens, it masterfully deconstructs and updates the classic scholar house and garden, blending a deep affinity for classical architectural styles with the modernist streak that influenced Pei's controversial glass pyramid outside the museum of the Louvre in Paris.

PRACTICAL INFORMATION

Getting There and Around Catch a CRH bullet train from Shanghai Station (35 mins). Local buses, rickshaws and taxis make it easy to get around Suzhou.

Where to Eat De Yue Lou (43 Taijian Xiang, Guanqian Lu; tel. +86 512 6522 2230) is a good place to sample Suzhou's speciality, seafood.

Where to Stay Pingjiang Lodge (www.the-silk-road.com/hotel/pingjianghotel/index.html) combines 4-star facilities with classic Suzhou architecture, designed around traditional landscaped courtyards.

When to Go Spring (Apr–May) and autumn (Sep–Oct) are best.

Budget per Day for Two £60–80

Dazzling neon illuminating the streets of Chongqing by night

CHONGQING

Known primarily as the departure point for Yangtze river cruises to the Three Gorges, Chongqing is a fascinating city too often overlooked by those who arrive just in time to set sail. With a total land area the size of Austria, and a population larger than that of Malaysia, China's World War II capital is sometimes called the "world's largest city". This is a misnomer – Chongqing is actually a municipality, not a city at all. The hilly downtown area is built around the convergence of the Yangtze and Jialing rivers, and at night the undulating neon skyline is an impressive spectacle – especially viewed from the old cable car that spans the river. It is growing at an astonishing pace, and its designs for the future are on display at the Planning Exhibition Gallery, which features virtual video presentations, interactive maps, and a vast scale model of Chongqing as it is predicted to be by the year 2020. The city's troubled history – it was repeatedly bombed by Japanese fighter planes during World War II – is documented with interactive exhibits at the Three Gorges Museum on People's Square. A 20-minute taxi ride from the city is Ciqikou, a pretty riverside village with an old hilltop temple.

PRACTICAL INFORMATION

Getting There and Around Chongqing (www.travelchinaguide.com/cityguides/chongqing/) can be reached by air, rail, sea or road. It has three airports, with links to all of China's provincial capitals as well as some Asian and European capitals. In town, there is a comprehensive bus system and cable cars to link those districts separated by the city's rivers.

Where to Eat Try Chongqing's famous spicy hotpot dishes at Chongqing Prince Restaurant (www.prince-catering.com/en/Stra_Chongqing6.php).

Where to Stay The 4-star Hongyadong Hotel (56 Cangbai Road, Yuzhong District; tel. +86 23 6399 2888) is well located near the Chaotianmen dock.

When to Go It is hot and humid all year, but especially in summer (Jun–Sep).

Budget per Day for Two £50–60

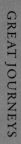

Elaborate traditional dress worn by Miao villagers, Guizhou province

TOP The imposing Catholic cathedral of Xi Kai, Tianjin **ABOVE** Eclectic wares for sale on Tianjin's market street, Shenyang Lu

TIANJIN

Known affectionately as the "Shanghai of the North", Tianjin has much in common with its more famous east coast cousin: similar historic architecture, a trading and shipping history, and an urban layout curved around a broad river. One of China's largest ports, the city is bisected by the Hai river, and tour boats glide along its waters offering fine views of the skyline. Tianjin's main attraction, however, is the varied architectural legacy of its 19th-century construction boom. Its Italian concession is graced by Tuscan-style villas, while Jiefang Bei Lu, the avenue which linked the French and British concessions, is lined with an impressive array of grand former banking headquarters and municipal buildings. There are also some fine churches, notably Xi Kai Cathedral, based on the church of Notre-Dame de la Garde in Marseille, France. At

weekends, an antiques street market on Shenyang Lu parades an eclectic assortment of paintings, clocks, Chinese musical instruments and Mao-era memorabilia. Tianjin is also revered for its steamed dumplings, and no trip here would be complete without a visit to the Goubuli Dumpling Restaurant.

PRACTICAL INFORMATION

Getting There and Around The CRH bullet train travels to/from Beijing South Station in 27 minutes, making Tianjin an easy day trip from the capital. Tianjin Binhai Airport (13 km/8 miles from the city centre) is well served by domestic airlines. The city has an excellent public transport system, including a subway, light railway and city buses.

Where to Eat The Goubuli Dumpling Restaurant (www.tjgoubuli.com) has been serving Tianjin's popular steamed buns since 1848.

Where to Stay Built in 1863, the colonial New World Astor Hotel (33 Taier Zhuang Road, tel. +86 22 2331 1688) is one of the city's oldest hotels.

When to Go Spring (Apr–May) and autumn (Sep–Oct) have the most pleasant temperatures.

Budget per Day for Two £80–90

GUIZHOU

Guizhou is one of China's poorest regions and remains relatively unvisited by foreign travellers. It is, however, stunningly beautiful. Nicknamed the "Switzerland of China", its jagged alpine peaks – clothed in pine forests, fruit trees, tea plantations and intricate agricultural terracing – are lusciously green in summer and decorously snow-capped in winter. Travelling here isn't easy: infrastructure is basic and a good phrase book is essential; but the highland landscapes, colourful Miao costumes worn by villagers, and delicious local cuisine give a real sense of unexplored China. Heading east from the provincial capital of Guiyang is particularly rewarding. In a deep valley below Thunder God Mountain lies Xijiang, an ethnic Miao village known as the Village of One Thousand Homes, where visitors can stay with local families in traditional two-floored wooden lodges built into the hillside. From here, numerous hiking trails lead over the hills and into picturesque adjacent valleys where agricultural communities adhere to time-honoured principles and crop-pickers carry large baskets of fresh herbs and vegetables on thick bamboo poles. The hills are also a rich source of precious metals and minerals, and the local female headdresses and jewellery are made from high-grade silver.

PRACTICAL INFORMATION

Getting There Guiyang, capital of Guizhou Province, has an airport with flights to/from all major Chinese cities. From the airport, catch a bus to the town of Kaili (3 hrs), and then to another Xijiang (3–4 hrs), or bargain hard for a taxi to take you all the way to Xijiang (5–6 hrs).

Where to Eat Xijiang's cafes serve hot Guizhounese mutton noodles and spicy stews made from fresh vegetables, and powerful warmed rice wine.

Where to Stay Xijiang Li Family Inn (tel. +86 855 334 8084 – Chinese only) has no formal address, but ask for the "Li Jia Jiudian" in the village and you will be pointed in the right direction.

When to Go Spring (Apr–May) and autumn (Sep–Oct) offer the best weather.

Budget per Day for Two £30–40

LESS-TRAVELLED
INDIA

*The magic of India, this most fascinating and colourful of countries, only begins with icons such as the Taj Mahal;
a less conventional tour will reveal wonders of nature, artistry and humanity in every corner of every state*

NEED TO KNOW

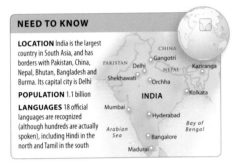

LOCATION India is the largest country in South Asia, and has borders with Pakistan, China, Nepal, Bhutan, Bangladesh and Burma. Its capital city is Delhi

POPULATION 1.1 billion

LANGUAGES 18 official languages are recognized (although hundreds are actually spoken), including Hindi in the north and Tamil in the south

When it comes to iconic images and unmissable attractions, India is a veritable tourist dream, and traditional tours of the country can feel as if they've been designed exclusively to yield a string of visual superlatives. On a typical journey you might travel from the bazaars of Old Delhi to the Taj Mahal and the great desert forts and palaces of Rajasthan, scouting for tigers in Ranthambore National Park en route. You might drift through the backwaters of Kerala, or tour the tea gardens of Darjeeling. Or follow the traditional temple trail to the world-famous shrines at Khajuraho or the ghats of Varanasi. All spectacular and unmissable, but also strangely one-dimensional.

The trouble with the great tourist attractions of India is that they're just that. Visiting the Taj or the Varanasi ghats, you'll be surrounded by fellow visitors as well as souvenir-wallahs, touts, guides and opportunistic rickshaw drivers, all looking to make a quick buck.

In fact, there's a great deal to be said for turning your back on the A-list sights entirely, and following an alternative route through the country. As soon as you get off the tourist trail your experience will be completely different – and probably a lot more enjoyable. Much of the fun of the place lies in simply being out in the streets, hanging out at local tea stalls, riding buses, meeting people and experiencing the never-ending variety of life on display here. Beauty, in India, is as much in the details as in the big sights: the sudden flash of a brilliantly coloured sari in a dusty street; the quaint, hand-painted signs of a local bazaar; the smell of freshly ground spices drifting out of a market. As for the sights themselves, even the country's "lesser" attractions are often every bit as fine as more-vaunted tourist destinations. You could start in the former colonial capital, Kolkata, then venture northeast to the wild, peaceful national park at Kaziranga – every bit as rewarding as the famous Ranthambore. From there, you might head northwest to follow the pilgrims up to the remote Himalayan village of Gangotri, before exploring the flamboyant desert towns of Shekhawati or the atmospheric abandoned city at Orchha, south of Delhi. The temples of Tamil Nadu, in the far south, are just as magical as those at Khajuraho. Best of all, you can probably visit all these without anyone trying to sell you a T-shirt or a model Taj Mahal with a built-in alarm clock.

PRACTICAL INFORMATION

Entry Requirements
All visitors require a visa, except citizens of Nepal and Bhutan.

When to Go
The best time to visit most parts of the country (apart from the Himalayas) is during the cool, dry months from November to March. The monsoon arrives on the south coast around June, and then sweeps up the country, taking around a month to reach Delhi. It lasts until September.

Air Travel
India has an extensive and continually expanding network of domestic flights run by about ten local airlines. You can now fly to virtually every corner of the country. Fares on busier routes can be a real bargain. Those to more unusual destinations can be relatively pricey.

Train Travel
India's legendary railway system (67,000 km/42,000 miles of track, 14,000 locomotives and around 12 million passengers daily) covers almost every area of the country, apart from the mountains, and even today is often the quickest and most comfortable way to get around. You have various travel options, from a private, air-conditioned first-class compartment to a packed third-class carriage with wooden bench seats. Fares are inexpensive, especially in second and third class.

Road Travel
Buses go absolutely everywhere, though they're generally less comfortable than the trains, and the driving can be rather hair-raising at times. Hiring a car and driver is relatively affordable. Given the fairly chaotic roads, few visitors drive themselves.

Climate
The climate varies greatly in India: temperatures soar in the Gangetic Plains of the north, though the Himalayan belt remains cool; the centre and south have a tropical monsoon climate; and the coastal belts are humid and warm.

Website
www.incredibleindia.org

FORGET INDIA'S TOURIST TRAIL?

THE BUILD-UP India is one of the most remarkable and captivating countries in the world: a constant festival of colour, crowds and organized chaos; sometimes maddening, and often plain mad, but never dull.

THE LETDOWN Rushing around iconic sights, getting on and off a tour bus and only meeting the Indians who work in your hotel or who try to sell you a carpet or a toy elephant leaves many visitors feeling like a piece of cargo. If you stick exclusively to the big tourist attractions, you are likely to see India at its worst.

DOING IT ANYWAY? India is more like a continent than a country, so concentrate on one particular area and try not to rush. Enjoying it in small bites – a state or two at a time – will give you the chance to get the most out of the place and meet the people who make it so interesting. Ensure you mix in one or two less well-known destinations along with the major tourist attractions.

ABOVE Hindus bathing and paying obeisance to the holy Ganges river at Varanasi

MAIN IMAGE Minakshi Sundareshvara Temple, Madurai, Tamil Nadu
BELOW (left to right) Intricate frescoes in a palace at Shekhawati; lively flower market, Kolkata; preparing offerings at a shrine

Rickshaw driver waiting for fares outside the Roxy cinema, Kolkata

KOLKATA (CALCUTTA)

Few cities suffer from as bad – and unjustified – an image problem as Kolkata. Its reputation has plagued it ever since 1756, when its unfortunate European residents were imprisoned in the notorious "Black Hole" by the Nawab of Bengal's troops. Despite such setbacks, Kolkata can plausibly claim, in its own rather grubby way, to be the most charismatic city in India. It is without doubt among its most cultured, boasting a vibrant literary, arts and cinema scene which has produced such world-famous luminaries as the Nobel Laureate writer Tagore and the filmmaker Satyajit Ray. As the former capital of British India, it is also a fascinating monument to the pretensions of the Raj, with a fine array of colonial-era relics ranging from the superbly bombastic Victoria Memorial to the vast Howrah Bridge. For many, the city's greatest pride may be the vast Eden Gardens cricket stadium, the national shrine to India's number-one sporting obsession.

Practical Information

Getting There and Around Kolkata airport is served by many international airlines. There are also direct flights from most major cities in India.

Where to Eat Head to 6 Ballygunge Place (tel. +91 33 2460 3922) for traditional Bengali food at its finest.

Where to Stay The Victorian Oberoi Grand (www.oberoihotels.com) is one of Kolkata's landmark hotels, offering a full range of five-star facilities.

When to Go Between October and March.

Budget per Day for Two £250

Buffalos viewed up-close on an elephant safari, Kaziranga National

KAZIRANGA NATIONAL PARK

Sprawling along the south bank of the majestic Brahmaputra river, in the remote northeastern state of Assam, lies the Kaziranga National Park. Although foreign visitors remain few and far between, the park is one of India's most spectacular wildlife destinations. Its combination of swamps and grasslands makes it the ideal habitat for elephants, deer, wild buffalos and boar, and a host of smaller creatures, as well as a considerable number of somewhat elusive tigers. It also attracts a wonderful range of birdlife, particularly during the winter migration months. Above all, though, the park is famous as the homeland of the great Indian one-horned rhino. Numbering around 1,800, the rhinos here make up two-thirds of the world's surviving population, and sightings are virtually guaranteed. You can explore the park by jeep, but the favoured method for rhino-spotting is to ride by elephant, allowing you to approach much closer than you would be able to in a vehicle – a unique and memorable twist on the traditional Indian safari.

Practical Information

Getting There and Around The park is around 220 km (135 miles) east of the city of Guwahati, in the state of Assam, which can be reached by plane from many parts of India, or by train from Kolkata (Calcutta).

Where to Stay and Eat Bon Habi Jungle Resort (www.bonhabiresort.com) offers comfortable rooms and friendly service in a forest setting close to the park. Its restaurant serves an excellent range of international dishes.

When to Go The park is open between November and early April.

Budget per Day for Two £100 including park entrance fees.

Stunning scenery at Garhwal, source of the Ganges and Yamuna rivers

GANGOTRI

High in the Himalayas in the state of Uttarakhand, the small town of Gangotri sits at the heart of the sacred region of Garhwal. One of the most physically beautiful and spiritually important areas in northern India, Garhwal is revered as the source of both the Ganges and Yamuna, India's two mightiest rivers. Gangotri is traditionally regarded as the spiritual source of the Ganges, and its small but vibrant temple attracts a steady stream of pilgrims and colourfully attired *sadhus* (holy men), who mingle with the few western tourists and trekkers who make it this far into the mountains. Much of the town's appeal is drawn from its magnificent setting. The surrounding countryside offers beautiful walks through deodar cedar forests, with dramatic views of snow-capped peaks. Two of the most rewarding trails are those that lead to the spectacular (though steadily retreating) Gangotri Glacier and the high-altitude oasis of Chirbasa. There are also longer hiking routes leading deeper into the mountains, including an overnight trek to the ice-cave of Gaumukh ("Cow's Mouth"), the official source of the Ganges, which is best visited at sunrise.

Practical Information

Getting There and Around Gangotri is beautifully remote and the journey requires several changes. Travel by air to Delhi, then by bus 225 km (140 miles) to Rishikesh, in Uttarakhand. You can take a further bus, or hire a jeep, to travel the last 250 km (155 miles) to Gangotri.

Where to Stay and Eat Accommodation in Gangotri is very limited, but the GMVN Tourist Bungalow (www.gmvnl.com) is a comfortable place both to stay and to eat.

When to Go Between May and October.

Budget per Day for Two £25

Historic murals in one of Shekhawati's extravagant mansions

Royal cenotaphs on the banks of the Betwa river, Orchha

Painted ceilings and carved pillars in Minakshi Sundareshvara Temple

SHEKHAWATI

Just a few hours' drive from Jaipur and other Rajasthani tourist hotspots, the magical region of Shekhawati offers all the attractions of its more famous neighbours, with a fraction of the visitors. In the latter days of the Raj this was one of the richest regions in India, thanks to enterprising local traders who made vast fortunes in places like Bombay and Calcutta, and sent the profits back to Shekhawati's dusty little towns. Their riches funded the construction of hundreds of extravagant *havelis* (mansions), each flaunting elaborate façades and flamboyant painted exteriors. Though some have been restored, most are now falling into slow decay, an atmospheric memorial to the wealth and fashions of a past era. Many of the *havelis* are also notable for their remarkable murals, their walls covered in a quirky array of eclectic paintings depicting traditional religious subjects alongside the latest European fashions and inventions – anything from representations of Krishna to images of new-fangled railways and hot-air balloons.

Practical Information

Getting There and Around Travel by air or rail to Jaipur, from where there is a good bus service to Shekhawati, 150 km (95 miles) away. There are also direct train services to Shekhawati from Delhi, 250 km (155 miles) away.

Where to Stay and Eat Among the nicest options is Apani Dhani (www. apanidhani.com), a gorgeous, eco-friendly rural retreat in the town of Nawalgarh, offering well-equipped rooms and delicious vegetarian cuisine.

When to Go Between October and March.

Budget per Day for Two £60

ORCHHA

Hidden away in peaceful wooded countryside in the central Indian state of Madhya Pradesh, the abandoned city of Orchha is one of the country's most atmospheric attractions. Capital of the local Bundela rulers for over 200 years, the city was founded by Raja Rudra Pratap, but his untimely death in 1531 (while allegedly trying to rescue a cow from the claws of a tiger) prevented him from completing his grand designs. His successors took up the challenge, adding embellishments until Mughal and Maratha attacks forced them to abandon the city in the 18th century. Most of its magnificent buildings have lain empty ever since. Many survive in remarkably good condition – a fascinating tangle of temples, palaces, *havelis* and cenotaphs. Among the highlights are a pair of sumptous palaces: the Raj Mahal, adorned by rich murals, and the Jahangir Mahal, built as a present to welcome the great Mughal emperor Jahangir, its fanciful roofline topped with dozens of domes and cupolas. Nearby soar the towers of the great Chaturbhuj temple, while a stately line of 14 royal cenotaphs, constructed for successive rulers of the city, stand imposingly alongside the banks of the tranquil Betwa river.

Practical Information

Getting There and Around Travel by train from Delhi to the town of Jhansi. From here local buses make the 25-km (16-mile) journey to Orchha.

Where to Eat The restaurant in the Sheesh Mahal hotel (tel. +91 7680 252624), set in Orchha's old fort, is particularly atmospheric.

Where to Stay Try Amar Mahal (www.amarmahal.com), an elegant, Mughal-style resort set amid spacious gardens.

When to Go Between November and February.

Budget per Day for Two £50

MADURAI

Located in the far southern state of Tamil Nadu, Madurai is one of India's oldest and most characterful cities, offering a heady taste of the subcontinent at its idiosyncratic and unspoilt best. The city is dominated by the enormous Minakshi Sundareshvara Temple, one of the most spectacular in the country. Its massive towers, alive with a riot of colourful statuary, have a powerful presence, their thousands of many-headed gods and goddesses, splay-toothed demons, lions, bulls and guardian figures keeping permanent watch over the city streets. The interior reveals a virtual city-within-a-city: a fascinating labyrinth of shrines, bathing tanks, courtyards and columned halls, thronged day and night with pilgrims who come here to pay homage to Shiva and his wife, the triple-breasted goddess Minakshi. Outside, the narrow, colourful streets of old Madurai offer an unforgettable taste of southern Indian life, dense with crowds, cows, and weaving rickshaws, all ploughing their way through the city amidst a cacophony of traffic horns and temple bells.

Practical Information

Getting There and Around The main gateway is Chennai, in Madras, 445 km (275 miles) away. From here there are daily flights to Madurai as well as direct train services.

Where to Eat The excellent, inexpensive banana-leaf thalis at Anna Meenakshi (West Perumal Maistry Street) are not to be missed.

Where to Stay A good choice is the Gateway Hotel (www.tajhotels.com), offering slick five-star service in a beautifully converted colonial mansion.

When to Go Between January and March.

Budget per Day for Two £125

CORSICA'S NORTHWEST COAST
VS THE AMALFI COAST

Typically Mediterranean, Corsica's northwest coast, with its unique savage beauty, is more relaxing than Italy's traffic-ridden Amalfi Coast where coach parties dominate

NEED TO KNOW

LOCATION The journey runs down the northwest coast of Corsica, France

LENGTH OF ROUTE 50 km (31 miles)

DAYTIME TEMPERATURES
Jan: 13°C (55°F);
Apr: 17°C (63°F);
Jul: 20°C (68°F);
Oct: 26°C (79°F)

So much stunning natural beauty is concentrated in this part of northwestern Corsica that the long stretches of dizzy cliff scenery will elicit "oohs" and "aahs" with every blind corner you turn on the hair-raising road through the rugged mountainsides.

On the wild coast, the route is 50 km (31 miles) from Calvi to Cargèse as the crow flies, but you'll clock up at least 112 km (70 miles) by driving along the winding road. All around are slopes smothered with aromatic maquis shrubs whose scents waft on the sea breeze. There is no evidence of crowds, in glaring contrast to the Amalfi Coast, where

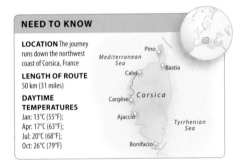

truckloads of tourists are common and long-term habitation has translated into urbanization.

Along the way, a host of highlights offer ample excuse for a rest from driving. You begin the journey at the small but bustling port of Calvi, occupying a picturesque promontory with a trademark citadel. Then, once out on the D81, if you turn inland from Galéria village, you'll see the crystal-clear waters of the Fango river and its bright-red porphyry rock gorge, spanned by the elegant Genoese bridge (Ponte Vecchiu).

The Bocca a Croce Pass demands a halt for the sweeping views it affords over the rugged shores of the Scandola headland reserve. Close by, a path drops through Mediterranean bush to the fishing hamlet of Girolata and a sheltered beach, where a seafood lunch or swim can be enjoyed.

Porto, a tiny clutch of hotels in an inlet, is another recommended stopover. Inland, the photogenic hamlet of Ota has a cluster of traditional stone houses above the cool Spelunca Gorge.

Next comes this coast's absolute highlight, Les Calanche, a weird wonderland of eroded pink granite, called "a haunting nightmarish menagerie" by French novelist Guy de Maupassant. Immersed in sweet-smelling pine forest and a UNESCO World Heritage Site, Les Calanche can be visited on foot thanks to many marked paths leading off the road.

Nearby, the beautifully placed village of Piana makes an excellent base. Sandy beaches beckon, as does the divine Capo Rosso headland, its old watchtower a lookout for marauding pirates, long-gone raiders of the Mediterranean coast.

This journey can also be a memorable adventure for hikers, who can enjoy the vistas on the long-distance walking path, Mare e Monti. The route begins at Calenzana outside Calvi, and ends in Cargèse in 10 days. There are stopovers at *gîtes d'étape*, or walkers' hostels.

ABOVE Genoese arched bridge in the Spelunca Gorge near Ota, Corsica

FORGET THE AMALFI COAST?

THE BUILD-UP Overlooking the Gulf of Salerno just south of Naples, the Amalfi Coast offers breathtaking scenery at every turn of the tortuous road. Photogenic villages cling to vertiginous mountainsides, clad with ingenious terraces where juicy lemons flourish on trellises.

THE LETDOWN Driving on the narrow winding roads is stressful even in light traffic, but once the cruise ship season has commenced, coach jams are the name of the game and frustrating delays the norm. Prices at glamorous resorts such as Positano and arty Ravello are aimed at the millionaire set. The few public beaches are cramped and pebbly, so consider shelling out for a private deckchair.

GOING ANYWAY? Try to avoid late spring to mid-summer. In winter, many hotels slash prices. Plan to arrive by train at either Salerno or Sorrento, and continue your journey by public bus or use the private ferries that link villages. Choosing accommodation and eateries off the seafront will help keep budgets manageable.

ABOVE Coaches squeezing past each other on the narrow roads around the Amalfi Coast

PRACTICAL INFORMATION

Getting There and Around
The closest airport is Calvi's Sainte Catherine, 8 km (5 miles) from town with scheduled flights via France. There are also charter flights to and from the UK between Apr–Oct. From Calvi, arrange a rental car to explore the coastal road. Buses run to Porto May–Sep. If you wish to take your own vehicle, then a car ferry from the mainland port of Nice or Marseille is feasible, but book ahead for the high season.

Where to Eat
Just outside Porto on the Calvi road, Restaurant Le Porto is reasonably priced, and you can enjoy your meal on a lovely terrace (www.hotel-leporto.com; tel. +33 4 95 26 11 20).

Where to Stay
Porto's Hotel Monterosso is on the waterfront, with rooms and terraces overlooking the wonderful gulf (www.hotel-monterosso.com).

When to Go
Spring is divine with the aromatic scent of Mediterranean plants, but the sea is still a trifle cool. The onset of summer heat — and perfect bathing conditions — is offset by cool breezes on the west coast, though the number of visitors is highest then.

Budget per Day for Two
£130 including accommodation and food.

Website
www.corsica.net

MAIN IMAGE A car driving along the winding route through towering Les Calanche **BELOW (left to right)** The port of Calvi on a fortified promontory; boats moored in the harbour at Porto

4 MORE JOURNEYS TO RIVAL THE AMALFI COAST DRIVE

CINQUE TERRE IN LIGURIA, ITALY Access is by train, burrowing through precipitous cliffs. Pastel-tinted houses cascade down steep hillsides where Vernaccia wine is grown.

COAST OF MADEIRA, OFF AFRICA The sheer cliffs that surround this route are the result of volcanic beginnings followed by water erosion. The route of this Portuguese island alternates between mountain roads and breathtaking scenery.

TASMAN PENINSULA, AUSTRALIA Travelling around the peninsula at the storm-battered southern tip of Australia, takes in a remarkable procession of natural rock formations, such as the soaring Tasman Arch and the Devil's Kitchen. The Arthur Highway leads to Cape Raoul, where 165 million-year-old dolerite columns stand on the seafront.

COSTA SMERALDA, SARDINIA Turquoise water washes onto dramatic headlands and immaculate white sandy bays on this coast, which also has upmarket resorts such as Porto Cervo.

ABOVE A group of trekkers crossing the partly snow-covered lava fields of Russia's Kamchatka Peninsula, with the smoking Mutnovsky volcano in the distance

KAMCHATKA PENINSULA TREK, RUSSIA The landscape of Kamchatka is bleak and powerful, with towering volcanoes throwing up plumes of ash and smoke, and surreal terrain that has been twisted over time by fierce lava flows. A trek through this region of contrasts will take you over rolling pasture land, alpine tundra, glittering glaciers, huge lava fields, crater lakes, waterfalls and snowy, conical peaks. Lumbering bears, marmots and foxes are not uncommon sights alongside the salmon-filled Asacha river. Looking down the steep rock walls into the caldera of the Mutnovsky volcano is a highlight.

WAINWRIGHT'S COAST-TO-COAST WALK, UK Alfred Wainwright described this route as "the grandest territory in the north of England". The 305-km (190-mile) trail runs from western Cumbria, through the Lake District and Yorkshire Dales, to Robin Hood's Bay on the east coast.

FRANKINCENSE TRAIL, OMAN This trail was carved out by camel caravans leaving Salalah over 7,000 years ago in search of the *Boswellia sacra* – a gnarled tree whose resin was once more valuable than gold. The UNESCO-protected route takes in mountains, beaches and a "lost city".

BEIJING/SHANGHAI–LHASA TRAIN, CHINA AND TIBET The world's highest railway averages 4,000 m (13,120 ft) in elevation, but you'll have plenty of time to acclimatize on the 48-hour trip. Enjoy fabulous bird's-eye views of the Loess Plain and Tangula Mountains on the way.

MILFORD TRACK, NEW ZEALAND Running from Glade Wharf to Milford Sound, this trail ascends from beech forest to sub-alpine scrub, crossing swinging bridges over roaring creeks along the way. Take in views of the twinkling fjords, plunging valleys and snowy peaks below.

HA LONG BAY BY JUNK, VIETNAM You may have a picture in your mind of Ha Long Bay, with its jutting limestone mountains that rise so dramatically from the Golf of Tonkin, but one thing's for sure – nothing can prepare you for its awesome beauty. Around 3,000 of these islands pierce the sky, their reflections shimmering in the emerald water of the bay. Rock arches, pristine lagoons, sheer cliffs, coves and stretches of white-sand beach adorn the dramatic islets, while junks pass between them, tending to fishing hatcheries. Cruises can last from one to ten days aboard a refitted wooden Chinese-style junk.

ANTARCTIC ICEBREAKER VOYAGE During the brief Antarctic summer, boats with strong hulls and powerful engines, known as icebreakers, plough through the ice to keep channels open for navigation in these inhospitable waters. Trips ashore allow a glimpse of this remote and extreme land, where the weather can change in an instant. Keep your eyes peeled for seals, grey whales and emperor penguins.

CANAL DU MIDI, FRANCE This 240-km (150-mile) canal, running from Toulouse to the port town of Sète, was built in the 17th century as a shortcut from the Atlantic to the Mediterranean. Hire a narrow boat and navigate your own way, or charter a more luxurious barge and put your feet up. Along the way, you'll pass ancient villages, magnificent châteaux and vineyards, and through 91 locks.

THE BLUE TRAIN, CAPE TOWN TO PRETORIA, SOUTH AFRICA This 27-hour journey covers 1,610 km (1,000 miles) and passes through some extraordinary scenery; from lush valleys, vineyards and farms, to towering mountain backdrops and bleak, high-altitude plains. The train is luxurious: its opulent suites are fitted with thick carpets and marble tiles, and the food and service are impeccable.

CURZON TRAIL, UTTARAKHAND, INDIA Skirting the western edge of the Nanda Devi Reserve, this challenging hike follows the route taken by Lord Curzon, Viceroy of India, in 1905. One of the best views of the Himalayas is visible from the Kuari Pass. You'll travel through local communities and past a number of ruined temples. The high meadow of Bedni Bugyal must be one of the world's most spectacular picnic spots.

GIBB RIVER ROAD DRIVE, WESTERN AUSTRALIA The Gibb Road is a dusty route that passes through some of the Kimberley's wildest terrain. Constructed in the 1960s as a cattle path, this 660-km (410-mile) dirt track can only be tackled in a 4WD. Creeks, gorges and waterfalls make good stop-off points along the way, and bush hikes bring you to deep pools that are perfect for getting the dust out of your hair.

ICEFIELDS PARKWAY DRIVE, CANADA This 230-km (145-mile) route from Lake Louise to Jasper takes in the spectacular Canadian Rockies, home of the vast ice fields of Columbia and Athabasca, as well as extensive flora and fauna. It's hard to believe that this scenic highway, now the main north-south route through this inhospitable range, was built in 1930 as part of an unemployment relief project.

ABOVE Trekking with llamas on a mountain slope in the Cordillera Real, Bolivia
RIGHT Colourful floating market, Mekong Delta, Vietnam

LLAMA TREK, BOLIVIA The magnificent Cordillera Real stretches for 160 km (100 miles) and encompasses sheer granite cliffs, snow-capped peaks, shimmering lagoons and glaciers. Starting with a 3-hour drive from La Paz, this high-altitude trek takes you to heights of up to 4,500 m (14,765 ft), where you need to take things slowly in the rarefied air. The path follows pre-Inca trails and your equipment is carried by mules and llamas, which are led by an *arriero* (muleteer). You are likely to come across the indigenous Aymara people in their stone houses or herding alpacas on the mountain slopes.

MEKONG RIVER, VIETNAM AND CAMBODIA At Cai Be floating market in Vietnam, small wooden boats bursting with fruits and flowers jostle for position, and the incessant calls of traders attempting to sell their wares fills the air. Life along the Mekong is all about the river: villages on stilts rise out of it, splendid temples and pagodas emerge from its banks and miles of rice paddies are flooded by its water every summer. The Mekong begins in the mountains of Tibet and descends through China, Burma, Laos, Thailand, Cambodia and Vietnam; but it's this last bustling stretch of the river that makes for the best trip.

SAHARA CAMEL CARAVAN, MOROCCO
The red-gold of this desert is best seen from atop a camel; their stately pace allows you to take in the changing colours in the searing heat. This is the way that Bedouins have travelled for thousands of years, working their way to Marrakech.

E&O EXPRESS, BANGKOK TO SINGAPORE Watching the changing Asian scenery from the Observation Car conjures up an image of a more romantic era of travel, as this half-kilometre (quarter-mile) string of immaculate cream carriages sweeps from Thailand into Malaysia, crossing wooden viaducts and scenic bridges as it goes. You'll pause at the Kwai river for a short cruise, and again at George Town for a rickshaw ride around the city. Cultural and geographical diversity are features of this epic ride, which begins with the bustle of Bangkok and terminates in Singapore, a melting pot of Chinese, Indian and Malay cultures.

KAYAKING IN THE SEA OF CORTEZ, BAJA CALIFORNIA, MEXICO The combination of calm, turquoise waters, unremitting sunshine and abundant wildlife makes a kayaking trip in the Sea of Cortez truly unforgettable. Watch out for manta rays, which surface gracefully beside you as you paddle. Nights are spent under the stars on white-sand beaches, with the craggy, cacti-studded landscape of Espíritu Santo Island as a backdrop. From here, it is a short trip to the sheltered lagoons of Magdalena Bay where, every year, grey whales arrive from more than 8,050 km (5,000 miles) away in the Arctic, to calve and nurse their young in the shallow waters. For safety's sake, jump off your kayak and onto a skiff to get a close view of these powerful creatures, which often breach so close to the boat that you could reach out and touch them.

DARJEELING HIMALAYAN RAILWAY, INDIA Every day for the past 130 years a steam engine has wound its way through the hill stations of northern India, under the gaze of Kanchanjenga, the world's third-highest mountain. The UNESCO World Heritage-protected "toy train", which once transported rice and tea, now takes passengers to Darjeeling. There are fabulous views along the way.

CHE GUEVARA'S MOTORCYCLE ROUTE, SOUTH AMERICA Icons don't come more swashbuckling than Ernesto "Che" Guevara, and South America's dramatic scenery is hard to beat too. The U-shaped loop from Buenos Aires to Santiago is breathtaking. The towns have changed since the 50s, but the ever-present Andean spine hasn't; cross it in the Lake District as Che did, and swap Argentina for Chile.

LYCIAN COAST BY GULET, TURKEY
Olive groves, sheer limestone cliffs, deep inlets, pristine beaches and ancient Greek and Roman ruins characterize Turkey's "coast of light". Explore it in a *gulet* – a two-masted wooden boat once used for trade and later styled into a luxury vessel. Bask in the sun and take in the mesmerizing, ever-changing littoral from the *gulet*'s comfortable deck.

NEW YORK STATE CANALS, USA
The 19th-century Erie Canal, a feat of engineering that established New York as America's commercial capital, connected the city with the Northwest Territories in Canada, which were rich in minerals. Erie, and New York State's three other canals – Oswego, Cayuga-Seneca and Champlain – can be explored by boat, and all have museums dedicated to their history.

STEVENSON TRAIL, CÉVENNES, FRANCE In *Travels with a Donkey*, Robert Louis Stevenson recounts his epic 210-km (130-mile) walk along the spine of the Cévennes in south-central France, with only his donkey for company. This gentle route can be taken as one or in shorter segments, and runs through meadows, medieval villages and lush woodland. Hire a donkey to help with your luggage.

ABOVE Gauchos herding cattle in Patagonia, Argentina
RIGHT The Ghan passing through Australia's dry and dusty Red Centre

HORSEBACK CATTLE DRIVE, PATAGONIA, ARGENTINA Galloping across wild rolling prairie, with the snowy peaks of the Andes rising up ahead, is one of the most exhilarating experiences South America has to offer. Accompanied by native gaucho horsemen, you'll assist in herding cattle from their winter estancia to their highland summer grazing land, traversing icy rivers, rocky gorges, flower-filled grasslands and dense forest, and scattering deer and guanacos along the way. You'll sleep under the twinkling stars of the southern hemisphere and feast alfresco on mouth-watering beef and freshly caught trout.

THE GHAN, AUSTRALIA From Adelaide in the south of the country through the scorching desert of the centre and on to tropical Top End (the northerly peninsula of land on which Darwin sits) runs one of the longest train journeys in the world. The Ghan covers 2,980 km (1,850 miles) in 54 hours and takes in the stunning diversity of the outback. The agricultural south gives way to vast stretches of desert and an interminable sun around Alice Springs. The journey ends in lush, swampy terrain as it nears Darwin. The train, while not luxurious, has comfortable berths, and kangaroo and barramundi are often on the menu.

SOUTH DOWNS WAY, UK Stretching for 160 km (100 miles) along the hills between Winchester in Hampshire and Eastbourne in Sussex, this path takes in two Areas of Outstanding Natural Beauty. It is open to hikers, horse-riders and cyclists, and links pretty villages with wide coastal vistas.

DOURO VALLEY WINE CRUISE, PORTUGAL This 8-day cruise in the world's oldest wine-making region begins among the gabled houses of Porto and turns around in Salamanca, Spain's fantastically preserved medieval city. Lush hills and pretty terraced vineyards flank the river.

CASCADE LOOP DRIVE, WASHINGTON, USA This 645-km (400-mile) journey along the North Cascades Scenic Highway takes in some of the state's most spectacular scenery, including the sheer, craggy walls of the Tumwater Canyon, the churning rapids of the Wenatchee River and the deep, narrow expanse of water at Lake Chelan. The landscape is dotted with vineyards, lakes and mountains, and is magnificent in autumn, when copper and gold maple leaves litter the valley floors. The forested islands of Whidbey and Fidalgo merit a few days' exploration, as do the horse enclosures in the Methow River Valley.

VANUATU ARCHIPELAGO CRUISE, SOUTH PACIFIC Tall ships, sloops and motorboats cruise between these 83 lush volcanic islands, taking in the thick jungle of Ambae Island, Maewo's fresh springs and waterfalls, the black sand of Ambrym, and the pristine white Champagne Beach on Espíritu Santo. There will be ample opportunity for diving, snorkelling and kayaking in the crystal-clear water.

TUNDRA BUGGYING FOR POLAR BEARS, CANADA When the Hudson Bay freezes in October and November, polar bears come out onto the ice to hunt for seals. Explore the icy landscape in a tundra buggy – a large, heated vehicle that allows close-up views of these powerful creatures from grated observation platforms. Dainty arctic foxes and arctic hares also pick their way across the snow and ice here.

KHYBER PASS STEAM SAFARI, PAKISTAN This 19th-century railway line begins in Peshawar and works its way between the Sulaiman Hills, passing through 34 tunnels and over 92 bridges, and climbing 1,200 m (3,940 ft) along the way. The coaches, which are pulled by two oil-fired engines, wheeze and shudder as they cross this rugged landscape. The scenery from the train is starkly beautiful.

NATCHEZ TRACE PARKWAY DRIVE, MISSISSIPPI AND TENNESSEE, USA The National Scenic Byway snakes its way from the Tennessee Valley to Natchez, and showcases the antebellum charm of the South. Tall colonnades front grand historic homes in Natchez; Raymond is rich in Civil War history; and Leipers Fork resonates with the sounds of country fiddle and banjo from its open-air theatre.

REINDEER MIGRATION, SWEDEN The frozen landscape of Laponia is white and still, but each spring it comes to life when thousands of reindeer are herded 200 km (125 miles) across it. Join the local Sámi herdsmen, who will lead you as you travel on skis or snowmobiles through dense forest and alongside ice-covered lakes. Nights are spent in a *kata* (tent), with a central stove for warmth.

DRÂA VALLEY DRIVE, MOROCCO Through craggy cliffs and steep canyons, the Drâa river has carved out a shady path between Agdz and Zagora in Morocco's High Atlas Mountains. The valley is full of date-palm plantations, oases and *ksour*, old fortified towns. Hire a 4WD for this 95-km (60-mile) journey, which takes in some of the country's most spectacular scenery.

ABOVE Bright red boat hut at L'Anse aux Meadows, at the end of the Viking Trail, in Newfoundland, Canada
LEFT The vivid gold and bronze of Colorado's autumn foliage, with the Rocky Mountains in the distance

SAN JUAN SKYWAY DRIVE, COLORADO, USA A drive through Colorado's southwestern San Juan Range is spectacular at any time of year. Follow this 380-km (235-mile) route and you'll pass gushing streams and waterfalls in spring, blankets of wildflowers in summer and precipitous slopes thick with snow in winter. But the landscape is at its most spectacular in autumn, when the cottonwood and aspen trees take on a palette of fiery hues. The towns along the road were established after the discovery of precious metals in the area, and remnants of the precarious railway that ran to and from the mines are still visible.

THE VIKING TRAIL, CANADA If the idea of exploring wild tundra landscapes with few people and herds of roaming caribous appeals to you, then make for Newfoundland's Viking Trail. This stunning route, which runs along a narrow sliver of highway that has been carved out of a spectacular landscape, is perfect for nature enthusiasts. It takes you from the dramatic coastal mountains and fjords of Gros Morne National Park north, along an unforgettably wild coastline, to the remote northern tip of Newfoundland. This is where Leif Erikson and a handful of other Viking settlers landed 1,000 years ago.

MONGOLIA ON HORSEBACK There is no better way to explore Mongolia than on horseback. This is a country of diverse landscapes, from the rolling dunes and vast steppes of the Gobi Desert in the south, to the forests of the Siberian north and fast-flowing rivers of the centre.

WALKING MONT BLANC'S HAUTE ROUTE, FRANCE AND SWITZERLAND With a backdrop comprising 10 of the 12 highest mountains in the Alps, including mighty Mont Blanc and the Matterhorn, the Haute Route is breathtaking. The trail leaves Chamonix and crosses forested valleys, ascends passes and traverses glittering ice-slopes to arrive in Switzerland at the picturesque village of Zermatt. Nights are spent in mountain huts. There is also a more challenging Haute Route, which takes in glaciers and requires more technical experience. Never attempt this second option without an experienced guide.

THE GOLDEN ROAD TO SAMARKAND, UZBEKISTAN The great trade route from China to the West, known as the Silk Road, was opened in order to satisfy ancient Rome's demand for silk in the 1st century BC. It saw a constant stream of merchants, laden with silk, spices, perfumes and gems. The Golden Road, Uzbekistan's stretch of the route, made a remarkable impact on the cities through which it passed. Their architecture is a heady amalgam of cultures and ideas, from the jumbled streets and high-walled citadel of Samarkand to the clay city walls of ancient Khiva and the delicate mosque of Bukhara. The intervening landscape is stark, inhospitable and spectacular, with jutting mountains, fertile valleys and bleak, high plains. The highlights can be seen in an 8- or 10-day trip by bus or 4WD, and there is a slow but reliable train.

YANGTZE RIVER CRUISE, CHINA Also known as Chang Jiang (Long River), the Yangtze flows 6,300 km (3,910 miles) from the Tibetan Plateau to the East China Sea, passing ancient temples, remote villages and the controversial Three Gorges Dam, soon to be the world's largest hydroelectric power plant. At Qutang Gorge, the shortest of the Three Gorges, low mist hangs eerily over triangular peaks.

ZAMBEZI CANOE SAFARI, AFRICA Elephants douse themselves on the riverbank as your canoe cuts silently through the water. This kind of close encounter is common on a river safari, with hippos and buffalos gathering around the region's lifeblood, and crocodiles occasionally slinking by. The largest concentration of game is found on the Lower Zambezi.

PACIFIC CREST TRAIL, USA AND CANADA This 4,265-km (2,650-mile) trail from Mexico to Canada passes through the diverse scenery of the western USA. The chaparral-covered slopes of Southern California give way to the steep valleys and high passes of the Sierra Nevada. In Oregon, the landscape is forested and dotted with crater lakes, while Washington offers dramatic canyons and snowfields.

SKELETON COAST DRIVE, NAMIBIA This remote stretch of coast, often shrouded in a thick sea mist caused by currents from the Antarctic, is riddled with shipwrecks. The region has a hostile beauty, with windswept sand dunes, black lava ridges and fiery granite massifs. Desert elephants, black rhinos and springboks live here, but the only human inhabitants are the Himba, who eke out a living in the interior.

MARLBOROUGH WINE TOUR BY BIKE, NEW ZEALAND The lower Wairau Valley, on New Zealand's South Island, is blessed with gentle sunshine, which makes the area ideal for growing Sauvignon Blanc and Chardonnay grapes, and also for biking. Take in the vineyards as you go, weighing down your basket with bottles. The route is flat and quiet, with views over neat rows of vines sloping up into misty foothills.

CAMINO REAL TREK, PANAMA Hike the ancient Royal Road 65 km (40 miles) from Panama's Pacific coast to the Caribbean, and you'll be on the most genuine of treasure trails, following in the footsteps of the bounty-laden conquistadors who carved the route as a shortcut for their homeward-bound Inca spoils. You'll trek through virgin rainforest, rich in flora and fauna, and camp on riverbanks.

ARCHITECTURAL MARVELS

Spectacular cupola inside the Reichstag, Berlin, Germany (p142)

ABOVE Hordes of tourists – and pigeons – outside Basilica San Marco, Venice, Italy

HAGHIA SOPHIA
VS BASILICA SAN MARCO

Haghia Sophia, built to proclaim the might and majesty of the Eastern Roman Empire, dwarfs Venice's Basilica San Marco in age, scale and artistic achievement

NEED TO KNOW

LOCATION Haghia Sophia is in the district of Sultanahmet, in the heart of Old Istanbul, northwestern Turkey

DATE OF CONSTRUCTION
AD 532–7

VISITORS PER YEAR
Around 2.2 million

For nearly 1,000 years, Haghia Sophia was thought to be the most glorious church in Christendom. Filled with treasures and decked out in gold, marble, semi-precious stones and sumptuous mosaics, the church unashamedly showed off the status of Constantinople, the capital of the Byzantine Empire. When its founder, the Emperor Justinian, saw the church completed for the first time, he compared it to King Solomon's splendid First Temple in Jerusalem, built 1,500 years earlier, exclaiming: "Oh Solomon, I have outdone you!"

Haghia Sophia has served different purposes over the centuries: it was converted into a mosque by Sultan Mehmet the Conqueror following his capture of Constantinople in 1453, and became a museum under Atatürk in 1935. Despite these incarnations, the building remains Istanbul's most iconic monument and one of the great religio-historic wonders of the world. Venice's better-known Byzantine treasure, Basilica San Marco, might attract more visitors, but when it comes to atmosphere and architectural splendour, Haghia Sophia wins hands down.

The building's spectacular, soaring dome and four graceful minarets dominate the city skyline, and enclose one of the largest interiors in the world. Stepping inside this majestic building can be rather an overwhelming experience. As you leave behind the swirling dust, street smells and

din of traffic and traders in Sultanahmet, you enter an extraordinary, vast sanctuary of diffused light, coolness and peace.

Though much of the original material used to decorate Haghia Sophia has been looted over the centuries, many treasures remain. Don't miss the dazzling 9th-century wall and floor mosaics, the 18th-century Sultan's Loge, which allowed Sultan Ahmet III to pray unseen, and the impressive work of the master-calligrapher Mustafa İzzet Efendi, seen on the roundels that sit at the base of the dome. Also found here is the Weeping Column, which, legend has it, once belonged to St Gregory the Miracle Worker, and which many people believe still retains powers of healing. This majestic building, which has withstood earthquakes and wars, is an enduring tribute to Byzantine art and one of the finest surviving buildings of antiquity.

PRACTICAL INFORMATION

Getting There and Around
Istanbul's main airport, Ataturk International Airport, lies 24 km (15 miles) west of Sultanahmet. Local trains, trams, airport buses and taxis connect the airport with Sultanahmet.

Where to Eat
Istanbul boasts one of the best dining scenes in the world. Restaurants, bistros, taverns, cafés, fast-food stalls and food and spice markets are found everywhere here. For atmosphere and authenticity, follow the locals to the *meyhanes* (taverns) in Nevizade Sokak, one of Beyoğlu's narrow streets, where you'll find fresh fish and mouth-watering *meze* aplenty. If you're looking for a restaurant with a view, head

for Hamdi Et Lokantası (tel. +90 212 528 0390), which has been an Istanbul institution since the 1970s.

Where to Stay
The famous Four Seasons Hotel Istanbul (www.fourseasons. com) is hard to beat for its central location in Sultanahmet and luxurious interiors. The service here is also renowned.

When to Go
Spring (Apr–May) and autumn (Sep–Oct) are the most pleasant times weather- and crowd-wise.

Budget per Day for Two
From £120 depending on your choice of hotel and restaurants, and including transport.

Website
http://whc.unesco.org/en/list/356

FORGET SAN MARCO?

THE BUILD-UP This awesome 11th-century basilica, designed as the final resting place of St Mark the Evangelist, is one of the world's most lavishly decorated churches. Among its many treasures are the saint's tomb itself, the Byzantine mosaics adorning the ceilings, the Pala d'Oro altar screen, which has over 2,000 enamelled panels studded with precious stones, and the San Marco Museum.

THE LETDOWN Basilica San Marco, the third church to be constructed on this site, postdates Haghia Sophia by 500 years. Disappointingly, many of its famous treasures are not the original church decorations, but were looted from other buildings around the world. San Marco is also one of the most visited sights in Europe, and the queues here are enormous, so don't come for peace and quiet.

GOING ANYWAY? If a visit to San Marco is still a must-do for you, try to come outside the main European holidays and avoid the hotter months, when Venice's lagoon can reek. Arriving early in the morning will give you a head start on the cruise-ship and guided-tour groups.

MAIN IMAGE The magnificent interior of Haghia Sophia, Istanbul
BELOW (left to right) Haghia Sophia illuminated at night; mosaic of the Virgin Mary and Christ Child with two Byzantine rulers, Haghia Sophia

3 MORE RELIGIOUS MONUMENTS TO RIVAL BASILICA SAN MARCO

ST CATHERINE'S MONASTERY, MOUNT SINAI, EGYPT

Dating from the 6th century, St Catherine's is one of the oldest functioning monasteries in the world. It is set spectacularly at the foot of Mount Sinai, where Moses is said to have received the Ten Commandments, and contains a priceless collection of religious art, icons and manuscripts.

MOUNT ATHOS, MACEDONIA, NORTHERN GREECE

The semi-autonomous monastic state of Mount Athos has altered very little since Byzantine days. Its 2,000 monks continue their 1,000-year-old tradition of study and prayer, and no female – human or animal – is permitted entry. The only access is by boat.

RAVENNA'S BYZANTINE CHURCHES, ITALY
Ravenna, once the western capital of the Byzantine Empire, is home to a number of beautiful churches dating from the 5th to the 7th centuries. These churches are famous for their stunning mosaics, which are considered among the finest in Western art.

MAIN IMAGE Fine mosaicwork within the dome at the Imam Mosque
BELOW (left to right) Portal to Imam Mosque; a minaret towers above the city of Isfahan; striking tilework on the dome of the Imam Mosque

IMAM MOSQUE
VS ST PETER'S BASILICA

*Isfahan's Imam Mosque is an architectural masterpiece of almost overwhelming loveliness,
and a far cry from the hustle and bustle of St Peter's in Rome*

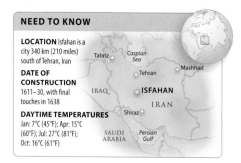
Few buildings in the world can match the refined
proportions and exquisite decoration of Isfahan's
Imam Mosque. In contrast to the vast, marble-clad
interior of St Peter's Basilica, the entrance of the
Imam Mosque leads the visitor to a sun-filled open
courtyard, surrounded on three sides by enormous,
vaulted chambers, the largest of these framed by
slender minarets and backed by a monumental
dome. Almost every visible surface is covered with
the dazzling blue tiles with which, for many, Islamic
architecture is synonymous. It is almost as if the
building had been turned inside-out (or outside-
in). Viewed from the outside, against a medley of
sun-baked ochre rooftops and low, jagged hills
rising beyond the city's edge, only the mosque's
lovely dome and its towering entrance give any
inkling of the mesmerizing beauty of the interior.

The Imam Mosque is the crown jewel of the
Meydan-e Imam – a huge square also known by
the more poetic name of Naqsh-e Jahan or
"Ornament of the World". Now a designated
UNESCO World Heritage Site, it was commissioned
by Shah Abbas I as part of a massive building
programme intended to transform his capital,
Isfahan, into one of the most splendid cities in the
world. The square itself was originally planned as a
space for military parades and polo matches and,
at over 500 m (1,640 ft) on its longest side, is
among the largest public squares in the world.
Each side is set with an architectural gem: on the
west side, the Ali Qapu palace; to the north, the
entrance to the great Bazar-e Bozorg; the exquisite
Sheikh Lotfullah mosque to the east and to the
south, the enticing doorway to the Imam Mosque.

The mosque is entered by way of a magnificent
portal, some 27 m (88 ft) high and encased entirely
in superb mosaic tilework. Framed by twin minarets
even taller than the portal, and festooned with
stalactite-like mouldings, the scale of this entrance
utterly dwarfs the visitor.

Although the gateway faces squarely onto the
Meydan, the interior of the mosque is offset from
this so that the main prayer hall faces towards
Mecca. The dome has a double-shelled construction,
its exterior rising to a height of 52 m (170 ft). In
spite of its size, the dome almost gives the illusion
of floating, a yellow arabesque pattern meandering
lazily across the pale blue surface. Its twin shells
produce a remarkable acoustic effect, replicating
individual sounds in a series of clear echoes.

FORGET ST PETER'S BASILICA?

THE BUILD-UP St Peter's Basilica is justifiably famous,
its spectacular design and decoration incorporating the successive
talents of Bramante, Michelangelo, Maderno and Bernini, among
others. Its scale is staggering by any standards, and its dome,
at 136 m (446 ft), is the highest in the world.

THE LETDOWN The problem is that St Peter's, like Rome as a
whole, attracts an enormous number of visitors, tourists and
pilgrims. The grand architectural design cannot help but lose
something of its impact when seen amid a sea of bodies and voices.
Expect long queues and security checks before you get in, and
crowds once you're inside. Michelangelo's exquisite sculpture,
the *Pietà*, is now surrounded with bullet-proof glass, after a visitor
attacked it with a geologist's hammer in the 1970s.

GOING ANYWAY? If you do plan to visit St Peter's, try to arrive
early in the day, to miss the worst of the queues. There is no shade in the square, so it's a good idea
to carry a hat and some water. It is best to visit outside of July and August, and to avoid Easter.

ABOVE Summer crowds throng the hot, unshaded
square outside St Peter's Basilica in Rome

The dazzling interior of the Süleymaniye Mosque, Turkey

The splendid dome of the mosque at Tilla Kari Madrasah, Uzbekistan

The light and airy space of the British Museum's Great Court, UK

SÜLEYMANIYE MOSQUE

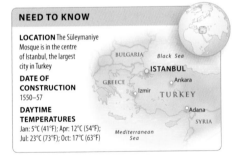

NEED TO KNOW

LOCATION The Süleymaniye Mosque is in the centre of Istanbul, the largest city in Turkey

DATE OF CONSTRUCTION 1550–57

DAYTIME TEMPERATURES Jan: 5°C (41°F); Apr: 12°C (54°F); Jul: 23°C (73°F); Oct: 17°C (63°F)

The Süleymaniye – the imperial mosque of the great Ottoman sultan Süleyman I (also known as "the Lawgiver", but better known in the West as Süleyman the Magnificent) – commands a superb location atop one of the Ottoman capital's many hills. It is one of two master works by the architect Sinan (the other is the Selimiye Mosque in Edirne). The vast, apparently unsupported, space of the interior is achieved through the use of semi-domes on either side of the main dome, and by disguising the massive supporting buttresses, which are incorporated within the walls. It is beautifully decorated with Iznik tiles, used more extensively here than ever before.

Practical Information

Getting There and Around From Istanbul airport buses and a metro serve the city centre. International train services run to Sirkeci station. The nearest tram stop is Beyazit.

When to Go April, when the tulips are in full bloom, is particularly pretty. September is also a pleasant month to visit.

Website www.tourismturkey.org

TILLA KARI MADRASAH

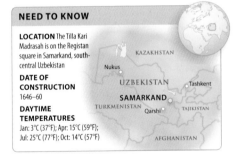

NEED TO KNOW

LOCATION The Tilla Kari Madrasah is on the Registan square in Samarkand, south-central Uzbekistan

DATE OF CONSTRUCTION 1646–60

DAYTIME TEMPERATURES Jan: 3°C (37°F); Apr: 15°C (59°F); Jul: 25°C (77°F); Oct: 14°C (57°F)

The Tilla Kari Madrasah is one of the three great *madrasahs*, or Islamic colleges, on Samarkand's Registan Square. The magnificent dome of its mosque rises from the rectangular plinth of the prayer hall, via two octagonal levels supporting a high cylindrical drum whose polychrome bands of Arabic calligraphy form a lovely counterpoint to the pure turquoise colour of the dome itself. Tilla Kari means "gold-covered", and the whole building is lavishly decorated, inside and out, with gilded inscriptions from the Koran.

Practical Information

Getting There and Around There are flights to Samarkand from Russia. Alternatively travel by air to Tashkent, then make the 4–5-hour trip by bus or taxi on to Samarkand. Trains run from Tashkent and Moscow on the Turksib Railway.

When to Go Best visited in spring (Apr–Jun) or autumn (Sep–Oct)

Website www.pagetour.org/samarkand/Registan.htm

BRITISH MUSEUM

NEED TO KNOW

LOCATION The British Museum is in the Bloomsbury district of central London, England

DATE OF CONSTRUCTION First opened to the public 1759; Great Court reopened 2000

DAYTIME TEMPERATURES Jan: 4°C (39°F); Apr: 10°C (50°F); Jul: 18°C (64°F); Oct: 11°C (52°F)

Although it is not technically a dome, the British Museum's Great Court, with its spectacular glass roof, is a magnificent interior space. Hidden since 1857, it was opened again in December 2000, following extensive redesign by British architect Norman Foster and the transfer of the museum's library collection to the new British Library premises at St Pancras. It now constitutes the largest covered square in Europe. A new south portico, pierced by three portals, leads visitors into the enormous court, at the centre of which is Sydney Smirke's round Reading Room, restored to its 1857 decorative scheme. The elaborately constructed roof is made up of 315 tonnes of glass, held together by 478 tonnes of steel.

Practical Information

Getting There and Around Travel into the city centre by train or tube from one of London's airports, or by international rail from Europe to London St Pancras. The museum is easily accessible by bus or tube. The nearest tube stations are Holborn and Tottenham Court Road.

When to Go Open all year but check and book ahead for major exhibitions.

Website www.britishmuseum.org

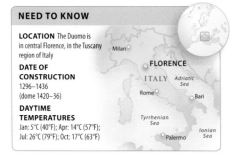

Florence's Duomo, rising majestically over the city, Italy

DUOMO, FLORENCE

NEED TO KNOW

LOCATION The Duomo is in central Florence, in the Tuscany region of Italy

DATE OF CONSTRUCTION 1296–1436 (dome 1420–36)

DAYTIME TEMPERATURES Jan: 5°C (40°F); Apr: 14°C (57°F); Jul: 26°C (79°F); Oct: 17°C (63°F)

The Basilica of Santa Maria del Fiore in Florence, better known as the Duomo, is without doubt an architectural masterpiece of the Italian Renaissance. The magnificent dome, which dominates the Florentine skyline, was designed by Filippo Brunelleschi. His distinctive octagonal design required some four million bricks. The building of the cathedral began in 1296, under Arnolfo di Cambio, and was continued by a succession of architects after his death. By the time work began on the dome itself, the cathedral had already been under construction for over 100 years, and the lantern that crowns it was not completed until 1461. The interior decoration is 16th-century, depicting scenes from the Last Judgement.

Practical Information

Getting There and Around Travel by air to Florence airport, then by bus or taxi to the city centre. The international train station is a 10-minute walk from the Duomo. The city is easily explored on foot.

When to Go Avoid high summer (Jul–Aug), which can be stiflingly hot and humid.

Website www.firenzeturismo.it

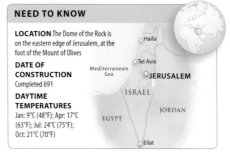

The elaborately tiled entrance to the Dome of the Rock, Israel

DOME OF THE ROCK

NEED TO KNOW

LOCATION The Dome of the Rock is on the eastern edge of Jerusalem, at the foot of the Mount of Olives

DATE OF CONSTRUCTION Completed 691

DAYTIME TEMPERATURES Jan: 9°C (48°F); Apr: 17°C (63°F); Jul: 24°C (75°F); Oct: 21°C (70°F)

The Dome of the Rock is the earliest Islamic building to have survived in its original form to the present day. Intended as a shrine for pilgrims, it was completed under the Umayyad caliph Abd al-Malik, and stands near the centre of the Haram al-Sharif ("The Noble Sanctuary"), or Temple Mount, a site important to both Muslim and Jewish faiths. Its octagonal form is derived from local Christian church architecture, and the interior is decorated with glittering mosaics that reveal Byzantine influence. It has undergone several restorations, notably in the 1540s by Süleyman the Magnificent, who replaced the colourful tiles on the exterior. The central dome was originally covered in pure gold, but this has now been replaced by anodized aluminium, coated in gold leaf.

Practical Information

Getting There and Around Fly to Tel Aviv, from where there are buses and train links to Jerusalem. Temple Mount is accessible by bus or taxi.

When to Go Spring (Mar–May) is usually dry, sunny and pleasantly warm.

Website www.sacred-destinations.com/israel/

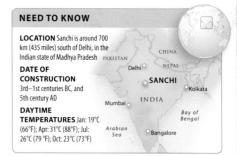

Worshipper at one of the gateways to the Great Stupa of Sanchi, India

GREAT STUPA OF SANCHI

NEED TO KNOW

LOCATION Sanchi is around 700 km (435 miles) south of Delhi, in the Indian state of Madhya Pradesh

DATE OF CONSTRUCTION 3rd–1st centuries BC, and 5th century AD

DAYTIME TEMPERATURES Jan: 19°C (66°F); Apr: 31°C (88°F); Jul: 26°C (79°F); Oct: 23°C (73°F)

Sanchi is one of the most important Buddhist sites in the Indian subcontinent. Its centrepiece is the Great Stupa, a huge hemisphere crowned with a stone umbrella. It encases a smaller stupa built by the Emperor Ashoka in the 3rd century BC to shelter the relics of Buddha. The present stupa is encircled by stone balustrades, beautifully carved with human and mythological figures, flowers and animals. Four elaborate gateways, one facing each entrance, were added in the 1st century BC. Depicting scenes from Buddha's life, they are among the finest carvings of their kind in India.

Practical Information

Getting There and Around Fly to Delhi or Mumbai, and continue to Bhopal by train or air. From Bhopal there are regular bus and train services to Sanchi, which lies 46 km (28 miles) to the east.

When to Go Visiting between October and March avoids the humid summer as well as the monsoon season.

Website www.cultural-heritage-india.com

MAIN IMAGE Aerial view of San Gimignano **BELOW (left to right)**
fresco of pilgrims in Sant'Agostino church; costumed, parading drummers
during the Fiera delle Messi; Piazza della Cisterna with its central well

SAN GIMIGNANO
VS THE LEANING TOWER OF PISA

Famed for its tourist-pleasing tilt, the Leaning Tower of Pisa attracts busloads of camera-toting tourists. However, the equally ancient but totally vertical towers of San Gimignano invite the truly curious to explore a preserved medieval community

NEED TO KNOW

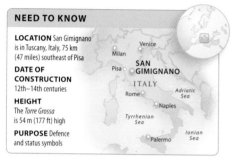

LOCATION San Gimignano is in Tuscany, Italy, 75 km (47 miles) southeast of Pisa

DATE OF CONSTRUCTION 12th–14th centuries

HEIGHT The *Torre Grossa* is 54 m (177 ft) high

PURPOSE Defence and status symbols

Unlike the bustling conurbation of Pisa, San Gimignano closes its gates to the modern world. Both car and 21st-century attitudes must be left outside as you enter this charming hilltop town with its deep medieval roots. Named after the Bishop of Modena credited with saving the town from marauding Huns in the 10th century, this turreted Tuscan gem elevates rather than entertains.

Situated on the Via Francigena route to Rome (*see pp96–7*), San Gimignano emerged and flourished for centuries as a waypoint for pilgrims on their journey to the Holy City. But increasing prosperity and a growing desire for autonomy demanded fortification, and the first defensive towers were built. By the beginning of the 13th century San Gimignano was a powerful and independent community, and its wealthy (and feuding) families vied with one another in the construction of ever taller tower-houses, to protect them from threats from without and within the city.

For medieval pilgrims headed to Rome, San Gimignano was an architectural anomaly in the rich farmland of Tuscany. Its 72 towers created an almost metropolitan skyline on the hill overlooking the Elsa valley, a sight which must have been both awe-inspiring and fear-inducing for weary travellers.

Sadly, the autonomy of San Gimignano was destroyed in the mid-14th century, in part due to its strategic location. Waves of the Black Plague pandemic ravaged the once-populous town, wiping out over two-thirds of the residents and leaving behind a destabilized society. In its weakened state it soon fell under the control of nearby Florence, and its power and status faded fast.

The period of domination by Florence, and later by Siena, saw many of the mighty towers tumble from neglect, and San Gimignano drifted further into obscurity. But it was this fall from grace that saved the town from losing its medieval Tuscan charm.

The *Torre Grossa*, nearly as tall as the tower in Pisa, but without the slant, dominates the town and is the only one of the 14 remaining towers that can be ascended. A climb up its stairs transports you back in time, as the view from the top reveals an ancient patchwork of carefully tended vineyards and farmlands spread across the Elsa valley.

The palaces, churches and squares within San Gimignano give a sense of what city life must have been like in its heyday. The Piazza della Cisterna, for example, with a public well in the centre, has been a gathering place for over 1,200 years. A visit to the town's museums offers insights into its cultural heritage and, in June, the *Feria delle Messi* festival brings knights, acrobats and medieval musicians to its streets. But your first glimpse of its tower-crowned hilltop is a thrill that you will never forget.

FORGET THE LEANING TOWER OF PISA?

THE BUILD-UP There is an inexplicable fascination with anything that is large and unstable, and in the case of the Leaning Tower of Pisa, people have been gathering and gawking for over 800 years. Bonano Pisano, commissioned in 1173 to design a bell tower to accompany the cathedral next door, never intended for it to lean. But only a few years into the construction, the foundations began to sink on one side.

THE LETDOWN By 1990, the tower was in real danger of collapsing and structural engineers were brought in to stabilize it. Even though the tower itself is an architectural and historical marvel, its celebrity status depends on its appearing to be on the verge of collapse, so the engineers anchored the tower at the best possible angle in order for this iconic structure to continue drawing huge crowds of visitors.

GOING ANYWAY? If you don't want a long wait for one of the limited places on a guided walk up the tower, buy a ticket in advance. To miss the crowds and get a clear photo of the tower, try to visit early in the day.

ABOVE One of a countless stream of tour groups poses for a photo in front of the tower.

PRACTICAL INFORMATION

Getting There and Around
The closest international airport is at Florence (70 km/43 miles). Poggibonsi is the nearest station (15 mins by bus). Trains and buses run there from Florence and Siena. From Pisa airport (73 km/45 miles), car hire is preferable to rather complicated public transport. The drive is quite slow but very scenic.

Where to Eat
Housed in a 14th-century building between the Duomo (cathedral) and the Piazza della Cisterna, Ristorante Dorando (www.ristorantedorando.it), with its vaulted ceilings and stone walls, hung with works by local artists, makes the perfect setting in which to experience the very best of Tuscan cooking.

Where to Stay
Set in a palace dating back to the 12th century, and ideally located in the heart of town overlooking the Piazza della Cisterna on one side and the Elsa valley on the other, Hotel Leon Bianco (www.leonbianco.com) has lovely double rooms from £100.

When to Go
The town is busy almost all year, but it's best to avoid the peak summer and weekend crowds. The many summer festivals are great fun but the narrow streets get packed with revellers.

Budget per Day for Two
£125–175 depending on choice of accommodation and dining.

Website
www.sangimignano.net

HUQIU TOWER

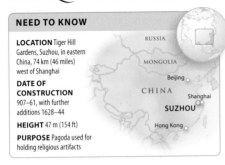

NEED TO KNOW

LOCATION Tiger Hill Gardens, Suzhou, in eastern China, 74 km (46 miles) west of Shanghai

DATE OF CONSTRUCTION 907–61, with further additions 1628–44

HEIGHT 47 m (154 ft)

PURPOSE Pagoda used for holding religious artifacts

Also known as the Yunyang Pagoda or the Tiger Hill Pagoda, the "Leaning Tower of China" is an octagonal seven-storey brick construction. Part of the foundations are on a rock base and the rest on soil, which, after more than 1,000 years, has resulted in an angle of tilt of some three degrees. Some interior columns have cracked, further weakening the structure. The tower has no staircase (movable ladders are used to reach upper levels), so cannot be climbed by the public. Huqiu Tower is set on a hilltop within the ancient gardens of Tiger Hill, where a legendary white tiger is said to guard the tomb of King He Lu, who died in 600 BC.

Practical Information

Getting There and Around Suzhou's nearest international airport is at Shanghai, 120 km (75 miles) away, with regular, fast bus and train links.

When to Go The humid, subtropical climate means that Apr–May and Oct–Nov are the most pleasant times to visit the gardens.

Website www.cnto.org/suzhou.asp

Strikingly ornate Huqiu Tower, rising magnificently above the lush landscape of Tiger Hill Gardens , China

LEANING TOWER OF TELUK INTAN

NEED TO KNOW

LOCATION Teluk Intan, 85 km (53 miles) south of Ipoh, the state capital of Perak, in peninsular Malaysia

DATE OF CONSTRUCTION 1885

HEIGHT 26 m (85 ft)

PURPOSE Water tower, clock tower, marker for ships

Fairly modern as leaning towers go, the circular Tower of Teluk Intan was originally known as the High Clock Tower due to the large upper-storey clock – still ticking – made by J W Benson of London, watchmaker to Queen Victoria. The tower was built by a Chinese contractor who incorporated many of his country's traditional architectural elements into the design. Initially intended as a water tower in case of drought or fire, and built on soft soil, it first started to lean under the sheer weight of the water. Later, floods submerged the base of the tower and increased the angle of tilt to nearly two degrees.

Practical Information

Getting There and Around Kuala Lumpur is the closest international airport, 100 miles (165 km) southeast, with bus connections.

When to Go This is a wet equatorial zone with little seasonal variation. The tower is open all year and is free to ascend.

Website www.perak.info/Hilir_Perak/Leaning_Tower_Teluk_Intan.htm

Colourful tower of Teluk Intan, the only tall building in the city and a landmark sight for miles around, Malaysia

KOUTOUBIA MINARET

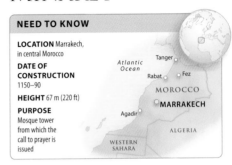

NEED TO KNOW

LOCATION Marrakech, in central Morocco

DATE OF CONSTRUCTION 1150–90

HEIGHT 67 m (220 ft)

PURPOSE Mosque tower from which the call to prayer is issued

The beautiful Koutoubia Minaret adjoins the largest mosque in Marrakech, and is the oldest of the world's three remaining Almohad-dynasty minarets. The mosque had to be rebuilt soon after completion because it did not align properly with Mecca, but the minaret was able to remain in its original form. The stately minaret became an influential model for other towers in the Moorish world, including the Hassan Tower mausoleum in Rabat, and the Giralda in Seville, Spain. Construction commenced shortly after the Almohad conquest of Marrakech in 1150 and was completed during the reign of Sultan Yacoub el-Mansour. The minaret is topped with 4 copper balls, one of which was a gift from the wife of the Sultan as penance for breaking her fast during Ramadan.

Practical Information

Getting There and Around The minaret is in central Marrakech overlooking Djemaa el Fna square, 15 mins by taxi from Marrakech-Menara Airport.

When to Go Marrakech is sunny all year round. The weather is at its best in spring, early summer and autumn, without extremes of temperature. Only Muslims are allowed access to the mosque and minaret.

Website www.marrakech-cityguide.com

Delicately carved Islamic stone- and tilework ornamentation on the Koutoubia Minaret, bathed in late-afternoon sunlight, Morocco

GIOTTO'S BELL TOWER

This exquisite masterpiece of the Florentine Renaissance is the perfect accompaniment to Brunelleschi's basilica dome on the Piazza del Duomo in Florence. An accomplished painter as well as an architect, Giotto di Bondone created a tower designed to look as if it were painted, incorporating his *chiaroscuro* ("light and shade") style and perspective. The tower is decorated in geometric designs of multicoloured marble and adorned with sculptures. Giotto was 67 when construction began and at the time of his death three years later, only the first level was complete, but his design was carried forward by Pisano, Talenti, Donatello and other master craftsmen and artists to glorious completion 22 years later.

Practical Information

Getting There and Around Florence has a regional aiport but most visitors arrive from Pisa's international airport (1hr by train).

When to Go April and May are delightful in Florence, while July and August bring the biggest crowds. The campanile can be climbed all year.

Website www.firenzeturismo.it

Giotto's magnificent bell tower, flanked by the Basilica di Santa Maria del Fiore on Piazza del Duomo, Italy

QUTB MINAR

The world's tallest brick minaret, the Qutb Minar is set in peaceful gardens along with funerary buildings and other masterworks of Indo-Muslim architecture dating from the 12th to the 14th centuries. It is a tapering cylindrical tower, with alternating angular and circular flutings, covered with fine engravings and Koranic quotations. Construction was begun under Qutub-ud-Din Aibak, the first ruler of the medieval Delhi Sultanate, and founder of the Slave Dynasty, using sandstone from demolished Jain temples. It was extended by his son-in-law and has been repaired several times since, but it has withstood the pull of gravity, leaning only 60 cm (24 inches).

Practical Information

Getting There and Around The Qutb Minar is the centrepiece of the Qutb Complex in Mehrauli, 15 km (9 miles) south of central Delhi.

When to Go The complex is open year-round (though the Minar cannot be climbed), but the heat and pollution of Mar–Jun, and the monsoons of Jul–Sep make late autumn to early spring (Oct– Feb) the best time to visit.

Website www.asi.nic.in/asi_monu_whs_qutbminar.asp

Elaborately carved, tapering Qutb Minar, viewed from the Quwwat-ul-Islam Mosque in the complex, India

ST MARK'S CAMPANILE

The elegant bell tower of St Mark's Basilica is as recognizable and treasured a Venetian icon as the gondolas of the Grand Canal. The red brick shaft, with its arched belfry and pyramidal spire, is topped by a 3-m (10-ft) golden weathervane depicting the angel Gabriel with outstretched wings. Venetians believe that when the angel is facing the Basilica, high tides are on the way. Fires, floods and earthquakes all took their toll on the campanile. Even after repeated restoration, ominous cracks reappeared and on 14 July 1902 at 9:45am the original tower collapsed into rubble. Miraculously, the only fatality was the caretaker's cat. A wisely reinforced reconstruction was inaugurated on St Mark's Day, 25 April 1912.

Practical Information

Getting There and Around Busy public water buses take 45 mins from Marco Polo Airport to St Mark's Square, site of the campanile.

When to Go Summer is hot and crowded. Winter can see flooding but the Carnival (Feb) is a magical time. The campanile may be climbed all year.

Website www.basilicasanmarco.it

The Campanile, dominating St Mark's Square, seen from the perfect vantage point of the Grand Canal, Italy

CHICAGO
VS MANHATTAN

Manhattan's soaring skyline dazzles, but Chicago is the birthplace of the skyscraper

ABOVE Art Deco façade of the Chicago Board of Trade building
BELOW The impressive Chicago skline viewed from a riverboat cruise

New York's skyscrapers may be the most famous in the world but, in the architectural race to the top, Chicago has always had the Big Apple beat, literally, from the ground up. The first skyscrapers were erected, not in the great eastern metropolis, but here on the edge of the Midwestern prairie, and present-day Chicago offers a fascinating visual history of the rise of the modern urban landscape.

The Great Chicago Fire of 1871 completely devastated the heart of this wealthy industrial city, but it also created a blank slate. As Chicago was rebuilt, talented architects rushed in from Europe and the east coast, eager to try out new forms and ideas unfettered by traditional styles and constraints. Among them were Louis H Sullivan, John Root, Daniel Burnham and William le Baron Jenney. The "father of the skyscraper", Jenney invented the metal-frame construction method that made such high-rise buildings possible.

While New York so often tore down its old buildings to make room for the new, in Chicago you can still see some of the earliest skyscrapers ever built. The Rookery, Marquette, Monadnock and Reliance buildings were all erected between 1885 and 1895. They sport such features as decorative terracotta façades and Jenney's trademark Chicago windows with narrow opening side panels. Their distinctive style has become known as the Chicago School of Architecture.

You'll trek miles to take in New York's landmark buildings, but many of Chicago's architectural gems lie within The Loop, the historic city centre beneath the "El". The clattering of this elevated train system adds to the urban buzz as workers and visitors bustle between shiny new office blocks, grand old hotels and department stores, cosy corner bars and art-decked public plazas.

The Chicago Architecture Foundation leads a wide range of tours of this vibrant downtown area as well as a skyscraper-spotting riverboat cruise. Highlights include Sullivan's ornate Carson, Pirie, Scott & Company building (1899); the striking Art Deco skyscraper of the Chicago Board of Trade (1930); and the minimalist "glass box" Federal Center by Ludwig Mies van der Rohe (1959–74).

The 442-m (1,450-ft) Willis – formerly Sears – Tower (1973) is currently the nation's tallest building, beating the Empire State Building by 61 m (200 ft). From its Skydeck observatory on the 103rd floor, you can see four states. Under construction on the lakefront nearby is Santiago Calatrava's Chicago Spire. When completed, this elegant, spiralling residential tower will stand 610 m (2,000 ft) high. Take a water taxi up the Chicago River for more fine skyline views on your way to Navy Pier, on Lake Michigan. In summer, this entertainment and dining centre offers everything from a fairground to a Museum of Stained Glass, as well as year-round live events.

FORGET NEW YORK?

THE BUILD-UP The Empire State Building is an American legend. The Chrysler Building spire, Rockefeller Center, and the Flatiron Building are among many other skyscrapers known the world over from movies and TV.

THE LETDOWN New York's architectural icons are scattered over several miles, from the tip of Lower Manhattan to the top of Central Park. The best features of many are at the top, only clearly visible from the upper floors of other skyscrapers. Few of these are open to the public, so expect long queues, security searches and costly admission to observation decks.

GOING ANYWAY? Pack comfortable shoes, binoculars and extra patience. Pre-purchase Empire State Building tickets online and, if time is tight, consider an Express Pass.

ABOVE Visitors who have made it to the 86th-floor Observation Deck of the Empire State Building

9 DE JULIO
VS CHAMPS-ELYSÉES

*Buenos Aires takes on Paris as home to
the world's greatest thoroughfare*

NEED TO KNOW

LOCATION Avenida 9 de Julio runs
north–south through the centre of
the Argentinian capital, Buenos Aires

VISITORS PER YEAR
2,342,000

WEATHER Summer (Dec–Feb)
can be very hot and humid. Autumn
and spring are warm and sunny

DIMENSIONS
2.6 km (1.6 miles) long and
140 m (460 ft) wide

ABOVE Dazzling interior of the Teatro Colón
BELOW Avenida 9 de Julio ablaze with light after the sun has set

ABOVE Packed pavement cafés along the Champs-Elysées

FORGET THE CHAMPS-ELYSÉES?

THE BUILD-UP The Champs-Elysées, Paris's
most prestigious avenue, is celebrated for its
tree-lined beauty and elegant fountains and
statues. Called "*la plus belle avenue du monde*"
by Parisians, it is marked at its eastern extreme
by the stately Place de la Concorde and at its
western limit by the glorious Arc de Triomphe.

THE LETDOWN Once synonymous with high
style and grand living, the Champs-Elysées has
sacrificed its reputation in recent times. In a
trend decried as "*banalization*" by the Paris
authorities, global chain stores and themed
restaurants now throng an avenue increasingly
seen as a commercialized tourist trap.

GOING ANYWAY? Focus your visit on the less
money-driven section of the avenue, east of
Rond-Point, where the majestic Grand Palais
and Palais de l'Elysée overlook lovely gardens.
To eat well and cheaply in true French style, try
the side streets for little bistros and *crêperies*.

Step out onto the Avenida 9 de Julio and you can't
fail to appreciate that you are on one of the world's
greatest, most thrilling thoroughfares. Twenty lanes
of roaring traffic stand between you and the other
side of an asphalt canyon claimed by Argentinians
as the widest avenue in the world. Gouged through
the centre of Buenos Aires in the 1930s to link the
city's northern and southern limits, this extraordinary
feat of urban planning renders even the Champs-
Elysées a mere side street in comparison. Not only
does it extend for over half-a-kilometre further
than Europe's most celebrated boulevard, but it is
also, incredibly, twice as wide.

It is not simply the dimensions of the 9 de Julio
that amaze. Visitors walking its length soon realize
they are on one of the world's greatest patriotic
thoroughfares, named in honour of Argentina's
Independence Day (9 July 1816) and studded with
monumental architecture. Most iconic of all is the
soaring Obelisco, a 65-m (213-ft) needle that
reaches skywards at the Avenida's midpoint. It was
built in 1936, to mark the 400th anniversary of the
city's founding. From its base, broad sidewalks of
fancy statuary and ornate fountains strike out for
the southern and northern extremities of the
Avenida; to the British-built Estación Constitución
(railway station), the vast, vaulted interior of which

echoes the grandeur of the great Roman baths;
and to the Palacio Ortiz Basualdo, whose exquisite
Beaux-Arts architecture recalls the palaces of Paris
and which houses the French Embassy.

No visit to the Avenida should overlook its single
greatest highlight, the magnificent Teatro Colón
opera house. Built in 1908, this world-class venue's
beautiful main entrance, fashioned in the French
Renaissance style, conceals a still more ornate
interior. Fascinating tours reveal marbled halls, a
majestically domed auditorium and labyrinthine
subterranean workshops. Underground, amidst the
relics of performances past, not a whisper is heard
of the urban highway that roars just metres away.

Whether you stroll down the Avenida or zip
along it at breakneck speed in a taxi, the influence
of Europe is ever-present on an avenue built in the
image of Paris's great boulevards. But linger awhile,
sip a leisurely cup of coffee at a pavement café,
and still more vibrant images emerge – children
splashing in ornate fountains; huge neon billboards
glowing atop crumbling *belle époque* façades –
all accompanied by the sound of tango music
drifting from open doors and windows. It is this
heady mix of South American vitality and European
grandeur that makes the 9 de Julio, like Buenos
Aires itself, a uniquely intoxicating place to be.

PRACTICAL INFORMATION

Getting There and Around
International flights to Buenos
Aires land at Ezeiza Airport,
22 km (35 miles) from the city
centre (45 mins by shuttle bus or
taxi). All subway lines stop at the
9 de Julio and numerous buses
run its length. The best way to
get around is on foot, but take a
taxi ride down the avenue at
night to see the neon billboards
and an illuminated Obelisco.

Where to Eat
Buenos Aires is world-famous
for its steakhouses. Try a sizzling
lomo (tenderloin) with a bottle
of Malbec, Argentina's best red
wine. El Mirasol de la Recova
(tel. + 54 11 4326-7323),
just off the Avenida, serves
king-sized cuts.

Where to Stay
There are numerous top-quality
hotels on the Avenida 9 de Julio.
Easily the most luxurious is the
Four Seasons Hotel, an elegant
main tower and an adjacent
Belle-Epoque mansion, set in
classical gardens with a Roman
pool (www.fourseasons.com).

When to Go
Springtime (Sep–Nov) is
beautiful in Buenos Aires.
The weather is warm at 17°C
(64°F) and the trees lining the
9 de Julio gorgeously green.

Budget per Day for Two
£160 including four-star
accommodation and food.

Website
www.bue.gov.ar

PUNING TEMPLE
VS TEMPLE OF HEAVEN

The Temple of Heaven is one of China's most iconic symbols, but it lacks the profound air of reverence that lures Buddhist pilgrims from across the land to Puning Temple

NEED TO KNOW

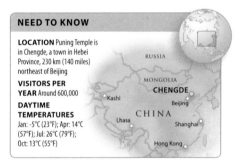

LOCATION Puning Temple is in Chengde, a town in Hebei Province, 230 km (140 miles) northeast of Beijing

VISITORS PER YEAR Around 600,000

DAYTIME TEMPERATURES
Jan: -5°C (23°F); Apr: 14°C (57°F); Jul: 26°C (79°F); Oct: 13°C (55°F)

The Temple of Heaven (Tian Tan), more accurately translated as the Altar of Heaven, might be one of China's most photographed sights, but it is obscure in its symbols, esoteric in function and essentially in religious disuse. In fact, this over-visited collection of buildings has little of the vitality and atmosphere of Chengde's Puning Temple (Puning Si).

While the Confucian orderliness and lifelessness of Beijing's famous altar points to a ceremonial purpose to which visitors can't easily relate, the day-to-day vibrancy of Puning Temple intoxicates pilgrims and travellers alike. This is a living, breathing, active place of worship, where the full panoply of Buddhist ritual is played out by resident lamas and incense-carrying worshippers.

The architecture and surroundings of the two temples reflect their different characters. The Temple of Heaven is a paradigm of Chinese architectural balance and symbolism. The site is perfectly flat, which accentuates the harmony of its layout and reinforces a certain monotony. Its buildings are an exercise in restraint, so there is an absence of spontaneity and natural wildness. Puning Temple, on the other hand, is a synthesis of Chinese and Tibetan architectural styles, built on the side of a mountain. Frequently associated with myths, spirits and magical happenings, mountains in China are characteristic refuges for Buddhist temples. This spectacular backdrop changes colour dramatically

from season to season, and frames the temple within the context of the natural world, which is inherently untamed and unmanaged.

Wreathed in devotion, the magnificent temple encloses a series of halls stacked against the slope that serve as sacred portals to the powers of Guanyin, the Buddhist Goddess of Mercy, who inhabits the religious imagination of the nation. Her legendary home may be on the island of Putuo Shan, off the Zhejiang coast hundreds of miles to the southeast, but the UNESCO-protected temple in Chengde is China's most impressive shrine to this deity.

The intangible but boundless energy of Guanyin is represented in the temple's most astounding treasure: a colossal effigy standing in the Mahayana Hall, a towering space with several viewing galleries. If you only have time for one Buddhist effigy in the whole land, this must be it. Standing at over 22 m (72 ft) high, the "1,000-arm and 1,000-eye" Guanyin, reputedly the world's largest wooden statue, presides over a wide-eyed assembly of the devout and awestruck. Gazing up at this giant figure, which sports an eye in each hand, could possibly be the most powerful experience China can impart.

PRACTICAL INFORMATION

Getting There and Around
The nearest international airport is in Beijing. Buses leave Liuliqiao and Sihui bus stations hourly for the 4-hour trip to Chengde. Trains can take over 4 hours.

Where to Eat
Imperial hunting traditions have left Chengde with a taste for wild game. Try the fowl in the Dadi Beijing Roast Duck Restaurant (tel. +86 314 202 2979).

Where to Stay
Chengde accommodation cannot compare with the choice in Beijing,

but the 4-star Yunshan Hotel (tel. +86 314 205 5888) has the best rooms and service in town.

When to Go
Avoid summer and winter, when temperatures are extreme. The temple's galleries sometimes shut in the afternoon, so get there early.

Budget per Day for Two
£70 including accommodation, food, transport and admission fees.

Website
www.world-heritage-tour.org/ asia/china/chengde/puning-si-up

FORGET THE TEMPLE OF HEAVEN?

THE BUILD-UP Beijing's Temple of Heaven is a picture-postcard emblem of China's capital. Venue of the heavily ritualized imperial sacrifices to heaven during the Ming and Qing dynasties, this collection of buildings gives visitors a unique insight into China's dynastic past. With its blue-tiled, triple-eaved umbrella roof, the beautiful Hall of Prayer for Good Harvests remains a paragon of Ming dynasty design.

THE LETDOWN Temple of Heaven park is alive with people and t'ai chi practitioners in the early morning, but the temple structures themselves are functionless. The halls and altar were reserved for imperial use during the Ming and Qing dynasties, and although the complex is now fully open to the public, no one comes here to worship. Neither Buddhist nor Taoist, the Temple of Heaven has little meaning for China's devout, and has an atmosphere of Confucian reserve.

GOING ANYWAY? Try to get to Temple of Heaven Park early in the morning, when you can watch it coming to life, and take time to explore the grounds. The cheapest and quietest time to visit is from November to March. Opt for the inexpensive and informative audio tour.

MAIN IMAGE The towering wooden statue of Guanyin, with her magnificent jewels and many arms **BELOW (left to right)** Monks in prayer; one of the temple builldings from the outside, with the Mahayana Hall on the right

4 MORE CHINESE TEMPLES TO RIVAL THE TEMPLE OF HEAVEN

DAFO TEMPLE In the walled town of Zhengding, in China's Hebei province, is the renowned Dafo Temple, home to a 21-m (69-ft) bronze statue of Guanyin, dating from AD 970. The town's charming streets are overlooked by temples and pagodas.

LAMA TEMPLE Beijing's largest Buddhist temple is a majestic Tibetan Buddhist shrine. The centrepiece is a magnificent 17-m (56-ft) statue of the Maitreya Buddha, but don't forget to explore the surrounding maze of *hutongs* (traditional Beijing alleyways).

JOKHANG TEMPLE Lhasa's ancient and venerable Jokhang Temple is the most sacred in Tibet, and the focus for an endless stream of worshippers. The doors and frames of the Chapel of Chenresig are among the few remains of the original temple.

MENCIUS TEMPLE China's largest Confucius temple lies at the heart of Qufu, in Shandong province, but it's perhaps the little-visited Mencius Temple in nearby Zoucheng that you should explore instead for authentic flavours of old China.

Walt Disney Concert Hall, Los Angeles vs Sydney Opera House

A classical music venue in step with the 21st century, the Walt Disney Concert Hall provides a captivating modern alternative to older venues like the Sydney Opera House

NEED TO KNOW

LOCATION South Grand Avenue, downtown Los Angeles, USA

CONSTRUCTION 1999–2003

ACCESS Auditorium is ticket only; guided tours of building available

DAYTIME TEMPERATURES Jan: 13°C (55°F); Apr: 16°C (61°F); Jul: 22°C (72°F); Oct: 18°C (64°F)

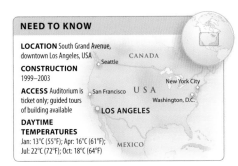

Upon stepping inside the Walt Disney Concert Hall, one cannot help but be swept up in its architectural grandeur. Full of odd angles, seductive curves and yawning windows that draw in the California sunshine, this gleaming metal-clad building looks every inch the world-class cultural centre. First-time visitors often regret arriving so close to show time, wishing they had more time to explore the labyrinthine corridors and breathtaking features of Frank Gehry's metallic wonderland. By comparison, with its white-tiled exterior and repetitive curves, the Sydney Opera House seems better suited to the 1970s, the decade of its contruction.

ABOVE The concert hall in downtown Los Angeles lit up at night

Upon its completion in 2003, the Disney revitalized downtown Los Angeles, taking the focus away from its faded municipal buildings and making it a key stop on the international classical music circuit. But for those who prefer Madonna to Mozart, the building also holds plenty of pop culture significance, having featured in such movies as *Iron Man* and *Get Smart*. Designed by Frank Gehry, the Disney is commonly thought of as a smaller version of his iconic Guggenheim Bilbao *(see p134)*. The concert hall provides its visitors with the opportunity to experience a key work of this modern architectural master. The Sydney Opera House's architect, Jørn Utzon, has unfortunately seen his legacy limited only to that project.

As much as its architectural splendour, the Disney is also admired for its superb acoustics. Classical music aficionados leave the concert hall raving about the Disney's sound qualities, which simply cannot be matched by the Opera House, which was completed some 30 years earlier. Gehry consulted the Los Angeles Philharmonic during the design process, and the results are sonically breathtaking. Even those sitting in the upper reaches of the hall's 2,265 seats enjoy crystal-clear acoustics, with sound perfectly reverberating off custom-designed Douglas fir and oak planks.

You don't need to attend a performance to appreciate the building's cultural and architectural significance. Free guided tours, offered nearly every day, encourage the public to come and study the complex – one of LA's biggest cultural bargains.

The Disney is at the forefront of a new breed of concert halls, where a visitor is just as likely to see a school group roaming the halls as a gaggle of dressed-up patrons. With its progressive programmes and foothold in LA's cultural scene, the Disney beckons visitors who want to stay ahead of the curve. It surely won't be long before the Disney takes its rightful place among the world's premier concert halls.

FORGET THE SYDNEY OPERA HOUSE?

THE BUILD-UP Perhaps the most recognizable symbol of an entire continent, the Sydney Opera House is, without question, one of the world's most famous performing arts venues. Perched majestically on Sydney Harbour, the complex is the city's most-visited tourist spot, with crowds snapping photos at all hours.

THE LETDOWN A visit to the Opera House is rarely a relaxing experience. With roughly 1,500 performances held annually throughout the complex's five main venues, it is clogged with tourists and concert-goers at most hours. Visitors taking one of the facility's tours are not guaranteed a glimpse of the Concert Hall or Opera Theatre, as accessibility depends on performance schedules.

GOING ANYWAY? For unhurried photo ops, visit during the early morning, when tourists are still not about and performances are rarely held. Opt for the more economical lunch at one of the venue's five eateries, over the pricier dinner service.

ABOVE Visitors gathered outside one of Australia's most popular tourist sights, the Sydney Opera House

PRACTICAL INFORMATION

Getting There and Around
International flights to Los Angeles land at LA International Airport (LAX), which is 26 km (16 miles) from downtown. If you take a cab, the Walt Disney Concert Hall is 30 minutes away, depending on traffic. If, however, you prefer to use the city's efficient Metro Rail service, the concert hall is located just a short walk from the Red Line Civic Center Metro stop.

Where to Eat
The complex's primary restaurant, Patina (tel. +1 213 972 3331) serves gourmet French-Californian fare amid undulating walls and ceilings. Chef's menus are available, there is both a lunch and dinner service, and seasonal tasting sessions.

Where to Stay
Downtown Los Angeles provides numerous hotel options; the Hilton Checkers Hotel (www.hilton.com) is conveniently located on South Grand Avenue, a short walk from the Disney.

When to Go
LA enjoys perfect weather through the year. Visitors keen to enjoy the Disney should check the venue's events schedule to see when Philharmonic performances or other special events will be taking place.

Budget per Day for Two
£350, including 4-star accommodation, dining out and performance tickets.

Website
www.laphil.com

MAIN IMAGE Walt Disney Concert Hall **BELOW (left to right)** The pipe organ and ceiling of the hall's auditorium; an abstract sculpture outside; a performance of *Tristan und Isolde* by the Wagner Opera

Exterior of the Michael Lee-Chin Crystal building at the Royal Ontario Museum, Toronto, Canada

ROYAL ONTARIO MUSEUM, CANADA

NEED TO KNOW

LOCATION The Royal Ontario Museum is on the northern side of Queen's Park, Toronto

CONSTRUCTION 1912–14

ACCESS Open to visitors with tickets

DAYTIME TEMPERATURES Jan: -5°C (23°F); Apr: 6°C (43°F); Jul: 21°C (70°F); Oct: 9°C (48°F)

Canada's largest museum, affectionately called the "ROM" by locals, has seen dozens of world-class exhibits, most involving world culture or natural history, pass through its halls since its construction in 1912. But with the recent Renaissance Royal Ontario Museum project wowing critics all over the world, it is the museum's ability to reinvent itself that has impressed connoisseurs of architecture. This massive renovation and expansion initiative is highlighted by the Michael Lee-Chin Crystal, a new angular facing designed by the highly respected architect Daniel Libeskind. By stepping into the 21st century with such an wonderful renovation, the museum is a shining example of how modern architecture can reinterpret and reinvigorate even the oldest of buildings.

Practical Information

Getting There and Around Located in downtown Toronto, the museum is easily accessible by car, bus or train.

When to Go Visit during Ontario's moderate spring (Mar–May) and autumn (Sep–Nov). Check the museum's calendar of events for special exhibits.

Website www.rom.on.ca

One of the three extraordinary buildings of the Neue Zollhof (New Customs House) in Düsseldorf, Germany

NEUE ZOLLHOF, GERMANY

NEED TO KNOW

LOCATION The Neue Zollhof is on the Rhine river waterfront, downtown Düsseldorf, Germany

CONSTRUCTION 1996–9

ACCESS Closed to the public

DAYTIME TEMPERATURES Jan: 2°C (35°F); Apr: 8°C (47°F); Jul: 17°C (63°F); Oct: 51°C (11°F)

A Frank Gehry masterpiece, Neue Zollhof sees the architect's whimsical – and some would say deconstructionist – touch applied to commercial office space. Three highly unique buildings are tightly packed together in a densely populated part of the city. Each of the Neue Zollhof's buildings sports a different exterior: one is outfitted in metal panels, another is finished in plaster, and the third is covered in bricks. Instead of yet another dour block of offices to pass by, locals can now stop and marvel at the complex.

Practical Information

Getting There and Around There are several flights into Düsseldorf from most of Germany's major cities. You also have the option of making the journey by bus, train or car.

When to Go Düsseldorf experiences harsh winters (Dec–Feb), with milder temperatures the rest of the year.

Website www.duesseldorf-tourismus.de

An example of modern, minimalist architecture, the Guggenheim Bilbao, Spain

GUGGENHEIM BILBAO, SPAIN

NEED TO KNOW

LOCATION The Guggenheim is in downtown Bilbao, northern Spain

CONSTRUCTION 1993–7

ACCESS Open to visitors with tickets

DAYTIME TEMPERATURES Jan: 9°C (48°F); Apr: 12°C (54°F); Jul: 21°C (70°F); Oct: 16°C (61°F)

On its completion in 1997, Frank Gehry's Guggenheim Bilbao forever changed the way critics viewed museums, providing a striking intersection between art and architecture. Overnight, the industrial city of Bilbao appeared on everyone's radar, with visitors coming from all over the globe to see the museum's soaring curves and funky angles. Situated along the Nervion river, the structure is made of glass, titanium and limestone, reflecting light off its many odd angles. Visitors to the main entrance are greeted by *Puppy*, a 13-m- (43-ft-) tall topiary terrier by artist Jeff Koons, which has also become a symbol of the city. Truly a benchmark in modern architecture, the Guggenheim Bilbao is a visceral reminder of the power of the medium.

Practical Information

Getting There and Around The airport is located 12 km (7 miles) outside Bilbao. From there, you can hire a car or take a bus to reach the downtown area.

When to Go Visit during special performances and exhibitions, though they bring additional ticket costs and extra visitors.

Website www.guggenheim-bilbao.es

The top of 30 St Mary Axe, or the "Gherkin", the sixth tallest building in London, England

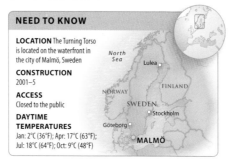

The spectacular Turning Torso in Malmö, Sweden supposedly modelled on a sculpture of a twisting human being

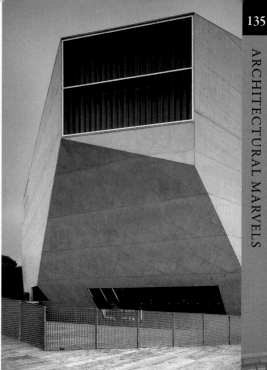

The mismatched angles and concrete façade of the Casa da Música, Porto, Portugal

30 St Mary Axe (The Gherkin), UK

NEED TO KNOW

LOCATION The Gherkin is in London's financial district (the City), England

CONSTRUCTION 2001–4

ACCESS Ground floor and outdoor plaza only

DAYTIME TEMPERATURES Jan: 4°C (39°F); Apr: 10°C (50°F); Jul: 18°C (64°F); Oct: 11°C (52°F)

Since its construction in 2003, the "Gherkin", as the 30 St Mary Axe office tower is affectionately known, has been a welcome addition to the London skyline. British architect Sir Norman Foster had a hand in its design. The 180-m (590-ft) skyscraper is a response to those who associate office towers with boring, rectangular shapes. Notable for its eco-friendly design, the building employs a natural ventilation system, as well as other energy-saving features. One can't help but gawk at the swirling glass patterns that soar up the building's sides, creating an eye-catching effect that demands attention from even the most casual observer.

Practical Information

Getting There and Around London's financial district is easily accessible by any mode of transport.

When to Go Avoid the wet, cold winter (Dec–Feb).

Website www.30stmaryaxe.com

Turning Torso, Sweden

NEED TO KNOW

LOCATION The Turning Torso is located on the waterfront in the city of Malmö, Sweden

CONSTRUCTION 2001–5

ACCESS Closed to the public

DAYTIME TEMPERATURES Jan: 2°C (36°F); Apr: 17°C (63°F); Jul: 18°C (64°F); Oct: 9°C (48°F)

Sometime in the 21st century, admirers of world-class architecture began to clamour for buildings that they could live in. Enter Santiago Calatrava's mind-blowing Turning Torso, a 190-m (623-ft) residential tower that has redefined urban living. The tower has nine, five-storey segments stacked on top of one another in a twisting fashion. The uppermost segment is turned a full 90 degrees from the base. Situated on the Malmö waterfront, this is one of Europe's tallest residential buildings, with 149 luxury apartment units. The "helicoidal" building itself is the pride of Malmö.

Practical Information

Getting There and Around You can fly into Malmö airport from any European city, or take a ferry or train across the Øresund Strait from Denmark.

When to Go With no public access to the building, visitors must contend with the waterfront's windy conditions. It is best avoided during Sweden's freezing winters.

Website www.turningtorso.com

Casa da Música, Portugal

NEED TO KNOW

LOCATION The Casa da Música is located alongside Rotunda da Boavista, one of Porto's major roundabouts, Portugal

CONSTRUCTION 1999–2005

ACCESS Open to visitors with tickets

DAYTIME TEMPERATURES Jan: 9°C (48°F); Apr: 14°C (57°F); Jul: 20°C (68°F); Oct: 16°C (61°F)

The work of the master Dutch architect Rem Koolhaas, the Casa da Música provided the city of Porto with a new icon. A concrete cube of mismatched faces and angles, the building is full of imagination. It was a modern rebuke to critics who felt that classical music performances were best enjoyed in the stately, straightforward halls of "Old Europe". The main performance hall is framed by a huge window, allowing natural light to flood the room. Even those who come here without a ticket feel engaged by the building, walking around its perimeter to admire its unique shape and unusual touches.

Practical Information

Getting There and Around Fly to Francisco Sa Carneiro airport. It is also possible to travel to Porto by train or bus, either from Lisbon, Madrid or Paris.

When to Go Summer months bring searing conditions, but any visit should be made with the performance schedule in mind.

Website www.casadamusica.com

PONTE DELLE TORRI VS PONT DU GARD

While Pont du Gard stands isolated, with only a visitors' centre and a car park, Ponte delle Torri leads you over a breathtaking chasm into the heart of medieval Spoleto

NEED TO KNOW

LOCATION Ponte delle Torri is located on the eastern side of the Italian town of Spoleto in Umbria, north of Rome

DIMENSIONS Length 236 m (774 ft); height 90 m (295 ft)

CONSTRUCTED Between the 12th and 14th centuries

DAYTIME TEMPERATURES
Jan: 3°C (37°F); Apr: 13°C (55°F); Jul: 26°C (79°F); Oct: 17°C (63°F)

Pont du Gard, the most spectacular section of a 50-km (30-mile) aqueduct, was built to bring water to the Roman city of Nîmes in France. Emerging fully formed from the Mediterranean scrub, it runs for 140 heroic metres (459 ft) before disappearing again into the scrub. After walking its length, all that's left to do is turn around and head back to the coach-filled car park.

Conversely, a narrow, unpeopled track near Ponte delle Torri guides you through the forested hills of Monteluco. The path edges warily round a ravine, and then the great aqueduct stands before

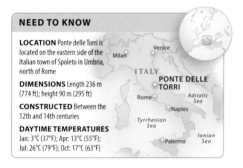

you, its slender columns spanning a seemingly impossible chasm. Continue past the ruins of the castle guarding this end and head, breath held, along the narrow walkway across the bridge. The fearsome Rocca, a medieval fortress, looms ahead. Turn left and within a few steps you're in the heart of Spoleto, one of the most beautiful towns in Italy.

No one is sure exactly when the magnificent Ponte delle Torri was built. It's possible that it was built on top of a long-vanished Roman aqueduct, but it's more likely to have been entirely constructed in the 13th century. Either way, it was used to bring water from the mountains to the upper part of Spoleto, while simultaneously providing access to Monteluco. There are castles at both ends of its 236-m (774-ft) span and two of its supporting columns are actually hollow, presumably to house guardrooms and storerooms. The view over the thickly wooded Tessino Valley from the middle of the bridge is breathtaking.

The 10 pillars divided by nine slender and graceful arcades are magically lit from below, yet the narrow path across the gorge heads into impenetrable darkness. Come here at night and chances are a courting couple will be somewhere ahead of you, arm-in-arm, incapable of resisting seclusion and the bridge's romantic appeal.

From the bridge you can either climb up to the medieval Rocca or head into the centre of Spoleto, where, within minutes, you'll be in the maze of narrow streets that cut through the town. There's a Roman theatre, several early Christian basilicas and the lovely Cathedral of Santa Maria dell'Assunta, which houses the final fresco cycle created by well-known Florentine painter Fra Filippo Lippi. But it's Ponte delle Torri that will draw you back. While you stand on the bridge, contemplating the silent Apennines, it seems impossible to believe that a thriving medieval town lies just yards behind you.

ABOVE Cathedral of Santa Maria dell'Assunta, Spoleto

FORGET PONT DU GARD?

THE BUILD-UP Pont du Gard is without doubt one of the Wonders of the Ancient World. Whether it's the first or fiftieth time you've seen it, the 2,000-year-old aqueduct never ceases to amaze. A gorgeous yet supremely practical piece of engineering, the aqueduct probably says more about Roman civilization than any other structure in the Classical World.

THE LETDOWN Your introduction to Pont du Gard is likely to be the enormous car park. Then there's the stroll down the carefully constructed gravel path in the company of that day's quota of the aqueduct's two million-plus annual visitors. Then it's past the visitor centre, restaurant and finally the bridge itself.

GOING ANYWAY? To avoid the hordes in cars, there are regular bus services from Avignon and Nîmes to Remoulins, a short walk from the entrance. You can swim in the river beneath the bridge; better still, hire a canoe from nearby Collias and glide beneath the aqueduct in style.

ABOVE Crowds gathered on the walking path along the Pont du Gard, Nîmes

PRACTICAL INFORMATION

Getting There and Around
Spoleto's nearest airport is 50 km (30 miles) away in Perugia, but most international airlines fly into Rome, which is a 1½-hour train journey away from Spoleto.

Where to Eat
There are many fine restaurants in Spoleto, with the popular *tartuffo nero* (black truffle) featuring prominently on the menu. The Apollinare (tel. +39 074 322 3256; www.ristorante apollinare.it) is housed in a converted 12th-century monastery, around a 10-minute walk from the aqueduct. It also has tables laid out in the tiny piazza behind. The vineyards of Montefalco are within sight of the city.

Where to Stay
The Hotel Gattapone (www.hotelgattapone.it) is spectacularly perched at one end of the aqueduct. Almost every room offers a stunning view. Doubles start at £100.

When to Go
Spoleto is worth visiting year round, despite the hot summers and cold winters. But it is hard to find accommodation during July's music festival *(see p268)*, so be sure to book in advance.

Budget per Day for Two
£200, including accommodation at Hotel Gattapone and the train ride on Eurostar Italia from Rome, which is about £10 one way.

Website
www.english.regioneumbria.eu

MAIN IMAGE Visitors on Ponte delle Torri, contemplating the drop
BELOW (left to right) A performance at the Roman theatre; the Rocca fortress; Fra Filippo Lippi's *Coronation of the Virgin*, Spoleto

SEGOVIA'S ROMAN AQUEDUCT, SPAIN

NEED TO KNOW

LOCATION The aqueduct is located in Castilla y León, 83 km (50 miles) north of Madrid

DIMENSIONS Length: 730 m (2,394 ft); height: 29 m (95 ft)

CONSTRUCTED AD 100

DAYTIME TEMPERATURES Jan: 4°C (39°F); Apr: 13°C (55°F); Jul: 25°C (77°F); Oct: 13°C (55°F)

The story goes that a young Segovian woman, tired of lugging water from the river, sold her soul to the devil on condition that he would bring water right to her front door. When you see the aqueduct he built for her (in truth built by the Romans), it's hard not to believe that there is something of the devil in it. Not a drop of mortar was used in the aqueduct's construction, which runs into the heart of Segovia. Made from 20,000 huge granite blocks sitting tightly on each other, it is the world's most spectacular 3-D jigsaw.

Practical Information

Getting There and Around A 35-minute bullet train connects Segovia to Madrid. There are regular buses as well. Several low-cost airlines also fly to nearby Valladolid, which has good bus and train connections to Segovia.

When to Go Perched at 1,000 m (3,280 ft) on the Spanish mesa, Segovia has extreme temperatures and is best visited in Jun–Sep.

Website www.turismodesegovia.com

The spectacular Roman Aqueduct in Segovia, made from massive blocks of granite simply stacked on top of each other

PONTCYSYLLTE AQUEDUCT, WALES

NEED TO KNOW

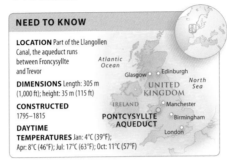

LOCATION Part of the Llangollen Canal, the aqueduct runs between Froncysyllte and Trevor

DIMENSIONS Length: 305 m (1,000 ft); height: 35 m (115 ft)

CONSTRUCTED 1795–1815

DAYTIME TEMPERATURES Jan: 4°C (39°F); Apr: 8°C (46°F); Jul: 17°C (63°F); Oct: 11°C (57°F)

Without doubt, this is Thomas Telford and William Jessop's finest work. Faced with the problem of getting canal barges over the River Dee, the two engineers built a 35-m- (115-ft-) high aqueduct, complete with a towpath and a sheer drop down the other side. The water is carried along a cast-iron trough perched on 19 hollow columns, all bound together with a mortar of lime, water and ox blood. The aqueduct is still used by canal boaters, and links the village of Froncysyllte with its neighbour Trevor. The view over the River Dee, if you can bear to look, is magnificent.

Practical Information

Getting There and Around You can cruise across the aqueduct on a barge or narrow boat – the 68-km (41-mile) stretch of the Llangollen Canal takes around 3 days. There is a regular bus service from Wrexham to Trevor, which is a short walk from the aqueduct. Wrexham can be reached by train from Cardiff and Birmingham. For those who would rather walk, Offa's Dyke, a long-distance footpath, also passes nearby.

When to Go The canal is open year round but July to September is the best time to visit. However, it can get very crowded in August.

Website www.canaljunction.com

A traditional narrowboat crossing the Pontcysyllte Aqueduct on the Llangollen Canal

CAESAREA MARITIMA, ISRAEL

NEED TO KNOW

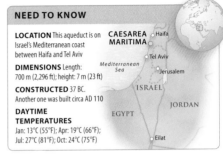

LOCATION This aqueduct is on Israel's Mediterranean coast between Haifa and Tel Aviv

DIMENSIONS Length: 700 m (2,296 ft); height: 7 m (23 ft)

CONSTRUCTED 37 BC. Another one was built circa AD 110

DAYTIME TEMPERATURES Jan: 13°C (55°F); Apr: 19°C (66°F); Jul: 27°C (81°F); Oct: 24°C (75°F)

There are few more seductive sights than bronzed bodies playing beach volleyball against the backdrop of this Roman aqueduct, built by Herod the Great for his new port of Caesarea Maritima. The lack of fresh water at the site forced the city's architects to bring water from Mount Carmel. You can see traces of that aqueduct on the road between Caesarea and Haifa and even walk a section that goes beneath Mount Carmel almost 17 km (10 miles) away. However, the most impressive section lies west of Caesarea, rolling for several (interrupted) miles over golden sands and almost taking a dip in the Mediterranean.

Practical Information

Getting There and Around Caesarea Maritima is a 40-minute train ride from both Tel Aviv and Haifa, but it's a long walk to the area. You may want to consider an organized tour.

When to Go May and June offer the most pleasant temperatures and you can swim in the white, sandy lagoons almost all year round. Avoid July and August, the months of the major holidays in Israel, October festivals and Passover week (usually in April).

Website www.goisrael.com

An arch of the Roman aqueduct at Caesarea Maritima, the civilian and military capital of Judaea

ÁGUAS LIVRES AQUEDUCT, PORTUGAL

NEED TO KNOW

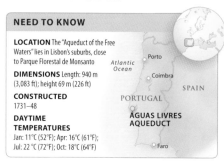

LOCATION The "Aqueduct of the Free Waters" lies in Lisbon's suburbs, close to Parque Florestal de Monsanto

DIMENSIONS Length: 940 m (3,083 ft); height 69 m (226 ft)

CONSTRUCTED 1731–48

DAYTIME TEMPERATURES Jan: 11°C (52°F); Apr: 16°C (61°F); Jul: 22 °C (72°F); Oct: 18°C (64°F)

With the highest pointed arch in the world, the 69-m (226-ft) Águas Livres Aqueduct is an 18th-century engineering marvel. It survived the 1755 earthquake that destroyed most of Lisbon, and was still bringing water to the city in the 1960s. After walking the length of the aqueduct over the Alcântara Valley with the Sintra Express hurtling beneath, visit the nearby Water Museum. It encompasses an 18th-century cistern – the Mãe D'Água Amoreiras – and the newer Boiler Room, housing exhibits of Lisbon's water system.

Practical Information

Getting There and Around Lisbon's airport is very close to the city centre. There are also buses and overnight trains from Madrid, Spain. To see the aqueduct's finest section, take a bus (2) or a taxi from the city centre.

When to Go The best months to walk the aqueduct are Mar–Jul and Sep. There are tours on Wed and Fri.

Website www.visitlisboa.com

The elegant arch of the Águas Livres Aqueduct looming over Lisbon's traffic

ACUEDUCTO DE LOS MILAGROS, SPAIN

NEED TO KNOW

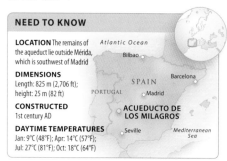

LOCATION The remains of the aqueduct lie outside Mérida, which is southwest of Madrid

DIMENSIONS Length: 825 m (2,706 ft); height: 25 m (82 ft)

CONSTRUCTED 1st century AD

DAYTIME TEMPERATURES Jan: 9°C (48°F); Apr: 14°C (57°F); Jul: 27°C (81°F); Oct: 18°C (64°F)

As you descend into the bowl of the city of Mérida, you'll pass through a particularly featureless set of suburbs. Then, suddenly, you come upon the towering remains of the Acueducto de los Milagros (Aqueduct of the Miracles), stranded heroically amid the tangle of peripheral roads. The effect of its alternating granite and brick structure is striking, especially in spring when the storks nest where the water once flowed. The aqueduct stands proudly aloof in its own parkland, acting as a superb appetizer for the rest of Roman Mérida. No other place in Spain boasts such a wealth of classical remains.

Practical Information

Getting There and Around The aqueduct is a short walk from Mérida's old centre. There is an airport at nearby Badajoz, but your best bet is Seville or Madrid. There are five trains a day from Madrid and one from Seville.

When to Go Mérida is at its best mid-Mar–mid-Jun (though avoid travelling in Spain at Easter) and mid-Sep–early Nov.

Website www.spain.info/TourSpain

The remains of the towering Acueducto de Los Milagros, illuminated at night

AQUEDUC ST-CLÉMENT, FRANCE

NEED TO KNOW

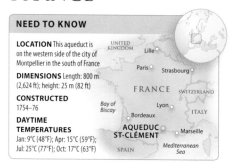

LOCATION This aqueduct is on the western side of the city of Montpellier in the south of France

DIMENSIONS Length: 800 m (2,624 ft); height: 25 m (82 ft)

CONSTRUCTED 1754–76

DAYTIME TEMPERATURES Jan: 9°C (48°F); Apr: 15°C (59°F); Jul: 25°C (77°F); Oct: 17°C (63°F)

The view of the St-Clément Aqueduct from the Château d'Eau is one of the most spectacular in France. Stretching far into the distance against the dramatic backdrop of the mountains of the Massif Central, this aqueduct was modelled on Pont du Gard by engineer Henri Pitot de Launay. It no longer brings water to the city, but the aqueduct is still in use, with a chic neighbourhood, Les Arceaux, beneath its arches. As well as a food market, several boutiques have sprung up alongside, and table-tennis tables and pétanque courts now take advantage of the shade.

Practical Information

Getting There and Around Montpellier has an international airport and is easily reached by TGV. To get to the aqueduct, head west to the flower-lined Promenade de Peyrou, which ends abruptly at the Château d'Eau.

When to Go Early spring is a great time to visit, as is October, when most of the tourists have left.

Website www.ot-montpellier.fr

A length of the Aqueduc St-Clément with the 11th-century Château d'Eau at one end

NOTRE-DAME D'AMIENS
VS NOTRE-DAME DE PARIS

The queen of Gothic religious architecture is not the Parisian cathedral that Hugo's hunchback called home, but another grande dame *in unassuming little Picardy*

ABOVE The façade of Notre-Dame de Paris

FORGET NOTRE-DAME DE PARIS?

THE BUILD-UP England's Henry IV was crowned, Napoléon declared himself Emperor, and Joan of Arc was canonized in Notre-Dame de Paris. It has an impeccable architectural as well as historical pedigree, wonderfully creepy gargoyles, a near-perfect setting on an island in the Seine, and an iconic supporting role in movie and literary history.

THE LETDOWN The expectation, gleaned from photos, films, books and your imagination, set against the hordes of camera-wielding tourists, buskers and street vendors, can be hard to reconcile. And – there's no Quasimodo!

GOING ANYWAY? Notre-Dame de Paris is open every day of the year, and it's free. Get there early to avoid the crowds. For spectacular Paris views and an up-close gargoyle encounter, you can ascend one of the towers. Entrance is outside the cathedral on the left. There are visits from 10am daily, for which there's an entry fee.

NEED TO KNOW

LOCATION Amiens is in the Picardy region, 130 km (80 miles) north of Paris

VISITORS PER YEAR 800,000

WEATHER Summer is usually warm, and spring and autumn mild with chilly nights. Winters are cold and damp, but rainfall may occur any time of year

The iconic cathedral of Notre-Dame in central Paris has welcomed pilgrims and visitors through its ornate portals for hundreds of years, drawn here by its dazzling rose windows, elegant flying buttresses and menacing gargoyles, as well as by its deep religious sigificance. But, not far to the north of the capital, towering over a city at the heart of the Somme in Picardy, lies another strong contender for the title of most outstanding Gothic church: the cathedral of Notre-Dame d'Amiens.

France's largest and tallest cathedral, Notre-Dame d'Amiens dominates the skyline of the city, and has been hailed as a Gothic masterpiece by UNESCO, who awarded it World Heritage status in 1981. It was built between 1220 and 1270, to house the alleged skull of St John the Baptist, brought back from Constantinople after the Fourth Crusade by Wallon de Sarton, Canon of nearby Picquigny.

Boasting a 42-m- (138-ft-) high ceiling, an enormous nave, four aisles and many radiating chapels, the cathedral is intensely luminous inside, making its counterpart in Paris look rather sombre. As a result, the array of statuary contained within its walls, such as the *Stone Encyclopedia of the Bible* and the much-loved *Angel of Sorrow*, as well as the 16th-century carved choir stalls and Flamboyant Gothic screen, are bathed in light. A sacred labyrinth of 1288, in effect, an intricate black-and-white marble road to God, is laid into the floor of the cathedral. The idea of it is that, as in life, believers negotiate their way, straying from and returning to the true path, until they reach the righteous centre.

While the interior of Amiens is strikingly simple, the exterior is embellishment gone into overdrive, with three portals celebrating biblical figures – saints, apostles, magi and angels. Christ *(le Beau Dieu)* reigns in the centre, while St Firmin, the first bishop of Amiens, occupies the left portal, and the Virgin Mary *(la Vierge Dorée)* is in residence in the right. Above them are 22 stony, life-size kings, stretching across the entire façade beneath the 16th-century rose window. Every element of the carving is of the highest craftsmanship.

A laser cleaning of the façade in the 1990s revealed traces of the polychromatic paint that had once enlivened its 13th-century statues, helping them act as a visual bible to illiterate pilgrims. Today, in the summer and at Christmas, laser illuminations replicate the breathtaking effect on France's Gothic cathedral *par excellence*.

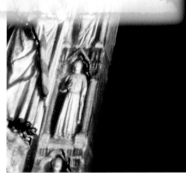

PRACTICAL INFORMATION

Getting There and Around
The cathedral is in the heart of Amiens, which is just over an hour by car from Paris via the A16, A29 and A1. Regular trains run from Paris (1 hr 30 mins), or the TGV Haute-Picardie station is 45 mins by bus from Amiens. Use buses or the self-service bike network, Vélam, to get around.

Where to Eat
Le Quai (www.restaurant-le-quai.com) on the waterside in the historic Quartier St-Leu, serves seafood fresh from the Picardy coast and vegetables grown in the Hortillonnages, the nearby "floating" market gardens.

Where to Stay
The Mercure Amiens Cathédrale (www.mercure.com) has stylish modern rooms, reserved parking, and is very close to the cathedral and the Quartier St-Leu.

When to Go
The illuminations are after dark, mid-Jun–Sep and in Dec, when there is also a superb Christmas market. Gregorian chanting takes place each Sun at 10:15am.

Budget per Day for Two
Around £100 including meals and accommodation.

Website
www.visit-amiens.com

MAIN IMAGE Central portal of Notre-Dame d'Amiens during the laser illuminations **BELOW (left to right)** Lofty central nave of the cathedral; *Angel of Sorrow* sculpture; the magnificent western façade

3 MORE CHURCHES TO RIVAL NOTRE-DAME DE PARIS

STEPHANSDOM, VIENNA, AUSTRIA Vienna's St Stephen's Cathedral is another Gothic beauty, famed for its diamond-patterned tiled roof. Don't miss the fabulous Wiener Neustadt altarpiece of 1477, the pulpit rail crawling with lizards and toads, or the tomb of Emperor Frederick III with its gruesome creatures trying to revive the defunct ruler.

CATEDRAL DE SANTA MARIA, BURGOS, SPAIN This Spanish cathedral was a long time in the making; it was started in 1220 but was not finally completed until 1795. The resulting vast edifice melds Gothic, Renaissance and Baroque styles, and houses the tomb of the Spanish national hero, El Cid.

KERIMAEN KIRKKO, KERIMAEKI, FINLAND The small town of Kerimaeki, in Finland's lakeland region, is home to Kerimaen Kirkko – not a Finnish racing car driver but the largest timber-built Christian church in the world. Built in 1837, it is 45 m (148 ft) long, 42 m (138 ft) wide and 27 m (88 ft) high.

ABOVE Imposing bulk of the Great Mosque of Djenné, Mali, the largest adobe building in the world
RIGHT Shiny aluminium cladding lends a futuristic air to the Esplanade arts complex, Marina Bay, Singapore

GREAT MOSQUE OF DJENNÉ, MALI In the 13th century Djenné was an important centre of Islamic study, and there has been a mosque on this site ever since. Although it looks ancient, the present mosque was only completed in 1907, replacing the original which fell into disrepair during the 19th century. With a capacity of 3,000, it is the largest adobe building in the world, making use of local building techniques to combat heat and humidity, its thick walls helping to keep the interior prayer hall cool. Its *qibla* (prayer wall), dominated by three minarets, overlooks the marketplace, facing east towards Mecca.

ESPLANADE - THEATRES ON THE BAY, MARINA BAY, SINGAPORE Work began on this 4-ha (10-acre) entertainment complex in 1992, on reclaimed land at the mouth of the Singapore River. The design is said to express harmony with nature, reflecting the balance of Yin and Yang. However the spiky cladding on the aluminium sunshades that cover the glass casing of the theatre and the concert hall have led the centre to be nicknamed "The Durian", owing to its resemblance to the skin of a local fruit. Fortunately, it doesn't have the fruit's pungent smell, which led to a ban on eating durian on public transport.

PANAMA CANAL, PANAMA This colossal feat of engineering, completed in 1914, provides a way through the 80-km- (50-mile-) wide Central American isthmus. It enables access from the Atlantic to the Pacific within hours, and accounts for 5 per cent of the world's trade.

PUENTE DE LA MUJER, BUENOS AIRES, ARGENTINA The "Women's Bridge" was built in 1998 by Spanish architect Santiago Calatrava in a bid to rejuvenate the city's docks. Angular yet graceful, it resembles a couple dancing the tango, bestowing the area with a unique cultural symbol.

THE GOMATESHWARA STATUE, SHRAVANABELAGOLA, INDIA Once every 12 years, pilgrims from all over the world flock to Shravanabelagola for the Mastakabhisheka festival, when the monolithic statue of Lord Gomateshwara, a revered Jain saint, is covered in ghee, coconut milk, turmeric, saffron, gold and flowers. The statue, more than 17 m (56 ft) tall and carved from a single block of white granite, was commissioned in the 10th century by Chavundaraya, a commander in the Ganga dynasty. Beautiful engravings representing the commander and his daring exploits are carved on the base.

HEDDAL STAVKIRKE, HEDDAL, NORWAY Built in the mid-13th century with know-how handed down by Viking boat-builders, Heddal's "wooden cathedral" is the largest stave church in Norway. Named after the wooden corner-posts on which it is based, its walls and beams are fastened with wooden nails, and the outer walls covered with tar. Inside are some 14th-century wall paintings.

DAILY NEWS BUILDING, NEW YORK, USA This 37-storey, flat-topped skyscraper was the inspiration for the fictional *Daily Planet*, where Superman worked as journalist Clark Kent. Built in 1930, it is characterized by vertical window strips separated by patterned brickwork. The bronze doors of the stunning Art Deco entrance are set beneath a bas-relief of hurrying office workers under a sunburst.

PARLIAMENT HOUSE, CANBERRA, AUSTRALIA A spirit of optimism is captured in Parliament House, set amid sweeping lawns on the city's Capital Hill. Designed by Italian architect Romaldo Giurgola in 1988, it is recognizable from afar by its boomerang-shaped roofs and the colossal national flag raised on four towering legs above it, but much of the 4,700-roomed building is underground.

SOLOMON R. GUGGENHEIM MUSEUM, NEW YORK, USA Completed in 1959, the Guggenheim is the last major work of architect Frank Lloyd Wright and its shell-like façade is one of the city's landmarks. Inside, displayed along walls that curve gently down the spiral ramp from the top, is one of the finest collections of modern and contemporary art in the world.

REICHSTAG, BERLIN, GERMANY When the seat of parliament moved from Bonn to Berlin following Germany's reunification in 1990, British architect Norman Foster was tasked with giving the Reichstag building a facelift worthy of its new occupants. Its most striking element is the iconic glazed cupola, intended to reflect values of clarity and transparency. The dome's roof terrace affords city views.

FALLINGWATER, PENNSYLVANIA, USA In the 1930s the Kaufmann family, owners of a grand department store, flaunted their wealth by having Frank Lloyd Wright design a house for them. Jutting out over a waterfall, it appears to be part of the landscape, with wide windows and low ceilings designed to turn your attention to the wilderness outside. Stairs lead to a tiny platform in the middle of the stream.

ABOVE Gleaming steel spheres of the Atomium, Brussels, the striking showpiece of the city's 1958 World's Fair
LEFT Sinuous design of the Fred and Ginger building, Prague, recalling the movement of a pair of dancers

FRED AND GINGER BUILDING, PRAGUE, CZECH REPUBLIC Also called The Dancing House, Frank Gehry's building beside the Vlatva river, finished in 1996, really does resemble a man and woman dancing together. In the sinuous shapes of the façade known as "the glass dress", Ginger, leaning against her more upright partner, is more evident than Fred. The irregularly spaced windows appear to be doing a dance of their own and, as the sun reflects off the glass, the whole building seems to be moving, which may explain its local nickname: The Drunk House.

ATOMIUM, BRUSSELS, BELGIUM The Atomium in Brussels' Heysel Park was built for the 1958 World's Fair. Resembling a giant executive toy, it represents an iron crystal molecule, with each of the nine steel spheres symbolizing individual atoms. The spheres, each 18 m (59 ft) in diameter, are connected by tubes containing escalators, and the topmost one, at a height of 102 m (335 ft), offers visitors a panoramic view over the city and surrounding area. The structure underwent renovation in 2006, financed in part by selling as souvenirs pieces of the metal sheeting that originally covered the spheres.

HOLOCAUST MEMORIAL, BERLIN, GERMANY Unveiled in May 2005, 60 years after the end of World War II, Peter Eisenman's monument comprises 2,711 concrete slabs, bearing no names or dates. Some are tiny, some towering, and the effect, seen from above, is that of a gently swelling sea.

SHIBAM, YEMEN Anyone stumbling unexpectedly on Shibam, glimmering in the sun, might think they were seeing a mirage. Set in the Valley of Hadhramaut this city of skyscrapers, known as the Manhattan of the Desert, has stood here for around 2,000 years, although most of the buildings date from the 16th century. The narrow streets are lined by six-storey, mud-built houses embellished with finely engraved wooden doors and latticed windows. Although it is UNESCO-protected, this is not a museum but a living city, home to around 7,000 people, whose families have lived here for generations.

ENNIS HOUSE, CALIFORNIA, USA Used as a backdrop for several films, including *Blade Runner*, Frank Lloyd Wright's pre-cast concrete house sits in the Santa Monica mountains overlooking Los Angeles. Built in 1924, its design is heavily influenced by ancient Mayan temples, with great halls, monumental columns and recurring geometrical decoration. It has recently been restored after earthquake damage.

MADRASAH MIR-I-ARAB, BUKHARA, UZBEKISTAN Built around 1535 in the historic centre of Bukhara, the madrasah is named after the Yemeni sheikh who financed it, and whose tomb lies under its northern dome. In the Shaybanid style (the dynasty descended from Genghis Khan), its façade is dominated by two luminous blue-tiled domes. It remained a working Islamic school until 1920.

CASA BATLLÓ, BARCELONA, SPAIN With its sinuous curves and swirling shapes, Casa Batlló looks like a fairytale castle. While the balconies and pillars are said to resemble skulls and bones, the overall effect of the façade is far from gloomy. Built in the 19th century, it was remodelled in 1905–7 by Antoni Gaudí, one of the fathers of Catalan Art Nouveau, and some consider it his masterpiece.

SHUKHOV TOWER, MOSCOW, RUSSIA Erected in the 1920s, this broadcasting tower should have been 350 m (1,150 ft) tall, but never made it past 150 m (490 ft) due to a shortage of steel during the Civil War. Its designer, Vladimir Shukhov, was the first engineer to use the lattice-style technique to make the steel shell subject to minimum wind load, the main design challenge for high-rise structures.

CHURCH OF ST FRANCIS, BELO HORIZONTE, BRAZIL Oscar Niemeyer's glistening white church, with four parabolic arches, commands a striking position on Pampulha Lake. It was finished in 1943 but consecrated only in 1959, due to opposition from the archbishop, who described it as "the devil's bomb-shelter". A tiled mural on the north façade depicts scenes from the life of St Francis of Assisi.

CN TOWER, TORONTO, CANADA Built in 1976 as a communications tower, the CN Tower is a structure of superlatives. At 555 m (1,815 ft) it is the tallest freestanding structure in the Americas, has the world's longest metal staircase, and its second highest public observation deck. It also holds the dubious distinction of having been struck by lightning more times than any other building in Toronto.

AACHEN CATHEDRAL, GERMANY Dating from AD 805, Aachen is the oldest cathedral in Northern Europe, and a worthy celebration of Charlemagne's coronation as Roman Emperor – his throne is just one of its medieval treasures. The *capella vitrea* (glass chapel), built in the early 15th century to accommodate vast numbers of pilgrims, is flooded with light from its coloured glass windows.

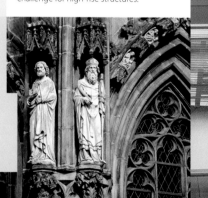

ABOVE The quirky church of Notre Dame du Haut, strikingly situated on a hilltop in Ronchamp, France
RIGHT Sir Norman Foster's towering, elegant Millau Bridge spanning the Tarn Valley, southwest France

NOTRE DAME DU HAUT, RONCHAMP, FRANCE Le Corbusier's snowy-white Notre Dame du Haut church was built on the crest of a hill in 1955 on the site of a pilgrimage chapel destroyed during World War II. "Here we will build a monument dedicated to nature and we will make it our lives' purpose", said the architect. Constructed mainly of reinforced concrete, with thick walls punctuated by irregular stained-glass windows, the curvaceous building is topped by an upturned roof resembling a billowing sail. Among its quirky details is an outdoor pulpit, used during open-air services.

THE MILLAU BRIDGE, TARN VALLEY, FRANCE Sir Norman Foster, architect of the Millau Bridge, said that it was designed to have "the delicacy of a butterfly". And so it has, particularly when emerging from the morning mist, a perfect combination of strength and subtlety. Seven slender piers support the road bridge, soaring up to align with seven graceful steel pylons. Rising to 345 m (1,125 ft) at its highest point, this is the world's tallest road bridge. It was built with practicality in mind, to ease traffic and shorten the journey to the Mediterranean, but it could stand simply as a beautiful piece of engineering.

HIROSHIMA PEACE CENTER, JAPAN This is an awesome sight, a reminder of the horror of nuclear devastation and hope for a peaceful future. Its centrepiece is the Genbaku Dome, which was the closest structure to withstand the atomic explosion on 6 August 1945. It has been preserved just as it was immediately after the bomb hit, the cladding of the dome melted away to reveal its raw steel skeleton. It is complemented by architect Kenzo Tange's Peace Center, a rectangular building raised on pillars, and the Peace Monument, a parabolic arch beneath which fresh flowers are constantly replenished.

TAIPEI 101, TAIPEI, CHINA Hailed as one of the Seven New Wonders of the World, this 101-floor tower rises 510 m (1,670 ft) above the city. Made from pliant steel, its slender pagoda-like structure combines ultra-modernity with references to traditional Chinese culture.

WORLD'S FAIR SITE, NEW YORK, USA If anything symbolized the flamboyant, optimistic attitude of the 1964 World's Fair, it was the Unisphere. Celebrating the dawn of the Space Age, the huge model of Earth stands in a pool surrounded by fountains, at the end of an avenue of national flags.

THE OMAYYAD MOSQUE, DAMASCUS, SYRIA This is one of the oldest mosques in Islam and one of the most beautiful. Built in the 8th century, during Omayyad rule, it was originally a place of worship for both Muslims and Christians: Muslims prayed at the eastern side, Christians at the west. Besides its fine courtyard, the most stunning features are the glorious decorative mosaics that cover the walls.

CRYSTAL CATHEDRAL, GARDEN GROVE, CALIFORNIA, USA This huge evangelical church, which opened in 1980, is constructed of mirrored glass and built on a steel frame in the shape of an elongated four-pointed star. The interior can accommodate 3,000 worshippers. A section of the walls opens to allow people to see and hear the services from their cars.

KREMLIN, KAZAN, RUSSIA The word "kremlin" actually means citadel, and Kazan's is a splendid example. Enclosed by white stone walls, it was begun under Ivan the Terrible in the mid-16th century. Its oldest building is the five-aisled Annunciation Cathedral, but its newest may be the finest: the Kul Sharif mosque, dating from 2005, with its gleaming blue-green cupola and delicate minarets.

RYUGYONG HOTEL, PYONGYANG, NORTH KOREA Resembling a huge space rocket, the Ryugyong has been nicknamed the "Hotel of Doom". It was begun in 1987, when it was intended to be the world's tallest hotel at 330 m (1,085 ft), but has never been finished. Construction started again in 2008 but, due to structural defects and the enormous cost of completion, it's unlikely to open soon.

WIELICZKA SALT MINE, POLAND Dating from the 13th century, this unusual UNESCO-listed site remained a working mine until 1996. Its 300 km (185 miles) of galleries are home to a depiction of Leonardo Da Vinci's *Last Supper*, a statue of Pope John Paul II, and a "crystal" chandelier, all carved in rock salt. The Chapel of St Kinga, patron saint of Poland, is one of several underground chapels.

UNAM LIBRARY, MEXICO CITY, MEXICO The library of Mexico's National University, built in the early 1950s, houses its books in a solid, windowless tower illuminated by artificial light. Wishing to imbue the building with truly Mexican character, designer Juan O'Gorman had the external walls covered with intricate figurative mosaic murals in bold colours, depicting Latin American themes.

ABOVE The intricate filigree design of Beijing's Bird's Nest Stadium, icon of the 2008 Olympic Games, shown off to dramatic effect when seen at night, illuminated from within

BIRD'S NEST STADIUM, BEIJING, CHINA With its filigree shell and twig-like structural elements, the Beijing National Stadium, which became so familiar to so many during the 2008 Olympic Games, really does resemble a giant bird's nest. One of the many unusual features of the design involved filling the spaces between the "twigs" with inflatable cushions to regulate the effects of wind and weather. The building has won environmental plaudits for incorporating a rainwater collection system and a translucent roof that permits sunlight to penetrate so that the grass beneath can flourish.

KUWAIT TOWERS These three towers are the lavish result of the 1970s oil boom. The highest, at 187 m (615 ft), is adorned with two huge spheres, the upper one with a revolving viewing deck. The second tower holds a water tank, and the shortest illuminates its taller neighbours.

MUSEU OSCAR NIEMEYER, CURITIBA, BRAZIL Oscar Niemeyer, Brazil's best-known architect, has had a long career; this museum opened in 2002 when he was 95 years old. The annexe resembles a great almond-shaped eye balanced atop a broad yellow plinth, reflected in the pool in which it stands. Behind this stands the long, low exhibition space, its smooth, clean lines typical of Niemeyer's work.

MELNIKOV HOUSE, MOSCOW, RUSSIA Russia's great Constructivist architect Konstantin Melnikov built this house for his family in the late 1920s, before ceasing work in protest at having to conform to Stalinist style. One of his last projects, it comprises two intersecting cylindrical towers: one admits light via a flat glazed wall; the other is illuminated by a pattern of hexagonal windows.

TWA FLIGHT CENTER, NEW YORK, USA The graceful, free-flowing curves of Eero Saarinen's futuristic Terminal 5 at JFK Airport (now occupied by JetBlue airlines) are a potent symbol of flight. Every aspect of it, from the wide windows overlooking the tarmac to the cool outlines of the sweeping staircases leading to elegant passenger lounges, recalls the days when flying was romantic.

VILLA MAJORELLE, NANCY, FRANCE A combined effort of outstanding Art Nouveau craftmanship, the villa was commissioned by furniture-maker Louis Majorelle; Lucien Weissenburger and Henri Sauvage designed the house, and Jacques Gruber the beautiful stained glass. Majorelle himself produced the furniture and the grand staircase, and there are delightful details throughout.

REGISTAN, SAMARKAND, UZBEKISTAN The centrepiece of historic Samarkand (see p122) is the Registan, a beautifully proportioned group of *madrasahs* (schools) adorned with majolica and mosaics. In the archway above the door of the 17th-century Sher Dor Madrasah are mosaics of lions attacking deer – rare in Islamic art, which does not usually portray animals or human figures. Opposite stands the the sublime Ulughbek Madrasah, with its soaring columns and astronomical motifs. A third madrasah is named Tilla-Kari – "coated with gold" – for the gilding covering its dome and walls.

KREMLIN, VELIKY NOVGOROD, RUSSIA Enclosed by red-brick walls, the Kremlin, also known as the *Detinets*, sits at the heart of this ancient city on the banks of the Volkhov river. Built mainly in the early 16th century, it was one of the most impregnable citadels in Russia. It now encloses a selection of buildings from various eras, ranging from the Gothic Granovitaya Palata (Chamber of Facets), dating from 1433, to the 19th-century, bell-shaped Millennium of Russia Monument, which is crowned by a cross and the figure of a woman representing Russia.

SALINE ROYALE, ARC-ET-SENANS, FRANCE The Saline Royale (Royal Saltworks) is a valuable example of early industrial architecture. Construction of the huge semicircular complex began in 1775 under Louis XVI, financed by a salt tax so unpopular it is said to have been one cause of the French Revolution. It was intended as the first step in creating an ideal city, but the plan was never realized.

SEA RANCH CHAPEL, GUALALA, CALIFORNIA, USA Resembling a huge seashell, the non-denominational Sea Ranch Chapel, dating from 1984, is a quirky place. Appealing but slightly kitsch, it has a swooping cedar roof crowned with a wavy spire resembling a peacock's plumage, lots of native redwood, and delicate stained-glass inserts in the roof, doors and windows to filter the light.

SAADIAN TOMBS, MARRAKECH, MOROCCO The tombs were built by Ahmad al-Mansur in the late 16th century, but when Moulay Ismail came to power a century later he had the entrances sealed, and they remained so until 1917. Now visitors can see what was hidden for so long: two stunning mausoleums housing more than 60 royal tombs, with intricate carvings and beautiful mosaic tiles.

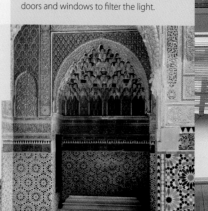

NATURAL WONDERS

Victoria water lilies in the Pantanal, Brazil *(p182)*

MAIN IMAGE Striking Devils Tower bathed in afternoon sunlight
BELOW (left to right) Rock-climbers scaling a channel between two columns in the rock; porcupine; aerial view of the rock's summit

DEVILS TOWER
VS ULURU

In the world of really big rocks, Devils Tower might not be the biggest (and neither is Uluru), but its extraordinary, upreaching tree-stump profile consistently attracts and amazes admirers

NEED TO KNOW

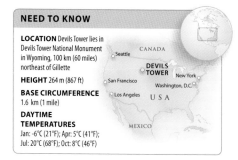

LOCATION Devils Tower lies in Devils Tower National Monument in Wyoming, 100 km (60 miles) northeast of Gillette

HEIGHT 264 m (867 ft)

BASE CIRCUMFERENCE
1.6 km (1 mile)

DAYTIME TEMPERATURES
Jan: -6°C (21°F); Apr: 5°C (41°F);
Jul: 20°C (68°F); Oct: 8°C (46°F)

Devils Tower, an imposing stack of rock that stands guard over Wyoming's Black Hills, is one of nature's finest sculptures. The soaring monument, formed some 50–60 million years ago from magma that was forced up from beneath the earth's surface, was originally concealed by a layer of sedimentary sandstone and silt. Erosion over millions of years

wore away this material to reveal the geological marvel we see today – a flat-topped monolith made up of hexagonal columns that look like a cluster of giant pencils standing on end. The rock is sacred to the area's indigenous people, who believe its many rifts and channels to be the ancient claw marks of a giant bear. Devils Tower might not be as large as Uluru, but it certainly vies with Australia's fabled red rock when it comes to spirit-stirring allure.

Devils Tower is made up of hard volcanic rock called phonolite porphyry – a substance so dense that it rings when even a small piece is struck. This solidity, along with its countless cracks, makes the sheer rock face ideal for climbing. It was first scaled in 1893 by a rancher who used ladders hung from pegs that were driven into the cracks. Today, 4–5,000 people attempt the ascent every year, but only about half make it to the summit – a deceptively small plateau that is actually the size of a football

field, where you'll find mice, chipmunks and snakes in abundance and fantastic views in every direction.

Those who have no plans to dangle on a rope from Devils Tower will find their own brand of fun just watching the rock in all its majestic, solitary glory, as it catches and reflects sunlight from infinite angles throughout the day. A walk along the trail that circles the base of the tower offers hikers the opportunity to spot the deer, pronghorn antelopes, coyotes and porcupines that inhabit the surrounding ponderosa pine forests and plains.

At the base of the tower lies the rubble of the stone columns that have fallen over time. Although geologists estimate that the last collapse occurred around 10,000 years ago, the tower is still slowly being eroded and the sedimentary base carried bit by bit into the Belle Fourche River – a subtle reminder to visitors that even something as timeless as Devils Tower is forever changing.

FORGET ULURU?

THE BUILD-UP Uluru (also known as Ayers Rock) is Australia's most recognizable natural feature. As impressive as its 348-m (1,140-ft) height and 10-km (6-mile) circumference are, it's even more astounding to think that most of its bulk lies underground. Uluru's sandstone surface changes shade throughout the day, glowing a dazzling, fiery red at sunset.

THE LETDOWN Although the great red rock is still a popular tourist attraction, visited by around 350,000 people every year, climbing Uluru is now officially discouraged. The local Anangu people have a spiritual connection to Uluru and ask visitors to respect their beliefs and culture. While in 1990 about 74 per cent of visitors followed the chain handhold to make the hour-long climb to the summit, today only about 38 per cent of people attempt the climb.

GOING ANYWAY? If you still want to visit Uluru, then do so with a purpose other than climbing it. Photograph the rock from a distance, visit the Cultural Centre to discover the richness of Anangu history, culture, language and religion, walk around the rock's enormous base or participate in a ranger-guided walk.

ABOVE A tour group at Uluru, Australia

PRACTICAL INFORMATION

Getting There and Around
From Gillette, where there is a regional airport with connecting services to major airports, the best way to get to Devils Tower National Monument is to hire a car and take Highway I-90 east to Moorcroft. Devils Tower is only 48 km (30 miles) north of here.

Where to Eat
One of the best restaurants in Hulett, which is 15 km (9 miles) to the north of Devils Tower, is Ponderosa Cafe and Bar (www.theponderosacafe.com), known for its tasty steaks and prime rib.

Where to Stay
There are several places to stay in Hulett, but for a more atmospheric experience, head to Devils Tower

Lodge (www.devilstowerlodge.com), which has four rooms and a hot tub. At just 700 m (766 yards) away from the tower, this is a great place to watch the moon rise over the rock or see it bathed in light at sunrise.

When to Go
Devils Tower National Monument is open all year, but the visitor centre is only open from mid-April to November. Visitors are asked not to climb the tower in June, when tribal ceremonies take place.

Budget per Day for Two
£130 including entrance to the park, accommodation and food.

Website
www.nps.gov/deto

Mount Augustus with wild flowers in foreground, Australia

Magnificent Half Dome beside Tenaya Creek, Yosemite National Park, USA

Hiker beside a mountain lake in Torres del Paine National Park, Chile

HALF DOME

NEED TO KNOW

LOCATION Half Dome
is in Yosemite National Park
in California, USA

HEIGHT
1,440 m (4,730 ft)

BASE CIRCUMFERENCE
Around 8 km (5 miles)

DAYTIME TEMPERATURES
Jan: 2°C (35°F); Apr: 10°C (50°F);
Jul: 21°C (69°F); Oct: 12°C (53°F)

Half Dome, the exquisite granite sentinel at the eastern end of Yosemite Valley, has become something of an icon in California, its image having found its way onto postcards, coins and several company logos. Even in Yosemite, which is home to more granite domes than anywhere else on earth, Half Dome cuts a commanding profile. Millions of years ago, glaciers undercut a much larger dome that stood here, weakening and eroding it to expose the sheer rock face we see today. Once declared "perfectly inaccessible", the rock's summit can today be reached by handrails and wooden planks placed in the stone. The ascent is one of the most popular hikes in the park.

Practical Information

Getting There Yosemite is a 4-hour drive to the east of San Francisco in California. Half Dome is located at the head of Yosemite Valley.

When to Go Half Dome can be viewed from Yosemite Valley all year round. Climbing on the cable track is only available from mid-May to mid-October.

Website www.nps.gov/yose

TORRES DEL PAINE

NEED TO KNOW

LOCATION Torres del Paine National
Park is in Chile's Patagonia region

HEIGHT The highest rock
is 1,000 m (3,280 ft)

BASE CIRCUMFERENCE
Around 5 km (3 miles)

DAYTIME TEMPERATURES
Jan: 13°C (57°F); Apr: 8°C (48°F);
Jul: 1°C (34°F); Oct: 8°C (48°F)

Set against the glacial lakes and windswept steppes of Patagonia, Torres del Paine National Park *(see p85)* offers some of the most breathtaking mountain scenery on the planet. The three colossal towers *(torres)* at the centre of the park provide intimidating and challenging rock climbs, with the central tower being the crown jewel. But for mere mortals, the park's rugged trekking routes are a better option. These will lead you around enormous glaciers, beside deep-blue lakes and across scenic valleys where guanacos and rheas roam freely. The great views here more than compensate for the fierce winds and wet weather.

Practical Information

Getting There and Around Torres del Paine National Park can be accessed by bus from Punta Arenas, which is 400 km (250 miles) to the southeast. Once in the park, the towers are normally viewed as part of a 10-day trek.

When to Go The best time to visit is in spring and summer (Oct–Apr).

Website www.torresdelpaine.com

MOUNT AUGUSTUS

NEED TO KNOW

LOCATION Mount Augustus
is in Western Australia, 490 km
(300 miles) east of Carnarvon

HEIGHT 860 m (2,823 ft)

BASE CIRCUMFERENCE
Around 32 km (20 miles)

DAYTIME TEMPERATURES
Jan: 32°C (89°F); Apr: 25°C (77°F);
Jul: 15°C (60°F); Oct: 23°C (74°F)

This spectacular solitary peak, which is known as Burringurrah by the local Aboriginal people, rises above an arid plain of shrubland dotted with emu bushes, river gums and wattles. Red kangaroos, emus, snakes and small rodents are common in the area. Surrounding the rock are trails and dirt roads that lead to Aboriginal rock engravings, pools and caves, and there is a 12-km (8-mile) round-trip summit trail for fit hikers. The visible part of this sandstone mountain, which lies on a subterranean granite base, might look very like Uluru, but it's more than twice as large as its more famous Northern Territory rival, with a summit ridge measuring 8 km (5 miles).

Practical Information

Getting There From Carnarvon on the west coast of Australia, go east to Gascoyne Junction and continue on a gravel road for a total of 490 km (300 miles) until you reach Mount Augustus National Park.

When to Go The national park is accessible all year round, but it's most pleasant between April and October

Website www.dec.wa.gov.au

Towering Peña de Bernal, Mexico

PEÑA DE BERNAL

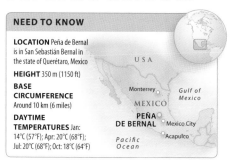

When Peña de Bernal was formed some 135 million years ago, during the Jurassic period, it was three times the size of the eroded – but still impressive – mountain you see today. This is one of the tallest monoliths in the world, and while it's a popular attraction for walkers and pilgrims who follow the trail to the chapel halfway up the mountain, the vertical route to the summit is the domain of expert rock climbers. The inhabitants of San Sebastián Bernal believe that the rock bestows a calming and life-enhancing energy to those living in its shadow. Each year at the spring equinox the villagers take part in an ancient ritual that involves dressing in white and forming a human chain around part of the monolith. There is also a five-day Christian festival here every May. This event culminates in a procession of villagers who bear a 45-kg (100-lb) cross to the mountain chapel, from where climbers carry it on to the summit.

Practical Information

Getting There The best way to get to Peña de Bernal is to hire a car in Mexico City. Take Highway 57 northwest for 200 km (120 miles) towards Querétaro and then go east for 50 km (30 miles) to San Sebastián Bernal, which lies at the base of the mountain.

When to Go The weather is good at any time of year.

Website www.penadebernal.com

Smooth-sided, soaring Pedra Azul, Brazil

PEDRA AZUL

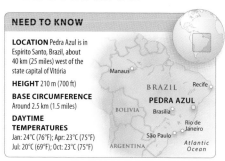

Pedra Azul (Blue Rock) is an exposed dome with an exquisite blue-grey hue resulting from the algae, lichen and mushrooms covering its surface. The rock's colouring alters subtly throughout the day, moving between charcoal grey and shades of mauve and blue, depending on the changing light. Although an ascent of this mighty rock would promise spectacular views towards the coast, climbing here has been prohibited in recent years in order to protect the bromeliads, orchids and other vegetation that lives on and around the rock. Near the base of Pedra Azul's north side you'll find a large granite tower that resembles a giant lizard scaling the dome, which is aptly named Pedra do Lagarto (Lizard Rock). Trails within the state park are accessed in the company of a naturalist guide and lead to nine natural pools and wildlife-viewing opportunities.

Practical Information

Getting There Hire a car in Vitória and travel along Highway BR 262 in the direction of Belo Horizonte for about 40 km (25 miles). From the road, the rock is clearly visible and the park entrance is well signed.

When to Go The warm tropical climate means you can visit at any time of year.

Website www.pedraazul.com.br

Stone Mountain with its enormous carving, Georgia, USA

STONE MOUNTAIN

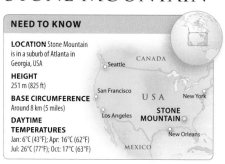

Stone Mountain, a beautifully rounded, immense piece of exposed granite, is a geological wonder, the centrepiece of Stone Mountain Park and the most popular tourist attraction in the state of Georgia. The rock was created underground 300 million years ago during the formation of the Appalachian Mountains. Friction from the shifting crust of the earth caused the rock to melt, and as it cooled, it hardened again, only to lie beneath the surface for millions of years before being exposed in the form we see today. Originally called New Gibraltar, the rock was renamed Stone Mountain in 1847. On the side of the mountain is the world's largest bas-relief, a memorial depicting three Confederate leaders of the US Civil War on horseback. The sculpture is the size of three football fields and in the summer becomes the backdrop for an evening laser show. The top of the mountain can be reached by a steep, 2-km (1.3-mile) footpath or by an aerial tramway.

Practical Information

Getting There The best way to see Stone Mountain is to hire a car in Atlanta and head east along Highway 78 for 26 km (16 miles) to the park entrance.

When to Go You can visit at any time of year, although the best weather is between March and October.

Website www.stonemountainpark.com

THE ORINOCO
VS THE AMAZON

The Orinoco symbolizes all that is mysterious, wild and wonderful in South America, and makes for a spectacular alternative to the over-visited Amazon

NEED TO KNOW

LOCATION Originating in southern Venezuela, the river runs north along the border with Colombia and then east across Venezuela to the sea

LENGTH 2,735 km (1,699 miles)

CLIMATE Temperatures range from 27°C (81°F) to 31°C (88°F); the Orinoco is much less humid than most tropical rivers

Caribbean Sea
Caracas
San Cristóbal · VENEZUELA · Ciudad Guayana
ORINOCO RIVER
COLOMBIA
BRAZIL

The Orinoco will not fail to delight even the most jaded traveller. The Amazon may be bigger and better known, but it doesn't provide direct access to the continent's most astonishing wildlife and scenery the way the Orinoco does. This mighty river system is home to some of the world's most biodiverse ecosystems, and runs a breathtaking topographical gamut, from tall mountains and tropical forests to humid *llanos* (plains) and marshy deltas, before finally emptying into the Atlantic.

For centuries this mysterious river has intrigued explorers and adventurers. The mouth of the Orinoco was sighted by Columbus in 1498, but it was not until the 1950s that explorers finally stumbled upon its headwaters at Cerro Delgado-Chalbaud, one of the most remote spots in the western hemisphere, located high up in the Parima Mountains on the border between Brazil

and Venezuela. Even now there remains some doubt about the river's true source, and several of its tributaries have yet to be explored.

What makes the Orinoco so impressive is the incredible diversity of microclimates, fauna, flora and terrain, which fall within its enormous basin – an area of more than 880,000 sq km (340,000 sq miles). Though the Amazon boasts remarkable biological richness, much of the river is either inaccessible or prohibitively expensive to reach, while the Orinoco – which is navigable for most of its length, unlike the Amazon – is easily seen and explored. Keep your eyes peeled and you're likely to spot alligators, pink dolphins, boa constrictors, herons, howler monkeys and pumas. The Orinoco protects one of the last pristine ecosystems on the planet, and boasts the highest biodiversity rate of any river system. Nearly a dozen new species are discovered along its banks every month. And the river's mouth, the Orinoco Delta, is thought to be the continent's richest area in aquatic biodiversity. At last count, this still largely uncharted river was home to more than 10,000 plant species, 1,400 bird species, 1,200 fish species, and at least 340 different types of mammal. You won't find those numbers anywhere else on earth.

PRACTICAL INFORMATION

Getting There and Around
Many travellers choose to start their trip at the mouth of the river, which is northeast of Ciudad Guyana in Venezuela, and stock up on provisions in the city. There are many reputable tour operators here, who will take you around some remarkable sights, including picturesque waterfalls and pools, before you get to the river.

Where to Eat
On a river excursion like this you will probably have your own food on board. However, it's likely that you will stop off at several towns along the river, where you'll have the chance to sample local food ranging from traditional chicken- and rice-based dishes to more exotic flavours, including ostrich and even piranha.

Where to Stay
Although you'll probably spend most nights on the boat, the town of Caicara de Orinoco, 600 km (373 miles) southwest of Ciudad Guyana, is a perfect stopover point. The Hotel Miami (tel. +58 35 67 587) here is comfortable and inexpensive, and is also only a stone's throw from the town's best restaurant, Caicara de Orinoco.

When to Go
The best time to visit is in September, when humidity is at its lowest and you have a good chance of seeing wildlife.

Budget per Day for Two
Roughly £100, depending on your tour operator.

Website
www.miamisci.org/orinoco

ABOVE The Orinoco meandering through lush forest, Venezuela

FORGET THE AMAZON?

THE BUILD-UP There's no doubt that the Amazon, a long-time favourite with explorers, remains a big draw for travellers. It is, after all, a superlative among rivers: it is the longest river in South America (some say the world), has the largest drainage basin on earth, and, by dint of its sheer size, is home to a staggering array of flora and fauna.

THE LETDOWN But what will you really have a chance to see here? The few towns teem with tour operators and travel agencies, all of which charge top-end prices, but few of which deliver. Hardly any of these tour operators are located on the river. And then there's the Amazon itself – unlike the Orinoco, parts of it are literally impassable, and the foliage is often so dense that you may not be able to see much of anything.

GOING ANYWAY? For those who feel they must see the Amazon at all costs, one option is to fly to Manaus in Brazil, and start the journey there. The city's central location and innumerable tour operators will make your planning easier.

MAIN IMAGE Dramatic Llovizna Falls, on an Orinoco tributary
BELOW (left to right) Orinoco turtle with a butterfly on its head;
paddling on the river; vividly coloured scarlet ibis

4 MORE RIVERS TO RIVAL THE AMAZON

RÍO PARAGUAY The 2,550-km (1,550-mile) Río Paraguay, another legendary South American river and gateway to Brazil's Pantanal and Mato Grosso ecosystems, makes for a fascinating alternative for those who want a little less jungle and a lot more open space.

HUANG HO For stunning mountain scenery and a chance to see ancient and modern civilizations side by side, head for China's lifeline, the Huang Ho. The river runs east for 5,500 km (3,400 miles) from the Bayan Har Mountains in western China.

ALLAGASH RIVER This 150-km (95-mile) waterway in the northeast USA might be comparatively short, but it's thrilling to explore. With its rapids, black water and deceptively placid appearance, the Allagash commands respect at every bend.

NIGER RIVER Coursing for 4,200 km (2,600 miles) through the southern Sahara, the Niger river, with its combination of relentless heat, surprise sandstorms and serpentine curves, will test even the most experienced navigator.

MAIN IMAGE The town of Puerto Varas with Osorno volcano in the background
BELOW (left to right) Patio at Hotel Antumalal in Pucón; the smouldering summit of Villarrica volcano; Geométricas Hot Springs, Villarrica National Park

THE CHILEAN LAKES
VS THE ITALIAN LAKES

Italy's magnificent lakes are synonymous with moneyed elegance, yet when it comes to natural splendour, they are no match for Chile's spectacular volcanic wonders

NEED TO KNOW

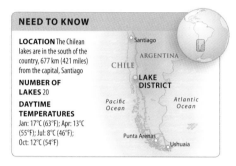

LOCATION The Chilean lakes are in the south of the country, 677 km (421 miles) from the capital, Santiago

NUMBER OF LAKES 20

DAYTIME TEMPERATURES
Jan: 17°C (63°F); Apr: 13°C (55°F); Jul: 8°C (46°F); Oct: 12°C (54°F)

Beautiful though the lakes of northern Italy are, ringed by tall mountains and overlooked by luxurious villas and medieval castles, their allure pales when compared to the dramatic lakes of southern Chile. Travel to the world's end and you'll discover a fairy-tale region of shimmering blue water, emerald forest, Andean peaks and steaming hot springs that bubble beneath smouldering volcanoes. Italy's lakes may have inspired the Romantic poets, but Chile's

beautiful land of fire and sapphire water has been a source of legend for millennia.

Journey through Chile's Lake District, anchored in its north by Temuco and in its south by Puerto Montt, and you'll encounter rare primordial beauty. The region takes its name from the magical lakes that spread across its entirety, their expansive, deep-blue waters lying serenely at the feet of soaring volcanoes. Picturesque towns, dotted with plazas and the spires of churches built by the German communities that settled here in the 19th century, overlook the lakeshores and make for romantic stopovers. Trails run from these towns to lakeside beaches of black volcanic and fine white sand, skirting around lush forest along the way. A barefoot walk across the sand, beneath green forest and dramatic smoking peaks, inspires a childlike delight; a sensation of closeness to nature that intensifies on sinking into the warm, mineral-rich lake water.

This sense of being in an untamed, elemental place is accentuated on the volcanic slopes that overlook the lakes. Roads lead to mountain spas,

ABOVE Monkey-puzzle trees on a hillside in the Chilean Lake District

where you can laze in hot springs that bubble up from beneath the earth's crust. Horse-rides on these slopes reveal virgin forest with hidden waterfalls, gushing streams and ancient woods of monkey-puzzle trees. Hiking trails lead to the summits of the great Villarrica and Osorno volcanoes, sacred to the Mapuche, the proud native people of the Lake District. Peering into their bubbling craters at spitting gases and glowing magma, the sensation is one of gazing into the very heart of the earth.

FORGET THE ITALIAN LAKES?

THE BUILD-UP Loved by everyone from Roman emperors and the Romantic poets to Hollywood actor George Clooney, who owns a villa on Lake Como, Italy's lakes have seduced visitors for centuries. Classical villas and turreted castles dot the perimeters of the lakes here and picture-perfect towns spill down to their shorelines. Close to Milan and Verona, they are easily accessed.

THE LETDOWN The region's easy access means that it swarms with tourists come high season, when restaurant prices soar higher than the surrounding peaks, driving tours of the lakes turn into gruelling ordeals and cafés have standing room only. Wordsworth described Italy's lakes as "a treasure the earth keeps to itself". Unfortunately, this is no longer the case.

GOING ANYWAY? The best time to visit the lakes is outside the high season, which runs from early June to September. If you're booking a stay at one of the bigger lakes, choose a small town with authentic Italian appeal rather than a resort – Maclesine on Lake Garda or Varenna on Lake Como are recommended. Consider too a smaller lake destination, such as picturesque Lake Iseo.

ABOVE The sandy shore of Lake Garda heaving with sun-worshippers, Italy

PRACTICAL INFORMATION

Getting There and Around
International flights land at Chile's capital city, Santiago, from where flights depart daily for Temuco. Maquehue Airport is a 7-km (4-mile) taxi ride from Temuco's city centre. Buses are a good way of travelling around the region, but a car is essential if you want to explore more freely. Bikes are great for exploring towns and lakeshores and horse-riding through forests can be breathtaking.

Where to Eat
Delicious regional specialities include freshwater trout and salmon, game and, in coastal cities, seafood. Have a quality Chilean wine or a local bock beer with your meal, followed by a German dessert and a glass of Pisco Sour, Chile's national drink. In Pucón,

La Maga (tel. +56 45 444 277) serves some of the region's best cuisine.

Where to Stay
Overlooking Lake Villarrica in Pucón, Hotel Antumalal (www.antumalal.com), built in the Bauhaus style, boasts a luxury spa and suites with stunning lake views.

When to Go
Visit between December and February, the southern hemisphere's summer, when days are long and warm and the lakes look magnificent.

Budget per Day for Two
£230 per day, to cover luxury hotel and spa accommodation, food, car hire and excursion costs.

Website
www.sernatur.cl

THE GLACIAL LAKES OF SLOVENIA

NEED TO KNOW

LOCATION Lakes Bled and Bohinj lie in northwest Slovenia, 45 km (28 miles) from Austria and Italy and 55 km (34 miles) from the capital, Ljubljana

NUMBER OF LAKES Two big lakes and many smaller pools

DAYTIME TEMPERATURES
Jan: -1°C (30°F); Apr: 11°C (52°F); Jul: 19°C (66°F); Oct: 7°C (45°F)

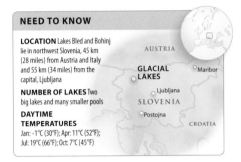

If you think the Italian lakes are romantic, you'll love the picture-book prettiness of Slovenia's glacial lakes. With the majestic Julian Alps as its backdrop, Lake Bled, a vivid turquoise tongue of water ringed by thick forest and stunning snow-streaked mountains, is the must-see here. There are superb views across the lakeshore to a fairy-tale castle of medieval turrets and ramparts. At the centre of the lake, a 17th-century "floating" church stands on a tiny island reached by gondola. It's a romantic place, and should be coupled with a trip to nearby Lake Bohinj, a body of crystal-clear water overlooked by woodland and jagged peaks.

Practical Information

Getting There and Around International flights arrive at Ljubljana. Trains and buses run from the airport to Triglav National Park, where the lakes are found. The motorway journey from the airport takes an hour. An hourly bus service runs between the two lakes, which are 25 km (16 miles) apart.

When to Go Visit in June and July for long days and blissfully few tourists.

Website www.bled.si

Church of the Assumption of Mary on Lake Bled, Slovenia

PLITVICE LAKES, CROATIA

NEED TO KNOW

LOCATION Plitvice Lakes National Park is 110 km (68 miles) southwest of Croatia's capital city, Zagreb

NUMBER OF LAKES 16

DAYTIME TEMPERATURES
Jan: -1°C (30°F); Apr: 11°C (52°F); Jul: 22°C (72°F); Oct: 13°C (55°F)

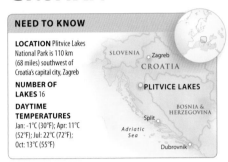

Nature's own champagne pyramid, Croatia's Plitvice Lakes are arranged on stepped limestone terraces that are linked to one another by a series of rapids and waterfalls. The views across these overflowing pools and sparkling white cascades to Eden-like emerald forest are mesmerizing. The lakes change hue constantly, from deep blue to azure, green and grey, according to sunlight and changing mineral content. These tumbling pools lie in Plitvice Lakes National Park, a UNESCO World Heritage Site, which is also home to threatened fauna, including bears, wolves and lynx.

Practical Information

Getting There and Around International flights arrive at Zagreb, from where buses and coaches run to the national park. The best way to get around the lakes is by hiking, but there are also boat and bus services.

When to Go Aim to travel here in late September, when temperatures are pleasant and the autumn colours truly amazing.

Website www.np-plitvicka-jezera.hr

The tumbling aquamarine waters of the Plitvice Lakes, Croatia

LAKE BALATON, HUNGARY

NEED TO KNOW

LOCATION Lake Balaton is 95 km (59 miles) southwest of Hungary's capital, Budapest

NUMBER OF LAKES One main lake and countless crater lakes

DAYTIME TEMPERATURES
Jan: -2°C (28°F); Apr: 15°C (59°F); Jul: 28°C (82°F); Oct: 10°C (50°F)

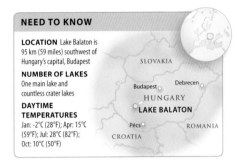

Affectionately known as "the Hungarian Sea", beautiful Lake Balaton is the largest of all central Europe's lakes, and also one of the most diverse. A 170-km (105-mile) shoreline fringes this expanse of green water, offering something for everyone. The southern shore boasts sandy beaches, shallow water, family-friendly resorts and lively beachside nightclubs. But it's the northern shore that utterly beguiles, its volcanic hills studded with geyser cones, crater lakes and wine caves. Nearby, pretty medieval towns and the centuries-old spas of the Tihany Peninsula beckon.

Practical Information

Getting There and Around FlyBalaton International Airport lies on the shore of the lake. Shuttle buses run from here to the lakeside towns. Regular ferries and buses serve the lake, though car hire is wise if you want to explore more freely.

When to Go Visit between June and August for summer sun and warm water.

Website www.gotohungary.co.uk

Rowing boats moored on the shores of Lake Balaton, Hungary

BAND-E AMIR LAKES, AFGHANISTAN

NEED TO KNOW

LOCATION The Band-e Amir Lakes are in Afghanistan's Hindu Kush mountain range, 309 km (192 miles) from the capital, Kabul

NUMBER OF LAKES Six

DAYTIME TEMPERATURES
Jan: -3°C (27°F); Apr: 9°C (48°F); Jul: 18°C (64°F); Oct: 9°C (48°F)

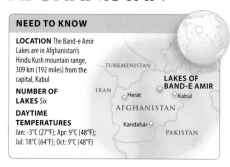

ABOVE Pilgrims at the lake of Band-e Haibat, Afghanistan

Few bodies of water can match the stunning, otherworldly beauty of the Band-e Amir Lakes. Set high in the Hindu Kush mountain range of central Afghanistan, this chain of deep-sapphire lakes lies across a desolate landscape of bone-dry canyon rock like shiny jewels on the fingers of a withered hand. Spread out across natural terraces, the enormous, interconnected ice-cold pools flow into one another, from the highest to the lowest in the chain, via a series of sparkling waterfalls and gushing rapids.

The lakes owe their unique beauty to the carbon-dioxide-rich water that oozes from fractures in the earth's crust deep beneath them. So rich in minerals are the lakes that they change colour regularly throughout the day, alternating between deep sapphire, turquoise, green and grey according to the light and motion of the water, which moves the minerals with it. White travertine dams, formed naturally by limestone deposits, edge each of the lakes and add yet another striking feature to this barren desert.

The Band-e Haibat dam is usually the focal point of a trip to the lakes. This is the deepest and largest of the Band-e Amir Lakes, and sinks to an awesome depth of 150 m (492 ft). Stunning vistas along its shores reveal rugged golden cliffs towering above turquoise water, beneath the distance gaze of the Hindu Kush peaks, which glow almost pink on the horizon. Not much disturbs this magnificent scene: the lakes, once a romantic haven for nomads and hashish-smoking hippies, do not receive many visitors despite being an oasis of peace in war-torn Afghanistan. The people who do visit are pilgrims who believe that the cold lakes have great powers of healing. Few places on earth are more serene.

Practical Information

Getting There and Around Flights to Kabul from Europe and North America go via Dubai. Minibuses make the 240-km (149-mile) bone-shaking journey across dirt roads from Kabul to Bamiyan, the gateway city to the Band-e Amir Lakes. Privately hired cars and minibuses carry visitors on to the lakes, which are 75 km (47 miles) away. Local drivers are essential as several of the roads in the region remain heavily mined. Once at the lakes, hike their banks or hire a pedalo to take in vistas from water level.

When to Go Aim to visit between September and November, when daytime temperatures are pleasant and mountain nights are cool.

Website http://afghanistan.saarctourism.org/band-e-amir.html

One of the Band-e Amir Lakes in its arid setting, Afghanistan

KERALA'S LAKES AND BACKWATERS

NEED TO KNOW

LOCATION Alleppey, in the heart of Kerala's backwaters, is about 65 km (40 miles) south of Cochin and 145 km (90 miles) north of Trivandrum

NUMBER OF LAKES Five lakes and thousands of backwaters

DAYTIME TEMPERATURES
Jan: 26°C (79°F); Apr: 29°C (84°F); Jul: 26°C (79°F); Oct: 27°C (81°F)

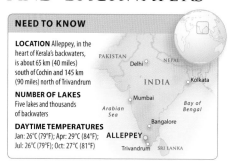

At the southwestern tip of India, the magnificent Keralan lakes and backwaters are a shimmering tropical labyrinth of five lakes and more than 1,000 km (621 miles) of rivers, canals, rivulets and lagoons. Trips aboard houseboats – converted barges once used to transport rice – depart for the backwaters from lakeshore towns. Using long bamboo poles, oarsmen slowly steer you through a maze of silent channels dotted with isolated hamlets and fringed with coconut palms, dazzlingly green paddy fields and plantations of banana and yam. Plan your trip around Alleppey, known as the "Venice of the East" for its myriad canals.

Practical Information

Getting There and Around International flights arrive at Bangalore, Delhi or Mumbai, where connecting flights go to Cochin and Trivandrum. Take a train, car or, best of all, boat on to Alleppey and the other lakeshore towns.

When to Go December to May is the best time to visit Kerala – this way you avoid the monsoon season and southern India's unbearably hot summer.

Website www.keralatourism.org

Houseboats on one of Kerala's verdant backwaters, India

ABOVE Crowds of tourists at Mather Point on the Grand Canyon's South Rim, Arizona

BRYCE CANYON
VS THE GRAND CANYON

Utah's dazzling Bryce Canyon is a unique, extraordinary wonderland, on a much more human scale than Arizona's huge and intimidating Grand Canyon

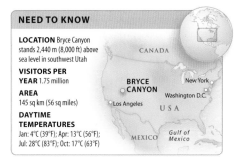

NEED TO KNOW

LOCATION Bryce Canyon stands 2,440 m (8,000 ft) above sea level in southwest Utah

VISITORS PER YEAR 1.75 million

AREA 145 sq km (56 sq miles)

DAYTIME TEMPERATURES Jan: 4°C (39°F); Apr: 13°C (56°F); Jul: 28°C (83°F); Oct: 17°C (63°F)

Map showing CANADA, USA with BRYCE CANYON, New York, Washington D.C., Los Angeles, MEXICO, Gulf of Mexico

Nothing can prepare you for your first sight of Bryce Canyon. It's as though the top layer of the earth has been ripped back to reveal a landscape full of incandescent orange, yellow and red columns jostling for position beneath the surface. It is such a splendid sight that even the colossal Grand Canyon pales in comparison. The local Paiute people called Bryce Canyon *Unkatimpe-wa-Wince-Pockich* – "red rocks standing like men in a bowl-shaped recess" – but its modern name comes from a 19th-century Mormon rancher, Ebenezer Bryce, who laconically observed that his new home was "a helluva place to lose a cow".

Despite its name, Bryce is not actually a canyon at all, but a succession of spectacular natural amphitheatres chiselled out of a high, pine-forested plateau by eternities of ice, water and wind erosion. Most visitors get their first glimpse of Bryce from the rim on its western edge, and, because there is no corresponding rim opposite, the views from this point are breathtaking. Below you lies the canyon, decorated in a palette of lurid hues. Many of its sandstone forms are *hoodoos* – extraordinary pillars created over thousands of years as soft rock has crumbled away from hard rock, leaving sturdy boulders balanced precariously atop pencil-thin shafts of petrified sand. Beyond the canyon, a desolate plain stretches as far as the eye can see.

A level walkway along the edge of the largest amphitheatre at Bryce makes it easy for people to admire the awesome rock formations en masse. Specific look-out points identified along this path boast particularly good views at sunset and sunrise, when the landscape seems to glow like a vast furnace. Unlike the Grand Canyon, an hour-long hike here can lead you into the very heart of the monolithic labyrinth. Several straightforward trails thread their way down to and among the most dramatic *hoodoos*. Walking in the perpetual shade of the canyon's floor, along narrow footpaths squeezed between looming orange rocks and implausibly slender pinnacles, is a truly mind-boggling experience. In many places, the trails cut right into the rock, through dramatic tunnels and underneath archways, leading you to new and astonishing vistas at every turn.

PRACTICAL INFORMATION

Getting There and Around
The nearest major airports to Bryce Canyon are at Las Vegas, 435 km (270 miles) to the southwest, and Salt Lake City, the same distance to the north. The only way to get here is to drive, though free shuttle buses tour the park itself. The park's entrance is at its northern end.

Where to Eat
Typical American diners are found near the park entrance, but the best place to eat is in the rustic dining room at the Bryce Canyon Lodge (*see Where to Stay*), which serves three meals daily. Steaks and chops are the speciality here.

Where to Stay
The comfortable Bryce Canyon Lodge (www.brycecanyonlodge. com), still kitted out in its original

1920s furnishings, has luxury suites, individual log cabins and motel rooms. It is set back 100 m (328 ft) from the rim, and is open in summer only (Apr–Oct).

When to Go
Unlike much of Utah and the Grand Canyon, Bryce remains cool enough in summer for hiking to be a pleasure. While in-park facilities close in winter, the park itself remains open, and looks more surreally beautiful than ever when veiled in snow.

Budget per Day for Two
Anything from £75 to £135 for food, accommodation and park entry (which is £17 per car). Car rental is a further £20 per day.

Website
www.nps.gov/brca

FORGET THE GRAND CANYON?

THE BUILD-UP The Grand Canyon deservedly ranks among the most famous sights on earth. It was formed over millions of years and measures a huge 446 km (277 miles) long, up to 29 km (18 miles) wide and 2 km (1 mile) deep.

THE LETDOWN Five million visitors flock to the Grand Canyon every year, but sadly almost all head to the same crowded, commercialized spot on its South Rim, known as Grand Canyon Village. Crammed into the hectic look-out points and dwarfed by the colossal, silent chasm, they experience the canyon as a remote spectacle. Those few who hike into it face a very challenging task – getting down to the Colorado River and back requires a two-day backpacking expedition.

GOING ANYWAY? If you're determined to go, consider visiting the quieter North Rim, where a lovely lodge stands at the canyon's edge. Alternatively, take a 193-km (120-mile) trip down dirt roads to remote Toroweap Point, where you can stare straight down a sheer 914-m (3,000-ft) cliff to the river.

MAIN IMAGE Bryce Canyon in all its fiery glory
BELOW (left to right) Snow atop a natural archway; hikers on the Mossy Cave Trail

4 MORE CANYONS TO RIVAL THE GRAND CANYON

COPPER CANYON, MEXICO Northern Mexico's spectacular Copper Canyon is deeper in parts than the Grand Canyon. The Copper Canyon Railway, which climbs alongside the precipice en route from Los Mochis to Chihuahua, affords fabulous views.

ZION CANYON, UTAH, USA Bryce's near-neighbour is a pretty, lush spot thanks to the Virgin River that flows through its centre. The canyon lacks the bizarre rock formations of Bryce, but boasts magnificent red-rock cliffs and fine hiking trails.

WAIMEA CANYON, HAWAI'I The so-called "Grand Canyon of the Pacific", which almost cuts the verdant island of Kaua'i in half, holds an amazing, ever-changing panoply of colours and offers magnificent views out over the ocean.

CANYON DE CHELLY, ARIZONA, USA Canyon de Chelly, another spellbinding red-rock canyon, is occupied by indigenous Navajo farmers and filled with the evocative cliff dwellings left by the Ancient Puebloan people of the region.

ABOVE A boat sailing past a mountain of ice, part of the Darwin Mountains, Tierra del Fuego, Chile

THE PATAGONIAN FJORDS

VS THE NORWEGIAN FJORDS

A magical world of water and ice, Patagonia's fjords eclipse Norway's famous waterways

NEED TO KNOW

LOCATION The fjords form part of the archipelago at the southernmost tip of the American continent, Tierra del Fuego, shared between Chile and Argentina

VISITORS PER YEAR
12,000

DAYTIME TEMPERATURES
Jan: 11°C (52°F); Apr: 7°C (45°F); Jul: 2°C (36°F); Oct: 7°C (45°F)

Santiago
ARGENTINA
CHILE
Pacific Ocean
Atlantic Ocean
Punta Arenas **PATAGONIAN FJORDS**

At the bottom of the Earth lies a dazzling world of hanging glaciers, floating icebergs, gushing waterfalls and towering peaks that rise sheer from blue-green seas. The Patagonian Fjords may sound fantastical but their existence is real, and the drama of their unspoiled beauty eclipses even that of Norway's well-visited waterways. Accessible by luxury sailboat only, these haunting wonders receive just 12,000 visitors each year – a fraction of the number that descends on their Norwegian rivals. For the few that sail their waters southwards to mythical Cape Horn (Cabo de Hornos) and the world's end, the sensation is one of awe.

The Patagonian Fjords experience begins in the city of Punta Arenas in Chile, from where cruise ships cross the legendary Magellan Strait (Estrecho de Magallanes) and float south to the Cape

through a labyrinthine network of channels, islets and inlets. As you sail, the extreme beauty of the fjords reveals itself. Mountains rise precipitously out of the sea, glacier after gorgeous glacier cascades down rock faces and waterfalls plunge into deep channels. Boat excursions magnify this thrilling drama that unfolds at water level – approaching the great Glaciar Pía, visitors can watch in wonder as one giant block of turquoise ice after another calves from the glacier's face into the Pía Fjord in a concerto of thunderous cracks and booms.

Small boat excursions also bring you incredibly close to some spectacular marine wildlife. In the escort of playful dolphins, you skirt the shorelines of coves and islets where enormous elephant seals slumber and smaller sea lions bask. Onshore, hikes reveal lush forest and cross-sheltered beaches where thousands of cute Magellanic penguins and cormorants form their nesting colonies.

After four days of navigating sheltered waters, you reach the desolately beautiful Cape Horn. Here, looking out across the Cape to where the Atlantic and Pacific oceans collide, one is struck by the utter remoteness of the place. Ice-floes pepper the powerful sea and the howling winds that once thwarted so many expeditions here lash against steep, ragged cliffs. It's not difficult to believe that Antarctica and the ends of the Earth are just 830 km (500 miles) away.

ABOVE A sea lion perched on a rock, Beagle Channel

FORGET THE NORWEGIAN FJORDS?

THE BUILD-UP Designated a UNESCO World Heritage Site, Norway's fjords are some of the world's longest and deepest, including Sognefjord, Hardangerfjord and Geirangerfjord. The beautiful, rugged landscape is also a big draw to this region.

THE LETDOWN Having fallen victim to their own beauty, these fjords play host to thousands of tourists each year. Sightseers throng them, kayakers paddle them, base-jumpers chuck themselves into them and the plain lazy drive through them. Search for silent majesty and you find cruise ships. The landscape is marred by a new power line – the world's second longest – straddling Sognefjord.

GOING ANYWAY? Head for Norway's less-visited Naeroyfjord and Lysefjord. The latter is overlooked by the stunning 600-m- (1,970-ft-) high Pulpit Rock.

ABOVE Queues of vehicles lined up for loading into car ferries at Hella, Sognefjord

PRACTICAL INFORMATION

Getting There and Around
There are daily flights from Santiago to Punta Arenas in southern Chile, the departure point for cruises to the Patagonian fjords. Four-night cruises sail to Cape Horn before disembarking at Ushuaia in Argentina. Seven-night cruises return to Punta Arenas.

Where to Eat
La Leyenda del Remezón (tel. +56 61 241 029) in Punta Arenas offers fresh seafood. Meals on board are four-course affairs served with Chilean wines.

Where to Stay
In Punta Arenas, stay at Hotel Nogueira (www.hotelnogueira. com). *Mare Australis* boats have three cabin categories. Book ahead for cheaper options.

When to Go
January or February, when days are long and wildlife abundant.

Budget for Two
£4,200 for a 7-night cruise including boat excursions and onboard activities.

Website
www.australis.com

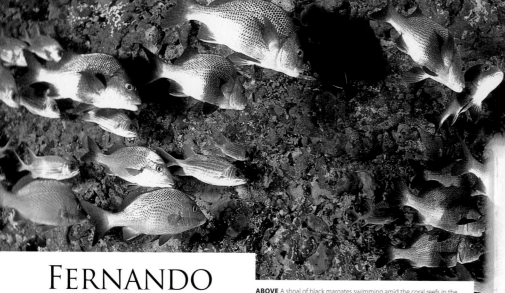

ABOVE A shoal of black margates swimming amid the coral reefs in the depths around Fernando de Noronha, Brazil

FERNANDO DE NORONHA

VS GALAPAGOS ISLANDS

Fernando de Noronha is a near mirror-image of the Galapagos, with a unique appeal

NEED TO KNOW

LOCATION This island in the Atlantic Ocean is to the south of the Equator and 360 km (216 miles) east of Natal

VISITORS PER YEAR
70,000

DAYTIME TEMPERATURES
Jan: 27°C (81°F); Apr: 27°C (81°F); Jul: 26°C (79°F); Oct: 26°C (79°F)

The **Atlantic twin** to the Pacific Ocean's world-famous Galapagos, the Fernando de Noronha archipelago of 21 volcanic islands and islets lies just south of the Equator, some 360 km (216 miles) from mainland Brazil. Like the Galapagos, this lesser-known island enclave is famous for its fabulous wildlife encounters.

Fernando de Noronha, however, offers a far more robust experience, with wonderful accommodation, fine restaurants, fortress ruins and other historic attractions, plus active adventures from biking and hiking to sea-kayaking and surfing.

While the Galapagos are best visited on cruises that last at least a week, Fernando de Noronha is a great place to settle into a *pousada* (hotel) on the main island and make daily forays by boat to neighbouring isles. This is easy to do on organized excursions or aboard hired wooden fishing boats.

The islands are gloriously scenic, with rugged pinnacles piercing the sky, and sheer-faced cliffs spilling onto snowy beaches such as Praia do Leáo, where marine turtles crawl ashore to lay their eggs. Migratory birds flock in their teeming thousands, joining permanent residents, including the

ABOVE Colourful wooden boats in Fernando de Noronha's harbour

magnificent frigatebird, red-billed tropicbirds and the endearing brown, masked, red-footed and blue-footed boobies. In fact, Fernando de Noronha is home to the largest concentration of tropical seabirds in the western Atlantic.

It's no wonder that the entire chain is protected as a UNESCO World Heritage Site. The Baía dos Golfinhos has the highest concentration of resident dolphins in the world. Post-dawn, spinner dolphins can be seen leaping and frolicking in the morning sunshine. Whales are also often seen close to shore. And the enthralling underwater world is considered the best in Brazil.

The main island, Ilha Fernando de Noronha, is graced by the lovely colonial village of Vila Remédios, with its pretty yellow-and-white Baroque Nossa Senhora dos Remédios church, built in 1772, overlooking a quiet cobblestone plaza. You can clamber the crumbling remains of Forte dos Remédios, completed in 1737, and admire the panoramic views. The Memorial Noronhense serves as a charming history museum. And the island is dotted with romantic *pousadas* where you might chance upon Brazil's hottest models and movie glitterati, for whom little-visited Fernando de Noronha is becoming hip.

The trails and dirt roads that lace the island are good for horse-riding and mountain-biking. And, unlike the Galapagos, you can even rent cars, which means a dune-buggy here, for exhilarating off-road rides to pristine beaches.

FORGET THE GALAPAGOS ISLANDS?

THE BUILD-UP These volcanic isles in the Pacific Ocean 1,000 km (600 miles) west of Ecuador, are renowned for their remarkable island ecosystems. Nowhere in the world would one have quite the same up-close-and-personal encounters with wildlife, with the intimacy of travelling between islands by boat.

THE LETDOWN The number of visitors to the islands has increased tenfold since 1980. Many of the popular trails are overcrowded, pollution is on the rise, implementation of regulations is lax and visits are increasingly costly.

GOING ANYWAY? The best way to explore the Galapagos is on an organized boat charter with a licensed guide. Preservation of this ecosystem is every traveller's responsibility. When hiking, stick to established trails and don't touch or, worse, feed the wildlife! Take only photographs, leave only footprints.

ABOVE A crowd of tourists watching sea lions sunning themselves at Sullivan Bay, Galapagos islands

PRACTICAL INFORMATION

Getting There and Around
The Aeroporto Fernando de Noronha, in the centre of the island, is served by flights from Natal and Recife. Dune-buggy taxis run around the island at bargain prices. You can also explore the main island on rented buggies. Budget hounds can take a public bus that runs along the main highway.

Where to Eat
For lobster and other seafood of mouthwatering quality, visit Ecologiku's Restaurante (tel. +55 81 3619 1807).

Where to Stay
Eco-sensitive resort, Pousada Maravilha (tel. +55 81 3619 0028; www.pousadamaravilha.com.br) has eight bungalows which offer comfort and superb vistas.

When to Go
Visit during the low season between Aug and Nov, when prices are reduced.

Budget per Day for Two
£175 per day for food, travel and accommodation.

Website
www.noronha.pe.gov.br

MAIN IMAGE Mountain gorilla, Bwindi Impenetrable National Park
BELOW (left to right) Nile river-boat cruise, Murchison Falls National
Park; African elephant, Queen Elizabeth National Park; shoebill

WESTERN UGANDA RESERVES
VS KRUGER NATIONAL PARK

The wide waterways, tangled jungles and open plains of Western Uganda make up Africa's most biodiverse safari destination, an unspoilt alternative to the more famous Kruger

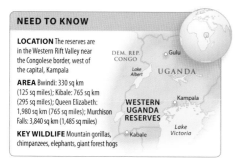

NEED TO KNOW

LOCATION The reserves are in the Western Rift Valley near the Congolese border, west of the capital, Kampala

AREA Bwindi: 330 sq km (125 sq miles); Kibale: 765 sq km (295 sq miles); Queen Elizabeth: 1,980 sq km (765 sq miles); Murchison Falls: 3,840 sq km (1,485 sq miles)

KEY WILDLIFE Mountain gorillas, chimpanzees, elephants, giant forest hogs

Western Uganda receives far fewer tourists than Kruger, but it surpasses all other safari destinations for sheer biodiversity. Here, where the East African savanna meets the West African rainforest – or less prosaically, where Hemingway's safari country meets Tarzan's jungle – a quartet of superb national parks promises visitors close-up encounters with some of Africa's most iconic wildlife. Imagine hiking to within metres of mighty mountain gorillas and chimpanzees, navigating tropical waterways dense with hippos and elephants, and exploring the open plains where lions eye herds of grazing antelopes.

In the south of the region is the dense mountain rainforest of Bwindi Impenetrable National Park, which protects about half the world's remaining mountain gorillas. Staring into the deep brown eyes of one of these gentle giants is a uniquely fulfilling experience. Consider heading further north to the lowland forest of Kibale Forest National Park, one of Africa's top chimp-tracking destinations. Its dense canopy is also home to the continent's highest concentration of monkeys, including the acrobatic red colobus and black-and-white colobus.

On the Rift Valley floor between Bwindi and Kibale lies Queen Elizabeth National Park, where savannah, forest and aquatic habitats converge to create a riot of biodiversity attested to by a bird checklist of 600-plus species, the most recorded in any African national park. Boat trips on the Kazinga Channel, with the snow-capped Rwenzori Mountains looming high on the horizon, bring nature-lovers face to face with hippos, buffalos, elephants, pelicans and waterfowl, while the fringing woodland is one of the most reliable places on earth to spot giant forest hogs. The remote Ishasha Plains are justly renowned for their tree-climbing lions, while elsewhere patches of dense forest enclose saline crater lakes tinged pink by thousands of flamingos.

To the far north lies Murchison Falls National Park, which is Uganda's largest national park. Daily boat trips follow the Nile, its banks lined with grunting hippos and gaping crocodiles, to the base of Murchison Falls, where the world's longest river erupts through a cleft in the Rift Valley escarpment in a deafening white plume. Lions, giraffes, elephants, buffalos and various types of antelope inhabit the palm-studded grassland north of the delta where the Nile flows into Lake Albert, which is also a famous haunt of the distinctive-looking shoebill, one of the most eagerly sought birds in Africa.

FORGET KRUGER?

THE BUILD-UP The size of a small European country, Kruger is South Africa's largest national park, and one of the most famous wildlife sanctuaries in the world. The mammal checklist of 150 species exceeds that of any other African park, and its scrubby plains are home to more than 13,000 elephants and 25,000 buffalos, alongside high concentrations of lions, leopards, rhinos and other safari favourites.

THE LETDOWN Organised safaris to this immense park almost invariably focus on the southern quarter, which is the closest sector to Johannesburg and intensely developed for tourism. As a result, the roads carry too much traffic and big-cat sightings attract dozens of vehicles jostling for the best place, transforming what should be a wilderness into something more like a car park.

GOING ANYWAY? The crowds can be avoided in Kruger if you hire your own car and use dirt side roads in favour of surfaced trunk roads. You can also focus your attention on the under-explored central and northern regions, and stay in low-key camps such as Letaba, Shingwedzi and Punda Maria.

ABOVE Safari vehicles clogging the road, Kruger National Park, South Africa

PRACTICAL INFORMATION

Getting There and Around
Entebbe International Airport, 30 km (19 miles) south of the capital Kampala, is the main port of entry to Uganda. From here, most visitors explore the western parks by road over one or two weeks – private safaris can be arranged through several operators in Kampala. Bwindi, Kibale Forest and Queen Elizabeth can also all be reached via public transport.

Where to Eat
The camps and lodges in the national parks all serve food. The best à la carte restaurant in any of the parks, with a cuisine reflecting its Indian ownership, is at Mweya Lodge (www.mweyalodge.com) in Queen Elizabeth National Park.

Where to Stay
The park's lodges and camps tend to be small and intimate in character. Popular options are Mweya Lodge *(see Where to Eat)*, Kibale Primate Lodge (www.ugandalodges.com), Volcanoes Bwindi Lodge (www.volcanoesafaris.com), and Paraa Lodge in Murchison Falls (www.paraalodge.com).

When to Go
Any time, though the wettest months (Apr, May, Oct, Nov) make gorilla- and chimp-tracking hard.

Budget per Day for Two
£200–300 for an all-inclusive organized safari. Gorilla-tracking permits cost US$500.

Website
www.uwa.or.ug

Black rhino, Hluhluwe-Imfolozi Game Reserve, South Africa

A bare-branched baobab tree drenched in evening sunlight, Ruaha National Park, Tanzania

Gerenuks feeding in Samburu National Reserve, Kenya

HLUHLUWE-IMFOLOZI GAME RESERVE

NEED TO KNOW

LOCATION Hluhluwe-Imfolozi Game Reserve is in the north of South Africa's KwaZulu-Natal province, about 50 km (30 miles) inland of St Lucia Village

AREA 1,000 sq km (385 sq miles)

KEY WILDLIFE Black rhinos, white rhinos, nyalas, elephants

The largest and most alluring of several under-rated game reserves in the Zululand region of South Africa, Hluhluwe-Imfolozi is a key strong-hold for Africa's endangered rhino. More than 1,000 white rhinos and 500 black rhinos roam these rolling green slopes, alongside elephants, buffalos, nyala antelopes and a varied cast of predators, including lions, leopards and endangered African wild dogs. The legendary four-day wilderness trails that run during winter are once-in-a-lifetime experiences, but for those with less time, the guided game walks are a great option.

PRACTICAL INFORMATION

Getting There A good road network makes Hluhluwe-Imfolozi ideal for self-drive safaris. St Lucia village is the nearest place to rent a car, and local operators also offer organized day trips into the reserve.

When to Go The dry winter (May–Sep) is the best time for game viewing, since vegetation thins and wildlife tends to congregate around water.

Website www.kznwildlife.com

RUAHA NATIONAL PARK

NEED TO KNOW

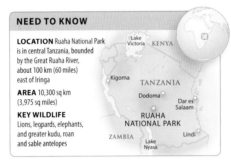

LOCATION Ruaha National Park is in central Tanzania, bounded by the Great Ruaha River, about 100 km (60 miles) east of Iringa

AREA 10,300 sq km (3,975 sq miles)

KEY WILDLIFE Lions, leopards, elephants, and greater kudu, roan and sable antelopes

Tanzania's second-largest national park has a rugged, remote and austere character. Baobab trees litter the landscape, their bare branches reaching skyward from the semi-arid plains. This is the sort of place where you can drive for hours without seeing another vehicle. Game viewing can be exceptional and cat-lovers are in for a treat, with a good chance of spotting cheetahs, leopards and large lion prides. More than 12,000 elephants and a diverse selection of antelopes, including the majestically horned greater kudu, also roam here.

PRACTICAL INFORMATION

Getting There Most visitors book an all-inclusive package with a camp, and fly in from Dar es Salaam or Selous Game Reserve. Most safaris start from Dar es Salaam, and are best broken by a night in Mikumi National Park.

When to Go Any time, though the dry season (May–Dec) is best for mammal spotting and the wet season (Jan–Apr) is best for bird-watching.

Website www.tanzaniaparks.com

SAMBURU NATIONAL RESERVE

NEED TO KNOW

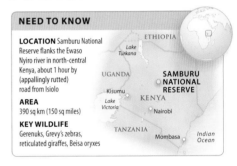

LOCATION Samburu National Reserve flanks the Ewaso Nyiro river in north-central Kenya, about 1 hour by (appallingly rutted) road from Isiolo

AREA 390 sq km (150 sq miles)

KEY WILDLIFE Gerenuks, Grevy's zebras, reticulated giraffes, Beisa oryxes

Samburu lies in the parched badlands that divide Kenya's central highlands from the Ethiopian border, and protects the most unusual fauna of any African savanna reserve. Here lives the gerenuk, an extraordinary gazelle-like creature distinguished by its long neck, freakishly small head, and habit of standing on its hind legs to feed on leaves. Other oddities include the densely striped Grevy's zebra, the geometrically marked reticulated giraffe and the regal Beisa oryx. All of these make the reserve attractive to regular safari-goers, but first-timers have plenty to enjoy too – elephants and lions abound, and the forest fringing the Ewaso Nyiro river is one of the best places in East Africa for spotting leopards.

PRACTICAL INFORMATION

Getting There The best way to visit Samburu is with a recognized safari operator or in a private 4WD. These can be rented in Nairobi, which is about 250 km (155 miles) to the south.

When to Go It is good all year round, but wildlife concentrations along the river are highest in the late dry season (Jun–Oct).

Website www.kenya-information-guide.com/samburu.html

Leopard lazing in a tree at night, South Luangwa National Park, Zambia

A mandrill with its characteristic nasal colourings, Lopé National Park, Gabon

A distinctive-looking ring-tailed lemur in the lush rainforest of Madagascar

LUANGWA VALLEY

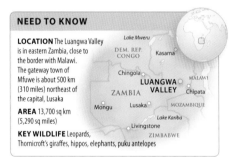

NEED TO KNOW

LOCATION The Luangwa Valley is in eastern Zambia, close to the border with Malawi. The gateway town of Mfuwe is about 500 km (310 miles) northeast of the capital, Lusaka

AREA 13,700 sq km (5,290 sq miles)

KEY WILDLIFE Leopards, Thornicroft's giraffes, hippos, elephants, puku antelopes

Africa at its most primal, this southern extension of the Great Rift Valley, named after the Luangwa river, is rendered inaccessible by flooding for several months each year. Its spectacular concentrations of buffalos, hippos, zebras and elephants, and some 14 antelope species, are protected in two national parks, South and North Luangwa. The larger and more developed southerly park is notable for night drives, which repeatedly strike gold when it comes to leopards, genets, civets and other nocturnal creatures. North Luangwa, though not accessible on a budget, is one of Africa's greatest wilderness areas, studded with a few small camps that specialize in walking safaris.

PRACTICAL INFORMATION

Getting There Fly in to Mfuwe, where you will be met by someone from your lodge, or the operator running your safari.

When to Go The dry southern winter (May–Sep) is best for game viewing and also the most comfortable time of year temperature-wise. The parks usually close in the southern summer due to flooding.

Website www.zambiatourism.com

LOPÉ NATIONAL PARK

NEED TO KNOW

LOCATION Lopé National Park is in Central Gabon, in the province of Ogooué-Ivindo, some 200 km (125 miles) from the capital, Libreville

AREA 4,910 sq km (1,895 sq miles)

KEY WILDLIFE Western gorillas, mandrills, forest elephants and buffalos, sitatungas, monkeys

One of the oldest, largest and most ecologically significant reserves in West Africa, Lopé National Park – inscribed as a UNESCO World Heritage Site in 2007 – is also one of the most accessible to moderately intrepid travellers. Primates are the main point of interest. The rainforest in the park is the world's most important refuge for the mandrill, a large baboon-like primate with a striking red-and-white nasal pattern and fangs that would make a vampire recoil. Lopé also supports around 4,000 western gorillas, high densities of chimpanzees and 400 bird species.

PRACTICAL INFORMATION

Getting There The gateway village to the park is Lopé, which is accessible by surfaced road, rail or chartered light aircraft from the capital, Libreville.

When to Go July and August are the best months for mandrill viewing, and August and September are best for gorillas and most other wildlife.

Website www.wcs.org/international/Africa/gabon/lope

MADAGASCAR

NEED TO KNOW

LOCATION Madagascar is the fourth-largest island in the world, and lies in the Indian Ocean off the southeast coast of Africa

AREA 587,040 sq km (226,655 sq miles)

KEY WILDLIFE Lemurs, fossas, leaf-tailed geckos, panther chameleons

Madagascar is one of the world's most important biodiversity hotspots. Once linked to Africa and the Indian subcontinent, the landmass became an island some 60 million years ago, and since then its wildlife has evolved in virtual isolation. Almost 1,000 vertebrate species are unique to Madagascar, the most famous of which are its 68 species of lemur – small, gentle, wide-eyed primates that include the indri (whose distinctive call sounds like a banshee), the dancing Verreaux's sifaka, and the demonic-looking aye-aye. Other bizarre species unique to the island are the tomato frog, nymphomaniac vasa parrot, giant hissing cockroach, 0.6-m- (2-ft-) long Oustalet's chameleon, fossa, giraffe-necked weevil and the astonishingly camouflaged leaf-tailed gecko.

PRACTICAL INFORMATION

Getting There The main point of access is the capital, Antananarivo, which has an international airport and many operators that organize countrywide tours. Public transport is an option for those with lots of time.

When to Go The driest months (Jun–Nov) are the best for walking and wildlife viewing. The cyclone season (Feb–May) should be avoided.

Website www.visitmadagascar.com

CHERRY BLOSSOMS IN JAPAN
VS NEW ENGLAND'S FALL

As beautiful as New England's fall but with far fewer foreign tourists, the coming of the cherry blossom in Japan is celebrated by everyone, from children to haiku poets

NEED TO KNOW

LOCATION Good places for viewing blossoms include Ueno Park, Tokyo; Dankazura, Kamakura; Heian Shrine, Kyoto; Himeji Castle, Himeji; Dogo Park, Matsuyama

VISITORS PER YEAR
Most of Japan's population

DAYTIME TEMPERATURE
Apr: 14°C (57°F) in Tokyo

The arrival of cherry blossoms brings to life an iconic image of Japan past and present. Each year, the pinkish-white clumps of blossom appear, as if fluted through the branches by some benevolent underground spirit – a timeless view, but also a fleeting one, since the fragile flowers perish almost as soon as they arrive.

While the fiery colours of New England's falls attract "leaf-peepers" by the bucketload, springtime

ABOVE Locals enjoying the *hanami* festivities in Ueno Park, Tokyo

in Japan sees the whole country getting in on the act; not only are tourists in the substantial minority – unlike New England – but they're actively encouraged to join in with the local celebrations and not just spectate.

Many Japanese assume cherry trees, known as *sakura,* to be unique to their homeland, or at least to the East. While this is far from the case, only in Japan is the arrival of the trees' blossoms taken so seriously as to constitute a national obsession. Followed assiduously on national weather reports, the *sakura-zensen* – cherry-blossom frontier – sweeps a pink wave across the country from south to north, with locals frolicking in its wake at flower-viewing parties known as *hanami.*

There are many popular places for a *hanami* – Tokyo's Ueno Park is a favourite spot, as is Takada Park in Jōetsu – but the truth is that you'll rarely be far from one if the *sakura-zensen* is sweeping by. With paper lanterns strung across the trees and mats laid out under the blooms in the manner of a kindergarten picnic, it's time for the serious business of food and sake consumption – in such a conservative society, the opportunity to let one's hair down is often taken with aplomb. Though many now follow the more practical modern maxim of *hana yori dango* (dumplings over flowers), there remain those who maintain the *hanami's* centuries-old purpose, a silent contemplation of the transient nature of beauty, and of life itself – rare feelings indeed, in one of the world's most hyperactive societies.

The samurai may be long gone and the geisha incongruous in neon-soaked streets, but the fragile, ephemeral spirit of the cherry blossom continues to live on.

FORGET NEW ENGLAND'S FALL?

THE BUILD-UP New England has worldwide renown as a place of autumnal beauty. Fiery hues form the backdrop to a quaint, small-town atmosphere brought about by the fact that most places in New England are quaint, small towns. Friendly locals, fantastic scenery and enjoyable drives make leaf-peeping hugely popular.

THE LETDOWN Once the leaves start to turn, in come the leafers – many visitors own a New England cottage for the sole purpose of leaf-viewing – and the sheer numbers make bona fide tourist towns out of settlements that otherwise lie empty. The typical tourist sees the leaves, then races off to buy Chinese-made trinkets sold by shop owners who live out of state – providing little benefit to the local economy.

GOING ANYWAY? Beat the crowds by eschewing the tourist traps such as Bar Harbor, Cape Cod or North Conway. In addition, many towns and states now tag locally made goods – "Made In Maine" being one example – ensuring that the bulk of your cash goes to the locals.

ABOVE Crowds gathered at the Fall Festival, Massachusetts

PRACTICAL INFORMATION

Getting There and Around
Though a *hanami* can be enjoyed almost anywhere in Japan, most international visitors will touch down at Narita Airport, located 57 km (35 miles) from downtown Tokyo. Foreign tourists will be able to make use of the Japan Rail Pass, though this rare Japanese travel bargain can only be bought outside the country (www.japanrailpass.net).

Where to Eat
Tokyo's Sasanoyuki restaurant dates back to the Edo period. Try its famous silky tofu at affordable prices (tel. +81 3 3873 1145).

Where to Stay
Chisun Hotel Ueno is a good-value option. Located right

next to Ueno Park, the hotel is Tokyo's cherry blossom focal point (www.solarehotels.com).

When to Go
The *sakura-zensen* spreads right across Japan from the south to the north, usually starting in Okinawa in late February and hitting Hokkaido in May. Given the vagaries of weather forecasting, it's hard to plan in advance, though those arriving in Tokyo or Kyoto for a couple of weeks in April should catch the *hanami* action.

Budget per Day for Two
£200 per day for food, travel and accommodation.

Website
www.jnto.go.jp/eng

MAIN IMAGE Cherry blossoms by Takada Castle in Takada Park, Jōetsu city **BELOW (left to right)** Sweets at a shrine served during *hanami*; colourful lanterns adorning the streets in spring

4 MORE FLORAL LANDSCAPES TO RIVAL NEW ENGLAND

THE WILD FLOWERS OF THE DRAKENSBERG MOUNTAINS, SOUTH AFRICA The South African summer sees a carpet of rare flora burst forth from the earth all around this sumptuous and highly distinctive mountain range *(see also pp252–3)*.

SPRING FLOWERS, CRETE Anemones, crocuses and over 100 endemic species of orchid can be seen during Crete's magnificent flower season, at its peak in April and May.

WILD RHODODENDRONS IN THE HIMALAYAS Nepal's jagged, roof-of-the-world ambience is given a pink, photogenic booster shot each April thanks to the arrival of its colourful national flower.

ORCHIDS IN MOYOBAMBA, PERU There are few better places to savour the delights of one of the world's most venerated flowers than in Moyobamba, also known as the City of Orchids. It is home to over 3,000 species of the plant.

ICELAND
VS YELLOWSTONE

If it is natural fountains and geothermal heat you desire, consider this sub-Arctic destination in the middle of the North Atlantic over the ever-popular Yellowstone

NEED TO KNOW

LOCATION Iceland is located in the North Atlantic Ocean just south of the Arctic Circle

VISITORS PER YEAR Less than one for each of the 300,000 citizens

DAYTIME TEMPERATURES Jan: 2°C (36°F); Apr: 7°C (45°F); Jul: 16°C (60°F); Oct: 7°C (45°F)

Greenland Sea

Husavik

Akureyri

ICELAND

GEYSIR

Reykjavík

North Atlantic Ocean

Apart from the fact that both Yellowstone and Iceland feature awesome geothermal wonders, the differences between the two destinations could hardly be greater. The highlights of world-renowned Yellowstone nestle amidst the forested hills and snow-capped peaks of North America's Rocky Mountains. Those of Iceland occupy a windswept and nearly treeless island just south of the Arctic Circle in the stormy North Atlantic.

Given its less-than-perfect climatic conditions, one might wonder what makes Iceland a worthy alternative to Yellowstone. To any first-time visitor, it is immediately clear that its landscape is alive

ABOVE Visitors enjoying the natural hot springs at Landmannalaugar

and dynamic. While Yellowstone's geothermic activities are derived from its underlying mega-volcano, Iceland's are created by the Mid-Atlantic Ridge. Along this mostly undersea ridge, tectonic movement between the European and North American plates is literally ripping the island in two. The resulting rift, which slashes across the island, allows volcanic materials to nudge upward from the centre of the earth and, in places, form volcanoes, geothermal fields, a kaleidoscope of colourful rock formations and plenty of other surprises. Visitors will find countless ways to experience these throughout Iceland.

Perhaps the most impressive destination is Landmannalaugar, in the desolate interior. Here, those who are prepared for outdoor adventure can lounge in natural outdoor hot springs or hike across spectacular rhyolite hills to crater lakes, fumaroles and mounds of natural obsidian glass. Alternatively, ferries link the Icelandic mainland with the steaming Vestmannaeyjar Islands, where the town of Heimaey was almost buried beneath lava in 1973. It was also the spot that saw the new volcanic island of Surtsey emerge from the sea as recently as half a century ago.

An easy day trip east of Reykjavík lies Geysir, a geothermal area after which all other spouting hot springs, or geysers, are named. Here, you'll find the Great Geysir which can send a blast of steaming water up to 40 m (130 ft) into the air. However, it is not very reliable, so to pass the time, enjoy the nearby dependable Strokkur Geysir, which erupts every few minutes with 20-m (65-ft) blasts. Combine these geysers and their empty landscapes with pristine Þingvellir National Park and the serene and beautiful Gullfoss waterfall and you have Iceland's Golden Circle of attractions – more than a match for bustling Yellowstone.

FORGET YELLOWSTONE?

THE BUILD-UP As the world's first national park, Yellowstone ranks high on most travellers' must-see lists, and with good reason. This magnificent wilderness, sitting atop one of the world's few mega-volcanoes, features numerous lakes and waterfalls, vast forests, a menagerie of North American wildlife, and an impressive collection of colourful hot springs, bubbling mud pots, steaming rivers and dramatic geysers.

THE LETDOWN A visit to Yellowstone will be hampered by sheer tourist numbers. Most campgrounds and other accommodation are fully booked through the temperate summer months, so advance reservations are essential, thwarting hopes of spontaneous travel. Without resorting to a guided tour, visitors will need to hire a car or private vehicle to explore the park.

GOING ANYWAY? The best time of year to beat the biggest crowds is September, when the autumn colours emerge, but late-season visitors risk snow and sub-freezing temperatures. Determined summer visitors will find detailed information on www.nps.gov/yell.

ABOVE Crowds gazing out over Artist Point overlooking the Grand Canyon of Yellowstone National Park

PRACTICAL INFORMATION

Getting There and Around
Flights from Europe and North America arrive at Keflavik, which is about an hour's bus ride from Reykjavík. Iceland can also be a stopover destination on a trans-Atlantic flight. Geysir and other geothermal spots are accessible using local buses or on a range of locally organized guided tours.

Where to Eat
Inexpensive Icelandic meals are largely forgettable, but the fresh – and very pricey – local seafood can be superb. Iceland's finest and most imaginative gourmet seafood dishes are found at Sjávarkjallarinn in Reykjavík (www.sjavarkjallarinn.is).

Where to Stay
Hotel Geysir (www.geysircenter. com) at Geysir offers a range of options, from camping

accommodation to comfortable double rooms.

When to Go
The best time to visit is Jun–Aug, when daylight is almost perpetual. There are few tourist services at other times, although winter does allow the possibility of watching the aurora borealis, a natural light phenomenon that occurs in the northern polar regions.

Budget per Day for Two
Around £300 including restaurant meals, hotel accommodation and bus travel. Eating at cafés and staying in hostels, "sleeping-bag accommodation" or farmhouse accommodation will bring down the expenses.

Websites
www.icetourist.is
www.geographia.com/iceland

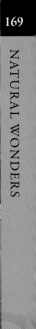

MAIN IMAGE Stream running between the rhyolite hills of remote
Landmannalaugar BELOW (left to right) Lava following an eruption
at Surtsey; Strokkur erupting in the Geysir area

4 MORE GEOTHERMAL SITES TO RIVAL YELLOWSTONE

SOL DE MAÑANA, BOLIVIA This geothermal field sits at an elevation of nearly 5,000 m (16,400 ft), in one of the wildest landscapes on earth. Nearby, you'll find vast salt flats, steaming volcanoes and colourful, flamingo-filled lagoons.

TONGARIRO NATIONAL PARK, NEW ZEALAND Head to this park if you're looking for superb hiking and extensive geothermal features. The popular Tongariro Crossing takes hikers through an amazing volcanic landscape. Nearby Rotorua offers a token geyser field.

KAMCHATKA PENINSULA, RUSSIA A visit to this wild and ragged hard-to-reach corner of the fiery Pacific Rim may well prove to be the trip of a lifetime. It is best accessed by organized tour *(see also p215)*.

BEPPU, JAPAN A popular Japanese resort on the island of Kyushu, Beppu is for those who appreciate tamed geysers and hot springs with a dose of carnival atmosphere.

CROATIA'S ISLANDS
VS THE GREEK ISLANDS

Combining breathtaking beauty and incredible diversity, Croatia's islands surpass those of Greece for unspoiled natural splendour – and they're also far more accessible

NEED TO KNOW

LOCATION The islands are situated in the central part of the Adriatic Sea just off Croatia's coast

POPULATION
4.5 million

NUMBER OF ISLANDS
1,085 but only 47 are inhabited

DAYTIME TEMPERATURES
Jan: 12°C (54°F); Apr: 17°C (63°F);
Jul: 29°C (84°F); Oct: 21°C (70°F)

SLOVENIA · Zagreb
CROATIA
CROATIA'S ISLANDS
BOSNIA & HERZEGOVINA
· Split
Adriatic Sea
· Dubrovnik

Forming a unique archipelago over 300 km (180 miles) long, Croatia's 1,000 or so islands and islets are spattered like paint along the length of the country's coastline. It's as though an artist has dipped a brush deep into greens and browns and flicked it at the cobalt-blue canvas of the Adriatic.

Unlike the Greek Islands, many of which are blighted by eyesore tourist resorts, Croatia's best and most unspoiled islands are easily accessible from the mainland without long and expensive ferry trips. The communities benefit from tourism, but at the same time continue to carry on with their traditional island life. Some of the highlights include beautiful Brac, with its magical, curving spit of golden sand, Zlatni Rat, which moves with the

tides; secret Solta's dense woods flavoured with mulberry, olives and rosemary; and Hvar, whose busy riviera nightclubs and restaurants are patronized by the beautiful, the rich and the tanned. But there's a whole lot more to Venetian-flavoured Hvar than cool nightlife. The island's interior, too, buzzes by day – from the hives tended by small farmhouses, the precious boxes loaded with delicious lavender-flower honey. And off the beaten track, you'll find perfect, deserted bays, inlets and even a quiet fishing village.

There's a vast choice of islands that you can visit, but don't miss Vis. Once the base for Allied forces during World War II, the craggy island with fabulous views, quaffable wine and unspoiled seas was closed to visitors until 1989 due to its status as a strategically important spot. It is dotted with clumps of pines and carob trees among a low scrub strewn with many varieties of herbs, cloaking the island in an invisible fragrant cloud. This magical perfume should be enough to convince you of the superiority of the Croatian Islands to the Greek. If not, a short boat ride to the Blue Cave, suffused with iridescent blue light at midday, a hike through Greek and Roman ruins, visits to sleepy fishing villages and dining in some of the country's best restaurants should clinch the deal.

Further south, towards Dubrovnik, get away from the mainland crowds on Mljet, a national park with karst caves, emerald-green saltwater lakes and the tiny Sveta Marija monastery on an island within an island. On this green island, ancient Aleppo pines and oaks ring with birdsong and provide shelter for mongooses, an exotic import brought from India to control the snake population and who were then reluctant to leave. The quieter eastern end of the island is perfect for exploring on foot or by bike and is home to some of Croatia's rare sandy beaches. If you can, stay overnight – you'll feel the same way as the mongooses.

ABOVE Zlatni Rat, the golden spit of sand, slicing the Adriatic at Brac

FORGET THE GREEK ISLANDS?

THE BUILD-UP There are approximately 1,400 Greek islands, of which only 227 are inhabited. They occupy a huge area of the Ionian and Aegean seas, stretching from Greece all the way to the coast of Turkey. Many are graced by fine, sandy beaches and sun through the year.

THE LETDOWN Several million tourists are brought each year by monster ferries, cheap flights and package holidays. Uncontrolled building legislation in the past means purpose-built resorts now litter the islands. Any authentic local economy or lifestyle has disappeared from most islands. Tourism is the only game in town, transforming the islands into theme parks.

GOING ANYWAY? Avoid the peak months of late-June, July and August. Don't choose an island with an airport – it makes getting there harder, but also means that the island will not have been developed for the tourist market. Instead, take a ferry from Piraeus, near Athens.

ABOVE Hordes of tourists soaking up the sun at a crowded beach in Malia, Crete

PRACTICAL INFORMATION

Getting There and Around
Split has an airport and is the best point of entry for the islands of Brac, Solta, Hvar and Vis. Mljet is most easily accessible from Dubrovnik, but it is also a good entry point for the other islands as well.

Where to Eat
Generally, the food available on the islands is simple fare such as baked or grilled fish, crab, lobster, octopus and grilled meat. However, Hvar and Vis islands have some select restaurants offering excellent food. One of the best places to dine on Vis is Jastozera (www.jastozera.com), a *konoba* (tavern) decorated with lobster pots and fishing paraphernalia. Lobster rules here.

Where to Stay
Hotel San Giorgio on Vis (www.hotelsangiorgiovis.com), or Hvar's luxury Riva Hotel (www.slh.com/rivahotel).

When to Go
As with all of Europe, it's best if you can avoid the peak summer months (Jul-Aug), when tourist and yacht traffic increases.

Budget per Day for Two
£250 should be enough if you stay in the smarter hotels and dine in quality restaurants. Otherwise, if you prefer the more standard accommodation and simple *konobas*, £150 should be sufficient.

Websites
www.croatia.hr
www.croatiafortravellers.co.uk

MAIN IMAGE Monastery and secluded beach at Bol on Brac island
BELOW (left to right) Couple inside the Blue Grotto Cave near Vis island; diners on the main square of Hvar

4 MORE ISLAND GROUPS TO RIVAL THE GREEK ISLANDS

AEOLIAN ISLANDS, ITALY These seven volcanic outcrops south of Sicily feature black-sand beaches, smoking craters and hot mud baths. Visit the smaller islands to avoid peak-season crowds. And there's the chance that Stromboli will blow its top.

STOCKHOLM ARCHIPELAGO, SWEDEN Just pick up an Island Hopper card and enjoy this pristine environment and extraordinary natural spectacle. The pace of life is slower on the islands, and involves cycling, hiking and kayaking.

AZORES, PORTUGAL Europe's most western outpost has nine islands with landscapes of rocky valleys studded with blue-green lakes and cloaked in lush vegetation. Famous for their wildlife, the islands are good for whale- and dolphin-watching.

FIJI, SOUTH PACIFIC Over 300 islands and islets form a paradise of palm-fringed beaches, idyllic lagoons and Robinson Crusoe landscapes. You can go scuba diving, windsurfing or kayaking – or just string up a hammock in the shade.

MAIN IMAGE Magnificent Iguaçu from above **BELOW (left to right)**
Jet boats heading to the foot of the mighty cascades; walkway guiding
visitors into the heart of the falls; brightly coloured toco toucan

IGUAÇU FALLS
VS NIAGARA FALLS

With an amazing 275 cascades in an unspoilt tropical rainforest setting, Iguaçu Falls is a breathtaking alternative to its famous North American rival, Niagara

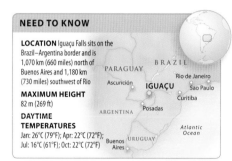

"**Poor Niagara!**" exclaimed Lady Eleanor Roosevelt on first seeing Iguaçu Falls, and few subsequent visitors to one of South America's most stunning natural marvels have found any reason to disagree with her. Niagara is impressive, but Iguaçu is unforgettable. Widely considered to be the planet's finest set of waterfalls, Iguaçu comprises a complex system of no less than 275 cascades spanning a 3-km (2-mile) stretch of the Iguaçu river, on the border between Brazil and Argentina. While Niagara reaches a modest height of 53 m (174 ft), many of Iguaçu's falls exceed 60 m (197 ft), with the highest cascade of all standing at a lofty 82 m (269 ft). And the sheer volume of water tumbling over the precipice at Iguaçu is usually about three times that of its North American rival.

But it's not just the size of the cataracts at Iguaçu that is compelling. The sheer number of cascades means that a trip to the falls offers constantly varying vistas and dramatic perspectives on the great torrents of water. Nowhere is this more apparent than around the celebrated Garganta del Diablo, a staggering U-shaped formation measuring 700 m (765 yards) long and 150 m (492 ft) wide. Standing beside this monumental cascade, the spectator is surrounded by roaring cataracts throwing plumes of spray up to almost twice the height of the waterfall, while boat trips to the lovely Isla San Martín, in the middle of the river, offer more majestic views.

The experience of the falls is immeasurably enhanced by the tropical rainforest that envelops

ABOVE Ring-tailed coatis balancing on branches in the rainforest surrounding Iguaçu Falls

them. The UNESCO World Heritage Sites of Parque Nacional Iguazú in Argentina and Parque Nacional do Iguaçu in Brazil provide refuge for a wealth of fauna, from woodpeckers, toucans and caciques to capuchin monkeys and coatis, as well as more than 2,000 species of flora – it's all a far cry from the high-rise hotels and casinos of Niagara.

FORGET NIAGARA?

THE BUILD-UP Ask someone to name a famous waterfall and nine times out of ten the answer will be Niagara. As one of America's most celebrated natural wonders, Niagara has lodged firmly in the popular imagination. People have dived into the falls, ridden over them in barrels and walked tightropes across them, and they have appeared in countless television programmes and Hollywood films. Each year the falls attract astonishing numbers of tourists.

THE LETDOWN Niagara might be spectacular, but it is far from being the world's largest – or most memorable – waterfall. Although the falls are impressively wide, there are at least a dozen broader and more powerful cataracts elsewhere in America and Africa. What's more, for those looking to commune with nature, Niagara is not the place to be. The recent rash of development has created such huge changes to the flow of air that many of the viewing areas are now obscured by mist.

GOING ANYWAY? Although you can't escape the crowds at Niagara, you are at least guaranteed spectacular views by taking the famous "Maid of the Mist" boat trip to the base of the falls, which brings you as close to the cataracts as it's possible to get, short of actually diving over them. Just don't forget to bring your waterproof.

ABOVE Hordes of tourists packed onto a viewing deck at the Horseshoe Falls, Niagara

NATURAL WONDERS

Glorious Angel Falls cutting through the forested mountainside, Canaima National Park, Venezuela

Visitors watching the torrential Dettifoss Falls as it crashes over the canyon side, Jökulsárgljúfur National Park, Iceland

ANGEL FALLS

NEED TO KNOW

LOCATION Angel Falls is 725 km (450 miles) southeast of the Venezuelan capital, Caracas, in Canaima National Park

MAXIMUM HEIGHT 979 m (3,212 ft)

DAYTIME TEMPERATURES Jan: 27°C (81°F); Apr: 29°C (84°F); Jul: 27°C (81°F); Oct: 28°C (83°F)

Tumbling in a single, delicate cascade that is almost a kilometre (half-a-mile) from top to bottom, Angel Falls is far and away the world's tallest waterfall, and a staggering 15 times the height of Niagara. It is so high, in fact, that much of the water turns to mist before reaching the bottom. It's not just the waterfall's size that is impressive, but the setting, too. The water plunges over the edge of a majestic, sheer-sided table mountain, known as Auyan-tepui (meaning "Devil's Mountain"), which rises up out of the lush Venezuelan jungle. Here you'll find giant anteaters, porcupines, three-toed sloths, jaguars, tapirs and poison arrow frogs.

Practical Information

Getting There Visitors must fly from Caracas or Ciudad Bolívar to the village of Canaima, which is 50 km (30 miles) from the falls. There's no road access from here to the falls: you can get to them either on a canoe trip (although this is only possible from June to November or December) or on a 40-minute flight for an aerial view.

When to Go Visit at the end of the rainy season in early December, when skies are clear and the falls are at their most spectacular.

Website www.salto-angel.com

The four cascades that make up Jog Falls, Karnataka State, India

JOG FALLS

NEED TO KNOW

LOCATION Jog Falls is located in Karnataka State, southern India, about 330 km (205 miles) northwest of Bangalore

MAXIMUM HEIGHT 253 m (830 ft)

DAYTIME TEMPERATURES Jan: 26°C (79°F); Apr: 29°C (84°F); Jul: 27°C (81°F); Oct: 28°C (83°F)

The grandest waterfall in Asia is hidden away in a remote forest setting among the craggy hills of the Western Ghats. Here, the Sharavati river tumbles over an impressively high and wide precipice in four cascades – the Raja (king), Rani (queen), rocket and roarer. Although a large hydroelectric power station upriver has reduced the volume of water in the river, the falls remain a dramatic sight, especially during, and immediately after, the monsoon season. The unspoilt surrounding landscape is memorable at any time of year.

Practical Information

Getting There The easiest route to the falls is to fly to Mumbai and catch the Konkan Railway (or a bus) south along the coast towards Mangalore, alighting at Honavar, from where it's a 2½-hour bus ride. The journey from Bangalore is much more complicated.

When to Go Visit the falls any time from October to January, just after the monsoons when there's plenty of water in the river.

Website www.tourism-of-india.com/karnataka-tour/jog-falls-tour.html

DETTIFOSS FALLS

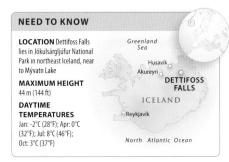

NEED TO KNOW

LOCATION Dettifoss Falls lies in Jökulsárgljúfur National Park in northeast Iceland, near to Mývatn Lake

MAXIMUM HEIGHT 44 m (144 ft)

DAYTIME TEMPERATURES Jan: -2°C (28°F); Apr: 0°C (32°F); Jul: 8°C (46°F); Oct: 3°C (37°F)

Situated in a remote area of northeast Iceland, almost 320 km (200 miles) from Reykjavík, Dettifoss Falls is nature at its wildest and most elemental. A great sheet of foaming water plummets dramatically into an enormous canyon, surrounded by a volcanic landscape of bleak basalt plains, where eruptions continued until as recently as 1984. This majestic waterfall sits on the Jökulsá á Fjöllum river, which is fed by water from Iceland's largest glacier, the Vatnajökull icefield, and boasts a staggering average flow of 200 cubic m (7,060 cubic ft) per second, making it the most powerful river in Europe.

Practical Information

Getting There Fly to Reykjavík, then take a bus or internal flight to Akureyri (there are also occasional direct international flights to Akureyri). Travel by bus or car from here to Mývatn, and then on to Dettifoss by car.

When to Go Visit between May and August. Temperatures can be bone-crunchingly cold during the rest of the year.

Website www.icelandvisitor.com

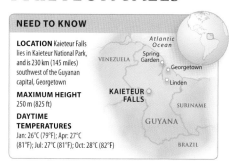

The thundering cascades of Kaieteur Falls shrouded in spray, Kaieteur National Park, Guyana

Dramatic Yosemite Falls plunging down the cliffs in Yosemite National Park, California, USA

Slender Tugela Falls gracefully bisecting the mountainside, Royal Natal National Park, South Africa

YOSEMITE FALLS

NEED TO KNOW

LOCATION Yosemite Falls is found in Yosemite National Park in California, USA

MAXIMUM HEIGHT 739 m (2,425 ft)

DAYTIME TEMPERATURES Jan: 3°C (37°F); Apr: 10°C (50°F); Jul: 24°C (75°F); Oct: 13°C (55°F)

The tallest waterfall in North America – and the seventh highest in the world – Yosemite Falls is one of the star attractions of the world-famous Yosemite Valley in the Sierra Nevada mountains of California. The falls plunge in three separate stages over a series of grey limestone cliffs. There's the spectacular 425-m (1,394-ft) Upper Falls, then the so-called "cascades" (a series of smaller drops), and finally the 97-m (318-ft) Lower Falls. Although it's not exactly undiscovered, of course (Yosemite is one of the world's most famous – and most popular – national parks), heading up the steep path to the Upper Falls is a great way of escaping the worst of the crowds, and there are superb views en route.

Practical Information

Getting There Fly into San Francisco and then either hire a car or take a bus to the park. The top of the Upper Falls can be reached by a 6-km (3.5-mile) trail.

When to Go Visit in April and May, when the falls are at their finest, the weather not too cold, and the crowds not too oppressive.

Website www.nps.gov/yose

KAIETEUR FALLS

NEED TO KNOW

LOCATION Kaieteur Falls lies in Kaieteur National Park, and is 230 km (145 miles) southwest of the Guyanan capital, Georgetown

MAXIMUM HEIGHT 250 m (825 ft)

DAYTIME TEMPERATURES Jan: 26°C (79°F); Apr: 27°C (81°F); Jul: 27°C (81°F); Oct: 28°C (82°F)

Kaieteur Falls is buried deep in the dense tropical jungles of central Guyana and, like Iguaçu, is memorable for its stupendous scale. The falls are five times higher than those at Niagara, and spew out water at a prodigious average rate of 663 cubic m (23,414 cubic ft) per second, making Kaieteur, statistically, one of the world's most powerful cascades and, visually, one of its most dramatic. The setting is unforgettable too – the waterfall lies in one of the continent's largest tracts of undisturbed rainforest. And despite being Guyana's leading tourist attraction, it still only attracts around 40,000 visitors a year – far fewer than Iguaçu, let alone Niagara.

Practical Information

Getting There There is no road access to the falls. They are best visited either by plane on a day trip from Georgetown, which is an hour's flight away, or on foot via a spectacular wilderness trek that takes between three and five days to complete.

When to Go Visit in January, June or July, during either of the country's two rainy seasons, when the falls are at their most powerful.

Website www.kaieteurpark.gov.gy

TUGELA FALLS

NEED TO KNOW

LOCATION Tugela Falls is found in Royal Natal National Park, in the KwaZulu-Natal Province of South Africa

MAXIMUM HEIGHT 947 m (3,107 ft)

DAYTIME TEMPERATURES Jan: 23°C (73°F); Apr: 16°C (61°F); Jul: 9°C (48°F); Oct: 18°C (64°F)

The highest falls in Africa and the second highest in the world (outdone only by Venezuela's Angel Falls), Tugela plunges in a single fine cascade from the topmost escarpment of the awesome Drakensberg Mountains. Surrounded by a great bowl of rocky red cliff faces known as the Amphitheatre, the falls boast one of the most memorable locations on the planet. Tugela can be seen from the road, but there are also two trails that lead right to the cascades. The first of these is the spectacular Mont-aux-Sources path, which climbs to the very top of the falls and the Drakensberg escarpment, while the second, less-strenuous trail heads to the base of the falls.

Practical Information

Getting There The best way to access Tugela Falls is to fly to Johannesburg and then drive to Royal Natal National Park.

When to Go Visit in the cool, dry months (Jun–Sep). Water volumes aren't part of the appeal of these falls, so it makes sense to avoid the wet season.

Website www.drakensberg-tourism.com/tugela-falls.html

MINDO-NAMBILLO CLOUD FOREST
VS COSTA RICAN RAINFORESTS

The Costa Rican rainforests, now largely co-opted by foreign tour operators, have less-than-pristine environments. Ecuador's Mindo-Nambillo cloud forest is the real thing

NEED TO KNOW

LOCATION The Mindo-Nambillo Cloud Forest is about 40 km (24 miles) northwest of Ecuador's capital, Quito

VISITORS PER YEAR Around 12,000

DAYTIME TEMPERATURES Jan: 25°C (77°F); Apr: 26°C (79°F); Jul: 28°C (82°F); Oct: 27°C (80°F)

MINDO-NAMBILLO CLOUD FOREST

Santa Marta • Quito
• Portoviejo
ECUADOR
• Guayaquil
Pacific Ocean
PERU
Loja •

Tucked away in the sloping hills northwest of Quito, and no more than a 90-minute drive from the capital, lies the extraordinary Mindo-Nambillo Cloud Forest or, to use its official title, the Bosque Protector Mindo-Nambillo. It's one of those places that will leave you doubly astonished – by its beauty and by the fact that it isn't more widely known, although that's changing fast. Covering nearly 20,000 hectares (49,000 acres), the reserve

ABOVE A visitor on a log bridge in the Mindo-Nambillo forest reserve

has a spectacular wealth of native-environment flora, including some of the world's rarest orchids, as well as fauna, especially tropical butterflies and birds – many of which were once thought to be extinct but actually manage to survive here.

The cloud forest is a truly magical place, filled with the sights and sounds of an ecosystem that still flourishes in this corner of Ecuador, free from 21st-century cares. In fact, to say that Mindo-Nambillo is a rejuvenating place is a huge understatement. For years a well-kept secret, or a largely ignored paradise, depending on who you ask, Mindo-Nambillo has come into its own only since 1982 and now falls under the protection of the Ecuadorean government. Unlike rainforests in Costa Rica and elsewhere, there are stringent regulations regarding who gets in and the purpose for the visit. You won't find tour guides hawking their services, nor five-star luxury hotels that undermine the forest's ecology. What you will find are increasingly rare flora and more than 500 species of birds in a pristine, natural environment. For those interested in outdoor activities, there are trails for walking and bird-watching, and if you're scrupulously careful, you may even be able to go rafting or rappel the beautiful La Isla Waterfalls.

The government wisely established a buffer zone within the park, the first of its kind in South America, where visitors can lodge or camp and stock up on supplies. Guides are allowed to set up shop only if they pass extensive tests.

Mindo-Nambillo also takes its commitment to family education seriously, so if you have the kids along, there's plenty for all to do and see, as much of the reserve is accessible to children.

FORGET THE COSTA RICAN RAINFORESTS?

THE BUILD-UP For years the rainforests of Costa Rica have been the destination of choice for travellers wishing to see and interact with Mother Nature on her own terms. Tall trees soar higher than the eye can see, tropical birds flit about with bright plumage and the sights and sounds of a pristine ecosystem are everywhere.

THE LETDOWN And so it was...but not so much anymore. What used to be a nearly intact rainforest has been splintered and chopped into small parcels throughout the country, many with little or no regulation. Now approaching the level of a mass tourism destination, these forests are crowded with vendors selling everything from Spanish-language instruction books to mass-produced souvenirs.

GOING ANYWAY? Rather than book an organized tour, visit one of the national parks and enlist the services of one of the certified guides there. It will be significantly cheaper, and you'll have less competition from other tourists.

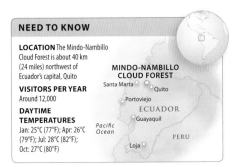

ABOVE Small shops and vendors lining First Beach at Manuel Antonio National Park, Costa Rica

PRACTICAL INFORMATION

Getting There and Around
Getting to Mindo-Nambillo couldn't be easier. It's less than a 2-hour drive over paved roads from Quito. There's a lot to do in the area, so hiring a car is recommended.

Where to Eat
On the way to the cloud forest, take the road to Calacalí and stop off at Pululahua to try El Cráter (www.elcrater.com), on the outskirts of town. It has excellent food and outstanding views of a volcanic crater and the surrounding landscape.

Where to Stay
In Mindo itself, the comfortable Mindo Garden (www.mindogardens.com) – situated in what may be the region's

prettiest setting – has excellent cabins and plenty of bird-watching opportunities of its own.

When to Go
June through September is the most pleasant period to visit. Avoid the rainy season from October to May. It is better to visit on weekdays as there are fewer tourists; weekends can be very busy with families.

Budget per Day for Two
Roughly £65 should do nicely, especially considering the lack of vendors and touts. Bring a bit more money if you plan to stay the night in Mindo.

Website
www.getquitoecuador.com/quito-natural-attractions/mindo_cloudforest.html

MAIN IMAGE Guarumos Waterfall, Mindo-Nambillo Cloud Forest
BELOW (left to right) Butterfly species, *Heliconius erato;*
birders in a forest hide; an Andean Emerald hummingbird

Bushwalkers admiring a cascading waterfall in the heart of the Blue Mountains, Australia

BLUE MOUNTAINS

NEED TO KNOW

LOCATION The Blue Mountains in New South Wales, Australia, are approximately 50 km (30 miles) northwest of Sydney

VISITORS PER YEAR
About 155,000

DAYTIME TEMPERATURES
Jan: 23°C (73°F); Apr: 16°C (61°F); Jul: 10°C (50°F); Oct: 17°C (63°F)

Australia's Blue Mountains range, set in arguably the continent's most beautiful region, defies classification. Comprising seven national parks and a UNESCO World Heritage Site, this remarkable area is a mix of everything Australia has to offer. The mountain ranges, referred to as Upper and Lower, are home to Australia's only temperate rainforest and a wealth of flora, including dozens of species found nowhere else in the continent. With numerous walking trails and out-of-the-way reserves just begging to be explored, there is something for everyone, served up against the backdrop of the Blue Mountains.

Practical Information

Getting There and Around The Blue Mountains are easily reached from Sydney by rental car, train or private bus.

When to Go The Australian winter, which occurs between Jun–Aug, is quite chilly. Dec–Feb is warmer and a better time to visit, though sees more visitors as a consequence.

Website www.bluemts.com.au

The thick canopy of lush green trees in a rainforest in the Cayo District of Belize

RAINFORESTS OF BELIZE

NEED TO KNOW

LOCATION Almost half of Belize is covered by rainforests; you're never more than an hour's drive by 4WD from one

VISITORS PER YEAR
More than 100,000

DAYTIME TEMPERATURES
Jan: 24°C (75°F); Apr: 27°C (80°F); Jul: 28°C (82°F); Oct: 26°C (79°F)

Costa Rica isn't the only country in Central America to lay claim to pristine rainforests. Its neighbour to the north, Belize, also boasts some of the continent's most marvellous expanses of these rapidly dwindling forests. An astonishing 65 per cent of the country's old-growth forests still remain and roughly half of the country is covered by rainforests. Long a proponent of sustainable tourism with an ecological twist, Belize has more protected land per square mile than any other Latin American nation. At the same time, the government has gone to great lengths to keep these forests free from urban development and has focused on their preservation. Around 44 per cent of Belize's forests are protected within national parks.

Of the many rainforests here, Cockscomb Basin, Crooked Tree, Western, Macal River Valley, Cayo and the Bladen Nature Reserve are particularly outstanding. All of them feature crystalline rivers coursing through blue-green valleys and hillsides, surrounded by untouched stands of tropical trees and myriad flora and fauna of every description. Birders from all over the world flock to the Belize rainforests, where more than 600 species of birds have been identified. If this wasn't enough to lure you, many of these forests are also home to magnificent Mayan ruins, while others border gorgeous, remote cays and inlets running along the country's coast.

The Belize rainforests for the most part are easily accessible and have a great infrastructure, as well as top-notch guides. So, whether you decide to stay a day, week, month or more, you're never far from what you need to be comfortable. For the many visitors who prefer to rough it a bit, there are campsites and tree lodges in most areas. Some of the private rainforests – yes, Belize has them as well, generally 200 hectares (490 acres) or less in size – even offer luxury accommodation carefully engineered to fit into

ABOVE A view of the main temple at Altun Ha, a Mayan ruin in the rainforest of Belize

the surroundings. But the one thing that most characterizes all of these Belize ecological jewels is the governmental commitment to ensure that these forests are maintained in their natural state – and it shows.

Practical Information

Getting There and Around Using Belize city as a base, it is easiest to reach the rainforests in a rented 4WD. Some can be accessed by boat.

When to Go The best time to visit is between Apr and Jun, although March is also an excellent month. Visitors wanting to spend time in the coastal regions arrive as early as December.

Website www.travelbelize.org

A **golden lion tamarin** on a tree in the Poço das Antas Reserve, Mata Atlântica, Brazil

MATA ATLÂNTICA

NEED TO KNOW

LOCATION The Mata Atlântica lies along Brazil's eastern coast, and extends inland as far as Paraguay and Argentina

VISITORS PER YEAR Fewer than 10,000

DAYTIME TEMPERATURES
Jan: 21°C (70°F); Apr: 19°C (66°F); Jul: 16°C (61°F); Oct: 23°C (73°F)

Taken as a whole, Brazil's once-gigantic Mata Atlântica (or Atlantic Forest) formerly represented the world's largest tree-covered region. This UN-mandated World Biosphere Reserve holds within more than 40 per cent of the world's known tree species. It also boasts thousands upon thousands of different kinds of flowers, plants and, of course, wildlife, many of them found nowhere else in the world. However, the deforestation of much of the country and unregulated development have put this forest – now estimated to be only a tenth of its original size – at great risk. Fortunately, reforestation efforts are underway and an increasing number of ecologically minded tourists are coming to see Mata Atlântica's great mangrove stands.

Practical Information

Getting There and Around Most travellers drive to the Mata Atlântica, located along eastern Brazil from Rio de Janeiro or São Paulo. Alternatively, visitors fly in from Manaus.

When to Go Nov–Mar is the best time to visit, as the days are generally warm and sunny (although it can rain in the western and southern forests).

Website www.biodiversityhotspots.org/xp/Hotspots/atlantic_forest

Longboats and tourists visit Clearwater Cave, Mulu National Park, in the state of Sarawak, Malaysia

BORNEO JUNGLE

NEED TO KNOW

LOCATION Almost the entire island of Borneo is covered by first-generation rainforests, all accessible from coastal settlements

VISITORS PER YEAR Fewer than 10,000

DAYTIME TEMPERATURES
Jan: 26°C (79°F); Apr: 28°C (82°F); Jul: 27°C (80°F); Oct: 27°C (80°F)

The island of Borneo is shared by three countries – Brunei, Indonesia and Malaysia – and has to rank as one of the most out-of-the-way places on earth. This is a truly exotic travel destination – expensive, hot, humid and primitive to the extreme. Yet for the adventurous, it can be a paradise. The rainforests here are still amongst the least explored anywhere, and some of the most biodiverse on the planet. And, despite suffering greatly from deforestation in the 1980s and 1990s, Borneo will still reward you like no other spot on earth.

Practical Information

Getting There and Around Borneo is about as remote as it gets, so you will most likely be met by your guide in Brunei or in one of Malaysia's coastal cities.

When to Go The weather is hot and humid throughout the year, but the best time to visit the rainforests is between March and October when there is less rain.

Website www.visitborneo.com

44 MORE BREATHTAKING NATURAL WONDERS

Aerial view of the dazzling sapphire lakes at Jiuzhai Gou, China

JIUZHAI GOU LAKES, SICHUAN PROVINCE, CHINA The lush mountainous area of Jiuzhai Gou is an earthly paradise known for its 90-plus crystal-clear lakes that sparkle with greens and blues ranging from sapphire to jade, and for its generously gushing waterfalls. Divided into three main valleys, the reserve is home to diverse vegetation, including bamboo forests that sustain the endangered giant panda population. Autumn is a good time to visit, when the leaves burn fiery shades of yellow, gold and red. The area is not easy to reach – it is 10 hours by road from Chengdu, the nearest big town.

AGGTELEK CAVES, HUNGARY These vast underground caves protect record-sized stalactites and stalagmites, as well as snails, beetles, worms and crabs. Just three of the hundreds of caves are open to the public, and the longest runs for 21 km (13 miles) into nearby Slovenia.

ARCHES NATIONAL PARK, UTAH, USA One of nature's seemingly random acts was to erode the rich sandstone of the high desert in Utah into arches – around 2,000 of them. You may want a guide in this dramatic landscape, where temperatures can fluctuate alarmingly in 24 hours.

BAKO NATIONAL PARK, SARAWAK, MALAYSIA Bearded pigs, mouse deer, flying lemurs, long-nosed monkeys and hairy-nosed otters are just some of the fabulous animals you're likely to spot on the jungle trails of Bako, the jewel of Borneo's national parks.

BEARA PENINSULA, IRELAND In the far southwest of Ireland, this toe of land dipping into the Atlantic is as wild and wonderful as the country gets. The great rocky peninsula, between Kenmare and Bantry bays, offers some spectacular scenery and wonderful walking country.

BLUE LAGOON, ICELAND This must be the ultimate bathing experience – and it could do you good, too. A steaming blue pool at a cosy 40°C (105°F), this surreal open-air bath, located 39 km (24 miles) from Reykjavík, is warm enough to swim in at any time of year. As clean as it is clear, the salt water is run-off from the neighbouring power station, which pumps it up from 1.5 km (1 mile) below the ground, where it is piping hot, harnesses its heat and then releases it into the lagoon, where it gradually cools. The water is said to be good for your skin, and health and beauty treatments are on hand.

BUCKSKIN GULCH, UTAH, USA Slot canyons are characterized by their narrow openings and great depth, and nowhere in the world are they as deep – or as long – as at Buckskin Gulch. The sunless depths of this 25-km (15-mile) canyon can be walked, although some people like to go canyoning too. The gulch is a tributary of the Paria River, which flows into the Colorado River.

VALLE DE LA LUNA, CHILE Upon arrival in the Atacama Desert's Valle de la Luna, you would be forgiven for thinking you had landed on the moon. Cavernous valleys and steep ridges sculpted entirely by nature cover a spectrum of changing hues. For somewhere so uninhabitable, there's a surprising amount to do, from trekking to sand-boarding, and a visit at sunset rewards you with breathtaking views.

COLCA CANYON, PERU Standing on the edge of this mighty canyon, which is twice as deep as the Grand Canyon, you'll see magnificent condors catching thermals that rise from the valley floor. Ancient terraces on the canyon's sloping sides maintain communities that farmed here before the Incas arrived. A good way to explore this magical place is on a white-water rafting trip of the Río Colca.

CURONIAN SPIT, LITHUANIA Europe's largest beach stretches for nearly 100 km (62 miles) along the Baltic Sea, and has the highest dunes in the northern hemisphere. If you visit on a sunny day, you may well think you have arrived in the middle of an Arabian desert. The sand bar encloses an enormous lagoon and has a fragile ecosystem, so obey the local rules to avoid causing erosion.

KAA-IYA DEL GRAN CHACO NATIONAL PARK, BOLIVIA This tropical forest gets so little rain that many of its animals have adapted so that they can go for days without water: deer and tapirs get their liquid from cacti, while big cats rely on fluids from their prey. The forest is also thought to be home to around 1,000 jaguars – the largest number in any protected area in the world.

FISH RIVER CANYON, NAMIBIA This magnificent canyon, one of the largest in the world, was created by the wear and tear of the river and the collapse of the valley bottom through a shift in the earth's crust. The best way to get to know it is on a five-day hiking trail, but you must come prepared, as there are no facilities. Try to visit in winter (May–Sep), when the river is less torrential than in the summer months.

ABOVE Glacier National Park combines rugged mountain beauty with verdant rolling meadows
RIGHT One of the four coral islands in the unspoilt Aldabra Atoll, Seychelles

GLACIER NATIONAL PARK, MONTANA, USA The beautiful mountainous landscape of Glacier National Park, which runs right up to the Canadian border, was formed thousands of years ago by dramatic glacial action. Its diverse terrain – which includes alpine forests, meadows, tundras and lakes – is still roamed by grizzly bears and wolves. You have to have a good idea of what you want to do before visiting, because there is so much on offer, from boating and fishing to horse-riding and cross-country skiing, not to mention the hundreds of miles of hiking trails. After a day in the clean mountain air you will sleep like a log.

ALDABRA ATOLL, SEYCHELLES Four idyllic coral islands encircling an enormous shallow lagoon make up this atoll, where humans have, by and large, kept away. Out of the way of shipping lanes and with no fresh water, this UNESCO World Heritage Site is one of the most remote and harsh environments on the planet. Despite this, the Indian Ocean's last flightless bird, the Aldabra rail, unlike the doomed dodo, has managed to survive here. Just as content are tens of thousands of turtles, while sharks, barracudas and countless manta rays bask in the beautifully clear turquoise waters.

LAKE BAIKAL, SIBERIA, RUSSIA Despite repeated attempts, nobody has ever got to the bottom of the world's deepest – and largest – freshwater lake. A spectacle all year round, the lake is frozen in winter and satin-smooth in summer, while autumn brings waves of oceanic proportions.

GLOW-WORM DISPLAYS, WAITOMO CAVES, NEW ZEALAND On the North Island of New Zealand, 3 hours' drive from Auckland, you'll find the labyrinthine limestone caves of Waitomo, which drip with the silken, sticky threads of the larvae of fungus gnats, otherwise known as glow-worms. Each worm hangs up to 70 glowing threads, 30–40 cm (12–16 in) long, from its ceiling nest to attract and trap midges, flies and moths. It's a magical display that resembles the Milky Way in microcosm. Tours include rides on rubber rafts through the underground waterways, black-water rafting trips and cave abseiling.

SAN JUAN ISLANDS, WASHINGTON STATE, USA Visitors boarding a ferry at Anacortes on the Washington mainland and gliding into the glorious San Juan archipelago for the first time might well feel that they are entering an enchanted land. Here, in a maze of inlets and channels, more than 450 islands – 172 of them named – emerge from the bright blue waters of the northern Puget Sound. Hills carpeted in old-growth Douglas fir rise from the shores, while the soaring snow-capped peaks of the spectacular Olympic Peninsula tower in the distance. It's an awesome scene. If so much natural beauty is too hard to take in at once, indulge in some whale-watching – either from a kayak or the Lime Kiln Point State Park on San Juan Island, where you might well catch a glimpse of the resident population of orca whales as they feed.

GORGES DU VERDON, PROVENCE, FRANCE One of the most picturesque spots in Europe, this canyon is not too daunting to explore. It is a wonderful spot for walking, and kayaking and white-water rafting are popular in the dazzling turquoise waters that seem to give the whole landscape its luminous, optimistic air. The limestone canyon walls also make this a centre for climbing.

FINGAL'S CAVE, ISLE OF STAFFA, UK On the ferry from Mull in Scotland to the Isle of Staffa, the chances are you will be serenaded by Mendelssohn's *Fingal's Cave Overture* over the boat's loudspeaker system. And when you reach the giant opening in the basalt rock that rises out of the sea like a huge stick of broccoli, you will see why the German composer was inspired to write his stirring piece.

KODACHROME BASIN STATE PARK, UTAH, USA It's no wonder this state park was named after America's most famous colour film – Kodak's Kodachrome – known for capturing "hot" colours well. The bright hues of the rocks are truly outstanding, especially on the "sand pipes" – chimneys of rock thought to be the sediment of extinct geysers that remained after the surrounding land eroded.

GOCTA FALLS, PERU These fabulous falls in Peru's Northern Highlands drop an astounding 770 m (2,530 ft) in two tiers. They were only "discovered" a few years ago, and until planned access roads are completed, you'll need to complete a 5-hour trek through dense jungle to reach them. But that trip itself, radiant with colourful birds and chattering monkeys, is worth the effort.

ERG CHEBBI, SAHARA, MOROCCO This is the desert at its most beautiful, but the footprints you leave here won't last long. An erg is a strange phenomenon – it's a mountain range of sand that drifts at the will of the wind. Watch the blazing sun cast weird and wonderful shapes and shadows over the pristine surfaces of the dunes, with their fluid, sensual curves and ripples created by the wind.

ABOVE Lighthouse in the azure, reef-speckled water off the southern coast of Grande Terre, New Caledonia
RIGHT Wattled jaçana walking across a Victoria water lily in a pond near Porto Jofre, northern Pantanal

NEW CALEDONIA BARRIER REEF, MELANESIA Second in length only to Australia's Great Barrier Reef, this coral formation in the southwest Pacific runs for nearly 1,600 km (1,000 miles) through the islands of New Caledonia, encircling a vast lagoon. Species found here are so diverse that many are still being discovered, though 1,000 kinds of fish are known. Turtles love the reef, as do dugongs – clumsy-looking marine mammals that can grow to the size of a cow. Dive in and see coral, sponges, molluscs and tropical fish; stay above water and glimpse many exotic birds, including the red-footed booby.

PANTANAL, BRAZIL The largest wetlands in the world don't sound particularly appealing. But this vast and incredibly fertile region of central-west Brazil has some of the most exciting – and easily seen – creatures in the world. The wet season runs from November to April, when it rains for several hours every afternoon and the aquatic flora rejoices; in the dry season, which runs from May to October, a huge variety of birds congregate here. Capybaras, giant otters and marsh deer are among the animals to be seen all year round. Stay on a local cattle farm and explore the region by boat or on horseback.

MONUMENT VALLEY, UTAH, USA Heading down dead-straight Highway 161 towards the backdrop of Monument Valley's broken crags, you might well get the feeling that you have been this way before. And in films, you have – this classic Western scene of unremitting desert scattered with the great, lonely fists of red rock known as "Mittens" has seen many a cowboy and stagecoach ride by. You can hire a horse or take a tour to reach those places that are off-limits to those on foot. For an authentic touch, consider staying in a hogan – a traditional home of the Native American Navajo people.

MANDAI ORCHID GARDEN, SINGAPORE Of all the world's cultivated flowers, none is so exotic as the orchid. And one of the best places to see it in all its exquisite glory is at Mandai's Vintage Garden in Singapore. This hillside plot has some 200 varieties of the flower in many fabulous shapes and colours, as well as a water garden and herb and spice enclosure.

RIO GRANDE GORGE, NEW MEXICO, USA Take in the view of this void from the Rio Grande Gorge Bridge on Highway 64, a piece of engineering to match the drama of the canyon itself. Way below is a river that promises white-water rafting *par excellence*. Underground volcanic activity still shows up in hot springs along the valley, and petroglyphs reveal human activity from centuries past.

SAMARIA GORGE, CRETE, GREECE A walk through this deep fissure of rock, running for 17 km (11 miles) from Omalos to Aghia Roumeli on the south coast of Crete, is not for the unfit. Once in the gorge, there's no turning back. It's a Dantean landscape of sheer rock rising towards the sun, which in high summer shines without mercy. Towards the end, the rock walls are 500 m (1,640 ft) high.

WADI EL-HITAN (VALLEY OF THE WHALES), EGYPT There was a time when whales wandered the earth. Well, an early type of whale – a four-legged creature called an archaeoceti. It's a scary, unlikely thought, but here the evidence is brought to light: the skeletons of land-whales on the point of losing their hind legs. This is the greatest concentration of prehistoric animal bones ever found.

PLAYA OSTIONAL, COSTA RICA One of nature's miraculous events is the arrival of thousands of turtles on this beach every few weeks from July to November. These amphibians lumber out of the surf to lay their eggs in such numbers that the beach can look like a rocky shore. A conservation deal with the locals allows them to collect eggs from the first batches, as long as they protect the later ones.

NORTHERN LIGHTS, GREENLAND Much mystery still surrounds the aurora borealis; scientists do not know, for example, why the geomagnetic storms behind the phenomenon are strongest during the equinoxes. But you don't have to understand the science to appreciate the most spectacular show on earth. Head to Greenland instead of the more touristy viewing spots in Alaska and Norway.

LUNAR RAINBOWS, VICTORIA FALLS, ZAMBIA/ZIMBABWE Victoria Falls is a spectacular sight at any time, not least because its spray, like rain, creates a rainbow when the sun is out. At night, this rainbow usually vanishes, except when there is a full moon and a clear sky, and when the Zambezi river is at its most thunderous (Jan–Jul). The combination of moon and rainbow is a very romantic one.

SEMENGGOH NATURE RESERVE, SARAWAK, MALAYSIA This is your chance to come face to face with the king of the swingers, the orang-utan. Many survive in the jungle here because of the successful work of the reserve's rehabilitation centre, where you can see these funny, intelligent primates. They spend most of their time foraging, but appear twice a day at feeding time.

ABOVE Two ring-tailed lemurs crossing a large rock in the late afternoon, Madagascar
LEFT Steller's sea eagles and white-tailed eagles on ice in the Nemuro Channel, Shiretoko Peninsula, Japan

SHIRETOKO PENINSULA, JAPAN In the far northeast of Hokkaido, Japan's most northerly island, lies a rugged finger of land jutting 65 km (40 miles) into the Sea of Okhotsk. Surprisingly, this peninsula, which is on about the same latitude as US state of Oregon or the French Riviera, freezes over in winter, and the snow remains in its shaded valleys until summer. A string of volcanoes – one of which, Iouyama, remains active – runs across this wild landscape, where bears live in ancient woodlands, eagles scour clear skies and sea lions bark on lonely shores. Shiretoko ("the end of the earth") is Japan's last wilderness.

PHOSPHORESCENT BAY, PUERTO RICO Anybody who has had a midnight swim in the sea on a moonlit night will know the excitement of seeing small phosphorescent bubbles spinning through their fingers. But that is nothing compared to snorkelling in Phosphorescent Bay, where microscopic organisms called dinoflagellates sparkle at the slightest disturbance. Even if you don't fancy diving in, you can easily see the effects. Just watch the wake of a boat or paddle your hand in the water, and you'll see twinkling. The best time to go is when there is a full moon or, most prettily, during a light rain.

TEIDE NATIONAL PARK, TENERIFE Spain's tallest mountain, which rises spectacularly from the island of Tenerife, is surrounded by the lava fields of the collapsed cone of an earlier volcano. It is a strangely exhilarating place, popular for fashion shoots and films about prehistoric monsters, including *Planet of the Apes* (1968). Snowcapped for much of the year, the peak is not all desolate: Teide broom and other brilliant flowers bloom with the first rains of spring.

WOLONG NATURE RESERVE, SICHUAN, CHINA With their big black eyes and deep-pile coats, giant pandas are the most appealing of bears. It's no wonder they were chosen as the emblem of the World Wildlife Fund. At the Wolong Giant Panda Breeding Centre in the highlands, you can watch these gentle creatures safe in the knowledge that the programme here is for their conservation and rehabilitation.

SKAGEN, DENMARK Walk along this sandy beach to Grenan, the most northerly tip of Denmark, and you will see the Baltic Sea on one side and the North Sea on the other, their waves hurtling towards each other and often colliding in such a tumult of spray that you expect white horses to jump out of the water. Remote and romantic, this shifting sandy headland has long been popular with artists.

TSINGY DE BEMARAHA NATURE RESERVE, MADAGASCAR The otherworldly landscape of this UNESCO World Heritage-listed reserve is a lush mix of mangrove swamps and emerald-green forests studded with fingers of limestone rock and riven by deep gorges. Make a special effort to see the dramatic Manambolo river canyon on the south side of the park. When it comes to wildlife, lemurs are the stars, particularly the endemic sifaka and ring-tailed varieties. Like these, many of the other creatures in the reserve have learned to adapt to the region's fiercely dry climate.

PAINTED CANYON, NORTH DAKOTA, USA Painted Canyon is one of the most awe-inspiring parts of the North Dakota Bad Lands. This phantasmagoric region lies on the southern edge of Theodore Roosevelt National Park, named after the former president, who owned a ranch here. It is a shockingly harsh landscape of rocks and buttes, where temperatures are extreme and bison and horses still roam freely. Roosevelt, who came here after the loss of his wife and mother on the same day, saw himself as a frontiersman, and in this remote and beautiful place, you are bound to feel like one, too.

SOSSUSVLEI, NAMIBIA Sunrise and sunset are the best times to see the magnificent sand dunes of Sossusvlei on the Namibian coast. But the only way to do so is to camp in the Namib Naukluft Park, which is otherwise closed at these times of day. These high dunes, which are blown as sheer as silk with razor-sharp edges, surround a *vlei* – a red-clay water hole that fills up every now and then.

KYUSHU AZALEAS, JAPAN In spring, the shade of pink that creeps across the slopes of Japan's most southerly island, Kyushu, is simply shocking. Kyushu azaleas are just one of 300 varieties native to Japan, and they spread like wildfire. It is a joy to see this shrub, so familiar as a tamed garden plant, completely untamed. Locals believe that the sight of them restores the human spirit, and they are surely right.

ANTARCTIC PENINSULA A setting of incomparable beauty, Antarctica is an unforgettable destination and one of the few untouched places in the world. Your days here will be spent cruising deep-blue waters known for their breaching whales and icebergs the size of ships. The region has some fascinating wildlife. Penguins are found in their thousands, along with whales, seals and a large number of birds.

FINGER LAKES, NEW YORK STATE, USA The 11 long, narrow, glacier-carved Finger Lakes are natural marvels ranging from 5 to 65 km (3 to 40 miles) in length, and surrounded by gorges brimming over with more than 1,000 waterfalls. Watkins Glen is a jewel, with its stunning gorge and a series of 19 waterfalls. Walking trails wind through it, including one that leads behind the roaring Central Cascade.

BEACHES

Aerial view of coral-ringed Kuata Island, Yasawa archipelago, Fiji *(p207)*

GRACE BAY
VS MAGENS BAY

*Sweeping in a spectacular arc as far as the eye can see and shelving into calm
turquoise water, breathtaking Grace Bay surpasses Magens Bay by leagues*

NEED TO KNOW

LOCATION Grace Bay is on
the north shore of the island
of Providenciales in the
Turks and Caicos Islands,
925 km (575 miles)
southeast of Miami

POPULATION 17,000

VISITORS PER YEAR 300,000

DAYTIME TEMPERATURES
Jan: 23°C (73°F); Apr: 25°C (77°F);
Jul: 29°C (84°F); Oct: 28°C (82°F)

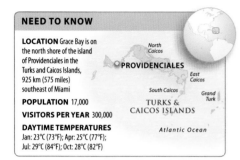

North
Caicos

PROVIDENCIALES

East
Caicos

South Caicos

Grand
Turk

TURKS &
CAICOS ISLANDS

Atlantic Ocean

For sugary, pristine sand that gently disappears
under clear, electric-blue water, Grace Bay is hard
to beat. This glorious beach dwarfs world-famous
Magens Bay in the US Virgin Islands in scale, beauty
and five-star appeal. And while its better-known
rival gets very busy with cruise-ship passengers
who surge down the hill to the beach like lemmings,
the frost-white curve of sand at Grace Bay unfurls
for a staggering 16 km (10 miles), making it well-
nigh impossible for the beach to get crowded.

Grace Bay is the jewel in the crown of the Turks
and Caicos archipelago's main island, Providenciales
(known by locals as "Provo"), and is consistently
rated among the world's top ten beaches. The
pristine ocean in the bay is part of Princess Alexandra
Marine National Park and is as still as a millpond
thanks to a protective coral reef that lies 500 m
(1,650 ft) off the coast. Not surprisingly, scuba-
diving, snorkelling and swimming conditions in
the bay are second to none. Horse-riding is
another popular activity at Grace Bay, where noisy
beach buggies, quad bikes and jet skis are banned.
Whether you want to try out every conceivable

ABOVE Thatched umbrellas on the beach at the Grace Bay Club

water sport, jump on a horse or simply relax on the
sand, where a near-constant breeze takes the edge
off the blazing sun, this blissful spot has it all.

While Magens Bay has no hotels, cosmopolitan
Grace Bay is blessed with a variety of plush
accommodation options that boast pampering
luxury, first-rate facilities and to-die-for settings.
These hotels are so swanky they even offer their
guests king-size canopied beds on the beach and
pretty thatched umbrellas to stand in for palm trees.
Atmospheric restaurants and casual but classy bars
on the beach give visitors the opportunity to sip
chilled beers or killer rum cocktails with the soft sand
between their toes. The bay's eco-friendly, ultra-
modern Leeward Marina, which opened in 2008,
beckons the super-rich in their floating party palaces.

Unlike Magens Bay, where you're trapped in a
bowl surrounded by steep forested hills and cannot
easily explore inland, Grace Bay is also the perfect
base for trips around Providenciales. It's no effort to
hop in a taxi to Conch Farm, which is home to about
2 million of the endangered molluscs, or the island's
National Environmental Center, where there are
fascinating exhibits on local marine life. You can even
get in the swing at the championship Provo Golf
Club, with its grass-fringed bunkers echoing the
silt-fine sands of Grace Bay. And Provo boasts plenty
of other beaches: at dusk, head west to lonesome
Malcolm Beach to savour the spectacular sunsets.

PRACTICAL INFORMATION

Getting There and Around
Provo International Airport is
served by daily flights from the
USA, Canada, the UK and other
Caribbean islands. From here,
take a taxi to Grace Bay, which is
just a 30-minute drive away.
Some hotels provide their own
airport shuttles. Taxi drivers are
usually happy to act as local
guides, but fares are expensive.
You can also rent cars and
scooters on the island.

Where to Eat
Grace Bay has some sensational
restaurants, with the focus on

fresh seafood. For sophistication,
try Anacaona at the Grace Bay
Club (www.gracebayclub.com).

Where to Stay
Try the luxurious all-suite
Seven Stars resort (www.
sevenstarsgracebay.com), the
largest hotel on the beach.

When to Go
The weather is best from
November to May.

Budget per Day for Two
Around £200.

Website
www.turksandcaicostourism.com

ABOVE Sun-worshippers crowd the beach at Magens Bay on
the island of St Thomas, US Virgin Islands

FORGET MAGENS BAY?

THE BUILD-UP This picture-postcard bay is
lined by a white-sand beach stretching for more
than 1 km (half-a-mile). It has virtually no tides
or waves, and the gentle slope into the azure
water, as well as the presence of lifeguards,
makes it perfect for children. Trees offer respite
from the sun, and a concession rents chairs and
lockers, has shower facilities and sells food.

THE LETDOWN Magens Bay can get very, very
busy, especially when the cruise ships have
docked and the tour buses spill out their hordes.
There's no coral reef here, and the big rock pools
boast only average snorkelling conditions. Alas,
the beach charges for the privilege of a visit:
there's a US$3 entrance fee plus US$1 for parking.
The road to the beach is also unnervingly steep.

GOING ANYWAY? If you like exercise, you can
hike to the beach via the Magens Bay Discovery
Trail. Try to time your arrival for when the cruise
ships aren't in port, or for late afternoon when
passengers have departed. No nude sunbathing
is allowed, but you can get an all-over tan at
Little Magens Beach, a short swim away.

MAIN IMAGE Local children racing towards the water at Grace Bay
BELOW (left to right) Windsurfers in the clear aquamarine water of the bay; colourful wooden huts on the beach

4 MORE ISLAND BEACHES TO RIVAL MAGENS BAY

PLAYA FLAMINGO, VIEQUES, PUERTO RICO This glorious 2-km (1-mile) scallop of pure-white sand is a little piece of paradise. It is studded with WWII tanks from the days when the US Navy used the island of Vieques for target practice.

SHOAL BAY, ANGUILLA With powder-fine sand, crystal-clear azure water, great beach bars, popular restaurants and pristine coral reefs offering sensational snorkelling, this beautiful beach has something for everyone.

SEVEN MILE BEACH, GRAND CAYMAN This scintillating stretch of sand runs for 9 km (6 miles) alongside a deep-blue sea, which is perfect for swimming and water sports. It is keen competition for Grace Bay as best beach in the Caribbean.

PINK SANDS, ELEUTHERA, THE BAHAMAS Yes, the beach here really is pink. It stretches for 5 km (3 miles) and boasts classy resorts that are popular with Hollywood stars.

COTTESLOE BEACH, PERTH
VS MIAMI BEACH, FLORIDA

They are both popular and beautiful, but Australia's Cottesloe Beach has a winning combination of loveliness and charm without the backdrop of a bustling high-rise city

NEED TO KNOW

LOCATION Cottesloe Beach is a suburb of Perth in the state of Western Australia

CITY POPULATION
Around 1.6 million

DAYTIME TEMPERATURES
Jan: 31°C (88°F);
Apr: 25°C (77°F);
Jul: 17°C (63°F);
Oct: 22°C (72°F)

Both Miami and Cottesloe beaches experienced a renaissance in the 1980s after years of fading from fashion. Miami's popularity grew from being the setting of the hit TV show *Miami Vice*; Cottesloe's from Australia playing host to the America's Cup international yacht race. However, their respective redevelopments took quite different paths and while Miami Beach is overshadowed by a high-rise city, Cottesloe has never lost its low-rise charm.

In the 1920s Miami Beach became a magnet for millions of Americans escaping to the coast for winter. The building boom that resulted has left a legacy in the now-restored Art Deco District. Then, as now, the beautiful and fashionable set flocked to its pastel palaces. With its British Raj-style Indiana Tea House, pine-fringed Cottesloe also has its share of celebrity fans (it was Heath Ledger's favourite beach and, sadly, the scene of his wake), but it retains a low-key, family feel. And while its popularity is clear from the crowds that flock here to soak up the sun, it is also quietly relaxed and exudes that laid-back atmosphere for which Australia is known.

Professional lifeguards patrol both beaches but Cottesloe has the iconic and much-photographed volunteer Surf Life Savers, founded in 1919, to keep an eye on things, too. Their newest members can be found on the beach on Sunday mornings, when local children participate in the "Nippers' program".

Families crowd the beach as the kids, in Cottesloe's surf-lifesaving colours of black, yellow and white, train in watersports and surf-lifesaving techniques.

Cottesloe's surf is one of its key attractions for many. A never-ending succession of waves roll across the Indian Ocean to rush up onto the long sweep of fine golden sand and entice surfers, who vie for the best position on each break. Quieter waters around the stone-built groyne are great for snorkelling.

By mid-afternoon the beach and its trendy bars are being colonized by the party crowd, a mixture of locals and tourists, enjoying a cold beer and light snacks at the end of another hot, sunny day. Later, the gourmet restaurants that fringe the beach begin to fill with appreciative diners savouring the fresh local produce and the spectacular views as the setting sun makes the world glow orange. Once again, numbers on west-facing Cottesloe Beach begin to swell, as everyone gathers to watch the sunset silhouette the surfers, the late swimmers and lovely Rottnest Island in the distance – a visual treat that the beachgoers of eastward-facing Miami can only dream about.

PRACTICAL INFORMATION

Getting There and Around
Perth International Airport is 12 km (7 miles) northeast of the city and linked by bus or taxi. Cottesloe Beach is 12 km (7 miles) southwest of Perth, 20 mins by train from Perth Station.

Where to Eat
With so many open-air cafés, bars with spectacular views and restaurant-lined Marine Parade, it is easy to see why so many people head to "'Cott" to dine. Try the Blue Duck Café (www.blueduck.com.au) for stunning views and great seafood.

Where to Stay
Rooms at the Ocean Beach Hotel (www.obh.com.au) range from ocean-view suites to budget dorms.

When to Go
In March, the beach becomes an outdoor gallery for the international art show Sculpture by the Sea.

Budget per Day for Two
£185 to include accommodation in a 4-star hotel, lunch at the beach and a gourmet dinner.

Websites
www.cottesloe.wa.gov.au
www.sculpturebythesea.com

FORGET MIAMI?

THE BUILD-UP Miami Beach, with its vast stretch of white sand, dotted with colourful lifeguard towers and scattered with bronzed bodies, is deemed one of the wealthiest beach resorts in America. The streets that border the beach include the famous and fabulous Art Deco Historic District, its chic boutiques, restaurants, hotels and nightclubs filled with the beautiful, rich and famous.

THE LETDOWN The place is fast-paced and expensive. Hotel prices have skyrocketed in recent years, as have the high-rises that loom over the beach. If you want to venture far from your base you will need to hire a car. And, because it's such a popular beach, there are crowds wherever you go; there's no point searching for a secluded spot of sand here.

GOING ANYWAY? Start at "SoBe" (South Beach) for a swim and, while in that area, take a look inside Art Deco hotels such as The Delano – the lobbies are simply stunning. Head to Lincoln Road for dinner and people-watching in the evening.

ABOVE Miami Beach, lined with high-rises and barely visible for the crowds of holiday-makers on its sands

MAIN IMAGE Cottesloe Beach, with its historic Indiana Tea House
BELOW (left to right) Sculpture by the Sea exhibit; , uncrowded, dune-fringed beach; fishermen on the Cottesloe groyne at sunset

Stunning white sand beaches curving round the headland at Al-Mamzar, close to the centre of Dubai, UAE

View across the dunes at Amager Beach Park, with wind turbines in the distance, Copenhagen, Denmark

Deserted, pristine sands of Non Nuoc Beach, washed by South China Sea breakers, Vietnam

AL-MAMZAR BEACH, DUBAI

NEED TO KNOW

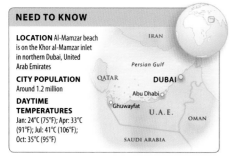

LOCATION Al-Mamzar beach is on the Khor al-Mamzar inlet in northern Dubai, United Arab Emirates

CITY POPULATION Around 1.2 million

DAYTIME TEMPERATURES Jan: 24°C (75°F); Apr: 33°C (91°F); Jul: 41°C (106°F); Oct: 35°C (95°F)

Al-Mamzar Beach is more than just a succession of beautiful, curving, white sandy beaches, it is also a park and recreational area that covers over 100 ha (247 acres) on a small headland to the north of central Dubai. Opened in 1994, the parklands include beaches, swimming pools, a stunning amphitheatre, picnic areas, barbecue facilities and children's playgrounds, set amongst acres of lush green lawn, palms, coconuts and other trees. The five beaches together make up the longest beach area along the coast of Dubai and there is always a lifeguard on duty on at least one. Al-Mamzar Beach and Park is open daily but Wednesdays are for women and children only.

Practical Information

Getting There and Around Dubai is the international flight hub of the UAE, and its airport is just 4 km (2.5 miles) from both the city centre and the Al-Mamzar Beach and Park. The easiest way of getting around Dubai is by taxi, with non-metered ones offering negotiable, often cheaper, rates.

When to Go Since summer maximum temperatures can reach unbearable extremes, the period from late autumn to early spring (Oct–Apr) is the best time to visit.

Website www.dubai.com

AMAGER BEACH PARK, COPENHAGEN

NEED TO KNOW

LOCATION Amager Beach is 5 km (3 miles) from central Copenhagen, Denmark

CITY POPULATION Around 500,000

DAYTIME TEMPERATURES Jan: 2°C (36°F); Apr: 10°C (50°F); Jul: 22°C (72°F); Oct: 12°C (54°F)

Amager Beach Park is made up of a series of beaches and a 2-km- (1-mile-) long artificial island, opened in 2005 and linked to the original Amager Beach by three bridges. The mainland beach is divided by a headland. The northern area has a natural, untamed feel and its broad, sandy shoreline is backed by low-lying, grassy dunes. The beach to the south, known as the "city beach", has more facilities, including coffee shops, a pier and a marina. The addition of the island has created a natural lagoon which is popular for water sports, and the shallow waters are calm and safe – perfect for children.

Practical Information

Getting There and Around Copenhagen's international airport is 8 km (5 miles) south of the city. The beach is 8–10 mins by Metro from Nørreport or Kongens Nytorv stations.

When to Go Jun–Aug is ideal for a Danish beach visit (water temperatures reach a comfortable 19°C/66°F), but it is also high season.

Website www.visitcopenhagen.com

NON NUOC BEACH, DANANG

NEED TO KNOW

LOCATION Non Nuoc Beach is just outside the major port city of Danang, on the central coast of Vietnam, 600 km (375 miles) south of the capital city Hanoi

CITY POPULATION Around 800,000

DAYTIME TEMPERATURES Jan: 24°C (75°F); Apr: 30°C (86°F); Jul: 34°C (93°F); Oct: 28°C (82°F)

Just south of Danang, at the foot of the Marble Mountains, Non Nuoc (also known as China Beach) stretches for 5 km (3 miles) in a white, sandy arc that slopes gently into the clear blue waters of the South China Sea. The beach is lined in part with an ancient forest of casuarina trees, and there are restaurants serving local seafood specialities. A day at the beach can be combined with a visit to the nearby village of Non Nuoc (where skilled craftspeople have been carving white, rose and grey marble since the 15th century), or a trip to the spectacular mountains.

Practical Information

Getting There and Around There are flights from Hanoi, Ho Chi Minh City, Bangkok and Singapore. Take a motorbike-taxi or cycle-rickshaw to the beach. Bargain hard and have the waiting time and return fare included.

When to Go The dry season (Feb–Aug) is the ideal time; temperatures are more comfortable and, from May to Jul the sea is at its calmest.

Website www.danang.gov.vn

Hang-glider's-eye-view of the idyllic setting and tranquil waters of Cheltenham Beach, Auckland, New Zealand

Quirky beach huts adding a splash of colour to Cape Town's lovely Muizenberg Beach, South Africa

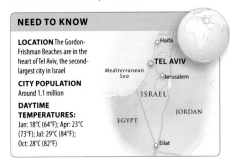

Lifeguard's station on the stretch of sands at Gordon–Frishman Beaches, Tel Aviv, Israel

CHELTENHAM BEACH, AUCKLAND

NEED TO KNOW

LOCATION Cheltenham Beach is situated to the east of Devonport, a suburb of Auckland on the north island of New Zealand

CITY POPULATION
Around 1.3 million

DAYTIME TEMPERATURES:
Jan: 23°C (73°F); Apr: 19°C (66°F); Jul: 13°C (55°F); Oct: 17°C (63°F)

A series of beaches extends north on the eastern side of Devonport, each with its own merits, but Cheltenham Beach is the closest. Popular with families on a day out from Auckland, it is a safe, tidal beach with picnic grounds. It is worth a walk to North Head, a headland that actually lies at the southern end of the beach. From here, the spectacular panoramic views extend through 360 degrees across the sweeping length of Cheltenham Beach, the harbour, Rangitoto Island and back across to Auckland. As lovely as the beach is, be sure you leave enough time to enjoy the trendy town of Devonport, with its beautiful architecture and great cafés.

Practical Information

Getting There and Around Auckland's international airport is 45 mins by road from the city. Ferry is the easiest way to get to Devonport from central Auckland, then the beach is a short walk. Boats leave approximately every 30 mins from early morning until late each day, from Ferry Building to Devonport Wharf.

When to Go Summer and early autumn (Dec–Mar) are the best times for a visit to New Zealand.

Website www.tourismnorthshore.org.nz

MUIZENBERG BEACH, CAPE TOWN

NEED TO KNOW

LOCATION Muizenberg a beach-side suburb on False Bay, 25 km (15 miles) south of Cape Town

CITY POPULATION
Around 3.5 million

DAYTIME TEMPERATURES
Jan: 26°C (79°F); Apr: 22°C (72°F); Jul: 17°C (63°F); Oct: 21°C (70°F)

This once-popular and prestigious destination for Capetonians is experiencing a renaissance. The beach lies on the Indian Ocean side of the Cape Peninsula, so the waters are much warmer here than at the beaches on the Atlantic Ocean side. The wide sweep of white sand and gentle surf is ideal for families as well as surfers. Look out for the dolphins that sometimes come in quite close to the shore, and the whales that pass during their migration season. At lunchtime, stroll up to the popular picnic area at the northern end of the beach, in the Zandvlei Nature Reserve.

Practical Information

Getting There and Around The international airport is 22 km (14 miles) southeast of central Cape Town. Metro trains run from the Main Station to Muizenberg.

When to Go Summer (Nov–Mar) has the lowest rainfall and the warmest weather. But the best time for whale-watching is from mid-August to mid-October.

Website www.tourismcapetown.co.za

GORDON-FRISHMAN BEACHES, TEL AVIV

NEED TO KNOW

LOCATION The Gordon-Frishman Beaches are in the heart of Tel Aviv, the second-largest city in Israel

CITY POPULATION
Around 1.1 million

DAYTIME TEMPERATURES:
Jan: 18°C (64°F); Apr: 23°C (73°F); Jul: 29°C (84°F); Oct: 28°C (82°F)

The whole of Tel Aviv's west side is one long beach, facing west over the Mediterranean Sea. At its northern end is the Tel Aviv Marina and what was, at one stage, the Gordon Swimming Pool, which was famous as a meeting place for Tel Aviv celebrities and other notable figures. At the southern end is Frishman Beach, where you can rent lounging chairs and umbrellas. At weekends the beach is a gathering place for the city's young, hip crowd. Slim, suntanned bodies pack the bars, sands and volleyball courts, and can overwhelm tourists, older locals and families. During the week things are much more peaceful. After a day of sun and sand, take a stroll along the boardwalk, choosing a café or restaurant from which to enjoy a spectacular sunset view.

Practical Information

Getting There and Around Ben Gurion International Airport is 15 km (9 miles) from Tel Aviv. The beaches are steps away from most hotels.

When to Go Tel Aviv is at its best during summer (May–Sep), when the days are usually dry and hot, but not unbearable.

Website http://telavivguide.net/

HULOPOʻE
VS WAIKĪKĪ

Hawaiʻi's Hulopoʻe Beach has everything from gorgeous golden sands and idyllic swimming, to abundant marine life – and none of the crowds and high-rises of Waikīkī

NEED TO KNOW

LOCATION Hulopoʻe is on the south shore of the small island of Lānaʻi, 15 km (9 miles) west of Maui

VISITORS PER YEAR
100,000

DAYTIME TEMPERATURES
Jan: 22°C (71°F); Apr: 23°C (74°F); Jul: 26°C (79°F); Oct: 25°C (77°F)

Kauaʻi
Lihuʻe
Oʻahu
Honolulu
Molokaʻi
HAWAIʻI
Lānaʻi
Maui
HULOPOʻE BEACH
Pacific Ocean
Big Island
Hilo

Most mornings, you can stroll along the rich golden sands of delightful Hulopoʻe Beach, Lānaʻi and have the place to yourself. Oh, there'll be a fisherman perched out on the lava boulders of the headland, or you might spot a snorkeller burrowing in and out of the rock pools. Someone from the tiny campsite, tucked away in the nearby woods, might even wander down. And, of course, the local pod of spinner dolphins will probably swim by at some point, to play and cartwheel in the surf before heading back out to sea.

Now compare that with the scene at Waikīkī – picking your way through busy traffic simply to get

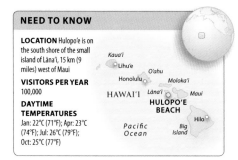

ABOVE Snorkellers in the waters off Lanaʻi

a glimpse of the ocean; the crowds of touts and tourists jostling for position on the beach, the wafting smells of the all-you-can-eat bacon-and-egg buffets just a few feet away from the water.

Lānaʻi is often called the "Private Island", as it is almost entirely owned by David H Murdock, the former chairman of Dole, the producer of fresh fruit and vegetables. After the company stopped growing pineapples here in 1992, Murdock re-directed the island towards tourism. While the island's image as an upscale resort is largely deserved, Hulopoʻe Beach is an exception. As with all Hawaiian beaches, it's always open to the public, and with regular ferries from Maui docking a few hundred yards east, access is easy.

The beach itself is a gem, a gentle curve of deep, thick sand, fringed by low kiawe trees, and demarcated to the east by the russet Mānele Cone, an extinct volcanic relic. The brisk slope of the sand into the ocean makes it ideal for swimming, while the offshore reef ensures that the surf seldom rises to threatening levels. By Hawaiian standards, the surfing conditions are relatively tame, making this a great spot to learn under safe conditions, or simply to play on a boogie board. Beach equipment can be rented from a small kiosk near the west end, and the park area set back from the centre holds public showers.

The whole bay forms part of a marine reserve – hence the dolphins – so the snorkelling conditions are superb, especially early in the day. In winter, when humpback whales are frequently visible out to sea, snorkellers are also able to hear their underwater songs. An ancient Hawaiian fishing village, inhabited for around 500 years, formerly stood at the west end of the beach; ruined stone homesites are still visible in the dunes, with explanatory placards alongside.

FORGET WAIKĪKĪ?

THE BUILD-UP Arguably the world's most famous beach, Waikīkī stretches for 3 km (2 miles) along the shoreline of southern Oʻahu. Its natural setting is magnificent, with the Koʻolau Mountains soaring to the rear, the extinct volcano of Diamond Head silhouetted to the southeast, and the sun descending each night into the Pacific Ocean straight ahead.

THE LETDOWN Waikīkī is, however, no timeless South Seas paradise; it is a hectic modern resort, whose high-rise hotels sleep 100,000 guests per night, and whose bars, clubs, restaurants and cafés remain open around the clock. Simply finding room to lie on the sand, or swim in the sea, can be a problem. And with busy Honolulu just 5 km (3 miles) west, traffic congestion is frequently horrendous.

GOING ANYWAY? To make the most of Waikīkī, throw yourself into the melee. Spend the day sunbathing or in the ocean, surfing or canoeing, then spend the night partying hard. And be sure to explore the rest of Oʻahu, which abounds in forests, beaches and cultural sights.

ABOVE Sunbathers crowding the golden sands of Waikīkī Beach, Honolulu

PRACTICAL INFORMATION

Getting There and Around
Fly into Honolulu International Airport on Oʻahu, from where you can take a connecting flight to Lānaʻi's airport, which is located 20 km (12 miles) northwest of Hulopoʻe Beach. Five ferries (www.go-lanai.com) ply daily from Lahaina on Maui to Mānele Bay, close to Hulopoʻe. A ferry-trip from Maui to Lānaʻi costs around £27.

Where to Eat
Lānaʻi City, 13 km (8 miles) from Hulopoʻe, has several appealing local restaurants, but the only place to eat near the beach is in the Four Seasons. Its open-air Hulopoʻe Court restaurant (www.fourseasons.com/manelebay) serves irresistible seafood dishes such as delicious fresh fish steamed in banana leaves (*laulau*).

Where to Stay
The Asian-influenced Four Seasons Resort Lānaʻi at Mānele Bay (www.fourseasons.com/manelebay) stretches upwards from near the west end of Hulopoʻe, and has a pool, luxury spa and plush rooms. Rates start at £250 per night. The plantation-style Hotel Lānaʻi is a cheaper option.

When to Go
It makes very little difference what time of year you visit Hulopoʻe Beach. From January to April, there is slightly more rainfall and the sea is a little rougher, but this is also peak whale-watching season.

Budget per Day for Two
£340 for food and accommodation at the Four Seasons Hotel.

Website
www.gohawaii.com

MAIN IMAGE Aerial view showing the curving Hulopo'e Beach
BELOW (left to right) Waves washing the golden sands of
Hulopo'e; spinner dolphins leaping out of the water

4 MORE HAWAIIAN BEACHES TO RIVAL WAIKĪKĪ

HAPUNA BEACH, BIG ISLAND OF HAWAI'I A magnificent
stretch of pure white sand, perfect for boogie-boarding in
winter or gentle swimming in summer, far from any town but
with a luxury hotel nearby.

KAILUA BEACH, O'AHU Nowhere in Hawai'i is the ocean such
a dazzling turquoise as on O'ahu's finest beach, a fabulous day-
trip from Waikīkī.

NAPILI BAY, MAUI This delightful little beach in West Maui
offers exhilarating swimming for the entire family and, very
unusually for Hawai'i, is lined with numerous low-key,
inexpensive hotels.

KĒ'Ē BEACH, KAUA'I Located at the western end of Kaua'i's
ravishing North Shore, this lovely little beach offers superb
snorkelling and unforgettable sunsets – the perfect way to end
your day after hiking on Hawai'i's finest trail, the Kalalau Trail,
which terminates alongside.

MAIN IMAGE Fishing boat anchored in the clear blue water of Turtle Bay
BELOW (left to right) Green turtle, from which the bay gets its name;
archaeological site of Gedi; a mushroom-like coral formation, Turtle Bay

TURTLE BAY
VS MOMBASA'S BEACHES

Clear turquoise water, fantastic coral gardens, lush jungles stretching inland and a minimum of hassle make Turtle Bay East Africa's most complete beach experience

Picture a classic tropical paradise, all soft white sand, swaying palms and glittering aquamarine water, enhanced to spectacular effect by a succession of fantastic ragged coral outcrops that explode from the water like surrealist mushrooms. This is Turtle Bay, one of the most glorious spots on East Africa's long Indian Ocean coastline, where stunning natural assets and a peaceful atmosphere upstage Mombasa's more famous beaches at every turn.

The extraordinary coral formations that adorn this stretch of coast are above-surface extensions of Kenya's finest and most accessible coral garden, which lies only 300 m (328 yards) from the shore.

This breathtaking underwater landscape teems with more than 600 fish species, including brightly coloured parrot fish, butterfly fish, surgeonfish and snappers, which dance around the corals giving a dizzying performance, and making Kenya's legendary landlubbing wildlife seem positively drab by comparison.

Unsurprisingly, the bay is a snorkellers' paradise and suitable for nervous novices thanks to nearby protective reefs, which ensure reliably calm water conditions. Meanwhile, the deeper reefs further offshore support healthy populations of whale sharks, giant sea bass and green turtles, and boast superb scuba-diving conditions. Deep-sea game fishing is popular in the open water beyond the reefs, where anglers can try their hand at catching tuna, sailfish, marlin and wahoo.

From the sea to the land, the exploring continues with a day trip to Arabuko-Sokoke National Park, which lies only 5 km (3 miles) inland. This park, which can easily be enjoyed on foot, protects East Africa's largest remaining tract of coastal forest and presents great opportunities for wildlife observation – scores of monkeys, baboons, antelopes and elephants live here, alongside the

ABOVE Sokoke scops owls on a branch, Arabuko-Sokoke National Park

bizarre, twitchy-nosed, golden-rumped elephant shrew, and several unique bird species, including the endangered Amani sunbird, East Coast akalat, Sokoke scops owl and Sokoke pipit.

Hidden in the park's tangled forest is Gedi, a "lost city" and Kenya's most important and impressive archaeological site. Its broodingly enigmatic mosques and palaces and eerie tombs and archways are all that remain of a medieval Swahili city-state, thought to have been home to 2–3,000 people in its heyday.

FORGET MOMBASA'S BEACHES?

THE BUILD-UP The beaches that stretch either side of the ancient island-bound port of Mombasa – Nyali and Bamburi to the north, Diani and Tiwi to the south – are the stuff of brochure-writers' dreams. Here you'll find idyllic arcs of white sand, calm blue waters, offshore reefs swirling with fish, and beach after beach refreshingly uncrowded by comparison to their Mediterranean counterparts.

THE LETDOWN In a nutshell: beach boys. One of the reasons the beaches around Mombasa are so uncrowded is that most visitors step out onto them once, and – having deflected a swarm of pushy hustlers and chancers – opt to spend the rest of their holidays lounging around the hotel swimming pool instead.

GOING ANYWAY? The hotel swimming pools are mostly very nice, and there's usually a good range of other activities to keep things interesting – everything from table tennis and diving excursions to day trips to Mombasa's old town or the Mwaluganje Elephant Sanctuary.

ABOVE A local trying to sell his wares to tourists on a Mombasa beach

PRACTICAL INFORMATION

Getting There and Around
The closest international airport is in Mombasa, from where there are domestic flights to Malindi, which is 15 km (9 miles) north of Watamu. Shared taxis head into Watamu from both Mombasa and Malindi, and private taxis are also available. Most sites around Watamu can be reached on foot or by a short taxi ride.

Where to Eat
There are no stand-alone restaurants of note in Watamu, but all the resort hotels serve good meals, with seafood being the speciality. Particularly recommended are the à la carte lunch menu and sumptuous themed buffet dinners at Hemingways (www. hemingways.co.ke).

Where to Stay
Watamu village has a good selection of budget accommodation, and the main beach running south of this is serviced by four medium-sized resort hotels. The pick of these is Hemingways *(see Where to Eat)*, which has a superlative setting and offers a great range of marine activities.

When to Go
Visit at any time except the wettest months (Feb–May).

Budget per Day for Two
£150–200 – far less than this if you're prepared to rough it in a local guesthouse, but a lot more if you want to charter a boat for game fishing.

Website
www.watamu.net

A local woman carrying a heavy load in the traditional manner along the beach at Busua, Ghana

The magnificent beach at Rocktail Bay in iSimangaliso Wetland Park, South Africa

Busua

NEED TO KNOW

LOCATION Busua is on the coast of Ghana, 20 km (12 miles) west of the main port of Sekondi-Takoradi

BEACH FRONTAGE About 3 km (2 miles), though there are many other beaches in the area

KEY WILDLIFE Green turtles, monkeys, marine birds, dolphins

ACTIVITIES Swimming, walking, boat trips, visits to Dixcove Castle

The small Atlantic coastal village of Busua is dominated by a beautiful, sweeping beach that boasts safe swimming conditions and a laid-back vibe rooted in the hippy heyday of the early 1970s. A favourite spot with villagers and the occasional savvy traveller, the beach remains one of West Africa's most unspoilt spots. If you tire of the beach, take a trip to the nearby fishing town of Dixcove, which has some elegant colonial architecture, or the remote estuarine villages of Butre and Akwidaa.

PRACTICAL INFORMATION

Getting There The closest international airport is at Accra, the capital of Ghana. From here you can take a bus to Takoradi, then catch a small shared "tro-tro" (van) to Busua via Agona junction and Asane.

When to Go The most comfortable period covers the relatively cool and less humid months (Oct–Apr). Avoid the wettest months (May–Jun).

Website www.touringghana.com

iSimangaliso Wetland Park

NEED TO KNOW

LOCATION iSimangaliso is between St Lucia village and the Mozambique border, 275 km (171 miles) north of Durban, South Africa

BEACH FRONTAGE 250 km (155 miles)

KEY WILDLIFE White rhinos, green turtles, blue monkeys, humpback whales

ACTIVITIES Snorkelling, scuba diving, whale- and dolphin-spotting

iSimangaliso is the largest and most ecologically varied coastal sanctuary in Africa, protecting a vast subtropical wetland system that stretches from the wildly beautiful St Lucia Estuary in the south to the pristine Kosi Bay in the north. A succession of spectacular and largely undeveloped beaches fringe the park's eastern edge, including the popular swimming spots around St Lucia village and the semi-deserted Cape Vidal, Sodwana Bay and Rocktail Bay – wide arcs of peach-coloured sand hemmed in by the world's tallest forested dunes.

It would be easy to spend a fortnight in iSimangaliso, beach-hopping from south to north with a stash of paperbacks, a collapsible umbrella and a large towel. But this would be missing the point of a trip here. The beaches, beautiful though they are, are only part of the appeal of this extraordinary wilderness, the rich biodiversity of which left Nelson Mandela spellbound when he came here in 2001 (a fate from which few visitors to the park can escape).

iSimangaliso became South Africa's first ever UNESCO World Heritage Site in 1999. It is a living Eden where rhinos, elephants, leopards, sharks and whales thrive in a remarkable mosaic of natural habitats, from beach and coral reef to swamp, forest and savanna. More than 500 bird species exist here, as well as high densities of hippo and crocodile, especially around the mangrove-lined St Lucia Estuary, which is easily explored by boat. The open waters offshore are legendary among game fishers, while the coral reefs around Sodwana – the most southerly reefs in the world – are lauded by snorkellers and divers. The beaches in the north of the park are a vital breeding ground for marine turtles, and on a clear day, hikers might well be treated to the distant sight of breaching whales from the tops of the sand dunes.

PRACTICAL INFORMATION

Getting There The nearest international airport is in Durban. From here, St Lucia village is accessible on public transport (buses, coaches and mini-bus taxis), and operators within the village offer a good range of day trips. Otherwise, the best option is to rent a car in Durban.

When to Go The dry southern winter (May–Sep) is more comfortable than the sweaty summer. Whale-watching is best from June to October, and bird-watching from November to March.

Website www.kznwildlife.com

Balcony at the Peponi Hotel, Shela Beach, Lamu Island, Kenya

SHELA BEACH, LAMU ISLAND

NEED TO KNOW

LOCATION Lamu Island is in the Lamu archipelago, just off the Kenyan coast, 350 km (217 miles) north of Mombasa

BEACH FRONTAGE 12 km (7 miles)

KEY WILDLIFE Dolphins, turtles, carmine bee-eaters

ACTIVITIES Snorkelling, diving, exploring old towns, island-hopping, bird-watching

The focal point of Lamu Island is the eponymous town, a UNESCO World Heritage Site with a rich architectural heritage and cultural integrity that make it unique among the medieval Swahili ports that survive into the modern era. Only a 45-minute walk from town lies Shela Beach, a fabulous sweep of bone-white sand that fulfils every expectation of a tropical beach nirvana. This is one of the few East African beaches to lack a protective reef, and although swimming is usually safe here, the sea is refreshingly lively. The nearby Peponi Hotel, which has been run by the same family for 40 years, is the ideal place for a drink or a fresh seafood meal after a day on the beach.

PRACTICAL INFORMATION

Getting There Regular scheduled and chartered light aircraft flights link Nairobi, Mombasa and Malindi to Lamu Island. The airstrip is on nearby Manda Island, from which point motorized dhows cross the channel to Lamu itself. The town and beach are easily explored on foot.

When to Go After the rainy season in May and June, the weather gets progressively finer. Christmas and New Year offer constant sunshine and pleasant offshore breezes.

Website www.lamuheritage.com

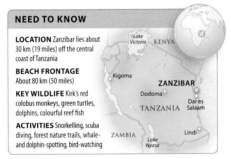

Bwejuu Beach on the island of Zanzibar, Tanzania

EAST COAST OF ZANZIBAR

NEED TO KNOW

LOCATION Zanzibar lies about 30 km (19 miles) off the central coast of Tanzania

BEACH FRONTAGE About 80 km (50 miles)

KEY WILDLIFE Kirk's red colobus monkeys, green turtles, dolphins, colourful reef fish

ACTIVITIES Snorkelling, scuba diving, forest nature trails, whale- and dolphin-spotting, bird-watching

The east coast of Zanzibar isn't the place to go for bland, international beach-resort luxury. Although its sandy palm-lined beaches are as idyllic as they come, the east coast offers visitors much more than just pretty beaches. The seafront is studded with traditional Swahili villages, including Bwejuu, Paje and Jambiani, each one smaller and more rustically somnambulant than the one before, making it a great place to experience rural Africa on its own terms. In keeping with this, accommodation tends to be low rise, low key, low impact and low cost – it's the ideal place to relax after a costly safari. Look out for the endangered Kirk's red colobus, a fringed monkey endemic to Zanzibar.

PRACTICAL INFORMATION

Getting There Several flights connect Dar es Salaam and Arusha, both of which are on the mainland, to Zanzibar Town, from where it is easy to arrange a transfer or taxi to the east coast. Ferries also depart every day for the island between Dar es Salaam and Zanzibar Town.

When to Go Any time except the rainy season (Mar–May).

Website www.tanzaniatouristboard.com

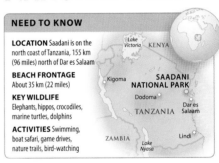

Seating area made from an old dhow at the beachside Saadani Safari Lodge, Saadani National Park, Tanzania

SAADANI NATIONAL PARK

NEED TO KNOW

LOCATION Saadani is on the north coast of Tanzania, 155 km (96 miles) north of Dar es Salaam

BEACH FRONTAGE About 35 km (22 miles)

KEY WILDLIFE Elephants, hippos, crocodiles, marine turtles, dolphins

ACTIVITIES Swimming, boat safari, game drives, nature trails, bird-watching

Long, lush and serviced by just two small and exclusive tented camps, the seafront of Saadani National Park boasts dozens of beautiful beaches and is a great spot for swimming, snorkelling and sunbathing. There really is no better destination for discerning travellers looking for a true African beach wilderness – a stunning palm-lined beach where you have a good chance of encountering creatures as diverse as eagles and giant turtles, lions and dolphins, seagulls and hippos, and giraffes and jellyfish. What makes Saadani – which bills itself as "where the beach meets the bush" – even more special is that it is one of the only places on the planet where snoozing sunbathers might conceivably be interrupted by a beachcombing elephant.

PRACTICAL INFORMATION

Getting There Most visitors fly here either from Dar es Salaam or Zanzibar. The park can be approached by rough roads from Tanga via Pangani or from Dar es Salaam via Chalinze. Activities in the park are organized by the camps.

When to Go Visit Saadani at any time of year, though the rainy season, which runs from March to May, is best avoided.

Website www.tanzaniaparks.com

ABOVE Columns of the Temple of Isis towering over the ruins of Sabratha beside the Mediterranean, Libya

SABRATHA
VS TULUM

Sabratha's beaches, lined with ancient temples, are a quiet contrast to Tulum

NEED TO KNOW

LOCATION Sabratha lies 80 km (50 miles) east of the Libyan capital, Tripoli, along the Mediterranean coast of northwestern Libya

VISITORS PER YEAR Around 60,000

DAYTIME TEMPERATURES Jan: 10°C (54°F); Apr: 19°C (66°F); Jul: 28°C (82°F); Oct 24°C (75°F)

If Sabratha were anywhere but in Libya, this pristine coastline would be overrun by resorts of the kind that spoil your view at almost every turn in Tulum, Mexico. This is Tulum as it used to be, before it was discovered by the package-holiday crowd – a sweeping coastline of white sand and waters of transparent turquoise.

All along the coast from Tripoli to Zuara, with Sabratha at its midpoint, empty roads lead down to empty beaches. There are built-up areas and even occasional half-hearted approximations of resorts, but such places are rare and overflow in summer with Libyan families, not sun-starved Europeans. Elsewhere along this often-deserted coast, you could spend an entire day on the beach and not see another living soul.

The only exception to this rule is a pretty special one. In Sabratha itself, the Roman city of the same name dominates the Mediterranean shoreline, a forest of columns in light sandstone rising from the sandy soil where other, more famous beaches have palm trees. Temples to the

full pantheon of Roman divinities, traces of the city's Phoenician origins and ancient Greek inscriptions litter the site within its Byzantine-era wall. Together they form an extraordinary seaside monument to the great civilizations of Mediterranean antiquity.

It was from Sabratha's port, alongside its small beach, that ships set sail for ancient Rome, laden with olive oil destined for Roman tables and elephants earmarked for gladiatorial conquests. Sabratha ranked among Rome's most prosperous cities on African soil, and for all its claims of fealty to the gods, was known for its devotion to the cult of excess – in the Seaward Baths that overlook the beach and the broad sweep of coastline, fragments of mosaic and marble peer out from beneath centuries' accumulation of sand and footprints.

On the sandy beach itself, it doesn't take much imagination to visualize yourself surrounded by toga-clad Romans enjoying the warm, southern Mediterranean sun. Once in the water, the view is exceptional – here stand the impressive Corinthian columns of the Temple of Isis, the goddess of seafarers, on a promontory away to the east; there, the three-storey fortress-like walls of Sabratha's theatre, one of the most exquisite structures in the ancient Roman empire.

As the Romans knew, swimming here is one of the great bathing experiences on earth, not least because Sabratha is how all seaside resorts once were, albeit a very long time ago.

ABOVE Detail of the floor mosaic in the Seaward Bath ruins

FORGET TULUM?

THE BUILD-UP It's not difficult to see why the crowds first flocked to Tulum with its picturesque stretch of coastline and evocative Mayan ruins overlooking the Caribbean Sea.

THE LETDOWN An astonishing 11 million visitors arrive every year in the small Mexican state of Quintana Roo, a sizeable proportion of whom visit Tulum to view the Mayan ruins, Mexico's third-most-visited archaeological site. Tulum may not be Cancún, that poster child for over-developed Caribbean resorts, but the latter is just a short drive away and its tour buses spill daily into Tulum. You'll spend most of your time lamenting the fact that you didn't visit before everyone else discovered it.

GOING ANYWAY? Whatever you do, stay in Tulum itself. Once the day-trippers return to Cancún, find a secluded vantage point in the expansive Mayan ruins of Zamá, close to sunset – this is the moment when you'll most understand Tulum's charm.

ABOVE Visitors touring the archaeological site of the Mayan ruins at Tulum, Mexico

PRACTICAL INFORMATION

Getting There and Around
The nearest international airport is at Tripoli. Although buses and shared taxis run regularly between Tripoli and Sabratha, visas for Libya are only possible as part of a guided tour in which all transport is included.

Where to Eat
Restaurants catering to tourists across Libya serve banquet-style meals that include soup, salad and a local main course, usually rice or couscous with meat or fish. Mat'am Bawady (tel. +218 24 620 224) is a good option. The best place to eat in the capital is Tripoli's fish market – you simply select your fresh seafood and have it cooked in a popular restaurant in the market area.

Where to Stay
Most travellers visit Sabratha as a day trip from Tripoli, not least because the former has few habitable hotels. A fine choice among many in Tripoli is Zumit Hotel (www.zumithotel.com).

When to Go
May–Sep offers great swimming weather, but the heat outside the water can be oppressive. Milder temperatures make Oct–Apr more agreeable.

Budget per Day for Two
Your visit to Sabratha, including accommodation and meals, will be included in the cost of your guided tour while in Libya.

Website
www.arkno.com

MANZANILLO BEACH
VS MONTEZUMA BEACH

Manzanillo, with its youthful edge, is replacing Montezuma as a hotspot for offbeat travel

NEED TO KNOW

LOCATION Manzanillo is located on Costa Rica's Caribbean coast, close to the Panama border

POPULATION 1,000

VISITORS PER YEAR 35,000

DAYTIME TEMPERATURES Jan: 25°C (77°F); Apr: 26°C (79°F); Jul: 26°C (79°F); Oct: 26°C (79°F)

The fishing hamlets of Montezuma, on the Pacific Coast, and Manzanillo, on the Caribbean, are gateways to two of Costa Rica's premier wildlife reserves. Montezuma has been the nation's unofficial offbeat travel capital for more than two decades. But Manzanillo now has the more youthful edge, and its taupe, palm-shaded beach backed by forested mountains is more than equal in beauty to the legendary sands of Montezuma.

Manzanillo was virtually unknown until barely a decade ago, when a road finally linked this sleepy village to the outside world. The pavement peters out here, close to the border with Panama and abutting the Gandoca-Manzanillo Wildlife Refuge, a tropical fantasia protecting a precious rainforest, mangroves and swamps.

Four species of marine turtles crawl ashore to lay their eggs in the soft sands of the beach. The lagoons and estuaries are a habitat for endangered manatees, and a rare dolphin species – the *tucuxí* – cavorts in these waters. Tapirs often wallow in the swampy pools, where crocodiles and caimans slosh about in the mud. Toucans and parrots are

ABOVE Idyllic, palm-fringed Punta Uva beach, located between Puerto Viejo and Manzanillo, Talamanca province, Costa Rica

among at least 350 bird species here. And you're sure to see coatis, sloths and monkeys galore. The refuge extends out to sea, protecting coral reefs teeming with colourful fish, a treat for snorkellers and divers. The watery world is also a breeding ground for tarpons and snooks – feisty gamefish that give anglers a rod-bending thrill to remember. There's even a fishing lodge in the heart of the refuge. A local cooperative offers guided hikes and horse-riding along well-marked trails, as well as canoe trips through the snakelike creeks.

Although accommodation in Manzanillo is budget-focused, the access road from Puerto Viejo is lined with several diverse options, from safari-style tent camps to deluxe modernist eco-lodges with spas and fine-dining restaurants. Surfers are drawn to the challenge of nearby Salsa Brava, where massive waves can reach heights of up to 10 m (33 ft). And the Crazy Monkey Canopy Ride is guaranteed to give you an adrenaline boost as you whizz through the forest along a zipline slung between trees.

Unlike on the Pacific Coast, local inhabitants include Afro-Caribbeans, descendants of Jamaican immigrants who have infused local culture with reggae music and spicy cuisine, and the local dialect with a lilting patois. Uniquely, Manzanillo is also a base for exploring the indigenous reserves of the Bribrí and Cabecar native people.

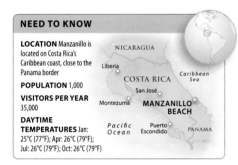

ABOVE A cluster of green turtles on the soft sands of Manzanillo

FORGET MONTEZUMA?

THE BUILD-UP A favourite of budget travellers, this laid-back village is an idyll for those who love paradise on a budget. The once sleepy fishing hamlet fronts a rocky cove and has a gorgeous wave-washed beach to the east. Visitors can choose from a variety of activities, from ATV rides to waterfall rappels. Cabo Blanco Absolute Nature Reserve is nearby.

THE LETDOWN With so many backpackers, Montezuma has a bit of a "hippy" aura, and much of the budget accommodation leaves a lot to be desired. Swimming in the ocean is dangerous due to riptides. Much of Cabo Blanco Absolute Nature Reserve is off-limits, and if you miss the bus, it's a long walk.

GOING ANYWAY? Carry sturdy footwear for hiking the trails in Cabo Blanco Absolute Nature Reserve and come prepared for rain. Do not clamber up La Cascada, the waterfall west of Montezuma, as several people have slipped and died doing so.

ABOVE Backpackers on a colourful street in the village of Montezuma

PRACTICAL INFORMATION

Getting There and Around
Juan Santamaría International Airport is 20 km (12 miles) west of San José. From here, regular buses connect to Puerto Viejo de Talamanca on the Caribbean coast. Buses depart Puerto Viejo for Manzanillo four times daily. Jeep taxis can also be hired.

Where to Eat
The beachfront Restaurante-Bar Maxi (tel. +506 759 9086) serves seafood and *típico* (Costa Rican) dishes on the sands.

Where to Stay
The best accommodation in Manzanillo is Almonds & Coral

Tent Camp (tel. +506 759 9056), with safari-style luxury huts on stilts in the forest behind the beach.

When to Go
Rain is a possibility at any time of the year, but September to November and February to April are the best times to pay a visit, when the chances of rainfall are less.

Budget per Day for Two
£100 includes accommodation, food and travel.

Website
www.visitcostarica.com

IHURU
VS KO PHI PHI

They may have filmed The Beach *on Ko Phi Phi, but it can't be a fantasy island getaway if you have to share it with a crowd – Ihuru is the real desert-island deal*

NEED TO KNOW

LOCATION Ihuru lies in the Kaafu Atoll, in the northern Maldives, 13 km (8 miles) from the capital, Malé

SIZE Ihuru is only 150 m (490 ft) in diameter

DAYTIME TEMPERATURES
Jan: 30°C (86°F); Apr: 31°C (88°F); Jul: 31°C (88°F); Oct: 30°C (86°F)

Ihavandippolhu Atoll · Horsburgh Atoll · Faadhippolhu Atoll · Indian Ocean · Ari Atoll · IHURU · Malé · MALDIVES · Kolhumadulu Atoll · Hadhdhunmathi Atoll · South Huvadhu Atoll · Indian Ocean

When you close your eyes and picture the perfect island paradise, do you imagine an ocean of beach towels and the thumpety-thump of outboard motors? Almost certainly not. There are four essential ingredients for an island retreat – sand, sea, peace and seclusion – and Ihuru has them all. This is a proper desert island: the only noise comes from surf breaking over the distant reefs and the rustle of palm fronds, and the only reason to stir is the incoming tide. Thailand's Ko Phi Phi has the surf and the palm fronds, of course, but the constant flow of tour boats is the nautical equivalent of rush hour in downtown Bangkok.

Formed from the tip of a submerged volcano, Ihuru is not so much an island as a beach with shade. Set in its own mini-atoll, the island is a single copse of palm trees, ringed by icing-sugar sand. Ihuru does not have beaches (plural) – the whole island is a beach, fringed by a turquoise lagoon of warm water and encircled by a sheltering curtain wall of reefs. You may well want to explore its breathtaking undersea world, or you might just prefer to doze beneath a palm tree or stroll along the sand. There's no pressure – which is rather the point of coming here.

Under the Maldives' unique model for tourism, every developed island is home to a single, self-contained resort. Compare that to Ko Phi Phi, where poorly-planned resorts are springing up like mushrooms after April showers. On Ihuru, the accommodation is as private and secluded as you can get. Basking beneath the palm trees, the swish villas of the Angsana Maldives Ihuru Resort & Spa are a favourite of the fashion set, who come here to be pummelled or pampered by expert practitioners in the spa, or left alone to rock gently on a Maldivian swing in front of an empty stretch of sand.

There is an interesting parallel between the two islands. Both saw visitor numbers dive after the 2004 tsunami but, while Ko Phi Phi responded to the disaster with yet more resort developments, Ihuru stayed true to its desert island roots. It is luxurious, certainly, but the resort buildings and villas are scattered like fallen coconuts between the palms, and the first footprints on the beach every morning will probably be your own. The whole purpose of an island getaway is being able to get away from it all – who wants to get away from it all with everybody else?

PRACTICAL INFORMATION

Getting There and Around
Fly to Malé International Airport on Hulhule island. From here it's a 20-minute speedboat ride to the island.

Where to Eat
The chefs here prepare delicious dishes using local fish and seafood combined with sauces from the Maldives, Asia and the Mediterranean. The Riveli restaurant is spread out under the stars, but you can go one step further with your own private table beside the surf.

Where to Stay
Guests at the Angsana Maldives Ihuru Resort & Spa (www. angsana.com/EN/Properties/ Ihuru) stay in elegant but understated thatched villas that spill out onto the beach beneath a canopy of palm trees.

When to Go
The seasons in the Maldives are dictated by the southwest monsoon, which soaks the islands with rain from May to October. December to March is the most popular time to visit, but those in the know choose the "shoulder" season (Apr and Nov) when the weather is balmy and the water as clear as Evian.

Budget per Day for Two
Assume on paying around £400, including accommodation and three gourmet meals. Alcoholic drinks, pampering in the spa and dive trips around the atolls are extra. For example, a 2-hour aromatherapy massage is £60.

Websites
www.visitmaldives.com

ABOVE Holiday-makers flock into the azure waters of Maya Bay on Ko Phi Phi, while tour boats buzz back and forth

FORGET KO PHI PHI?

THE BUILD-UP When travellers first started combing the Thai islands for the perfect beach, Ko Phi Phi ticked all the right boxes. Hidden by a curtain of cliffs, Maya Bay was the perfect place to escape from prying eyes and indulge in some island escapism.

THE LETDOWN *The Beach* was the fantasy – Maya Bay is the reality. These days, its enclosed lagoon is a magnet for sea-borne litter and tour boats whizz across the short stretch of water between Ko Phi Phi and Phi Phi Leh all day, undermining the castaway vibe.

GOING ANYWAY? Ko Phi Phi has bounced back impressively from the Christmas 2004 tsunami. Reconstruction and new build has focused on smaller, more intimate bays, rather than the heavily-developed beaches along the sandy central isthmus of the island. Among the best of the new developments are secluded resorts on Hat Laem Thong and Ao Lo Bakao.

MAIN IMAGE Thatched jetty of the Angsana Resort on Ihuru
BELOW (left to right) Colourful coral reef, ideal for diving and snorkelling; relaxing in a hammock at the beach; small boat on the shore

4 MORE ISLAND GETAWAYS TO RIVAL KO PHI PHI

RADHANAGAR BEACH, HAVELOCK ISLAND, ANDAMAN ISLANDS, INDIA Brigands and British governors used to walk the sands of this tiny dot in the Bay of Bengal. You just might encounter a swimming elephant as you snorkel round the reefs.

GOLDEN BEACH, NORTH CYPRUS Little has changed in North Cyprus since the island was divided in 1974. More turtle tracks than footprints mark the sands on this 17-km (10-mile) stretch of beach on the remote Karpas peninsula.

SANDAY, ORKNEY, SCOTLAND Imagine an island 2 km (1 mile) wide by 20 km (12 miles) long, encircled by white sand and the warm waters of the Gulf Stream. . . in Scotland. Remote Sanday comes into its own in summer – think of it as Hawaii with haggis.

KO TARUTAO, THAILAND Preserved as an island prison, and now a national park, wonderful Ko Tarutao has seen none of the development that has marred other Thai islands. Apart from national park bungalows, all you'll find here is jungle and beach.

ISLE OF HARRIS BEACHES
VS COAST GUARD BEACH, CAPE COD

Coast Guard Beach is the most stunning of Cape Cod beaches, but for a peaceful experience in an equally spectacular location, seek out the Isle of Harris in Scotland's Outer Hebrides

NEED TO KNOW

LOCATION The Isle of Harris is in the Outer Hebrides, off the coast of northwest Scotland, UK

VISITORS PER YEAR
26,000

DAYTIME TEMPERATURES
Jan: 4°C (37°F); Apr: 8°C (46°F); Jul: 16°C (61°F); Oct: 8°C (46°F); Summer temperatures occasionally exceed 30°C (86°F)

Coast Guard Beach in Cape Cod, USA, may well be blessed with mile upon mile of golden sand and brushed by Atlantic breezes, but for much of the year, it heaves beneath the weight of urban weekenders and hordes of tourists traipsing along the New England trail. If you truly want to get away from it all, then head for the Outer Hebrides in the extreme west of Scotland – you can't get much more remote than these rugged islands.

Like Cape Cod, the Isle of Harris has some of the finest beaches you'll see, yet the Scots manage to keep theirs relatively secret. Strung out along the island's southwestern coast, these jewels shimmer beside the roaring Atlantic Ocean – and one of the biggest diamonds in the chain is Seilebost. Approaching by road from the fishing port of Tarbert, Harris's main town, you traverse a glaciated moonscape of ancient rock exposed between peat bogs and clumps of heather, passing only the occasional stone crofter's cottage. At the tiny settlement of Seilebost, a seemingly endless spit flanked by high tufted dunes and a

broad expanse of machair (coastal grassland) comes into view. Beyond is the wide Luskentyre Estuary backed by brooding mountains. On a clear summer's day, the scene takes on the colours of a Caribbean island, the pale-cream sand gleaming in the clear sunlight beside a turquoise ocean broken by rolling surf. This being Scotland, it won't be as warm as the Caribbean, nor even Cape Cod, but the fresh breeze will feel invigorating, and chances are you won't see a soul here all day.

If you can tear yourself away from Seilebost, it's worth exploring the island. Across the bay from Seilebost is the beautiful Luskentyre Beach, and further south along the west coast are Scarista and Northton. Stop off to see the interesting medieval St Clement's Church at Rodel, the megalithic MacLeod standing stone at Nisabost and Seallam Genealogy Research Centre, where Celtic expats can rediscover their roots. Alternatively, drive north along a spectacular coastal road towards Hushinish, which takes you right past the front door of Amhuinnsuidhe Castle (pronounced "avan-soo-ee"), a stately baronial manor nestled between the ocean and mountains. Continue north and you reach the Isle of Lewis, where the highlights include the magnificent Callanish standing stones.

Harris is an outdoor enthusiast's dream. It offers some of the best climbing, hiking, fishing and surfing in the UK. There is a wonderful golf course beside Scarista Beach, and it harbours a dazzling array of wildlife, including whales, dolphins, seals, puffins and golden eagles. But whether you are an active type or a sedentary beach-lover, a trip to Harris will be more than a match for Cape Cod.

FORGET COAST GUARD BEACH?

THE BUILD-UP Coast Guard Beach near Eastham is Cape Cod's finest stretch of beach and is regularly ranked as one of USA's best. This broad, windswept beach, bounded by large dunes and marshes and overlooked by a historic Coast Guard Station, is a favourite seaside retreat with Bostonians.

THE LETDOWN The peak season extends from the last Monday in May to the first Monday in September, but it can also be busy in spring and autumn. In summer, prices can shoot sky high and the car park is closed, so you have to rely on a shuttle bus to get here. 4WD drivers have to apply for an ORV sticker.

GOING ANYWAY? Brace yourself for the crowds and you can have a good holiday. Coast Guard Beach is a great place for the family, with lifeguards on hand. It is also one of the cape's best surfing beaches. The spit offers excellent hiking, with walking paths revealing stunning scenery and rich wildlife. The end of the spit is ideal for bird-watching and seal-spotting.

ABOVE Sunbathers crowding the sands of Coast Guard Beach in Cape Cod

PRACTICAL INFORMATION

Getting There and Around
Getting to Harris can seem like a pilgrimage. You can fly to Stornoway Airport on the Isle of Lewis, then hire a car (www.stornowaycarhire.co.uk) and drive the 44 km (27 miles) to Tarbert, Harris. Flights depart from Edinburgh, Glasgow, Aberdeen, Inverness and Benbecula. Alternatively, take your car across on the ferry from Uig, on the Isle of Skye, to Tarbert, or from the Isle of Berneray to Leverburgh in the south of Harris (Caledonian MacBrayne: www.calmac.co.uk)

Where to Eat
Though they're readily available, Scottish food isn't all haggis, neeps and tatties. Other dishes made from local produce include

superb seafood. Try Scarista House, Scarista (www.scarista house.com) – also a hotel – for wonderful traditional cuisine.

Where to Stay
Accommodation includes B&Bs, guesthouses, cottages, self-catering and boutique hotels. Privately owned Hotel Hebrides in Tarbert (www.macleodmotel.com) has plush rooms and is an ideal base to explore the island.

When to Go
July and August are the warmest months. Many places and facilities close during Oct–Apr.

Budget per Day for Two
£230, including accommodation, car hire and food.

Website
www.visitscotland.com

MAIN IMAGE Waves breaking on a beach on the coast of the Isle of Harris in the Outer Hebrides, Scotland **BELOW (left to right)** A pair of puffins native to the region; stately Amhuinnsuidhe Castle

4 MORE BEACHES TO RIVAL COAST GUARD BEACH

OCRACOKE ISLAND, NORTH CAROLINA, USA This 27-km- (16-mile-) long island on the east coast is one of the most remote on the Outer Banks. It can only be reached by ferry or private plane so its windswept beaches are blissfully empty.

WINEGLASS BAY, TASMANIA, AUSTRALIA A brilliant azure bay on the east coast of Tasmania, Wineglass Bay is scooped out in a perfect semi-circle from pink granite mountains. Temptations for outdoor adventurers include bushwalking, fishing, sea-kayaking and wilderness camping.

SOPOT BEACH, GDANSK, POLAND In summer, locals flock to this Baltic wonderland close to the city of Gdansk to soak up the sun and hang out before partying in nearby bars and clubs.

DOG'S BAY, COUNTY GALWAY, IRELAND Tucked away in wild Connemara, this sheltered bay is one of Ireland's undisputed gems. Its dazzling white-shell sand seems to have been made for taking a solitary stroll.

MAIN IMAGE Sailing boats on a white-sand beach at Punta del Este
BELOW (left to right) The distinctive, whitewashed Casa Pueblo; aerial view of the beach-lined resort

4 MORE PARTY BEACHES TO RIVAL COPACABANA

PUERTO ESCONDIDO, OAXACA, MEXICO Tired of the mega-hotels and commercialism of Vallarta and Acapulco? Puerto Escondido (meaning "hidden port") is, as its name implies, off the beaten track, but it still boasts a great party scene.

SOUTH BEACH, MIAMI, USA The young and beautiful now call South Beach home more than any other beach in the USA. The nightlife (and beach life) here is second to none and the time to visit is now, before it achieves superstar status.

COZUMEL, YUCATÁN PENINSULA, MEXICO If you want (or can stand) non-stop partying for the 30-and-under set, then look no further than this year-long party island, which is on the "quiet" side of Mexico's most famous resort, Cancún.

SALINAS, SANTA ELENA PROVINCE, ECUADOR A relative newcomer to the beach-party sweepstakes, Salinas is an up-and-coming South American destination for those who want fun in the sun, away from the usual suspects.

PUNTA DEL ESTE
VS COPACABANA

Thanks to myriad things to do in addition to the ever-present party scene, Uruguay's elite Punta del Este has the lead over fabled Copacabana when it comes to attracting the fun-loving set

NEED TO KNOW

LOCATION Punta del Este occupies a peninsula in southern Uruguay, which is 139 km (86 miles) east of the capital, Montevideo

POPULATION
70,000

DAYTIME TEMPERATURES
Jan: 25°C (77°F); Apr: 20°C (68°F); Jul: 14°C (57°F); Oct: 17°C (63°F)

For decades, **Punta del Este** has been a haven for the rich and famous. This glamorous resort – a collection of fabulous beaches, elegant hotels and stylish restaurants, clubs and bars – has long been synonymous with champagne, celebrities and fashion chic, but at the same time has remained firmly grounded, attracting visitors from all walks of life. Unlike Rio de Janeiro's Copacabana beach, which these days has few cards to play, Punta del Este manages to combine serious partying and a carefree attitude with plentiful things to see and

do. Activities range from sailing and surfing to horse-riding, archery and volleyball. There's a casino, a lighthouse and the iconic Casa Pueblo, an extraordinary house and "living sculpture" built over a 36-year period by the Uruguayan painter and sculptor Carlos Páez Vilaró. Close by there's also an aquarium, a zoo, several quaint seaside towns and picturesque hills that boast fantastic trekking routes. In fact, it's likely that there are more things to do in and around Punta del Este than any other resort in Latin America.

But don't let these sights and activities distract you for too long from the resort's stunning beaches. It is here, perhaps more than anywhere else, that Punta del Este really shines. There are more than a dozen beaches on this fashionable peninsula, all of which have a very different character. Take your pick from white- and golden-sand beaches, sheltered coves and wave-battered shores, water-sports hubs and sunbathing areas, secluded bays and party beaches. Even the rowdiest beaches are clean and safe, day and night, and all boast excellent facilities. It's no surprise that savvy Brazilians,

Argentinians, North Americans and Europeans looking for the good life now head to Punta del Este instead of their own resorts, which aren't exactly second-class spots themselves.

Punta del Este has year-round appeal. In the high season, which runs from December to March, the resort's classy clubs and popular beaches host endless parties, which rarely begin before midnight, and the atmosphere is electric. There's no shortage of glitterati types here, drawn by the alluring beach and party lifestyle. The crowd is a mix of the young and beautiful, who frequent the beaches and bars, a wealthy, older generation in their yachts, and energetic types, who spend their time on the water and in the hills. In the off-season, the resort might be quieter, but it remains enticing. Those who long for the wild nights of summer should not despair – there's still plenty of partying to do at this time just up the coast in Buenos Aires and Montevideo. Whether you're in search of high times and endless nights, solitude and surf, or anything in between, you can't do better than Punta del Este.

FORGET COPACABANA?

THE BUILD-UP Rio de Janeiro's Copacabana, known for its golden arc of sand and glitzy beach lifestyle, is probably the most famous beach on the planet. Other beaches boasting fun, sun and sand have to compete with its legendary reputation, and more often than not come up short.

THE LETDOWN In recent years, Copacabana's reputation has suffered greatly. It has rampant crime (generally theft), polluted water, beach vendors who are difficult to fend off, overcrowding and – for women – a likelihood of receiving male attention, whether desired or not.

GOING ANYWAY? If you do go, choose the right stretch of beach for you. Some spots are ideal for surfing but nothing else, others are family-oriented and others are good just for sunbathing, but none are chic and all are crowded. Leave your jewellery, watches, mobile phones and cameras in your hotel.

ABOVE Aerial view of the crowds on Copacabana, Rio de Janeiro, Brazil

PRACTICAL INFORMATION

Getting There and Around
It couldn't be easier to reach Punta del Este. Rent a car in Montevideo, which has an international airport, and head east on the motorway. You'll be there in 2 hours or less.

Where to Eat
Punta del Este has restaurants for every budget and taste. For the best international cuisine and people-watching in an elegant, hip setting, try the award-winning Novecento (www.bistronovecento.com), but reserve well ahead.

Where to Stay
The epitome of luxury in Punta del Este these days is the sophisticated Mantra Resort (www.mantraresort.com).

It's everything you could imagine and more, right on the coast and yet tucked away from the crowds. Book at least three months in advance.

When to Go
Punta del Este's high season is between December and March, when it is most crowded. A better option is to visit in either October and November or April and May, when it is less expensive and less crowded.

Budget per Day for Two
You should allocate at least £200 per day to travel here in style; Punta del Este may not be cheap, but it's worth every penny spent.

Website
www.vivapunta.com/en/index

44 MORE STUNNING BEACHES

ABOVE Aerial view of the bright-turquoise Aitutaki Lagoon, Cook Islands
RIGHT The smooth grey rocks and calm water of Anse Source d'Argent, La Digue, Seychelles

AITUTAKI, COOK ISLANDS At one corner of a triangular lagoon in the South Pacific sits Aitutaki, the most idyllic of the Cook Islands. The lagoon is peppered with 14 *motu* – small volcanic and coral islets – which offer some great snorkelling and diving opportunities. There's plenty to do away from the beaches, too. Attempt the spectacular climb up Munga Poo, Aitutaki's highest point, enjoying the renowned local hula dancing and local grilled fish at villages along the way. There is plenty of affordable accommodation next to the pristine beaches on the island, and a boat tour around the lagoon is a must.

ANSE SOURCE D'ARGENT, LA DIGUE, SEYCHELLES Probably the most photographed beach in the world, Anse Source d'Argent is the stuff of tropical-island fantasy. A series of small, crescent-shaped, pink-sand beaches are separated by huge, smooth granite boulders worn into weird and wonderful shapes by the waves and the wind. The water is turquoise and shallow and protected by an offshore reef, so it is safe for children and non-swimmers. A ferry takes you from the main island, Mahé, to a nearby jetty, and from here a 10-minute bike or ox-cart ride will bring you to the start of a short footpath leading to the beach.

ANSE LA ROCHE, GRENADA, CARIBBEAN An unspoiled curve of sand with wooded hills rising up behind it, Anse la Roche is an idyllic place. Here, your only company will be the pelicans that sit on a rocky outcrop offshore, diving elegantly every now and then in search of fish.

ARAMBOL BEACH, GOA, INDIA The atmosphere at Arambol is distinctly laid back: wake up in a bamboo hut just footsteps from the shore and share the sunrise with a few scuttling crabs. Don't miss the beach's freshwater lake and mud baths with purported healing properties.

BAAN MAI, KOH LONE, THAILAND Traditional long-tail boats cross the water south from Phuket to Koh Lone Island (the trip takes 15–20 minutes), where a small boutique hotel is nestled within dense tropical foliage. There are also wooden bungalows a stone's throw from the shore, with verandas from which you can watch spellbinding sunsets. The atmosphere at Baan Mai is quiet and relaxing. Should you want to rouse yourself into some activity, there are kayaks for hire and snorkelling trips to a nearby coral island. There is also a boat service to an adjacent beach, which is very good for swimming.

BARLEYCOVE BEACH, CORK, IRELAND Between two craggy headlands on the Mizen Peninsula, Barleycove is a remote horseshoe of golden sand. A bracing walk in the fresh Atlantic air takes you to nearby Mizen Head, Ireland's most southwesterly point. The region has some of the country's best weather, but the beach is rarely busy, though the sea is sometimes flecked with surfers enjoying the large waves.

BANGARAM BEACH, LAKSHADWEEP ISLANDS, INDIA This teardrop of lush green coconut palms fringed by creamy sand in the warm waters of the Indian Ocean is uninhabited, with the exception of one low-key resort. Bangaram Island is surrounded by a lagoon, and its main beach boasts wonderful snorkelling, with abundant puffer, parrot, angel and clown fish, as well as manta rays and moray eels.

QUEEN'S BEACH, MONTENEGRO Queen Milena of Montenegro so loved this beach that it was named after her. Sheltered by pine-clad cliffs and lapped by the clear waters of the Adriatic Sea, the beach affords the ultimate rose-tinted view every evening as the sun sets on its pink-sand shores. Unspoilt and relatively inaccessible, this is one of the Mediterranean's more appealing refuges.

CATHEDRAL COVE, NEW ZEALAND North Island's Coromandel Peninsula is an ecological paradise renowned for its marine wildlife and beaches, the most beautiful of which is Cathedral Cove. Whether taking the coastal path from Hahei or arriving by boat or kayak, time a visit here with low tide for the essential photo opportunity under the spectacular limestone archway that divides the beach.

WHITE BEACH, BORACAY, THE PHILIPPINES This 5-km (3-mile) stretch of pristine sand lined with swaying palms is frequently voted one of the world's best beaches. Boracay, which is 6 km (4 miles) long and 1 km (half-a-mile) at its narrowest point, has many other bays scattered along its shores. There are fantastic views of the beaches and the deep ocean beyond from Mount Luho, the island's highest point.

BIG BUDDHA BEACH, KO SAMUI, THAILAND This 3-km (2-mile) stretch of beach gets its name from the 4-m- (12-ft-) tall statue that watches over it from the east. The temple here is a pilgrimage site, but most visitors come for the sand, sea and nightlife. Big Buddha Beach slips down into clear, protected waters and is backed by low palms and hotels, restaurants and bars, which come alive at night.

ABOVE Sixteenth-century Lindisfarne Castle, romantically perched atop a rocky bluff known as Beblowe Crag at Holy Island, Northumberland, UK

HOLY ISLAND, NORTHUMBERLAND, UK Holy Island, also known as Lindisfarne, lies off the coast of northeast England and is accessible only via a paved causeway at low tide. It's a wild, remote place, fringed by miles of golden beaches with fascinating rock pools and rolling dunes. The main beach is lined with upturned fishing vessels, which were once part of a 19th-century herring fleet and now serve as work sheds. Also on the island are the ruins of a 7th-century Benedictine priory and a 16th-century castle, built in defence of England against the Scots. Only 160 people live here, and the pace of life is slow.

LLANDUDNO BEACH, CAPE TOWN, SOUTH AFRICA Shy neighbour of glitzy Clifton and Camps Bay beaches, Llandudno is the local in-the-know choice for post-work sundowners. The picturesque sandy sweep is heaven for surfers and the perfect spot for a cold beer as the sun sets.

MAJAHUITAS, MEXICO Majahuitas is just a short boat ride off Mexico's coast, but it feels like another world. This palm-fringed beach is backed by wooded hills and accessible only by boat. Here, manta rays and dolphins swim gracefully, pelicans dive for food and parakeets sit in mango trees.

LOPES MENDEZ, ILHA GRANDE, BRAZIL Lopes Mendez, a stunning 3-km (2-mile) stretch of white sand that is so bright you have to squint as you make your way across it, is the highlight of this lush island. The beach is buffeted by the Atlantic, but the water is shallow and safe for bathing.

MONKEY BAY, TIOMAN ISLAND, MALAYSIA Tioman, the largest of the volcanic islands off the east coast of peninsular Malaysia, comprises 115 sq km (44 sq miles) of dense jungle and three towering peaks. A hike through the rainforest from the main tourist hub at Salang will lead you to Monkey Bay; you're likely to see the eponymous monkeys, who can get a little territorial, along the way. This secluded yellow-sand beach is a great place to spend the day snorkelling or picnicking. Many visitors choose to arrive by ferry from Mersing on the mainland, a 1–2 hour journey, depending on the boat.

INGONISH BEACH, CANADA Ingonish Beach on Cape Breton Island in Nova Scotia is not your average beach, but a temporary bank of sand that is swept away every winter by waves and redeposited in the spring, creating a barrier between the sea and a lake. Time your trip right (Mar–Apr), and expect both salt- and fresh-water swimming, and access to a wealth of marine life, including lobsters, salmon and trout – rich pickings for anyone keen on fishing. The unusual beach is part of Cape Breton Highlands National Park, a wilderness area that provides opportunities for many outdoor pursuits, such as hiking, canoeing and whale-watching. And it goes without saying that this majestic place is a camper's dream – Cape Breton Island sits on the dramatic eastern seaboard and offers visitors a surprising amount to do for somewhere so far off the beaten track.

JOST VAN DYKE ISLAND, BRITISH VIRGIN ISLANDS The south of this island is home to coconut-fringed White Beach and the Soggy Dollar Bar – the perfect place to sip a rum cocktail at sunset. The north is craggy and deep and great snorkelling territory. Just 200 people live on the island, principally in Great Harbour, where smells of freshly baked banana bread waft down the streets.

NOIRMOUTIER, FRANCE The west coast of this island is dominated by great curves of golden sand, while its northern Atlantic shores are home to craggy cliffs, secluded bays and creeks. This small island lies 5 km (3 miles) from the mainland and can be reached by the Passage du Gois, which becomes submerged at high tide. Don't miss the island's 12th-century castle and church, once a Benedictine priory.

KUATA ISLAND, FIJI Southernmost in the Yasawa archipelago, tiny Kuata Island is technically the easiest one to reach from Fiji's main island, Viti Levu. However, most maps of the Yasawas don't even feature Kuata and it certainly isn't what you'd call overcrowded. The best beach is at Likunivisawa Point, but the whole island is enchanting, with its fine-white sand, dramatic volcanic ridges and caves.

BOSLUISBAII, NAMIBIA It's sand upon sand as beach meets desert in the north corner of Namibia's Skeleton Coast, so-called because of its treacherous currents and resultant shipwrecks (see also p115). As you'd imagine, swimming is impossible here, and because special permission is required to access Bosluisbaii, your party will be the only one there. This is a beach for fans of rugged, raw beauty.

PLAYA DE CABO DE GATA, ALMEÍRA In contrast to much of Spain's overcrowded coastline, the southeast coast of Almería remains relatively neglected by tourists. The region has volcanic terrain, and many undiscovered beaches lie tucked beneath its craggy cliffs. Most impressive is Playa de Cabo de Gata, a 5-km (3-mile) beach that is buffeted by open sea. You're unlikely to see many other people here.

ABOVE Picturesque Nungwi in Zanzibar, with its clear, bright-blue water and elegant dhows
RIGHT Lone bather in the calm, shallow sea at Palawan, the Philippines

NUNGWI, ZANZIBAR The twinkling sapphire water of the Indian Ocean tempts you on the long, hot drive to Nungwi, which lies on the northernmost tip of Zanzibar. But it'll be worth the uncomfortable journey; the sand is so fine it squeaks between your toes as you walk and the calm water off the beach stretches out to a wide coral reef. Most visitors are happy just to kick back on the beach, watching from beneath a shady palm as fishermen cast their nets from wooden dhows. But if you want a change of scene, visit nearby Stone Town, with its winding streets and eclectic architecture.

PALAWAN, PHILIPPINES Palawan, an island province comprising one main island and thousands of smaller islets and outcrops, is located between Mindoro in the Philippines and Borneo in Malaysia. It is an area of extraordinary natural beauty, its sloping white-sand beaches slipping down into still turquoise waters, and towering forested cliffs jutting dramatically into the ocean. The main island is long and narrow, and surrounded by coral and limestone offshore reefs. With over 1,600 km (1,000 miles) of coastline here, you are bound to find your own little piece of paradise.

DAYMER BAY, CORNWALL, UK Pretty Daymer Bay lies in a sheltered position at the mouth of the Camel Estuary, and is a great place for swimming and windsurfing. Walk along the nearby coast path from Polzeath to St Enodoc, passing the church where poet John Betjeman was laid to rest.

CORONADO BEACH, SAN DIEGO, CALIFORNIA, USA Swimming, volleyball and kite-surfing are the popular activities on this wide stretch of sand. Crowds gather here to watch fiery-red sunsets and, from January to March, the grey-whale migration south to Baja California.

CAPE MAY, NEW JERSEY, USA Visitors always fall in love with Cape May, a resort with a lovely, blustery beach met by the cool waters of the Atlantic, and rows of Victorian town houses that recall a bygone era of holidaying on the coast. The town was settled by fishermen and whalers in the mid-19th century, and it became a popular resort for city-dwellers on summer weekends. This is still the case today, though the area has remained remarkably unspoilt. Beach-goers come here to relax on the sand, try their hand at sailing and watch dolphins playing in the gentle surf.

MATIRA BEACH, BORA BORA The lush island of Bora Bora, which juts impressively into the South Pacific, is fringed on the south and east with white sandy beaches. Matira, with its shallow turquoise water protected by an offshore lagoon, is undoubtedly the most scenic of these. Stop at one of the beach bars to try the delicate local *poisson cru* – raw fish marinated in lime and coconut milk.

DON DAENG ISLAND, LAOS Sit sipping coconut milk on the sandy, quiet beaches of this river island, beneath steeply rising mountains. Don Daeng, on the Mekong, is an enclave of traditional culture, where locals go about their work fishing, farming and weaving. Staying as part of the community is a highlight; local families put guests up in their simple homes and serve up steaming portions of fresh fish.

EMERALD BAY, PANGKOR LAUT, MALAYSIA Just off the west coast of Malaysia, in the Straits of Malacca, lies the picture-postcard island of Pangkor Laut. On its western shores lies Emerald Bay, a flawless white-sand beach, with bowing palms and tepid green waters. Trace turtle footprints in the sand and watch crabs scuttle across the beach from one of the comfortable sun loungers here.

ESSAOUIRA, MOROCCO The laid-back charms of this small coastal town attracted a hippie crowd during the 1970s, and today pulls in backpackers and windsurfers. Essaouira is known for its 10-km (6-mile) beach, popular with locals for barefoot football and evening strolls. The town also has a lively fishing port. Spend a day in the medina here, or walking along the ramparts overlooking the bay.

GRAYTON BEACH, FLORIDA, USA The Florida Panhandle Gulf Coast stretches for 320 km (200 miles) and boasts beautiful white-sand beaches, freshwater lakes and undulating dunes. Grayton Beach, a broad sweep of quartz-white sand lapped by calm, warm Gulf waters, regularly features high in rankings of the nation's top beaches. Grayton Beach State Park offers nature trails, hiking, biking and camping.

MORNE ROUGE, ST GEORGE'S, GRENADA Pretty Morne Rouge is one of the most secluded beaches in Grenada. There is plenty of natural shade beneath palms here, and the water is warm, calm and shallow. Boss Reef, 3 km (2 miles) offshore, is popular with snorkellers, but otherwise there are few activities on offer; it's a place to relax. The nearest town of L'Anse aux Epines is only a short walk away.

ABOVE Beautifully sculpted natural archway in the shallow water at Spiaggia del Principe, Sardinia
LEFT The dazzling, bright-white moonscape and vivid azure sea at Sarakíniko Beach, Mílos, Greece

SARAKÍNIKO BEACH, MÍLOS, GREECE The volcanic island of Mílos might be best known for the ancient statue of *Venus de Milo* that was found here in 1820 (now housed in the Louvre in Paris), but it also has a dramatic landscape and over 70 glorious beaches. The spectacular island forms a horseshoe around a clear central gulf in the Aegean Sea. The bay at Sarakíniko, on the north coast, is formed of great white pumice rocks, which have been smoothed by wind and rain over millions of years. There is a small sandy beach here, and it's a popular spot for swimming and snorkelling.

SPIAGGIA DEL PRINCIPE, SARDINIA, ITALY Sardinia's Emerald Coast, or Costa Smeralda, is known for being home to some of the best beaches in the Mediterranean. A drive along the winding coastal road, stopping occasionally to take in the wind-sculpted rocks that emerge from the glittery turquoise sea, is a great way to see the coast. Linger at Spiaggia del Principe, a white-sand bay sandwiched between pink granite rocks and divided into two sheltered beaches by a rock wall. The beach may have become an exclusive holiday spot, but it remains relatively hidden, accessible only by a 10-minute walk down a dirt track.

PORTO DE GALINHAS, BRAZIL This low-key resort in sunny Pernambuco is known for its natural tide pools that form in the reefs just a short distance offshore. These heat up in the sun and are ideal for swimming and snorkelling. To the south is Maracaipu, a great beach for surfing.

HANALEI BAY, KAUA'I, HAWAI'I Hawai'i is not short of great beaches, but Hanalei Bay, on Kaua'i, is one of the most beautiful. This 3-km (2-mile) crescent stretches from the base of a sheer cliff at one end to a craggy bluff at the other, and is backed by lush mountains that collect the morning mist.

JOATINGA BEACH, BRAZIL As the coast stretches south of Rio de Janeiro, the beaches become more beautiful and secluded. Dense Atlantic forest dips into the ocean at Joatinga, which is sheltered on both sides by towering rocky outcrops. Surfers come here for the big swell.

TAYRONA, COLOMBIA Take a taxi to the Tyrona National Park visitor centre, and from there, travel on horseback along a dense jungle path, teeming with swinging titi monkeys. You'll soon emerge on Arrecife Beach, a crescent of cream sand, where the wild ocean crashes against huge boulders. This is a magnificent beach, but a dangerous place to swim. Follow a series of precipitous paths through the forest, over rickety bridges, and you'll come to some calmer bays where you can submerge yourself in the Caribbean. Despite a recent tourism boom, the infrastructure in Tayrona remains undeveloped, and you are unlikely to see many other visitors. The nearest town is Santa Marta, a half-hour drive away, and flights from Bogotá take just over an hour. There are some budget *cabañas* on the beach, and a more upmarket eco-resort in the mountains.

MURI LAGOON, RARATONGA, COOK ISLANDS Surrounded by a lagoon that stretches to an offshore reef, and with forest-clad mountainous ridges, Raratonga is the most dramatic of the Cook Islands. Muri Lagoon, to the southeast of the island, boasts a beautiful stretch of pristine sand. From here, you can paddle into the shallow water to the uninhabited islets beyond, which are excellent for snorkelling.

LUKA KORCULANSKA, CROATIA The sandy beach at Luka Korculanska protrudes into the clear waters of the Adriatic on a wooded peninsula. It bustles with local families, the air filled with smells from open-air grills and food stalls. The beach is a leisurely 15-minute walk or a short boat ride from Korcula. This picturesque town, with its winding flower-filled alleys, is encircled by 14th-century fortress walls.

LAS ISLAS CIES, GALICIA, SPAIN These three granite islands are a far cry from the Costa del Sol. They are isolated, wildly beautiful and buffeted by the Atlantic at the mouth of the Vigo river. The steep cliffs on their western shores feel the full force of the ocean, while the eastern coast is gentler, with rolling sand dunes and calm waters. Glorious Praia das Roadas is found here, its dunes sheltering a lagoon.

OFU BEACH, AMERICAN SAMOA The jagged, forested peaks of Piumfa and Sunuitao mountains loom over the 3-km (2-mile) stretch of coral sand on Ofu Island's south coast. The offshore reef is home to 150 species of coral and 300 species of fish, but you'll need to bring your own snorkelling equipment if you want to see them – there is little in the way of tourist infrastructure here.

OXWICH BAY, GOWER, UK The Gower Peninsula in Wales, which juts into the Bristol Channel, has a coastline pitted with secluded bays, rocky bluffs and sweeps of golden sand. Oxwich is a 4-km (2½-mile) sandy stretch, backed by dunes and a salt marsh, and is popular year-round for windsurfing, sailing and water-skiing. The quietest part of the bay is on the eastern side, at Nicholaston Burrows. If you have time, walk on the coast path to Oxwich Point, from which point there are great views back over the bay.

SPORTS AND ACTIVITIES

Sea kayaking in the calm, glacier-studded waters of Prince William Sound, Alaska *(p238)*

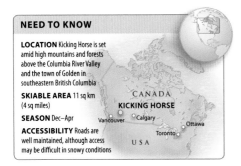

KICKING HORSE
VS WHISTLER

If you want your skiing steep, deep and powdery, forget the oft-visited, rain-drenched ski runs of Whistler and head east into the frosty splendour of Kicking Horse, Canada's coolest ski resort

NEED TO KNOW

LOCATION Kicking Horse is set amid high mountains and forests above the Columbia River Valley and the town of Golden in southeastern British Columbia

SKIABLE AREA 11 sq km (4 sq miles)

SEASON Dec–Apr

ACCESSIBILITY Roads are well maintained, although access may be difficult in snowy conditions

For years, Whistler has been the big boy of the Canadian ski scene, and with its hosting of the 2010 Winter Olympics, that situation is unlikely to change soon. Yet, on the opposite side of British Columbia (BC), there is a far smaller resort which proves that big isn't necessarily best.

Kicking Horse, in the Canadian Rockies, has skiing that will challenge the very best, is surrounded by classic mountain wilderness and, to top it all,

even has the finest mountain restaurant in Canada, when you need a break from the action. You can sit in said Eagle's Eye Restaurant at a height of 2,350 m (7,700 ft), gaze out across the snow-draped Selkirk, Purcell, Kootenay and Rocky Mountain ranges and wonder about all the fuss over the big guy to the west.

Whistler may have vast amounts of terrain and the famous big vertical, but who wants to ski if it's raining on the lower slopes and draped in clouds on the upper slopes? Kicking Horse is the skier's ski resort – the focus is on those wanting to push themselves on challenging terrain, where the skiing comes first and everything else, from nightlife to ease of access, is secondary. And, because of its ideal location, you often get the light, dry snowfall referred to as "champagne powder", which is great for skiing.

Just getting here is a mini adventure in itself – the spectacular drive from Calgary takes you through the kind of scenery that was made for

Mounties and grizzly bears. The resort's satellite town of Golden may not live up to its name, but it is a utilitarian blue-collar logging town that is far removed from the glamour that defines much of Whistler (so much the better, some might say).

The real gold however, lies 11 km (7 miles) uphill from Golden, where Kicking Horse's small selection of recently built hotels, bars and restaurants greets you, and the powder-white bulks of the 2,450-m (8,035-ft) Blue Heaven and 2,410-m (7,900-ft) Terminator Peak loom above. From these radiate a series of ridges from which deep chutes descend, attracting keen skiers from all over the world. Almost every run off the two main ridges, CPR and Redemption, is a double black diamond and the exciting descents that they offer take you into snowy bowls, where a good, hard turn will see the powder arcing over your shoulder into a long, dry plume that hangs in the air for several seconds after you've passed by.

Who wouldn't travel to the other side of British Columbia for all that?

FORGET WHISTLER?

THE BUILD-UP Huge vertical, a massive off-piste area, great lift system and buzzing nightlife make Whistler one of the world's most popular ski resorts – you'll literally encounter skiers and boarders from every corner of the globe on the resort's slopes.

THE LETDOWN Being so popular means it's often busy on the lifts, on the slopes and in the bars and restaurants. So if you like peace and quiet, this may not be for you. Whistler is located relatively close to the Pacific Coast, which means the frequent snowfalls here can be heavy in every sense of the word. While bluebird days and powder are not uncommon, you may also spend day after day under leaden skies and maybe even rain.

GOING ANYWAY? Travel outside peak holiday periods to avoid the crowds; plan for alternative activities, should the weather turn bad. Fortunately, Whistler has heaps of options.

ABOVE Skiing enthusiasts parking their skis outside a busy mountain restaurant at Whistler

PRACTICAL INFORMATION

Getting There and Around
The nearest international airport is at Calgary, about a 3-hour drive to Golden. Shuttle services from the airport to the resort are also available. The road is well maintained but the drive may be difficult in heavy snow.

Where to Eat
The dining is just adequate, except at Eagle's Eye Restaurant (www.kickinghorseresort.com). Located at the mountaintop and only accessible via the Golden Eagle Express Gondola, this is an absolute must for its sensational locally produced food and magnificent views.

Where to Stay
The award-winning Copper Lodge (www.kickinghorseresort. com) is boutique hotel accommodation at its best, and it's just a short walk from the Golden Eagle Express Gondola.

When to Go
The season runs Dec–Apr. Skiing is possible before and after the "official" season, but there will be no lift access.

Budget per Day for Two
£200 including food, lift pass, ski hire and lessons.

Website
www.kickinghorseresort.com

MAIN IMAGE Skier enjoying the view from one of Kicking Horse's ridges **BELOW (left to right)** Scenic view of Kicking Horse River with mountain; a steep ski run; interior of the Eagle's Eye Restaurant

5 MORE SKI RESORTS TO RIVAL WHISTLER

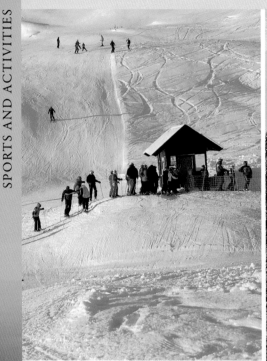

People queuing up for the ski lift on a snow-covered mountain slope at Voss resort, Norway

VOSS

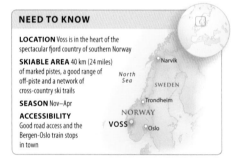

NEED TO KNOW

LOCATION Voss is in the heart of the spectacular fjord country of southern Norway

SKIABLE AREA 40 km (24 miles) of marked pistes, a good range of off-piste and a network of cross-country ski trails

SEASON Nov–Apr

ACCESSIBILITY Good road access and the Bergen-Oslo train stops in town

Voss is a relatively small resort, but there's enough here to occupy anyone for a week. The mix of downhill runs accessed by the cute red cable car from the centre of the town is surprisingly varied and offers sublime sunset views across the region's pastel-shaded whaleback mountains, which have a real "call of the wild" feel about them. There is also a vast network of cross-country trails emanating from the town.

As well as skiing, visitors can also enjoy a spectacular winter rail journey to the shores of mighty Sognefjord. With so much to do, you won't easily get bored at this lakeside resort.

Practical Information

Getting There and Around There are regular trains to and from Bergen (approximately 1 hour) and Oslo (5–6 hours). Road access from Bergen is also good in all but the worst weather.

When to Go Nov–Apr. It is possible to ski after this but lift access may not be available.

Website www.visitvoss.no

Skiing through glorious powder past a stand of snow-covered trees, Record Ridge, Red Mountain Ski Resort, Canada

RED MOUNTAIN

NEED TO KNOW

LOCATION Red Mountain is in southern British Columbia (BC), above the former mining town of Rossland

SKIABLE AREA 7 sq km (3 sq miles)

SEASON Nov–Apr

ACCESSIBILITY Vancouver is 8 hours away by road and Calgary 6. The nearest airports are at Spokane in Washington and Kelowna, BC

Red Mountain is something of a testing ground – say you've skied here and your coolness coefficient rises exponentially (no need to mention the fact that you fell down the steep slope and bounced off the trees).

Along with its steeps and, more especially its trees, Red is also famous for the lavish helpings of British Columbian powder that it gets. There's an apocryphal tale of the local who once found the perfect tree run here, but was never able to discover the exact line again. So blessed with perfect lines is Red Mountain, that it's easy to believe the story.

The hill sits perfectly with the resort's satellite town of Rossland, a characterful old gold-mining town populated by equally colourful characters. The hill is slowly being developed, but there has been a genuine effort on behalf of the owners to maintain its old-school feel.

Although growing in popularity, Red Mountain is still an overlooked destination. If you want a challenge and like to wallow in knee-deep powder, a skiing trip here is a must.

Practical Information

Getting There and Around The most convenient access is from Spokane International Airport, which is about 2½ hours south. There's a shuttle service from Rossland.

When to Go Nov–Apr. February is the busiest. It's quite feasible to ski well after April if you don't mind hiking up the mountain.

Website www.redresort.com

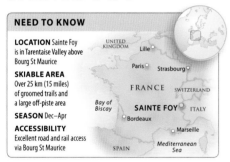

A group of visitors enjoying the natural hot springs in the freezing winter at Kamchatka, Russia

A snowboarder performing a stunt spinning over mountain peaks at Sainte Foy, France

Skiers on the magnificent snow-covered slopes of Åre, Sweden's number-one ski resort

SAINTE FOY

NEED TO KNOW

LOCATION Sainte Foy is in Tarentaise Valley above Bourg St Maurice

SKIABLE AREA Over 25 km (15 miles) of groomed trails and a large off-piste area

SEASON Dec–Apr

ACCESSIBILITY Excellent road and rail access via Bourg St Maurice

Don't be fooled by the fact that Sainte Foy has a mere 25 km (15 miles) of pistes, for the off-piste in this recently developed Alpine resort is extensive, challenging and relatively crowd-free, especially compared to popular neighbours such as Les Arcs and Tignes. And it's great for snowboarders.

It pays to get in with the locals in order to discover the best riding. Many of them will hike from the top of the lifts to lay down fresh tracks far away from skiers who are not in the know. But even without local knowledge, you'll enjoy some of the finest and most open terrain in the Alps here, especially late in the season.

Practical Information

Getting There and Around There are excellent road links to the nearest airports, Chambéry and Lyon, although the journey may take longer in bad weather. Eurostar service to Bourg St Maurice operates through the winter.

When to Go Dec–Apr. Late season has almost empty pistes, longer days and warmer weather.

Website www.saintefoy.net

KAMCHATKA

NEED TO KNOW

LOCATION Kamchatka is in the volcanic "Ring of Fire" region on the Pacific Ocean's edge in Eastern Siberia, Russia

SKIABLE AREA About 250,000 sq kms (96,500 sq miles), although most of the terrain is unexplored

SEASON Apr–May

ACCESSIBILITY Slopes can be accessed by helicopter or long hikes

Skiing in Kamchatka is an almost surreal experience. Many of the peaks your battered Mi-8 helicopter will drop you on have steam issuing from cracks in their flanks; active volcanoes dot the landscape and at the end of your run, you might find yourself on a black-sand beach that is being pounded by Pacific breakers. You may spot grizzly bears and sea eagles while skiing, and can easily clock up over 11,000 m (36,000 ft) of vertical per day. And it's not unusual to wind it all up at the end of the day sipping Russian "champagne" in a natural hot spring, easily making Kamchatka the ski trip of a lifetime.

Practical Information

Getting There and Around The only practical means of accessing Kamchatka is from the Petropavlovsk-Kamchatsky international airport, which is 9 hours from Moscow. Accommodation is in the regional capital of Petropavlovsk-Kamchatsky. Hotels are basic by western standards. You will have to bring all your own ski gear and spares as nothing is available in the town.

When to Go Apr–May, as midwinter weather is too unpredictable.

Website www.eaheliskiing.com

ÅRE

NEED TO KNOW

LOCATION Åre is 630 km (390 miles) north of Stockholm and 350 km (210 miles) south of the Arctic Circle, and sits above a collection of linked villages

SKIABLE AREA Around 100 km (60 miles) of pistes, and extensive off-piste

SEASON Early Nov–early May

ACCESSIBILITY Good road, rail and air links

Above Åre's attractive pastel houses and shining lake lies the best lift-accessed skiing in Scandinavia, with something for everyone. Those skiers wanting to head off-piste, in particular, will love the options here, including a great snowcat-accessed run from the 1,420-m (4,660-ft) summit of Åreskutan. There's also a fine array of novice and intermediate runs, allowing skiers and snowboarders of all abilities to enjoy a trip to Scandinavia, the home of skiing.

Late-season skiing can be sublime as the sun rarely sinks beneath the horizon. And if you like to party hard, Åre provides plenty of entertainment.

Practical Information

Getting There and Around Östersund airport is 1 1/2 hours away and there are good road and rail links with all Sweden's major cities. However, snow may make road access difficult.

When to Go February onwards – midwinter has short days and is very cold. Late season is often best due to longer days and uncrowded slopes.

Website www.skistar.com

THE PARIS MARATHON
VS THE LONDON MARATHON

Running the Paris marathon instead of London means broad boulevards instead of narrow streets – and an inspiring start in the looming shadow of the Arc de Triomphe

NEED TO KNOW

ROUTE Head down the Champs-Elysées, around the Place de la Concorde and east, looping around the Bois de Vincennes. Return to the centre and finish on Ave Foch, behind the Arc de Triomphe

ENTRY DEADLINE End Jan

RACE DATE First Sun in April

NUMBER OF ENTRANTS 37,000

London may be host to one of the most famous marathons in the world, but Paris can offer runners the same big-city buzz without the uncertainty of getting a place. Unlike London, which sometimes has as many as eight applicants for each place, any potential participant will virtually be guaranteed a place in the Paris marathon. Both races take place in April, with similarly mild weather, so many runners who unsuccessfully tried for London head to Paris instead.

ABOVE Athletes racing out of the Alma Tunnel in Paris

Blessed with a beautiful setting, with its broad avenues ideal for mass runners, Paris is certainly no second-best alternative to London. Unlike London, which starts on the eastern outskirts, the Paris marathon begins and ends in the city centre, so you'll be running along wide boulevards and passing famous Parisian landmarks. What could match the excitement of beginning a marathon at the top of the Champs-Elysées, with the Arc de Triomphe behind you and an endless wave of some 35,000 runners before you as you set off into the rising sun?

As you head east, the surreal sight of an artificial mountain at the Bois de Vincennes zoo looms on the horizon. Twists and turns through leafy parkland here give a welcome break from the long straight avenues. The crowds are thinner too; a few suburban dog-walkers look on bemused as you bound – or by now trudge – through the trees.

This of course, being Paris, refreshments are plentiful; bananas and oranges are the official offering, though look out for the wine and cheese stand at around the 35-km (21-mile) mark. Supporters en route are numerous, though they are, for the most part, markedly laid-back in typical Parisian style. It's the entertainers who provide more risqué fun: from a gay mariachi band – men in fake moustaches wearing pink tutus – to cheerleaders in giant squirrel costumes.

Your 42-km (26-mile) tour takes you past some famous Parisian landmarks, including the Place de la Concorde, Rue Rivoli, Place de la Bastille, and Avenue de Versailles, ending up back near the Arc de Triomphe.

Here, at last, you can stop, enjoy the free massage and wait while your loved ones do their own jostling through the pack to find you.

FORGET THE LONDON MARATHON?

THE BUILD-UP London is undoubtedly one of the world's top marathons, in terms of its number of competitors, and for the top-ranking runners it attracts. Begun in 1981, it has since built up a huge following, with the streets lined with cheering supporters from start to finish.

THE LETDOWN London has become a victim of its own success. Competition for getting in is high – almost 100,000 applicants for 50,000 accepted places. Moreover, as most of the course is on relatively narrow roads, you become hemmed in, which can be frustrating and energy-sapping when you're trying to get into a rhythm and keep up your planned pace.

GOING ANYWAY? If you don't get into London at first, keep trying, as they guarantee a place if you apply five years in a row. To get around the congestion problem, try to worm your way to the front of your section. When the race starts, zig-zag through firmly but sportingly. Or wear a giant hedgehog suit – that'll soon clear the pack!

ABOVE The streets of London crowded with thousands of runners at the London Marathon

PRACTICAL INFORMATION

Getting There and Around
Paris' main airport is Roissy Charles de Gaulle, some 27 km (17 miles) north of the city. International train links to Paris are excellent; Eurostar (www.eurostar.com) serves the UK via the EuroTunnel, with a 2 ½-hour journey from London's St Pancras to Paris Gare du Nord. On the morning of the marathon, the nearest Métro station is Charles de Gaulle Etoile; if it's too packed, try Argentine or George V.

Where to Eat
If you are planning on eating out, go for the *plat du jour* at lunchtime, the main meal of the day in France. It is usually a good-value and tasty option. Try Chez Gladines, which serves excellent meals (tel. +33 1 45 80 70 10).

Where to Stay
Résidence Lord Byron is located two blocks from the Champs-Elysées (www.escapade-paris.com/fr).

Budget per Person per Day
Approximately £100, including food, accommodation and transport.

Website
www.parismarathon.com

MAIN IMAGE Participants running along the Champs-Elysées
BELOW (left to right) Runners beside the Seine; competitors at Place de la Bastille

4 MORE MARATHONS TO RIVAL LONDON

EVEREST MARATHON, NEPAL The highest marathon in the world at 5,180 m (17,000 ft). Runners even have to walk up to the start at Gorak Shep, which helps acclimatize to the oxygen-depleted air. Held in November (www.everestmarathon.org.uk).

ATHENS, GREECE The original first run, from Marathon to the Greek capital held in 490 BC. Unlike the heroic Phidippides, today's runners don't do this marathon in full military gear. Hot and hilly, every November (www.athensmarathon.com).

ICE MARATHON, ANTARCTICA Try running 42 km (26 miles) in -20°C (-4°F), buffeted by katabatic winds, at a 3,050-m (10,000-ft) altitude and a few hundred miles from the South Pole. Madness, every December (www.icemarathon.com).

TWO OCEANS, SOUTH AFRICA This 56-km (35-mile) ultra-marathon, the "world's most beautiful marathon", links both the Atlantic and Indian Oceans. Held on the Saturday of Easter weekend (www.twooceansmarathon.org.za).

SALSA IN HAVANA
VS TANGO IN BUENOS AIRES

Tango in Buenos Aires pales in comparison to the spicy-hot salsa popular in Havana, with an evocative colonial ambience and vivacious nightlife as the perfect backdrop

NEED TO KNOW

LOCATION Havana is on the northern coast of western Cuba, 150 km (90 miles) south of Key West, Florida

POPULATION 2.1 million

VISITORS PER YEAR 800,000

DAYTIME TEMPERATURES
Jan: 22°C (72°F); Apr: 25°C (76°F); Jul: 28°C (82°F); Oct: 26°C (79°F)

Lovers of Latin music and dance could be forgiven for thinking that Buenos Aires, with its passion for tango, is unrivalled as a place to learn dance. But anyone who has spent time in Havana would beg to differ – Cuba's capital city is considered to be the global destination for Afro-Latin dance.

From the sentimental *son* to sizzling salsa, music and dance are the pulsating undercurrents to Cuban life. Everywhere you go in Havana, you are surrounded by melodious rhythms. The soft notes of Spanish guitars echo along cobbled streets full of the romance of history, while the throbbing beat of brassy salsa tunes rises above the wheezing of patched-up cars from the 1950s clattering past centuries-old cathedrals and castles.

The Cuban love of salsa reflects an instinct for gaiety that turns material adversity on its head. Couples dance in the street to overtly sexual numbers and by night, younger Cubans flood the city's nightclubs. Women are whisked onto the dance floor and whirled around to thrilling *timba*, a

ABOVE Musicians on the street playing guitars, Habana Vieja

recent salsa craze that's both energetic and innovative. Buenos Aires and tango seem tame in comparison. If salsa whets your appetite for dance, why not also try rumba, the African soul of Cuban music. Its dance rhythms can be either sensual and dynamic, or slow and sad.

And who better to teach you the complicated steps than Cubans themselves, deemed the world's finest dancers? Several hotels in Havana offer classes, as do local troupes and freelancing tutors. You can also sign up for package tours that teach you how to swivel your hips like the Cubans. After class, you can sip *mojitos* and smoke fine cigars in bars such as El Floridita and La Bodeguita del Medio. Then, you can up the ante and let your hair down dancing on stage at famously colourful cabarets, such as the Tropicana.

Add to that the city's simmering pre-revolutionary allure. Habana Vieja (Old Havana) is a treasure-trove of magnificent colonial buildings, many of which have recently emerged from restoration as hotels, restaurants and museums. Dance classes are taught in Vedado, an early 20th-century district imbued with effusive Art Deco, Beaux Arts and Modernist structures with a tropical twist. Most of the venues, hardly changed since the 1950s, offer a glimpse of a once-gilded era.

PRACTICAL INFORMATION

Getting There and Around
Havana's José Martí International Airport on the outskirts of Havana is served by flights from Europe, Canada and Latin America. The city has an efficient and inexpensive, albeit crowded, bus system. Taxis are plentiful, although the main tourist spots can be explored on foot.

Where to Eat
Dining is not a strong point, and the best bargains are in *paladares* (private restaurants). The best of these is La Guarida (Concordia 418; tel. +53 786 37351; www.laguarida.com), which

gets packed. The area is unsafe to walk at night, so take a taxi.

Where to Stay
The atmospheric Hotel Raquel, (Calles Amargura and San Ignacio; tel. +53 786 08280; www.habaguanexhotels.com) is an Art Deco masterpiece.

When to Go
Oct–Apr are the coolest months; summer can be stiflingly hot.

Budget per Day for Two
£120 for food, travel and accommodation.

Website
www.salsa-in-cuba.com

FORGET TANGO IN BUENOS AIRES?

THE BUILD-UP The capital of Argentina has plenty of European sophistication and style, and tango, the melancholic dance that evolved in the brothels of 19th-century Buenos Aires, draws many visitors to the city. Several first-class restaurants host tango shows in the evening, dancers perform in the streets of San Telmo and many studios teach you the moves.

THE LETDOWN Tango in Buenos Aires feels like a well-worn cliché. The dance form's explosion of popularity has resulted in a flood of foreigners. The *barrio* (quarter) of San Telmo gets crowded with gawking tourists, especially when cruise ships are in town. And dance studios are often packed with tourists on learn-to-dance package vacations.

GOING ANYWAY? When you're done watching public tango in San Telmo, just pick up a free copy of *El Tangauta* for a listing of tango clubs. Take time to browse the *barrio's* antiques markets. In summer, sit out the midday heat in one of the city's shady parks.

ABOVE A crush of people watching a couple performing the tango on a San Telmo street

MAIN IMAGE Musicians travelling in a 1950s American car **BELOW (left to right)** La Bodeguita del Medio bar, with signed walls; couples dancing salsa at the Salon Rosado; Plaza de la Catedral, Habana Vieja

4 MORE DANCE DESTINATIONS TO RIVAL BUENOS AIRES

DOMINICAN REPUBLIC, CARIBBEAN The locals of this Caribbean hotspot move to merengue, a high-energy, frantic, fast-paced dance characterized by slow turns.

SALVADOR DE BAHÍA, BRAZIL This city situated in northern Brazil is the capital of thumping samba beats and is famous for its annual carnival, when hordes of revellers descend on the city to join in the celebrations.

CALIFORNIA, USA West Coast Swing is synonymous with southern California. All connoisseurs of the dance can sign up for a class in Los Angeles to perfect the swing patterns which number more than 5,000.

THE LEVANT AND ISTANBUL, TURKEY The Levant, an area that encompasses the Eastern Mediterranean region, gyrates and swivels to the sinuous beats of belly-dancing, and Istanbul is an alluring place to learn this mesmerizing Middle Eastern dance.

MOUNT STANLEY
VS MOUNT KILIMANJARO

Those who climb Mount Stanley are promised a breathtaking variety of flora, fauna and terrain that puts Africa's more famous giant, Mount Kilimanjaro, to shame

ABOVE Trekkers heading towards the summit of Africa's legendary Mount Kilimanjaro

FORGET MOUNT KILIMANJARO?

THE BUILD-UP Mount Kilimanjaro, which is the highest peak in Africa, is the tallest mountain in the world that is accessible to hikers, and requires no technical mountaineering expertise. Rising above the Serengeti, the broad, snowcapped summit is an alluring fixture on the horizon throughout much of Kenya and Tanzania. And the opportunity to visit some of Africa's finest game parks before climbing the fabled mountain has undeniable appeal.

THE LETDOWN The major ascent routes are consistently crowded, and on the most popular of these, dubbed the "Coca-Cola Route", you'll find camps selling drinks and snacks. Wildlife sightings, even at lower levels, are rare and the terrain at higher levels is often less than picturesque. There are many inexperienced climbers here who shortcut acclimatization, are unfit for the challenge and never see the summit.

GOING ANYWAY? If seeing Mount Kilimanjaro's steadily shrinking glacier before it disappears is still on your must-do list, make sure you go with a reputable operator that is committed to your safety and the fair treatment of porters. These operators are likely to recommend less-congested routes offering gradual acclimatization and, therefore, a better chance of summit success.

NEED TO KNOW

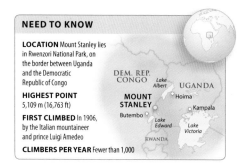

LOCATION Mount Stanley lies in Rwenzori National Park, on the border between Uganda and the Democratic Republic of Congo

HIGHEST POINT 5,109 m (16,763 ft)

FIRST CLIMBED In 1906, by the Italian mountaineer and prince Luigi Amedeo

CLIMBERS PER YEAR Fewer than 1,000

DEM. REP. CONGO · Lake Albert · UGANDA · MOUNT STANLEY · Hoima · Kampala · Butembo · Lake Edward · Lake Victoria · RWANDA

Explorers returning from Africa to Europe in the mid-19th century were met with scepticism when they claimed to have seen ice and snow atop Mount Kilimanjaro and Mount Kenya, both of which stand just miles from the equator. But by the time the British explorer Henry Morton Stanley returned home in 1889 with tales of a dazzling set of six glaciated summits in central Africa's Rwenzori Mountains – the tallest of which was named Mount Stanley in his honour – the extraordinary reality began to sink in. Today, thousands of people travel to Africa's equatorial peaks for their challenging climbs, picturesque scenery and to experience the strange existence of near-Arctic conditions in the tropics. But while some 20,000 people flock to fabled Mount Kilimanjaro every year, fewer than 1,000 people visit Mount Stanley, which boasts all the majesty, much more wildlife and none of the crowds of its more famous rival.

One of the most spectacular features of tropical mountains is the wealth of different ecosystems and extraordinary biodiversity found on their slopes. Mount Stanley is no exception. You'll climb from rainforest and moorland up to mossy forests and bogs, and finally onto glaciated alpine terrain. The mountain's abundant rainfall gives rise to weird and wonderful plants, including heather that grows up to 6 m (20 ft) high and giant groundsels and lobelia, which look more like miniature trees than ground cover. Wildlife-spotting on Mount Stanley is also superb, and far superior to that of Mount Kilimanjaro. Over 70 mammal species inhabit the

Rwenzori Mountains, including colobus and blue monkeys, which chatter in the forest canopies, bushbucks and antelopes, which graze near lakes and meadows, and mountain elephants, golden cats and leopards. And nearly 200 species of endemic and migratory birds, from colourful turacos to bee-eaters, reside in the lowland jungles.

The terrain on Mount Stanley, Africa's third highest peak, is tougher than that found on either Mount Kilimanjaro or Mount Kenya. The Rwenzori Mountains – also known as "The Mountains of the Moon" because of their rocky white peaks – are sliced with deep-cut gorges, rivers and ravines. Once you get near the summit, you'll need to rope up and use an ice axe and crampons to traverse the Elena Glacier, before making the final push towards the summit. In addition to the challenging landscape, be prepared for more rain and lower visibility than you might find on other African peaks, along with some dicey river crossings and knee-deep mud. But the rewards are spectacular. The mountain's tricky terrain and near-constant wet weather explain why this UNESCO World Heritage Site is so unspoilt, lush and full of life.

PRACTICAL INFORMATION

Getting There and Around
The Rwenzori Mountains are best accessed from Kasese in southwest Uganda, which is about 300 km (185 miles) – or a 5- to 6-hour journey on paved roads – from Kampala's Entebbe International Airport. From Kasese, you can arrange your trek into Rwenzori National Park, which will include an ascent of Mount Stanley.

Where to Eat
Meals included in trekking packages to the Rwenzori Mountains.

Where to Stay
Accommodation also comes part and parcel with your trekking

package, and is usually in simple wooden huts along the circuit.

When to Go
Due to its equatorial setting, Mount Stanley can be climbed at any time of year, but July to mid-September and December to February do offer slightly drier conditions.

Budget per Day for Two
An eight-day guided trek in the Rwenzori Mountains, including a climb of Mount Stanley, meals, accommodation and porters is about £500 for two people.

Website
www.rwenzorimountaineering services.com

MAIN IMAGE Lake Bujuku beneath Mount Stanley, with moss, giant groundsels and lobelias in foreground **BELOW (left to right)** Bushbuck; porter on a walkway over a bog; climbers near the top of Mount Stanley

MOUNT WILHELM

NEED TO KNOW

LOCATION Mount Wilhelm is in the Bismarck Mountains of Papua New Guinea

HIGHEST POINT 4,509 m (14,793 ft)

FIRST CLIMBED In 1938 by Australian Leigh Vial, who became a World War II patrol watcher in Papua New Guinea

CLIMBERS PER YEAR Fewer than 1,000

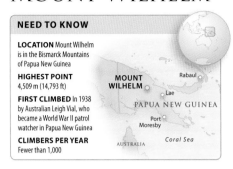

The jagged granite summit of Mount Wilhelm, the highest peak in Papua New Guinea, is quite a departure from the highland route that leads you there, which ascends through dense rainforest, temperate mountain forest and open grassland before breaking out into rugged alpine terrain. The trek to the top of the mountain takes three to four days and although it isn't technical, it involves some steep scrambling near the top. The snowfields that used to carpet the mountain no longer exist, but the air in the higher elevations is still cool and crisp. From the summit on a clear day there are spectacular views north to the Pacific Ocean and small coastal islands.

Practical Information

Getting There and Around Fly into Goroka, which is in the centre of Papua New Guinea. Here you can join an organized trekking group and travel by shuttle bus to a base camp on Mount Wilhelm.

When to Go The best climbing conditions are from May to November.

Website www.pngtrekkingadventures.com

The barren rocky summit of Mount Wilhelm, Papua New Guinea, set against a brilliant blue sky

MAUNA LOA

NEED TO KNOW

LOCATION Mauna Loa lies in Hawai'i Volcanoes National Park on the Big Island of Hawai'i, USA

HIGHEST POINT 4,169 m (13,679 ft)

FIRST CLIMBED In 1794 by Scotsman Archibald Menzies

CLIMBERS PER YEAR Fewer than 1,000

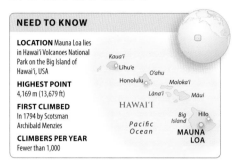

Rising over 9,000 m (30,000 ft) from the ocean floor, Hawai'i's Mauna Loa is both the largest volcano and mountain in the world. Yet from a distance, its gently sloping sides and apparently flat summit belie this magnitude. The volcano's 63-km (39-mile) circular trekking route cuts across a spectacular landscape of different types of exposed lava, and although it's virtually lifeless here – there are no plants, animals or birds in sight – the surreal rock formations provide a fascinating backdrop to the trail. As you approach the summit caldera, cinder cones, gas emissions and ground swelling serve as a constant reminder that this is an active volcano, with plenty of punch still remaining.

Practical Information

Getting There and Around Fly into Hilo and either rent a car or catch a shuttle bus from there to Hawai'i Volcanoes National Park, which is a 45-minute drive away.

When to Go Mauna Loa can be climbed at any time of year, though the weather is best between June and August.

Website www.nps.gov/havo

Lone hiker on top of the expansive, gently sloping summit of Mauna Loa, Hawai'i, USA

COPA

NEED TO KNOW

LOCATION Copa is located in the Cordillera Blanca, a mountain range in the Peruvian Andes

HIGHEST POINT 6,188 m (20,302 ft)

FIRST CLIMBED In 1932 by a German expedition team led by Erwin Schneider

CLIMBERS PER YEAR Fewer than 200

Less than 10 degrees south of the equator lies the world's highest tropical mountain range, Peru's Cordillera Blanca (see also p85). These mountains, which cradle hundreds of glaciers and form part of South America's continental divide, contain no less than 27 rugged summits that are higher than Mount Kilimanjaro and are cut sharply by plunging glacial valleys. It's a mountaineer's dream. The most accessible of these towering peaks is Copa, which can be climbed up and either climbed or skied down. Burros carry your equipment to a base camp, from which point you will follow the tongue of a glacier that leads to a route up the mountain's western ridge.

Practical Information

Getting There and Around From the Peruvian capital, Lima, it's an 8-hour bus ride to Huaraz, where you can acclimatize before taking a 2-hour ride by local bus or private shuttle to the trail head.

When to Go The best time to climb Copa is in the dry season, which is from May to September.

Website For general information on the Cordillera Blanca visit www.peaksandplaces.com

The dramatic snowcapped summit of Copa, Cordillera Blanca, Peru

MOUNT KINABALU

NEED TO KNOW

LOCATION Mount Kinabalu National Park is located in the Malaysian state of Sabah on the island of Borneo

HIGHEST POINT 4,095 m (13,435 ft)

FIRST CLIMBED In 1858 by British naturalist Sir Hugh Low

CLIMBERS PER YEAR Around 50,000

On anyone's list of bizarre flora, a carnivorous plant that can eat small mammals would certainly be near the top. On the same list you would also expect to find the parasitic Rafflesia plant, which has the largest flower in the world and is also known as the "corpse flower" because it smells and looks like rotting flesh. These are just two of the extraordinary plants found in the jungles of Borneo, where the ascent of mighty Mount Kinabalu begins in a shuttle bus carrying trekkers to the trail head. The jungle also boasts more than 800 orchid species and 600 fern species – to put this in context, there are only 500 fern species in

Climbers roping up for the challenging ascent of Mount Kinabalu's rocky summit, Borneo

Africa. This is one of the most biodiverse places on the planet and a hotbed of endemism thanks to its tropical climate and abundant rainfall.

The three-day climb of this giant granite dome begins at the Timpohon Gate, which lies at an elevation of 1,800 m (5,900 ft). Accompanied by mandatory guides, trekkers rise through forests of conifer and oak, cloud forest and subalpine meadow. Like the rainforest below it, the mountain boasts a wealth of unusual fauna, including giant red leeches that prey on giant earthworms, extraordinary rhinoceros hornbills – birds that look as if they have a shoe attached to their heads – and the threatened orang-utan, one of the four great apes. Pygmy squirrels, fruit bats and brightly coloured tropical birds share the forest canopy on the steep mountain slopes. Hand-carved stone steps, moss-covered wooden stairs and fixed ropes assist trekkers on the trail's steeper sections. The final leg of the climb emerges onto a slippery surface of exposed granite that leads to the summit and boasts fantastic panoramas.

Practical Information

Getting There and Around A 3-hour bus journey takes you from Kota Kinabalu Airport to Kinabalu National Park, where you join your tour group.

When to Go Mount Kinabalu can be climbed at any time of year, but is most enjoyable in the dry season, which is from February to April.

Website www.sabahparks.org.my

COTOPAXI

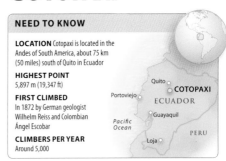

NEED TO KNOW

LOCATION Cotopaxi is located in the Andes of South America, about 75 km (50 miles) south of Quito in Ecuador

HIGHEST POINT 5,897 m (19,347 ft)

FIRST CLIMBED In 1872 by German geologist Wilhelm Reiss and Colombian Ángel Escobar

CLIMBERS PER YEAR Around 5,000

Cotopaxi, which is known locally as "the neck of the moon" because of its near-perfect symmetrical cone that seems to stretch forever upwards, is one of the highest active volcanoes in the world. Its last eruption, in 1877, sent pyroclastic rivers of fire streaming down all sides of the mountain, melting glaciers along the way and carving deep valleys with scorching mudflows that ran as far as the Pacific Ocean, 100 km (60 miles) to the west. Today, trekkers either camp or stay in huts on the mountain, where the most popular route to the summit can be climbed in a long day from a hut at 4,800 m (15,800 ft). Though not a terribly difficult climb, it should only be attempted by experienced mountaineers with appropriate climbing kit.

Practical Information

Getting There and Around From Quito, local and shuttle buses run to Cotopaxi National Park, which is an hour to the south.

When to Go Cotopaxi can be climbed at any time of year, although January, June, July and December offer particularly clear, dry days.

Website www.moggely.com

Snowcapped Cotopaxi, Ecuador, with its sharply pointed peak

REYKJAVÍK GOLF CLUB, ICELAND
VS ST ANDREWS, SCOTLAND

Frustrated by the lottery for the Old Course's balloted tickets at St Andrews? Swap bracken, ferns and heather for the glacial home of Reykjavík's prestigious Icelandic PGA Open

NEED TO KNOW

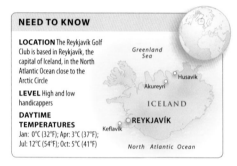

LOCATION The Reykjavik Golf Club is based in Reykjavik, the capital of Iceland, in the North Atlantic Ocean close to the Arctic Circle

LEVEL High and low handicappers

DAYTIME TEMPERATURES
Jan: 0°C (32°F); Apr: 3°C (37°F); Jul: 12°C (54°F); Oct: 5°C (41°F)

Greenland Sea
Husavik
Akureyri
ICELAND
REYKJAVIK
Keflavik
North Atlantic Ocean

St Andrews in Scotland may have been synonymous with golf since the 15th century, but it might come as a surprise to learn that Iceland has twice as many golf courses per capita than Scotland – the so-called "home of golf". Fifteen 18-hole courses are open to visiting players, together with almost 50 nine-hole facilities – that's a staggering 700-plus holes and counting. What's more, unlike at St Andrews, golf can be played round-the-clock in the summer months.

Established in 1934, the RGC is the oldest and largest golf club in Iceland. It boasts two exceptional 18-hole courses, Grafarholt and Korpa, in an otherworldly landscape of volcanic crags, glaciers, gushing ravines and rugged mountains.

ABOVE Women on a putting green in Laugardalur, Reykjavík

The country's awe-inspiring terrain features some of Mother Nature's greatest triumphs, from tremendous ice caps and mammoth spouting geysers to gnarled lava chasms and cascading waterfalls. Just half an hour from the fairways, glacial lagoons and gin-clear sparkling pools beg exploration with deep-dives into an exhilarating underwater world. Summer golfers can enjoy 24-hour daylight from mid-June to mid-July each year, when Iceland's midsummer "White Nights" encourage playing all night.

The 45-year-old Grafarholt layout is recognized as the nation's premier championship venue. As the host of European and Nordic tournaments, Grafarholt is arguably the toughest test of golf in Iceland, with lava-hemmed fairways suited to big-hitters. However, the par-71, 6,026-m (6,590-yard) 18-hole course has more than rounded curves to contend with, as its stunning mist-shrouded panoramas over Reykjavík can prove to be a serious distraction.

Since it opened in 1997, the 18-hole Korpa has satisfied the golf-hungry with two distinct nines hugging the Atlantic coastline overlooking the Esja Mountain's peaks. On the back nine, the par-4 12th and par-5 15th along the Korpa river's banks require concentration. Designed by Iceland's premier golf-course architect, Hannes Thorsteinsson, the par-72 course stretches for 6,035 m (6,600 yards), with innocuous looking holes inflicting the maximum punishment on high handicappers. Acres of diabolical molten rock provide the rough from hell, though locals refer to this as *vinur í hrauninu* (a friend in the rocks) – as the phenomenon often sends wayward shots back into play when errant balls ricochet off the magma.

The golf courses in Iceland peak in condition in mid-July to the end of August. Though the RGC's courses attract many visitors, it would be a shame to miss out on some of the country's other courses, some set in spectacular locations. You can even play a round by Vatnajökull, Europe's largest glacier.

FORGET ST ANDREWS?

THE BUILD-UP As the self-proclaimed "home of golf", St Andrews has welcomed golfers for more than six centuries. Though commonly referred to as a single course, St Andrews is actually seven separate courses, each open to the public. You can follow in the footsteps of golfing legends, from Old Tom Morris and Bobby Jones, to Jack Nicklaus and Tiger Woods.

THE LETDOWN To walk the fairways of the Old Course at St Andrews, golfers must enter a ballot for a chance to tee off the following day. Demand is high, with over 42,000 rounds played each year, so a prayer to the site's religious relics by the West Bay are common as a last-ditch attempt in prompting a tee time.

GOING ANYWAY? Hand in a ballot card or call the ballot line by 2pm. Highly coveted tee times are hugely oversubscribed with inevitable disappointment for most. The good news is the New Course is usually offered as a consolation prize. The greens are much smaller than the Old but there are still plenty of deep sod bunkers to provide a decent test of golf.

ABOVE Golfers and spectators at the Royal and Ancient Golf Club of St Andrews, Scotland

PRACTICAL INFORMATION

Getting There and Around
Keflavik International Airport (Leifur Eiríksson International) lies on the Reykjanes Peninsula about a 40-minute drive southwest of Iceland's capital Reykjavik. Taxis and airport bus shuttles, known as Flybus, connect the city centre hotels with the terminal building.

Where to Eat
The art of preserving food is endemic to Icelandic culture, so it's no surprise that pickles and cured and salted produce remain at the heart of local cuisine. Classic dishes centre on lamb, chicken, veal and game. However, fish is the mainstay in Reykjavik, such as at the Seafood Cellar (www. sjavarkjallarinn.is).

Where to Stay
As an alternative to the city's bland, mainstream chain hotels, book a room at the ultra-stylish 101 Hotel, where 30 rooms and suites boast quirky one-off designs with a contemporary twist (Hverfisgata 10; tel: +354 580 0101; www.101hotel.is).

When to Go
Iceland's golf season runs for five months a year, peaking in summer when tee times are offered round-the-clock.

Budget per Day for Two
Allow £200 to include accommodation, food and green fees of £20–40.

Website
www.goiceland.org

MAIN IMAGE The 18-hole Grafarholt golf course, with sweeping mountain views **BELOW (left to right)** Aerial view of a course in Vifilsstadir; golfers with Vatnajökull Glacier in the background

3 MORE GOLF COURSES TO RIVAL ST ANDREWS

ANTALYA PGA SULTAN COURSE, TURKEY Until recent years, nobody would ever have associated golf with Turkey. However, by 2008, Turkey's Antalya PGA Sultan Course had hosted the PGA National Pro-Am Championship, Europe's largest Pro-Am for the second year running (www.antalyagolfclub.com.tr).

ROYAL COUNTY DOWN, NORTHERN IRELAND Boasting a 100-year golfing tradition, this 18-hole facility with gorse-lined fairways that weave through tussock-faced bunkers is set in spellbinding scenery along Dundrum Bay's shores. It is also one of US golfer Tiger Woods' favourite courses (www. royalcountydown.org).

LJUNGHUSEN GOLF CLUB, SWEDEN Jutting out into the Baltic Sea on the Falsterbo Peninsula, this 40-year-old club's course sits within a protected marshland area. Its 27 holes are blasted by fearsome winds – little wonder several that heroic coastal holes have earned it a regular ranking in Sweden's top five.

MAIN IMAGE Diver exploring the colourful reef at Christmas Island
BELOW (left to right) Secluded beach on the island; dragon moray
eel; thousands of red crabs crossing the road as they migrate

CHRISTMAS ISLAND
VS THE GREAT BARRIER REEF

The rarely seen coral reefs that surround Christmas Island in the Indian Ocean are just as splendid as those of the Great Barrier Reef in Australia – only they're far more isolated and far less spoilt

NEED TO KNOW

LOCATION Christmas Island is in the Indian Ocean, 360 km (225 miles) south of Java

SCUBA DIVING Christmas Island boasts steep walls, shallow reefs and safe cave dives

DAYTIME TEMPERATURES Jan: 25°C (77°F); Apr: 26°C (79°F); Jul: 24°C (75°F); Oct: 25°C (77°F)

Your first descent into the crystal-clear blue water surrounding Christmas Island will be nothing short of breathtaking. Beneath the surface lies the most luxurious of hard coral reefs – a colourful, lush display that is almost ostentatious in its beauty. The view goes on forever, way down to the depths of the Indian Ocean. Brilliant rays of sunlight cast stripes of turquoise through the sea and highlight the flapping motion of a distant wing. Pause mid-water and wait for the manta ray as it approaches

effortlessly, rotates slightly to ponder on the ungainly nature of the intruder suspended before it, and then slides on by. A pod of spinner dolphins follows in its wake, mother and babies playfully enclosing you, running rings around you and hoping for a new playmate. And in all this time there is no one else in sight other than your diving buddy and a divemaster. It's a far cry from the more famous, but eternally crowded, Great Barrier Reef.

Christmas Island is actually best known not for its scuba diving, but for its extraordinary red-crab migration – a spectacle that takes place every year when millions of the scarlet creatures emerge from the rainforest and walk en masse down to the sea to spawn. At this time, the shallow water turns pink with eggs, but beyond that the sea remains aquamarine, completely pristine and utterly deserted except for its wealth of marine residents. The island has more indigenous species than anywhere else on the planet except the Galapagos Islands, and some of the marine creatures are unique too, including the exotic-looking dragon

moray eel, which frequently pokes its nose up from deep inside hard coral formations to view divers as they pass by its lair.

Rising up from the depths of the Indian Ocean, this rainforest-clad island is actually the tip of an ancient volcano. Its tortuous limestone base has been shaped over millions of years by the waves that lap the island and by rainwater that sinks into the porous rock, creating a honeycomb effect beneath the surface. This rugged, potholed landscape continues into the ocean, where countless underwater caves coax you back into your diving gear and beneath the surface. You enter the splendid Thundercliff Cave, on the shore side of the immaculate fringing coral reef, at a depth of 16 m (53 ft) and through a series of pitch-black grottoes that are decorated with stalactites and stalagmites. A little further on, you ascend to an extraordinary subterranean beach where you can take off your dive gear and continue exploring on foot. It won't be long before you see that you're inside an enormous cavern that is as beautiful and grand as any Gothic cathedral.

FORGET THE GREAT BARRIER REEF?

THE BUILD-UP Often touted as the top must-see-before-you-die attraction, Australia's Great Barrier Reef is the most famous coral reef on the planet, due mostly to its overwhelming size. Swim with minke whales, dive with sharks and snorkel with rainbow-hued fish along 3,000 individual reefs that traverse the coast for 2,300 km (1,430 miles).

THE LETDOWN Thousands of people arrive at the Great Barrier Reef every year hoping to find a pristine underwater world teeming with fascinating marine life. Instead, they find a coral reef that has been damaged by crowds of unthinking visitors, many of whom trample on it at low tide and grab hold of fragile pieces while snorkelling and diving.

GOING ANYWAY? For the best diving, take a liveaboard boat to distant reefs well away from the day-trip regions. Never forget that the reef is a living entity. Help ensure its longevity by using ecologically minded operators.

ABOVE A group of divers preparing to jump into the sea at the Great Barrier Reef, Australia

PRACTICAL INFORMATION

Getting There and Around
Weekly flights arrive at the island's small international airport from either Singapore or Kuala Lumpur, Malaysia, depending on the season. There are also twice-weekly flights from Perth in Australia. There is no public transport on the island, so it's vital that you rent a car, preferably a 4WD, to negotiate the roads through the rainforest.

Where to Eat
The handful of restaurants on Christmas Island, including Australian bistros and Malay and Chinese restaurants, reflect its multicultural population. Indulge in Cantonese cuisine with a twist at Yoong Chong in Poon San (tel. +61 9164 8133).

Where to Stay
Try the Captain's Last Resort (tel. +61 9381 54576), a cosy self-catering cottage with fantastic views of the ocean.

When to Go
Christmas Island sits just below the equator, so its climate is tropical. Try to avoid February and March, which are the wettest months.

Budget per Day for Two
£280 for a day's diving, food, accommodation and transport.

Website
www.christmas.net.au

TUFI, PAPUA NEW GUINEA

NEED TO KNOW

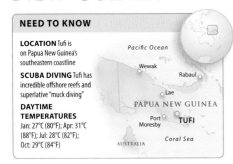

LOCATION Tufi is on Papua New Guinea's southeastern coastline

SCUBA DIVING Tufi has incredible offshore reefs and superlative "muck diving"

DAYTIME TEMPERATURES Jan: 27°C (80°F); Apr: 31°C (88°F); Jul: 28°C (82°F); Oct: 29°C (84°F)

Papua New Guinea is one of tourism's last frontiers. Many areas of the country, it is said, have never been visited by Westerners. The village of Tufi sits on a rugged, fjord-like coastline, its dive centre nestled in the crook of an inlet that was used for decades as a rubbish dump. It doesn't sound alluring, but this mucky environment attracts unusual creatures that use the discarded objects as camouflage. Blennies retreat inside old cola bottles, harlequin shrimps hide beneath rusting 40-gallon drums and hairy robust ghost pipefish mimic red algae as it grows on ageing driftwood. At a depth of 45 m (148 ft) you'll also see an intact torpedo and a shell gun – reminders that this was an American forces station during World War II.

Practical Information

Getting There Fly to Port Moresby, the capital of Papua New Guinea, and then hop on a small aircraft for the 40-minute transfer to Tufi. You'll land on the village football field. The resort is a short walk from here.

When to Go Visit at any time – the weather is great all year round.

Website www.pngtourism.com

A harlequin shrimp in the bay at Tufi

GULF OF AQABA, JORDAN

NEED TO KNOW

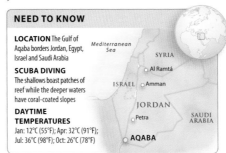

LOCATION The Gulf of Aqaba borders Jordan, Egypt, Israel and Saudi Arabia

SCUBA DIVING The shallows boast patches of reef while the deeper waters have coral-coated slopes

DAYTIME TEMPERATURES Jan: 12°C (55°F); Apr: 32°C (91°F); Jul: 36°C (98°F); Oct: 26°C (78°F)

The city of Aqaba sits at the top of Jordan's small share of the Red Sea coast, but drive a short way towards the Saudi border and you'll find pretty and uncrowded coral reefs that run right up to the shore. "Bommies" (coral outcrops) decorate the sand here like flowerbeds. Anthias, damselfish and lionfish are common sights, while prehistoric slipper lobsters are more unusual. The wreck of the cargo vessel *Cedar Pride*, which sank in 1982, adds a fascinating dimension to diving in the area. And for those who like a dash of ancient history to balance their days at sea, nowhere is quite like Jordan. Emerge from the reefs at the top of the Gulf of Aqaba and head inland to the rose-red city of Petra – the perfect foil for the underwater realm.

Practical Information

Getting There and Around Flights land at Aqaba airport but few are direct – most go via the capital city, Amman. Aqaba is small enough to explore on foot. Dive centres provide transport to the sites.

When to Go Diving is available all year round, but July and August can be unbearably hot, with temperatures reaching up to 50°C (122°F) at times.

Website www.aqaba.jo

Orange lyretail anthias swimming on the reef, Gulf of Aqaba

LIGHTHOUSE REEF, BELIZE

NEED TO KNOW

LOCATION Lighthouse Reef is 80 km (50 miles) southeast of the capital, Belize City

SCUBA DIVING Gently shelving lagoons are divided from the ocean here by small, raised reefs

DAYTIME TEMPERATURES Jan: 27°C (81°F); Apr: 30°C (85°F); Jul: 30°C (86°F); Oct: 29°C (84°F)

Lighthouse Reef's famous Blue Hole, explored by Frenchman Jacques Cousteau on his *Calypso* expedition of 1972, is the jewel in Belize's diving crown. This barren circular tunnel, which drops to a depth of 450 m (1,475 ft), has stalactites hanging from a shelf at 40 m (130 ft), indicating that it was once dry land. The only fish you'll see are reef sharks and groupers, but venture into other areas and you'll find livelier spots, where bottom-feeding rays dwell in sandy lagoons, pastel-toned sea plumes cover the raised barrier reef and pelagic species, including turtles, patrol the steep walls.

Practical Information

Getting There and Around Flights to Belize City are available from most major American cities. On arrival, your dive operator will arrange transport to the sites, but Lighthouse Reef is best seen from a liveaboard boat.

When to Go This is an all-year destination, but from August to October there is more rain and a higher chance of hurricanes.

Website www.belizetourism.org

Aerial view of the awe-inspiring Blue Hole at Lighthouse Reef

BANDA ISLANDS, INDONESIA

NEED TO KNOW

LOCATION The Banda Islands are in the Spice Islands in Indonesia

SCUBA DIVING Deep pinnacles here contrast with shallow channels

DAYTIME TEMPERATURES Jan: 30°C (86°F); Apr: 30°C (86°F); Jul: 28°C (82°F); Oct: 30°C (86°F)

The Banda Islands, at the centre of the Spice Islands, were long fought over for their wealth of nutmegs, once worth far more than gold. This small brown nut is still the lifeblood of the islands, but running a close second are its dazzling coral reefs, which have long been protected against marauding fishermen. When you descend through the warm, clear water, swim to the edge of the sheer wall and look down into the abyss, you won't see far. Blocking your view will be shoal after shoal of colourful fish darting around in ribbon-like waves, like a bizarre three-dimensional screensaver. Indian Ocean triggers occupy the top layer, pyramid butterflies sit below and rainbow runners beneath them. Don't miss the fan corals, lower down the wall, which dwarf divers, or the harbour, famed for its rare bottom-dwelling creatures.

Practical Information

Getting There and Around Although Banda Neira has a small airport, most divers arrive on the island via a liveaboard boat from Ambon Island.

When to Go The water is calmest and clearest between October and April.

Website www.divingmaluku.com

Shoal of reef fish around a bright red sea fan, Banda Neira

PEMBA, TANZANIA

NEED TO KNOW

LOCATION The island of Pemba is in the Indian Ocean, 50 km (30 miles) from the African mainland

SCUBA DIVING Coral-ringed islands dot the western coast and steep walls lie on the eastern coast

DAYTIME TEMPERATURES Jan: 28°C (82°F); Apr: 26°C (80°F); Jul: 24°C (75°F); Oct: 26°C (80°F)

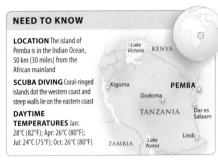

A little piece of Africa that time almost forgot, Pemba was once a spice-growing centre run by the Sultans of Oman. Today, the island is known for its clear water and vibrant marine life. Its east coast, which drops away sharply from mangrove-lined shores, has deep walls. Strong currents on this side might restrict the growth of corals, but they also attract big pelagic species, such as grey reef sharks and hammerheads. On Pemba's west coast, which is much calmer, you'll find masses of tiny islands that create nooks and crannies for divers to explore. The coral here is richer and larger, and the reef fish more plentiful. To the south of the island lies the eerie but well-preserved wreck of a steam freighter that sank in a storm in 1967.

Practical Information

Getting There Fly to Pemba from Tanzania's capital, Dar es Salaam, or fly to Mombasa in Kenya and reach the island by car and boat across the channel.

When to Go This is a year-round destination, although the rainy season is between March and May.

Website www.tanzaniatouristboard.com

Diver exploring the wrecked steam freighter off Pemba

BLUE CORNER, PALAU

NEED TO KNOW

LOCATION Located in the western Pacific, Palau is often incorrectly regarded as part of nearby Micronesia

SCUBA DIVING Palau is best known for big marine animals and rocky reefs

DAYTIME TEMPERATURES Jan: 27°C (81°F); Apr: 28°C (82°F); Jul: 27°C (81°F); Oct: 27°C (81°F)

In ancient times a matrilineal society regarded as one of the wealthiest in the Pacific, Palau is today a magnet for those few divers who are prepared to travel a long distance for their sport. And often they come just for one very famous dive known as Blue Corner. Strong currents sweep up a perfectly vertical wall to a flat reef top where guides position divers, who hover above the reef using specially designed hooks that attach to rocks or rubble. It can be a battle staying still in these currents – a challenge that doesn't seem to affect the massive numbers of fish that come to the wall to feed. Huge schools of barracuda block the sunlight as they approach. They are followed by even larger schools of jacks, while grey reef and whitetip sharks patrol just below, waiting for an easy meal.

Practical Information

Getting There The most frequent and convenient flights to Palau depart from Manila in the Philippines, although there is also a route available from the USA via the Pacific island of Guam.

When to Go There is year-round diving here, although visibility is said to be at its lowest in September.

Website www.visit-palau.com

A mesmerizing shoal of Bigeye trevally fish at Blue Corner

CAPPADOCIA
VS THE SLICKROCK TRAIL

For head-over-wheels mountain biking, Cappadocia's extraordinary rock formations rival Utah's Slickrock Trail – and 4,000 years of human history is just part of the ride

ABOVE Mountain bikers on the famous Slickrock Trail, Utah, USA

NEED TO KNOW

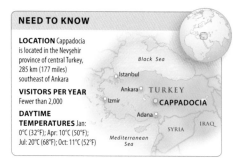

LOCATION Cappadocia is located in the Nevşehir province of central Turkey, 285 km (177 miles) southeast of Ankara

VISITORS PER YEAR Fewer than 2,000

DAYTIME TEMPERATURES Jan: 0°C (32°F); Apr: 10°C (50°F); Jul: 20°C (68°F); Oct: 11°C (52°F)

Cappadocia has been at the crossroads of history for thousands of years – Hittites, Persians, Greeks and Romans all had their day here, but they didn't have mountain bikes with thick tyres to make this fantasy landscape more enjoyable. The dazzling setting comprises volcanic rock cones, spires and pinnacles, known collectively as "fairy chimneys", which form natural pillars that are ideal for darting and skirting around on two wheels. Both a playful pursuit and a great way to explore the area, riding among these surreal forms is a far more exhilarating and picturesque alternative to the well-worn routes of Utah's Slickrock Trail.

But this breathtaking, otherworldly scenery is just the start of the mountain-biking experience in Cappadocia. There are also dozens of man-made wonders to take in along the way, giving the trip a fascinating cultural and historical dimension. You'll pass ancient cave dwellings that are still in use, intricately carved pigeon lofts and monasteries with stunning frescoed walls and Byzantine art, all of which invite inspection. As you ride through Göreme National Park, a UNESCO World Heritage Site known for its towering 40-m- (130-ft-) high fairy chimneys, be sure to visit the centuries-old rock dwellings and underground villages, as well as the informative Open-Air Museum, which boasts ten rock-hewn Byzantine churches.

Another rewarding day trip is a ride through the Ihlara Valley, which is one of several sites in the area where 4th-century Christians hid in rock-hewn buildings and natural caves to escape persecution.

Along the course of the river that runs through this 14-km- (9-mile-) long valley are more than 100 ancient churches chiselled out of the stone. Other bikers rarely visit this peaceful, rural spot, which is shaded by apricot, walnut and Russian olive trees.

Even though Cappadocia is a mountainous region where elevations range from 1,000 to 1,700 m (3,280 to 5,580 ft), the trails are never jarring or brutal, and a full-suspension bike, although useful, isn't essential for most recreational riders. The dramatic terrain is, in most places, ideally suited to first-time mountain bikers, but it also dishes out enough contours, twists and turns to keep professionals entertained for days. On the international mountain-biking scene, Cappadocia is an up-and-coming destination – in 2007 it hosted the European Mountain Biking Championships and it now features an annual festival dedicated to the sport, which takes place in June. And judging by the smiles on the faces of riders moving gracefully about this bewitching, bizarre landscape, mountain biking in Cappadocia is here to stay.

PRACTICAL INFORMATION

Getting There and Around
From Istanbul, fly into Kayseri, which is 70 km (44 miles) northeast of Ürgüp, a town in the heart of Cappadocia. A shuttle-bus service is available from Kayseri Airport to hotels in the major towns of Cappadocia.

Where to Eat
Turkish food is a delight, and Cappadocia's signature cuisine of dishes slow cooked in clay pots is no exception. Here you'll find a good variety of small, traditional restaurants and fine-dining options. Somine Restaurant in Ürgüp is one of the top restaurants in Cappadocia (www.sominerestaurant.com).

Where to Stay
You don't need to be a troglodyte to enjoy the famous cave

accommodation of Cappadocia. These intimate and welcoming inns are carved into the limestone and are well furnished, equipped with electricity, plumbing and air conditioning, and offer a high standard of comfort. One of the best is the Esbelli Evi Cave Inn in Ürgüp (www.esbelli.com).

When to Go
The best riding conditions are in May, June, September and October, when the weather is at its coolest and driest.

Budget per Day for Two
Budget £75–100 for food and accommodation. Bicycle rentals and guided tours can be an extra £100–150 a day for two.

Website
www.cappadociaexclusive.com

FORGET THE SLICKROCK TRAIL?

THE BUILD-UP This sinuous track, which winds around sculpted red-rock formations on a desert plateau in Utah overlooking the Colorado River, is the world's most popular mountain-biking trail. It is rugged terrain, to be sure, and dishes out some dizzying twists and turns along with some quad-burning climbs. The famed "slickrock" is actually a sandpaper-like surface that grips tyres at gravity-defying angles and makes for a thrilling and challenging ride.

THE LETDOWN Slickrock attracts over 100,000 mountain bikers every year. Among the throngs, though, are many with an attitude – aficionados who are more interested in showing off their US$7,000 carbon-frame bikes than in just getting out there and having a great time.

GOING ANYWAY? The Slickrock Trail is open all year round, but to avoid the searing summer heat, plan on tackling it from February to May or from September to November. The nearby town of Moab is the gateway to two national parks – Arches and Canyonlands – and offers easy access to miles of additional mountain-biking trails and many other outdoor pursuits.

MAIN IMAGE Mountain biker on a daring downhill run near Ürgüp, Cappadocia **BELOW (left to right)** Distinctive-looking fairy chimneys; interior of the Byzantine St Anna's Church at Göreme Open-Air Museum

4 MORE MOUNTAIN-BIKING ROUTES TO RIVAL SLICKROCK

TRAIL 401, COLORADO, USA Colorado's best mountain-biking trail is 23 km (14 miles) long and boasts breathtaking views of the two-peaked mountain known as the Maroon Bells, as well as stands of flickering aspens and meadows full of wild flowers.

APOLOBAMBA ROAD, LA PAZ DEPARTMENT, BOLIVIA Check your brake pads before you begin this hair-raising descent on what has been called "the world's most dangerous road". Here, sheer drop-offs, towering mountains and misty waterfalls make for an exhilarating and intense 5-hour downhill run.

FREEDOM TRAIL, SOUTH AFRICA Set your sights on this 2,300-km (1,450-mile) route from Durban to Cape Town and expect weeks on end of dirt roads and bike trails that traverse wilderness areas, national parks and nature reserves.

SKYLINE TRAIL, SWANSEA, UK With over 2,000 m (6,600 ft) of roller-coaster ascents and drops, this 46-km (29-mile) loop delivers stunning views. Not for the unfit or faint of heart.

TREKKING IN BHUTAN
VS TREKKING IN CHIANG MAI

The fascinating Kingdom of Bhutan receives only 20,000 visitors a year – about as many as plod through Chiang Mai in four days

NEED TO KNOW

LOCATION Bhutan is a Himalayan kingdom bordered by Tibet to the north and India to the south

VISITORS PER YEAR About 20,000

DAYTIME TEMPERATURES Jan: 5°C (41°F); Apr: 14°C (56°F); Jul: 16°C (61°F); Oct: 16°C (61°F)

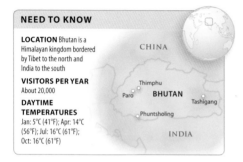

CHINA

Thimphu
Paro • ● BHUTAN
Phuntsholing ● Tashigang

INDIA

Considered to be a modern-day Shangri-La, Bhutan is tucked below the southern slope of the eastern Himalayas, with Tibet to the north and India to the south, and is one of the most remote and protected lands on the planet. The country is slightly larger than Switzerland with a population of about 2 million people, almost all of whom are connected to the land through agriculture. From the tops of the 7,000-m (22,960-ft) Himalayan peaks, the land descends into high alpine slopes grazed by yaks and goats, into forests of spruce and oak which cover about 70 per cent of the country, and further down into fertile valleys and a low, subtropical southern strip. Although only 10 per cent of the land is arable, the soil is so rich and the climate so favourable it can grow almost any crop. It's no wonder that the country is completely self-sufficient in its food production.

Bhutan remains preserved as one of the least deforested countries in the world, and hunting is prohibited by law and religion. In this predominantly Buddhist kingdom, traditional culture is rigorously preserved in a society where myth and legend are inseparable from the land and people. Since tourism is limited and unguided travel is not permitted, you won't find armies of budget backpackers, banana pancakes in every teahouse, cluttered campgrounds and legions of bars as in Chiang Mai and other places where trekking is the lifeblood of the economy.

Trekking in Bhutan is decidedly not adventure on a shoestring, but it is an exquisite journey into a diverse natural environment and a captivating culture. Bhutan can cater to a wide range of interests, including mountain scenery, birding, agriculture and architecture. But regardless of the itinerary or the duration of the trek, being immersed in the rich cultural heritage of Bhutan is always a highlight. Even extended treks into high mountain regions will see you spend much of the time in the lower-elevation villages, walking through rice terraces, fields of millet and apple orchards before ascending to higher elevations where semi-nomadic yak herders roam the hills.

Dotting the landscape are medieval fortresses known as *dzongs* and elegant monasteries – the Tiger's Nest Monastery (Taktshang Goenmba) is the best known – all composed in a unique, almost mystical architectural style. Wearing colourful traditional dress with knee-length gowns and draping cuffs is common among the locals, as is practising traditional sports, such as archery, tug-of-war and *digor*, a kind of shot put.

After the trek, if time permits, spend a few days in Thimphu, perhaps the only capital city in the world with no traffic lights. What Bhutan lacks in modern conveniences and tourist amenities, it more than makes up for with its gracious people, fascinating culture and diverse scenic appeal.

PRACTICAL INFORMATION

Getting There and Around
There are only two ways to enter Bhutan. You can either enter from India along a single road that crosses the border, or you can fly into Bhutan's only airport in Paro, on the country's flagship airline, Druk Air. Be sure you have made prepaid travel arrangements and have secured a visa in advance. Independent travel is not permitted in Bhutan.

Where to Eat
Be forewarned – Bhutanese food is spicy hot, but the Bhutan Kitchen (tel. +975 233 1919) in Thimphu offers a pleasing setting with a well-prepared local cuisine that can be tempered to the Western palate.

Where to Stay
With rooms heated by iron stoves and hot-water bags placed in your bed, the Dewachen Hotel (tel. +975 244 2550; www.dewachenhotel.com) in Gangtey is a wonderfully traditional experience. Set in a pine forest, it offers convenient trekking options in the area.

When to Go
Mar–May and Sep–Nov are ideal for trekking.

Budget per Day for Two
Around £200 including the services of a guide, meals and accommodation.

Website
www.tourism.gov.bt

FORGET TREKKING IN CHIANG MAI?

THE BUILD-UP Located 700 km (435 miles) north of Bangkok, Chiang Mai is the undisputed trekking hub for Thailand's mountainous northern interior. Trekkers find easy access to lush tropical vegetation, hill-tribe villages and unspoilt nature. It is also a great place to find handcrafted goods, woodcarvings and jewellery. Other options, from elephant riding to whitewater rafting, also abound.

THE LETDOWN Over the past 30 years, Chiang Mai has become increasingly modern and more congested, with a crowded city centre. It hosts about 2 million tourists annually. Even though it has a more relaxed atmosphere than Bangkok, Chiang Mai has lost much of its appeal to trekkers in search of a remote forest trail.

GOING ANYWAY? Chiang Mai can still be an appealing getaway, provided you make a quick exit for the hill country. Look for a reputable local operator – as well as in Chiang Mai, many can be found in nearby communities like Pai. Opt for a trek that includes different hill-tribe villages so that you become familiar with varied – and sometimes colourful – ethnic groups.

ABOVE Crowds visiting Wat Phrathat Doi Suthep, a highly revered Buddhist temple near Chiang Mai

MAIN IMAGE Tiger's Nest Monastery, perched on a cliff
BELOW (left to right) Village houses between Thimphu and Wangdi; a procession at Paro Dzong Monastery; on the trail, Bhutan

4 MORE TREKKING TRAILS TO RIVAL CHIANG MAI

HIGH ATLAS MOUNTAINS, MOROCCO As you hike from one Berber village to the next, you'll pass grazing sheep, and find rarely visited valleys and remote mountain trails.

THE COORG, KARNATAKA, INDIA The Western Ghat mountains combine jungle flora and cascading waterfalls with coffee and tobacco plantations. Local festivals, tantalizing food and historic shrines complete a memorable experience.

SINAI DESERT, EGYPT Travel through this unforgiving wilderness with a Bedouin guide who will find sinuous canyons and hidden springs in an otherwise barren landscape. In the evening, share a camp with local Bedouin goat herders.

PAPUA NEW GUINEA The steep tracks and dense jungles make for challenging trekking, and this is one of the last places on earth where you can meet primitive tribes who still maintain stone-age lifestyle and use tools made from bone and stone. Best undertaken with an experienced local operator.

TANDRAGEE 100
VS TT RACES

For elbow-to-elbow, death-defying motorcycle racing on narrow, bumpy roads the Tandragee 100 is the full-flavour taste sensation compared to the half-fat TT

NEED TO KNOW

LOCATION Tandragee is on the edge of the Glebe Hills along the River Cusher in Co Armagh, Northern Ireland

WHEN First Sat in May; free entry

NUMBER OF VISITORS 13–15,000

DAYTIME TEMPERATURES May: 17°C (62°F) and below freezing at night; rain is always a possibility

Motorcycle racing is not all about the biggest being best. Tandragee is a small unassuming town in Northern Ireland that is probably not on anyone's holiday destination wish-list. Scratch below the surface, though, and you will find a town of friendly people who know how to squeeze the very pips out of life. They love to party hard and know their motorcycle racing like the backs of their hands. It is a way of life for the town's residents, as much as the Sunday visit to church.

The TT Races held on the Isle of Man are the biggest tourist attraction of the year, backed by big

ABOVE A duelling pair of racers rounding a bend at Tandragee

budgets, the Department of Tourism and local business. Tandragee has none of that – riders race and families visit for the love of the sport.

The race takes place on a 9-km (5-mile) open-road circuit which, put simply, you would be mad to race on at 80 kmph (50 mph), never mind the 240 kmph (150 mph) the racers reach and exceed. Scars of tractor tyre imprints mix with dripped remains from slurry tankers to create a slippery slime. The narrow roads boast spectacular motocross-style jumps, projecting man and machine into the air at over 160 kmph (100 mph). If there is an edge, then the riders are right on it. One mistake and it is likely to be their last.

The TT Races boast a purpose-built, ticket-controlled complex of paddock buildings where bikes and competitors prepare. At Tandragee, the paddock is a more charming open-access field, where, in the past, buckets of water have been supplied to scrub mud from slick tyres.

Half-a-dozen races entertain the appreciative crowds, with everything from the buzzing 192-kmph (120-mph) 125 cc "smoke burners" to the 320-kmph (200-mph) Superbikes. Visitors burrow into hedgerows and climb trees that line the circuit. When the bikes go by at speed, the true fan is only a few inches away in the undergrowth, camera in hand and heart beating fast in case the rider is off-line and on a collision course.

The riders all set off at once, not in a time trial one-at-a-time format as in the TT. Perhaps part of the appeal of watching the massed start of the race is the close association with danger and death – it is as tangible as the smell of two-stroke oil.

The TT offers a certain amount of danger and excitement in a sanitized-health-and-safety controlled sort of way; Tandragee is back to basics, raw by comparison and all about passion. Which would you prefer?

FORGET THE ISLE OF MAN TT RACES?

THE BUILD-UP The Isle of Man TT, with 100 years of racing history behind it, is the ultimate challenge for any pure road-racer – it is the Everest of the biking world. It is held once a year, with practice during the last week of May and the race during the first week of June.

THE LETDOWN The Isle of Man is a costly event to travel to. Accommodation can also be a problem unless you book almost a year in advance. Each lap lasts around 17 minutes, so there is a limited number of opportunities to see your favourite riders in action. Racing takes place every second day, so to make it worth-while, you need to stay at least for a few days.

GOING ANYWAY? Book as far in advance as possible, as it fills up as soon as the previous TT ends. You may be able to find a room with the residents of the Isle of Man, who, as part of a "Home Stay" project, rent out spare rooms to visitors. Hire a vehicle to get to the vantage points on the 63-km (38-mile) circuit.

ABOVE Bikers preparing for the Isle of Man TT races in the purpose-built paddocks

PRACTICAL INFORMATION

Getting There and Around
The airport closest to Tandragee is in Belfast (Belfast City Airport), which is about 50 km (30 miles) from the town. From there, it is best to hire a car, as Tandragee is a little off the beaten track. However, if you plan on travelling by motorbike, you can take the ferry from Stranraer, situated in western Scotland, to Belfast. Alternatively, you can board the ferry from Holyhead to Dublin, located 133 km (80 miles) from Tandragee.

Where to Eat
Moneypenny's Restaurant in the Montagu Arms (www.montagu-arms.com) offers a cosmopolitan menu along with traditional "Ulster fayre". You should try the steak,

prepared from local beef cattle, and the salmon, which is served fresh from the coast.

Where to Stay
Self-catering accommodation is available in the form of a quaint gate lodge (tel. +44 28 3752 4256) located on Tandragee Road, which is a short drive from both Tandragee and another town called Markethill.

Budget per Day for Two
£100, including car hire, food and accommodation for 3 nights at the gate lodge located in Tandragee.

Websites
www.realroadracing.com
www.discovernorthern ireland.com

MAIN IMAGE Riders tackling the jumps at the Tandragee Motocross Circuit **BELOW (left to right)** Spectators waiting for the start of a race; bikers racing through the streets at Tandragee

4 MORE RACES TO RIVAL THE ISLE OF MAN TT RACES

SKERRIES, REPUBLIC OF IRELAND Head to Ireland for the spectacular racing Skerries has to offer. The fact that the people are extremely friendly and it isn't far from Dublin provides an additional motivation to visit.

THE MACAU GRAND PRIX, MACAU, CHINA This is an unusual alternative to Irish road-racing. The race is held on the Guia Street Circuit and sees riders actually race through the city. Instead of fields on each side of the road, there are walls and barriers.

SCARBOROUGH, NORTH YORKSHIRE, UK Another unusual "road race", these races are held in a park with the riders racing on a narrow lane which makes up the Oliver's Mount Circuit.

LANDSHAAG, AUSTRIA The only pure road race in Austria is this awesome one held sometime in mid-April. The race takes place on a mountain course which is short but narrow, bumpy and very difficult.

THE SOUP BOWL
VS BONDI BEACH

The Soup Bowl, on the rugged east coast of Barbados, offers year-round warm-water surfing and tube rides that put super-crowded Bondi Beach in the shade

ABOVE Sun-worshippers crowding the sand – and the sea – at Bondi Beach, Australia

NEED TO KNOW

LOCATION The Soup Bowl is about 16 km (10 miles) northeast of Bridgetown, the capital of Barbados

VISITORS PER YEAR Around 600,000 people visit Barbados

DAYTIME TEMPERATURES Jan: 28°C (82°F); Apr: 29°C (84°F); Jul: 29°C (84°F); Oct: 30°C (86°F)

Speightstown

THE SOUP BOWL

Atlantic Ocean

BARBADOS

Bridgetown   Marchfield

Oistins   Seawell

The fact that Kelly Slater, who is considered to be the world's greatest surfer, counts the Soup Bowl as one of his favourite breaks is a fair indication of the oceanic riches awaiting its visitors. There are crystalline barrels galore as perfect waves reel over a limestone reef, the palm-fringed village of Bathsheba providing an old-world backdrop. In contrast to most people's experience of riding the waves at Australia's over-hyped Bondi Beach, the Soup Bowl only exceeds expectations. This is a surfing paradise to set the heart racing, and better still, it has a fraction of the Bondi crowds.

But make no mistake – surfing the Soup Bowl will test your mettle. With Bathsheba, which is adored by non-surfers for its warm-water rock pool bathing, facing northeast, the Soup Bowl picks up any swell the Atlantic throws at it. Even on calm days, waves can rear up at the last minute, as if from nowhere, and when the swell gets bigger, this is a place for experts only, as waves reaching up to 4.5-m (15-ft) high detonate on the reef. Paddling out is

easy enough, thanks to a conveniently situated rip that ferries surfers to the optimum wave-catching position. But once there, the hard work begins, with constant motion required to keep you in position and prepare you for rogue sets that can appear at any moment. That's tough enough, but it pales into insignificance when compared with the ride: a fast, vertical descent, as if from a cliff edge, into shallow water where urchins lurk on rocks. Get it wrong and you will wish you'd opted to idle in the rock pools.

Get it right, though, and you'll be racing down the face, tucked under the lip of a giant wave. The Soup Bowl's tubes are the stuff of legend, and, unlike those at Bondi Beach, can be surfed on all but a few days of the year. Depending on the size and direction of the swell, they can be elegant, smooth walls suitable for carves, slashes and aerials, as much as they are a barrel-rider's dream.

Back on the beach, sipping coconut juice with the laid-back Bajan locals after a day in the water, the chances are that you'll agree with Kelly Slater and count this as one of the best waves in the world. And despite its upsides, that isn't something many people could say about Bondi Beach.

FORGET BONDI BEACH?

THE BUILD-UP Surfing didn't start at Bondi Beach, but sometimes it feels like it. This beach is steeped in Australian surfing history, and no wonder: its 1-km (half-mile) stretch of golden sand often has classic beach-break surf, offering fun waves for surfers of all levels. There are year-round surfing contests and when the swell is big, Bondi can produce good left- and right-breaking waves of up to 2.5 m (8 ft) high – enough to challenge the very best surfers. A shark net keeps the ocean's top predators out.

THE LETDOWN Bondi Beach is busy. Tourists flock to the Sydney suburb in their thousands every year, many to try their hand at surfing. This means that there are near-constant crowds on and around the beach, especially at weekends. There are also some severe rip currents here, with the infamous "Backpackers' Express" ensuring that the lifeguards are always on their toes.

GOING ANYWAY? If surfing at Bondi Beach is your thing, then plan to arrive at sunrise to beat the crowds. Check the tide times beforehand, either at local surf shops or with the lifeguards, because this will affect the swell.

PRACTICAL INFORMATION

Getting There and Around
Flights arrive at Sir Grantley Adams International Airport in Seawell, which is 13 km (8 miles) southeast of Bridgetown. Beware: some airlines will not allow you to take your surfboard. The best way to get around the island is by car. Car-hire companies are found all over the island.

Where to Eat
Bajan cuisine, which features seafood and spices, is served at the island's restaurants and at the outdoor stalls of Oistins, a fishing community on the south coast. Nearby, overlooking Miami Beach, is Café Luna (www.littlearches. com/dining-overview) – the beef tenderloin here is to die for.

Where to Stay
Zed's Surfing Adventures (www. zedssurftravel.com), run by local surf guru Zed Layson, is a surf school that boasts a range of comfortable one- and two-bed apartments on the beach at Surfers' Point, which is 30 minutes' drive south of Bathsheba.

When to Go
Barbados has good surf all year, but the Soup Bowl comes alive between October and April.

Budget per Day for Two
Up to £100, including food and accommodation. Car rental is around £15–20 a day.

Website
www.barbados.org/surfing.htm

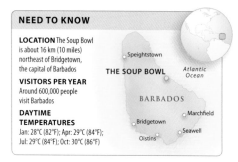

ABOVE Surfers walking down to the beach at Bathsheba, Barbados

MAIN IMAGE Surfer riding a large, perfectly formed wave, the Soup Bowl, Barbados **BELOW (left to right)** Surf shack in Bathsheba; heading to the beach in a buggy; vibrant mural on the wall of Bathsheba Community Centre

4 MORE SURF BREAKS TO RIVAL BONDI BEACH

JEFFREYS BAY, EASTERN CAPE, SOUTH AFRICA On the south coast of South Africa lies the surfing paradise that is Jeffreys Bay, which boasts one of the best waves in the world – a long, tubing, super-fast right-hander.

CHICAMA, LA LIBERTAD, PERU The isolated and remote port of Chicama is home to the longest left-breaking wave in the world. Rides of over 2 km (1 mile) are possible here, and better still, this relatively mellow break is not just for experts.

G-LAND, BAY OF GRAJAGAN, EAST JAVA G-Land was first surfed in 1972 after a surfer saw the break from an aeroplane window. It has since gone on to be justly regarded as one of the most perfect waves on the planet.

THURSO EAST, CAITHNESS, SCOTLAND The north shore of Scotland might not seem to be the obvious choice for surfing, but it is home to countless excellent reef breaks, including the world-class Thurso East. Situated in the shadow of a ruined castle at the mouth of the River Thurso, this break is widely thought to be the best wave in the UK, but be warned – it's very cold.

ABOVE Invigorating whitewater rafting along the Karnali river in Nepal
RIGHT Dogsleds racing through the snow-covered landscape, Lapland, Finland

RAFTING THE KARNALI, NEPAL Nepal is home to the highest mountains on earth, and the rivers that run down them are fast, deep and brimming with whitewater as a result. The Karnali is Nepal's longest river, and a multi-day trip along it marries tricky, adrenalin-charged early sections with calmer moments towards its end. The route also takes in some of Nepal's most dramatic scenery, including jagged mountains, lush jungle and rare pockets of savanna. The river runs through remote Bardia National Park, offering the chance to see rhinos, wild elephants and crocodiles.

SPHEREING, ROTORUA, NEW ZEALAND People had tried rolling around in giant balls before of course – and hamsters have been doing it for years – but the sulphurous, activity-mad town of Rotorua is where sphereing (or "zorbing", as the locals call it) really took off. Participants clamber into giant cushioned balls, wobble their way through a starting gate and then careen down a 200-m (656-ft) hill or zig-zag course, spinning head over heels in a breathless and completely undignified rush. A "wet" ride adds soapy water to the equation, for the full spin-cycle experience.

DOG SLEDDING, FINLAND Forget Father Christmas – Lapland's real draw is its awesome scenery and tangible sense of remoteness. Winters are long and dark, summers short and magnificent, and the sky seems impossibly vast. The husky dogs here are fascinating, charismatic creatures, blending the enthusiasm typical of domestic dogs with otherworldly looks and phenomenal strength and stamina. Enter a tug-of-war with one and you'll be yanked off your feet, but taking the reins is a wonderful sensation, and speeding through the snow on a sled an achingly beautiful experience.

SEA KAYAKING, PRINCE WILLIAM SOUND, ALASKA You may have paddled down rivers or lakes, but kayaking on the sea really is something else. The ocean seems to breathe beneath you, its vast expanse making you feel at once utterly insignificant and connected to something very big indeed. And if it's scale you want, this southern dent in Alaska's great bulk is the place to be. Its calm waters mean even beginners can paddle past icebergs, watch glaciers calve and spot whales and sea otters; experts can range far and wide, packing gear into canoe bags and camping on remote stretches of the coast.

PLANICA SKI JUMP, SLOVENIA Skiing is Slovenia's national sport, and more records have been set at these jumps than anywhere else in the world. It's unlikely you'll fancy braving any of them yourself (the drops look utterly intimidating) but the annual World Cup event, held in late March, attracts hordes of spectators – there for the party and the sight of the daring athletes.

FISHING, DENMARK Denmark's complex coastline is dotted with islands, fjords and beaches. Nowhere in the country is more than 53 km (33 miles) from the sea, and sea-fishing trips to catch cod, mackerel, sea trout and eel are justifiably popular. Permits are easy to obtain and well-stocked rivers and lakes inland ensure that there's plenty to keep anglers happy too.

KLOOFING, SOUTH AFRICA While most of the world calls it canyoning, South Africans have their own word for the practice of throwing oneself off cliffs into pools, sliding down rivers and scrambling up wet rocks. There are bigger drops elsewhere, but Cape Town's Table Mountain National Park offers the finest collection of *kloofs* (ravines) so close to a major city.

WRESTLING, MEXICO CITY Faster, more dexterous and more reliant on aerial stunts than their American cousins, Mexico's wrestlers would create a spectacle even without the culture that has grown up around them. In *lucha libre* (free fighting) most competitors don masks and adopt fake identities: some are *técnicos* (the skilful good guys), others *rudos* (the bullyboys and cheats).

BUSHWALKING THE OVERLAND TRACK, AUSTRALIA There are some stellar alternatives, but the king of Australia's bushwalking destinations is in laid-back Tasmania. The Overland Track takes five to six days, and you'll have to carry enough food to see you through. Tramping past shimmering tarns and grand peaks you may see wombats, Tasmanian devils and even platypuses.

SKI-JORING, SWITZERLAND If simply going with the slope's flow in one of Switzerland's many ski resorts is getting a little boring, you may want to consider ski-joring, in which horses drag skiers along the flat in a shower of snow. Regular spectator races will give you an idea of what's involved – in St Moritz you can even watch experts whizzing along behind galloping reindeer.

ABOVE Sailing the Adriatic off the Dalmatian Coast

SAILING THE ADRIATIC The sparkling blue sleeve of the Adriatic skirts Italy's eastern shore on one side, and those of Croatia, Montenegro and Albania on the other. Croatia's dusty coast and charming islands are increasingly popular stops for sailors – whether they're trying the activity for the first time or taking their own boats on epic routes around the Med. Picturesque Hvar and lively Split make fine stops, but if you want to venture further off the beaten track, Albania is becoming increasingly hip, its classical sites and mountainous interior as appealing as its developing beach scene.

CYCLING THE LOIRE, FRANCE Take advantage of the "Loire-à-Vélo" scheme to explore the glorious châteaux and vineyards of the Loire Valley. You can wend your way along the river on over 300 km (190 miles) of designated cycle routes between Orléans and the Atlantic.

HOT AIR BALLOONING, TURKEY The ancient volcanic landscape of Cappadocia (see pp230–31) is at its most fantastical seen from above, as dawn creeps up over its weird and wonderful rock formations. Balloons take flight from the town of Göreme.

CAVING, PUERTO RICO In the wild heart of Puerto Rico is a compelling subterranean world of vast caves, submerged rivers and huge stalagmites. Sightseeing tours around Río Camuy give you a taste, while organized expeditions in the hills nearby include abseiling, canyoning and stunning hikes.

MOUNTAINBOARDING, ITALIAN DOLOMITES Mountainboards are not the most graceful pieces of sports kit, their flexible bodies set off by four oversized rubber tyres. Riding them, twisting your body into turns and crouching down over bumps, can feel even more ungainly. The gear isn't cheap and the sport is still in its early stages, but week-long instruction courses are a fine way to hone your skills. The resort town of Cortina offers rolling slopes on which to bust those fly moves – and some rather flash shopping opportunities if you feel the need to regain some elegance after class.

HORSE SAFARIS IN THE MASAI MARA, KENYA The mind-boggling Great Migration, in which zebras, wildebeests and gazelles sweep across the savanna, looks sensational on TV and thrilling from the safety of a vehicle. However, to really get an eye on the action, try making your own way across the Serengeti on horseback. Riders can join tour groups in Kenya on trips lasting a week or longer, cantering alongside and amongst the herds, while spotting lions, hippos and elephants along the way. You do need previous experience in the saddle (most companies will only take skilled riders), but the area's altitude means that neither the temperature nor the mosquitos are too troubling and, while the days can be exhausting, expeditions generally come with luxuries such as chefs, beer and ice cubes.

WATCHING JAI ALAI, THE PHILIPPINES Often claimed to be the fastest game on earth – the handmade rubber balls can fly at over 240 kph (150 mph) – jai alai was imported to the Philippines from Spain's Basque country. It's a furious spectacle, vaguely related to handball, in which players sling the ball from basketed hands against a massive wall, cheered on by fanatical crowds.

SCRAMBLE UP TRYFAN, WALES Two legends are attached to this mountain. The first is that it's the only mountain in Wales you can't climb without using your hands – the scramble up its jutting crags requires considerable concentration and a head for heights. The second is that by making the leap between two pillar-like rocks at its summit (915 m/3,000 ft) you earn the "Freedom of Tryfan".

WATCHING THAI BOXING, THAILAND Strongly ritualistic, shockingly violent and followed with real passion throughout Thailand, Muay Thai is one hell of a spectacle. Catch a fight in Bangkok, where clamorous, hard-gambling crowds and hammering percussion serve as the backdrop for nightly fights. You can even undertake training yourself – with no obligation to actually step into the ring.

WINDSURFING, PENGHU ISLANDS, TAIWAN Lying around 50 km (30 miles) west of the mainland, the Penghu Archipelago is a popular retreat for Taiwanese holiday-makers. The winds that eroded its distinctive stacks and cliffs also make it a world-famous windsurfing destination – home both to international competitions and numerous rental outfits offering lessons to beginners.

KITESURFING, PREÁ, BRAZIL First things first: kitesurfing is not easy, and all too often you end up wrestling with the wind and cursing. Yet while it has a tricky learning curve (lessons for beginners are almost essential), kitesurfing is not a world away from windsurfing, and Preá beach, with its warm waters and almost constant breeze, is a superb place to learn.

ABOVE Tour skaters on frozen Nordreälvs fjord near Gothenburg, Sweden
RIGHT Locals performing a dazzling *capoeira* move on a beach in Bahia, Brazil

TOUR SKATING, SWEDEN Skating rinks, whether you zoom round them with poised efficiency or wobble your way along the barriers, are fine for a few sessions. But if you don't want to be restricted to such a small area, there are alternatives. Tour skaters use longer, thinner blades, often attached to skiing boots, which are far more stable than figure skates, meaning that even beginners can cover around 10 km (6 miles) on a lake, river or canal. Sweden presents a wealth of clubs that can point you in the right direction; for the more experienced, forays onto frozen stretches of the Baltic Sea are possible.

CAPOEIRA, BRAZIL Like many martial arts, *capoeira* came into existence because of the limitations placed on the poorer members of society – in Brazil's case, slaves who were forbidden from carrying weapons or practising formal fighting techniques. Couched in the movements of dance, the kicks, spins, cartwheels and blocks of modern *capoeira* are generally backed by the beat of the single-stringed *berimbau*. The relaxed coastal city of Salvador is regarded as the activity's heartland, and as well as the displays on the city's streets, visitors are welcome at the various schools around town, either to watch or learn.

LUMBERJACK WORLD CHAMPIONSHIPS, USA Wisconsin's vast pine forests make it an obvious base for this three-day festival of sawing, chopping and climbing, which features several hundred competitors, 12,000 spectators and a whole lot of wood.

HORSE-RIDING, KYRGYZSTAN Follow part of the Silk Road, Central Asia's ancient trade route, on horseback through Kyrgyzstan. Canter across the wide, open steppes dotted with traditional *yurts* (felt tents) and over the high passes of the awesome Tien Shan mountains.

WALKING THE CHORO TRAIL, BOLIVIA Peru's Inca Trail is, of course, magnificent – but it's also busy, and hikers are restricted to joining organized groups. Landlocked Bolivia arguably has better trekking and mountaineering opportunities, many close to its sprawling high-altitude capital, La Paz. The Choro Trail follows Inca paths past ancient remains, over mountain passes and into thick cloud forest, and should take three or four days. It's a fine way to experience Bolivia's unique environment, with impossibly blue, broad skies, rare birdlife and glimpses of the Altiplano's ancient civilizations.

CRICKET IN THE TROBRIAND ISLANDS, PAPUA NEW GUINEA The inhabitants of the remote Trobriand Islands play their own unique form of cricket. The Trobriands come to life during the Milamala Festival, usually in July or August, when cricket combines with raucous festivities – presumably not what the missionaries who introduced the sport had in mind.

PLAYING CARAMBOLE POOL, THE NETHERLANDS Of all the takes on everyday billiards, carambole pool is one of the more unusual. It dispenses with pockets entirely; instead, you *carom* your cue ball into other balls, and rebound off the table edges. In Amsterdam's numerous bars, experts put impossible amounts of spin on their shots – and most will be delighted to give you a lesson.

SKIING IN YONGPYEONG, KOREA It's not the most obvious haven for snow hounds, but South Korea's substantial mountains and freezing winters have put the country in the running for several Winter Olympics. Yongpyeong (or Dragon Valley) is the country's largest resort, and the 31 runs here offer a variety of terrains, lined with trees and often blessed with sharp blue skies.

KAYAKING IN GWAII HAANAS NATIONAL PARK, CANADA The archipelago that makes up Gwaii Haanas National Park, miles off the coast of British Columbia, is untouched by roads and joint-run by the government and the Haida people. A kayaking expedition is the ideal way to experience its thermal pools, fjords, and traditional villages characterized by longhouses and totem poles.

SINGAPORE GRAND PRIX September 2008 saw Singapore host its first Grand Prix – and Formula One hold its first night-time event. The race exceeded all expectations and is to become a regular event. The tight, bumpy track, illuminated by over 3,000 lights, threads through the city streets past colonial buildings and a crowd delighted to see motor racing's biggest series taking place on their doorstep.

KAYAKING THE ARDÈCHE, FRANCE The limestone of the Ardèche valley in France's grand Massif Central provides the raw material for some wonderful features, including the photogenic rock arch of Pont d'Arc. It's the start of a series of dramatic gorges, pockmarked with stalactite-riddled caves and surrounded by epic cliffs and thick forest that are best seen from a kayak.

ABOVE Gymnasts performing at one of Beijing's amazing acrobatic shows, China
LEFT Players jostling for the ball during an elephant polo match in Nepal

ELEPHANT POLO, NEPAL It started as an expat joke, but elephant polo makes for a serious spectacle. Meghauli, in the flat, agricultural western Terai, hosts the tournament on its airstrip every December, with teams coming from Britain, India, Australia, Hong Kong and beyond. The pitch is slightly smaller than standard, due to the elephants' slower pace, while two people ride each mount, a mahout directing the elephant and a stick-wielding player hitting the ball. The action is surprisingly fast-paced and passionate, with group stages preceding a knock-out contest.

ACROBAT DISPLAYS, BEIJING, CHINA Acrobatics in China go back to 500 BC, and Beijing has some of the best venues. Today, you can see high-wire acts, cycling, juggling, conjuring, gymnastics and animal dances based on folk traditions – all in the same evening's entertainment.

DEEP SEA FISHING, CAPE TOWN, SOUTH AFRICA The waters off the coast of Cape Town, where the Atlantic and the Indian Oceans meet, offer some of the best big-game fishing in the world. Hook yellow-fin tuna, swordfish or, if you're lucky, a whopping 450-kg (1,000-lb) blue marlin.

CAMEL-TREKKING, MOROCCO Graceless and hard to ride, camels are not natural mounts but they are the best way to travel in the desert. On an organized trek, your camel will follow ancient trade routes through shifting sands to reach massive dunes and the vast empty spaces of the Sahara.

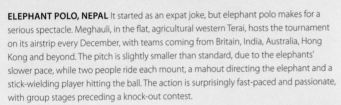

DIVING AT NINGALOO, AUSTRALIA The hot, dry North West Cape might not seem Australia's most alluring destination, but poke your head under the water and there's all manner of life to see. Hundreds of species of coral and fish support a vast ecosystem, topped by turtles, manta rays, sharks and whales, but while there are growing tourist facilities, Ningaloo Marine Park is far more low key than the Great Barrier Reef. Its stunning, deserted beaches offer perfect chill-out opportunities, while Coral Bay is a dazzling playground for both casual snorkellers and experienced divers.

HIKING IN WYOMING, USA Yellowstone and the Teton Range may be Wyoming's main trekking areas, but if you want to get away from the crowds, head for the state's highest, longest and often most stunning range. In the Wind River Mountains, hikers can follow the scenic Glacier Trail or the lovely route from Lander to Valentine and Washakie lakes. There are fishing and geyser trips for the footsore.

LAWN BOWLS, UK Despite its reputation for attracting Britain's grey-haired elders, lawn bowls is a lot of fun for all ages. The aim of this skilful game is to roll a black ball, or "bowl", across a smooth grass lawn to hit a small white ball, or "jack". Sounds easy? Not so. The bowls are biased (weighted) on one side and in the case of crown-green bowls, the lawn has a slightly convex surface. Runaway balls are not uncommon.

ISLAND-TO-ISLAND SWIMMING, GREECE The Cyclades can be swamped with tourists in summer, but a swim tour will let you really immerse yourself in the Aegean – far away from the crowds. The tours take in uninhabited islands and open water, and even involve treks up hills. Boats accompany groups on most trips, although you need to be a decent swimmer to sign up.

VOLCANO CLIMBING, GUATEMALA With its fertile flood plains, rainforest, buzzing cities and Pacific and Caribbean coastlines, Guatemala is not short of attractions, but its epic chain of volcanoes takes top billing for most adventurous visitors. At 2,250 m (7,380 ft) Pacaya is the classic climb, while Tajumulco, at 4,220 m (13,845 ft), is the highest point in Central America and has views to Mexico.

MARATHON DES SABLES, MOROCCO The toughest foot race in the world is over 254 km (158 miles) long – more than five times the length of a regular marathon. Competitors carry all their kit and run over energy-sapping dunes; temperatures can edge over 50°C (122°F); and most runners take six days of pain to reach the finish line. Incredibly, some athletes complete the route in less than 24 hours.

A DAY AT THE RACES, IRELAND With its dressing up and reputation as a boozy day out, it can be easy to forget that horse-racing is a sport. In Ireland, Kildare is home to the Curragh Racecourse, named after the grassy plain on which it sits. The track hosts many of Ireland's greatest flat races, including the Irish Derby in late June or early July, with its boisterous atmosphere and serious competition.

GOLF IN EDINBURGH, SCOTLAND Scotland may be the home of golf, but most visitors are totally unaware that they can play on a historic course a few minutes' walk from Edinburgh's centre. The Bruntsfield Links may have been used for the sport as early as the 15th century, and are a lovely, relaxed setting for a pitch and putt, overlooked by the craggy Arthur's Seat.

ART AND CULTURE

Pre-historic rock paintings depicting women, ostriches and cattle at Jebel Acacus, Libya *(p254)*

SMALLER PARISIAN MUSEUMS
VS MUSÉE DU LOUVRE

The illustrious Louvre is an undisputed crowd-puller but, if you prefer a little breathing space with your culture, Paris has a host of lesser-known art museums with equally commendable credentials

It is one of the world's greatest art collections, some 13 km (8 miles) of Egyptian, Greek, Etruscan, Islamic, French, Italian, Flemish and Dutch treasures marshalled into an impossibly sumptuous royal palace. And it has something for everyone: Renaissance masterpieces by Botticelli, Raphael and da Vinci; the Rubens-filled Medici Gallery; the *Winged Victory of Samothrace*; the *Venus de Milo*; sphinxes and mummies; and the 2,490-diamond-studded crown of Empress Eugénie. But, let's face it, 35,000 works of art can be downright daunting. Where to begin? Where to finish? How to stay on your feet? Don't feel guilty, you can love the Louvre but you can leave it, too. For beyond its imposing walls lie smaller, more accessible collections, some of them housed in mansions that also permit you a glimpse of long-vanished lives and lifestyles.

The extraordinary Musée National du Moyen Age combines the remains of an ancient thermal spa, a Gothic mansion, and a vast collection of medieval art and artifacts. The most highly prized exhibits in the museum are a set of six radiant wool-and-silk tapestries, and the carved stone (noseless) heads of the Kings of Judah.

The Institut du Monde Arabe reaches even further back in time, showcasing Arabic history and culture with exhibits such as urns and carpets dating from prehistory to the present day. Interestingly, these relics of the ancients are housed in an ultra-modern building, acclaimed for its architectural innovation.

The exquisite good taste of an art-adoring 19th-century couple, Edouard André and Nélie Jacquemart, is in evidence in their former family home. Here, English portraits are displayed with Tiepolo friezes, French tapestries with Van Dycks, and their assembled collection of Early Italian Renaissance paintings is breathtaking.

The collections in the Musée Cognacq-Jay, amassed by another prosperous husband-and-wife team, favour the 18th century, with outstanding French Rococo paintings, and Sèvres porcelain far too beautiful to eat off.

Despite its loveliness, the Musée Nissim de Camondo is founded on sadness. On the death of his aviator son Nissim, in World War I, Count Moïse de Camondo, a passionate collector of 18th-century French furniture and art, retreated from society and bequeathed his lavishly furnished house to the State in memory of his son.

In the 1930s, a group of artists campaigned to save the home of Eugène Delacroix from demolition. Today, it houses a wide range of his works, along with his easel, palette and other memorabilia.

FORGET THE LOUVRE?

THE BUILD-UP The Louvre was founded in 1793 to display the royal collection and, as that grew, so did the museum. Subsequent rulers added their flourishes to create this marvellous architectural amalgam, filled to its pitched rafters with art from all over the world.

THE LETDOWN More than eight million visitors a year means crushing crowds and, once inside, little in the way of crowd control. Catching a glimpse of the *Mona Lisa* devoid of flashing, whirring cameras is impossible, and she's behind a thick shield of bullet-proof glass. The cut-off point for the collection is 1848, disappointing for fans of modern art.

GOING ANYWAY? As a rule, there are fewer crowds in the evening but, if this is not convenient, buy a ticket online in advance (www.louvre.fr). You can't see everything in one visit, so plan ahead and make a hit list, or be spontaneous and enjoy what you find.

ABOVE Crowds of visitors gather round the *Mona Lisa*, probably the most famous and most popular painting in the Louvre

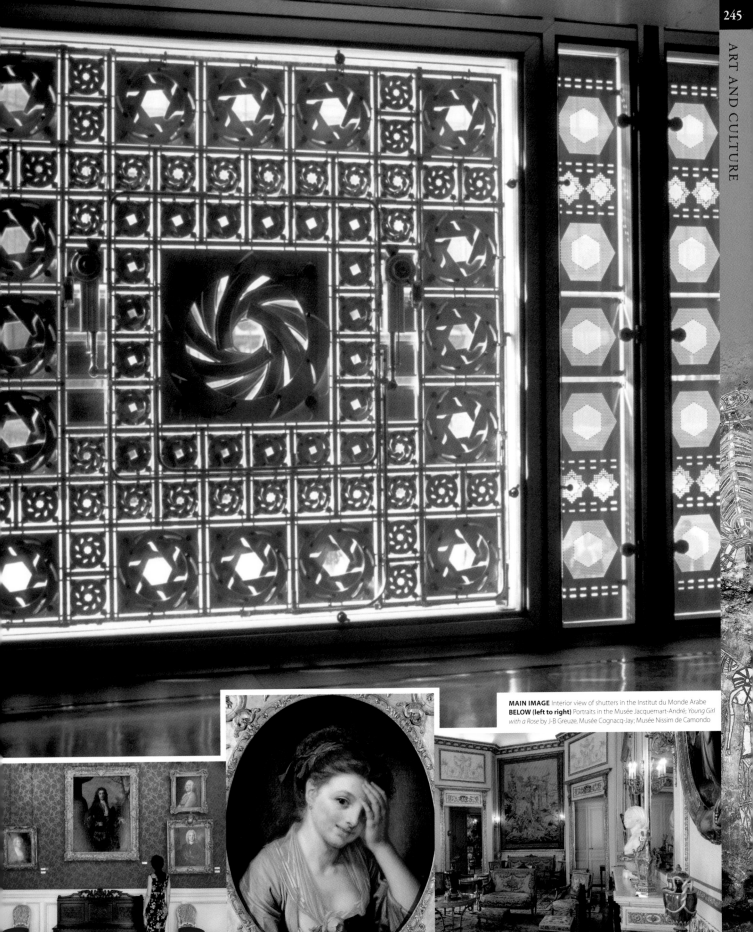

MAIN IMAGE Interior view of shutters in the Institut du Monde Arabe
BELOW (left to right) Portraits in the Musée Jacquemart-André; *Young Girl with a Rose* by J-B Greuze, Musée Cognacq-Jay; Musée Nissim de Camondo

6 PARIS ART MUSEUMS TO RIVAL THE LOUVRE

"To My Only Desire" tapestry from the *Lady and the Unicorn* series

Wall of solar shutters on the Institut du Monde Arabe

Elegant Winter Garden of the Musée Jacquemart-André

MUSÉE NATIONAL DU MOYEN AGE

Amusingly, the most famous inhabitant of the flamboyant ex-home of the Abbots of Cluny is female – the captivating *Lady and the Unicorn*. Six 15th-century Flemish tapestry panels, full of charm and hidden symbolism, are housed in an impressive circular room here. Five of the elegant images are believed to portray the senses – taste, hearing, sight, smell, touch – while the meaning of the sixth, bearing the inscription "To my only desire", remains a mystery. Elsewhere, there are glorious 7th-century crowns; stained glass; armour; Limoges enamels; a medieval waffle iron; travel chests; shoes; and textiles from Iran, the Byzantine Empire, Italy and England. Stone heads of the Kings of Judah, ripped from the façade of Notre-Dame during the Revolution by angry crowds, are the treasures of the sculpture section. These were discovered in 1977, along with a host of other damaged statues and fragments, in the basement of a Parisian bank. Outdoors there's a flourishing medieval physic garden, with a "unicorn forest" and "carpet of 1,000 flowers", as well as the ruins of the Thermes de Cluny (thermal baths), from the 2nd to 3rd centuries. The frigidarium (cold bath) retains traces of remarkable mosaics, including the delightfully named "Love Riding a Dolphin".

Practical Information
Address 6 Pl Paul Painlevé, Latin Quarter; tel. +33 1 45 62 11 59; www.musee-moyenage.fr

Getting There Métro: Cluny-La Sorbonne, St-Michel; Odéon; bus: 21, 27, 38, 63, 85, 86, 87.

Opening Times 9:15am–5:45pm Wed–Mon.

INSTITUT DU MONDE ARABE

Traditional Arab style meets high-tech here, in the hundreds of solar-activated shutters which cover the Institut's southern façade. These lovely geometric apertures, that open and close according to the intensity of the light, were designed by celebrated French architect Jean Nouvel to echo the intricate wooden balconies of Moorish palaces. Opened in 1987 with the aim of fostering exchange between Western and Arab cultures, the Institut houses a library, cultural centre, exhibition spaces and the "Museum of Arab Museums". This displays several hundred items, many on long-term loan from Syria and Tunisia, that trace the history and art of Arabic-Islamic civilization. There are terracotta urns; slabs from ancient Carthage; frescoes from the Kairouan Mosque and stuccoes from the palace of Sabra al-Mansouriya, both in Tunisia; a mesmerizing array of gold astrolabes; costumes and jewellery; ancient manuscripts donated by Yemen; and a magical collection of carpets. Temporary exhibitions showcase Arab life and culture, and have included paintings of Algeria by 19th-century French artists; Napoleon Bonaparte's travels in Egypt; Venice and its relationship with the Arab world; and Arabian horses and their riders.

Practical Information
Address 1 Rue des Fossés-St-Bernard, Latin Quarter; tel. +33 1 40 51 38 38; www.imarabe.org

Getting There Métro: Jussieu, Cardinal Lemoine, Sully-Morland; bus: 24, 63, 67, 86, 87, 89.

Opening Times 10am–6pm Tue–Sun.

MUSÉE JACQUEMART-ANDRÉ

Banker Edouard André and his society painter wife, Nélie Jacquemart, travelled the world amassing their treasures. Their splendid 19th-century town-house – which, when glimpsed from the sweeping Boulevard Haussmann, looks quite unremarkable – positively drips with art and atmosphere. The library is hung with Dutch paintings, including portraits by Rembrandt and Van Dyck, while the superb upstairs "Italian Museum" boasts Uccello's *St George and the Dragon*, Botticelli's *Virgin and Child*, Mantegna's *Ecce Homo*, and sculptures by Donatello and Della Robbia. The penetratingly pink Venetian Room is crowned with a grand coffered ceiling by Murano-born Mocetto. Other rooms house works by French artists Boucher, David, Chardin and Nattier, and the double spiral staircase is presided over by Tiepolo frescoes depicting the arrival of Henri III in Venice. The Smoking Room displays Nélie's eclectic collection of curios picked up on her passages through India, Persia and the British Isles, and the private apartments include Edouard's anteroom, housing his portrait painted by his wife ten years before they were married.

Practical Information
Address 158 Bd Haussmann, Champs-Elysées; tel. +33 1 45 62 11 59; www.musee-jacquemart-andre.com

Getting There Métro: Miromesnil, St-Philippe-du-Roule; bus: 22, 28, 43, 52, 54, 80, 83, 84, 93.

Opening Times 10am–6pm daily.

François Boucher's *The Beautiful Kitchen Maid*, Musée Cognacq-Jay

Sculptures in the grand stairwell of the Musée Nissim de Camondo

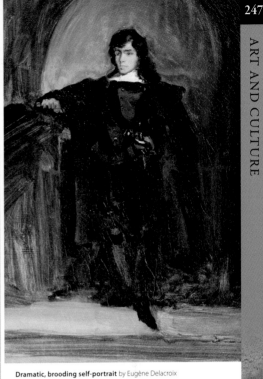

Dramatic, brooding self-portrait by Eugène Delacroix

MUSÉE COGNACQ-JAY

While Ernest Cognacq and Marie-Louise Jay owed their considerable fortune to factory-made goods (he founded the department store La Samaritaine in 1869), their personal tastes were anything but modern and middle-of-the road. They preferred the 18th century, and spent an impressive amount of time (around 25 years) and corresponding coinage amassing their collection. Works by French Rococo artists La Tour, Fragonard, Van Loo, Boucher, Greuze and Watteau decorate the beautifully restored 16th-century Hôtel Donon. Twenty rooms, over four floors, chart the aesthetic acumen of the couple. There are Louis XVI chairs, panelling from the Château d'Eu (King Louis Philippe's summer residence in Normandy), and paintings by Rembrandt alongside works by lesser-known artists such as Lavreince. A gallery of sculptures features Rococo works by Falconet (a favourite of Madame de Pompadour), Houdon and Clodion, along with porcelain from Saxe and Sevrès. There's also a remarkable royal bed, with coiling leaves and garlands carved into its posts, and lavish folds of damask descending majestically from an ornate crown; a writing table inlaid with ivory, conjuring up images of perfumed letters and wax seals; and display cabinets brimming with everyday objects such as snuff boxes and pocket watches.

Practical Information

Address Hôtel Donon, 8 Rue Elzévir, Marais; tel. +33 1 40 27 07 21; www.paris.fr/portail/Culture/Portal.lut?page_id=6466

Getting There Métro: St-Paul, Chemin Vert, Rambuteau; bus: 29, 69, 76, 96.

Opening Times 10am–6pm Tue–Sun.

MUSÉE NISSIM DE CAMONDO

Once settled into the vast Right Bank mansion that he modelled on Marie Antoinette's Petit Trianon in Versailles, Count Moïse de Camondo, former banker to the Ottoman Empire, indulged his passion for the 18th century. Today, it almost feels as if the Count has just stepped out: the table in the dining room is sumptuously set for a dinner, while photographs of his fallen son, Nissim, nestle amid other precious keepsakes. Six Aubusson tapestries line the walls of his study, and the grand reception rooms brim with exquisite items – country scenes painted by Jean-Baptiste Huet in 1776, Louis XV and Louis XVI furniture, portraits by François-Hubert Drouais, and Sevrès and Meissen porcelain. However, the aptly named Grand Salon is the most spendid of all, with its Aubusson upholstered chairs, sculptures by Houdon and Clodion, a Savonnerie carpet from 1678, and exquisite commodes by master cabinetmaker Adam Weisweiler. Interestingly, the trappings of modern life – kitchen, offices and bathrooms – lie hidden behind fine wooden panelling. The Count died in 1935 and, while his house survived World War II intact, tragically all his remaining family members perished in Auschwitz.

Practical Information

Address 63 Rue de Monceau, Champs-Elysées; tel. +33 1 45 63 26 32; www.lesartsdecoratifs.fr/francais/nissim-de-camondo

Getting There Métro: Monceau, Villiers; bus: 30, 84, 94.

Opening Times 10am–5pm Wed–Sun.

MUSÉE NATIONAL EUGÈNE DELACROIX

While it's true that the most famous work of France's leading Romantic painter – the bare-breasted *Liberty Leading the People* – resides in the Louvre, Delacroix's former home and studio is worth a visit for its artistic insight. Here, you'll find small oil paintings; drawings and pastels; lithographs; and his only three attempts at fresco; as well as the tools of his trade – palette, brushes and easel. Also on display are items collected on his travels to Morocco, including ceramics, jewellery, sabres and kaftans. There are also letters from friends, including George Sand and Charles Baudelaire. Indeed, he had a quite a band of admirers, including now-legendary artists such as Cézanne, Manet and Van Gogh, all of whom copied his compositions. In 1849 Delacroix began work on several large murals themed around good and evil for the Chapelle des Anges in St-Sulpice. In 1857, seriously ill and unable to manage the trip across town, he moved his home and studio here to be nearer to the church. His notebooks on the project, along with studies for the murals, form part of the museum's collection. Impressionist painter Paul Signac was one of the founding members of the Société des Amis d'Eugène Delacroix, a group established in 1935 to save this studio from being demolished.

Practical Information

Address 6 Rue de Fürstemberg, St Germain-des-Prés; tel. +33 1 44 41 86 50; www.musee-delacroix.fr

Getting There Métro: St-Germain-des-Près, Mabillon; bus: 39, 63, 70, 86, 95, 96.

Opening Times 9:30am–5pm Wed–Mon.

MAIN IMAGE A vineyard in the Tupungato Valley with the Andes in the distance, Mendoza **BELOW (left to right)** Vintage bottles in a winery cellar, Mendoza; harvesting Malbec grapes

4 MORE WINE REGIONS TO RIVAL NAPA VALLEY

COLUMBIA GORGE, OREGON, USA Take in the awesome splendour of this towering river canyon as you sip sweet whites and luscious reds at one of its small vineyards. Then cool off beneath a gushing waterfall or take to the water by kayak.

CAPE WINELANDS, SOUTH AFRICA A trip to the Cape promises cloudless African skies, lush green mountain valleys and azure seas. While you're here, head to nearby game reserves and vibrant townships or take in the delights of Cape Town.

MARLBOROUGH, SOUTH ISLAND, NEW ZEALAND Marlborough, ringed by rugged mountains on New Zealand's South Island, grows some of the world's best Sauvignon Blanc grapes. Enjoy tours and tastings before heading to the nearby coast to swim with dolphins and watch whales.

TOKAJ WINE REGION, HUNGARY The world's only UNESCO-protected wine region, Tokaj boasts over 1,000 years of wine-making, and its wines still age in 700-year-old rock cellars.

WINE-TASTING IN MENDOZA
vs WINE-TASTING IN NAPA VALLEY

In the shadow of the magnificent snowcapped Andes in Argentina, the high-altitude vineyards of Mendoza are a stunning alternative to the well-trodden wine trails of California's Napa Valley

NEED TO KNOW

LOCATION Mendoza lies in the foothills of the Andes in western Argentina, 710 km (440 miles) northwest of Buenos Aires

NUMBER OF WINERIES 700

DAYTIME TEMPERATURE During the autumn harvest festival in March, expect a daytime average of 28°C (82°F)

MENDOZA · Córdoba
Buenos Aires
ARGENTINA
CHILE
Pacific Ocean
Atlantic Ocean

Whatever happened to the romance and charm of Napa Valley? It's an all-too-familiar lament, and one with a simple answer: they've been put in the shade by Mendoza, Argentina's premier wine-growing region. Likened to the pre-boom Napa Valley of the early 1980s, Mendoza is an emerging destination of empty roads and fabulous, exotic wines. And the vineyards here, set against a splendid backdrop of the soaring, white-tipped Andes, are some of the most scenic in the world.

Mendoza's roads, many of which are prettily lined with poplars and sycamores, gently wind their way up to 1,700 m (5,577 ft) above sea level. They cross deep fertile valleys and high plains and skirt around enormous vineyards that sweep for miles across the picturesque foothills, boasting fabulous Andean panoramas at virtually every turn. This dramatic landscape has hundreds of vineyards, from large, family-owned estates to state-of-the-art boutique wineries and little rustic bodegas.

A lazy vineyard walk is the perfect prelude to intimate tastings with wine experts who speak passionately about their produce. There is little show here, only great wine. Stop at a high-end estate for an evening rooftop tasting. Watching the sun set behind the towering Andes as aromatic premium varietals roll across your tongue is an exquisite experience. Stay overnight at a luxury wine spa before visiting a small bodega that has remained unchanged for a century, with cobbled courtyards that open directly onto the vineyard. Here, sweating mules still plough between the vines, grapes are pressed by hand and ice-cold run-off from the Andes irrigates the fertile land.

Mendoza's wines have at last won the global recognition they deserve. The region produces

ABOVE Bunches of bluish grapes on the vine, Mendoza

abundant varietals, but its most outstanding wine is a deep, rich red, made from the Malbec grape, which flourishes in the dry air and high altitude. Malbec enthusiasts can attend gourmet lunches hosted by winery owners who pair the wine with local cuisine, or travel on horseback to vineyards where the grape thrives. The riding routes skirt herds of guanacos beneath the gaze of Andean condors gliding high in the sky. Ahead, among a whirl of soaring rock faces, is Aconcagua, the highest peak in the world outside Asia. It's a dizzyingly beautiful scene.

FORGET NAPA VALLEY?

THE BUILD-UP Napa Valley, which is just an hour north of San Francisco by car, is renowned for its world-class wines. Each year, hundreds of thousands of enthusiasts visit its 300 or so wineries by bicycle, luxury 4WD, hot-air balloon or aboard the Napa Valley Wine Train. Rolling green hills provide a picturesque backdrop to wine crawls in the area.

THE LETDOWN Napa has sadly shed much of its original charm. Tours emphasize entertainment over wine and tastings have a happy-hour feel, led by volunteers that are more like bartenders than wine experts. Highway 29, the region's main road, is bumper to bumper with cars during the high season.

GOING ANYWAY? Try to visit outside the peak season. Spring is a great time to go, when the weather is warm, there are fewer tourists and the winery owners are less busy. If you plan on travelling in the high season, aim for a midweek stay and book early-morning tastings to avoid the crowds. Try the wineries on the Silverado Trail, a more scenic, less-travelled alternative to Highway 29.

ABOVE A busy picnic spot at the V Sattui Winery, St Helena, Napa Valley, California

PRACTICAL INFORMATION

Getting There and Around
There are regular flights from Argentina's capital, Buenos Aires, to Mendoza City. Shuttle buses run from Mendoza's airport to the city centre. The region's three main wine-growing areas — Luján de Cuyo, Valle de Uco and Maipú — are only a short drive away. Tour agencies run tours of varying lengths and provide itineraries should you wish to explore alone.

Where to Eat
Housed within the Escorihuela Winery — one of Mendoza's oldest wineries — is the sumptuous Francis Mallman 1884 restaurant (www.escorihuela.com), which serves classic Argentinian cuisine. Order a succulent steak or *chivita* (kid goat), a local speciality, and accompany with a rich Malbec.

Where to Stay
Nestled at the foot of the Andes in its own vineyards, Cavas Wine Lodge (www.cavaswinelodge.com) boasts luxury suites and a spa with wine-therapy treatments.

When to Go
Visit during the harvest season from February to March, when visitors help with grape-picking and take part in Vendimia, the area's lively wine-harvest festival.

Budget per Day for Two
£270 including accommodation, wine tours and dining out.

Website
www.welcomeargentina.com

ABOVE The giant sculpture of Crazy Horse from below, USA

CRAZY HORSE VS MT RUSHMORE

The world's largest sculpture in the making stands head and shoulders above Mt Rushmore

NEED TO KNOW

LOCATION The Crazy Horse Memorial is in the Black Hills of South Dakota near Custer, about 65 km (40 miles) southwest of Rapid City

VISITORS PER YEAR 1 million

DAYTIME TEMPERATURES
Jan: -6°C (22°F); Apr: 7°C (45°F); Jul: 22°C (72°F); Oct: 9°C (48°F)

Carved into a granite outcrop in South Dakota's Black Hills, Mount Rushmore is one of America's most patriotic landmarks. Here, the 18-m (60-ft) faces of George Washington, Thomas Jefferson, Abraham Lincoln and Theodore Roosevelt gaze out across the Great Plains. Journey 25 km (17 miles) to the southwest, however, and you'll see a newer, larger and equally impressive sculpture slowly being carved out of another mountain.

The monument depicts Native-American hero Crazy Horse, the Lakota warrior who defeated General Custer at the 1876 Battle of the Little Bighorn, and is chiselled out of Thunderhead Mountain, a site considered sacred by some tribes. The figure sits astride a galloping horse and has an

outstretched arm pointing towards the southeast – a gesture that is meant to recall his poignant words: "My lands are where my dead lie buried".

Work on the sculpture started in 1948 when Lakota Chief Henry Standing Bear asked Korczak Ziolkowski, a Polish-American sculptor who had worked on Mount Rushmore, to design a monument honouring Native American people. Crazy Horse never allowed himself to be photographed, so rather than being an exact likeness, this sculpture represents the spirit of Native America. The face, measuring 27 m (87 ft) high, was completed in 1998. Workers are now blocking out the horse's head, and depending on what is happening on the day you visit, you may be able to see and hear the explosive blasts used to shape the rock before carving begins. When it is completed, the sculpture of Crazy Horse will be 172 m (563 ft) high and 195 m (641 ft) long, dwarfing Mount Rushmore.

The enormous sculpture was unfinished when Ziolkowski died in 1982, and his wife and sons have continued his work. Ziolkowski refused to accept government funds, believing it would compromise the project's cultural and educational mission, so this work-in-progress is entirely funded by donations and admission fees.

ABOVE Model showing what the finished monument will look like

FORGET MT RUSHMORE?

THE BUILD-UP Mount Rushmore, which was completed in 1941, is one of the most iconic images in America. Whether or not its patent nationalism appeals, the sheer scale of the monument is impressive. So too is the story of how 400 workers blasted and carved it out of a granite ridge at a height of 1,745 m (5,725 ft). You can't help marvelling at such details as George Washington's nose or Theodore Roosevelt's moustache, as well as at the beautiful scenery of the Black Hills.

THE LETDOWN The presentations given to visitors are staunchly patriotic in tone, and some of the monument's symbolism may be lost on those who aren't familiar with American history. Mount Rushmore is highly popular in summer, so expect crowds.

GOING ANYWAY? Bring binoculars to better see the sculpted details and to spot mountain goats clambering around the noble faces. Arrive early to beat the crowds and catch the clear morning light. Observe how the faces appear to change with the movement of the sun.

ABOVE The heads of four US presidents carved out of the rock at Mount Rushmore, USA

PRACTICAL INFORMATION

Getting There and Around
Flights go from major US cities to Rapid City Regional Airport, which is 65 km (40 miles) away from Crazy Horse. You will need a car to drive to the monument. Several car-rental companies are located at the airport.

Where to Eat
Diners, cafés and steakhouses in the area serve regional fare, such as burgers, steaks and buffalo. The Steak 'n Ribs Place (www. steaknribsrestaurant.com) in nearby Custer is set in a handsome bank building dating from 1881.

Where to Stay
The Victorian gabled Custer Mansion Bed and Breakfast (www.custermansionbb.com) has charming rooms with four-poster beds and serves hearty breakfasts.

When to Go
Spring and autumn have the most pleasant temperatures and fewer crowds than the summer.

Budget per Day for Two
£135 including accommodation food, transport and admission.

Website
www.crazyhorsememorial.org

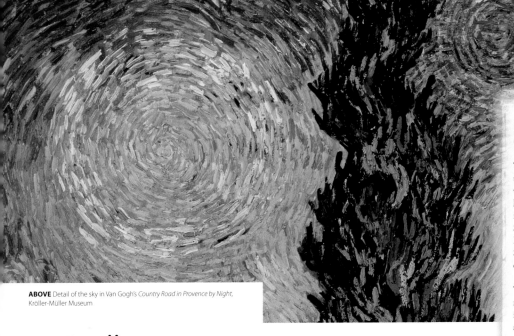

KRÖLLER-MÜLLER
VS THE VAN GOGH MUSEUM

For the best of Van Gogh, leave the city behind and head into the Dutch countryside

NEED TO KNOW

LOCATION The Kröller-Müller Museum is 80 km (50 miles) southeast of Amsterdam in the centre of Hoge Veluwe National Park

VISITORS PER YEAR Around 260,000

DAYTIME TEMPERATURES
Jan: 4°C (39°F); Apr: 12°C (55°F); Jul: 22°C (72°F); Oct: 13°C (57°F)

North Sea

Groningen

NETHERLANDS

Amsterdam

KRÖLLER-MÜLLER MUSEUM

The Hague

GERMANY

Eindhoven

BELGIUM

Art-lovers anxious to get their fix of Van Gogh should bypass the popular Van Gogh Museum in Amsterdam, with its overcrowded rooms and long queues, and head instead to the fascinating Kröller-Müller Museum, located in the heart of Hoge Veluwe National Park in the eastern Netherlands. Here you'll find an extensive collection of the great man's work in an idyllic rural setting of woodland, heathland, grassy plains and sand drifts.

This fine, isolated museum is named after Helene Kröller-Müller, a 20th-century art enthusiast who built up a large collection of works, including many Van Gogh paintings, with the support of her wealthy industrialist husband. But when his business was hit hard during the Great Depression, Helene feared for the future of her collection, and in 1935 she gave all 11,500 pieces to the Dutch state on the condition

that a museum be built to house them. Her wish was granted, and in 1938 the Kröller-Müller Museum opened on the family estate at Hoge Veluwe.

Helene's favourite artist was Van Gogh, who she believed "created modern Expressionism". She purchased 91 of his paintings and 175 drawings, and, while this is less than half the number owned by the Van Gogh Museum in Amsterdam, it represents a more digestible helping for one visit. Look out for the arresting *Self Portrait* of 1887, in which the artist's face emerges from a thunderous, swirling background and seems to stare right at you, and *Four Cut Sunflowers*, with its fiery yellow petals that appear to flicker on the canvas. The paint has been applied so thickly in *The Sower* (1888) and *Country Road in Provence by Night* (1890) that the works have a shimmering quality, the energy from the bright stars and the sun somehow radiating far beyond the edges of the canvases. The famous piece *Café Terrace at Night* (1888) is also on display. Some critics believe this is part of a trilogy that includes *Starry Night* (1889) and *Starry Night Over the Rhone* (1888), both of which are exhibited elsewhere.

The Kröller-Müller collection also has a major collection of 19th- and 20th-century French paintings and a sculpture garden with distinctive works by Auguste Rodin and Henry Moore.

ABOVE Van Gogh's vivid work *The Sower*, Kröller-Müller Museum

FORGET THE VAN GOGH MUSEUM?

THE BUILD-UP The Van Gogh Museum boasts the largest collection of the artist's work in the world and offers visitors the chance to compare his style to that of other 19th-century artists, including Toulouse-Lautrec, Gauguin and Seurat. It is conveniently located close to the Rijksmuseum on Museumplein (Museum Square) in Amsterdam, which has an extensive collection of the work of other Dutch masters.

THE LETDOWN The temptation to view so many great works of art all together can be irresistible. But how much can the brain absorb at one viewing, especially when you're vying for viewing space with so many visitors? Nearly 2 million people visit the museum every year.

GOING ANYWAY? Amsterdam is undoubtedly one of the most popular and interesting cities in Europe, and its museums are renowned the world over. The Van Gogh Museum has a very good English-language website that is essential reading if you wish to make the most of your visit. It is better to visit off-season and at either end of the day (particularly at opening time) to avoid the worst of the crowds.

ABOVE Visitors at the Van Gogh Museum, Amsterdam

PRACTICAL INFORMATION

Getting There and Around
Schiphol Airport, located on the outskirts of Amsterdam, is 95 km (60 miles) from the Kröller-Müller Museum. You can travel to the museum by car, train or bus.

Where to Eat
Amsterdam boasts a good variety of places to eat, from basic cafés to sophisticated restaurants. For a unique dining experience try De Kas Restaurant (www.restaurantdekas.nl), with its glass conservatory. At the museum, there's a very good self-service café called Monsieur Jacques.

Where to Stay
Try the small and friendly Hotel Multatuli (www.multatulihotel.nl), located in the centre of Amsterdam and named after a 19th-century Dutch writer.

When to Go
The driest, warmest months are from April to September.

Budget per Day for Two
£200 including accommodation, food, transport and entrance to the museum.

Website
www.kmm.nl

ROCK ART OF THE DRAKENSBERG
VS THE CAVE PAINTINGS OF LASCAUX

The breathtaking mountain wilderness of Southern Africa's Drakensberg offers ancient art on a grand scale, dwarfing the skilful artifice at France's Lascaux

ABOVE Tourists cluster in the shade around the entrance to the Lascaux cave complex

NEED TO KNOW

LOCATION South Africa's uKhahlamba-Drakensberg Park skirts the border of Lesotho, 325 km (200 miles) south of Johannesburg

DATING FROM
1,000 BC to 1880s

DAYTIME TEMPERATURES
Jan: 26°C (79°F); Apr: 22°C (72°F); Jul: 18°C (64°F); Oct: 24°C (75°F)

The Zulu call it *uKhahlamba*: "Barrier of Spears". Dutch settlers, encountering its formidable reptilian spine in the 1830s, named it the Drakensberg, or "Dragon's Mountain". By either name, the jagged series of peaks over 3,400 m (11,000 ft) rising within uKhahlamba-Drakensberg Park – Africa's largest tract of protected mountain wilderness – is an immense and imposing sight, beside which the replica caves at Lascaux cannot help but seem contrived in comparison.

Below these wild craggy peaks stands a giant open-air gallery of prehistoric rock art – a full 500 individual painted shelters and caves, remarkable both for the fine quality of their workmanship and for their excellent state of preservation. The most complex panels are simply giddying, depicting a mysterious dreamscape populated by naturalistic or distended people, a menagerie of wild animals, and surreal antelope-headed human figures known as therianthropes.

Among the sites that stand out for quality and accessibility is Game Pass Shelter, which features a beautifully executed main frieze of a herd of elands (Africa's largest antelope) interspersed with various human figures. Dubbed the "Rosetta Stone" of the uKhahlamba-Drakensberg, it was here that the scholar David Lewis-Williams "cracked the code" of religious symbolism that underlies the area's rock art, revealing it to depict figures in a state of shamanic trance, and hunters absorbing the qualities of the animals they killed.

At Giant's Castle, the prosaically named Main Cave hosts 500 human and animal figures, ranging from the ubiquitous eland to big cats and snakes. Here, a life-size replica of the so-called "bushmen" serves to introduce the artists responsible for this ancient tradition. While the oldest paintings in the Drakensberg may be 3,000 years old, the most recent are only about 150 – they depict the first ox-wagons to roll across the escarpment, carrying the European settlers who took possession of the land, shooting the local "bushmen" population on sight.

UKhahlamba-Drakensberg ranks among the elite group of 26 UNESCO World Heritage Sites to be inscribed on both cultural and natural grounds. Boasting spectacular scenery and abundant wildlife, its wild beauty is a world away from the landscaped walkways of Lascaux. You can ramble through lush green foothills, brave a hike up to the escarpment, or snake your way by jeep up the sole pass that breaches the Barrier of Spears' otherwise impregnable border with Lesotho. Far from being stage-managed, the Drakensberg still hosts a profusion of the elands so beloved of the bushmen, while quarrelsome baboons bark shrilly from the cliffs, vying to be heard above the calls of 300 species of birds.

PRACTICAL INFORMATION

Getting There and Around
Fly to Johannesburg or Durban. From the airport, rent a car, set up a customized tour, or catch the inexpensive Baz Bus (www.bazbus.com) to one of the backpacker hostels that organise hiking trips from the foothills.

When to Go
October–March is hot and wet; June–August drier and colder.

Where to Eat
All hotels, backpacker hostels and resorts serve adequate to good meals, mostly at very reasonable prices. To splash out,

head to the award-winning Cleopatra Mountain Farmhouse (www.cleomountain.com).

Where to Stay
The Orion Mont-Aux-Sources (www.oriongroup.co.za) is the most scenic hotel, but Cathedral Peak (www.cathedralpeak.co.za) beats it for rock art access. For good value, try one of the national park's rest camps.

Budget per Day for Two
Up to £100.

Website
www.kznwildlife.com

FORGET LASCAUX?

THE BUILD-UP Dubbed the "Sistine Chapel of Prehistory", Lascaux is the most famous of 25 painted caves in France's Vézère Valley, containing around 1,800 individual figures – horses, stags, bulls and other animals – whose rich colour and lifelike detail belie their antiquity, estimated at 15–35,000 years old.

THE LETDOWN Opened to the public in 1948, Lascaux had to close 15 years later when it was noted that changes to the subterranean microclimate associated with human traffic and artificial lighting would soon destroy the paintings. The original cave has never re-opened to the public, and the replica "faux-Lascaux" a short walk away can feel touristy.

GOING ANYWAY? Touristy it may be, but faux-Lascaux is devoutly faithful to the original. The two finest galleries – the Chamber of Bulls and Central Corridor – have been reproduced down to the last contour and brushstroke using identical natural pigments such as ochre, charcoal and iron oxide.

MAIN IMAGE Vibrant frieze in Game Pass Shelter, in the Kamberg area
BELOW (left to right) Drakensberg mountains; eland in Drakensberg National Park; models depicting traditional bushmen, Giant's Castle

ART AND CULTURE

JEBEL ACACUS

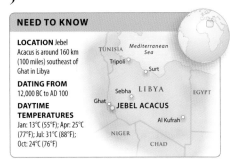

NEED TO KNOW

LOCATION Jebel Acacus is around 160 km (100 miles) southeast of Ghat in Libya

DATING FROM 12,000 BC to AD 100

DAYTIME TEMPERATURES Jan: 13°C (55°F); Apr: 25°C (77°F); Jul: 31°C (88°F); Oct: 24°C (76°F)

Tucked away in Libya's remote southwestern corner, the Jebel Acacus region (also known as Tadrart Akakus, *tadrart* being the Berber word for "mountain") is home to one of the world's greatest collections of prehistoric art. There are thousands of rock and cave paintings here in a wide range of styles, dating from 12000 BC to AD 100 and showing changing ways of life in the Sahara, along with depictions of local flora and fauna. The area's fantastical desert scenery is another major attraction, with sweeping sand dunes, rock arches, the stumps of eroded mountains and a labyrinth of twisting *wadis* (dry river valleys).

Practical Information

Getting There and Around Fly to Libya's capital, Tripoli, then take an onward domestic flight to Ghat (925 km/575 miles away). Domestic transfers must be arranged through a Libyan tour operator.

When to Go The cooler winter months (Oct–Feb) can be surprisingly temperate, although nights can be teeth-chatteringly cold.

Website http://looklex.com/libya/acacus.htm

Delicately painted figures at Wadi Anshal appearing to depict musicians, dancers and feasting as well as hunters and animals, Libya

CRESWELL CRAGS

NEED TO KNOW

LOCATION Creswell is 35 km (22 miles) north of Nottingham in the East Midlands of England

DATING FROM Around 8000 BC

DAYTIME TEMPERATURES Jan: 4°C (39°F); Apr: 8°C (46°F); Jul: 16°C (61°F); Oct: 11°C (51°F)

England is not particularly known for its rock art, so there was considerable excitement in 2003 when prehistoric paintings showing bison, birds and an ibex were discovered at Creswell Crags, the only example of Ice Age rock art so far discovered in the country. Paintings apart, the Crags offer a rich insight into life during the last Ice Age, between 50,000 and 10,000 years ago. The caves here, carved by centuries of erosion out of the flanks of a beautiful limestone gorge, were used by hunters as a temporary camp during their seasonal pursuit of herds of migrating mammoths, bison and reindeer. Creswell is one of the most northerly points they ever reached.

Practical Information

Getting There and Around The nearest international airport is the East Midlands airport near Nottingham. London to Nottingham by train takes about 2 hours. There are train and bus links from Nottingham to Creswell station and the Crags respectively.

When to Go May to September offers the best chance of good weather, though it may rain at any time of year. Book in advance for cave tours.

Website www.creswell-crags.org.uk

Dramatic limestone cliffs riddled with caves and crevices, typical of the scenery at Creswell Crags, UK

GOBUSTAN

NEED TO KNOW

LOCATION Gobustan is around 50 km (30 miles) southwest of Baku, capital of Azerbaijan

DATING FROM Around 8000 to 3000 BC

DAYTIME TEMPERATURES Jan: 4°C (40°F); Apr: 12°C (54°F); Jul: 26°C (79°F); Oct: 16°C (61°F)

The Gobustan (or Qobustan) State Reserve has an estimated 6,000 petroglyphs, scattered amidst the rocky outcrops and caves that dot the desert landscape southwest of Baku. Carvings include depictions of hunters, animals, battles and dancers, as well as a famous image of a reed boat which led Norwegian ethnologist Thor Heyerdahl to suggest that Scandinavians might originally have come from this region. Gobustan is also known for its belching cold mud volcanoes, and for curious musical stones, which produce strange sounds when struck with a smaller stone, often compared to the noise of a tambourine.

Practical Information

Getting There and Around Fly to Baku, then continue by bus to Gobustan town, some 50 km (30 miles) away. Alternatively, hire a vehicle with a driver to take you to the site.

When to Go From April to June the weather is pleasant but not too hot.

Website www.window2baku.com/eng/Ancient/9gobustan.htm

Striking petroglyphs at Gobustan, showing what seem to be hunters in pursuit of a horned animal, Azerbaijan

CUEVA DE LAS MARAVILLAS

NEED TO KNOW

LOCATION The cave is around 50 km (30 miles) east of Santo Domingo, in the Dominican Republic

DATING FROM Around AD 1000

DAYTIME TEMPERATURES: Jan: 24°C (75°F); Apr: 26°C (79°F); Jul: 27°C (81°F); Oct: 27°C (81°F)

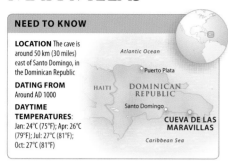

Discovered in 1926, the Cueva de las Maravillas ("Cave of Miracles") is a veritable subterranean art gallery. The walls of the single huge grotto, over 800 m (2,625 ft) long, are decorated with almost 500 quaintly stylized and perfectly preserved pictographs and petroglyphs, created by the Taino people around 1,000 years ago. The cave is also home to an impressive quantity of stalactites, stalagmites, columns and other unusual crystalline formations. With guided tours lasting an hour, it is well set up for visitors and is one of the few caves in the world accessible to wheelchairs.

Practical Information

Getting There and Around Fly to Santo Domingo. From here, catch a taxi or bus to the caves, or take an internal flight to Cueva Las Maravillas airport at San Pedro de Macoris. The caves lie east of here, on the La Romana highway.

When to Go November to April is dry season. The caves are open all year.

Website www. gocaribbean.about.com/od/attract4/gr/LaRomanaCaves.htm

Spectacular stalactites descending in curtains from the cave roof at the Cueva de las Maravillas, Dominican Republic

MURUJUGA

NEED TO KNOW

LOCATION Murujuga begins at Dampier, around 1,265 km (785 miles) north of Perth, Western Australia

DATING FROM Around 8000 BC

DAYTIME TEMPERATURES Jan: 33°C (91°F); Apr: 34°C (93°F); Jul: 28°C (82°F); Oct: 33°C (91°F)

The remote Burrup Peninsula, or Murujuga, of northwestern Australia, is part of the Dampier Archipelago. It is home to what is claimed to be the world's largest array of rock carvings, dating back some 10,000 years or more. According to estimates there are as many as a million carvings to be found here, showing an astonishing range of images including animals (kangaroos, emus, snakes, dogs, turtles and whales) and humans, some depicted carrying traditional objects such as boomerangs and wearing ceremonial head-dresses. The threat of industrial development to the archipelago's archaeological treasures has become a *cause célèbre* for conservationists and, in 2007, most of the area was added to Australia's National Heritage list. There are ongoing appeals for it to be given UNESCO World Heritage status.

Practical Information

Getting There and Around Fly to Perth, then catch a connecting flight to Karratha Airport, from where you can rent an off-road vehicle for the 42-km (25-mile) drive to the Burrup Peninsula.

When to Go The cooler winter months from May to October are best.

Website www.burrup.org.au

Bird tracks etched into the stone at Deep Gorge on the Burrup Peninsula of Western Australia

FONT-DE-GAUME

NEED TO KNOW

LOCATION The caves are in the Dordogne region of southwest France, 125 km (78 miles) from Bordeaux

DATING FROM Around 12,000 BC

DAYTIME TEMPERATURES Jan: 6°C (42°F); Apr: 11°C (52°F); Jul: 21°C (70°F); Oct: 14°C (57°F)

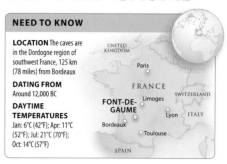

There are very few prehistoric painted grottos still open to the public. The finest is Font-de-Gaume, with some 240 paintings and engravings dating from around 12000 BC. As at Lascaux, the paintings were created using colour-blowing techniques, as well as employing the natural contours of the karst cave walls to lend shape and volume to figures. There's a positive menagerie of animals on display here: bison, mammoths, deer and horses appear most often, but you can also make out a wolf, a bear and two rhinoceroses. Together with enigmatic hand outlines and geometrical shapes, they offer a rare and fascinating glimpse into the lifestyle of a remote Paleolithic era.

Practical Information

Getting There and Around The caves are on the D47 road, 1 km from the town of Les Eyzies. The nearest airport is Bordeaux (90 mins drive away) and the nearest train station at Périgeux (20 mins drive away). You will need your own transport to explore the local area. Note that only 200 visitors are allowed to enter the caves each day. Advance booking is essential in peak season.

When to Go Easter holidays and July–August are particularly busy. May, June and September offer good weather and fewer crowds.

Website www.francethisway.com/heritagesites/fontdegaume.php

Contours of the cave wall lend volume to images of bison at the caves of Font-de-Gaume, France

The menu boards visible in the image:

MENU DU BOUCHON 15€

MENU à 12€

MENU à 18€

LE MENU ETE à 15€

SPECIALITE LYONNAISE À LA CARTE

VINS
COTEAUX DU LYONNAIS
MACONNAIS
BEAUJOLAIS
COTES DU RHONE

LE POT BEAUJOLAIS

MAIN IMAGE Diners at a traditional Lyonnaise *bouchon*
BELOW (left to right) A fresco paying tribute to local chef Paul Bocuse; the unmissable Les Halles de Lyon-Paul Bocuse market

4 MORE GASTRONOMIC HOTSPOTS TO RIVAL PARIS

CAPE TOWN, SOUTH AFRICA Where there's good wine, there's bound to be good food and, with 200 vineyards within striking distance of the city, Cape Town has plenty of both.

ALEPPO, SYRIA The oldest continually inhabited city in the world, Aleppo is also a gourmet capital, famed for its barbecued meatballs with black cherries, and pastries flavoured with orange blossom.

MONTREAL, CANADA A little slice of France in North America, Montreal is devoted to good eating and has a fabulous selection of eateries, from high-end restaurants to homely bistros. The city's markets are pretty vibrant, too.

MELBOURNE, AUSTRALIA With its fresh food markets, upscale restaurants, trendy cafés and cool bars, Melbourne is hailed by many as the country's culinary hub.

LYONNAISE CUISINE
VS PARISIAN CUISINE

Paris has an enviable gastronomic reputation, but Lyon has a great deal of culinary credibility, too.
In fact, where food is concerned, France's second city has the edge

NEED TO KNOW

LOCATION Lyon is in the Rhône-Alpes region of France, 290 miles (465 km) southeast of Paris

VISITORS PER YEAR 6 million

DAYTIME TEMPERATURES Jan: 4°C (39°F); Apr: 14°C (57°F); Jul: 22°C (72°F); Oct: 17°C (63°F)

Map: UNITED KINGDOM, Lille, Paris, Strasbourg, FRANCE, SWITZERLAND, Bay of Biscay, LYON, Bordeaux, ITALY, Marseille, SPAIN, Mediterranean Sea

The battle for gastronomic supremacy between Lyon and Paris has long been waged. Sure, Paris has the tower, the museums, the shops and myriad eateries in every neighbourhood, but it's Lyon that's top when it comes to food, with the highest ratio of restaurants to people in the whole of France.

Unique to Lyon is the *bouchon* – a traditional bistro dishing up 100% Lyonnaise food. Think herring and potatoes soused in oil, sausages in all their guises (including tripe *andouillettes*), chunky terrines, lentils and pork, juicy chicken and buttery-

rich apple tarts – simple home-style cooking at its rustic best, washed down with a glass or two of Beaujolais. This is, after all, the wine's heartland. In fact, in Lyon the third Thursday of November sees a serious celebration of the arrival of Beaujolais Nouveau – the new season's wine. Come midnight on the Wednesday, the Place Bellecour is alive with music, fireworks and people hanging out to taste the new vintage. It's an event that's been dubbed "the Beaujolympics".

In addition to its down-to-earth eating establishments, Lyon has its stellar performers. Veteran super-chef Paul Bocuse, a proud local, has his Michelin 3-star restaurant here. (He also runs a string of brasseries, so the great man's tastes are available to all pockets.) As revered as Bocuse are the nearby Côtes du Rhône vineyards, home to the famed Condrieu, Château Grillet, Saint Joseph and Côteaux de l'Hermitage wines.

If you're still in any doubt about the gastronomic wonders on offer in the city, take a wander around the Halles de Lyon–Paul Bocuse market to see creamy clouds of cheese at Maréchal, briny oysters

ABOVE Panoramic view of Lyon from Fourvière Hill

at Pupier, silky foie gras at Rolle, glossy meat at Maurice Trolliet and plump *andouillettes* at Bobosse. Sample the lemon verbena or strawberry and basil macaroons at Sève. And then, sustained by *coussins* (pillows of almond paste filled with chocolate ganache), roam the charming passageways of Vieux Lyon and salute the city and its cuisine from one of the floating bars on the banks of the Rhône.

FORGET PARISIAN CUISINE?

THE BUILD-UP The French passion for food is a huge part of life in Paris, with bistros and regional restaurants, from modest to upscale, proudly flying the French flag. Also on offer are Japanese, North African, Caribbean, Vietnamese and Chinese cuisine, as well as that from every part of the Mediterranean. And, of course, Paris is the headquarters of *haute cuisine*.

THE LETDOWN You can spend a lot of money on food in Paris without even trying. And without a recommendation, finding a good-value eatery can be hit and (mostly) miss. The city is a tourist mecca and prices are heavily inflated in popular areas, where the food rarely corresponds to the bill.

GOING ANYWAY? Book ahead at famous or popular restaurants, and confirm the reservation the day before. Read up on where to eat before you visit. And bear in mind that many places that are hard to get into in the evening are sometimes much easier to get a table at for lunch.

ABOVE A rare opportunity for good-quality food at economical prices – Chartier, in Paris's 9th arrondissement

PRACTICAL INFORMATION

Getting There and Around
TGV trains run regularly from Paris to Lyon. Lyon-Saint Exupéry airport is 16 miles (25 km) from the town centre. A shuttle bus runs every 20 minutes. To get around Lyon city centre, take trains, trams or buses. Bicycle hire is another option.

Where to Eat
Head for the atmospheric La Meunière (www.la-meuniere.fr) *bouchon* for its Lyonnaise salad buffet table, including *cervelle de canut* (cream cheese with shallots and herbs), shredded beef with lentils and Beaujolais drawn straight from the cask. The Michelin 2-star Nicolas Le Bec (www.nicolaslebec.com) serves an original take on regional

and French classics: pigeon cooked in Dijon mustard, poached quince with fresh figs and almond cream.

Where to Stay
The all-white, very modern Collège Hôtel (www.college-hotel.com) in Vieux Lyon used to be a university dormitory and still has a fun, school theme.

When to Go
Try to visit in June or September; July and August get very crowded.

Budget per Day for Two
If you eat in *bouchons* and stay in a mid-range hotel, expect to spend £180 per day. Any splurges on Michelin-starred restaurants will significantly add to the cost.

Website
www.lyon-france.com

CLEMENS XI P. M.

MAIN IMAGE Roman statuary in the courtyard of the Palazzo dei Conservatori, part of the Capitoline Museums **BELOW (left to right)** Piazza del Campidoglio; head of Constantine; Hall of the Horatii and Curiatii

CAPITOLINE MUSEUMS
VS VATICAN MUSEUMS

Light and spacious, the Capitoline Museums make an elegant setting for some of the finest art of the antique world.
Across the Tiber, meanwhile, the exhibits at the Vatican Museums seem suffocated by the great press of visitors

NEED TO KNOW

LOCATION The Capitoline Museums sit atop the most sacred of ancient Rome's seven hills – the Capitoline Hill

VISITORS PER YEAR
520,000

DAYTIME TEMPERATURES
Jan: 10°C (50°F); Apr: 14°C (57°F); Jul: 26°C (79°F); Oct: 19°C (66°F)

A **magnificent flight of steps** (the Cordonata) leads you up the gently rising Capitoline Hill. At the top lies Michelangelo's Piazza del Campidoglio, flanked on one side by Palazzo Nuovo and on the other by Palazzo dei Conservatori. Together, the two buildings form the main body of the Capitoline Museums, home to exceptional collections of classical sculpture and paintings. The architecture of the square is bold, geometric and harmonious. And with no traffic, it's relatively quiet here. The Vatican Museums across the river seem aloof and inhuman in scale by comparison.

As befits a modern European capital, Rome has its share of idiosyncratic museums, from one dedicated to mental illness to another exploring the history of crime. But in truth these are only sideshows to the city's unimaginably vast hoard of paintings and antique sculptures, which are exhibited in a hundred or more public and semi-public palaces. The Vatican Museums attract the lion's share of tourists to the city – more than 4 million go there each year – leaving Rome's other galleries in relative peace. The Capitoline Museums may not be quite so off the beaten track as the Galleria Nazionale d'Arte Antica (*see p260*), but the number of visitors is never overwhelming.

The main entrance to the museums is in the cool, white marble façade of the Palazzo Nuovo, on the left of the Piazza del Campidoglio. Busts of philosophers and statues of river gods lead you down the Hall of the Philosophers to an octagonal room, where Venus awaits you, modestly covering her marbled nakedness. In the Hall of the Galatian, the dying Gaul, proud yet bowed by the pain of defeat, evokes genuine pathos. In the Hall of Doves, mosaics from Hadrian's Villa are on show.

An underground passageway then takes you to the Galleria Lapidaria, with its collection of epigraphs, and the Tabularium (the former records office), where the remains of the Temple of Veiovis can be seen. Stairs lead back to the light, and at the end of the long corridor is the museum's greatest surprise – not an exhibit, but the best view of the Roman Forum. From this height, much of its confused archaeology falls neatly into place.

Returning to Michelangelo's piazza, you pass into the courtyard of the Palazzo dei Conservatori, where you're greeted by a jumble of fragments from a colossal statue of Emperor Constantine. The tour then heads upstairs to one of the museum's most helpful exhibits – the story of Rome told in a sequence of 16th- and 17th-century frescoes in the Hall of the Horatii and Curiatii. The picture gallery is next and, after the acres of marble you've just seen, your eyes feast on the vivid reds of Titian's *Baptism* and Garofalo's *Annunciation*. Also on show are Caravaggio's *St John the Baptist*, Veronese's *Rape of Europa* and some fabulous portraits by Van Dyck. The visit finishes on a high, with the famous equestrian statue of Marcus Aurelius.

FORGET THE VATICAN MUSEUMS?

THE BUILD-UP The Vatican Museums not only have the two most beautiful rooms in the world (the Sistine Chapel and the Room of the Segnatura), their vast corridors also contain all the vanity, devotion and sheer financial clout of the greatest collectors the world has ever known. The picture gallery houses one of the best art collections in Rome.

THE LETDOWN The Vatican Museums can feel like purgatory. They are positively overwhelmed with visitors, and the usual start to a visit here is an hour queuing in the hot Roman sun.

GOING ANYWAY? Book a group tour (www.myvaticantour.com) and you'll sail past the long lines. With a good guide, you'll also get a better handle on the collection in 3 hours than you might in days of dazed wandering on your own.

ABOVE Jostling for a better view, some of the 4.3 million visitors to the Vatican Museums each year

PRACTICAL INFORMATION

Getting There and Around
The nearest metro stop is Colosseo, a 10-minute walk away. Dozens of buses from Rome's main station, Termini, stop nearby. Get off at either the Via dei Fori Imperiali or the Via del Plebiscito.

Where to Eat
Swanky restaurants abound, but the real food of Rome is *la cucina povera* – the tripe, salt cod, beans and artichokes of the traditional trattorias. The Asinocotto (www.asinocotto.com), just over the river in Trastevere, is a great example. Stuffed courgette flowers and veal tongue are just two of the dishes on offer.

Where to Stay
The Inn At The Roman Forum (www.theinnattheromanforum.com) has a quiet courtyard, a roof terrace and its own Roman crypt. And, as the name suggests, it's right next to the forum.

When to Go
Rome has a mild Mediterranean climate. May is the nicest month. The period from December to February is the nearest the city has to a low season.

Budget per Day for Two
Resist the shops and you could get away with £200.

Website
www.museicapitolini.org

Rape of Persephone (1621–2) by Bernini at the Galleria Borghese

Pope Innocent X (c. 1650) by Velázquez at the Galleria Doria Pamphilj

Palazzo Barberini, part of the Galleria Nazionale d'Arte Antica

GALLERIA BORGHESE

Cardinal Scipione Borghese had money, taste and, most importantly, a pope for an uncle. He started collecting paintings and sculptures for his villa in the (then) outskirts of Rome in 1605, and over the course of a lifetime amassed a truly awe-inspiring collection. His smartest move was hiring the young artist Bernini to work for him. His second smartest was to kick off his collection by confiscating a hundred wonderful canvases from Caravaggio's teacher, the painter Cavalier d'Arpino.

The Galleria Borghese has only 20 rooms, but there isn't a single one that won't make you gasp in delighted recognition. You have to book a 2-hour slot in advance, but this makes the whole experience much more civilized. On the ground floor there's sculpture, including some of Bernini's finest statues. When you see the fingers of the god Pluto pressed into the impossibly soft marble flesh of Proserpina, you'll understand what a sharp eye for talent the cardinal had. On the first floor the collection of paintings is so rich, so full of chocolate and cream, that an aesthetic tummy ache may force you to leave before your 2 hours are up: Titian, Raphael and six (count them, six!) Caravaggios.

Practical Information

Address Piazzale Scipione Borghese 5; tel. +39 06 32810; www.galleriaborghese.it

Getting There The Galleria Borghese is on the eastern side of the Parco Villa Borghese. The Spagna metro stop, on Line A, is at the other end of the park, 1.5 km (1 mile) away.

Opening Times 8:30am–7:30pm Tue–Sun. Visits must be booked in advance. You will be given a 2-hour slot.

GALLERIA DORIA PAMPHILJ

Alongside the Windsors and the Gettys, the Doria Pamphilj family has the best private art collection in the world, boasting works by most of the great names of the Renaissance. This Roman dynasty has been marrying, inheriting and buying its way towards the collection since the 16th century.

On entering the museum, you're immediately transported far from the traffic on the Via del Corso. The Poussin Room, filled with sensual landscapes, drops you into an entirely new world. And it gets better, with a ballroom the producer of a costume drama could only fantasize about, a chapel with a family mummy and then, at the very heart of the palace, the four gilded galleries that run round the light-filled courtyard. Velázquez's portrait of Pope Innocent X (a member of the family) is the star, the light splashing on his crimson sash against the lightless depths of the damask drapery behind. Then there's Titian's Salomé, a girl far too virtuously beautiful to be carrying the head of St John the Baptist on a plate. Other treasures of the collection include works by Raphael, Filippo Lippi, Caravaggio, Titian and a bewitching landscape with dancing figures by Claude Lorrain.

If you can, visit the Galleria Doria Pamphilj at dusk, just as the lights come on, and marvel as the light dances between the ornate glass chandeliers and the gilded mirrors.

Practical Information

Address Via Corso 305; tel. +39 06 679 7323; www.doriapamphilj.it/ukhome.asp

Getting There The nearest metro stop is Colosseo, on Line B. The Via Corso is used by dozens of bus routes.

Opening Times 10am–5pm daily.

GALLERIA NAZIONALE D'ARTE ANTICA

Split between two exquisite *palazzi*, the Galleria Nazionale d'Arte Antica has hundreds of enthralling paintings and a few genuine masterpieces, yet it barely sees a soul from one day to the next. You might easily have a room full of Sienese Masters or a couple of Filippo Lippis to yourself. On the flip side, you might equally get Caravaggio's spine-tinglingly ruthless decapitation of Holofernes – not a painting to see on your own.

Perhaps even more rewarding than the paintings are the buildings themselves. Palazzo Barberini had Bernini, Borromini and Maderno as its designers. Its epic centrepiece is the swirling, angel-filled fresco by Pietro da Cortona in the main salon. It's as masterfully outrageous as anything the notoriously over-the-top Baroque era could muster. On the other side of the Tiber, Palazzo Corsini must be the most shamefully ignored beauty in Rome. The palace, standing next to the old Botanical Gardens, has works by Rubens, Van Dyck and Giordano, all waiting patiently while the ghosts of the Corsini family drift through the quiet corridors.

Practical Information

Address Palazzo Barberini, Via delle Quattro Fontane 13. Palazzo Corsini, Via della Lungara 10; tel. +39 06 4201 0066; www.galleriaborghese.it

Getting There Palazzo Barberini is a few steps from the Barberini metro stop, on Line B, while Palazzo Corsini is in northern Trastevere, a good walk from the San Pietro metro stop. It's easier to take the 23, 28 or 65 bus there.

Opening Times 8:30am–7:30pm Tue–Sun.

Sarcophagus of a married couple at the Etruscan Museum

Fourth-century mosaics at the Museo Nazionale Romano

The Decumanus Maximus road at Ostia Antica

ETRUSCAN MUSEUM, VILLA GIULIA

In the middle of Rome, there's a park with a lake, a zoo, several Roman ruins, countless fountains and two of the world's finest museums – the Galleria Borghese and, in the Villa Giulia, the Etruscan Museum.

When the Romans were still scrabbling around in the mud up on their seven hills, their neighbours to the north, the Etruscans, were already building aqueducts, paving roads and decorating their exquisite temples with Asian-style Medusas. Though their art was archaic and occasionally inscrutable, the laughing eyes of the Apollo of Veii or the easy affection between the Bride and Groom in the 2,500-year-old funerary sculpture evoke more genuine warmth than a thousand Roman statues. There are also distinctly unsettling works, like the frieze depicting Tydeus gorging himself on the brains of his rather shocked archenemy Melanippus.

The very best works in this former papal villa are also the tiniest. The Etruscans were fabulous goldsmiths, and some of the jewellery from the Castellani collection is amazing. There's nothing in the shops on the swish Via dei Condotti that can match this stuff.

Practical Information

Address Piazzale di Villa Giulia 9; tel. +39 06 320 1951; www.romaturismo.com

Getting There The Villa Giulia is at the northern end of the Parco Villa Borghese, a pleasant 15-minute walk from the Flaminio metro stop, on Line A. Alternatively, take the 19 or 3 tram.

Opening Times 8:30am–7:30pm Tue–Sun.

MUSEO NAZIONALE ROMANO

If your experience of classical art is rows of anonymous and noseless marble busts, headless torsos and incomprehensible labels, the Museo Nazionale Romano will make a refreshing change and reveal the vitality of so much Classical sculpture. There's the proud Seleucid prince, more confident in his bronze nakedness than the rest of us could ever feel fully clothed, and a disconcerting bust of Julius Caesar with his toga pulled over his head. Best of all is the famous Olympian, every sinew tensely balanced as he prepares to unleash his discus.

Upstairs, you'll get a tingle of excitement when the guide unlocks a double door and takes you to the gallery on the top floor. Entire rooms from the Villa of Livia on the Palatine Hill have been faithfully reconstructed. The mosaics and frescos have been so vividly realized, it's as if the artist has only just finished work.

The collection in the Palazzo Massimo is the best part of Rome's Museo Nazionale Romano, but your ticket will also get you into the nearby Baths of Diocletian, which includes the Aula Ottagona with its two bronze sculptures of great beauty. Both museums are near Rome's Termini station, and would definitely top any list of good ways to kill time before your train.

Practical Information

Address Palazzo Massimo, Largo di Villa Peretti 1; tel. +39 06 328101; www.romaturismo.com

Getting There The museum is 5 minutes' walk from Rome's principal train station, Termini. It's also very close to the Repubblica metro stop, on Line A.

Opening Times 9am–7:45pm Tue–Sun.

OSTIA ANTICA

Although Ostia Antica is outside Rome, you can ride the metro to the ruined city and be sitting in the theatre in the time it takes to queue for the Vatican Museums. Ostia Antica was Rome's port for 600 years and, after Herculaneum and Pompeii, it's the best-preserved Roman town in Italy. You walk in on the Decumanus Maximus, passing the warehouses, the baths (posh and not so posh) and the pub on the way to the theatre. All these sites can be readily recognized without a degree in archaeology. Most impressive of all is the Forum of the Corporations, where 61 maritime offices are ranged around a great temple, each identified by its own descriptive mosaic. Further into the city are more signs of how rich and poor rubbed along together. There's the meat market, the latrines and a whole host of temples, including the 2nd-century remains of the city's synagogue.

If you can afford the time, take a cruise out to Ostia from the Marconi Bridge in Rome. If not, at least try to hang on until dusk, when the sun glances off the sea and bathes the umbrella pines and ancient buildings in a glorious warm glow.

Practical Information

Address Viale dei Romagnoli 717, Ostia Antica; tel. +39 06 5635 8099; www.ostia-antica.org/visiting.htm

Getting There Take metro Line B to Piramide or EUR Magliana, then get the Ostia Lido train to Ostia Antica. You could also take a Battelli di Roma boat (www.battellidiroma.it) from the Marconi Bridge.

Opening Times 8:30am–6pm Tue–Sat; 8:30am–noon Sun (8:30am–5pm Mar and Oct; 8:30am–4pm Nov–Feb).

SAN SEBASTIÁN
VS CANNES FILM FESTIVAL

Cannes is a duty for cineastes but, at San Sebastián, Spain's premier film festival offers the movies, the stars and the high life – without the hype

NEED TO KNOW

LOCATION San Sebastián is in the Basque region, on Spain's northern coast, 450 km (280 miles) northeast of the Spanish capital, Madrid

WHEN The festival runs for ten days from mid- to late September

VISITORS PER YEAR Over 175,000

Atlantic Ocean
Bilbao
SAN SEBASTIÁN
Barcelona
PORTUGAL
Madrid
SPAIN
Seville
Mediterranean Sea

"Oh, I don't come here to see films." Overheard in a bar on Cannes' Boulevard de la Croisette, this throwaway line sums up the frustrations of the world's number one festival for the true cineaste. Cannes is full of people who are here to buy, to sell, to schmooze, to party; sometimes one gets the distinct impression that the films screening in and out of competition are just a sideshow.

San Sebastián, on the other hand, is very much a movie buff's festival. It may not have the number of weighty world premieres offered by its French cousin, but it has a good eye for new directors – many of them Spanish or Latin American – and has developed strong links with Scandinavian and Asian filmmakers over the past few years. It also has great retrospectives, with recent subjects ranging from Japanese noir to director Terence Davies to films dealing with migration.

Crucially, there's time to see such classics, as this is a much more laid-back festival than manic, sleep-deprived Cannes. It's also more democratic: in San Sebastián, with a little forward planning, you can buy tickets for any movie on the schedule, whereas in Cannes, only films in the parallel Quinzaine section and Cinéma de la Plage beach screenings are accessible to the general public.

The Spanish festival, which runs for nine days at the end of September, is not without its glamorous side, either. Talent attending the 2008 event included Meryl Streep, Antonio Banderas, Woody Allen, Javier Bardem, Ben Stiller, Robert Downey Jr

and John Malkovich – and San Sebastián manages a similar roster most years, regularly outpunching other European festivals such as Rotterdam or Locarno. Even better, because things are on a more human scale here, and everyone tends to stay in the same hotels, you're much more likely to find yourself elbow to elbow with Penélope Cruz at the bar than you ever would in Cannes.

The festival's relaxed schedule also allows time to explore San Sebastián (Donostia in the local Euskara language) itself. It's an elegant, hedonistic and good-looking seaside resort with a vibrant eating and drinking scene, mostly concentrated in the old town. The walk from the Kursaal Centre (the futuristic skewed cube that is the festival hub) to the *belle époque* Cinema Principal, where many press screenings take place, should take 5 minutes but the gauntlet of tempting *pintxos* (the Basque version of *tapas*) bars on the way can turn it into an hour-long gourmet ramble.

PRACTICAL INFORMATION

Getting There and Around
San Sebastián's small airport, 16 km (10 miles) east of town, is served by internal flights from Madrid and Barcelona. The closest international and low-cost hub is Bilbao, 105 km (65 miles) west. Central San Sebastián is easily explored on foot, but there is also an efficient local bus network.

Where to Eat
San Sebastián is one of Spain's top gastronomic centres. Even bar snacks, or *pintxos*, tend to be bite-sized gourmet treats. The town has its fair share of award-winning restaurants but, to sample creative Basque cuisine without breaking the bank, head for Bodegón Alejandro (www. bodegonalejandro.com) in the

old town, the most affordable of celebrity chef Martín Berasategui's group of superb restaurants.

Where to Stay
The Hotel Londres (www. hlondres.com) is a beautiful *belle époque* building facing the main La Concha beach. Rooms are spacious, classic and comfortable.

Daytime Temperature
19°C (66°F) in September, when the festival takes place.

Budget per Day for Two
Allow £220 for accommodation, meals and tickets for screenings.

Websites
Film festival:
www.sansebastianfestival.com
Tourist information:
www.sansebastianturismo.com

FORGET CANNES?

THE BUILD-UP There's no denying that Cannes is the world's most important film festival. Founded in 1946 as a small event on France's beautiful Côte d'Azur, it has grown to become a glamorous 10-day celebration of film, with everybody who's anybody in the industry in attendance, and a solid programme of world premieres in the official selection.

THE LETDOWN All-singing, all-dancing Cannes sometimes gets all too much to bear. Brash and cynical, the marketing and fashionista side of the festival can torpedo its claims to art. And the pressure of numbers is such that getting into screenings – or even just securing a table in a restaurant – is a major feat.

GOING ANYWAY? If you're still set on Cannes, plan your visit like a military campaign. Hotel rooms need to be booked at least six months in advance and, if you're planning to see any competition films, you'll need to apply for accreditation – the general public are not admitted to most of the festival's screenings.

ABOVE Crowds swarming to catch a glimpse of arrivals on the red carpet at the Cannes Film Festival

MAIN IMAGE La Concha beach in San Sebastián **BELOW (left to right)** Aerial view of the bay of San Sebastián; Teatro Victoria Eugenia, one of the festival venues; Meryl Streep accepting the Donostia Award

4 MORE FILM FESTIVALS TO RIVAL CANNES

BERLINALE Berlin is not the warmest place in February, but this festival generates plenty of energy with an eclectic mix of low-budget world cinema and quality commercial films.

VENICE FILM FESTIVAL Opening the autumn awards season at the beginning of September, Venice has given Cannes a run for its money in recent years, with world premieres of Oscar contenders such as *Brokeback Mountain* and *The Queen*.

FILM FESTIVAL LOCARNO This Swiss festival, held in August, is perhaps the closest to San Sebastián in its mix of great setting, small-but-interesting competition line-up and enthusiastic local participation. The open-air gala screenings are justly famous.

MOTOVUN FILM FESTIVAL Of Europe's scattering of "village film festivals", this one, held each July in a pretty Croatian hill town, is among the most enjoyable. Intelligent indie programming and a loyal following of tent-dwelling young film fans has led to it being called "a cross between Glastonbury and Sundance".

MAIN IMAGE Piazza della Signoria Gubbio during Festa dei Ceri
BELOW (left to right) Main square, Perugia; a fresco at Orvieto
Cathedral; a musical performance at Spoleto *(see pp268–9)*

UMBRIA
VS TUSCANY

A land of atmospheric ancient towns, lingering mists and long lunches, Umbria gazes serenely across its western border at its Tuscan neighbour, watching as it suffocates beneath the weight of mass tourism

Umbria is well used to tourists. However, unlike its next-door neighbour Tuscany, it has not yet grown weary of them. While Tuscany's San Gimignano orders urgent measures to stop the hordes clogging its precious medieval streets, Umbria's Gubbio enacts its centuries-old rhythms barely conscious of the tourists strolling wide-eyed in wonder through its equally ancient thoroughfares.

If Italy really was a booted leg, then Umbria would be somewhere around the calf muscle.

Flanked by Lazio, Tuscany and the Marche, this beautiful region has some of the finest landscapes in Italy. But, beyond its natural charms, Umbria also has a hundred towns and villages blessed with outstanding works of art. Places like Trevi, Narni and Montefalco, which anywhere else in Europe would be mobbed like rock stars, are left largely alone on their lofty hilltop perches.

Then there are the region's heavy hitters, prominent on the tourist itinerary. The frescoes in the Basilica di San Francesco d'Assisi paint vivid stories. The cathedral at Orvieto crowns a tufa crag, reflecting shafts of golden light across the valley. Pinturicchio and Perugino seduce with the silver-blue haze of their landscapes, framing Madonnas as beautiful as any in Florence, while Roman and Etruscan remains watch proudly over the plains.

But what really distinguishes this region from others in Italy is its spirit of "campanilismo", the idea of bearing allegiance to the church bells of your mother town. The people of this region scarcely regard themselves as Umbrians at all, but as Perugini, Spoletani and Assisiati. However, this parochialism hasn't fostered a sense of inwardness as it might elsewhere in Italy, but a fervent desire to outdo one's neighbours. This is manifested in *ragús* (meat-based sauces) that change flavour from one valley to the next and towns outbidding each other to put on world-class music festivals. More dramatically, the evidence of this proud, republican spirit lies before you in some of the finest secular buildings in the world. The town halls of Perugia, Gubbio, Todi and Città di Castello are all signs in pink and grey stone of a spirit of independence nurtured since the Dark Ages.

Mention Umbria to an Italian and they'll say approvingly "You'll eat well there", a grudging mark of respect from this most parochial of nations. And you can be assured of a feast – from Castellucio's tiny sweet lentils and hams from Norcia that melt on your tongue, to wild boar hung for days, and simmered to tenderness in a rich Sagrantino wine.

FORGET TUSCANY?

THE BUILD-UP Without Tuscany, there would have been no Renaissance, fewer Merchant-Ivory movie adaptations and fewer places for your maiden aunt to go on holiday. Some of man's greatest artistic achievements are here, from Brunelleschi's Dome to Michelangelo's *David* and it has magical landscapes and stunning towns that look down from their rounded hilltops.

THE LETDOWN Unfortunately, someone forgot to keep quiet about Tuscany. Camera-wielding crowds ruthlessly tick off lists of endangered statues, leaning towers, famous frescoes and historic squares. Then there are the costs, which have sky-rocketed in the last 20 years.

GOING ANYWAY? Thankfully, parts of Tuscany still remain unknown, from the mysterious lands of the Etruscans in the southwest to the majestic marbled mountains above Lucca. But if it is San Gimignano or Pisa you want to visit, then go in winter, when you can enjoy them without hordes of tourists spoiling your view.

ABOVE Snap-happy visitors surrounding the majestic sculpture of *David* in Santa

Detail of the Franconia fountain outside the former residence of prince bishops, Würzburg

The pueblo blanco, or white village, of Cómpeta, overlooking the Andalucian landscape

Manicured cypress trees lining the banks of the lake in the charming city of Lugano

LOWER FRANCONIA, BAVARIA, GERMANY

NEED TO KNOW

LOCATION Lower Franconia is in southern Germany, just east of Frankfurt. Würzburg is the region's main city

AREA 8,560 sq km (3,300 sq miles)

DAYTIME TEMPERATURES Jan: 1°C (34°F); Apr: 11°C (52°F); Jul: 20°C (68°F); Oct: 10°C (50°F)

The air really does get sweeter in Franconia. The hills soften their hard outlines and acres of pines give way to the deciduous forests of the Odenwald. The candyfloss Baroque architecture that festoons Germany is replaced by a far more refined style in Franconia, most evident in the Residenz, a palace in Würzburg. Here, the greatest of all Baroque architects, Balthasar Neumann, built a staircase that climbs to the Tiepolo frescoes above. Inside Würzburg's Cathedral are two of sculptor Tilman Riemenschneider's finest works. West of the city, the Veitshöchheim Palace boasts Europe's most gorgeous Rococo garden.

Practical Information

Getting There and Around Most of Lower Franconia can be reached by public transport from Frankfurt or Nuremberg airports. Numerous river boats also cruise up the Main from the Rhine and the Danube.

When to Go August is busy throughout Franconia, especially on the famous Romantische Straße highway. Visit in spring or autumn.

Website www.bayern.by

ANDALUCÍA, SPAIN

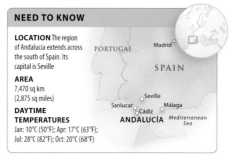

NEED TO KNOW

LOCATION The region of Andalucia extends across the south of Spain. Its capital is Seville

AREA 7,470 sq km (2,875 sq miles)

DAYTIME TEMPERATURES Jan: 10°C (50°F); Apr: 17°C (63°F); Jul: 28°C (82°F); Oct: 20°C (68°F)

Just west of the Costa del Sol, the wind picks up, blowing away the flotsam of mass tourism. The tangled streets of the great sherry towns of Jerez and Sanlucar de Barrameda are home to white horses and the mixed blood of a centuries-old Anglo-Spanish aristocracy. Head inland, and the *pueblos blancos* rise above the stunning Andaluz landscape. A hundred castles of the Spanish Reconquista in turn rise above them, cruel reminders of a 700-year-long clash of civilizations. Then there's the city of Cádiz. Spectacularly situated on a slim spur of sand, it self-consciously stretches away from Spain's reactionary past. At its heart, a golden-domed cathedral shines over the elegant streets and squares of the old town.

Practical Information

Getting There and Around Fly to Cádiz, Seville or Málaga. There are also high-speed trains to Cádiz from Madrid. The local Al Andaluz express cuts through the region in vintage coaches.

When to Go This is one of the sunniest regions in Europe. But summer in the interior makes travelling hard, so visit in early spring or late autumn.

Website www.andalucia.com/province/cadiz

TICINO, SWITZERLAND

NEED TO KNOW

LOCATION The canton of Ticino is in southern Switzerland, hemmed in by Italy on three sides. The Ticino river joins Lake Maggiore before heading into Italy

AREA 2,820 sq km (1,085 sq miles)

DAYTIME TEMPERATURES Jan: 2°C (36°F); Apr: 12°C (54°F); Jul: 22°C (72°F); Oct: 12°C (54°F)

Over the mountains north of the fog-bound Po river, there lies a land of kinder temperatures and bluer skies. You'll find some of Europe's most elegant towns in Switzerland, with Renaissance and Baroque buildings clustered around Italianate piazzas or lining the shores of lakes Maggiore and Lugano. The *belle époque* grandeur of Locarno rivals laid-back Lugano, a city that seduces the fussiest with its ancient churches, alleys and Villa Favorita, home to one of the world's greatest private art collections.

Practical Information

Getting There and Around Ticino is accessible from main cities such as Zurich, Geneva and Milan. Transport options in Ticino include post-buses, cable cars, funiculars, trains and ferries. Avoid taking cars as parking is a problem.

When to Go April and October are ideal times to visit.

Website www.ticino.ch

The **Romanesque nave** of the Basilica of Vézelay with sunlight spilling through the tall windows

The **686-step grand staircase** of Lamego's Nossa Senhora dos Remédios decorated with azulejo tiles

The famous *trulli* of Alberobello, curious structures with rounded conical roofs found in Puglia

BURGUNDY, FRANCE

NEED TO KNOW

LOCATION Burgundy is a region in eastern France. Its main towns are Dijon, Châlons-sur-Saone and Auxerre

AREA 31,700 sq km (12,240 sq miles)

DAYTIME TEMPERATURES
Jan: 2°C (36°F);
Apr: 11°C (52°F);
Jul: 21°C (70°F); Oct: 11°C (52°F)

The vineyards of Burgundy, nestled against the strong, straight ridge of the Côte d'Or, give the region its fame. But far from the traditional touring routes lie the most beguiling landscapes in France. In the Middle Ages, the Court of Dijon was Europe's wealthiest, and artists such as Roger van der Weyden travelled from the Low Countries to paint for the dukes. But Burgundy's real soul lies in its monasteries – Cluny, Montigny and Citeaux, and, towering above them, the Basilica of Vézelay, the last great survivor of western monasticism.

Practical Information

Getting There and Around Burgundy lies on the main motorway and railway routes between Paris and Lyon. Dijon has a small international airport, but private transport is required in much of the countryside.

When to Go In spite of the long, cold winters, Burgundy is a pleasure to visit right through the year, summer's warmth lasting until October.

Website www.burgundy-tourism.com

THE DOURO VALLEY, PORTUGAL

NEED TO KNOW

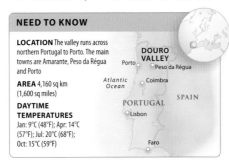

LOCATION The valley runs across northern Portugal to Porto. The main towns are Amarante, Peso da Régua and Porto

AREA 4,160 sq km (1,600 sq miles)

DAYTIME TEMPERATURES
Jan: 9°C (48°F); Apr: 14°C (57°F); Jul: 20°C (68°F); Oct: 15°C (59°F)

As you leave the harsh lands of the Upper Douro Valley, the curves of the river valley soften, and the sunburnt Port grapes give way to white Vinho Verdes and the cap-doffing majesty of the red Barca Velha. Just out of sight of the river valley, a cluster of Visigothic churches and ghost-like Cistercian monasteries still populate the hills. The Douro bears ever westwards, passing near Lamego with its monumental Baroque staircase, then Amarante, dominated by the monastery and church of São Gonçalo, before finally flowing into the Atlantic beneath the city of Porto.

Practical Information

Getting There and Around Porto, at the mouth of the Douro Valley, has a large international airport. Trains also run regularly from Lisbon and Madrid. Along the river, there are boat cruises and the Linha do Douro train.

When to Go Winters can be wet, though the rainfall reduces dramatically away from the Atlantic coast. Summer becomes increasingly brutal the further east you travel. Spring is the best time to visit.

Website www.visitportugal.com

PUGLIA, ITALY

NEED TO KNOW

LOCATION Puglia stretches along the Adriatic coast to the tip of Italy. Its main cities are Bari, Brindisi and Lecce

AREA 19,420 sq km (7,470 sq miles)

DAYTIME TEMPERATURES
Jan: 9°C (48°F); Apr: 14°C (57°F); Jul: 26°C (79°F); Oct: 18°C (64°F)

Along the back of Italy's famous "heel", which juts out into the Adriatic Sea, stretches a line of Puglia's remarkable Romanesque churches, gazing out to sea from Trani, Molfetta and Bari. Further south is the village of Alberobello with its astonishing *trulli* – conical structures made using a prehistoric building technique, and Brindisi, an ancient Roman port joined to the imperial capital by the 580-km (350-mile) Appia Antica. But don't stop here, or you will miss Europe's most spectacular city, Lecce (see p323). Inside its medieval walls, a hundred overwrought façades shine against azure skies. Further south, and beyond the barren Salentine peninsula flanked by a bleached-white coast, are the town of Otranto, with its famous mosaics, and the golden fortress of Gallipoli.

Practical Information

Getting There and Around Puglia has two international airports, at Bari and Brindisi. Brindisi is also the main passenger ferry point for arrivals from the eastern Mediterranean.

When to Go Winters are mild in Puglia, but the vibrant colours of spring make this the best time to visit. Summers are long, hot and crowded, and by autumn the colour has been all but drained from the land.

Website www.italyheaven.co.uk/puglia

FESTIVAL DI SPOLETO
VS THE PROMS

*At the Festival di Spoleto, the last note of each performance hangs in the air;
stepping out from the Proms, it fades fast back into the tuneless roar of London's traffic*

NEED TO KNOW

LOCATION Spoleto is a large medieval town in Umbria, central Italy, 130 km (80 miles) north of Rome

WHEN Late June/early July

NUMBER OF VISITORS 20,000 spectators attend 95 different performances

DAYTIME TEMPERATURE 28°C (82°F) in July

For 16 glorious days each summer, Spoleto transforms itself for a performing arts extravanganza: the town's Roman theatre shakes off any dust and fills with the echoes of its orchestra; the medieval *duomo* (cathedral) becomes a backdrop for the finest operas; and the Teatro Nuovo polishes its exquisite 19th-century boxes.

In contrast, at London's Royal Albert Hall, BBC technicians fiddle and fuss in front of the audience, intent on relaying the music to far-flung television viewers. At the end of each performance, the flushed crowds file out into a city that barely pauses to take note of the extraordinary music pouring from its heart.

In creating the Festival di Spoleto in 1957, the Italian composer Gian Carlo Menotti wanted to bring together the best young performers of the day, and to encourage directors, choreographers and composers to share ideas in order to re-invigorate old classics and to find ways to perform innovative new works. Menotti scoured Italy for a suitable venue. He came upon Spoleto, a slumbering storehouse of Roman remains and medieval buildings which was already blessed with several theatres and a supportive mayor.

The festival, dedicated to theatre, music and dance, grew to be one of Europe's finest. In its early years, unknown artists including Rudolph Nureyev and Margot Fonteyn danced here, and Jacqueline du Pré and Jessye Norman gave debut performances.

Each summer, Spoleto's cafés fill with the sounds of rehearsals and the cathedral square is transformed into a stage. You may rub shoulders again with your neighbour from last night's Row B during the evening *passeggiata* or see a young ballerina bounding up Via Apollinare for her rehearsal at the Roman theatre. It sure beats queuing on Kensington Gore for tickets to the Proms.

ABOVE Cecilia Bartoli during her recital with pianist Jean Yves Thibaudet at Teatro Caio Melisso, Festival di Spoleto

PRACTICAL INFORMATION

Getting There and Around
Spoleto's nearest airport is in Perugia, 48 km (30 miles) to the northwest, but most international airlines fly into Rome – a 1½-hour train ride away. There is an excellent network of buses in the Valle di Spoleto, and small shuttle buses operate between the train station and the historic centre.

Where to Eat
There is a big emphasis on simple, local ingredients in Umbrian cuisine and even the most basic dishes can vary from village to village. One of Spoleto's best restaurants is the Tempio del Gusto (www.iltempiodelgusto.com).

Where to Stay
You will need to book very early, or consider staying outside of town. In Spoleto itself, the Hotel Residenza d'Epoca Palazzo Dragoni (www.palazzodragoni. it) is right in the middle of town. Its dining room has breathtaking views over the medieval city.

When to Go
The Festival di Spoleto is a 16-day event, starting on the last weekend of June (or first week of July) and finishing in mid-July. It's well worth keeping an eye on the official website for dates and venues.

Budget per Day for Two
With inflated hotel prices and watching two shows a day, you will need at least £300.

Website
www.festivaldispoleto.com

FORGET THE PROMS?

THE BUILD-UP The BBC Proms is a unique event. No other music festival can compete with the sheer scale of performances put on over the eight weeks. World-class orchestras and soloists, newly commissioned works, and pieces too expensive to stage elsewhere are all performed in one of the world's most striking concert venues.

THE LETDOWN There is something unsatisfying about the Proms. The BBC's lighting rigs can push the temperatures close to unbearable. The domed hall's acoustics flatter only the largest-scale works. Then there are the Promenaders: rarely young and rarely stylish, their greatest distinction may be their status as the most civilized queuers in the world.

GOING ANYWAY? Don't even think about driving. There are two underground stations within 10 minutes' walk, and several buses stop just outside. Seats for the most popular concerts may sell out, but you can queue on the day for standing tickets. If you plan to watch a lot of performances, think about a £190 season ticket.

ABOVE A high-spirited audience waving flags at the Royal Albert Hall on the Last Night of the Proms

MAIN IMAGE The town of Spoleto with the *duomo* in the foreground
BELOW (left to right) A medieval street; a ballet at the Roman theatre; a musical event in Cathedral Square

4 MORE ARTS FESTIVALS TO RIVAL THE PROMS

BREGENZER FESTIVAL, AUSTRIA Each summer, this festival takes over the attractive Austrian town of Bregenz. It combines drama, operetta and obscure works with magnificent operas staged on the shores of Lake Constance.

AIX-EN-PROVENCE FESTIVAL, FRANCE Already the most fashionable city in France, Aix becomes even more so in July. Theatres and grand palaces are commandeered for performances of generally lesser-known classical works.

TANGLEWOOD MUSIC FESTIVAL, MASSACHUSETTS, USA For three glorious months each summer a vast estate becomes home to the Boston Symphony Orchestra, which puts on large-scale performances every night, providing a musical score to one of the most beautiful corners of New England.

EDINBURGH INTERNATIONAL FESTIVAL, UK Late summer brings three weeks of world-class opera and dance to the city's theatres, while the festival's once humble sidekick, the "Fringe", bursts onto its streets. It's the perfect festival if you fancy some offbeat stand-up comedy between symphonies.

NEW YORK'S INDEPENDENT GALLERIES
VS MOMA

New York's Museum of Modern Art is as famous as it's massive, but for more eclectic offerings, browse the city's unique cutting-edge galleries, where progressive art is on show and often on sale

NEED TO KNOW

LOCATION New York City is in New York State on the east coast of the USA

POPULATION Around 8.3 million

VISITORS PER YEAR Around 40 million

DAYTIME TEMPERATURES Jan: 0°C (32°F); Apr: 12°C (54°F); Jul: 25°C (77°F); Oct: 14°C (57°F)

MoMA – the name alone has become a synonym worldwide for modern art. In 2004, after an ambitious building project, the Museum of Modern Art returned to its Manhattan home, reopening in a gleaming new space designed by Japanese architect Yoshio Taniguchi. The eye-catching building reveals spacious, sky-lit galleries and an elegant sculpture garden. The museum's collection features a great number of superstar paintings, from Picasso's *Les Demoiselles d'Avignon* to Vincent van Gogh's *Starry Night*. It's undoubtedly impressive. But if you're looking for a more eclectic art experience, make for the city's progressive art galleries, both in Manhattan and further afield in the city's boroughs.

Before – long before – an artist has a shot at showing at the Museum of Modern Art, it's likely they'll exhibit in one of New York's many independent galleries or art spaces. And a tour of these will give you the chance to check out up-and-coming artists before they make a name for themselves – to discover them as they're discovering themselves, as it were.

For budding buyers on a budget, these galleries can be a boon, with potentially high-value pieces selling for low prices. But above all, they make for a memorable visit. The art can be strange, sure. Bewildering? Probably. But boring? Rarely.

Anything's game – particularly in Brooklyn – from taxidermy in motel settings to marshmallow sculptures. That said, this being New York, plenty of the art could also well turn out to be a sound investment. As the saying goes: "If you can make it in New York, you can make it anywhere." It's not just artists who get their start here – artistic movements do, too.

The home of contemporary art in New York has long been Chelsea, on Manhattan's West Side, though SoHo to the south features a number of big-name galleries wedged between its plush shops. But the contemporary art scene is by nature migratory, and Brooklyn, with its high ceilings and low rents, has become the new artistic frontier. A visit to the DUMBO Arts Center, for instance, under the Manhattan Bridge, reveals a wealth of artist-friendly industrial structures and warehouses, while nearby Williamsburg is crammed with galleries. For a unique take on contemporary art in Manhattan, don't miss the glowing New Museum on the Bowery.

FORGET MOMA?

THE BUILD-UP MoMA offers a double draw: the world's largest collection of modern art and sculpture, along with a unique building that is a work of contemporary art in itself. The collection showcases most of the modern greats, from Matisse and Braque to Picasso and Klimt. Surrealist fans, take note – Dalí's *The Persistence of Memory* hangs here.

THE LETDOWN Sadly, art loses some of its appeal when you have to elbow others out of the way to view it properly. And the relatively steep entrance fee can be tough to justify for those on a budget.

GOING ANYWAY? Avoid the crowds by visiting the museum midweek or early in the day. You can get around the pricey entrance fee by going between 4 and 8pm on Fridays, when admission is free, though bear in mind that everyone else in the city will have exactly the same idea, so the place gets packed.

ABOVE Queuing to see one of the world's most comprehensive collections of modern art at MoMA

PRACTICAL INFORMATION

Getting There and Around
New York City is served by three major airports: JFK, LaGuardia and Newark. You'll find plenty of transport options within the city.

Where to Eat
Food in New York is very varied, from high-end Italian and French to fiery Latino, with plenty of all-American burgers and hot dogs in between. Union Square Cafe (www.unionsquarecafe.com), a favourite with New Yorkers, features Italian-influenced fare.

Where to Stay
New York City features a wide array of accommodation. For a Midtown hotel with a formidable literary and artistic history, stay at the comfortable, Edwardian-style Algonquin Hotel (www.algonquinhotel.com).

When to Go
Spring and early autumn usher in the finest weather – sunny yet breezy. For fewer crowds, aim for October and November.

Budget per Day for Two
The sky's the limit, but if you stay in a mid-range hotel, eat out once a day and take public transport and the occasional cab, £175–250 should be enough.

Website
www.nycvisit.com

MAIN IMAGE Futuristic lobby at the New Museum **BELOW (left to right)**
DUMBO Arts Center; installation by Tim Noble and Sue Webster at Deitch
Projects; Zach Feuer Gallery, an influential contemporary art space in Chelsea

The New Museum on the Bowery, with its precariously stacked levels

A temporary façade at the Deitch Projects' Grand Street venue

Dance performance at the Galapagos Art Space

NEW MUSEUM

The Bowery was once known for its flophouses – and those who frequented them. Wandering along this street, you'll still see vestiges of its gritty past, but also cutting-edge venues such as the aptly named New Museum. Designed by Japanese architects Sejima and Nishizawa, this seven-storey museum rises like a stack of glowing cubes, casting the Bowery in a new light – literally and figuratively. The changing collection features a wide range of art, from large-scale photographs of 1960s America to geometric abstracts of bright, jarring colours that seem to vibrate with movement.

In keeping with the Bowery's anti-establishment past, the museum's curators take an inclusive approach, featuring emerging artists along with established names. They also celebrate the artistic heritage of the neighbourhood with the Bowery Artist Tribute, an exhibition on the history of artists in the area, including such 20th-century figures as Mark Rothko and Roy Lichtenstein. The museum hosts a monthly performance series, "Get Weird: Experimental and Freaky Jams", which involves youth hip-hop shows by Brooklyn school students who are paired with independent musicians. Even the museum views are a departure: instead of the usual iconic cluster of skyscrapers, the top floors offer wide vistas of the rooftops of the Lower East Side, from its sooty chimneys to its fire escapes.

Practical Information
Address 235 Bowery, Lower East Side; tel. +1 212 219 1222; www.newmuseum.org
Getting There Subway: line 6 to Spring Street or lines N or R to Prince Street.
Opening Times Noon–6pm Wed, Sat & Sun, noon–9pm Thu–Fri.

DEITCH PROJECTS

Plush stores may have replaced many of SoHo's experimental galleries, but you'll still find several artistic stalwarts that have managed to withstand rising rents. The long-running Deitch Projects has evolved with the times, featuring ambitious exhibits that often blend art, music, design and performance. The galleries showcase work by Keith Haring, and recently featured a superb exhibit on Jean-Michel Basquiat's work from 1981, when the New York artist moved from creating graffiti art on the streets to working in the studio. They also present a wide range of multimedia projects made with high-profile artists and musicians, including Madonna, photographer Steven Klein and film-maker Michel Gondry. Some of Deitch Projects' more memorable works have included Yoko Ono's *Ex It* (1998), which featured trees growing out of 100 wooden coffins; the unique *Street Market* (2000), which depicted an apocalyptic urban street; and a project with New York artist Swoon in 2008 that involved the construction of seven boats in the form of floating sculptures that sailed down the Hudson River from upstate New York to one of the gallery's new riverfront spaces in Long Island City.

Every September, Deitch Projects also heats up the streets of SoHo with an audacious art parade involving naked cyclists, giant papier-mâché dolls of politicians and massive floating eyeballs.

Practical Information
Address 76 Grand Street, SoHo (note that the Deitch Projects has two other locations: 18 Wooster Street in SoHo and 4–40 44th Drive in Long Island, Queens); tel. +1 212 343 7300; www.deitch.com
Getting There Subway: line 1; lines A, C or E; lines N, R or W; or lines 4, 5 or 6 to Canal Street.
Opening Times Noon–6pm Tue–Sat.

GALAPAGOS ART SPACE

Ever in search of cheaper pastures, New York's contemporary art scene tends towards the nomadic. Its newest stomping ground is DUMBO (Down Under the Manhattan Bridge Overpass), where lofts and galleries dot the crooked streets under the bridge's steel span. The Galapagos Art Space, a high-ceilinged venue that is hung with enormous canvases and dotted with reflecting pools of water, is one of the first certified "green" art galleries in New York. Its wide range of eclectic exhibits and performances includes live music from neo-soul bands; Coney Island burlesque; gamelan Indonesian concerts; nights of spoken word and poetry by the contributors of *Poets & Writers* magazine; puppetry; and the 60 x 60 show, involving 60 works by 60 composers in 60 seconds or less, and featuring writhing dancers in leotards. It's modern performance art in all its earnest (and sometimes questionable) artistry – but you won't easily forget an evening here. Kids can also get their fill of entertainment, with kite-flying on the first Saturday of each month at the nearby Brooklyn Bridge Park. Kites are provided, and participants get the chance to fly them over the East River between the Brooklyn and Manhattan bridges, and compete for titles such as "longest-running kite."

Practical Information
Address 16 Main Street, DUMBO, Brooklyn; tel. +1 718 222 8500, www.galapagosartspace.com
Getting There Subway: line F to York Street or line A to High Street.
Opening Times Times vary, so call ahead.

Exhibition opening at the Agora Gallery in Chelsea

Colourful artworks inside Momenta Art

CHELSEA'S GALLERIES

New York's best-known gallery district is Chelsea, with 200-plus galleries within an eight-block radius on the west side of Manhattan. The breadth and range (and occasional audacity) of the art here is formidable, with powerhouse galleries like Gagosian sharing the windswept streets with plenty of up-and-coming spaces, where many emerging artists have their New York debuts.

The best way to experience Chelsea is by wandering and window-watching; before long, you'll be drawn in. The airy Agora Gallery, which has been here since 1984, features memorable local and international works, from Andalusian-style Art-Nouveau pieces depicting men in swirling capes and women draped in lacy shawls to moody paintings of the Scandinavian coastline bathed in the northern lights.

The long-running Barbara Gladstone Gallery, a model of industrial chic with its grey metal façade, cement floors and snow-white walls, showcases plenty of bankable artists, along with rising stars. Exhibitions here have featured works by 15 artists of different generations who explored themes of aspiration and frustration; an overview of the work of artist Mario Merz, a leading figure in the Arte Povera ("poor art") movement of the 1960s and 70s; and Jean-Luc Mylayne's large colour photographs of birds in their natural environments in New Mexico and Texas.

The risk-taking Zach Feuer Gallery is at the forefront of New York's art scene, introducing such artists as Dana Schutz, whose thought-

ABOVE Exterior of the Gagosian Gallery in Chelsea

provoking series "Self Eaters and the People Who Love Them" has made her a name to watch. Other exhibitions have included Tom McGrath's aerial paintings of the East Coast suburbs and urbanized southern California. Raise the entertainment value by touring Chelsea on a Thursday night, when galleries often celebrate the opening of new shows with plenty of free-flowing wine, nibbles and chatter. These lively events will offer you the chance to mingle with other art-lovers, meet artists and perhaps walk out with a signed work of art.

Practical Information

Agora Gallery 530 West 25th Street; tel. +1 212 226 4151; subway: C or E to 23rd Street; 11am–6pm Tue–Sat; www.agora-gallery.com

Barbara Gladstone Gallery 515 West 24th Street; tel. +1 212 206 9300; subway: C or E to 23rd Street; 10am–6pm Tue–Sat; www.gladstonegallery.com

Gagosian Gallery 555 West 24th Street; tel. +1 212 741 1111; subway: C or E to 23rd Street; 10am–6pm Tue–Sat; www.gagosian.com

Zach Feuer Gallery 530 West 24th Street; tel. +1 212 989 7700; subway: C or E to 23rd Street; 10am–6pm Tue–Sat; www.zachfeuer.com

MOMENTA ART IN WILLIAMSBURG

Space is at a premium in Manhattan, and spiking rents in SoHo and Chelsea have squeezed out many artists over the last couple of decades. Next stop? Brooklyn – and specifically the working-class neighbourhood of Williamsburg, which has become one of New York's most artistic districts thanks to its relatively inexpensive warehouses and lofts.

The progressive, friendly Momenta Art stands out as one of Williamsburg's more experimental venues, with every medium imaginable, from video satires set in South America to baskets woven entirely out of one-dollar bills. Other shows have included Seher Shah's Black Star Project, a portfolio of 25 prints that explore the geometry of the cube and its associations as an architectural element and religious symbol; Elisabeth Kley's ambitious drawings, ceramics and video featuring extravagant personalities and architecture, from Salvador Dali to Coco Chanel; and Arnold von Wedemeyer's unique video pieces, which have been known to present a vase of tulips withering or a slice of bread hardening. For those with an eye to buy, note that artwork here is generally far less expensive than in Manhattan galleries.

Practical Information

Address 359 Bedford Avenue, Williamsburg, Brooklyn; tel. +1 718 218 8058; www.momentaart.org
Getting There Subway: line L to Bedford.
Opening Times Noon–6pm Thu–Mon.

ABOVE Works from the Ancient Art Collection at the Musées Royaux des Beaux-Arts de Belgique, Brussels, Belgium
RIGHT Vivid 14th-century frescoes by the Florentine artist Giotto in the Capella degli Scrovegni, Padua, Italy

MUSÉES ROYAUX DES BEAUX-ARTS DE BELGIQUE, BRUSSELS, BELGIUM The poem *Musée des Beaux Arts*, written by W H Auden after a visit to this gallery, is a hymn of praise to old masters such as Hieronymus Bosch and Pieter Brueghel, famous for capturing daily life with wonderful realism. That was in 1938, when the museum occupied a former royal palace in the Belgian capital. Today the palace holds the Ancient Art Collection, while a new building houses work from the 18th century on, including a room devoted to local Surrealist René Magritte. The whole collection is one of the finest of its kind.

GIOTTO FRESCOES, CAPELLA DEGLI SCROVEGNI, PADUA, ITALY Here in this chapel, Giotto, the shepherd-boy painter from Florence, produced his most complete series of frescoes. Painted between 1303 and 1305, its depictions of the life of Christ and the Virgin Mary are full of human warmth and a sense of calm; honesty is imbued in the simple figures, and the vivid colours have endured. The barrel-vaulted chapel holds the tomb of its patron, Enrico Scrovegni. He commissioned the work to atone for his userer father, whom the Renaissance poet, Dante Alighieri, had just confined to hell in *The Divine Comedy*.

GARMA FESTIVAL, NORTHERN TERRITORIES, AUSTRALIA Every August thousands of Aboriginal and non-Aboriginal Australians are joined by foreign visitors in Garma in Arnhem Land, home of the Yolngu tribe, for this five-day event in celebration of the country's indigenous culture. Apart from the sale of art, and much revelling in music, song and dance, the festival provides a forum for discussion and debate on Aboriginal issues. Staged on the remote Gove Peninsula overlooking the Gulf of Carpentaria, it's a memorable spot in which to contemplate Australia's cultural heritage.

VILLA MAJORELLE, MARRAKECH, MOROCCO Villa Majorelle demonstrates the dramatic emotive effects of colour and design. With the sun radiating off piercing blue walls, it is impossible to walk through the villa's garden without feeling happy. The shade of blue is even named *bleu majorelle* after Jacques Majorelle, the painter who designed and built the property in French colonial days. More recently it belonged to the French couturier Yves St Laurent and his partner, Pierre Bourgé, whose collection of North African textiles is in the Islamic Art Museum of Marrakech, housed in the main building.

THE BOATHOUSE, LAUGHARNE, UK Tucked into a cliff, looking out across a Welsh river estuary, the Boathouse is an inspirational spot. Described as "sea shaken on a breakneck of rocks" by Dylan Thomas, who spent the last years of his life here, it is hard to imagine a better place for a writer in search of solitude. Up the road lies Laugharne, the town he fictionalized in his play *Under Milk Wood*.

BAUHAUS, DESSAU, GERMANY Walter Gropius's 1920s straight-lined Bauhaus Building, a powerhouse of art, design and architecture, is an icon of classical modernism. While still actively involved in experimental design, research and teaching, it also hosts exhibitions and events. Nearby Bauhaus gems include the Masters' Houses, the Törten Estate and the cool Kornhaus restaurant.

DOMAINE DES COLLETTES, CANNES, FRANCE In the hills behind Cannes lies a small farm where the Impressionist artist Pierre-Auguste Renoir spent the last 11 years of his life. Setting up his easel in its lovely ancient olive grove, he painted right to the end, his brushes strapped to his arthritic fingers. The original furniture is preserved in the house together with sculptures, paintings and memorabilia.

ALBA INTERNATIONAL TRUFFLE FAIR, PIEDMONT, ITALY In a region renowned for its food, this is the gourmet highlight. Every October, food experts from all over the world descend on the hilltop town of Alba to indulge in local delicacies such as chocolate, nougat, cheese and wine. The prized white truffles are sold in a special tent, at astronomical prices – a single truffle once sold for 95,000 euros.

EPIDAVROS THEATRE, GREECE Take centre stage in this 15,000-seat theatre and clear your throat – and you will be heard 50 rows back. The acoustics here are impeccable, and the setting, in the Peloponnese countryside, makes this the perfect Greek theatre. Watching a play here can still induce catharsis – the mental and emotional healing believed by Greeks to be achieved by watching a drama.

CÉSAR MANRIQUE FOUNDATION, LANZAROTE In Lanzarote, it can be hard to tell where nature ends and buildings begin. One man is responsible for this unusually sympathetic architecture, inspired by the island's folds of flowing lava and green, palm-filled valleys: César Manrique. His own home, built around five volcanic bubbles, is the best place to appreciate his philosophy and his art.

THE PHOTOGRAPHERS' GALLERY, LONDON, UK At its launch in 1971, this was the first independent photographic gallery in London. By 2008 it was drawing half a million visitors a year, and has moved into a new, purpose-built six-storey building due to be completed in 2011. It mounts popular exhibitions, encourages new talent and awards an International Photography Prize every year.

ABOVE Exterior of the National Museum of Mali, Bamako, a showcase for the country's cultural talent
LEFT Flamboyant European-style architecture at the grandiose Amazon Theatre in Manaus, Brazil

AMAZON THEATRE, MANAUS, BRAZIL One might well ask how this preposterously pink *belle époque* opera house came to be built in a port city in the middle of the South American rainforest. Step inside and you could be in any opera house in Europe: its decorations and furniture hail from France, its marble from Italy, its porcelain and glass from Venice, and its cast-iron columns and banisters from Britain. The international effort seems to have been worthwhile – more than a hundred years on, the venue is thriving, with a varied repetoire of opera, dance, music and film.

NATIONAL MUSEUM OF MALI, BAMAKO This is one of Africa's finest archaeological and ethnographic museums. Among several thousand cultural and art objects, perhaps the most interesting are the vast collections of photographs and musical instruments. Mali is renowned worldwide for its music, and here you can find out all about its roots: field research has produced hour upon hour of recordings. The museum puts on regular musical events as well as films and fashion shows, and plays host to the biennial African Photography Encounters exhibition of contemporary photographic work.

MUSEUM OF ISLAMIC ART, DOHA, QATAR This elegant, understated building, a late work by the American architect I M Pei, is set on an island in the bay of Qatar. With a wonderful domed atrium, it holds treasures from across the Islamic world, from Spain to India.

AMBER ROOM, CATHERINE PALACE, ST PETERSBURG, RUSSIA A glitzy show of wealth and craftsmanship, the Amber Room comprises six tons of amber. Today's room is a reconstruction. The original, a gift from Friedrich I of Prussia to Russia's Peter the Great, was looted in World War II.

BERLIN FILMMUSEUM, GERMANY This fantastic celebration of German cinema comprises four floors of cutting-edge design and effects in the Sony Centre on Potsdamer Platz. It shows what towering figures and films emerged out of the industry, from silent movies such as Fritz Lang's *Metropolis* and Marlene Dietrich's *Blue Angel*, to Werner Herzog and other stars of the German New Wave. Many black-and-white greats were made in Berlin's huge Filmpark Babelsber, the world's oldest large-scale film studios. Once employed to make Nazi propaganda films, they are now revitalized, back in use and open to visitors.

DALÍ THEATRE-MUSEUM, FIGUERES, SPAIN Decorated with bread rolls, this museum is no doubt the best place to see what the eccentric Spanish Surrealist artist would himself have described as his fantastic genius. Among trompe-l'oeil paintings and other visual jokes are a Cadillac with a raining interior and a sofa shaped like Mae West's lips. Dalí himself, ever the showman, is buried in the crypt.

GUGGENHEIM FOUNDATION, VENICE, ITALY For 30 years the wealthy American art collector Peggy Guggenheim lived in the fabulous Palazzo Venier dei Leoni on Venice's Grand Canal. A visit to the gallery established here after her death is worth it as much for the opportunity to step inside this intimate palace as to admire the 20th-century art she collected. The sculpture garden is especially delightful.

CARPET MUSEUM, TEHRAN, IRAN Persia is synonymous with carpets, and a visit to this museum helps to understand their history, beauty and craftsmanship, and their place at the centre of Middle-Eastern cultural life. The tradition goes back to 2,500 BC and continues to this day. The building, designed in 1978 by the then queen, Farah Diba Pahlavi, resembles a carpet loom.

MUSEUM OF BAD ART, BOSTON, USA "It's clear that many of these artists suffered for their art," says MOBA; "now it's your turn." With galleries in Somerville and Dedham Square, this is a collection of previously ignored or abandoned artworks garnered from piles of garbage and thrift stores. It pokes fun at the most pompous aspects of the art world, leaving you wondering: what is art *for*?

THREE CHOIRS FESTIVAL, UK Held every summer for nearly 300 years, this is one of the world's oldest classical choral festivals. It rotates between three of Britain's great cathedrals, at Worcester, Hereford and Gloucester, with the host organist acting as musical director. The week-long event is a choral extravaganza of chamber music, opera, organ recitals, theatre, talks and exhibitions.

TOULOUSE-LAUTREC MUSEUM, ALBI, FRANCE The episcopal palace in Albi offers an unlikely window onto the demi-monde of *belle époque* Paris. With a fine garden overlooking the Tarn river, this ancient palace-fortress houses the largest collection of works by Henri Toulouse-Lautrec, who grew up in the town. It has his famous Moulin Rouge posters as well as works by his contemporaries.

276

ART AND CULTURE

ABOVE Floral tributes decorating the statue of a saint in one of the shrines at Las Pozas, Xilitla, Mexico
RIGHT Keats-Shelley House, remembering England's great Romantic poets, Rome, Italy

LAS POZAS, XILITLA, MEXICO Rich, English, eccentric and friend of the Surrealists, Edward James sold his great collection of art to put his own taste to the test in his very own Garden of Eden. It was no small task. The garden is situated deep in the jungle, up in the mountains 7 hours north of Mexico City. Here, in the company of a menagerie of pets and wild animals, he spent more than 20 years nurturing exotic plants and creating houses, trails, bridges and dozens of ambitious concrete follies. Many display a Surrealist twist, such as the House on Three Floors Which Will in Fact Have Five or Four or Six.

KEATS-SHELLEY HOUSE, ROME, ITALY There are few figures in English poetry more romantic than John Keats and Percy Bysshe Shelley, and no more romantic a spot in which to contemplate their lives than this house by the Spanish Steps. For years the haunt of England's Romantic poets, it is filled with paintings and memorabilia in homage to them. Keats came here suffering from tuberculosis and this is where he died, aged 25, in 1821. A year later his friend Shelley, 29, drowned while sailing off the Italian coast. The awareness of their deaths, so close together in time and place, only adds to the romance.

WINE FESTIVAL, BURGUNDY, FRANCE The monks of Burgundy were masters of viniculture, and the feast of St Vincent (22 Jan) celebrates its grape-fuelled heritage. Each year, a different village defies the winter with processions and tastings amid paper-flower-decked streets.

STRATFORD SHAKESPEARE FESTIVAL, ONTARIO, CANADA Between April and November each year around 12 plays are staged in repertory in the city's four theatres. Shakespeare takes centre stage, but the programme also covers a variety of classical and contemporary drama.

MIHO MUSEUM, SHIGARAKI, JAPAN Visiting this museum, designed by I M Pei for textile heiress Mihoko Koyama, is like a trip to Alice's Wonderland. A peach-tree-lined path dives into a steel tunnel and over a bridge to a part-subterranean space full of Western and Asian antiquities.

PERGAMONMUSEUM, BERLIN, GERMANY One of the finest collections of ancient archaeological artifacts in the world, this imposing museum houses a wealth of Roman and Greek finds as well as treasures of the Near East such as the Pergamon Altar, to which it owes its name.

ANDERSON VALLEY VINEYARDS, CALIFORNIA, USA North of San Francisco, this bucolic, rolling valley is a tranquil enclave attracting artists and craftsmen, where grapes have nothing to do all day but ripen in the sun. Encircled by protective mountains, it's an idyllic spot to spend a few days acquainting yourself with the region's two dozen wineries, and dining out in civilized style.

BIBLIOTHECA ALEXANDRINA, ALEXANDRIA, EGYPT The new Alexandria Library, inaugurated in 2003, has set itself a challenging task: it aims to live up to the example set by its predecessor, the Ancient Library of Alexandria, widely recognized as the greatest library of classical times. Built on the harbour near what is thought to have been the site of the old library, the building itself is quite breathtaking. A giant glass disc, tilted towards the sea, it is a stunning complex in three parts: a conference centre, a planetarium and the new library itself, connected by a plaza. Outside, carved into its shield-like, curved granite walls, are letters in more than a hundred different scripts, intended to invite understanding between all cultures and nationalities. Inside, arranged over 11 cascading levels, there are reading rooms and enough shelf space to stack eight million tomes.

CARL HAMMER GALLERY, CHICAGO, USA To catch who's new and what's hot, visit this gallery on North Wells Street. Carl Hammer specializes in "Outsider Art", aiming to give a break to untrained – and unknown – artists. Much of the work he promotes is "social art", the art of the underdog, but he also puts on regular shows of known artists. Exhibitions change every month.

LA CHASCONA, SANTIAGO, CHILE La Chascona ("the uncombed") is the epitome of a poet's home, full of art and optimism. It was built by Pablo Neruda on a hill by a stream, after he discovered the spot with his lover, Matilde Urrutia. The place grew organically, and its fascinating complex of whimsical rooms is filled with art and found objects, including a portrait of Urrutia by Diego Rivera.

DENNIS SEVERS' HOUSE, LONDON, UK This cluttered, candlelit house, which belonged to the fictional Jervis family of Huguenot silk weavers, is a model of what it was like to live in the East End of London in the early 18th century. With a fire in the grate, and a half-eaten meal on the table, it is a theatrical time capsule of ten panelled rooms, brilliantly re-created by the late American artist Dennis Severs.

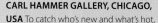

ABOVE Artifacts filling every nook and cranny of the Sir John Soane's Museum, London, UK
RIGHT Distinctive Giacometti figures outside the Fondation Marguerite et Aimé Maeght, France

SIR JOHN SOANE'S MUSEUM, LONDON, UK One of joys of the Sir John Soane's Museum (see p283) is watching visitors' faces as they enter each room. Their eyes widen, their jaws drop, and they invariably smile at the discovery of such a cornucopia of treasures. On the outside, this straight-laced Georgian terraced building gives no hint of what is in store. Sir John Soane was one of the founders of the British Museum, and his London home is like Dr Who's Tardis – it seems to contain more art and antiquities than such a house could possibly hold, much of it in specially made cabinets and display cases.

FONDATION MARGUERITE ET AIMÉ MAEGHT, ST-PAUL-DE-VENCE, FRANCE This privately run gallery is the best place to get a feel for post-war art in the south of France. Set in the countryside above the Riviera, the real star is the building. Designed by Catalan architect Josep Lluís Sert, the single-storey gallery is set around a courtyard peopled by Alberto Giacometti sculptures, and crowned with rooftop arrangements like nuns' cowls, which help to suffuse the rooms with light. Artworks are skilfully integrated into the building and gardens, including a labyrinth by Joan Miró and mosaics by Marc Chagall.

CENTRE BELGE DE LA BANDE DESSINÉE, BRUSSELS, BELGIUM Inspired by Belgium's favourite character, Tintin, this museum holds tens of thousands of comic books. From the first feature-film cartoons to the latest digital masterpieces, it shows how strips are made, and the people who made them.

GIARDINO DEI TAROCCHI, GARAVICCHIO, ITALY The cartoon-like figures populating this garden are a joyful flight of fancy, each based on tarot cards. Made of ceramics, mosaic and glass, they were assembled by French artist Niki de Saint Phalle over the last 20 years of her life.

STUDIO MUSEUM, HARLEM, NEW YORK, USA Dating from 1968, this was the country's first museum to chart black America's contribution to the arts. Today it showcases contemporary African-American artists, and its artist-in-residence programme has launched many careers.

THE STATE MUSEUM OF V V MAYAKOVSKY, MOSCOW, RUSSIA A visit to this museum helps to recall that the Russian Revolution was not just an overthrow of the political order, but a revolution in the arts, too. Here in this building lived the Russian Futurist poet and artist Vladimir Mayakovsky; one room has been furnished to look as it would have done when he moved in. His poetry, plays, film scripts and poster art gave a strident voice to the Revolution. Today the space is an inspired blend of crazy angles and colours, of photographs, manuscripts, art and memorabilia – the whole thing has been described as being like the inside of his brain. As for many, however, the Revolution under Stalin turned sour, and Mayakovsky became increasingly disillusioned, which may have contributed to his suicide here in 1930.

CHARLES HOSMER MORSE MUSEUM OF AMERICAN ART, FLORIDA, USA Founded by the granddaughter of Chicago industrialist Charles Hosmer Morse, this has the largest collection of work by Louis Comfort Tiffany, and represents the high point of America's Arts and Crafts movement. Exhibits range from familiar lamps and stained glass to paintings, pottery, jewellery and a glittering chapel.

FADO MUSEUM, LISBON, PORTUGAL Best heard live in the tiny bars of Lisbon's Alfama district, the haunting music of Portugal, Fado, evokes all the joy and tragedy of human experience. Alfama is also home to this intriguing museum, where you can follow the development of the style, see the Portuguese guitar and other instruments, and listen to recordings of Fado's great performers.

PRECITA EYES MURAL ARTS CENTER, SAN FRANCISCO, USA The streets of the Bay Area are striking for their murals. Many of these originated from the Mission District's Precita Eyes Mural Arts Center, a community organization that runs art classes and plans projects to beautify the neighbourhood. In a strange twist for street art, murals can only be reproduced with permission from the artist.

CAVE OF THE SWIMMERS, WADI SORA, EGYPT To the members of an expedition that stumbled on this cave in the 1930s, the black silhouetted figures painted on the rock walls appeared to be floating, suggesting swimmers. Nearby caves show white cattle and tethered calves, giraffes, archers and women in skirts, hinting at other aspects of the lives of their early inhabitants, dating from around 8000 BC.

ISLAMIC ART MUSEUM MALAYSIA (IAMM), KUALA LUMPUR, MALAYSIA This modern museum in Kuala Lumpur's leafy Lake Gardens is one of the best places to explore aspects of Muslim culture shared between India, China and Southeast Asia. Two extensive floors hold a permanent exhibition of jewellery, coins, armour, metalwork, ceramics, textiles and manuscripts, as well as a large library.

CITIES

The magnificent skyline of Sana'a, Yemen, bathed in afternoon sunlight *(p299)*

DELFT
VS AMSTERDAM

With none of the big-city problems associated with Holland's capital city, Delft offers a succession of charming canals edged with cafés, cobblestones and historic grandeur

NEED TO KNOW

LOCATION Delft is in the province of South Holland (Zuid Holland), 13 km (8 miles) from The Hague and 15 km (9 miles) from Rotterdam

POPULATION Around 100,000

VISITORS PER YEAR Around 850,000

DAYTIME TEMPERATURES Jan: 3°C (37°F); Apr: 16°C (61°F); Jul: 18°C (64°F); Oct: 16°C (61°F)

Delft is often referred to as "Mini Amsterdam", and it's easy to see why. Pretty stone bridges straddle tree-lined canals, and Gothic and Renaissance-style houses rub shoulders with flower-clad convents, ancient monasteries and ornate church spires. The market square (the largest in the Netherlands) is hemmed with dozens of cosy restaurants and pavement bars, while floating cafés on the canals provide views of the historic 700-year-old centre.

But the similarities largely end there. Unlike Amsterdam, Delft is one of Europe's most serene cities, unblemished by the noise, crowds, street-crime, drugs and prostitution that take the edge off the country's capital. It's a sea of bicycles that weave, wobble, race and screech around the puzzle of passageways and bicycle paths. Delft's cyclists favour battered Dutch-built boneshakers (their counterparts in Amsterdam opt for sleek, streamlined models), and these trademark single-gear Omas, with their solid handlebars, thick tyres and industrial-sized padlocks, are available to hire from the tourist office in Hippolytusbuurt. Simply ring your bell loudly to pass as a local.

Delft was put on the map for art-loving romantics around the world by Tracy Chevalier's international bestseller *Girl with a Pearl Earring*. Set in the household of the 17th-century painter Johannes Vermeer, it's the story of a peasant maid who becomes the artist's assistant and then his model. In the film adaptation of the book, several scenes were shot against the blood-red window shutters of Delft's Stadhuis, and there are guided walks *(see right)* that centre on Vermeer's status as one of the best-known artists of the Dutch Golden Age.

MAIN CITY SIGHTS

Royal Delft Blue-and-white Delft ceramics with Oriental-inspired patterns have been an important export for over 400 years. In the mid-17th century, the city had around 30 potteries. Today, Royal Delft (www.royaldelft.com) is the last remaining ceramics factory. It's open to visitors.

Museum Nusantara Like Amsterdam, Delft boasts a 400-year link with Indonesia, and the fine range of exhibits at Museum Nusantara (www.nusantara-delft.nl) depicts a fascinating shared history and culture. Founded by the colonial Indische Instelling company, the museum houses exotic collections of artifacts from all over Indonesia, including pottery and artworks, which chart an evocative relationship from the era of the Dutch East India Company.

Vermeer Cube Walk Having painted all his masterpieces in Delft, Vermeer is honoured in grand style throughout the city. You can follow a succession of rotating cubes along a dedicated Vermeer Cube Walk (www.essentialvermeer.com) that travels back to the artist's birth in 1632 and then chart his works, life, loves and death en route.

Nieuwe Kerk The crypts of the Nieuwe Kerk, on the market square, are testament to Delft's historic ties with the Dutch royal house. The mausoleum of the assassinated William of Orange (1533–84) – considered the founding father of the Netherlands – is to be found here.

PRACTICAL INFORMATION

Getting There and Around
Delft's nearest airport is Schiphol, near Amsterdam. A frequent train service links the two cities. The journey time is 50 minutes. Delft city centre is compact and easy to walk round, but if you'd like the real deal, hire a bike.

Where to Eat
There's something for everyone in Delft – from fast food to gourmet cooking. For the city's best pancakes, served on huge plates, head to Café Wapen van Delft (tel. +31 15 21 231 68).

Where to Stay
Blessed with 18th-century charm, the Hotel Coen Delft (www.hotelcoendelft.nl) is crammed with Delft pottery and antiques, and it's within walking distance of most attractions.

When to Go
June, July and August often bring sunshine, but don't bank on it.

Budget per Day for Two
Around £190.

Website
www.delft.nl

FORGET AMSTERDAM?

THE BUILD-UP Dubbed the "Venice of the North", Amsterdam is world-renowned for its extensive canal system: its waterways are cruised by tour boats and moored with brightly painted barges. Big on outrageous clubs and wild nightlife, Amsterdam is also a cultural and historical centre of great acclaim – its galleries, museums and exhibits attract discriminating art-lovers, romantics and shoestring travellers alike. The city's leafy parks are popular with picnickers in the summer.

THE LETDOWN But not that far from the art galleries, canalside cafés and flower-filled gardens, there's Amsterdam's red-light district, which can be a distasteful reminder of why many visitors come here. Adult-themed pubs, clubs and bars take sleaze to another level. It's an ugly world far removed from the city's sophisticated beauty.

GOING ANYWAY? To get the most from Amsterdam, rent a bicycle from any of the many MacBike Bicycle Rentals shops (www.macbike.nl). Then pick up a map of the dozen bicycle routes that weave their way around the city and hit the roads.

ABOVE A busker plying his trade outside a pavement café – a more palatable side of life in Amsterdam

MAIN IMAGE A canal with the towers of Delft's Oostpoort (East Gate) in the background **BELOW (left to right)** Classic blue-and-white Delftware; the spire of Nieuwe Kerk; *Girl with a Pearl Earring* (1665) by Delft-born artist Johannes Vermeer

3 MORE LOW-COUNTRY CITIES TO RIVAL AMSTERDAM

GHENT, BELGIUM The quaint cobbled streets, winding canals and grand buildings hark back to an affluent medieval era when, as a thriving textile centre, Ghent was Europe's largest city outside Paris. Today, it offers visitors a pleasing mix of past and present, with waterways lit by fairy-lights, gilded guild-houses and street stalls of trinkets and hippy kitsch.

ANTWERP, BELGIUM Like Delft, Antwerp has a pottery tradition, but it fuses its enthusiasm for tin-glazed tiles with an abundance of urban grit. This down-to-earth city, which has a rich mercantile and cultural past, is undergoing a spirited regeneration, seen in its trend-setting architecture and lively restaurant and pub scene.

THE HAGUE (DEN HAAG), THE NETHERLANDS The third-largest city in Holland boasts a buzzing energy like never before. Characterized by medieval cobbled streets, The Hague boasts handsome 18th-century mansions, paved courtyards, opulent palaces and an eye-popping collection of clock towers and spires.

LESS-EXPLORED
LONDON

Much more than just Big Ben and Buckingham Palace, London is Western Europe's largest and most vibrant city, a multi-ethnic melée, cultural hothouse and bastion of the new

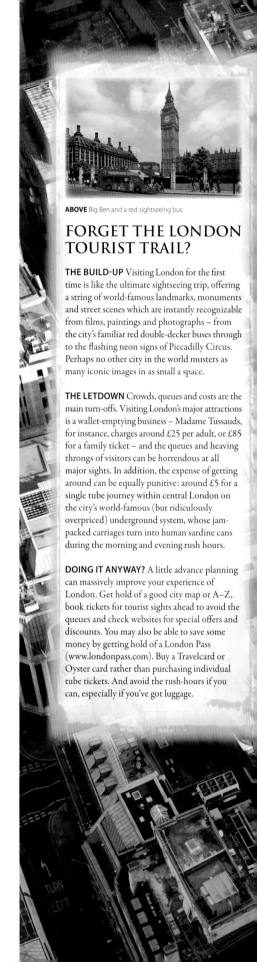

NEED TO KNOW

LOCATION London is situated on the River Thames in southeast England

POPULATION Around 7.5 million

VISITORS PER YEAR Around 25 million

DAYTIME TEMPERATURES Jan: 4°C (39°F); Apr: 10°C (50°F); Jul: 18°C (64°F); Oct: 11°C (52°F)

London is one of the world's most touristy cities, and little wonder. Seeing the place for the first time, many visitors experience a strange sense of *déjà vu*: Big Ben and the Houses of Parliament towering statesman-like above the serene waters of the River Thames; Nelson's Column rising out of the pigeon-infested expanse of Trafalgar Square; the voluminous dome of St Paul's Cathedral and the romantic outline of Tower Bridge; red double-decker buses and the regal façade of Buckingham Palace; Life Guards and Beefeaters in their ceremonial red tunics and unusual headgear – the list of clichés goes on. More than a city, London has become the universal symbol of Englishness and empire, from the lordly towers of Westminster Abbey to the royal pageantry of the Trooping of the Colour.

For many visitors, these emblematic sights are what London is all about. This is no surprise, given how imposing many of them are, or how much history and tradition they encapsulate. Having said that, there's a whole lot more to London than kings, queens, palaces and soldiers in silly hats. Indeed, a trawl through its small and less-touristed

ABOVE St Paul's Cathedral viewed from the Millennium Bridge

museums, such as the absorbing Geffrye Museum and the innovative Museum in Docklands, reveals all sorts of fascinating and little-documented stories about the city and the people who made it.

Modern London is one of the most extraordinary cities on the planet. It can confidently lay claim to being the world's most ethnically diverse and eclectic metropolis – a third of Londoners were actually born abroad, and the contribution of foreign nationals to the city's cultural and culinary make-up can hardly be underestimated, from the cafés of Chinatown to the Sikh and Hindu temples in Southall. It's a place of amazing cultural ferment, setting the global agenda in everything from fringe theatre and pop music through to avant-garde art and architecture, epitomized by the string of landmark new constructions that have appeared across the city during the past decade. These range from the spectacular London Eye through to the stunning new Swiss Re Tower, popularly known as "the Gherkin". And not forgetting Docklands, where clusters of towers, including the monumental Canary Wharf, have risen from nowhere over the past three decades to become a symbol of the modern city – built, appropriately enough, on the remains of its remarkable industrial and maritime past.

PRACTICAL INFORMATION

Getting There and Around
London is served by Heathrow, Gatwick, Stansted, Luton and London City airports. There is a sprawling underground (or "tube") system, plus extensive overground train and bus services, as well as plentiful taxis.

Where to Eat
London is a serious contender for world capital of food, offering every conceivable type of cuisine, from pie 'n' mash to glitzy eateries, such as Hakkasan (www.hakkasan.com) and Amaya (www.realindianfood.com), which showcase modern Chinese and Indian food. Gordon Ramsay's Hospital Road restaurant (www.gordonramsay.com), the capital's only triple-starred Michelin establishment, gets rave reviews for its French-influenced dishes.

Where to Stay
London's landmark hotels include the Dorchester, Ritz, Savoy and Claridge's. There is also a new generation of boutique hotels, such as the Conran-designed myhotel Bloomsbury (www.myhotels.com) and the mid-range but very hip Hoxton Hotel (www.hoxtonhotels.com). For something less flash, try the Premier Inn chain (www.premierinn.com).

When to Go
Late spring and early autumn when the weather can be good. The city is especially vibrant during the run-up to Christmas.

Budget per Day for Two
£200 for accommodation, food and travel.

Website
www.visitlondon.com

ABOVE Big Ben and a red sightseeing bus

FORGET THE LONDON TOURIST TRAIL?

THE BUILD-UP Visiting London for the first time is like the ultimate sightseeing trip, offering a string of world-famous landmarks, monuments and street scenes which are instantly recognizable from films, paintings and photographs – from the city's familiar red double-decker buses through to the flashing neon signs of Piccadilly Circus. Perhaps no other city in the world musters as many iconic images in as small a space.

THE LETDOWN Crowds, queues and costs are the main turn-offs. Visiting London's major attractions is a wallet-emptying business – Madame Tussauds, for instance, charges around £25 per adult, or £85 for a family ticket – and the queues and heaving throngs of visitors can be horrendous at all major sights. In addition, the expense of getting around can be equally punitive: around £5 for a single tube journey within central London on the city's world-famous (but ridiculously overpriced) underground system, whose jam-packed carriages turn into human sardine cans during the morning and evening rush hours.

DOING IT ANYWAY? A little advance planning can massively improve your experience of London. Get hold of a good city map or A–Z, book tickets for tourist sights ahead to avoid the queues and check websites for special offers and discounts. You may also be able to save some money by getting hold of a London Pass (www.londonpass.com). Buy a Travelcard or Oyster card rather than purchasing individual tube tickets. And avoid the rush-hours if you can, especially if you've got luggage.

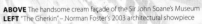

ABOVE The handsome cream façade of the Sir John Soane's Museum
LEFT "The Gherkin" – Norman Foster's 2003 architectural showpiece

SMALL MUSEUMS

London has enough museums – over 300 and counting – to exhaust even the most ardent culture-vulture. The city is home to some of the world's greatest collections, including the British Museum, the V&A and the Natural History Museum, to name just three. If the sheer scale of the major museums (and the density of the crowds thronging them) seems daunting, however, then there are plenty of more intimate establishments to explore, covering smaller slices of local or cultural history, such as the absorbing Geffrye Museum, which showcases changing fashions and lifestyles through a series of period interiors dating from 1600 to the present day.

Other museums have been dedicated to – or created by – famous individuals, lending them a sense of personality, and sometimes a decided quirkiness, which is generally missing from the larger public collections. Notable examples include the Freud Museum, occupying the rambling Hampstead house where the great Viennese psychoanalyst spent his final years and which has been preserved largely as Freud left it, complete with his book-lined study and original consulting couch. Or the equally enjoyable, if slightly less reverent, Sherlock Holmes Museum at 221b Baker Street, which lovingly recreates the home of the celebrated fictional detective, and features Holmes's violin, magnifying glass and chemical apparatus. Then there's the unique Sir John Soane's Museum in Lincoln's Inn Fields, an elegant old Georgian townhouse once owned by Sir John Soane, one of the foremost architects of his era, who filled it with an extraordinary array of artworks and antiquities collected from around the world, piled up around the atmospheric old house in a picturesque jumble.

Practical Information

Freud Museum 20 Maresfield Gardens, Hampstead; tel. +44 20 7435 2002; www.freud.org.uk

Geffrye Museum Kingsland Road, Shoreditch; tel. +44 20 7739 9893; www.geffrye-museum.org.uk

Sherlock Holmes Museum 221b Baker Street, Marylebone; tel. +44 20 7935 8866; www.sherlock-holmes.co.uk

Sir John Soane's Museum 13 Lincoln's Inn Fields, Holborn; tel. +44 20 7405 2107; www.soane.org

Sign outside the King's Head Theatre, Islington

Pub Theatre

London's theatrical scene can seem a bit moribund if judged by the touristy offerings served up in the innumerable West End theatres, with their wall-to-wall musicals and other populist shows. Despite appearances, there is a thriving fringe scene in many of the capital's pub theatres – London's equivalent to New York's off-off-Broadway. These "theatres" usually consist of a small room above a pub. They often have only basic equipment, forcing producers into prodigious feats of improvization and putting actors and audience more or less in one another's laps – all making for some intimate and electrifying drama. There's an eclectic repertoire on offer, too, taking in everything from new plays and adaptations to revues, cabaret and the occasional classic. Tickets are a snip compared to those at mainstream theatres.

London's oldest, and still the best-known, pub theatre is the King's Head Theatre, which has graced Islington's fashionable Upper Street since 1970. It has helped to launch the careers of some of Britain's most celebrated actors, notching up 30 West End and six Broadway transfers in the process. The nearby Old Red Lion Theatre, founded in 1979, also has an illustrious pedigree. Other notable venues include the Finborough Theatre in Earl's Court, which has developed a remarkably big reputation for such a tiny venue, and the Landor Theatre in Clapham, which is known for its offbeat musical productions.

Practical Information

Finborough Theatre Earl's Court; tel. + 44 20 7244 7439; www.finboroughtheatre.co.uk

King's Head Theatre & Bar Islington; tel. + 44 20 7226 8561; www.kingsheadtheatre.org

Landor Theatre Clapham; tel. + 44 20 7737 7276; www.landortheatre.co.uk

Old Red Lion Theatre Islington; tel. + 44 20 7837 7816; www.oldredliontheatre.co.uk

Boats on Regent's Canal in Little Venice

Hidden Green Spaces

Surprisingly for such a large metropolis, London is one of the world's greenest cities. From the myriad tree-filled squares that dot the heart of the city to the sprawling golf courses, reservoirs and woodlands that fringe the outer suburbs, nature is surprisingly close at hand. Meanwhile Hyde Park, Regent's Park, Hampstead Heath, Greenwich and Richmond are landmarks in their own right – great expanses of grass, heath and woodland that have somehow survived centuries of frantic urban development.

Many of London's town squares are effectively miniature parks themselves, such as Soho Square and Russell Square. The expansive Lincoln's Inn Fields is said to have inspired the creators of New York's Central Park. Some of the city's most beautiful green spaces today are, ironically, the result of its Victorian industrial heyday, such as the lovingly restored Regent's and Grand Union canals, which once thronged with coal barges but now offer long corridors of sylvan tranquillity through the eastern and northern suburbs. Abandoned railway lines also provide the city with pockets of unspoilt nature, such as the beautiful Parkland Walk in north London, which follows the line of the old train tracks from Finsbury Park to Alexandra Palace. A short way away lies the peaceful wooded parkland of Highgate Cemetery, famed as the final resting place of Karl Marx, George Eliot and many other local luminaries.

Practical Information

Grand Union Canal Brentford to Paddington Basin; www.visitlondon.com/areas/river

Highgate Cemetery Highgate; www.highgate-cemetery.org

Lincoln's Inn Fields Holborn

Parkland Walk Finsbury Park to Alexandra Palace; www.haringey.gov.uk

Regent's Canal Little Venice to Limehouse Basin; www.visitlondon.com/areas/river

Entrance to the National Maritime Museum, Greenwich

Maritime London

London is intimately connected to all things watery – indeed, the city owes its very existence to the River Thames. A boat trip to Greenwich from central London offers a unique view of the city. En route you will pass spectacular waterfront developments, the imposing Tower of London, HMS Belfast (which saw service during World War II) and a beautiful full-scale reconstruction of the Golden Hinde – the Tudor galleon on which Sir Francis Drake circumnavigated the globe in 1577–80.

Greenwich itself is a veritable showcase of all things nautical, including the National Maritime Museum and the Cutty Sark – a 19th-century tea clipper. Facing Greenwich across the river is the fascinating London Docklands area, once one of the most important ports in Europe, from where ships departed to all parts of the British Empire and beyond. The great Victorian docks fell into sudden decline during the 1960s but a massive regeneration project transformed the area into a thriving business district, with the monumental Canary Wharf tower – the UK's tallest building – at its heart. The absorbing Museum of London Docklands nearby traces the history of the docks from Roman times to the present.

Practical Information

Cutty Sark Greenwich (under restoration; due to reopen in 2011); tel. + 44 20 8858 2698; www.cuttysark.org.uk

The Golden Hinde Southwark; tel. + 44 20 7403 0123; www.goldenhinde.com

HMS Belfast Southwark; tel. + 44 20 7940 6300; hmsbelfast.iwm.org.uk

Museum of London Docklands West India Quay, Canary Wharf; tel. + 44 20 7001 9844; www.museumindocklands.org.uk

National Maritime Museum Greenwich; tel. + 44 20 8858 4422; www.nmm.ac.uk

Ornate gateway on Gerrard Street, Chinatown

WORLD FOOD

As befits the former capital of the world's largest empire, London's food scene has an overwhelmingly cosmopolitan slant, the legacy of the waves of immigrants who have settled in the city over the past century. Right in the middle of the West End lies Chinatown, one of London's most popular dining destinations. Although the area has a reputation for lame Anglo-Cantonese food and notoriously rude service, this notion has now been partly dispelled by a new generation of restaurants, such as the Baozi Inn, which specializes in Beijing- and Sichuan-style street food, and fragrantly spiced handmade noodles – all at bargain prices.

The most famous ethnic area is the Bengali enclave of Brick Lane, just east of the City of London, the capital's financial hub. The district is home to innumerable curry houses, though you'll find better Indian food in Southall, in the far west of London. Madhu's, famous for its unusual Kenyan-influenced cooking, is a good bet. For all things Turkish and Greek, head northeast to Stoke Newington and Haringey. They boast almost as much ethnic colour as Brick Lane, but with none of the tourists, along with an outstanding selection of places to eat, such as the popular 19 Numara Bos Cirrik, which has built up a cult following for its superb mezes and grills.

Most of the city's Arab community lives in the area to the west of the city centre, particularly in and around Queensway and Edgware Road where you'll find an abundance of Lebanese eateries. The classy Al Waha claims, with some justification, to dish up the juiciest *shwarma* in town.

Practical Information

19 Numara Bos Cirrik 34 Stoke Newington Road, Dalston; tel. + 44 20 7249 9111

Al Waha Notting Hill; tel. + 44 20 7229 0806; www.alwaharestaurant.com

Baozi Inn 25 Newport Court, Chinatown; tel. + 44 20 7287 6877

Madhu's Southall; tel. + 44 20 8574 1897; www.madhusonline.com

TOP Culinary delights in Borough Market **ABOVE** Browsing a stall at Camden Market **BELOW** Fresh flowers at Columbia Market

MARKETS

Markets are an enduring element of London street life, and the sound of local stallholders hawking their wares in piercing Cockney accents is a distinctive feature of the city's soundtrack. Old-fashioned markets abound, such as the archetypal Walthamstow Market, the longest outdoor market in Europe, and the colourful Columbia Road Flower Market, where endless lines of potted plants add a horticultural flourish to inner-city Shoreditch.

Some of the the city's old fish, fruit, vegetable and meat markets have been transformed into must-do shopping experiences. While Greenwich Market has become a major source of upmarket collectibles including fine art, antiques and arts and crafts, the most spectacular transformation is that of Borough Market, where an elegantly restored Victorian wrought-iron market building hosts myriad stalls serving up a fabulous array of gastronomic delights.

Finally, Camden Market's sprawling cornucopia of the weird, wonderful and downright tacky ensures that it remains the market haunt of choice for the capital's mohican-sporting punks, black-frocked Goths, and other alternative fashionistas.

Practical Information

Borough Market Borough; www.boroughmarket.org.uk

Camden Market Camden Town; www.camdenmarkets.org

Columbia Road Flower Market Shoreditch; www.columbiaroad.info

Greenwich Market Greenwich; www.greenwichmarket.net

ABOVE Wall relief in the Kom es-Shoqafa Catacombs, Alexandria, Egypt

ALEXANDRIA
VS CAIRO

Stately Alexandria makes for a much more satisfying urban break than brash Cairo

NEED TO KNOW

LOCATION Alexandria sprawls for 30 km (19 miles) along the Mediterranean coast of Egypt, 200 km (124 miles) from Cairo

POPULATION
Around 4.2 million

VISITORS PER YEAR
Around 131,000

DAYTIME TEMPERATURES
Jan: 15°C (59°F); Apr: 19°C (66°F); Jul: 26°C (79°F); Oct: 24°C (75°F)

Egypt's second city and largest port, Alexandria comes across as refreshingly unintimidating and orderly when compared to Cairo. This is a lovely city to explore on foot – it's hassle-free and endlessly rewarding, whether you follow the sweeping palm-lined corniche to the imposing medieval walls of the harbour-front Fort Qaitbey or wander the narrow backstreets through bustling markets to its many Roman ruins.

Contemporary Alexandria, set at the physical and cultural juncture of Africa, Europe and Arabia, is a difficult city to pin down. Though predominantly Islamic, it still remains the most important centre of the Coptic Church, founded here almost 2,000 years ago. Architecturally, the city has a distinctly Mediterranean character, while its aura of moderate affluence is decidedly atypical of urban Africa.

Alexandria's historical pedigree is second to none. It was founded in 334 BC by Alexander the Great and served as the capital of Egypt for 1,000 years. The city's original Bibliotheca Alexandrina

was the largest library ever assembled by the ancients, and the harbour-front Pharos Lighthouse, which collapsed in AD 700, stood taller than any ancient structure aside from the Pyramids of Giza. It was in Alexandria in around 30 BC that Cleopatra's suicide by snakebite marked the last gasp of the Pharaonic era, and, a century later, that the earliest incarnation of Christianity was first formally codified.

The illustrious past of the city named the "Capital of Memory" by the 20th-century British novelist Lawrence Durrell reveals itself in tantalizing glimpses. No trace remains of Alexandria's ancient founder, despite persistent rumours that his tomb lies beneath the Roman amphitheatre. The site of the original library was discovered as recently as 2004, and the ancient foundations of the Pharos Lighthouse now underpin the more recent Fort Qaitbey. And then there is the palace where Cleopatra had her dalliances with Julius Caesar and Mark Antony, which has long been submerged in the harbour and is currently being excavated.

MAIN CITY SIGHTS

Roman Amphitheatre The recently excavated amphitheatre is the city's most impressive surviving Roman structure. A selection of delicate mosaics can be visited *in situ* in the adjacent Villa of Birds.
Kom es-Shoqafa Catacombs These eerily brooding 2nd-century-AD relics of the Roman occupation are reached by a spiral staircase that burrows 35 m (115 ft) underground. After a trip here, visit nearby Pompey's Pillar, a 25-m- (82-ft-) tall Pharaonic column.
Bibliotheca Alexandrina This modern landmark, which evokes its legendary ancient namesake, was inaugurated in 2002, more than two millennia after the original building was razed to the ground by a Christian mob. The ancient building contained some 700,000 papyrus scrolls, and its modern-day replacement ranks among the world's largest libraries, with shelf space for eight million books.
Fort Qaitbey Built in the 1480s to guard the entrance to the harbour, this imposing fort stands on the foundations of the 150-m- (492-ft-) high Pharos Lighthouse, which was built in the 3rd century BC and collapsed 1,000 years later.

FORGET CAIRO?

THE BUILD-UP Modern Cairo was founded on the east bank of the River Nile in AD 969, but the area boasts a history stretching back to Pharaonic times, as evidenced by the iconic Pyramids of Giza and the Sphinx, which watch over its western outskirts. Often dubbed "the city that never sleeps", Cairo is Africa's largest metropolitan area. Attractions include the mind-boggling riches of the Egyptian Museum, the historic Coptic and Arabic quarters, the Cairo Opera House and the football stadium.

THE LETDOWN Sheer urban chaos. There's a 24-hour aural backdrop of horn-blasting traffic, a tangible aura of pollution, the world's most aggravating taxi drivers and, above all, crowds – caffeine-addled locals clogging up the pavements of Midan Tahrir, snap-happy tourists and touts thronging around the pyramids.

GOING ANYWAY? If you can adapt to this mayhem, Cairo soon asserts itself as one of the world's great cities. Fail to adapt, however, and there are always the outlying pyramid sites of Saqqara and Dahshur *(see pp12–13)* for relief.

ABOVE Crowds crossing a typically traffic-clogged road in Cairo, Egypt

PRACTICAL INFORMATION

Getting There and Around
International flights land at Al Nozha Airport, 7 km (4 miles) southeast of the city, or Borg al Arab Airport, 50 km (31 miles) to the west. Reliable train and bus services connect Alexandria to Cairo. The city centre is easily explored on foot. Taxis are cheap and a good option if you want to explore further afield.

Where to Eat
Eating out is one of the chief pleasures in this city. Local Egyptian fare is very tasty and inexpensive. Locals and visitors generally agree that there's no better place to sample the city's legendary fresh seafood than the unpretentious Kadoura Restaurant (tel. +20 3 480 0405).

Where to Stay
Built in 1929, the Sofitel Cecil Hotel (www.sofitel.com), whose former guests include Noel Coward and Winston Churchill, heads the list when it comes to historic ambience and a prime location on the corniche.

When to Go
There's no bad time to visit the city, but its temperate climate makes it a great winter destination. The sea keeps temperatures down in the hottest months (Jul– Aug).

Budget per Day for Two
Less than £30 if you want to keep costs down, but £100–200 if you're living it up.

Website
www.egypt.travel

ABOVE View across the rooftops of Potosí from the top of the San Francisco Church

POTOSÍ
VS CUSCO

With its colonial grandeur and air of mystery, Potosí has the edge on better-known Cusco

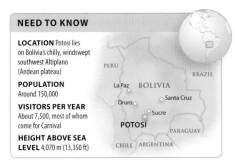

NEED TO KNOW

LOCATION Potosí lies on Bolivia's chilly, windswept southwest Altiplano (Andean plateau)

POPULATION Around 150,000

VISITORS PER YEAR About 7,500, most of whom come for Carnival

HEIGHT ABOVE SEA LEVEL 4,070 m (13,350 ft)

There's no shortage of people who have journeyed to Cusco in Peru and other cities along South America's "gringo trail", but very few have marvelled at Potosí – a city that takes your breath away, and not only because of its high altitude. This majestic place is today home to the descendants of those who laboured for the Spanish centuries ago, and has a colonial legacy to rival that of any other Latin American city. Cusco, Lima and Mexico City might all have their charms, but they also have plenty of drawbacks, not least their over-abundance of tourists. Much of Potosí is a peaceful treasure trove of colonial architecture, art and antiques, where the past lingers on in grand old buildings and on charming cobbled streets.

The city's proud motto – "I am rich Potosí, treasure of the world, king of the mountains, envy of kings" – coined by Charles I of Spain more than 400 years ago, only hints at Potosí's former glory. This was the world's first boom town and the richest city in the New World for nearly two centuries, thanks to its fabled Cerro Rico – the world's largest silver mine. Today, the mine's once-prodigious output is everywhere to be seen. It adorns ceilings and walls in every other building, gleaming unexpectedly from dimly lit corners. The brilliant metal covers the altar in the Baroque Church of San Lorenzo, dominates the collection at the Casa de Moneda (Royal Mint) and can be seen in no less than nine museums and as many convents around the city.

More than 2,000 colonial buildings have been identified or preserved in Potosí, which is more than in any other Latin American city – it's little wonder this remarkable place became Bolivia's first UNESCO World Heritage Site in 1987.

MAIN CITY SIGHTS

Casa de Moneda Potosí's first mint is now one of Latin America's finest museums. It boasts an art gallery full of priceless viceregal paintings, a large exhibition space with displays on everything from colonial coins to current smelting techniques, and a larger-than-life mask of Bacchus in the courtyard that must be seen to be believed.

Convento y Museo de Santa Teresa This 1691 wonder, which is the centre of all things Baroque in the city, does double duty as a museum and a convent – the nuns live next door. Here you'll find some of the continent's most impressive colonial and religious artworks, and exhibits on convent life.

Cerro Rico Words fail to describe this colossal monument to avarice, the silver mine, which has been a graveyard to more than a million miners over the centuries. A tour is an absolute must.

Churches of San Francisco, San Lorenzo, San Martín and the Jesuits These superb churches lie near each other in the heart of the city, and are widely considered to rank among the world's finest examples of colonial architecture. They also house some outstanding pieces of religious art.

FORGET CUSCO?

THE BUILD-UP Cusco, the former capital of the Inca, boasts a plethora of pre-colonial and colonial-era sights, and is a jumping-off point for trips to Machu Picchu and Lake Titicaca. It's small wonder this is the most-visited city in Peru, and its enormous selection of tours means that there's something for every type of visitor.

THE LETDOWN Most of Cusco's Inca heritage was destroyed centuries ago, and what is visible now is in ruins. Furthermore, sightseeing here can be daunting. The city is congested and rife with fly-by-night operators, with visitors often being handed back and forth between self-appointed "guides" and "experts" who frequently require a big cash outlay.

GOING ANYWAY? If Cusco is on your must-see list, opt for a trip to the city's outlying areas, many of which have more to offer in terms of local culture. Here you'll see more at your own pace, without the crowds and the pressure to buy yet another guided tour.

ABOVE Groups of holidaymakers taking a break on the historic Plaza de Armas in Cusco, Peru

PRACTICAL INFORMATION

Getting There and Around
Getting to Potosí is no hardship. The city is served by a high-altitude airport, which boasts fantastic views. Many travellers arrive via bus or 4WD from La Paz or Oruro, and enjoy equally impressive views on the way. The city is easy to walk around and taxis are plentiful and cheap.

Where to Eat
The cuisine in Potosí is similar to that found throughout the Andes, only it has more spice to it. There are myriad chicken- and potato-based dishes on offer, and warm soups are a traditional favourite. El Mesón, located on the main square (tel. +591 622 3087), is an excellent restaurant and a great place to sample local dishes at affordable prices.

Where to Stay
Try the comfortable, centrally located Hostal Colonial (tel. +591 622 4809). The friendly staff here have a well-deserved reputation for assisting travellers of all stripes.

When to Go
Potosí can be chilly all year round, but is most pleasant during the summer months, from June to August, when it is dry and sunny.

Budget per Day for Two
No more than £50. Much of the city can be seen on foot, which brings travel costs down. Prices here are among the lowest of anywhere on the continent.

Website
www.boliviaweb.com/cities/potosi.htm

LESS-EXPLORED
NEW YORK

Scratch the surface of the world's most iconic city and you'll find another side to this diverse, culture-crammed metropolis – and understand why the slogan is "I ♥ New York"

Even for first-time visitors, New York will seem as familiar as an old friend. It is, after all, one of the most filmed, photographed and written-about cities in the world, and its icons have achieved something of a superstar status. Wander the city, and celluloid images will flicker across your consciousness: Cary Grant waiting in vain for his love atop the Empire State Building in the 1957 classic *An Affair to Remember*; Audrey Hepburn strolling Fifth Avenue and gazing into Manhattan's most famous jewellery store in *Breakfast at Tiffany's* (1961); and Spiderman swooping towards the Brooklyn Bridge to save his dangling leading lady in the 2002 Hollywood blockbuster of the same name. And Central Park? This lush swath of green could practically apply for its own Actors' Union card, having been the verdant backdrop for lovers smooching, strolling and ice-skating, as well as plenty of chase scenes, in films from *Annie Hall* (1977) to *Ghostbusters* (1984). Even a subway grating has received top billing – remember Marilyn Monroe with her skirt flying up?

Without doubt, New York lives up to its name, but it's when you go from the legendary to the lesser known that the city really stirs to life. Roam the vibrant ethnic neighbourhoods, from the sizzling *taquerías* (taco stalls) of Spanish Harlem

to Italian Brooklyn, where white-haired *nonnas* (grandmothers) watch the world go by from their wooden chairs on shaded pavements. And bigger isn't always better: Fifth Avenue's fragrant, multi-tiered department stores make for splendid window-browsing, of course, but for local designers, hit downtown's quirky shopping district, where you can find everything from hand-sewn, sequined skinny jeans to custom cuff links and (because you know you want one) Yankees caps along Canal Street at a fraction of the uptown cost. As for avant-garde art, with such New York names as Warhol and Basquiat for inspiration, emerging artists from around the world introduce their collections at the city's galleries. And far from the chorus-line high kicks and feather headdresses of Broadway are the alternative theatres (or "off-off-Broadway", as they're called), with quirky shows from poetry slams to body-painting. The television show *Sex and the City* trained a spotlight on the city's flirty nightlife – where you can gaze at a sparkling view of Manhattan while sipping a drink of the same name. But explore the city's crooked backstreets and you'll come across rumpled, centuries-old bars with uneven floors, scarred wooden furniture and ruddy-cheeked regulars who'll fill you in on other local haunts.

ABOVE Central Park on a summer's day with skyscrapers in the distance

PRACTICAL INFORMATION

Getting There and Around
New York is served by three major airports: JFK and LaGuardia (both in Queens), and Newark (in New Jersey). To get from the airports to the city take the subway, a bus (www.mta.org), a shuttle bus (www.supershuttle.com) or a taxi.

Where to Eat
New York's cuisine is marvellously varied, from *haute* French to spicy Mexican. The Balthazar (www.balthazarny.com) serves up superb French fare, with an infectious vibe. For juicy burgers head to Corner Bistro (tel. +1 212 242 9502) and for Italian with a twist, fill up at Babbo (www.mariobatali.com), a popular restaurant with super-chef Mario Batali at the helm.

Where to Stay
The Pod (www.thepodhotel.com) has simple rooms within strolling

distance of Times Square and Grand Central Station. The Mayfair (www.mayfairnewyork.com) boasts boutique comfort in the thick of the Theater District. Head to SoHo for the 60 Thompson (www.60thompson.com), an elegant, soothing antidote to the city's accelerated pace.

When to Go
Spring and early autumn usher in the finest New York weather. But for fewer crowds, aim for October and November, after the summer, but before the December rush.

Budget per Day for Two
The sky's the limit for what you can spend in New York, but budget £175–250 for a mid-range hotel, a meal out and the occasional taxi.

Website
www.nycvisit.com

ABOVE Sightseers admiring the Statue of Liberty, New York

FORGET THE NEW YORK TOURIST TRAIL?

THE BUILD-UP New York's skyline is perhaps its most celebrated (and recognized) feature, so it's not surprising that most of the city's main sights are architectural, with many offering soaring views of the twinkling lights – and of each other. The Empire State Building and Statue of Liberty lead the pack, followed by the splendid span of the Brooklyn Bridge. Then there's the unmissable Museum Mile, which runs along Central Park, where you can peruse superb art collections and then take a breezy stroll through the world's best-known city park.

THE LETDOWN Two words: sweaty queues. Visiting the city's big-name sights – particularly in the heat-blasted summer months – is a practice in patience. The queues at the Empire State Building are notorious – you could spend the better part of your afternoon on the hot pavement. Another downer about the iconic sights is that they're, well, iconic: the hype, the crowds and the fact that you've probably seen them in photos and films ad nauseam can make the real thing somewhat anti-climactic.

DOING IT ANYWAY? To avoid the wait at the Empire State Building, buy your tickets online (www.esbnyc.com), or arrive when it opens at 8 am, or in the early evening. In general, a prompt morning arrival helps greatly in bypassing the crowds, particularly at popular museums such as the Metropolitan Museum of Art, MoMA and the Museum of Natural History.

ABOVE Accessories on display at the funky Kirna Zabete
LEFT Stylishly dressed mannequin in the Betsey Johnson window

UNIQUE BOUTIQUES

For fashion with a twist, stroll the streets of SoHo, NoHo and NoLita, where you'll find such whimsical clothing shops as Kirna Zabete, which features the work of home-grown designers and one-of-a-kind threads and accessories, from graffiti silk twill dresses to Flapper-style fringe scarves. Or pop in to sleek boutique Roni, where you can pick up unique yet affordable pieces including chic little black dresses, colourful, silky cocktail dresses and browse a great range of accessories. New York's popular gal-pal television show *Sex and the City* could just as easily have been called *Shoes and the City*, since the streets of New York are packed with sassy shoe shops, many of which sell styles that you won't find anywhere else. Check out the 1960s-inspired sandals and stilettos by local designers Sigerson and Morrison in their eponymous SoHo shop. And don't miss the sleek boutiques of New York couturiers who have since hit the big time, where you can often find one-off pieces from their collections. The spiky-haired, tattooed fashionista Betsey Johnson debuted her playful dresses and heels in her SoHo shop, and that's still the best spot to check out her latest offerings. Brooklyn-born Kenneth Cole, one of the leading designers to bring AIDS "awearness" to the fashion community, also has eye-catching downtown digs. His collection reveals an urban sensibility that pays homage to New York, including thick-soled shoes that can withstand the city's rugged streets, and weird and wonderful accessories inspired by skyscrapers.

PRACTICAL INFORMATION

Betsey Johnson 138 Wooster Street, SoHo; tel. +1 212 995 5048; www.betseyjohnson.com

Roni 119 Saint Marks Place, East Village; tel. +1 212 388 0038; www.roninyc.com

Kenneth Cole 597 Broadway, SoHo; tel. +1 212 965 0283; www.kennethcole.com

Kirna Zabete 96 Greene Street, SoHo; tel. +1 212 941 9656; www.kirnazabete.com

Sigerson Morrison 28 Prince Street, SoHo; tel. +1 212 625 1641; http://sigersonmorrison.com

TOP New Yorker walking beneath cherry blossoms in the Brooklyn Botanic Garden **ABOVE** Late afternoon stroll in Cloves Lake Park, Staten Island Greenbelt

Hidden Parks and Greenery

New York reveals a surprising number of green spaces where you can wiggle your toes in the grass and forget that you're in the concrete jungle. Central Park is, of course, *de rigueur* on every New York itinerary, but venture further afield and you'll find quiet pockets of greenery that you might share only with the chirping birds.

For a reminder that Manhattan is, in fact, an island, head to its southern tip. Tucked behind the sun-speckled promenade lies the petite, peaceful Robert F. Wagner, Jr. Park, with its gentle grassy slopes, pretty linden trees and sweeping views of the East River and the Statue of Liberty. For a romantic escape, roam the lush Brooklyn Botanic Garden, with their acres of fragrant foliage, from orchids to honeysuckle. New York's coastal areas have some splendid patches of greenery, including Fire Island's Sunken Forest, one of the few remaining maritime forests on the eastern seaboard. Its mist-soaked gnarled trees look like they've been plucked straight out of a Tolkien

novel. The ferry to Staten Island is one of the city's great deals, offering top-notch views of the Statue of Liberty and the city skyline – for free. Upon arrival, make for the centre of the island, where you'll find the Greenbelt, a lush nature reserve of verdant forest, streams and lakes. Staten Island also features a superlative: Todt Hill, the highest natural point in the five boroughs of New York (and also where the 1972 epic *The Godfather* was filmed). Trek to the top and gaze out at the rolling greenery that gives way to the sparkling Upper Bay. Standing here, you might just forget you're in New York.

Practical Information

Brooklyn Botanic Garden 1000 Washington Avenue, Brooklyn; subway: lines 2 or 3 to Eastern Parkway/Brooklyn Museum, lines B or Q to Prospect Park or line 4 to Franklin Avenue; www.bbg.org

Robert F. Wagner, Jr. Park Near Rector Place and the Esplanade in Battery Park, on the southern tip of Manhattan; subway: lines 1, R or W to Rector Street; www.bpcparks.com

Staten Island Greenbelt and Todt Hill Staten Island; public transport: take the ferry or the 11X, 12X or 13X express buses to get from Manhattan to Staten Island; www.nycgovparks.org

Sunken Forest On Fire Island, just to the south of Long Island; public transport: take the LIRR (Long Island Railroad) from Pennsylvania Station in Manhattan to Bay Shore, from where it's a 15-minute walk or a short taxi ride to the ferry (30 minutes to Fire Island); www.fireisland.com

Music Venues

New York's indie music legacy has included punk rock icons the Ramones, the New York Dolls, Talking Heads, Blondie and Sonic Youth. Many innovative jazz and blues musicians, such as freewheeling artist Ornette Coleman and Thelonious Monk, also made their start here. New York's alternative music scene continues to flourish, and you can groove to creative tunes throughout the city, from East Village haunts with cheap booze and tiny corner stages to low-lit Harlem jazz joints. Check out local bands seven nights a week at the lively Cakeshop in the Lower East Side. In the West Village, the cheery Cornelia Street Café showcases local music of all stripes, from improvisational quartets to "po'jazz", a blend of poetry and jazz. Tap your toes to jam sessions and Afro-Cuban and Latin jazz at the intimate lounge Smoke in Morningside Heights. The Brooklyn Academy of Music (BAM) has long been at the forefront of contemporary music, dance and theatre. Tune in to free live shows, from world music to modern vocalists, at the BAMcafé at weekends. Indie music fans might want to time a visit to New York for the CMJ Music Marathon in October, one of New York's largest musical events.

Practical Information

BAM 30 Lafayette Ave, Brooklyn; tel. +1 718 636 4100; www.bam.org

Cakeshop 152 Ludlow Street, Lower East Side; tel. +1 212 253 0036; www.cake-shop.com

Cornelia Street Cafe 29 Cornelia Street, Greenwich Village; tel. +1 212 989 9319; www.corneliastreetcafe.com

CMJ Music Marathon www.cmj.com/marathon/

Smoke 2751 Broadway, Morningside Heights; tel. +1 212 864 6662; www.smokejazz.com

Chinatown chef hard at work

TOP Exterior of the Bowery Poetry Club ABOVE Rapper Nas performing at the Bowery Poetry Club

OFF-BROADWAY THEATRE AND PERFORMANCES

From leotard-clad dancers writhing on stage to wine-fuelled audience-participation nights to political poetry slams, New York abounds with avant-garde theatre and performances. Downtown is home to many of the off-off-Broadway theatres, including the Public Theater, which showcases emerging playwrights, and also hosts the splendid Shakespeare in Central Park event every summer. The student-thronged Astor Place is a breeding ground for independent theatres, including Under St. Marks, a black-box-and-folding-chairs performance space. As its name suggests, the theatre space is under St Marks Place, a street that has long been known for its incense and zany performance art.

Poetry Slams (sometimes called spoken word) are recitals of free-form poems, rap and storytelling that are usually entertaining, unpredictable and raucous, but never boring. The Nuyorican Poets Cafe, located in Alphabet City and generally heralded as the progenitor of spoken word in New York, serves up a nightly mix of memorable acts. The Bowery Poetry Club also presents an eclectic range of performances, from poetry recitals to performance art. For a sassy night out, come by for a "Badass Burlesque" night. The club also puts on lively events for the neighbourhood, including puppet performances and bingo nights hosted by a popular local drag queen. Finally, for avant-garde improvizational comedy, check out the Upright Citizens Brigade (UCB). Keep your eyes peeled: amid all the emerging comics, big names will occasionally stop by, including Robin Williams and Tina Fey.

Practical Information

Bowery Poetry Club 308 Bowery, East Village; tel. +1 212 614 0505; www.bowerypoetry.com

Nuyorican Poets Cafe 236 East Third Street, East Village; tel. +1 212 505 8183; www.nuyorican.org

Public Theater 425 Lafayette Street, East Village; tel. +1 212 539 8500; www.publictheater.org

Under St. Marks 94 St Marks Place, East Village; tel. +1 212 868 4444; http://horsetrade.info/

Upright Citizens Brigade 307 West 26th Street, Chelsea; tel. +1 212 366 9176; www.ucbtheatre.com

WORLD FOOD

If America is a melting pot, then New York's diversity of cuisine is one of its finest manifestations. In the foodie capital of the USA, it's not so much a question of finding a cuisine, as trying to choose between them. The numbers say it all: over 180 nationalities – and counting – live in New York. You could find your way through the neighbourhoods by scent alone, from the smoky tang of caramel-skinned duck in Chinatown (Peking Duck House is one of its best restaurants) to the chunky tomato sauces that hark back to grandma's kitchen in Naples, ladled out at many of Little Italy's trattorias. And of course, New York-style pizza is a city obsession and the ultimate urban fuel, often wolfed down while on the run – try the thin-crust slices at Lombardi's. The city's Jewish heritage introduced such favourites as bagels with cream cheese, which have become synonymous with New York cuisine. You'll find old-world delis across town, particularly on the Lower East Side, where one of the best is Katz's Delicatessen. And if you're in the mood for spicy food, try some fiery salsa at the Mexican and Latin American *taquerías* (taco stalls) of Spanish Harlem, or head to Koreatown – or K-town – for *kimchi* (a spicy vegetable dish) and karaoke on and around West 32nd Street. Further afield, munch on grape leaves and tangy feta at the lively Greek restaurant Agnanti in Astoria, Queens, and for a vodka-fuelled Russian feast, make your way to the restaurants of Brooklyn's Brighton Beach, where nothing's done in moderation, from the velvet paintings to the bubbling vats of beef stroganoff.

Practical Information

Agnanti 19–06 Ditmars Boulevard, Astoria, Queens; tel. +1 718 545 4554; www.agnantimeze.com

Katz's Delicatessen 205 East Houston Street, Lower East Side; tel. +1 212 254 2246; www.katzdeli.com

Lombardi's 32 Spring Street, SoHo; tel. +1 212 941 7994; www.firstpizza.com

Peking Duck House 28 Mott Street, Lower East Side; tel. +1 212 227 1810; www.pekingduckhousenyc.com

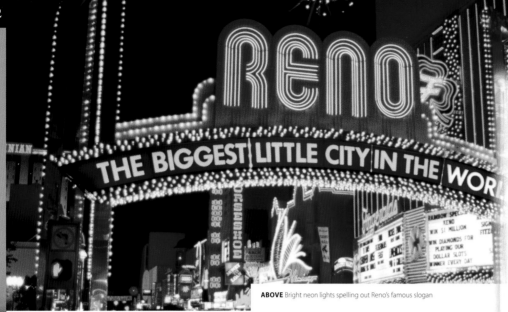

ABOVE Bright neon lights spelling out Reno's famous slogan

RENO
VS LAS VEGAS

Reno offers all the thrills and glitz of its big sister Vegas, but with a side order of charm

NEED TO KNOW

LOCATION Reno, Nevada, is 725 km (450 miles) northwest of Las Vegas, 290 km (180 miles) northeast of San Francisco

POPULATION 210,000

VISITORS PER YEAR Over 5 million

DAYTIME TEMPERATURES Jan: 1°C (33°F); Apr: 9°C (48°F); Jul: 21°C (70°F); Oct: 10°C (50°F)

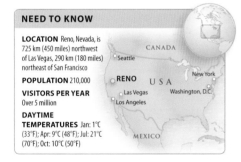

The "Biggest Little City in the World", Reno was already a mature gambling destination when Las Vegas was cutting its teeth. Founded in the mid-19th century as a crossroads settlement during the Comstock Lode silver- and gold-mining rush and construction of the transcontinental railroad, early Reno boomed as a divorce and, later, wedding capital well ahead of Las Vegas. By the 1930s, the back-room gambling dens that initially served transient miners had turned mainstream and legal, adding respectability to Reno at about the time that mobsters were developing Las Vegas as their own boomtown on Nevada's southeastern frontier.

Reno's city fathers have since been careful to preserve its quality of life and areas of old-world charm, avoiding the wilder excesses of Vegas. Sure, Reno's answer to The Strip, Virginia Street, is a sparkling river of neon at night, lined with casinos, and the city has plenty of lounge bars and cabaret shows. But, where Las Vegas is nothing if not over the top, Reno manages to remain endearing.

Set astride the Truckee River, Reno has a historic district and bucolic parks. The downtown Riverwalk is a setting for arts and craft shows and music festivals. Hire a bicycle and follow the Truckee River Bike Path or explore Newland Heights, where the millionaires of the great mining boom built gracious mansions. There are even hiking trails within the city limits. And, while culture vultures might feel starved in Las Vegas, Reno has a fistful of cultural venues and events, as well as world-class museums.

If all that's not enough to give this desert city the edge over its rival, it's surrounded by a sparkling wonderland of mountains and lakes. In winter, the snow-capped peaks glisten invitingly – skiing at nearby Lake Tahoe is barely a 45-minute drive away.

MAIN CITY SIGHTS

National Automobile Museum Set in a stunning Modernist glass building are over 200 of the world's rarest vehicles. "Cars of the stars" include James Dean's 1949 Mercury, and Elvis's 1973 Cadillac Eldorado.
Truckee River Arts District The Riverwalk is lined with galleries, boutiques and bistros. Visitors can take to the water at Truckee River Whitewater Park.
Nevada Museum of Art This black-clad, angular structure holds an impressive collection of works depicting nature and the desert environment.
Fleischmann Planetarium and Science Center Northern Nevada's crystal-clear night skies are perfect for stargazing. The planetarium's SkyDome has dazzling movies and 3D shows to inspire you.

ABOVE Skiing fresh powder in the mountains above Lake Tahoe

FORGET LAS VEGAS?

THE BUILD-UP The most flamboyant city street in the world, Las Vegas's 8-km (5-mile) "Strip" is a dazzling, non-stop extravaganza of casinos and hotels with fantastic themes and flamboyant, round-the-clock entertainment, offering something for every taste and age.

THE LETDOWN The glare of neon and the incessant tinkling of slot machines can get very wearing. Strip clubs and illegal prostitution further tarnish the sheen, as do horrendous traffic, gamblers committing financial suicide and losers seeking an instant divorce.

GOING ANYWAY? Visiting Vegas without gambling is like touring France without tasting the wine. But establish in advance the amount of money you're prepared to lose. When it's gone, walk away. And the gorgeous stranger you meet is almost certainly interested in one thing – your money. Whatever you do, stay sober. Las Vegas is mercenary and it's shockingly easy to marry on the spur of the moment.

ABOVE The neon sensory overload that is downtown Las Vegas at night

PRACTICAL INFORMATION

Getting There and Around
Reno-Tahoe International Airport is 3 km (2 miles) southeast of downtown Reno; shuttles and taxis are available to take you to downtown Reno. There is a well-developed and inexpensive public transport system within the city, and the old town centre is easy and pleasant to get around on foot. The South Tahoe Express (www.southtahoeexpress.com) offers a shuttle service from the airport to Lake Tahoe, and Sierra Nevada Stage Lines (tel. +1 800 822 6009) operates between downtown Reno hotels and Lake Tahoe.

Where to Eat
The elegant White Orchid (tel. +1 775 689 7178) serves top-notch American contemporary cuisine;

cozy Harrah's Steak House (tel. +1 775 788 2929) will satisfy carnivores with four-star dining.

Where to Stay
The sophisticated Eldorado Hotel & Casino (www.eldoradoreno.com) is highly regarded for its stylish rooms, great facilities and excellent location right by the "Biggest Little City" sign.

When to Go
Early April to late June are warm and sunny, while winter months are perfect for hitting the slopes at nearby Lake Tahoe.

Budget Per Day for Two
Allow under £100 per day to include accommodation, meals and local travel.

Website
www.visitrenotahoe.com

ABOVE Rooftops of the palace at Anapji, rising above a field of rapeseed

GYEONGJU
VS KYOTO

Japan's ancient capital has been spoilt, but the pride of Korea is still full of treasures

NEED TO KNOW

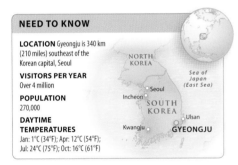

LOCATION Gyeongju is 340 km (210 miles) southeast of the Korean capital, Seoul

VISITORS PER YEAR Over 4 million

POPULATION 270,000

DAYTIME TEMPERATURES Jan: 1°C (34°F); Apr: 12°C (54°F); Jul: 24°C (75°F); Oct: 16°C (61°F)

When it comes to preserving ancient capitals, sometimes you just can't beat a bit of good, old-fashioned dictatorship. Kyoto lost much of its original genteel atmosphere after World War II, largely transforming into a modern Japanese city. In the 1970s, the same fate may have befallen Gyeongju, capital of the Silla empire (57 BC– AD 935), had Korea not been ruled at the time by a military strongman from the area. The city was shielded from the burgeoning Korean economy by a cap on building height. So, from just 22 m (72 ft) above ground level, one is able to see the whole city – something hard to imagine in present-day Kyoto.

The limit is based on the height of Gyeongju's largest burial mound, or tumulus. The city is dotted with these soft, grassy hillocks, evidence of a line of Silla kings that stretched unbroken for almost a millennium. Other royalty and assorted noblemen were afforded the same privilege, so there are a fair few such mounds to see, mostly in Tumuli Park in the city centre. Here, you are even allowed to walk inside one mound for a look at the way in which Silla royalty was entombed.

This period has left its mark in other ways, too. Sillan artisans were the envy of East Asia, and a glut of golden treasure has been hauled from the earth and displayed at the Gyeongju National Museum – a sight not to be missed. Also scattered around the city are some of the most jaw-droppingly beautiful temples in the land – most notable are sumptuously painted Bulguksa, the martial arts centre of Golgulsa and isolated Girimsa. Most visitors also take time to check out Namsan, a mountain just south of the town that still yields archaeological discoveries on a regular basis. It is best reached by bicycle and, on the way, you'll be amazed at how quickly the city gives way to farmland and bucolic landscapes – unthinkable in Kyoto.

Kyoto's jewels may be more highly polished, and certainly better known, but it's Gyeongju that better evokes the atmosphere of its bygone days as the capital of an advanced and noble culture.

MAIN CITY SIGHTS

Tumuli Park Containing almost two dozen burial mounds, this enclosed area is very picturesque. The Cheonmachong ("heavenly horse") tomb, named for an exquisite painting of a flying horse found inside, is open to the public as a museum.

Bulguksa In a country with no shortage of stunning temples, ornately painted Bulguksa is among the best. It is thoroughly deserving of its place on UNESCO's World Heritage list, as is Seokguram, the nearby mountaintop Buddhist grotto with breath-taking views, that can be reached via a steep but pleasant hiking trail or a winding shuttle-bus ride.

Anapji This pleasure garden and palace complex, centred around a charming lotus pond, was built for King Munmu in the 7th century. Many people opt to visit at night, when the surrounding trees and bamboo are delightfully illuminated.

Namsan This mountain lies just south of central Gyeongju. Surrounded by tombs and temples, and still yielding up its treasures to archaeologists, it can fill a whole day of hiking and sightseeing. Many visitors opt to explore by rented bicycle, on which you can also weave through the surrounding patchwork of farms and fields.

FORGET KYOTO?

THE BUILD-UP Having served as the imperial capital of Japan for more than 1,000 years, Kyoto boasts a suitably impressive collection of palaces, temples, shrines and gardens. Geishas still trip through streets lined with traditional inns and townhouses.

THE LETDOWN Kyoto was largely spared from bombing during World War II, but much of its magnificence has been destroyed by factories, traffic and high-rise apartment blocks. City planning has occasionally bordered on sabotage – the mammoth new train station (Japan's largest) being a case in point.

GOING ANYWAY? Its Zen gardens are among Kyoto's most appealing features. However, visitors are often required to carry their footwear around in a plastic bag, which somewhat spoils the atmosphere. It may be worth booking a tour around one of the more illustrious imperial villas instead, as these receive far fewer guests.

ABOVE The futuristic interior of Kyoto's gargantuan train station – in stark contrast to the city's traditional charm

PRACTICAL INFORMATION

Getting There and Around
Gyeongju can be reached directly by bus from Incheon, Korea's main airport (5 hours), but most travellers come here via Seoul, from where there are buses every half hour or so (4 hours). Gyeongju's tiny train station is also served by seven trains a day from the capital (4–5 hours).

Where to Eat
As in all Korean cities, you can eat excellent food for next to nothing in Gyeongju. The city is noted for its restaurants serving *ssam-bap*, a largely vegetable-based meal made up of over a dozen separate dishes. There are several places to eat on the road running along the eastern edge of Tumuli Park, but the most attractive is Sampo Ssambap (tel. +82 54 762 6148), which is decorated with photos and Korean bric-a-brac.

Where to Stay
There are numerous 5-star options around Bomun Lake, a few kilometres east of central Gyeongju, but those seeking something more homely should head to Sarangchae (tel. +82 54 773 4868), a budget gem of a guesthouse whose rooms are set around a traditional courtyard.

When to Go
Winters in Korea can be bitterly cold and summers stifling, so go in spring (Mar–May) or autumn (Sep–Nov).

Budget per Day for Two
£100 will be more than enough. Transport, food and admissions are cheap in Gyeongju, so your expenses will depend upon your choice of accommodation.

Website
www.gyeongju.go.kr

LESS-EXPLORED
HONG KONG

Hong Kong is a vibrant East-meets-West destination of world-class dining, shopping and nightlife, but its appeal reaches far beyond the showpiece Victoria Harbour

NEED TO KNOW

LOCATION Hong Kong is made up of a southern peninsula of China, plus a cluster of 236 islands

POPULATION
Over 7 million

NUMBER OF VISITORS
Over 28 million

DAYTIME TEMPERATURES Jan: 19°C (66°F); Apr: 25°C (77°F); Jul: 31°C (88°F); Oct: 28°C (82°F)

CHINA
New Territories
HONG KONG
Lantau Island
Kowloon
Hong Kong Island
South China Sea

Hong Kong is a city that raises expectations. Travellers' anecdotes frequently drop phrases like "cultural kaleidoscope", "gateway to China", "world-class hotels", and "amazing dining culture", while Hong Kong raised its own bar by rebranding itself as "Asia's world city". Even Chek Lap Kok airport, built on reclaimed land on Lantau Island, is regularly rated the world's best.

It is in the evening, sitting in a chic cocktail lounge overlooking Victoria Harbour, that Hong Kong really delivers. The harbour view – flanked by skyscrapers sculpted by leading global architects and set against a backdrop of undulating hills – is magnificent. The density of these vertical steel pinnacles explains why movie director Christopher Nolan chose Hong Kong to represent Gotham City in his Batman blockbuster *The Dark Knight*. When night falls, Hong Kong is a mesmerizing vision, whether viewed in the flesh or on the silver screen.

In addition to its glamorous appeal, classy tourism marketing and openness to globalization, Hong Kong is remarkably resilient. When the territory was returned by the British to Chinese rule in 1997, concerns were raised about its future as a tourist destination. Then the late 1990s Asian financial crisis and the 2003 SARS outbreak decimated its economy. On both occasions, the officially titled "Hong Kong

Special Administrative Region of China" (historically known as "The Fragrant Harbour'" in Chinese) bounced back and, since 2004, has seen booming visitor numbers, largely from mainland China.

Hong Kong's signature attractions span its irregular topography. At sea level, riding the ageing green-and-white Star Ferry that chugs heroically between the Kowloon Peninsula and Hong Kong Island remains a timeless pleasure. Crossing from Kowloon, gaze up into the hills behind Cesar Pelli's soaring Two IFC Tower, I M Pei's angular Bank of China headquarters and Lord Foster's meccano-like HSBC building. The futuristic Peak Tower atop Victoria Peak affords the city's best vantage point.

Day and night, visitors throng the harbourside malls, restaurants and bars. A nightly laser and light show adds an extra dimension of colour and drama. Hong Kong is a renowned destination for diners and, while locals choose the *dim sum* snacks and double-boiled soups of Cantonese cuisine, the city's food scene offers something for everyone, from a sumptuous array of mainland Chinese dishes to pan-Asian and global fare.

But there is much more to Hong Kong than its well-trodden tourist routes and, by leaving behind the delights of the harbour, you'll discover the city's culture, history and heritage, secluded spots and green spaces, and experience the real Hong Kong.

ABOVE Peak Tower building at twilight

PRACTICAL INFORMATION

Getting There and Around
Hong Kong's Chek Lap Kok airport (www.hongkongairport.com) is located on Lantau Island. Frequent Airport Express trains run to Kowloon and Central Hong Kong Island in 24 mins.

Where to Eat
Yung Kee (www.yungkee.com.hk) serves unfussy Cantonese *dim sum* and a splendid roast goose. Bo Innovation (www.boinnovation.com) offers more contemporary, deconstructed Chinese cuisine, while two-Michelin-starred French fare is the hallmark of L'Atelier de Joël Robuchon (www.robuchon.hk).

Where to Stay
The pride of Hong Kong is The Peninsula (www.peninsula.com) on the waterfront of Kowloon. Bishop Lei House

(www.bishopleihtl.com.hk) offers mid-range rooms in Central's Mid-Levels district. Hong Kong's most quirky design-led hotel is the Luxe Manor in Kowloon (www.theluxemanor.com).

When to Go
Mar–Apr and Oct–Nov offer the best climate. The long summer in between is very humid. Hotel accommodation is very hard to find during the week-long Chinese New Year (Jan/Feb) and National Day (1 Oct) holidays.

Budget per Day for Two
Hong Kong is not a cheap destination. Allow £175–250 for a mid-range hotel, meals and transport. Hotel rates rise significantly at peak times.

Website
www.discoverhongkong.com

ABOVE Parade at Disneyland Hong Kong

FORGET THE HONG KONG TOURIST TRAIL?

THE BUILD-UP Hong Kong's Victoria Harbour is a stunning inlet of the South China Sea, and is awash with sights familiar even to those who have never visited the city. On opposite banks are the high-rise districts of Kowloon and Hong Kong Island. From Central (Hong Kong Island), the Peak Tram chugs up to Victoria Peak for stunning panoramas across the harbour, city and hills beyond, while the Star Ferry has been a Hong Kong icon since the 1890s.

THE LETDOWN This is a high-octane city, and the urban pace is relentless. The huge influx of mainland Chinese tourists can result in long weekend and high-season queues, especially at Disneyland Hong Kong. Touts hawking tailored men's suits are persistent on Nathan Road and near the Star Ferry terminal. Hong Kong is also a major corporate events and conference centre, and hotels can get booked up far in advance.

DOING IT ANYWAY? Travelling between Kowloon and Central by taxi can be time-consuming. A multi-purpose Octopus card (www.octopuscards.com), valid on the subway, trams, trains, buses and even the ferry, is a speedy, more affordable way to get around Hong Kong.

ABOVE *Dim sum* dumplings on a Hong Kong street-food stall
LEFT Aerial view of the market stalls and crowds of shoppers in the
Temple Street night markets of Kowloon.

TASTES OF ASIA

It is said that Hong Kongers' two passions are shopping and food. The range of retailers may be impressive, but the dining is even better. "Asia's World City" boasts a truly globalized food scene. Cantonese *dim sum* is highly praised, but Hong Kong also serves up sublime cooking from across Asia. Exquisite hotel restaurants historically set the standard, but fine independent restaurants can now be found right across the city. At the other end of the scale, so can market stalls offering some of the most delicious – and cheap – street food.

The Mid-Levels district boasts an eclectic range of dining choices, while the boho-chic culinary styles of Star and Gough streets attract Central's smart set. In Kowloon, scores of reputable Cantonese restaurants line the streets around Nathan Road.

For traditional Chinese food, the venerable Tai Ping Koon, one of Hong Kong's oldest restaurants, dating from 1860, serves a much-appreciated roasted pigeon. Upscale and expensive Japanese restaurants abound, but for excellent-value *sushi*, *maki* rolls and *tempura*, Sushi Mata is a popular choice with in-the-know locals.

Across the water on Hong Kong Island, light and fragrant Vietnamese dishes are served with charming élan at Rice Paper in Causeway Bay. Non-meat-eaters need not feel left out: Life Café in Mid-Levels serves vegetarian, vegan and raw-food breakfasts, lunches, and a dinner menu including vegetable stir-fries and Indonesian *gado-gado*.

Practical Information

Life Café Shelley Street, Mid-Levels, Central; tel. +853 2810 9777; www.lifecafe.com

Rice Paper 413–8, 4F, World Trade Centre, 280 Gloucester Road, Causeway Bay; tel. +853 2890 3975.

Sushi Mata 61–5 Chatham Street, Tsim Sha Tsui; tel. +853 2191 4787.

Tai Ping Koon Several branches; www.taipingkoon.com

Appealing interior of G.O.D. (Goods Of Desire)

Striking façade of the Hong Kong Museum of Art in Kowloon

Hong Kong Park, a delightful urban oasis

ANTIQUES AND HOMEWARES

Hong Kong loves to shop, and boasts Asia's most exciting portfolio of glitzy malls and designer labels. But tucked discreetly away from the melee of big names and their insatiable shoppers is a world of more refined retailing, a refreshing alternative to the mall culture of Central, Kowloon and Causeway Bay and the over-touristed markets of Stanley and Temple streets.

Halfway between Victoria Harbour and the Peak is the aptly named Mid-Levels, where the sloping streets around Hollywood Road are home to elegant, authentic antiques shops and low-key art galleries. Since 1982, the Altfield Gallery has been a leading purveyor of fine 18th- and 19th-century Chinese furniture and artworks, and has also diversified into high-quality Southeast Asian artifacts. The Red Cabinet is another specialist dealer, showcasing antique furniture and accessories for private collectors and export dealers, as well as superior reproduction items.

Further afield, in Aberdeen, China Art sells exquisitely restored antique Chinese beds, cabinets, chairs, tables and soft furnishings.

Promoting a quirkier, contemporary angle on Asian home furnishings is G.O.D. (Goods of Desire), with shops in Central, Causeway Bay and Tsim Sha Tsui. Their stated aim is to promote unconventional and desirable furniture for modern consumers.

Practical Information

Altfield 248–9 Prince's Building, Chater Road, Mid-Levels, Central; www.altfield.com.hk

China Art Aberdeen; www.chinaart.com.hk

G.O.D. Several outlets; www.god.com.hk

Red Cabinet 1–3 Hollywood Road, Central; www.red-cabinet.com.hk

MUSEUMS AND GALLERIES

Often dismissed as a shopping-and-dining city that views culture with disdain, Hong Kong is seeking to emphasize its appreciation of history and the arts. An annual contemporary art fair has been launched, and the long-running Hong Kong Arts Festival draws an eclectic mix of creative talents.

But as well as importing global performers, Hong Kong is reassessing its own cultural and historic identity. Emerging from its recent slumber is the Hong Kong Museum of Art. Several guest curators have breathed new artistic life into this long-neglected museum – a space always imbued with potential. The Open Dialogues contemporary art series presaged bolder, more conceptual shows. Somewhat more cerebral is the often-overlooked University Museum & Art Gallery, which takes an intellectual but accessible approach to ancient Chinese art and archaeology.

Though not usually a topic to lure visitors, urban planning is critical to Hong Kong's future vision – especially as land reclamation alters the shape of its shoreline. The Hong Kong Planning & Infrastructure Exhibition Gallery offers a glimpse, via videos, models, maps and interactive exhibits, of the city of tomorrow. Going back in time, the Museum of Coastal Defence, located in a 19th-century former British fort, explores Hong Kong's military past.

Practical Information

Hong Kong Museum of Art Tsim Sha Tsui, Kowloon; www.lcsd.gov.hk/CE/Museum/Arts

Hong Kong Planning & Infrastructure Exhibition Gallery 3 Edinburgh Place, Central; www.infrastructuregallery.gov.hk

Museum of Coastal Defence Shau Kei Wan, Eastern District; www.lcsd.gov.hk/CE/Museum/Coastal

University Museum & Art Gallery Pok Fu Lam, Central; www.hku.hk/hkumag

PARKS AND NATURAL SPACES

Hong Kong is far more than a chrome-and-glass urban jungle – in fact, some 40 per cent of the terrain is dedicated as protected parkland. When the downtown temperature rises, Hong Kongers head for the hills for fine hiking and cycling trails, or to one of myriad national parks and beaches for family relaxation and convening with nature.

Even in the urban areas, pleasant parks and gardens can be found. The delicately landscaped Hong Kong Park sits on a grassy incline overlooking the Financial District. Paths weave between rocks and ponds, attracting city elders, schoolchildren, bank workers and families, while the fountains are popular spots for pre-wedding photo shoots.

Opened in 2006, the 61-ha (150-acre) Hong Kong Wetland Park in the Northern Territories is a modern ecotourism centre, demonstrating the dramatic diversity of the wetland habitat, which is often overlooked by city folk. Set in the heart of a picturesque rolling valley, the Kadoorie Farm & Botanic Garden is beautifully maintained and showcases new initiatives for sustainable living and improving wildlife habitats and biodiversity.

Keen walkers should head to Shek O Country Park. The undulating 4-km (2½-mile) Dragon's Back Peak trail, linking Wan Cham Shan and Shek O Peak, affords fine views of Big Wave Bay.

Practical Information

Dragon's Back Trail Southern District; http://www.afcd.gov.hk

Hong Kong Park 19 Cotton Tree Drive, Central, Hong Kong Island

Hong Kong Wetland Park Tin Shui Wan, New Territories; www.wetlandpark.com

Kadoorie Farm & Botanic Garden Tai Po, New Territories; www.kfbg.org.hk

Hong Kong tram making its way through Central after dark

TOP Star Ferry crossing Victoria Harbour **ABOVE** Sok Kwu Wan, Lamma Island **BELOW** Fish drying by the harbour on Cheung Chau Island

BOAT TRIPS

Hong Kong's history is tied to the sea. Made up of 236 islands, it is surrounded and defined by water. The urban centres of Kowloon and Central radiate back from Victoria Harbour, and the tradition of feng shui (literally, "wind and water") decrees that harmonious residences should face the sea.

So, naturally, the best way to discover Hong Kong's hidden treasures is by boat. The most visible option is the Star Ferry, which runs between Kowloon and Hong Kong Island, and also offers harbour tours and charter vessels for evening parties. For a more upscale experience, the Agua Luna, an 80-year-old junk, has been restored in style, with scarlet sails, for cocktails-and-canapés harbour parties.

Lamma Island's rising contours, lush vegetation and excellent seafood restaurants make for an alluring day-trip by boat. A scenic hike across from Yung Shue Wan to Sok Kwu Wan takes about 2 hours. From Sok Kwu Wan catch a 35-minute ferry back to Central. Another getaway option is Cheung Chau, a picturesque island with beaches, markets and great seafood. A ferry from the Central Ferry Terminal takes 45–55 minutes.

Practical Information

Aqua Luna Several sailings daily between Central and Tsim Sha Tsui (reservations essential); www.aqua.com.hk

Cheung Chau Central Ferry Terminal, Pier 5, Central; www.nwff.com.hk

Lamma Island Ferry Central Ferry Terminal, Pier 4, Central; www.nwff.com.hk

Star Ferry Star Ferry Pier, Kowloon Point, Tsim Sha Tsui, Kowloon; www.starferry.com.hk

ALTERNATIVE EVENINGS

Evenings in Hong Kong tend to revolve around eating, drinking and conviviality – with some snaps of the dazzling night-time skyline thrown in for good measure. Yet after-dark Hong Kong affords just as much diversity as during the day.

Floodlit horse-racing at the Happy Valley Racecourse is a time-honoured night out for locals, who take their racing and their betting extremely seriously, and great fun for visitors. Located in an urban bowl and surrounded by high-rise buildings, the racecourse itself is a spectacular sight. Be sure to study the form carefully before betting.

Visitors who prefer to play a sport rather than watch one can fine-tune their golf swing into the night at the City Golf Club. Located close to Tsim Sha Tsui, the upper level of the two-storey driving range affords fine views over the harbour.

Fast ferries, operating around the clock between Central and Macau, mean that a high-rolling evening in Macau's bars and glitzy super-casinos is relatively straightforward – provided you don't stake your return fare on the baccarat tables.

For a romantic and nostalgic trip, the venerable Hong Kong Tram plies a meandering route between Causeway Bay and Western via the Central Business District and Downtown. Jump on and off en route (there's a stop roughly every 250 m/275 yards), or just sit and snuggle up as your wooden carriage trundles through the heart of Hong Kong.

Practical Information

Causeway Bay–Western Tram www.hktramways.com

City Golf Club 8 Wui Cheung Road, Kowloon; tel. + 852 2992 3333

Happy Valley Racecourse Happy Valley, Hong Kong Island; www.happyvalleyracecourse.com

Hong Kong–Macau Ferry Shun Tak Ferry Terminal, Lai Chi Kok, Kowloon; www.turbocat.com

FEZ
vs MARRAKECH

Marrakech may set the city-break crowd's hearts aflutter, but Fez, Morocco's ancient spiritual capital, really makes hearts throb

NEED TO KNOW

LOCATION Fez is situated in northern Morocco, on the fertile plains at the base of the Middle Atlas Mountains

POPULATION
1 million

DAYTIME TEMPERATURES
Jan: 9°C (48°F); Apr: 14°C (57°F); Jul: 34°C (93°F); Oct: 18°C (64°F)

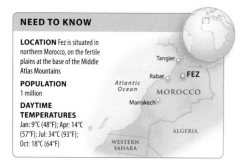

Morocco's capital city has shifted repeatedly over the centuries, according to the whim and power of the dynasty of the day. These days, Rabat might host the embassies and Marrakech the tourists, but the majority of Moroccans will still point to Fez as the country's spiritual and cultural heart.

Fez was Muslim Morocco's first capital, and in 2008 the city celebrated its 1,200th birthday with remarkable understatement. But unlike their glitzy Marrakechi rivals to the south, Fassis don't feel the need to shout about their city. Just one day in the buzzing warren of the old city is all most visitors need to be instantly hooked. Exploring the Fez medina is undoubtedly one of the Arab world's greatest travel experiences. Its dusty streets are gloriously alive, and its sights, sounds and smells have the force of a battering ram on the senses.

The city has changed very little over time, and is today the most complete and unspoilt medieval Islamic settlement in the world. Surrounded by hills on all sides, Fez has been unable to expand much

ABOVE The Bab Bou Jeloud Gate at dusk, Fez, Morocco

over the centuries and is almost entirely free of motor vehicles. Its bent and narrow lanes are far better suited to mules and donkeys, which still work hard carrying everything from bags of cement to televisions in and out of the medina. The medieval way of organizing a city also persists in Fez, with each quarter having its own mosque, fountains and communal bakeries, as well as areas dedicated to particular arts and crafts, such as slipper-making, leatherwork and the city's famous fine embroidery.

Ancient though it is, Fez isn't above learning a few new tricks. Scores of its old townhouses are being turned into the *riad* guesthouses beloved of foreign visitors, and a UNESCO-supported rehabilitation scheme has provided funding and expertise to help restore threatened and crumbling parts of this World Heritage city. Government plans to boost Moroccan tourist numbers past 10 million mean that there's not a lot of time left to get here before the crowds do.

MAIN CITY SIGHTS

Talaa Kebira The medina's main street leads visitors to the heart of the old city, from the Bab Bou Jeloud Gate past mosques, markets and fountains, and an unending stream of people and pack animals.
Bou Inania Medersa One of the finest buildings in Fez, this 14th-century theological college is a masterclass in Moroccan craftsmanship. Its sumptuous decorations include intricate mosaics, woodcarvings and decorative plasterwork.
Tanneries Moroccan leather is produced here the old-fashioned – and highly smelly – way, with skins submerged in open-air vats full of dyes made from indigo, poppies and saffron. The colourful results are on sale throughout the medina.
Batha Museum This museum, housed in a beautiful 19th-century palace with a classical Andalucian garden, holds a fine collection of Moroccan artifacts from the heyday of the great imperial dynasties.
Festival of World Sacred Music This cross-cultural musical festival was founded in response to the first Gulf War and is now a huge international success, attracting world-class performers for grand concerts and intimate recitals. The week-long festival takes place every year in June *(see p56)*.

FORGET MARRAKECH?

THE BUILD-UP Ever since the budget airlines started flying to Marrakech, the city has experienced a tourism gold-rush. With its colourful bazaars, year-round sun, fabulous palaces and designer-renovated *riads*, Marrakech quickly found itself billed as one of the world's most fashionable short-break destinations.

THE LETDOWN Marrakech is no longer the bargain destination it once was. The tourists that throng the souks – often inappropriately dressed for a Muslim country – are easy prey for shop owners, who quickly inflate prices according to customers' perceived wallet sizes.

GOING ANYWAY? Timing is all: avoid the hordes at the peak times of Christmas, New Year and Easter, as well as the scorching heat of high summer. Vary your clock once there too, hitting the main Djemaa el-Fna, the central square, late at night when it's a locals-only scene.

ABOVE Tourist searching for bargains in a busy souk in Marrakech, Morocco

PRACTICAL INFORMATION

Getting There and Around
Fez Saïss airport has direct connections to many major European cities, mainly through budget airlines. Other flights come via Casablanca, which is 87 km (54 miles) southwest of Rabat. Fez has excellent road and rail connections with the rest of Morocco.

Where to Eat
Fez is famous in Morocco for its culinary heritage, and is the home of *b'stilla*, a sweet-savoury dish of filo pastry stuffed with nuts and pigeon. The restaurant at La Maison Bleue hotel (www.maisonbleue.com) offers one of the city's best dining experiences.

Where to Stay
The boutique hotel *riad* scene is ever-expanding in Fez, offering visitors an excellent choice of accommodation for different budgets. Riad Lune et Soleil (www.riadluneetsoleil.com) is a charming and eccentrically decorated guesthouse, renowned for its excellent food.

When to Go
Spring and autumn are the most pleasant times to visit the city weather-wise. Winter is cold and rainy, while summer heat can be uncomfortable.

Budget per Day for Two
From £60 upwards, depending on accommodation. The best *riads* charge up to £110 per room per night.

Website
www.visitmorocco.com/index.php/eng/I-am-going-to/Fez

MAIN IMAGE Women shopping in a covered market, Fez, Morocco
BELOW (left to right) Vats of coloured dye at a tannery, Fez; mosaic-tiled stairway in the Bou Inania Medersa

3 MORE ARAB CITIES TO RIVAL MARRAKECH

SANA'A, YEMEN The centre of the Yemeni capital is a UNESCO World Heritage Site known for its concentration of ancient mud-brick tower houses – tall buildings built for defensive purposes. With traditional dress very much in vogue here – few men would dare be seen lacking their *jambiya* (dagger) in their belt – Sana'a is a true vision of old Arabia.

TUNIS, TUNISIA Tunis hosts another of north Africa's great medinas, but the city's origins far predate the arrival of Islam. The main mosque was built with columns stolen from Roman-era Carthage, which stood at the edge of the modern city. Further ruins add to the blend of ancient, medieval and modern.

ALEPPO, SYRIA Syria's second city is home to the country's greatest souks. Miles of bustling covered bazaars surround the stunning 8th-century Great Mosque and lead to the mound of Aleppo's imposing citadel, which withstood the armies of both the Crusaders and the Mongols.

LESS-EXPLORED
VENICE

No one can fail to be impressed by magical Venice, but it is the backwaters of the city, far from the tourist trails, where the real soul of the city lies undisturbed by crowds

NEED TO KNOW

LOCATION Venice is in the top northeast corner of Italy, on the curve of the Adriatic Coast

POPULATION 60,700

VISITORS PER YEAR 19 million

DAYTIME TEMPERATURES Jan: 4°C (39°F); Apr: 12°C (54°F); Jul: 23°C (73°F); Oct: 16°C (61°F)

Any trip to this waterborne city inevitably starts at Piazza San Marco, with its entourage of glittering monuments. Here are photo opportunities galore, including feeding pigeons and rooftop views from the Campanile (bell tower). A trip in a gondola rowed by a handsome gondolier, as you glide on the magnificent Grand Canal beneath the majestic Rialto arch, is about as delightfully stereotypical as it can get. But there is much more of Venice to be experienced, hidden away in the city's backwaters.

All it takes is a wrong turn, a detour from the tourist trails and the maddening crowds are left behind as you wander into the real Venice, where the locals live, work and socialize. In this maze of alleys, wonderful rewards come in the form of authentic neighbourhood cafés and canalside wine bars, or *osteria*, buzzing with the sounds of the local Venetian dialect. These are inviting places for a relaxed morning cappuccino, an unhurried alfresco lunch or a *spritz* apéritif, later in the day. Wander further to discover tiny squares where kids play football and neighbours settle down to chat beside Renaissance churches housing exquisite works of art. Then, unexpectedly, you emerge at the lagoon's edge in the company of wheeling

ABOVE Church of San Michele on San Michele, an island in Venice lagoon

seagulls to enjoy far-reaching views against a backdrop of the snow-spattered Alps.

The immense 550-sq-km (210-sq-mile) expanse of the Venice lagoon has much to offer visitors, too. Its waters are dotted with islands that have been inhabited since Roman times and through the Middle Ages. There are still hosts of monasteries (albeit abandoned), the famous *lazaretti*, or hospitals, constructed for plague victims and lepers, and small but thriving fishing communities. Barely navigable channels snake through shallows and salt marshes. The northern stretch harbours fish farms, market gardens and open spaces where herons, cormorants and flamingoes come to breed.

The public waterbus, or *vaporetto*, runs out to Murano, with its world-famous glass; Burano, known for its lace; and Torcello, where the first lagoon dwellers settled. The lagoon's southern end features islands with multiple uses, from being ancient ammunition dumps to havens for refugees. Just 20 minutes away by waterbus from St Mark's is the Lido, with its long stretch of sandy beach offering respite from the high culture of the city. Further south, joining the mainland, the lively fishing port of Chioggia is worth a visit for its sandy beach and fish restaurants.

A little off the beaten track, these backwaters of the "floating" city hide a uniquely Venetian allure.

PRACTICAL INFORMATION

Getting There and Around
Marco Polo airport is 10 kms (6 miles) northeast of Venice. Buses take 20 minutes to reach the city and launches about 45 minutes. The city is best explored on foot, although the public ferry or *vaporetto* makes for a relaxing cruise.

Where to Eat
Food in Venice centres on seafood. Exclusive Da Fiore (www.dafiore.net) in the San Polo district specializes in dishes made from seasonal ingredients. Or opt for La Caravella, where traditional fare is reinterpreted (www.restaurantlacaravella.com).

Where to Stay
Al Campaniel (www.alcampaniel.com) is a good

budget option, while Pensione La Calcina (www.lacalcina.com) falls in the mid-price category. Those looking for luxury should opt for Palazzo Abadessa (www.abadessa.com).

When to Go
Winter can be sunny and crisp, with fewer crowds. However, take heed that in the months of October, November and December, you are more likely to encounter flooding, known as Acqua Alta. Spring (Mar–May) is lovely, as a little warmth streams into the sun's rays.

Budget per Day for Two
£150 including food and accommodation.

Website
www.turismovenezia.com

FORGET THE VENICE TOURIST TRAIL?

THE BUILD-UP The dazzling array of must-see sights includes grandiose Piazza San Marco, and the intricately decorated Doge's Palace. Then there's the bejewelled Basilica of St Mark and its treasures, and the myriad museums and churches that showcase the glorious Renaissance art created here. Hours can be spent on the city's main water artery, the Grand Canal, lined with palaces and crossed by four major bridges.

THE LETDOWN You'll be hard put to have the famous square to yourself, day or night. Queuing and jostling become familiar pastimes at top sights and prices are sky high at every corner.

DOING IT ANYWAY? Careful planning is essential to ensure an enjoyable holiday, so go at a non-peak time, steering clear of European public holidays. Try and visit sights at lunchtime to avoid groups. Invest in a Venice Card travel pass covering boat transport and the main sights.

ABOVE A popular destination for visitors in Venice, the ever-crowded Piazza San Marco

ABOVE A *vaporetto* on the Grand Canal, Santa Maria della Salute in the background **LEFT** Colourful houses lined along the quiet canals of Burano

BOAT TRIPS

Armed with a 24-hour ticket or a Venice Card boat pass, you can take the weight off your feet and explore the city and its surrounds on a *vaporetto* or public ferry. Line 1 is the popular, all-stops service for the Grand Canal, passing under brand-new Constitution Bridge and the historic Rialto Bridge. By nightfall, it becomes a divinely romantic cruise, sliding past elegant palaces, their lights reflecting on the surface of the canal. Of a different nature, and much quieter, is Route 51/52, whose slimmer *motoscafo* craft circle the entire city, taking in the fascinating Arsenale and Castello districts.

A delightful day can be spent out on the northern lagoon on a sturdier *motonave* ferry if you take the LN line. After calling in at the islands of Murano and Burano, the ferry runs on to Punta Sabbioni. As it steams past the passages where the lagoon connects with the Adriatic Sea, passengers can witness the construction work under way for the Mose Floodgate Project, intended to protect Venice from the sea. Past monumental Forte di Sant'Andrea, its cannons mounted at water level to cripple enemy ships, the next stop is the city's beach resort, the Lido. Private lagoon trips with specialist guides, including marine scientists, can also be arranged through Context Travel.

It's worth making the effort to travel on the car ferry that shuttles between San Nicolò on the Lido and the Tronchetto car park. Known to the Venetians as the "ferry boat", it transits via the broad Giudecca Canal, the tall decks providing lovely views, and the on-board bar great drinks.

PRACTICAL INFORMATION

For ferry information www.actv.it

For the Venice Card www.hellovenezia.com

For boat trips on the northern lagoon www.contexttravel.com

A replica of the ceremonial Bucintoro barge displayed in the Naval History Museum

TOP Piazza San Marco as seen from the Grand Canal **ABOVE** Basilica di San Marco and San Marco district seen from the Campanile

SMALLER MUSEUMS

A host of little-visited but interesting museums and galleries are hidden around town, each with curious exhibits that shed light on the story of this magnificent city. On entering the Palazzo Querini Stampalia Museum, you are transported back to the 1700s for a glimpse of life in a Venetian palace of that period. Beautifully furnished rooms are decorated with rich fabrics, fine porcelain, famous Murano glass and period paintings by illustrious artists such as Longhi and Bellini.

The Naval History Museum (Museo Storico Navale) near the Arsenale has displays of ancient watercraft, which provide an excellent overview of life and work in Venice prior to the arrival of motor-powered boats. One highlight here is the replica of the Bucintoro ceremonial barge that had pride of place in the Sposalizio del Mare rituals symbolizing Venice "marrying" the sea – the original was put to the flames by Napoleon. Not to be missed is the Pavilion of Boats (Padiglione delle Navi), with a royal vessel complete with decorated oars and naval craft employed during World War II.

On Murano, the dusty old bishops' residence, Palazzo Giustiniani, now the Glass Museum (Museo del Vetro), is a treasure trove of priceless, fragile pieces of exquisite craftsmanship. One of the many highlights is a gigantic candelabra composed of 356 handmade pieces, weighing over 300 kg (660 lbs). Explanations of glass-working techniques covering beads, millefiori, mirrors and blowing accompany the visit. A ferry trip away, Burano has a showcase museum, Museo del Merletto, with exhibits that display the ancient art of lace-making, believed to derive from a magical veil of foam which was dreamt up by a fisherman.

VIEWPOINTS

After a while, Venice can feel claustrophobic with its narrow, sunless streets and swarms of people, but visitors in the know can enjoy spectacular vantage points high above the bustle. Queues usually build up outside the celebrated 99-m (323-ft) Campanile (bell tower) in Piazza San Marco, but it's worth the wait. In 1452 an impatient Frederick III, the Holy Roman Emperor, rode his horse up the ramp, but nowadays there's a lift.

A short boat trip across St Mark's Basin is the quiet monastery island of San Giorgio Maggiore. Here, at the back of the church designed by Andrea Palladio, one of the remaining Benedictine monks accompanies visitors by lift up to a little-visited bell tower that affords wonderful vistas. But the best place for memorable panoramas is the Skyline Terrace at the Hilton Molino Stucky hotel

on Giudecca island. A walkway around the hotel's pool affords stunning views over the vast sweep of the shipping canals and the layout of the majestic city backed by the mighty Alps. A bar overlooks beautifully laid-out gardens and residences, as well as tastefully converted industrial premises.

Finally, for unbeatable aerial views take a boat over to the Lido (see p301) and treat yourself to a helicopter ride. Visitors taking off or landing at the outlying Venice airport only get a fleeting glimpse of the lagoon, but from the chopper, the intricate system of channels, shallows, sandbanks and islands becomes crystal clear.

PRACTICAL INFORMATION

Campanile San Marco Piazza San Marco, San Marco; www.basilicasanmarco.it

Heliair Aeroporto G. Nicelli, Lido di Venezia, Lido; www.heliairvenice.com

Hilton Molino Stucky Hotel Giudecca 810; www.molinostuckyhilton.com

San Giorgio Church San Marco; Line 2

PRACTICAL INFORMATION

Museo del Merletto Piazza Galuppi 187, Burano; www.museiciviciveneziani.it

Museo Storico Navale Riva S Biasio, Castello; www2.regione.veneto.it/cultura/musei/inglese/pag462e.htm

Museo del Vetro Fondamenta Giustinian 8, Murano; www.museicivici veneziani.it

Palazzo Querini Stampalia Castello 5252; www.querinistampalia.it

The monastery of San Lazzaro degli Armeni surrounded by manicured gardens on San Lazzaro island

Doorway leading into the atmospheric 15th-century *osteria* Cantina Do Mori

Canal-side residences and vendors selling their wares on the promenade, Riva degli Schiavoni, in Castello

Lagoon Islands

Far-flung patches of marshy land transformed into fishing villages, monasteries, asylums, hospitals and market gardens, the islands in the Venice Lagoon are a marvellous world unto themselves. San Pietro in Volta, inhabited by hardy fisher-folk and rowing champions, is a photogenic village set on a slender strip of sand facing the Adriatic, and accessible from the Lido by car ferry, bus or bicycle. It comes alive in the summer months with a string of saints' festivities that see colourful processions and dancing in the streets. A bunch of excellent fish restaurants there includes Trattoria Da Nane.

A short distance north across the water on *vaporetto* Line 20, a dwindling community of Armenian monks on San Lazzaro degli Armeni continue as guardians of a historic library with numerous beautifully illustrated manuscripts. They also act as tour guides for visitors to their peaceful haven. The fascinating neighbouring island of San Servolo (guided tours available), erstwhile psychiatric sanatorium, now not only houses an international university but also hosts artisans' workshops.

Northwards, most visitors head for Burano for its brightly painted houses and lace shops, but next door is also pretty Mazzorbo, home to laid-back trattorias and vegetable gardens bulging with prize artichokes. A private taxi launch is needed to reach San Francesco del Deserto, a peaceful cypress-ringed retreat for a small community of Franciscan monks who happily show the curious around their island home, founded by Saint Francis himself.

PRACTICAL INFORMATION

For ferry information www.actv.it

Isola di San Francesco del Deserto www.isola-sanfrancescodeldeserto.it

Isola di San Lazzaro degli Armeni Line 20 from San Zaccaria; tel. +390 41 526 0104

Isola di San Servolo www.sanservolo.provincia.venezia.it

Trattoria Da Nane Via Laguna 282, Pellestrina; tel. +390 41 527 9110

Osterie

Found all over town, these traditional watering spots are convivial places for an *ombra* (glass of house wine) or a *spritz*, the local concoction of white wine and a generous dash of Campari or similar apéritif, embellished with a fat green olive and a slice of lemon. Perfect accompaniments are the omnipresent bowls of crisps or peanuts, but connoisseurs prefer *cicchetti*, flavoursome traditional bar snacks. Favourites include *crostino di baccalà* (creamed salt cod spread on crusty bread), *folpetti* (a saucerful of tender baby octopus) and *sarde fritte* (crispy fried sardines in light batter).

The Rialto market area boasts a great choice of atmospheric *osterie* including Cantina Do Mori, where the ceiling is hung with copper cooking pots. At Al Marca, customers clutching drinks and food spill out into the square mixing with shoppers laden with fresh fruit and vegetables.

A fine establishment on the opposite side of the Grand Canal in Cannaregio is low-ceilinged La Bottega ai Promessi Sposi, which does delicious things with anchovies and calamari. Frequented by the young crowd, bustling Osteria alla Botte located in the San Marco district has often been known to verge on the rowdy. A place worth hunting out near the Accademia Gallery is friendly Al Bottegon, where old-fashioned pickles, mortadella sausage and hard-boiled eggs on toothpicks are served along with wine. Bottles can be purchased from the ranks of impressive vintages lining this family-run bar.

PRACTICAL INFORMATION

Al Bottegon (Cantinone già Schiavi) Fondamenta Nani, Dorsoduro 992; tel. +390 41 523 0034

La Bottega ai Promessi Sposi Calle dell'Oca, Cannaregio 4367; tel. +390 41 241 2747

Cantina Do Mori Calle dei Do Mori, San Polo 429; tel. +390 41 522 5401

Al Marca Campo Bella Vienna, San Polo 213; tel. +390 03 992 4781

Osteria alla Botte Calle della Bissa, San Marco 5482; tel. +390 41 520 9775

Castello Walk

The less-visited Castello district that accounts for the city's far eastern section is perfect for a fascinating walking tour via quiet squares and neighbourhood cafés. A stroll along waterside Riva degli Schiavoni, named after Slav sailors from the Dalmatian Coast, leads past a procession of palaces and La Pietà, the church where Antonio Vivaldi used to give musical instruction. Then it's on past the stuccoed ochre Ca' di Dio, or House of God. Now a convalescent home, it once hosted pilgrims on their way to the Holy Land in the Middle Ages. Over a bridge is the huge Arsenale shipyard, where galleys and warships were assembled during the centuries of the Venetian Republic. Encircled by a high crenellated brick wall, the shipyard is open during art shows such as the Biennale extravaganzas.

Close to Castello's southern edge is broad Via Garibaldi, lined with eateries such as cheerful Trattoria Giorgione. Next to a lively market, the road forks, and you turn down a shady, tree-lined avenue constructed under the late 18th-century French dominion. Here a statue of Garibaldi towers over a pond crawling with terrapins, which have been released here by locals.

At the rear of Castello, accessible by a long wooden bridge, is the sleepy backwater of San Pietro, site of settlements dating back to the 7th century. Its handsome church of Palladian design, the Chiesa di San Pietro di Castello, was actually the cathedral of Venice up until 1807, when Basilica di San Marco took over. During the Venetian Republic years, the ecclesiastical authorities were all but confined here, well away from the city's seat of power at San Marco, to keep Church and State separate. Nearby, the public gardens of Sant'Elena and its playground are a good spot to relax with a book or enjoy a picnic.

PRACTICAL INFORMATION

Biennale Palazzo Giustinian Lolin, San Vidal, San Marco 2893; www.labiennale.org

Chiesa di San Pietro di Castello Campo San Pietro; www.chorusvenezia.org

Trattoria Giorgione Via Garibaldi 1533, Garibaldi; www.ristorantegiorgione.it

MAIN IMAGE Elegant, colourful Rīga from above **BELOW (left to right)**
Latvians in costume at the Open-Air Ethnographic Museum; street café in
the heart of Rīga's Old Town; House of Blackheads, Old Town

RĪGA
VS PRAGUE

Prague may have hogged the limelight since the Velvet Revolution of 1989, but the Baltic gem that is Rīga gives the Czech capital a run for its tourist money

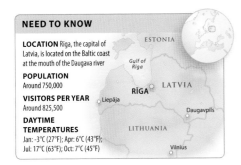

It would be hard to deny the fairy-tale appeal of Prague's Old Town, but as it attracts ever-growing hordes of tourists – and the touts who prey on them – the city risks losing its Cinderella glamour and being revealed as more of an ugly sister. It's hardly surprising that savvy travellers have been looking for "the new Prague" for some time now. With Rīga, they might just have found it.

Long the most lively and cosmopolitan of the Baltic capitals, and with a rich history as a mercantile centre, Rīga refused to let its merits go unnoticed when the Soviet Union collapsed in 1991, and instead plunged headlong into its new-found independence. Today, this medieval city, known for its pretty gables, turrets and steeples, is also a dynamic, thriving metropolis looking to the future, with a boisterous nightlife to match. Funky cafés, sophisticated restaurants and edgy boutiques line the cobbled streets here, where old and new come together with undeniable charm.

Rīga's beautiful, well-preserved Old Town serves as a constant reminder of the city's fascinating past. In the 13th and 14th centuries, under the rule of Baltic German crusaders, it became a member of the powerful Hanseatic League of trading cities, the legacy of which can be seen in the many medieval merchants' houses that line the streets. At this time, the city's administrative headquarters were based in three buildings: the magnificent Dome Cathedral (Doma baznīca), which represented the Catholic Church; the turreted Rīga Castle (Rīgas pils), which represented the German nobility; and

the Town Hall (Rātslaukums), which represented the merchants (the original building was destroyed in World War II and has since been replaced by a modern office block). By the late 19th century, Rīga was the third-largest city in the Russian Empire, and evidence of this prosperity can be seen in its many Art Nouveau buildings, which are regarded as the best in Europe. World War II saw much of the city devastated, but extensive restoration work has left the Old Town's streets and courtyards looking much as they did centuries ago.

An excellent collection of museums reflects the city's cultural standing, not least during the 19th-century growth of national sentiment, which culminated in the brief existence of an independent Latvia between the two world wars. Today, with this independence regained, Rīga finds itself capital of a nation eager to engage with the world around it – NATO and EU membership included – and to introduce visitors to its own brand of Baltic charm.

MAIN CITY SIGHTS

Town Hall Square This square is the focal point of the Old Town. Its step-gabled House of Blackheads, which was damaged in the war and rebuilt in the 1990s, once housed a guild of unmarried merchants. At the edge of the square is the sombre but fascinating Museum of the Occupation of Latvia.
Dome Cathedral The largest church in the Baltics was founded in 1211 and exhibits a variety of architectural styles due to various extensions over the centuries. The interior might be plain, but it boasts an ornate 17th-century pulpit.
Art Nouveau District Art Nouveau buildings are scattered around Rīga, but the best examples lie near the Old Town along Alberta, Strēlnieku and Elizabetes streets. The inventive and symbolic work of Mikhail Eisenstein – father of the renowned Soviet film director, Sergei – is particularly popular with visitors.
Open-Air Ethnographic Museum This site on the edge of the city draws together homesteads, churches and other buildings from all over Latvia, offering a fascinating glimpse of the country for visitors without time to go beyond Rīga.

FORGET PRAGUE?

THE BUILD-UP Prague needs no introduction. Widely considered to be one of the most beautiful cities in Europe, the Czech capital offers a fascinating blend of Bohemian, Germanic and Jewish cultural influences and serves as an enduring symbol of the rich and cosmopolitan history of Central Europe. Its captivating 18th-century streetscapes and majestic medieval churches, synagogues and mansions have survived largely untouched.

THE LETDOWN In many respects Prague's tourist industry is a victim of its own success: taxi drivers are notorious for overcharging, money-changers routinely misrepresent their rates and the Old Town Square is awash with tacky souvenir shops and postcard stalls. It is now the sixth most-visited city in Europe, and the elegant streets throng with tourists. The city has also, rather unfortunately, become a favourite destination for British stag parties.

GOING ANYWAY? The crowds are at their worst at Easter, Christmas and in the summer, so aim to go in autumn or winter. To avoid being scammed, change money in banks or use ATMs, and try to avoid using taxis altogether.

ABOVE Crowds of sightseers on the streets below the castle, Prague, Czech Republic

ČESKÝ KRUMLOV

NEED TO KNOW

LOCATION Český Krumlov lies in the Southern Bohemia region of the Czech Republic, 180 km (110 miles) southwest of Prague

POPULATION Around 14,100

VISITORS PER YEAR Around 1.2 million

DAYTIME TEMPERATURES
Jan: 3°C (37°F); Apr: 12°C (54°F); Jul: 21°C (70°F); Oct: 9°C (48°F)

A popular day trip from Prague, Český Krumlov is nestled scenically between two loops of the Vltava river and also boasts a very attractive medieval centre. The city's main draw is a castle complex on a rocky outcrop above the river, which offers visitors guided tours to its 18th-century Baroque theatre. But there is more to the city than its castle, and even with the trappings of modern tourism, it's a pleasure to explore streets lined with medieval, Renaissance and Baroque town houses. In the summer, tourists and locals alike take to the Vltava river on kayaks, rafts and even inner tubes.

Practical Information

Getting There The easiest way to get to Český Krumlov is to take a bus from Prague. You can also take a train from Prague, but you'll need to change at České Budějovice. If you're coming from the south, it may be best to take a train to Linz in Austria and from there, a shuttle bus.

When to Go Visiting in summer means sharing the town with thousands of other visitors, but it also brings the best weather for rafting on the Vltava river. Winter is cold, but the city can look very attractive at this time.

Website www.ckrumlov.info

The charming city of Český Krumlov beside the Vltava river, with idyllic wooded hills and fields in the background, Czech Republic

BOLOGNA

NEED TO KNOW

LOCATION Bologna lies in the Po Valley of northern Italy, between the Reno and Sàvena rivers

POPULATION Around 371,200

VISITORS PER YEAR Around 1.1 million

DAYTIME TEMPERATURES
Jan: 2°C (36°F); Apr: 13°C (55°F); Jul: 23°C (73°F); Oct: 14°C (57°F)

Italians call the city "Bologna la rossa" (Bologna the red) and it is not hard to see why – many of its buildings are painted in reddish hues, from vivid red to terracotta, although the epithet is also said to refer to the city's left-leaning politics. The Old Town, which sits on the site of a settlement dating from the 5th century BC, was damaged during World War II, but still impresses with its medieval, Renaissance and Baroque buildings. It is also home to one of the world's oldest universities. Today, the city is best known to Italians for its food, which is quite something in a country famed for its gastronomy.

Practical Information

Getting There Bologna's airport is connected to many cities in Europe and its train station has direct connections to other cities in Italy.

When to Go Spring is generally the best time to visit Bologna. Summers can be oppressively hot and many businesses close in August, while winters are usually very cold.

Website iat.comune.bologna.it

Fruit and vegetable market on a cobbled backstreet lined with distinctive russet-coloured buildings, Bologna, Italy

BRATISLAVA

NEED TO KNOW

LOCATION On the Danube river in southwestern Slovakia, on the edge of the Little Carpathian Mountains

POPULATION Around 426,000

VISITORS PER YEAR Around 686,200

DAYTIME TEMPERATURES
Jan: 0°C (32°F); Apr: 10°C (50°F); Jul: 20°C (68°F); Oct: 10°C (50°F)

It seems natural to compare Bratislava with Prague: from the end of World War I until the "Velvet Divorce" of the Czech Republic and Slovakia in 1993, the two cities were yoked together as part of Czechoslovakia. But historically speaking, Bratislava, which was once part of the Austro-Hungarian Empire, has more in common with Vienna or Budapest. Though the modern parts of the city will earn few devotees, the medieval Old Town is a treat. At its heart are two beautiful pedestrianized squares, Františkánska námestie and Hlavné námestie, with the distinctive Old Town Hall on the latter. The City Gallery of Bratislava, which is housed in three of the city's impressive palaces and also in the rebuilt castle overlooking the city, holds more than 35,000 artworks.

Practical Information

Getting There The airport is 12 km (7 miles) from the city and is mainly used by low-cost airlines. It is also easy to fly to Vienna's Schwechat Airport and then make the 50-km (30-mile) transfer by bus. Regular ferries run along the Danube river between Bratislava and Vienna.

When to Go Summer is the most pleasant time to visit the city, although it can look very attractive when it's covered in snow.

Website www.visit.bratislava.sk/en

St Michael's Gate, the only surviving original gateway to the medieval city, and street-side cafés, Bratislava, Slovakia

CARCASSONNE

It may be a highly regarded attraction today, but Carcassonne's walled city, known as "La Cité", was very nearly lost to history: in 1849, the French government announced that it was in such disrepair that it would have to be demolished. Following a public outcry, the architect Eugène Viollet-le-Duc, who was also responsible for work on Notre-Dame de Paris, was commissioned to restore the fortifications as a monument of historical importance. Today, it is possible to take tours of the castle and its ramparts, and the Romanesque and Gothic St Nazaire Basilica is a very popular sight. The Ville Basse (Lower Town), outside the walls, boasts two handsome 13th-century churches.

Practical Information

Getting There Carcassonne is linked by air to several cities in the UK and Ireland, including London and Dublin. The town is also easily reached by train from other cities in France.

When to Go The temperate climate means that Carcassonne can be visited throughout the year, but it is at its busiest in the summer months. Some attractions are closed in winter.

Website www.carcassonne.org

Aerial view of the walled city of Carcassonne, France

GDAŃSK

Although the historic centre of this port city was devastated during World War II, meticulous restoration has recaptured much of the former glory of its cobbled streets and Flemish architecture. Attractions include the vast St Mary's Church, said to be the largest brick church in the world, the Gdańsk Crane, the largest medieval port crane in Europe, and the elegant façades along Ulica Długa. This historic city saw the first shots of World War II fired in Gdańsk Bay in 1939, and was also the home of the 1980 Solidarity trade union, the formation of which is considered a key moment in the decline of the Soviet Union.

Practical Information

Getting There Lech Wałęsa Airport is 14 km (9 miles) from the city. Avoid taxi touts in favour of transfer buses into the centre. You can also get to the city by rail. Trains arrive at Gdańsk Główny train station on the edge of the Old Town – the station is a historic attraction in its own right.

When to Go Summer is the most popular time to visit Gdańsk, both for the warmer weather and for the city's extensive festival calendar – the Dominican Fair in July is a highlight.

Website www.en.gdansk.gda.pl

Close-up of the magnificent clock face on the red-brick St Mary's Church, Gdańsk, Poland

BRUGES

It is hard to describe the capital of the West Flanders province of Belgium without using the phrase "fairy tale", although it was not always that way. After its heyday from the 12th to 15th centuries, the port fell into decline when its river channel silted up, stifling trade. It was only in the early 20th century that the creation of the nearby port of Zeebrugge reinvigorated Bruges. The medieval walled city is circled by a canal and filled with charming step-gabled houses and attractive churches. Although the main squares – Markt and Burg – are usually bustling with tourists, it is still possible to find peace and quiet in the streets nearby. The canals are particularly appealing first thing in the morning, before the day-trippers arrive.

Practical Information

Getting There The nearest airports to Bruges are at Brussels and Charleroi in Belgium and Lille in France. Trains shuttle visitors from the airports to Bruges centre. Eurostar services go directly from London to Brussels, from which point you can take another train on to Bruges.

When to Go The Old Town is packed with tourists in summer, so visit out of season to avoid the crowds. Be prepared for cold weather in the winter.

Website www.brugge.be

The canal at dusk, with the towering Belfry illuminated in the background, Bruges, Belgium

LESS-EXPLORED
SAN FRANCISCO

For every well-trodden tourist trail, San Francisco offers an equally fascinating alternative, off the beaten track, for an authentic experience

NEED TO KNOW

LOCATION San Francisco is located along California's Pacific Coast

POPULATION 792,000

VISITORS PER YEAR 16.1 million

DAYTIME TEMPERATURES Jan: 14°C (57°F); Apr: 17°C (63°F); Jul: 19°C (66°F); Oct: 21°C (69°F)

CANADA — Seattle — SAN FRANCISCO — USA — New York City — Los Angeles — Washington, D.C. — MEXICO

San Francisco is everybody's favourite American city. It would be hard to find another with a more appealing combination of striking architecture, world-class cuisine, cultural attractions, vibrant communities and the laid-back, anything-goes lifestyle, gilded with a mild climate and a stunning setting on the northern California coast. This is a romantic city, and if you did nothing more than ride its antique cable cars, stroll along the waterfront, and watch the fog rolling in around the Golden Gate Bridge, you would come away happy.

There is, however, much more to this fascinating place. Since its meteoric rise during the 1849 Gold Rush, San Francisco has always been a free-thinking town. The rainbow slices of San Francisco's city life are apparent in its more than 40 neighbourhoods. Visit the Italian café-bars of North Beach, which were a hub for the Beat Generation writers of the 1950s, a legacy that still lingers. Get a nostalgic blast of flower power in the old hippie haven of Haight-Ashbury. Castro is the centre of the city's gay and lesbian community, and its lively bars and clubs welcome straight revellers too.

For every famous tourist-laden attraction, there's an equally good spot for an authentic experience nearby. Tired of the crowds and commercialism at Fisherman's Wharf? Stroll along to see the historic ships at Hyde Street Pier. Frustrated by queues at Coit Tower or Twin Peaks? A city with 43 named hills isn't short of impressive views. Try the ocean vistas from the windswept hills of the Presidio or the quiet footpaths around the northwest coast.

At Alamo Square you can admire the classic row of "Painted Ladies" (wooden houses), with the skyscrapers of the Financial District gleaming in the background. Then explore the surrounding streets, where you'll find more of these ornate Victorian homes. Brave the descent down crooked Lombard Street on Russian Hill, and seek out hidden cobbled lanes like Macondray Lane and Havens Place.

You can also visit outstanding art museums, such as the San Francisco Museum of Modern Art, the Legion of Honor, the Asian Art Museum and the de Young Museum in Golden Gate Park. But don't miss the smaller museums dedicated to cable cars, cartoon art, Jewish heritage, African diaspora, Chinese history and life in pioneer days.

And after you've admired the incomparable Golden Gate Bridge from every angle, drive across it and look back across the bay for an unforgettable view of this splendid city.

ABOVE Cars navigating the sinuous curves of Lombard Street

PRACTICAL INFORMATION

Getting There and Around
San Francisco International Airport is 25 km (15 miles) south of the city. Oakland International Airport across the bay is about 33 km (20 miles) from downtown. The city has good public transport links, so you don't need to hire a car.

Where to Eat
Combine the city's diverse ethnic cuisines and top chefs with the Bay Area's array of fresh produce, seafood and fine wines, and you get a rich dining scene. Try Ella's (www.ellassanfrancisco.com) for an all-American breakfast; R&G Lounge (www.rnglounge.com) for traditional Cantonese cuisine; or Farallon (www.farallonrestaurant.com) for a blow-the-budget seafood meal.

Where to Stay
A budget option is Grant Plaza Hotel (www.grantplaza.com). You can opt for the mid-range Hotel Boheme (www.hotelboheme.com) or spend on luxury at Palace Hotel (www.sfpalace.com).

When to Go
Autumn has the warmest temperatures. Summers can be chilly. Winter brings heavy showers, but the climate is mild year round. As the city is a popular convention destination, hotels can be busy year round.

Budget per Day for Two
£210 for accommodation and food at the recommended spots.

Website
www.onlyinsanfrancisco.com

ABOVE Tourists crowded along San Francisco's popular Fisherman's Wharf

FORGET THE SAN FRANCISCO TOURIST TRAIL?

THE BUILD-UP Most visitors come to the city armed with film-fuelled images of the Golden Gate Bridge rising out of the fog and boats bobbing alongside Fisherman's Wharf. And who can resist a ride on the romantic cable cars?

THE LETDOWN Fisherman's Wharf is a tourist trap, with overpriced food and shops. Trips to Alcatraz are often sold out. Parking is difficult at popular places and the streets to famous viewpoints can be clogged with traffic. There are only three cable car lines, so they are not a main mode of transportation in the city.

DOING IT ANYWAY? Book tickets in advance for Alcatraz. Go to Fisherman's Wharf early in the morning to spot a real fisherman. Use public transport whenever possible. Wear comfortable shoes and ride the cable cars at least once.

ABOVE Victorian ornamentation in Haight-Ashbury
LEFT Rows of "Painted Ladies" on Alamo Square

NEIGHBOURHOOD HANG-OUTS

The real heart of San Francisco lies in its neighbourhoods, and one of the best ways to enjoy the city is to skip the tourist areas and hang out where the locals do. No neighbourhood is more famous than Haight-Ashbury, the psychedelic hub of the counterculture of the 1960s on the edge of Golden Gate Park. These days, the die-hard hippies and head shops are joined by boutiques and restaurants and equally fashionable customers. Survey the scene from The Grind Café, a local favourite.

The Mission District is another edgy neighbourhood, where working-class Hispanic families, artists and cool youth create a vibrant atmosphere. Stroll along 24th Street to see some of the area's fantastic street murals – pick up a map at Precita Eyes Mural Arts and Visitor Center – then have lunch or dinner in one of the many Latino restaurants or hip eateries.

The adjoining neighbourhoods of Castro and Noe Valley are great for walking, thanks to the "golden fire hydrant" opposite Dolores Park that saved the beautiful homes here from the fires of the 1906 earthquake. Castro is home to San Francisco's large gay and lesbian community. The flamboyant Castro Theatre is a suitable landmark and a great place to catch a movie.

Richmond is a bustling residential district between the Presidio and Golden Gate Park, home to Russian descendants and Chinese immigrants who have formed a second Chinatown here. Next to the Civic Center, Hayes Valley has gentrified into a trendy neighbourhood of great bars, restaurants, galleries and boutiques. Try the popular Absinthe Brasserie and Bar to enjoy cuisine of top quality.

PRACTICAL INFORMATION

Absinthe Brasserie and Bar 398 Hayes St at Gough, Hayes Valley; www.absinthe.com

The Castro Theatre Market St, 429 Castro St, Castro; www.thecastro theatre.com

The Grind Café 783 Haight St, Haight-Ashbury; www.thegrindcafe.com

Precita Eyes Mural Arts and Visitor Center 2981 24th St, Mission District; www.precitaeyes.org

The pews and the altar in dimly lit Saints Peter and Paul Catholic Church

TOP A Chinese Pavilion standing amid lush greenery at the Golden Gate Park **ABOVE** The beautiful greens and fairways of Lincoln Park Golf Course awash in the first rays of the sun

GREEN SPACES

Covering more than 405 hectares (1,000 acres), Golden Gate Park is the city's most famous green space. You could spend days exploring its many attractions, from the Japanese Tea Garden and Botanical Gardens to the Conservatory of Flowers. But there are plenty more alternatives for getting away from it all.

Large areas of the northern and western shoreline are protected in the Golden Gate National Recreation Area. The Presidio encompasses woodlands, beaches, dunes, marshlands and grasslands that shelter a wealth of birds and wildlife. There are plenty of walking and biking trails and historic buildings to explore.

Lincoln Park, another part of the National Recreation Area, may have a golf course and major art museum, the Legion of Honor, but it also has wild, windswept cliffs and dramatic views, which you can see along the Coastal Trail. It adjoins Sutro Heights Park, where there are more stunning views from Cliff House, a restaurant overlooking Seal Rock. When the wind is right you can even hear the barking of the sea lions who inhabit these offshore outcrops.

The last thing you might expect to see in the downtown Financial District is a grove of giant redwood trees, but that's exactly what you'll find at the TransAmerica Redwood Park. The half-acre park on the eastern side of the TransAmerica Pyramid is a shady retreat, with playful fountains and statues. The redwoods are fitting green partners for the pyramid, which is San Francisco's tallest building.

Another hidden green space is Ina Coolbrith Park in Russian Hill, which has terraces carved into a steep hillside and benches to enjoy the flowers, trees and spectacular views.

PRACTICAL INFORMATION

Cliff House 1090 Point Lobos, Richmond; www.cliffhouse.com

Ina Coolbrith Park Taylor and Vallejo streets, Russian Hill

Lincoln Park Entrances off Clement Street at 34th and 48th avenues, Richmond

The Presidio Golden Gate National Recreation Area, Building 201, Fort Mason, Marina District; www.nps.gov/prsf

TransAmerica Redwood Park 600 Montgomery Street, Financial District

HEAVENLY HIGHS

In a hedonistic city like San Francisco, cathedrals, churches and other places of worship may not top your sightseeing list. But these establishments reveal the city's rich history and ethnic diversity.

Mission Dolores is the city's oldest building, founded by Spanish missionaries in 1776. Its adobe walls, cemetery and small chapel – which still has its original timber beams and colonial statues and altarpiece – are a tribute to the city's origins. It lends its name to the Mission District, home to a largely Hispanic population to this day.

By contrast, Nob Hill's Grace Cathedral was only completed in 1964. Beneath its soaring spire, a wealth of artworks create a spiritual retreat from the urban buzz, including artist Charles Connick's stained-glass windows and an altarpiece by Keith Haring. Two medieval labyrinths from the floor of Chartres Cathedral are replicated, while the gilded bronze doors are modelled after Ghiberti's Gates of Paradise on the baptistery in Florence.

In Chinatown, burn some incense and make an offering at the Kong Chow Temple, founded by immigrants in 1851. The god is said to bring good fortune in business, and you'll see his image in restaurants and shops throughout the district.

The ornate white-stone towers of Saints Peter and Paul Catholic Church are a North Beach landmark. Built for Italian immigrants in 1924, it now says Mass in Italian, English and Chinese. Finally, for an uplifting experience in the downtrodden Tenderloin district, you can sing and sway with the gospel choir at Glide Memorial United Methodist Church.

PRACTICAL INFORMATION

Glide Memorial United Methodist Church 330 Ellis St, Tenderloin; www.glide.org

Grace Cathedral 1100 California St, Nob Hill; www.gracecathedral.org

Kong Chow Temple 855 Stockton St, Chinatown

Mission Dolores 3321 Sixteenth St, Mission District; www.missiondolores.org

Saints Peter and Paul Catholic Church 666 Filbert St, North Beach; www.stspeterpaul.san-francisco.ca.us/church

Fresh fruit and local produce stalls at the Farmers Market set up on the Ferry Plaza

Antique streetcar, part of a vintage transportation system at a station near Embarcadero

Residential Telegraph Hill topped by the Art Deco 64-m (210-ft) Coit Tower

FOOD AND DRINK

With the bountiful produce of northern California and the fine wines of Napa Valley and Sonoma County close by, not to mention the culinary influence of the Pacific Rim, it's not surprising that San Francisco has one of the best dining scenes in the country. Top chefs shop alongside local food-lovers at the Ferry Building Marketplace, a gold mine of gourmet goodies, set inside a historic waterfront building on the Embarcadero. The Ferry Plaza Farmers Market operates outside on Tuesdays and Saturdays, selling everything from organic produce and flowers to artisan breads and cheeses.

Visit the Golden Gate Fortune Cookie Factory, tucked away down an alley in Chinatown, for a peek at how these traditional treats are made. Tours and samples are free, but few can resist buying a bag to take home.

Only in San Francisco would you find a non-profit restaurant founded by Zen Buddhists and serving some of the most acclaimed vegetarian food in the country. At Greens Restaurant, enjoy fabulous views of the marina and Golden Gate Bridge, along with the exquisite dishes made from organic produce grown on their Green Gulch farm.

Despite the vineyards just across the bay, wine isn't the only drink in town. Set in a 1907 saloon, the San Francisco Brewing Company is the city's original brewpub and the only bar from the wild days of the notorious Barbary Coast. Try their fresh, handmade beers brewed by traditional methods in a copper brew kettle and aged on site.

PRACTICAL INFORMATION

Ferry Building Marketplace Embarcadero; www.ferrybuildingmarketplace.com

Ferry Plaza Farmers Market Embarcadero; www.ferryplazafarmersmarket.com

Golden Gate Fortune Cookie Factory 56 Ross Alley, Jackson St, Chinatown; tel. +1 415 781 3956

Greens Restaurant Building A, Fort Mason Center, Marina District; www.greensrestaurant.com

San Francisco Brewing Company 155 Columbus Ave, North Beach; www.sfbrewing.com

TRANSPORT

A ride on the famous cable cars is a must in San Francisco, but there are plenty of other fun ways of getting around the city. The F-line streetcars are another vintage transportation system much loved by locals. Each of these colourful electric trolleys is different, with historic cars dating from the 1890s to the 1950s. They run 10 km (6 miles) each way, along Market Street from the Castro to the Embarcadero and on to Fisherman's Wharf.

With Silicon Valley at its doorstep, it's no wonder that there are also high-tech transport options. Take a City Segway Tour and glide along the waterfront on your own super-cool personal transporter. The 3-hour tour takes in many historic sites. Or you can let a talking car be your guide – a GPS-guided GoCar, that is. You can rent these jolly three-wheeled, two-seater yellow convertibles by the hour, and choose from several free GPS tours.

If climbing the hills becomes too much of a strain, take to the air for a bird's-eye view of the city with San Francisco Helicopters. Tours range from the 20-minute Vista Tour of the major city landmarks to a half-day tour which heads north for a delicious picnic lunch in Napa Valley.

You can also cycle across the Golden Gate Bridge. A bike path through Presidio National Park takes you along San Francisco Bay and safely across the 2-km (1¼-mile) bridge, allowing for photo stops. Blazing Saddles offers bike rentals, organized tours, self-guided tours and maps and information on other popular routes throughout the city.

PRACTICAL INFORMATION

F-line Streetcars 870 Market Street, Suite 803; www.streetcar.org

City Segway Tours 505 Beach Street, Suite 50; www.citysegwaytours.com

GoCar Tours Fisherman's Wharf, 2715 Hyde Street; www.gocartours.com

San Francisco Helicopters PO Box 280776; tel. 800 400 2404 (toll free); www.sfhelicopters.com

GRAND VIEWS

Rising over 274 m (900 ft), Twin Peaks is the most popular – and crowded – spot for sweeping city views. The road to the top is often clogged with traffic, and parking is limited to just 20 minutes. Check out some of the city's other, lesser-visited hilltop vistas instead.

South of Twin Peaks, near the city centre, Mount Davidson is San Francisco's highest peak at 282 m (925 ft). The surrounding hillside is part of a municipal park, covered in eucalyptus forest with ivy, ferns and brambles creating a wilder landscape. The peak offers grand views to the south and east.

Although it's smaller and lower in elevation, many locals rate Tank Hill, directly north of Twin Peaks, as having the best view of the city. You can see both the Bay Bridge and Golden Gate Bridge, the Presidio and Golden Gate Park. It is also a haven for 60 species of native plants.

Another wonderful, if windy, spot lies to the west on Grand View Hill, also known as Turtle Hill. Topped by remnants of dune habitat, it offers stunning ocean scenery and a panoramic view that takes in Golden Gate Park.

Buena Vista Park in Haight-Ashbury is one of the finest city parks for its large, beautiful trees and winding paths. The steep bits are worth the climb for the fine city views framed by lush foliage.

Beat the crowds at Coit Tower by walking up Telegraph Hill. Filbert Street leads to the Filbert Steps and Greenwich Steps, which take you past lovely old houses and gardens, and under leafy passages, opening on to splendid views of the bay.

PRACTICAL INFORMATION

Buena Vista Park Haight St and Buena Vista Ave East, Haight-Ashbury

Grand View Hill 14th Avenue at Moraga Street

Mount Davidson Access at Dalewood Way and Lansdale Avenue

Tank Hill Belgrave Avenue, Clarendon

Telegraph Hill Filbert Steps

ABOVE The rooftop pool at Thermae Bath Spa, UK

BATH
VS BUDAPEST

Budapest, with its healing waters, has just met its match in the rejuvenated spa city of Bath

NEED TO KNOW

LOCATION Bath is about 100 miles (160 km) west of London

POPULATION Around 80,000

VISITORS PER YEAR Nearly 4 million day visitors to the city

DAYTIME TEMPERATURES Jan: 9°C (48°F); Apr: 14°C (57°F); Jul: 22°C (72°F); Oct: 16°C (61°F)

Budapest is commonly seen as a kind of nirvana for spa-lovers. Since the invading Ottoman Turks introduced communal bathing to Central Europe in the 16th century, Hungarians have embraced the culture as their own. Such a mythology has built up around this city that it's easy to forget there are many equally great spa towns found around Europe. One example is the city of Bath in the heart of England's West Country, whose long history of bathing dates back almost 2,000 years to when the Romans built the first baths here. The city underwent a revival in the 18th century when people flocked to its reputedly healing waters, but gradually interest waned and in 1978 the baths were closed due to lack of funding and a health scare.

Today, the UNESCO World Heritage City of Bath is seeing another revival following the opening of a new spa that throws down the gauntlet to Budapest. Thermae Bath Spa, which opened in 2006, draws water from the same natural source used by the Romans, though it is cleansed of harmful bacteria –

and of the sulphurous smell that pervades Hungary's baths. It is a monument to luxury, with five floors of pools, steam "pods" and treatment rooms. Take its rooftop facility: on a cool evening, thick clouds of steam rise and part to reveal a clear pool dotted with swimmers immersed in its warm, mineral-rich waters. There's no better way to unwind than lingering in the gentle Jacuzzis here while surveying the rooftops of creamy Georgian buildings glowing in the sunset, as pigeons fly past at eye level.

It's not just thermal waters that make Bath one of Europe's great cities. This is a thriving place with fine theatres, cinemas, live music and great restaurants, shops, museums and art galleries. While the Danube is undeniably beautiful, this British university town has its own pretty river, the Avon, crossed by the charming Pulteney Bridge. Bath is also renowned for its splendid Georgian architecture, and has a thriving pub and club scene to which its Central European counterpart can only aspire.

MAIN CITY SIGHTS

Roman Baths and Pump Room The original Bath spa is fascinating to visit. Built as a temple and sanctuary in around AD 70, the ruins are in very good condition, with Roman plumbing that still works. The adjoining 18th-century Pump Room, once a rest centre for the sick, is now a daytime restaurant that offers spa water on the drinks menu.

Royal Crescent This sweeping semi-circle of elegant Georgian buildings is the architectural pride of Bath. Of the 30 Grade-I listed houses along the road, the two central buildings are now occupied by the luxurious Royal Crescent Hotel.

Bath Abbey The 15th-century Abbey Church of Saint Peter, with its 52 stained-glass windows and magnificent fan-vaulted ceiling, is the West Country's finest example of Gothic Perpendicular architecture. Climb the tower's 212 steps for fantastic city views.

Pulteney Bridge Built for businessman Sir William Pulteney by Robert Adam in 1773 to develop the Avon's east bank, this is one of only four bridges in the world that is lined with shop buildings. Below it, the river drops down an attractive weir.

FORGET BUDAPEST?

THE BUILD-UP The capital of Hungary, which boasts grand Baroque architecture and pretty tree-lined boulevards, is one of Europe's most beautiful cities. The majestic Danube river, which separates historic Buda from modern Pest, is spectacular at night when each bank is illuminated by a string of lights. There are many historic spas around the city.

THE LETDOWN Budapest has the air of having seen better days. The most popular spas are often packed with tourists, despite their crumbling appearance and sulphurous smell. The city seems to lack nightlife, with the centre all but deserted on a weekend evening. Food here is generally hearty but unsophisticated.

GOING ANYWAY? Visit a spa for a unique cultural experience. It is where locals gather to discuss the issues of the day and men play chess on the side of the pool. Head for Buda for its historic streets and a fantastic view of the city from the Fishermen's Bastion. In winter, don't miss the Christmas market on Vörösmarty Tér.

ABOVE Locals playing chess in a bath in Budapest, Hungary

PRACTICAL INFORMATION

Getting There and Around
The nearest airport is just outside Bristol, 32 km (20 miles) northwest of Bath, but most international visitors will come via London Heathrow Airport. Bath is well served by national trains and regional buses and is 16 km (10 miles) from Junction 18 of the M4 motorway.

Where to Eat
The food scene is well established in Bath, where there are several award-winning restaurants and a multitude of independent and chain restaurants serving all kinds of cuisine. The Hole in the Wall (www.theholeinthewall.co.uk) is a great choice offering modern British cuisine. Some of the country's top chefs trained here, yet it's remarkably good value, with meals for £30 per head.

Where to Stay
If you're in Bath for a pampering weekend, then choose a luxury hotel to match. The 4-star, boutique Queensberry Hotel (www.thequeensberry.co.uk) is in the city centre, a short walk from the Thermae Bath Spa.

When to Go
Any time of year, but avoid the height of summer, when Bath gets busy. Britain's weather is changeable, but in the Thermae rooftop spa, it doesn't matter too much what the weather is doing.

Budget per Day for Two
Around £340 for your hotel, a 2-hour spa session and meals. There are no travel costs as all sights can be reached on foot.

Website
www.visitbath.co.uk

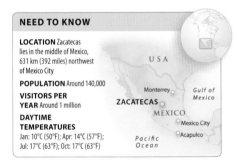

ABOVE Mexico City's enormous Zócalo and the imposing Catedral Metropolitana

ABOVE Colourful houses in Zacatecas, Mexico

ZACATECAS
VS MEXICO CITY

*The colonial city of Zacatecas beats heaving
Mexico City in just about every way*

NEED TO KNOW

LOCATION Zacatecas
lies in the middle of Mexico,
631 km (392 miles) northwest
of Mexico City

POPULATION Around 140,000

**VISITORS PER
YEAR** Around 1 million

**DAYTIME
TEMPERATURES**
Jan: 10°C (50°F); Apr: 14°C (57°F);
Jul: 17°C (63°F); Oct: 17°C (63°F)

Map showing: USA, Monterrey, Gulf of Mexico, ZACATECAS, MEXICO, Mexico City, Acapulco, Pacific Ocean

Ask most Mexicans what comes to mind when they think of Zacatecas, and you'll hear the word *paraíso* (paradise) more than any other. This jewel of a city, which is almost 500 years old and blessed with the best climate, finest architecture, lowest crime rate and highest quality of life in the country, is still a relatively well-kept secret. If you want gridlock, unimaginable levels of pollution and are willing to part with the contents of your wallet (sometimes unknowingly), stick with Mexico City. But if you want to get to know the real Mexico, head to Zacatecas.

The historic city was the first in Mexico to undergo a rigorous preservation programme, and it shows. A UNESCO World Heritage Site since 1993, the downtown area is a faithfully restored Spanish colonial city like no other. Here you'll find a richly decorated 18th-century cathedral, which is the finest example of Mexican Churrigueresque architecture in the world; many ex-convents that have been converted into first-rate museums; and a famous mint. These museums and the city's countless monuments explore the role Zacatecas played in both the War of Independence (1810–21) and the early-20th-century Mexican Revolution.

Zacatecas plays host to innumerable festivals and events each year. The most vibrant of these is a cultural celebration held during Semana Santa (Holy Week) that is unrivalled across Mexico. The city also boasts a national folklore festival, an impressive *charrería* (traditional display of horsemanship), a national fair that doubles as a drinking contest at night, hot-air balloon festivals, street theatre extravaganzas, re-enactments of ancient battles and centuries-old religious processions that are long-extinct elsewhere. Better still, most of these events are free to the public.

The city's central location makes it an ideal base for trips to nearby attractions. The Cerro de la Bufa, which is located just outside the centre behind the cathedral, is a beautiful hilltop with its own cable car – one of the only two cable cars in Mexico – and an enormous monument to the revolutionary general, Francisco "Pancho" Villa. The countryside nearby is home to archaeological sites, indigenous Huichol communities famed for their imaginative art and quaint villages that have remained virtually unchanged over the centuries. Zacatecas is also close enough to both coasts that Mexico's fabled beaches are only ever a day trip away.

MAIN CITY SIGHTS

Cerro de la Bufa Climb or take the cable car to the top of this hill for fabulous views of the city. At the top you'll find statues of revolutionary heroes, a chapel and a museum dedicated to the Revolution. Don't miss the Tomb of the Illustrious Zacatecanos, a marble mausoleum where the remains of several famous Zacatecanos are enshrined.
Cathedral of Zacatecas Even the most jaded traveller will be impressed by this soaring spiritual monument, with its magnificent pink-stone façade.
Mina El Eden A legacy of the silver mines on which Zacatecas grew rich, this mine is now a museum and, rather unexpectedly, a disco at night. A cable car runs from here to the top of the Cerro de la Bufa.
Rafael Coronel Museum In a beautiful converted convent, this museum exhibits artworks from all over the world, including pottery, masks and the largest collection of Miró works outside of Spain.

FORGET MEXICO CITY?

THE BUILD-UP Still a major tourist draw, Mexico City is a sprawling metropolis and the country's cultural, economic, political and social heart. It's been said that Mexico City has more to offer the visitor in one place than the rest of the country combined, and its historic centre is one of the most famous destinations in the world.

THE LETDOWN Four words: pollution, touts, crime and traffic. Mexico City has them all on an ever-increasing scale, and they take a huge toll on the city's enjoyment potential. And once you're outside the renowned city centre – which isn't all that well preserved to begin with – there's very little of interest to see.

GOING ANYWAY? If you're still keen on going, explore the city on foot and in daylight hours only. Start early, take in the grand Zócalo (central square) before it's impassable, and don't waste your time or money outside the centre, where the sights are fewer and farther apart.

PRACTICAL INFORMATION

Getting There and Around
Zacatecas is served by major and local airlines and also has excellent motorways from all major Mexican cities. The city is best explored on foot.

Where to Eat
The city boasts great restaurants, with French, Italian and Mexican cuisine predominating. Café Nevería Acrópolis (tel. +52 492 922 1284), with its museum-quality art collection and high-street views, is a perennial favourite whether you're after a Mexican or international dish.

Where to Stay
There's no question that the Quinta Real (www.quintareal.com/eng/idt/120/) is the leader here. The hotel, which is built into the ruins of a bullring, has a monastery-like subterranean bar and boasts five-star luxury.

When to Go
Zacatecas is gorgeous all year round, although its height above sea level – roughly 2,500 m (8,200 ft) – can mean chilly evenings. From March to August the temperatures are comfortable and the days long, sunny and free from humidity.

Budget per Day for Two
£120 a day inclusive of everything, though many travellers make do on considerably smaller budgets.

Website
www.turismozacatecas.gob.mx/

LESS-EXPLORED
PARIS

Lauded for its dizzying array of monuments, museums, sweeping boulevards and alluring cafés, the world's most romantic city still has a few surprises up its perfumed sleeve

NEED TO KNOW

LOCATION Paris is in the Île de France region of north-central France

POPULATION Around 2.2 million

VISITORS PER YEAR Around 28 million

DAYTIME TEMPERATURES Jan: 4°C (39°F); Apr: 11°C (52°F); Jul: 20°C (68°F); Oct: 12°C (54°F)

It's a long way from the plains of Africa, but Paris has its own "Big Five", and everyone who visits the City of Lights morphs into a modern-day big-game hunter, intent on bagging a glimpse. No trip to the French capital is complete without a safari around the mother of all museums, the Louvre, a gallop down the aisles of the gloriously Gothic Notre-Dame and a pause on the terrace of the sculptured cloud that is Sacré-Cœur. Gustave Eiffel's masterpiece of 19th-century engineering, the Eiffel Tower, with its extraordinary views across the city – and down into its magnificent belly – still provokes gasps of disbelief. And the exultant Arc de Triomphe, a monument to military might, is famed for its commanding view of the elm-lined Champs-Elysées and the other avenues that radiate from its base. All this, however, is just the tip of the iceberg.

The city is made up of 20 arrondissements (districts), and many of these are captivating sights in their own right. The Marais, to the east of the centre, is as bewitching as the *Mona Lisa*. Unique boutiques, slick art galleries, gay bars and Jewish falafel shops line the streets, while regal mansions-turned-museums recall the ancient aristocracy's penchant for this once-swampy piece of Paris.

A stroll through Belleville, one of the city's most multicultural and working-class quarters, provides an antidote (if you need it) to seriously stylish Paris, and its eccentric Parc des Buttes-Chaumont is a remarkable reinvention of an old gypsum pit. The neighbouring 10th arrondissement also harbours reminders of industrial Paris, with the imposing railway stations of Gare de l'Est and Gare du Nord, and the meandering Canal St-Martin, the banks of which are now home to cool cafés and quirky shops.

As the birthplace of couture, Paris knows a thing or two about shops – the department store was, after all, a French invention. But before these grand retail dames came the dainty *passages couverts* – glass-covered, iron-columned shopping arcades that still dazzle with their old-world atmosphere and eclectic, occasionally designer, tenants. Just as diverse are the city's many markets, each of which has a distinct personality and flavour, from vast flea markets brimming with glossy antiques and funky bric-a-brac to open-air food markets groaning with seasonal goodies.

Roam the city's serpentine backstreets, bustling bridges, *quais* and handsome boulevards and you'll chance upon the haunts of artists, writers, poets and photographers, dusty bookstores, gossipy bars and cafés, hidden squares and pretty gardens – the lesser-known side of this legendary metropolis.

PRACTICAL INFORMATION

Getting There and Around
Paris is served by two airports: Charles de Gaulle (CDG), 30 km (19 miles) northeast of the city, and Orly, 18 km (11 miles) south of the city. Trains and shuttle buses run from both into the city centre.

Where to Eat
The city's restaurants are reason enough to visit. Au Bon Accueil (tel. +33 1 47 05 46 11) dishes up tasty bistro fare and Eiffel Tower views, while Chez Michel (tel. +33 1 44 53 06 20) champions hearty food from the north. The classy Table de Joël Robuchon (www.joel-robuchon.com) serves modern French food with flair.

Where to Stay
The hip Hôtel Arvor Saint Georges (www.arvor-hotel-paris.com) is

within strolling distance of Sacré-Cœur and Opéra. The chic Hôtel Verneuil (www.hotel-verneuil.com) is located near to galleries, cafés and shops, while Le Meurice (www.lemeuricehotel.com), a plush hotel overlooking the Jardin des Tuileries, has a Michelin-starred restaurant and the most romantic of all rooms – the Marco Polo.

When to Go
For lovely weather and shorter queues, visit in spring or autumn.

Budget per Day for Two
Paris can be wildly expensive, but if you stay in a mid-range hotel, eat out once a day and take the Métro, expect to spend £175–250.

Website
www.parisinfo.com

ABOVE Tree-lined path on the bank of the Canal St-Martin, Paris

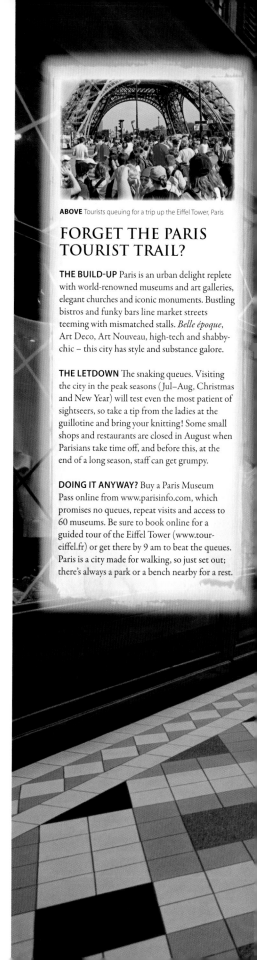
ABOVE Tourists queuing for a trip up the Eiffel Tower, Paris

FORGET THE PARIS TOURIST TRAIL?

THE BUILD-UP Paris is an urban delight replete with world-renowned museums and art galleries, elegant churches and iconic monuments. Bustling bistros and funky bars line market streets teeming with mismatched stalls. *Belle époque*, Art Deco, Art Nouveau, high-tech and shabby-chic – this city has style and substance galore.

THE LETDOWN The snaking queues. Visiting the city in the peak seasons (Jul–Aug, Christmas and New Year) will test even the most patient of sightseers, so take a tip from the ladies at the guillotine and bring your knitting! Some small shops and restaurants are closed in August when Parisians take time off, and before this, at the end of a long season, staff can get grumpy.

DOING IT ANYWAY? Buy a Paris Museum Pass online from www.parisinfo.com, which promises no queues, repeat visits and access to 60 museums. Be sure to book online for a guided tour of the Eiffel Tower (www.tour-eiffel.fr) or get there by 9 am to beat the queues. Paris is a city made for walking, so just set out; there's always a park or a bench nearby for a rest.

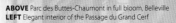

ABOVE Parc des Buttes-Chaumont in full bloom, Belleville
LEFT Elegant interior of the Passage du Grand Cerf

BELLEVILLE

Belleville has long been at odds with the polished, prosperous Paris of elegant façades and boulevards forged by Baron Haussmann in the 1800s. Tapering streets, old factories and tatty shopfronts proudly confirm the area's blue-collar history. Workers flocked to Belleville in the 1860s, attracted by its factory jobs and new housing projects, and the area became a hotbed of opposition to Emperor Napoléon III. This was the last part of the city to fall to government troops during the 1871 rule of the Paris Commune. Stroll along Passage Plantin to glimpse its neat row of old factory-worker cottages.

By the 1900s, music halls and cabarets had sprung up in the area, luring the mobs. The urchin-like singer Édith Piaf was born here in a hospital in 1915, not under a gaslight at 72 Rue de Belleville, as romantics would like us to believe. But she did sing for her supper on these streets. Waves of immigration from Africa, Eastern Europe, Asia and North Africa have spiced up the mix – North African, Chinese and Vietnamese shops and restaurants now line Rue de Belleville. Stop at Lao Siam for a Thai-style duck curry, or for coffee at La Vielleuse, where you can eavesdrop on the natterings of Armenians, Laotians or plain old Parisians. The area has a strong art vibe too, with contemporary exhibitions at the Atelier d'Artistes de Belleville. Ironically, Belleville does owe a debt to Haussmann: he commissioned Parc des Buttes-Chaumont, an old quarry-turned-verdant-haven with gushing waterfalls, Italian-style villas, a Greek temple and lodges at each entrance.

Practical Information

Atelier d'Artistes de Belleville 32 Rue de la Mare; tel. +33 1 46 36 44 09; www.ateliers-artistes-belleville.org

Lao Siam 49 Rue de Belleville; tel. +33 1 40 40 09 68

La Vielleuse 2 Rue de Belleville; tel. +33 1 43 58 06 38

Parc des Buttes-Chaumont Entrances on Rue Manin and Rue Botzaris

Colourful flower stalls at the President Wilson market

TOP Colourful shopfront with the St-Gervais–St-Protais Church in the background ABOVE Plush interior of the Hôtel Carnavalet

Marais Mansions

It's hard to believe that the Marais (which means marsh) started life as a soggy bog. In 1139 the Knights Templar built a fortified free town – a haven for tax dodgers – on the drained land here, but nothing of that remains nowadays. Instead, elegance and wealth loom large. When, in the 14th century, trendsetter Charles VII moved his court into the Hôtel des Tournelles, which sat on what is now Place des Vosges, a host of titled disciples and their magnificent mansions followed. Henri IV is responsible for the gloriously symmetrical Place des Vosges, the city's first planned square.

Just off Place des Vosges is the perfectly restored 17th-century Hôtel de Sully, home to France's photographic archives and a dainty French garden. The ardent 17th-century letter-writer Madame de Sévigné lived in the nearby Hôtel Carnavalet, so it's fitting that this Renaissance gem has been reborn as a museum devoted to the history of Paris. The Hôtel de Soubise, with its superlative Rococo interiors and paintings by Boucher and Van Loo, houses the national archives, including letters from Joan of Arc, while Hôtel Guénégaud, a superb mansion built by French architect François Mansart in around 1650, displays stuffed animals and weapons in its Museum of Hunting and Nature. In contrast to the other Marais mansions, the Hôtel

de Retz bears no signs of its patrician-era interiors, which have been replaced by a series of art exhibition spaces designed to echo the building's 19th-century spell as a furniture workshop and sculptor's studio.

Practical Information

Hôtel Carnavalet 23 Rue de Sévigné; tel. +33 1 44 59 58 58; www.paris.fr/musees/musee_carnavalet/

Hôtel Guénégaud 60 Rue des Archives; tel. +33 53 01 92 40; www.paris.org/Musees/AN/

Hôtel de Retz 9 Rue Charlot; tel. +33 1 48 04 37 99

Hôtel de Soubise 60 Rue des Francs-Bourgeois; tel. +33 40 27 60 00; www.paris.org/Musees/AN/

Hôtel de Sully 62 Rue St-Antoine; tel. +33 1 44 61 20 00

ABOVE A grand room in the Hôtel de Soubise

Street Markets

The city's richly coloured street markets offer an unrivalled taste of France. Melons picked in Provence, geese fattened in the Périgord, ruby-red cherries, milky cheeses, flour-dappled breads and earthy wild mushrooms are hauled to the city, snapped up and polished off while still at their peak. Roving *marchés volants* (street markets) set up twice a week at cockcrow and disappear by lunchtime, leaving in their wake happy customers and satisfied pigeons.

The Saxe-Breteuil market, in the shadow of the Eiffel Tower, attracts a discerning crowd who think nothing of lining up for 25 minutes to secure the most emerald lettuces and the creamiest cheese for Sunday lunch. Move onto the 16th arrondissement, where you'll find the President Wilson market; the casually slung Hermès scarves and bags worn by the glamorous shoppers here for a food run are bona fide. Under the gaze of a rampaging statue of George Washington, locals buy sweet carrots and Cabernet-coloured beetroots from the delightful Monsieur Thiébault, whose family has been selling vegetables since 1873. Head to the small, pavement-style Port de Vanves on weekends for 1950s jewellery and vintage glassware. Francophile bookworms should browse the weekend book market held under the metal rafters of a former horse slaughterhouse, now transformed into the pretty Parc Georges Brassens, for rare and second-hand tomes.

Practical Information

Marché Président-Wilson Ave du Président-Wilson, Chaillot; Métro: Iéna; opening times: Wednesday and Saturday morning

Marché Saxe-Breteuil Ave de Saxe, Invalides & Eiffel Tower; Métro: Ségur; opening times: Thursday and Saturday morning

Parc George Brassens Rue de Morillons, Montparnasse; Métro: Convention; opening times: 9am–6pm Saturday and Sunday

Port de Vanves Ave Georges-Lafenestre & Ave Marc-Sangnier; Métro: Porte de Vanves; opening times: 8am–7pm Saturday and Sunday

A couple on a bridge over the Canal St-Martin at dusk

A restaurant inside Galérie Véro-Dodat

CANAL ST-MARTIN AND THE 10TH

If you step away from the grinding traffic of the main boulevards and flurry of commuters at Gare du Nord and Gare de l'Est, the 10th arrondissement is a charmer. Its meandering Canal St-Martin, a 19th-century waterway bordered by swaying chestnut and plane trees and overhung by iron footbridges, has become a magnet for picnickers, café-goers, retro-shoppers and sun-seekers. You might even see a fisherman dangling a line. Mariners can take to the water on one of the cruise boats that chart the locks and tunnels up to the Bassin de la Villette, while film buffs can scout the spot where Amélie Poulain skipped stones in the quirky 2001 French film, *Amélie*.

Drift along Quai de Valmy for sustenance – a glass of wine with olive tapenade and taramasalata at supremely laid-back Chez Prune, or snap up a piece of colourful kitsch from Antoine & Lili. Follow Quai Jemmapes to Rue de la Grange aux Belles and on to the Hôpital St-Louis, which ranks with the buildings on Place des Vosges as one of the city's best examples of brick and stone architecture. Nearby Place Ste-Marthe boasts atmospheric streets lined with time-worn façades and a chirpy

ethnic vibe. Africa meets Paris on Rue du Château d'Eau, a strip of beauty shops and barbers touting braids, wigs, dyes, creams and all manner of *Afro-Carib* body magic, while at Passage Brady and Rue Cail, Indian and Pakistani restaurants and spice shops rule. Cool off at the Musée de l'Eventail, which showcases 800 fans, some centuries old, made by the Houguet family, France's only remaining fan manufacturer.

Practical Information

Antoine & Lili 95 Quai de Valmy; tel. +33 1 48 34 40 93; www.antoineetlili.com

Chez Prune 71 Quai de Valmy; tel. +33 1 42 41 30 47

Hôpital St-Louis 1 Ave Claude Vellefaux; tel. +33 1 42 49 49 49

Musée de l'Eventail 2 Boulevard de Strasbourg; tel. +33 1 42 08 90 20

ABOVE The picturesque Canal St-Martin

LES PASSAGES

In 19th-century Paris, the city's shopping arcades, or *passages couverts*, were as much a fashionable place to show off as they were to shop. The emerging bourgeoisie was enamoured by these glitzy glass-roofed galleries, not least because of their bright lighting, heating and shelter from the rain and careening carriages of the busy streets outside. They also had cafés and restaurants where ladies of leisure could linger and people-watch.

One such arcade is Galérie Vivienne, which has been deftly restored with vaulted arches and columns, and brims with smart bistros and high-end fashion boutiques, such as Jean-Paul Gaultier. One of the city's oldest wine stores, the enchanting Legrand Filles et Fils, is also found here. Another of the city's *passages* was fitted out in 1826 by two butchers, Véro and Dodat, with gaslights, mirrors and black-and-white marble floors, and crowned with a glass roof interlaced with painted panels. Today it's home to antiques shops, art galleries and personalized couture make-up. The Passage du Grand Cerf, with its three storeys and aerial bridges, is the highest Parisian arcade and the place to pick up funky 1950s furniture and pretty pearl necklaces. One of the oldest remaining arcades, Passage des Panoramas, was built in 1800 and is the home of the stamp-collecting trade. Peruse old postcards and stamps here, and visit the bijou Théâtre des Variétés. Last stop is Passage Jouffroy, known for its waxworks museum (Musée Grévin) and historical monument-cum-budget lodging at the Hôtel Chopin.

Practical Information

Galérie Véro-Dodat From 19 Rue Jean Rousseau to 2 Rue du Bouloi, Beaubourg and Les Halles; Métro: Louvre or Palais Royal

Galérie Vivienne From 4 Rue des Petits-Champs to 6 Rue Vivienne, Opéra; Métro: Bourse; www.galerie-vivienne.com

Passage des Panoramas From 10 Rue St Marc to 11 Bd Montmartre, Opéra; Métro: Richelieu-Drouot

Passage du Grand Cerf From 145 Rue St-Denis to 10 Rue Dussoubs, Beaubourg and Les Halles; Métro: Étienne Marcel; www.passagedugrandcerf.com

Passage Jouffroy From 12 Bd Montmartre to 9 Grange Batelière, Opéra; Métro: Richelieu-Drouot

LESS-EXPLORED
SYDNEY

*Images of Sydney's iconic cityscape and harbour may be imprinted on the mind,
but there are lesser-known – yet no less exciting – sides to this amazing city*

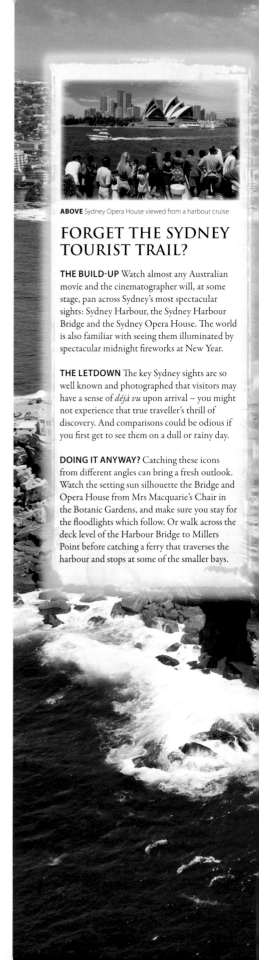

ABOVE Sydney Opera House viewed from a harbour cruise

NEED TO KNOW

LOCATION Sydney is 290 km
(180 miles) northeast of the
Australian capital Canberra

POPULATION
4,120,000

VISITORS PER YEAR
Over 10 million

**DAYTIME
TEMPERATURES**
Jan: 26°C (79°F); Apr: 22°C (72°F);
Jul: 16°C (61°F); Oct: 22°C (72°F)

Sydneysiders often claim they live in one of the
most spectacular cities in the world and, especially
on a sunny afternoon, it is not hard to see why. The
city clings to Sydney Harbour, an ancient, drowned
river system, which stretches for 20 km (12 miles)
inland, twisting and curving to create beautiful,
small bays tucked in between imposing headlands.

At its narrowest point, the Sydney Harbour
Bridge connects the northern and southern sides.
Known familiarly as the "coat hanger", this single-
arch bridge spans 503 m (1,650 ft) and is 134 m
(440 ft) high. Brave visitors can climb the steel arch
to the top for spectacular views, which include the
dramatic Sydney Opera House.

Poised like a diver on Bennelong Point, the white
"sails" of the Opera House stand in bold contrast to
the rich blues and greens of the Harbour beyond.
This architectural marvel took over 14 years to build,
amid great public controversy, but finally opened
in 1973 and is now a beloved symbol of the city.

These three icons of the city – Harbour, Bridge,
Opera House – are undoubtedly beautiful and
unquestionably worth the visit. However, Sydney
has much more to offer, too. On its seaward side,
there are 60 km (37 miles) of white sandy beaches
and towering sandstone cliffs that glow brilliant

yellows and oranges in the morning light. On the
other three sides, national parks rich in astonishing
flora and fauna surround the city in a vast green
wilderness of Australian bush, lush river valleys and
magnificent mountains with cascading waterfalls.

The area's history dates back 40,000 years, and
ancient drawings can be seen, carved into sandstone outcrops by the indigenous tribes that lived
here. But there are links within the city itself, and
you can get an insight into the living history of the
Aboriginal peoples by taking a tour with a local
guide. Reminders of Sydney's colonial past, too –
though centred on tourist-friendly The Rocks (the
early settlement area) – are scattered throughout
the city and beyond. There are places that will give
you a sense of the tough life and the tough people
that founded this amazing place – you can even
camp overnight on a former convict prison island.

The city's vibrant multicultural mix is reflected
in many ways, from authentic ethnic dining to local
festivals – it's possible here to attend a *corroboree*,
or parade for St Patrick's Day, or dance alongside
dragons at Chinese New Year.

Sydney's little neighbourhoods and hidden
corners must be explored to discover quiet parks
offering spectacular views; gems of modern art and
flamboyant counter-culture; chic restaurants and
quirky bars; and deserted coves and leafy lanes.

PRACTICAL INFORMATION

Getting There and Around
Sydney's Kingsford Smith
International Airport is 9 km
(6 miles) from the city centre.

Where to Eat
Sydney's multicultural heritage
has inspired an exciting fusion of
food traditions. Try Cafe Sydney
(www.cafesydney.com) on the
top level of Customs House, relax
on the open deck at Catalina
(www.catalinarosebay.com.au)
in Rose Bay or mingle with local
beachgoers at Speedo's (www.
speedoscafe.com.au) on Bondi.

Where to Stay
Blue Parrot Backpackers (www.
blueparrot.com.au) is a friendly
hostel located in trendy Potts
Point. The Lord Nelson (www.
lordnelsonbrewery.com) is the
city's oldest hotel, and is full of
character. The luxury Park Hyatt

(www.sydney.park.hyatt.com) is
next to the Bridge, with views of
the Harbour and Opera House.

When to Go
Sydney's weather can be rather
unpredictable. However, in
general, the summer (Dec–Feb)
is great for festivals and beaches
if you don't mind the holiday
crowds. Spring and autumn are
cooler, but spring is generally
drier and less humid. There may
be some cold snaps in winter
(Jun–Aug), but it's a good time
for indoor cultural events.

Budget per Day for Two
Allow at least £115 per day,
depending on accommodation,
excluding tours and admissions.

Websites
www.visitnsw.com
www.cityofsydney.nsw.gov.au

ABOVE Striking modern artwork on the Corso at Manly Beach

FORGET THE SYDNEY
TOURIST TRAIL?

THE BUILD-UP Watch almost any Australian
movie and the cinematographer will, at some
stage, pan across Sydney's most spectacular
sights: Sydney Harbour, the Sydney Harbour
Bridge and the Sydney Opera House. The world
is also familiar with seeing them illuminated by
spectacular midnight fireworks at New Year.

THE LETDOWN The key Sydney sights are so
well known and photographed that visitors may
have a sense of *déjà vu* upon arrival – you might
not experience that true traveller's thrill of
discovery. And comparisons could be odious if
you first get to see them on a dull or rainy day.

DOING IT ANYWAY? Catching these icons
from different angles can bring a fresh outlook.
Watch the setting sun silhouette the Bridge and
Opera House from Mrs Macquarie's Chair in
the Botanic Gardens, and make sure you stay for
the floodlights which follow. Or walk across the
deck level of the Harbour Bridge to Millers
Point before catching a ferry that traverses the
harbour and stops at some of the smaller bays.

ABOVE "Koalas crossing" road sign
LEFT World-famous Bondi Beach seen from a less-familiar viewpoint

WEEKEND RETREATS

To the south of Sydney, the sleepy coastal village of Sussex Inlet offers a unique glimpse of Australian life. During the day, take a fishing boat out on the tranquil waters, enjoy a round of golf (making sure you don't hit a kangaroo) or walk along the inlet to the entrance and then back across the wild, rugged beach to complete the loop. In the evening, join the locals for dinner at the Bamboo River Chinese restaurant in the RSL Club.

Situated on a scenic back road that leads to the Hunter Valley wine region, the small, historic town of Wollombi is the perfect destination for a romantic getaway. You can stay in charming guesthouses and visit local vineyards; awaken to the cry of bell birds, and stroll through misty valleys on your perfect weekend. Make sure to leave time for a counter lunch at the Settlers Arms Inn at St Albans on the way there or back.

At the end of a long and winding road is the historic Caves House, a beautiful Victorian-built, Tudor-style building with accommodation to suit every budget. Located within a World Heritage area, right on its doorstep are the Jenolan Caves, a labyrinth of limestone caves that, at 340 million years old, are by far the oldest yet discovered.

To really escape the city and soak up the peace of the Australian bush, hire a houseboat and enjoy Kur-ring-gai Chase National Park from the water. Clipper Cruises at Akuna Bay are only 40 minutes north of the city. Moor next to a deserted beach, cast a fishing line and try your luck, or head to Cottage Point Inn for a long, leisurely lunch.

Practical Information

Clipper Cruises at Akuna Bay www.clippercruisers.com.au

Cottage Point Inn www.cottagepointinn.com.au

Jenolan Caves Three hours' drive on the Great Western Highway via the Blue Mountains; www.jenolancaves.org.au; www.jenolancaveshouse.com.au

Kur-ring-Gai Chase National Park www.atn.com.au/pittwater/park.htm

Sussex Inlet Three hours' drive south of Sydney, 10 km (6 miles) off the Princes Highway; www.sussexinlet.info; www.sussexrsl.com.au

Wollombi Two hours' drive northwest of Sydney via the Great Northern Road and Wisemans Car Ferry; www.wollombivalley.com; www.settlersarms.com.au

Dee Why Beach surfer heads for the waves

Quarantine Station date-stone at North Head

Aerial view of Pittwater with Palm Beach in the distance

Quiet Beaches

When summer arrives, Sydneysiders flock to their beaches to escape the city heat and enjoy the warm waters. If the crowds on Bondi are a bit daunting then try one of the secluded, lesser-known beaches to be found along the coastline.

At the bottom of a steep, grassy hill in the South Head suburb of Vaucluse is tiny Milk Beach. A rocky outcrop protects the beach from most currents and provides great snorkelling. Its spectacular and uninterrupted views of the Opera House and Harbour Bridge make it ideal for New Year's Eve fireworks views. If the lack of shark netting is a concern, take the short Heritage Foreshore Walk to nearby Nielson Park Beach.

To the north, the surf beaches still have Bondi-style golden-white sands and rugged headlands, but without the crowds. A short way past charming Manly is the wide sweep of Dee Why Beach. Patrolled by lifesavers during summer, it is quite protected, has a tidal pool for the kids and a great selection of cafés nearby. From here, enjoy a leisurely stroll north along the deserted sands to Long Reef Beach and then out to the tip of the peninsula, from where there are gorgeous views.

A fair way further north (about 45 mins by car from Sydney), but well worth the trip, is Bungan Beach. Accessible only down a 400-m (1,300-ft) steep series of paths and steps, this wild and unspoilt beach is backed by a natural bushland reserve where bandicoots and owls may be seen.

Practical Information

Bungan Beach Mona Vale; numerous buses from Wynyard Station

Dee Why Beach Warringah; ferry from Circular Quay to Manly, then bus 136 from Manly Wharf

Long Reef Beach Warringah; ferry from Circular Quay to Manly, then bus 136 from Manly Wharf

Milk Beach and Nielson Park Vaucluse; bus 325 from Circular Quay

Historic Sydney

The Aboriginal-owned Tribal Warrior Association runs cruises that give a unique perspective of the Harbour and its history, including the traditional names of, and stories about, major landmarks. They demonstrate the fishing methods, food gathering techniques and coastal lifestyle of the tribes that lived in the area prior to colonization, before giving a cultural performance on Shark Island.

Further west, Cockatoo Island is the largest island in the harbour. Over the last 200 years it has been used as a prison, school, reformatory and shipyard. Take a self-guided audio tour around the convict sites, workshops and slipways, or camp overnight to experience it by moonlight.

For an eerie insight into the hardships of life in the early days of the colony, take an evening ghost tour of the Quarantine Station. Located on isolated North Head, it housed migrants from arriving ships who were suspected of having contagious diseases. Most passengers were free to leave after 40 days but over 500 died in harrowing circumstances and are now said to haunt the old buildings. Further along North Head are the World War II remnants of North Fort. Heavy artillery was built into tunnels in the sandstone cliff to protect the city from potential invasion. Tours take you through the fortifications and tunnels, the Defence of Sydney Memorial Park and the Memorial Walk.

Practical Information

Cockatoo Island Ferries depart Circular Quay; www.cockatooisland.gov.au

North Fort North Head, Manly; ferry to Manley, then bus 135; www.northfort.org.au

Quarantine Station North Head, Manly; water shuttle from Darling Harbour or ferry to Manly then bus 135; www.qstation.com.au

Tribal Warrior Association Tours depart Circular Quay; www.tribalwarrior.org

Bays & Harbours

Port Jackson, more commonly known as Sydney Harbour, may be the jewel in the crown but there are other fine bays on the doorstep of the city.

Most visitors to Sydney fly over Botany Bay as they descend towards Kingsford Smith Airport. Captain Cook originally landed here in 1770, just inside its southern headland, now a part of Botany Bay National Park. Close by is the Towra Point Nature Reserve, a significant wetland conservation area, while at Brighton-le-Sands you can mingle with Sydney's European community, picnicking in the sunshine on the Mediterranean-style beaches.

Port Hacking is situated between Sydney's outer suburbs to the north, and the Royal National Park to the south. Explore Cronulla Beach and take a ferry along Gunnamatta Bay and across the waterway to Bundeena, gateway to the park itself. Spend a day exploring to find Aboriginal rock carvings and lovely coastal walks, as well as a lively arts scene and buzzy cafés.

To the north of the city are Pittwater Harbour and Broken Bay. Surrounded by beautiful national parks and dotted with islands, these waters have all the beauty of Sydney Harbour but without the crowds or the urban landscape. On Pittwater's southerly headland is the popular and exclusive Palm Beach, with its chic restaurants and millionaires' mansions. From here you can hire a boat for the day and explore the bay's isolated beaches, islands and long inlets, landing occasionally to bushwalk to ancient Aboriginal carvings.

Practical Information

Botany Bay Sydney; bus 309 from Wynyard Station; www.environment.nsw.gov.au/NationalParks/parkHome.aspx?id=N0066

Pittwater/Palm Beach Upper North Shore; bus 190 from Wynyard Station; www.pittwater.nsw.gov.au/recreation

Royal National Park Bundeena; train from Central Station to Karingbah then 978 bus to Port Hacking; www.environment.nsw.gov.au/NationalParks/parkHome.aspx?id=N0030

Spectacular city skyline view from the Sydney Flying Squadron's deck

BEST PLACES FOR A DRINK WITH A VIEW

At the northern end of Bondi Beach, a huge wrap-around veranda buzzes with beachgoers and locals relaxing at the end of a long, hot day. "The Rats", more formally known as the North Bondi Returned Soldiers League Club, has uninterrupted views of the entire beach, and a bird's-eye view of the bronzed surfers and lifeguards that are so Bondi.

Located on the Bay Street Ferry wharf, the Australian 18 Footers League Club's floor-to-ceiling windows give a panoramic view of Double Bay. Relax in one of the huge lounges and watch the play of sunlight on water, or follow the 5.5-m-long 18 Footer skiffs as they skim down the harbour.

The Coast Golf Club sits in the midst of a green sanctuary of courses clinging to a rugged coastline at Little Bay, less than 12 km (8 miles) from the city. The members-only St Michaels and NSW Golf clubs are nearby, but at The Coast you can enjoy a quiet afternoon drink with scenic views of the coastline.

Sydney Flying Squadron's huge deck over Milsons Point captures the evening sun and makes it the perfect place for a pre-dinner drink. On a Saturday in summer, join the cruise which follows the skiffs around the harbour. Every fourth Sunday of the month is a little livelier with "Jazz at the Squaddy".

International visitors can sign into a club with identification, and club prices ensure a cold Aussie beer impacts only lightly on the travelling budget.

Practical Information

Australian 18 Footers League Club Double Bay; Watsons Bay ferry from Circular Quay; www.18footers.com.au

Coast Golf Club Little Bay; bus 392 or 399 from Circular Quay; www.coastgolf.com.au

North Bondi RSL Club North Bondi; bus 380 from Circular Quay; www.northbondirsl.com.au

Sydney Flying Squadron Milsons Point; Milsons Point ferry from Circular Quay; www.sydneyflyingsquadron.com.au

TOP Glamorous revellers at the Gay and Lesbian Mardi Gras **ABOVE** Dragon Boat race during the Chinese New Year festivities

FESTIVALS

Sydney's diverse multicultural identity ensures a never-ending array of fabulous festivals in which visitors can often participate alongside the locals. Neighbourhood festivals might celebrate anything from a local ethnic community to speciality food, the arts or a religious occasion, and they happen throughout the year. In Leichhardt, the Sydney Italian Festival takes place in May; at Redfern, the Dank Street Festival of culture and heritage is held in October; and Cabramatta's Moon Festival occurs at the moon's equinox, usually in September.

Starting with a traditional *corroboree* (traditonal Aboriginal gathering), Yabun is the indigenous celebration of Australia Day (26 January) by Aboriginal and Torres Strait Islanders. Held in Victoria Park, on the western edge of the city, the main stage hosts a diverse line-up of indigenous comedians, musicians and celebrities to entertain the crowds. Stalls offering crafts, food, face-painting and more line the park and add to the festivities.

Sydney's Chinese community rings in its New Year around early February. Over 3,000 paddlers compete in Dragon Boat races on Darling Harbour, a parade of floats and Chinese dragons dance through the city streets during the twilight parade, and Chinatown is decorated with red for good luck.

The Gay and Lesbian Mardi Gras *(see pp66–7)* is much more than just a colourful parade of floats and costumes. Held over three weeks in February and March, its diverse events include cabarets, film festivals, live theatre, history walks and a hugely popular picnic called Fair Day, all culminating in the riotous night-long Mardi Gras Party.

Practical Information

Chinese New Year www.cityofsydney.nsw.gov.au/cny

Dank St Festival Redfern; www.cityofsydney.nsw.gov.au

Gay and Lesbian Mardi Gras www.mardigras.org.au

Moon Festival Cabramatta; www.visitnsw.com/town/Cabramatta/Asian_Moon_Lantern_Festival_-_Cabramatta/info.aspx

Sydney Italian Festival Leichhardt; www.sydneyitalianfestival.com.au

Yabun Victoria Park, Camperdown; www.gadigal.org.au

44 MORE FANTASTIC CITIES

ABOVE Pavement cafés along Luzern's Reuss river, with the Baroque Jesuitenkirche in the background
RIGHT Aerial View of Helsinki, with the prominent Great Church and Senate Square in the foreground

LUZERN, SWITZERLAND A town and a lake, Luzern (Lucerne in French) is quintessential Switzerland: clean, quaint and prosperous, with clear fresh air. Half-timbered houses and ancient bridges on the Reuss river are among the sights you'll see as you stroll around the town. Visit the Picasso Museum, where most of the works on show date from the latter part of the artist's life. Plenty of entertainment is laid on, too, with regular music events (the town has its own orchestra) and a thriving nightlife. On Tuesdays and Saturdays, market stalls line the arcaded streets of the Old Town.

HELSINKI, FINLAND Helsinki seems too quiet, too tranquil to be a capital city. Spread across bays, peninsulas and islands, it has one of the lowest population densities of any major European city. Summer is lovely here, with a full 18 hours of daylight and temperatures that are moderated by the sea. The city is best known for its Art Nouveau, but it's also strong on contemporary architecture – expect clean lines. Classical composer Jean Sibelius (1865–1957) is the city's musical hero and his name is everywhere, but expect to hear a lot of jazz, too.

CORK, IRELAND For the independent-minded Corkonians, their hometown is a rival to Dublin, rather than standing in second place. A city of more than 20 bridges, Cork has at its centre a vibrant and compact island full of lively pubs, excellent restaurants and artistic venues.

LIJIANG, CHINA Up near the Tibetan and Burmese borders, Lijiang isn't the easiest place to get to, but China's best-preserved ancient town repays the effort. Beneath its rippling roofs, life goes on as it has for hundreds of years. And the climate here is pleasant 365 days a year.

TOLEDO, SPAIN There are few cities where getting lost is such a pleasure. The narrow twisting streets of medieval Toledo hold delights and surprises around every corner. You are never lost for long, however, because the rocky escarpment at the city's edge drops sheer away to a meander in the Tagus river, which acts as a natural moat. Just south of Madrid, Toledo was Spain's first capital. Romans, Moors, Christians and Jews have all left their mark on the city, which is as famous for forging the swords of Latin America's conquistadors as it is for the paintings of El Greco.

QUEENSTOWN, NEW ZEALAND Queenstown likes to see itself as the adventure capital of the world and, with some truly astounding scenery, it's easy to see why: the city lies on deep-blue Lake Wakatipu, and has mountains all around. It's popular for skiing in winter and has a real buzz in summer, when people flock here for skidiving and white-water rafting. Enjoy the local wines between adventures.

SPLIT, CROATIA Whether you're having a drink in the Peristyle café or visiting a market stall in Diocletian's Palace, on every side you are surrounded by Roman history. The emperor's buildings are still the focus of Croatia's second city. They lie beside the palm-tree-lined Riva, a pedestrianized promenade lapped by the Adriatic. On summer evenings, people gather here to stroll, to sit and to chat.

GRONINGEN, THE NETHERLANDS There's always something going on in Groningen, which is maybe why it was voted the country's best city centre. Night-times are as good as the days – there are many romantic spots in the old town, with its cosy restaurants and cafés and medieval streets and squares. The museums here house everything from comics to cutting-edge art.

TARTU, ESTONIA The centre of Estonia's second city is cobblestoned, pastel-coloured and peppered with museums and galleries. Tartu has been the country's intellectual and cultural centre since a university was founded here in the early 16th century. It's a friendly student town of inexpensive bars and restaurants, and makes a convenient base for exploring the rest of the country.

SIDI IFNI, MOROCCO This former Spanish colonial outpost brought Art Deco to Africa, and the characteristic tiles and ironwork are on display in many places around the city. Sidi Ifni is unexpectedly charming, with a big sandy beach where the Atlantic pounds (expert surfers head here when the waves really start to roll). The Sunday souk is authentically African and full of music.

SANTIAGO, CUBA Compact and noisy, Santiago sizzles with heat and music. It was here that Castro's revolution began in 1953, with a failed attack on the Moncada army barracks. Set on a beautiful bay, with a deep natural harbour, it's a city of narrow streets, crumbling colonial architecture and friendly people. It's also the place to hear the most vibrant music in Cuba.

ABOVE The richly decorated gateway to Hien Lam Cac temple within the Imperial City of Hue Citadel
RIGHT Chinese fishing nets looming over the water in Cochin like vast spiders perched upon their webs

HUE, VIETNAM Looking at the grand illuminated Ngo Mon Gate at night, it's hard to imagine the battering Hue Citadel received during the Vietnam War. Home of emperors from the mid-18th century until the end of World War I, its jumble of knocked-about monuments is still an impressive sight. Utterly tranquil now beside the Song Huong (Perfume River), the fortified citadel of the old imperial capital has quiet streets that are easy to find your way around. Better-preserved are the tombs of the emperors, which lie in temples, palaces and lakes to the south of the city. A sampan will take you there.

COCHIN, INDIA Cochin (also known as Kochi) is a melting pot of the many colonial cultures that have flourished in Kerala. There's a fascinating Jewish quarter and an English village green, as well as Portuguese and Dutch mansions and palaces. Keralan culture is vibrant and there are plenty of chances to see colourful Kathakali theatre and dance. Ferries ply the lovely harbour, allowing you to discover the many facets of the city's peninsulas and islands. Go for a tour of the tranquil backwaters in an elegant wicker rice boat and see traditional life continuing along the banks *(see p157)*.

SOZOPOL, BULGARIA Stuck out in the Black Sea like a crab's claw, Sozopol is Bulgaria's main fishing port. Life carries on much as always in the cobbled streets and wooden houses, though the arrival of tourists (and Hollywood stars fleeing the limelight) is bound to lead to changes.

LUANG PRABANG, LAOS Set on the Mekong river, the former royal capital of Laos is more like a village than a city, its traffic largely two-wheeled and often unmotorized. Buddhism is the dominant religion, and more than two dozen temples are home to around a thousand monks. Rise at dawn to watch them pass by, taking food offered by the community, their only meal of the day. The city is pleasantly warm all year round, and much of life is lived outdoors. The night market is a daily highlight. Take a trip on a long-tailed boat up the river to find further Buddhist sites, including the Pak Ou Caves *(see p39)*.

LECCE, ITALY If you stumble on Lecce by chance, you're in for a shock. In the poor, dry lands of Italy's "heel", this Baroque city erupts like a volcano out of the sea. Many façades are enriched with the lace-like patterns of the decorative Lecce Baroque style and look especially enchanting at night. Enclosed in a city wall, with a lively street life, this former Roman town is the most exuberant in southern Italy.

DARWIN, AUSTRALIA Most visitors to Darwin are en route to the nearby Kakadu and Lichfield national parks, but this energetic and cosmopolitan city has attractions of its own that are well worth seeking out. Take in the ocean views at Cullen and Fannie bays. Shop for classy Aboriginal crafts. And if you fancy a beer, you're in the right place – the city's alcohol consumption is notorious.

ALEPPO, SYRIA This is one of the oldest cities in the world – and it feels like it. Among its crumbling, sun-baked buildings is a wonderful souk surrounding the Great Mosque and ancient warehouses, which were used by merchants on this important stop on the Silk Road. At its centre is the citadel, where the beautiful Ayyubid Palace and Mameluke Throne Room hint at the wealth of the past.

SANTA FE, NEW MEXICO, USA There is a sizeable artistic community in the picturesque old Spanish town of Santa Fe, which lies in a green valley within sight of the ski slopes of the Sangre de Cristo range. Clear blue skies give the air a brilliant clarity, and it's warm all year round. Creative Native Americans were here first, and buyers come from all over the world for the Indian Market in August.

THESSALONIKI, GREECE With snowy Mount Olympus gazing down across the bay, Thessaloniki could not be better sited. Greece's ancient second city is a well-turned-out town, with buzzing cafés, bars and restaurants. Wonderful Byzantine churches have survived wars, earthquakes, occupations and a devastating fire, and the golden treasures of the tomb of Philip of Macedon are not far away.

SIEM REAP, CAMBODIA Most visitors to Siem Reap are here to see the great Khmer enclave of Angkor Wat and the scores of surrounding temples. But the town is worthy of appreciation, too. It started to boom when the temples were discovered in the early 20th century. The colonial architecture and Chinese-style buildings make it an attractive place. Take home local silks from the market.

SHIRAZ, IRAN This beautiful city lies on high ground, which keeps its temperatures moderate. It's a university town and has wide avenues shaded by trees. Many of the mosques, monuments and splendid gardens were either built or restored in the 18th century, when it was the Iranian capital, and take a good few days to explore. Within striking distance are the magnificent ruins of Persepolis *(see p44)*.

ABOVE Shimla, once a Raj hill station and now the fast-growing capital of Himachal Pradesh
RIGHT Sintra's Palácio Nacional de Pena, a fascinating mixture of different architectural styles

SHIMLA, INDIA The best way to travel to the mountain retreat of Shimla is the way British officers and their wives did during the Raj: aboard the panoramic narrow-gauge steam railway. Clinging to spurs way up in the northwest Himalayas, Shimla (then Simla) was the summer headquarters of the British government in India, a place to escape the intense heat of the plains. The Viceregal Lodge and Gaiety Theatre are reminders of those days, as are The Ridge and Scandal Point on the Mall – a road and a crossroads, respectively. The latter is still the town's main strolling and meeting area.

ADDIS ABABA, ETHIOPIA The name of this city, which means "new flower", is a fitting way to describe the rising star of Africa. Old meets new in Addis Ababa, where you'll find a museum housing 3.2-million-year-old human remains, historic monuments, hip bars and luxury hotels.

SIENA, ITALY Nobody who walks into Siena's Piazza del Campo can fail to be overwhelmed by the audacity of its space. This hilltop Tuscan town is much smaller and less busy than major tourist centres such as Florence, but is jammed full of rewarding corners and artistic highlights.

HEIDELBERG, GERMANY One of Germany's most romantic towns, Heidelberg owes a lot to its setting, high on a bank beside the Neckar river, with a a ruined Gothic castle looking down on it. Mark Twain wrote of the duels that took place here (you can still visit the duelling club for coffee or tea), but it's hard to imagine blood being spilled in such a genteel, well-preserved town.

SUCRE, BOLIVIA Although Sucre was once the country's capital, its core is sufficiently contained to walk around. Bolivians are the most colourfully attired of all Latin Americans, and they create a continual vibrancy beneath the white walls, balconies and red roofs of this old Spanish city. The exhibitions at the textile and modern-art museums are testament to the continuing taste for bright colours.

SEDONA, ARIZONA, USA Set between desert and mountain snows, Sedona is hauntingly beautiful. The city is known for its massive red sandstone rocks and rich cultural life, which includes the Sedona International Film Festival and various music events. Shops offer crystals, amulets and other healing devices that appeal to New Age visitors who are convinced the Native Americans are on to something.

SINTRA, PORTUGAL This is a charming town with fairy-tale appeal, where the kings of Portugal used to come to escape Lisbon's summer heat. Hidden among wooded hills above the Atlantic Ocean are a scattering of palatial retreats, their fanciful turrets peeking out. At their centre is the Palácio Nacional de Sintra. Begun by the Moors, it was a popular summer residence for some of Portugal's royal family for hundreds of years. Exploring Sintra by foot involves lots of walking, but take heart – you can always hop aboard one of the horse and carriage rides if you tire of climbing the town's steep hills.

SAVANNAH, GEORGIA, USA This is the American South at its most gracious. Come to sip sweet tea and enjoy the locals' renowned hospitality. Take a guided tour of the historic district – it's one of the largest and most elegant in the USA – to find out who lived where and how they made their money. River Street is among the main entertainment areas, lined with warehouse conversions housing seafood restaurants, souvenir shops and taverns. Walking is the best way to explore the city, but do go for a riverboat or harbour cruise – preferably in a paddle steamer.

ODESSA, UKRAINE Returning to the world stage after decades in the Soviet Union, this cosmopolitan port has rediscovered itself as the hotspot of the Black Sea. Summers here have a Mediterranean feel, the beaches are playgrounds and people stay up late. Palaces, a ballet theatre and an opera house are proof that the city's grandeur never entirely went away.

TOURS, FRANCE As a hopping-off place for the châteaux of the Loire, Tours is too often overlooked. Lying between the Loire and Cher rivers, the city has a half-timbered medieval centre with a first-rate art gallery, cathedral and sophisticated boutiques. Social activity centres around Place Plumereau, particularly at weekends, when commuters who take the TGV train to Paris find time to relax.

GRAZ, AUSTRIA The Habsburgs seem to live on in this sunny city in southeast Austria, with its old regime of grand palaces, spires and cobbled courtyards. Unblemished by war, its architectural mix – from Italian Renaissance to Baroque – gives the city a solid, confident air. But not all is old – there's a brand-new art gallery and an imaginative glass amphitheatre that sits in the middle of the Mur river.

ABOVE Hindus making offerings to the gods in a *puja* ritual on the banks of Lake Pichola in Udaipur
LEFT Canada, Quebec City, Saint Lawrence River in winter, Château Frontenac in the background

QUEBEC CITY, CANADA History runs deep in Quebec City. The French-speaking town on the St Lawrence River has North America's only fortified old town outside Mexico, and you can walk its walls. Dominating the old town is the French-style Château Frontenac, with its turrets, towers and steep green copper roof. The hotel's sumptuous public salons are an excellent place to enjoy an old-fashioned tea. Quebec City has a Parisian feel, and every tiny street is worth a visit. Conveniently, most of the sights are packed into one corner, above and below the Cap Diamant cliffs.

AIX-EN-PROVENCE, FRANCE As you wander Aix's fountain-filled streets, you can't help but be seduced by the *joie de vivre*. The town's ongoing love affair with art can be seen in the cathedral, with treasures such as the 15th-century *Burning Bush* triptych by French artist Nicolas Froment.

ISFAHAN, IRAN It's hard to think of a city centre as beautiful as Isfahan's Imam Square *(see pp120–21)*. Nor can there be bazaars more exciting nor mosques more exquisite than the brilliantly tiled examples here. A day's sightseeing is best ended on the two-storey Khaju Bridge, where young people meet to enjoy themselves on warm desert evenings.

KANAZAWA, JAPAN Nowhere in Japan can you feel so close to the days of its feudal lords. Little remains of Kanazawa Castle except a rebuilt gate and walls, but within its grounds lies the exquisite samurai Seisonkaku Villa. Nearby there are samurai mansions and two geisha districts of traditional wooden buildings, including a teahouse where you will be expertly waited on.

TAOS, NEW MEXICO, USA Surrounded by ski mountains and broad plateaus, Taos is a picturesque town that was a favourite with artists at the beginning of the 20th century. They were drawn here by the walled adobe Taos Pueblo, which dates back nearly a thousand years and is still inhabited by villagers today. Head for the Harwood Museum of Art to see the work of present-day artists.

VIENTIANE, LAOS As capital cities go, Vientiane feels little more than a country town. A broad, open community beside the Mekong river, it's largely on the flat and ideal for walking around (though a *tuk tuk* will help you through the traffic). The temples and stupas are the highlights, particularly Wat Si Saket and Pha That Luang. The place to chill is by the river in one of the café kiosks' gardens.

UDAIPUR, INDIA Resplendent with a score of maharajas' palaces, the "City of Lakes" in Rajasthan is one of the most beautiful, tranquil places on the whole subcontinent. Anybody who stays in one of the former palaces that are now hotels is liable to feel like a maharaja, too. City Palace is the largest in Rajasthan and dominates the town. Part museum, part hotel, it's full of artworks and antiques. Lake Palace, made entirely of white marble, has a magical setting on Lake Pichola. The impressive building has been a setting for film shoots, including the James Bond film *Octopussy*.

MONTEVIDEO, URUGUAY "The highest quality of life in South America" is a statement that's often made about Montevideo, and it's easy to see why. This is a prosperous, sophisticated and relaxed city, with wide avenues, handsome European-style buildings and all the trappings of modern life. The beaches are pretty wonderful, too. The best place for a stroll is the Rambla, the avenue that runs along the city's waterfront beside the Río de la Plata and Montevideo Bay. It's here that people gather to play, exercise and meet up for a *maté*, the local tea.

SALVADOR, BRAZIL More Caribbean in outlook than most of Brazil, Salvador is a laid-back town that likes to party. Music follows you wherever you go – on the beautiful palm-backed beaches or around the old district of Pelourinho, which has some of the finest colonial architecture in South America. This is the third-largest city in Brazil, and its carnival is the biggest street party in the world *(see pp50–51)*.

NANCY, FRANCE Stand in the middle of Nancy's Place Stanislas and at once you feel an exhilarating sense of style and space. Around you, the magnificent Hôtel de Ville, the theatre and the Musée des Beaux Arts are as fresh and dazzling as the day they were completed more than 250 years ago. This is a lovely place to sit in a café, and the medieval quarter has many delightful shops.

BRISTOL, UK Set on the River Avon in England's West Country, Bristol has a real buzz: its docks are tourist honeypots, its galleries and theatre are thriving, and the area of Clifton, beside Brunel's great suspension bridge, is as elegant as ever. Visit Brunel's *SS Great Britain* for an insight into how passengers used to have to make transatlantic journeys.

GEOGRAPHICAL INDEX

The geographical index below locates the main sights covered in this book on a map of the world. Every entry in the list has a grid reference, and the destinations in bold are also labelled on the map. The numbers in brackets refer to the pages on which the sights appear.

King penguins huddled for warmth with their chicks after a snowstorm, Antarctica *(see page 112)*

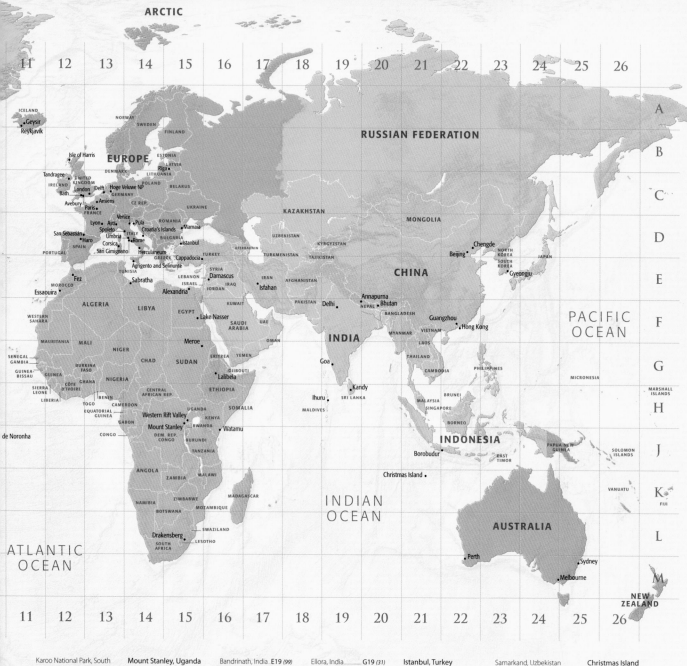

INDEX

ABOUT OUR AUTHORS

RUDOLF ABRAHAM

Rudolf is an award-winning writer and photographer, whose books include *Walking in Croatia* and *The Mountains of Montenegro*, as well as guides to the mountains of eastern Turkey and Patagonian Chile. He also writes on Islamic art and architecture. *"Where would I really like to go next? The island of South Georgia would be nice – although there are some remote corners of Patagonia calling me back for another visit."* Author of **pages 120–23.**

ERIC AMRINE

A Seattle-based writer, photographer and musician, Eric made the jump from technology to travel in 1999, and worked for the luxury travel consortium Virtuoso. He has written *Top 10 Seattle*, part of *Eyewitness Travel Guide Alaska* and has reviewed dozens of cruise-ship vacations for Expedia, but he really prefers kayaking in deserted seas and wild river rapids. *"While I have climbed the slopes of Mt Rainier, my dreams include summiting Mt Kilimanjaro before its glaciers melt."* Author of **pages 74–5.**

ALF ALDERSON

A keen surfer, skier and mountaineer, Alf worked as an oil field geologist, ski lift operator, cycle courier and journalist before finding his perfect job – travel writing. *"The place I'd most like to visit I've already been to once – Kamchatka, Russia. I visited in winter to ski down the region's active volcanoes. Next time I'd like to go in summer and see the grizzly bears – it has the largest population of them in the world."* Author of **pages 212–15.**

CHRISTOPHER BAKER

An adventurer by heart, Christopher P. Baker, the Lowell Thomas 2008 Travel Journalist of the Year, has been a professional travel writer and photographer for three decades and has written for many of the world's leading publications. *"Although Antarctica, South Africa and Chile are on my 'must visit soon' list, my real dream is to return to Cuba, where I'm never happier than when relaxing in a rocking chair with a mojito and a fine cigar."* Author of **pages 161, 186–7, 199, 218–19, 292.**

JOSEPH BINDLOSS

Joe caught the travel bug in the early 1990s on a grand tour of Asia, and he's been jumping onto trains, boats and planes ever since. When he's not roaming around India, Nepal and Southeast Asia for various guidebooks and magazines, he writes dining and travel guides in London. *"If I could be anywhere in the world this very second, it would have to be India – either drifting along the Brahmaputra River in Assam, or sipping butter tea high up in the Himalayas."* Author of **pages 70, 200–1.**

MARYANNE BLACKER

Maryanne has a taste for travel, from the cafés of Paris to the peaks of Peru, via Colombian cow farms and Argentine tango bars. Prior to moving to Peru in 2005, the Australian-born writer lived in Paris for nine years and is partial to a coconut macaroon or six. *"I'd like to hike Peru's Ausangate mountain trail, spending my days ambling through grassy valleys and ice fields to see one of the few herding communities left in the world, and spending my nights snug in eco-friendly lodges at altitudes around 4,500 m."* Author of **pages 66–7, 71, 140–41, 244–7, 256–7, 314–17.**

GARY BOWERMAN

As a Shanghai-based journalist, Gary's searches for offbeat stories have taken him from a gangland prison in San Salvador to the Harbin Ice Festival, and from a Bandung sculptor's homestead to the Qinghai-Tibet railway. *"Libya's ruins and the vineyards of Georgia top my 'to do' list, but living in China also presents great new opportunities, even in tried-and-trusted cities like Beijing or Xi'an."* Author of **pages 102–5, 294–7.**

PHILIP BRIGGS

A specialist in Africa, Philip wrote what were then – and in some cases still are – the only dedicated guidebooks to Tanzania, Uganda, Malawi, Ethiopia, Ghana, Mozambique and Rwanda. The author of DK's *Top 10 Cape Town* and co-author of *Eyewitness Travel Guide Kenya*, he recently spent time exploring the rainforests of Madagascar and deserts of Egypt. *"I am currently looking for a pretext to track mandrills and gorillas in Gabon and Cameroon."* Author of **pages 162–5, 194–7, 252–3, 286.**

PAUL CLAMMER

Paul started life as a molecular biologist, but in a gap between jobs picked up his rucksack and never quite managed to return to the lab. Having worked as a tour guide in Morocco, Turkey and Pakistan, he is now a full-time guidebook author. *"When I'm not at my Wiltshire home, I'm usually heading for the dustier climes of Africa and the greater Middle East."* Author of **pages 10–13, 298–9.**

JANE CORNWELL

Jane is an Australian-born, London-based writer, journalist and broadcaster specializing in arts and music. She is a World Music critic for London's *Evening Standard* newspaper and an arts correspondent for *The Australian* newspaper. *"My next travel adventure will be sashaying around the salsa clubs of Cali in Colombia, a city of painted bridges, cobblestone plazas and the occasional skyscraper."* Author of **pages 56–7, 62–5.**

DONNA DAILEY

An award-winning travel writer and photographer, Donna writes for magazines, newspapers and websites worldwide. She is the author of numerous travel guides and inspirational travel books, such as the recent *Travelers' Atlas North America*. *"For my next big road trip I'm planning to drive the Alaska Highway. My grandfather helped to build it during the Great Depression, and I'm keen to experience that great road through the wilderness."* Author of **pages 128, 250, 308–11.**

JENNIFER EVELAND

Jennifer will tell you that the best travel experiences can't be planned – often they're the spontaneous moments when things go completely off-course. For the bits that do need planning, she's co-authored DK's *Top 10 Singapore*. *"I'm currently intrigued by the many private islands around Singapore. Some owners have built gorgeous holiday villas that they hire out when they're not in residence. There's nothing like having an entire tropical island to yourself."* Author of **page 58.**

CAROLE FRENCH

Based in Cyprus, professional travel journalist Carole is often asked to cover her favourite places in Greece, Egypt, Jordan and the Middle East. She loves to travel further too. *"For a long time Jamaica was at the top of my next travel adventure list, but as I'm just back from that dazzling island my next trip has to be to see Belize's amazing Barrier Reef."* Author of **pages 100–1.**

JENNY GEAL

Jenny spent 6 months of her languages degree working hard at seeing as much of Mexico as possible, and has regularly returned to Latin America. She has eaten her way around South East Asia and loved every minute of a recent safari in the Selous, Tanzania. *"I hope to head for the pristine Adriatic beaches of Montenegro before the UK market discovers this tiny country's appeal. I work for a specialist tour operator and take every opportunity to write; I've always thought that the life of a travel journalist seems like a pretty good one!"* Author of **pages 40–1.**

GEOFF GROESBECK

Geoff writes and lectures extensively on Bolivia's remote and beautiful Chiquitania. Author and specialist contributor, his works have been translated into 12 languages. A leading researcher on the Jesuit missions of Chiquitos, his writing has appeared in some of the world's best-known publications. His recent works include guides to Bolivia and Mexico. *"My next destination? A trip to the secret archives of the Vatican."* Author of **pages 32–5, 84–5, 86–9, 152–3, 176–9, 204–5, 287.**

ERIC GROSSMAN

An experienced food and travel writer, Eric is committed to his goal of celebrating New Year's Eve in a different city every year. *"I can't wait to go back to West Texas. From the smallest of towns (artsy Marfais only 1.6 square miles) to big cities like El Paso (which has the same population as Boston), the entire area is shrouded in mystery."* Author of **pages 132–5.**

ANTHONY HAM

The empty spaces on maps are what really get Anthony excited. He likes nothing better than sharing a campfire with a Tuareg nomad or looking to the horizon and not seeing another living soul. *"I recently went to sand-buried Araouane (north of Timbuktu), and I'm already planning an expedition deep into the Algerian Sahara."* Author of **page 198.**

DAMIAN HARPER

With a degree in Chinese and an instinct for travel, Damian has been writing guidebooks about China for over a decade. *"My next trip is to return to the Hakka roundhouses of Fujian province. The landscape is gorgeous and the architecture astonishing, while the ambience of village life is what trips to China are all about."* Author of **pages 130–31.**

HUW HENNESSY

Huw caught his travel bug 25 years ago as a tour leader in South America. *"My earliest memories there are of vultures and the smell of sugar-cane fuel in Brazil."* Recently Huw has spent much time in Devon training for marathons. *"I'd love to go back to the Amazon, to flop in a hammock with a book and just gaze at the expanse of water."* Author of **pages 216–7.**

NICK INMAN

Nick has contributed to 50 travel guides on Spain and France. He is always sent to cover the same few places – the obvious destinations and world-famous sights. Despite receiving so much attention, these countries are packed with little known curiosities. *"Rather than go to spectacular new places, I prefer to look at familiar places afresh to see what surprises I can find."* Author of **page 59.**

DILWYN JENKINS

A veteran globetrotter with 33 years of travel and several books under his well-worn belt, Dilwyn specializes in South America, with particular emphasis on Peru, the Amazon, remote wildlife regions and sustainable development within tribal communities. *"My idea of relaxing is another visit to an area of lush protected rainforest, probably in the jungles of central Peru."* Author of **pages 50–53.**

JORDAN LANCASTER

Jordan first boarded a plane when she was three weeks old and has been on the go ever since. After growing up in Canada, she lived and studied in Italy for 11 years. She is the author of *In the Shadow of Vesuvius: A Cultural History of Italy*, and today works in London as a translator and interpreter. *"I've covered a lot of ground. Next stop: carnival in Salvador de Bahia!"* Author of **pages 72–3.**

FRANCES LINZEE GORDON

Bitten by the travel bug since visiting Venice on a scholarship at the age of 17, Frances has made travel writing her trade. Her work has included TV features, articles and first-edition guidebooks on Africa and also the Middle East, a region which particularly fascinates her. *"I plan to spend a year in Syria, from where I hope to get to Iran; arguably two of the most alluring but least understood destinations in the world."* Author of **pages 28–9, 118–19.**

LEE MARSHALL

Aware from an early age that he had been born in the wrong country, in 1984 Lee headed off to Italy from Bristol at the age of 23, and has lived there ever since. A film critic and travel writer, he is keen to go back to the hidden Vallée des Roses in southern Morocco. *"It's the most enchanting valley full of little villages and rosebeds, and the people are amazingly hospitable."* Author of **pages 262–3.**

JASON McCLEAN

With two young children, Gaelen (3) and Ariane (9 months), the furthest Jason travels these days is to kids' warehouses around the UK. *"While the children play I daydream of new destinations to visit, and I also long to visit the land of nod for some quality sleep… as well as a trip to the moon if at all possible in my lifetime."* Author of **pages 234–5.**

DECLAN McGARVEY

A travel writer and editor who specializes in South America, Declan has lived in Buenos Aires since 1999. *"My next big trip will have to be to the north-eastern tip of South America; to the tropical wetlands, vibrant towns and wonderful white-sand beaches of Surinam, Guyana and French Guiana. I am utterly fascinated by these three small non-Hispanic states."* Author of **pages 129, 154–7, 160, 248–9.**

JOHN OATES

Using the Guardian Young Travel Writer of the Year award as an excuse to disappear from the UK in 2002, John spent an adventurous year travelling solo from Turkmenistan to Nepal. He has contributed to numerous newspapers, magazines and guidebooks, including DK's *Eyewitness Travel Guide Estonia, Latvia and Lithuania.* *"I am currently developing a mild obsession with the former nation of Tuva."* Author of **pages 304–7.**

GILLIAN PRICE

Gillian admits to a weakness for anything Mediterranean – especially if it involves the outdoors. *"In the future I plan on exploring more of Italy's little-visited regions such as the Maritime Alps, a superb blend of sea and mountains."* Author of **pages 110–11, 300–3.**

PAUL SHAWCROSS

Paul has been a freelance travel journalist and photographer for nearly 20 years. Although his most recent work is a Paris guidebook revision, he much prefers to write about more remote locations. *"One of my next projects will be the almost tourist free, wide-open spaces of the fabulous Mercantour National Park in the hills above Nice."* Author of **page 251.**

JAMES SMART

In his career as an award-winning writer and editor, James has contributed to many publications. Upcoming activities include the Edinburgh marathon, an attempt to pull his first snowboarding 360° and a hiking trip to France's underappreciated Massif Central. *"Extinct volcanoes, plateaus and enormous slabs of cheese – I'm not sure if it gets any better."* Author of **pages 238–41.**

ANNELISE SORENSEN

Writer and reporter AnneLise Sorensen has penned (and wine-tasted) her way across four continents, from Barcelona to Belize and Copenhagen to Calcutta, contributing to magazines, guidebooks, radio and TV. Between trips, she samples the weird and wonderful secrets of New York, a city that continually satisfies her wanderlust. *"On my travel list are the Borneo longhouses and Istanbul's wine bars."* Author of **pages 270–73, 288–91.**

DEANNA SWANEY

Deanna has travelled the world as a freelance journalist and has an almost spiritual affinity with lonely places, especially Nevada, Namibia, Bolivia, the Arctic and the tiniest islands of the South Pacific. *"My next trip is likely to include the inspiringly isolated northern reaches of Laos."* Author of **pages 168–9.**

MATTHEW TELLER

Matthew is an award-winning author and travel journalist who specializes in the Middle East. *"I have return visits lined up to Jordan, Abu Dhabi and Oman, but I'd love to go back to Saudi Arabia. It's a beautiful country and I found the people fascinating, cultured and extremely hospitable."* Author of **pages 42–3.**

GAVIN THOMAS

A Londoner by upbringing and an incurable vagabond by inclination, Gavin has so far visited over 50 countries across the globe. He now works as a freelance travel journalist specializing in Arabia, India and Sri Lanka. *"I'd love to visit Iran, one of the world's most fascinating, neglected and misunderstood countries."* Author of **pages 24–7, 30–31, 36–9, 60–61, 92–5, 106–9, 172–5, 254–5, 282–5.**

HUGH THOMPSON

After 10 years as a food and travel editor, Hugh now enjoys time travel – favourite destination Ancient Egypt. *"The temples and tombs of Egypt are so well preserved, you're instantly transported back 2,000 years. And my next trip also involves time travel of a sort. I'm going on a family surfing holiday to Cornwall, just as I used to do over 20 years ago."* Author of **pages 170–71.**

BETH TIERNEY

After a long spell trekking in the tropics, Beth became hooked on the beauty of the underwater world. Since then, she and her husband Shaun have written several dive travel guide books. *"I experienced the ultimate adrenaline rush on a recent visit to the Revillagigedos Islands in Mexico, where I saw giant Pacific manta rays, five different endangered shark species and swam with pods of bottlenose dolphins."* Author of **pages 226–9.**

ALEX WADE

Alex is the author of books on surfing and boxing and writes a column on coastal life for *The Times* newspaper. He has surfed in places as diverse as Barbados, Costa Rica, California, Bali, France and Portugal. *"The next destination on my surfing wishlist has to be Chile."* Author of **pages 236–7**

ALISON WALFORD

Alison has travelled widely to far-flung places in Africa, Asia and the Pacific, but some of her favourite destinations are much closer to home, including the wilder corners of Scotland and Cornwall. However, her next adventure will either be *"a trek in the Ladakh region of the Indian Himalayas or a trip to Addis Ababa, one of Africa's coolest city destinations."* Author of **pages 202–3, 312.**

GREG WARD

Greg has been travelling and writing since the 1980s. Besides a dozen different guides to Hawaii, he has written books on the USA, the Southwest USA, the Grand Canyon, the Blues, American history, and many other topics. *"I'd love to see the Inca cities, high in the Peruvian Andes. The second I get over my fear of heights, I'm going!"* Author of **pages 158–9, 192–3.**

CILA WARNCKE

Music and travel writer Cila considers herself more of a colonizer than a traveller – since leaving her native United States she's pitched camp in London, Ibiza and Merida, in Mexico's Yucatan Peninsula. *"My next travel plan is to take my laptop and my pointed political opinions to the vestiges of the Red Menace: Cuba and China."* Author of **pages 54–5.**

CAROL WILEY

After completing a BA in Photography and an MA in Journalism, Carol set off to photograph the world for a while, living and working the winter seasons in both Austria and Australia. Today, her work appears in over 40 books as well as magazines, newspapers and other media. *"My favourite destination is Laos, where I seek out old men who are reviving ancient ceremonies and record their stories."* Author of **pages 188–91, 318–21.**

JOBY WILLIAMS

Joby has spent extended periods of time in Latin America, first as a teacher and later as a tour leader. Back in the UK, as well as contributing to numerous travel publications, she is now working on a PhD. *"Trekking to Colombia's Lost City to explore pre-Columbian ruins off the tourist radar is going to be my next big adventure."* Author of **pages 76–9, 112–15, 206–9.**

ROGER WILLIAMS

In 2007 Roger used a travel prize to find out more about Russia, Turkey, Egypt and Greece. *"I'd like to win it every year,"* says the author of *Lunch with Elizabeth David, High Times at the Hotel Bristol* and *Burning Barcelona.* *"Next time I'll do the Black Sea – Odessa, Crimea, Yalta, Sochi, Trebzon. All places with magic names."* Author of **pages 14–17, 18–19, 20–23, 44–7, 142–5, 180–83, 274–7, 322–25.**

GREG WITT

An adventure guide with encyclopedic knowledge, Greg leads treks worldwide, including his home turf of Utah's majestic mountains. *"I love venturing off into the unknown. My next stop is Borneo, where I'm determined to snap a photo of a flying snake or pygmy rhino before delving into the limestone chambers of Mulu Caves."* Author of **pages 82–3, 90–91, 124–7, 148–51, 220–23, 230–33.**

ADRIAN WOODFORD

In between taking tourists up mountains and writing, Adrian attempts to entertain his two children. *"This year I'm going to follow in the errant footsteps of Don Quixote, mapping his every misadventure with giants, windmills and dodgy innkeepers across the very real (but seldom seen) plains of La Mancha."* Author of **pages 96–9, 136–9, 258–61, 264–9.**

SARAH WOODS

Triple award-winning travel writer Sarah has been travelling the globe since the 1980s and has written extensively about South and Central America's indigenous tribes. *"I'm currently trekking in the Darien jungle and planning an Amazon expedition, but I'm also no stranger to luxury, having recently enjoyed Venice to London aboard the Orient Express."* Author of **pages 68–9, 224–5, 280–81.**

MARTIN ZATKO

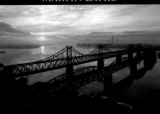

Martin has been travelling almost non-stop for over seven years, and has written or contributed to the *Rough Guides* to Korea, China, Vietnam and Europe. *"I'm saving up to get back to North Korea, the least visited country on earth and, at least in my tiny mind, the most fascinating."* Author of **page 166–7, 293.**

ACKNOWLEDGMENTS

DK would like to thank the following individuals: Mabel Chan (original concept design); Kate Leonard and Dean Morris (design assistance); Natasha Lu and Jamie McNeill (DTP); Rhiannon Furbear, Taiyaba Khatoon and Sarah Smithies (picture research); Tessa Bindloss and Meredith Smith (cover design); Caroline Elliker and Hugh Thompson (editorial assistance); Stewart J. Wild (proofreading); Helen Peters (index); Christopher Catling (consultancy). With special thanks to Greg Witt for reading through the entire book with boundless enthusiasm.

PICTURE CREDITS

The publisher would like to thank the following for their kind permission to reproduce their photographs:

Key: a–above; b–below/bottom; c–centre; l–left; r–right; t–top; d–detail; f–far

A Armstrong: 234bl, 234–5b, 235bc; **4Corners Images:** Stefano Amantini 268–9t; Massimo Borchi 44br; Olimpio Fantuz 236bl; Guido Cozzi 162bc, 318bl; Sladja Kisic 189bc; Paul Panayiotou 282bl; SIME/Reinhard Schmid 46tr, 156br, 230–1b, 304br; SIME/Stefano Cellai 124bl, 127bl; SIME/Franco Cogoli 159bc; SIME/Bruno Cossa 51bc; SIME/ Colin Dutton 136bl; SIME/FotoSa/Alexey Pavin 44clb; SIME/Giovanni Simeone 18–9t, 208tr, 261tr; SIME/Guido Baviera 46tl, 302tr; SIME/Gianni Iorio 58t; SIME/Johanna Huber 26bc, 44tl, 170–1t, 206tr; SIME/Kaos03 124–5, 256br; SIME/Manfred Mehlig 54br; SIME/Massimo Pignatelli 255br; SIME/Massimo Ripani 45c, 56bc, 209tr; SIME/ Bruno Morandi 38br; SIME/ Aldo Pavan 40bl, 164tc; SIME/ Marco Pavan 285tl; SIME/Maurizio Rellini 124br; SIME/Alessandro Saffo 150tc; SIME/Udo Bednarz 210–1; Amantini Stefano 30tl, 99tr, 258–9t, 291tr; **A3 Communication:** Pierre-Emmanuel Rastoin 56–7t, 57cra; **Africa Image Library:** Ariadne Van Zandbergen 162bl; **Africa Imagery:** Roger de la Harpe 252–3b, 253bc; **Agora Gallery NY :** 273tl; **Alamy Images:** AEP 110cr; Arco Images GmbH/B. Boensch 143br; Arco Images GmbH/R.Kiedrowski 60bl; ArkReligion.com 119bc; Peter Barritt 300bl; Mark Bassett 277br; Bildarchiv Monheim GmbH/Achim Bednorz 316bc; Jeffrey Blackler 274bc; blickwinkel/Lohmann 168bl; blickwinkel/McPhoto/zad 196tr; Anders Blomqvist 106bc; Tibor Bognar 38tr, 100cr, 293cr; G P Bowater 110bl; brianlatino 34tl; Lorenz Britt 115tl; Richard Broadwell 168cr; Claire Broomfield 198cr; Sean Burke 15bc; Buzz Pictures 236–7t; Felix Choo 16tl; TS Corrigan 90tr; Gary Crabbe 310cl; Chris A Crumley 186–7b; CuboImages srl/Bluered 73bc; CuboImages srl/Claudio Penna 72–3t; CuboImages srl/Federico Meneghetti 274tr; CuboImages srl/Ghigo Roli 137br; Tim Cuff 187bc; Danita Delimont/ Janis Miglavs 304bl; Danita Delimont./Charles Crust 74bc; Danita Delimont./John And Lisa Merrill 267tc; Danita Delimont/ Cindy Miller Hopkins 101bl, 280–1b; Danita Delimont/Kenneth Garrett 12–3t; Danita Delimont/Russell Gordon 313tr; Dattatreya 244bc; David Noton Photography 219bc, 284tr, 306bc; dbimages 13tc; dbimages/Allen Brown 61bc; dbimages/Derek Brown 310tr; DC Premiumstock 92bc; Reinhard Dirscherl 228bc; Eagle Visions Photography/Craig Lovell 35tc; Zeno Elea 176–7b; Sindre Ellingsen 286cr; eMotionQuest 277c; Extreme Sports Photo 215tl; Michele Falzone 33bc, 33br; FLPA 168–9b; Ian Francis 254bc; Michael Freeman 11br; Robert Fried 144br, 275tl; Johan Furusjö 135tc; Gareth McCormack Photography 238tl; angelo giampiccolo 194br; Artur Gora 166–7b; Tim Graham 149bc; Alex Griffiths 25br; guichaoua 173cb; Nick Hanna 285cla; Blaine Harrington III 48–9, 53tr, 114clb, 233bl, 326–335t; Martin Harvey 113c; Hemis/Jean Du Boisberranger 113br; Skye Hohmann 167bc; Andrew Holt 28–9b; Jeremy Horner 83bc; Peter Horree 281bc; D. Hurst 24tr; icpix_can 68–9t; imagebroker/Fabian von Poser 10–1b, 11bc; imagebroker/Florian Kopp 32–3t; Images of Africa Photobank/David Keith Jones 194bc; Images&Stories 160t; Imagestate Media Partners Limited – Impact Photos/Mike McQueen 58cr; INSADCO Photography/McPHOTO /ZAG 155bc; Rainer Jahns 24t; Michael Jenner 246tc; Andre Jenny 86–7t, 151tr; Joe Fox Motorsport 234–5t; Inge Johnsson 308–9c; Jon Arnold Images Ltd./Demetrio Carr 258bl; Jon Arnold Images Ltd/Doug Pearson 110–1t; Bjanka Kadic 95tr, 176–7t; Kim Karpeles 128tc; Art Kowalsky 126br, 267tl, 300br; Emmanuel Lattes 60–1b, 240br; Leslie Garland Picture Library 160cr; Yadid Levy 111bc; Jackie Link 311tl; Suzanne Long 255bc; LOOK Die Bildagentur der Fotografen GmbH 224cr; Dennis MacDonald 186tr; Alex Maddox 77tr; Manor Photography 15br; Marka/Giulio Andreini 198bc; Buddy Mays 179clb, 250t; Colby McLemore 250bc; mediacolor's 94tl, 241br, 254br; Middle East 13cl; Network Photographers 218cr; Ron Niebrugge 176cr; Martin Norris 40tr; Alan Novelli 138bc; Rolf Nussbaumer 177bc, 177br; Bernard O'Kane 75cra; original images 234cr; Paul Panayiotou 36tr; David Parker 302cl; Parks/Tina Manley 130tr; PCL 79tr, 132cr, 309tr; Peter Jordan 93bc; Luke Peters 298bl; Martin Phelps 15–5b; Photofrenetic 12tl; Picture Partners 125bc; Christopher Pillitz 204br; Chris Porter 175tc; Profimedia International s.r.o. 122tc; Rolf Richardson 92bl; Robert Harding Picture Library Ltd/Upperhall Ltd 178–9t; Robert Harding Picture Library Ltd/Guy Thouvenin 18tr; Robert Harding Picture Library Ltd/Jean-Pierre De Mann 145br; Robert Harding Picture Library Ltd/Lee Frost 197tc; Robert Harding Picture Library Ltd/Mrs Holdsworth 240clb; Robert Harding Picture Library Ltd/Richard Ashworth 179tr; Felipe Rodriguez 71cr; Roger Cracknell 14/Asia 70bc; Helene Rogers 190tl; Pep Roig 32cb, 35tr; Rolf Hicker Photography 115tr; Grant Rooney 200tr; Kevin Schafer 179tc; Scott Hortop Travel 316tr; SCPhotos/Dallas and John Heaton 192cr; Leonid Serebrennikov 232cr; Zoltan Serfozo 220tr; Slick Shoots – *Russian Puzzle* (aluminium) by Stuart Green 188–9b; Trevor Smithers ARPS 209br; Steve Davey Photography/ Charlie Stevens 284tl; StockImages 63bc; Bettina Strenske 216cr; Peter Titmuss 14cr; Top-Pics TBK 22tr; Travelscape Images 178tl; travelstock44 323tr; TTL Images 170bl; Ariadne Van Zandbergen 29bc, 164tr, 252–3t; Toni Vilches 97bc; Matthias Wassermann 136cr; Ken Welsh 194–5t; Tim Whitby 38bl, 207c; Wild Places/Chris Howes 252tr; Jim Wileman 82bc; Michael Willis 189br; World Pictures 195bc; WorldFoto 74br; Alan Wylie 270bc; Mark Zylber 78tr; **Amtrak Corporate Communications:** 95tc; **ArchivoLatino:** Diego Giudice 248br; **Arctic Images:** 169bc; **Ardea:** Auscape 226bc; Mark Boulton 165tl; Jean Paul Ferrero 226bl, 226br; Valertie Taylor 227bc; **Sebastian Arnoldt:** 83br; **The Art Archive:** Gianni Dagli Orti /Archaeological Museum Timgad Algeria 26br; **Auscape:** Tim Acker 222bl; David Messent 320tr; **Axiom Photographic Agency:** Timothy Allen 298cr; Sue Carpenter 91bl; David Constantine 109tr; Ian Cumming 170–1b; Doug McKinlay 180br; Mark Thomas 285tr; **Kedar Bhat:** 99tl; **Antonio Gomez Bohorquez:** 222br; **Melvin Bourne:** www.photographersdirect.com 191tl; **Gary Bowerman:** 105tr; **The Bridgeman Art Library:** Alinari/Galleria Doria Pamphilj, Rome, Italy – *Portrait of Pope Innocent X* (oil on canvas) Diego Rodriguez de Silva y Velazquez (1599–1660) 260tc; Giraudon/Musee Cognacq-Jay, Paris, France – *Young Girl with a Rose* (oil on canvas) Jean Baptiste Greuze (1725–1805) 245bc; Giraudon/Musee Eugene Delacroix, Paris, France – *Self Portrait as Hamlet*, 1821 (oil on canvas) Eugene (Ferdinand Victor) Delacroix (1798–1863) 247tr; Giraudon/Musee National du Moyen Age et des Thermes de Cluny, Paris *The Lady and the Unicorn: 'To my only desire'* (tapestry) 246tl(d); Musee Cognacq-Jay, Paris, France – *The Beautiful Kitchen Maid* (oil on canvas)Francois Boucher (1703–70) 247tl; **Cephas Picture Library:** Ted Stefanski 249bc; **Corbis:** 114tl; Theo Allofs 146–7; amanaimages/Walter Bibikow 172bc; Arctic-Images 174tr, 225bc; ART on FILE 244–5t; Yann Arthus-Bertrand 145c; Atlantide Phototravel/Massimo Borchi 72bl, 127tc, 274tl; Atlantide Phototravel/Stefano Amantini 258br, 259bc; Craig Aurness 299bc; B.S.P.I 201bl; Tom Bean 158tr; Beateworks/Tim Street-Porter 133bc; Jonathon Blair 24–5b; Christophe Boisvieux 123tr; Kevin Burke 74–5t; Comet/Dennis Degnan 102tr; Richard Cummins 30tr; Araldo de Luca 260tl, 261tc, 261tl; dpa/Horst Ossinger 28tr; EPA/How Hwee Young 58bc; EPA/Peter Endig 16tc; Macduff Everton 154bl; Eye Ubiquitous/Hugh Rooney 276tr, 277tr; Eye Ubiquitous/Paul Seheult 124bc; Sandy Felsenthal 86tr; J. Emilio Flores 133br; For Picture/Natacha Connan/ 262cr; Free Agents Limited 191tc; Richard Glover 320tc; Justin Guariglia 276tl; Peter Guttman 87br; Hemis/Franck Guiziou 80–1; Hemis/Philippe Body 47c; Jon Hicks 54cr; Arne Hodalic 96bl; Jeremy Horner 83bl; Kit Houghton 238br; George H. H. Huey 31tc; JAI/Michele Falzone 120bl; Gavriel Jecan 85tr; Mimmo Jodice 24–5t; Jon Arnold/Jane Sweeney 41bc; Wolfgang Kaehler 77cb; Catherine Karnow 290cla; Kuba 152tr; Robert Landau 132bl; Danny Lehman 322tr; Massimo Listri 260tr, 277tl; Ludovic Maisant 98tl; William Manning 20–1bc; Stephanie Maze 239c; Tim Mosenfelder 75bc; Kazuyoshi Nomachi 28–9t, 71t; Richard T Nowitz 27tc; Radius Images 87bc; Jose Fuste Raga 282tr; Redlink 335br; Robert Harding World Imagery/Bruno Morandi 323crb; Joel W. Rogers 239t; Bill Ross 13tr; Galen Rowell 148br, 175tl; Kevin Schafer 152br, 161cr; Ted Soqui 132–3b; Keren Su 335ca; Luca Tettoni 37bc; Henrik Trygg 240tl; Peter Turnley 219bl; Horacio Villalobos 216bl; Visions of America/Joseph Sohm 288tr; Karl Weatherly 292bc; WEDA/epa 37br; Clifford White 320tl; Staffan Widstrand 172br; Nevada Wier 334tc; Adam Woolfitt 14bl, 98tr, 231bc; Alison Wright 40–1t; zefa/Kevin Schafer 112clb; zefa/Roland Gerth 266tr; zefa/Ted Levine 238tr; **www.clubevents.info:** 55bc, 55bl; **Danita Delimont Stock Photography:** 232br; **www.daveheathphoto.com:** Dave Heath 213bc; **Courtesy of Deitch Projects:** *Contiguous Façade* Assume Vivid Astro Focus Deitch Projects 2003 272tc(d); Tom Powel Imaging – *I Love U*, Installation on Deitch Projects Facade by Tim Noble & Sue Webster, February 25 – March 25, 2000 271bc(d); **www.dinodia.com:** Johanna Huber 60 –1t, 61br; **DK Images:** 272tr; Demetrio Carrasco 303tc; Neil Lukas 129tr; Susannah Sayler 289tr; **Ricardo Donezar Vélez:** 59t; **Eyespice:** Jon Nickson 186–7t; **Festival d'Avignon:** Laurent Ziegler 64tl; **FLPA:** Minden Pictures/Hiroya Minakuchi 194bl; Minden Pictures/JH Editorial/Cyril Ruoso 165tc; Minden Pictures/Gerry Ellis 162–3t; Jurgen & Christine Sohns 220–1b; **fotoLibra:** David Turnbull 236br; **G.O.D.** Limited www.god.com.hk: 296tl; **Courtesy Gagosian Gallery:** 273c; **Getty Images:** AFP 66–7b; AFP/Aizar Raldes 78br; AFP/Andrew Ross 294tr; AFP/Antonio Scorza 50cb; AFP/Juan Barreto 52tl; AFP/Leo Caldas 53tc; AFP/Massoud Hossaini 157bl; AFP/Olivier Chouchana 321cla; AFP/Patrick Kovarik 217bc; Agence Zoom 238clb; altrendo images 153bl; Carlos Alvarez 263bc; Aurora/Corey Rich 85tc; Aurora/Greg Von Doersten 148bl; Aurora/Joanna B. Pinneo 86bl; Aurora/Robert Caputo 152bl; Axiom Photographic Agency/Ian Cumming 321tr; Scott Barbour 76tl; Philippe Bourseiller 84–5t; Paula Bronstein 70cr, 77tl; De Agostini Picture Library 18–9b, 26bl, 72tr, 72–3b; De Agostini Picture Library/G. Sosio 200–1t; Digital Vision/Jeremy Woodhouse 129b; Digital Vision/Keith Mcgregor 284tc; Digital Vision/Nicholas Pitt 123tl; Digital Vision/Peter Adams 76br; Sergio Dionisio 321tl; Discovery Channel Images/ Jeff Foott 148–9t; First Light/Yves Marcoux 68br; fStop/Catapult 140tr; Gallo Images/Travel Ink 281bl; Gallo Images/Wolfgang Kaehler 22tl; Tim Graham 319tr; Paul Hawthorne 291cla; Bill Heinsohn 17tc; hemis.fr/Franck Guiziou 23tr; hemis.fr/Stefano Torrione 218–9t; Iconica/Arctic-Images 224–5b; Iconica/Steffen Thalemann 128cr; The Image Bank/David Sanger 157br; The Image Bank/Eric Meola 76tr; The Image Bank/Gallup Pix 76clb; The Image Bank/Gary Yeowell 307br; The Image Bank/Jason Hawkes 282–3c; The Image Bank/joSon 36–7t ,258bc; The Image Bank/Peter Adams 107bc, 307bc; The Image Bank/picturegarden 249cr; John Kelly 233bc; Roger Kisby 290tr; Michael Langford 33bl; LatinContent/Ayrton Vignola 66trl; LatinContent/SambaPhoto/Araquem Alcantara 209c; Lonely Planet Images/ John Elk III 276clb; Lonely Planet Images/Holger Leue 78tl; David Madison 216–7b; Mambo photo/Sven Creutzmann 79br; Peter Mintz 134tl; Michael Nagle 60cr; National Geographic/ Skip Brown 91bc; National Geographic/Kenneth Garrett 89tr; National Geographic/Martin Gray 99c; Photodisc/Gary John Norman 248bc; Photodisc/Medioimages 19bc; Photodisc/Richard Ross 120br; Photographer's Choice RF/ Sami Sarkis 182tl; Photographer's Choice/Guy Vanderelst 156bl; Photographer's Choice/Michele Falzone 45t, 181br; Photographer's Choice/Mitchell Funk 311tr, 314tr; Photographer's Choice/Peter Pinnock 229bc; Photographer's Choice/Slow Images/ Simeone Huber 241c; Photographer's Choice/Stephen Studd 201bc; Photographer's Choice/Stuart Dee 205bc; Photographer's Choice/Travelpix Ltd 128b; Photographer's Choice/Tyler Stableford 1; Spencer Platt 291tl; Purestock 192–3b; Riser/Chris Simpson 200–1b; Riser/Gary John Norman 204–5t; Robert Harding World Imagery/Christian Kober 102–3c; Roger Viollet/Lipnitzki 275cb; Benjamin Rondel 212bc; Stone/David Hanson 170cr, 280cr; Stone/Hugh Sitton 8–9; Stone/Jeremy Woodhouse 156bc; Homer Sykes 268cr; Mario Tama 290tl; Tango Stock/Aldo Sessa 129tc; Taxi 250cr; Taxi/Peter Adams 46br; Ami Vitale 70t; Darwin Wiggett 88tl; Lisa Maree Williams 67bc; **Justin Gilligan Photography:** 226–7t; **Golfklúbbur Reykjavíkur:** 224–5t; **Great Southern Rail:** 95tl; **Curtis Hamilton:** 288–9c; **Hay Festival:** Daniel Mordzinski 64tc; **Hemispheres Images:** Christophe Boisvieux 77br; Thierry Borredon 51bl; Arnaud Chicurel 316cla, 317tr; Romain Cintract 56br, 262br; Matthieu Colin 120bc; Marc Dozier 118–9t; Patrick Escudero 98tc; Alain Felix 2–3; John Frumm 188cr; Bertrand Gardel 85cl, 123tc, 240tr; Frank Guiziou 79tl, 256bc, 257cr, 287t, 304bc, 316tl; Ludovic Maisant 245bl, 246tr; René Mattes 257bc; Bruno Perousse 164tl; Philippe Renault 292cr; Bertrand Rieger 245br, 247tc, 317bc; Sylvain Safra 51br; Paule Seux 107bl, 108tl; **imagequestmarine.com:** Takaji Ochi 229br; **International Festival of Art and Ideas:** Robert Day 65c; Elaine K. Ficarra 65tl; **iStockphoto.com:** Rob Broek 112tl; **Istrian Tourist Board:** Igor Zirojevic 21bc, 21br; **John Warburton-Lee Photography:** Amar Grover 39bl; Julian Love 42cr; Andrew Watson 66bl; **Julian James** www.julianjames.com: 7br; **Kicking Horse Mountain Resort:** 213br; **Harry Kikstra, ExposedPlanet.com:** 221br; **Kröller-Müller Museum:** 251bc, 251t(d); **Remo Kurka,** www.photographersdirect.com: 196tl; **Søren Lauridsen,** www.photographersdirect.com: 190tr; **Lonely Planet Images:** Jerry Alexander 206br; Anders Blomqvist 109tl; Jean-Bernard Carillet 223bl; Richard Cummins 118tr; Mark Daffey 52–3c, 53cl, 208tl; Krzysztof Dydynski 62–3t; Lee Foster 292t; Christer Fredriksson 108tc; Dan Gair 313t; Dan Herrick 271bl; Craig Pershouse 31tr; **LucasKane.com:** 230–1t; **La Mania:** Stefan Ciocan 54–5t; **Masterfile:** Peter Christopher 64tr; JW 118–9b; R. Ian Lloyd 39br; Freeman Patterson 86–7b; Ron Stroud 39bc; Westend61 182br; **Rudy Mateeuwsen:** 220–1t, 221bc; **Azizul Ameir Bin Md Redzuan:** 126bc; **Melbourne International Arts Festival:** Jeff Busby 62br; John Sones 62bc, 62bl; **Momenta Art:** Frank Schwere – Elisabeth Kley installation view Jan 2007 273tr; **MoreBeach.com:** 202cr; **National Geographic Stock:** Micahel Poliza 29br; **naturepl.com:** Peter Bassett 334cl; Georgette Douwma 229bl; Luiz Claudio Marigo 195tr; Pete Oxford 165tr; **Grazia Neri:** Roberto Serra 268bl; **New Museum:** Dean Kaufman 270–1t, 272tl; **NHPA / Photoshot:** James Carmichael JR 148bc; Martin Harvey 162br; **OnAsia:** Agustinus Wibowo 157tc; **PA Photos:** AP Photo/Bassem Tellawi 79c; AP Photo/David Zalubowski 78clb; **PBase:** Sunil Nallode 174tc; **Photolibrary:** ABPL/Gerald Hinde 163bc; Aflo Foto Agency/Yoshio Tomil Photo Studio 144clb; age fotostock /Alvaro Leiva 113tr, 199cr, 199t, 207br, 262–3t, 325tr; age fotostock /Jean-Marc Charles 140–1t; age fotostock /Kordcom Kordcom 154–5t; age fotostock /Walter Bibikow 132–3t; age fotostock/Aguililla & Marin 59crb; age fotostock/Alan Copson 139br; age fotostock/Atlantide SN.C. 25bc, 264bl; age fotostock/Blaine Harrington 232–3t; age fotostock/Bruno Morandi 267tr, 323tl; age fotostock/Dan Leffel 160bc; age fotostock/Eric Baccega 181c; age fotostock/Francisco Mora 275br; age fotostock/Javier Larrea 20cr, 59bc; age fotostock/JD. Dallet 100br, 286t; age fotostock/Jeronimo Alba 298–9b; age fotostock/Joan Mercadal 127br, 302tl; age fotostock/Jordi Cami 276bc; age fotostock/Jose Antonio Moreno 139bc; age fotostock/Jose Fuste Raga 142br, 143tl, 334cr; age fotostock/Jose Moya 190tc; age fotostock/Josu Altzelai 335tl; age fotostock/Kris Ubach 183cb; age fotostock/Leonardo Diaz Romero 151tl; age fotostock/Michel Renaudeau 197tl; age fotostock/Morales Morales 199bc; age fotostock/Nigel Dennis 88tc; age fotostock/P.Narayan 22tc, 266tl, 304–5t; age fotostock/Raymond Forbes 171bc; age fotostock/Robert F Campbell 88tr; age fotostock/Santiago Fdez Fuentes 23tl; age fotostock/Sergio Pitamitz 251cr; age fotostock/Sylvain Grandadam 27bl, 40br, 42–3b, 100–1t; age fotostock/Thomas Dressler 255bl; age fotostock/Walter Zerla 144tl; age fotostock/Werner Otto 139bl; age fotostock/Wojtek Buss 6–7, 47tl, 208clb, 263bl, 323c; age fotostock/Ximena Griscti 204bc; Animals Animals/David Boyle 150tl; Animals Animals/Roger de la Harpe 253br; Jon Arnold 138br; Asia Images RM/OTHK OTHK 297cla; Best View Stock 105tl, 145tl; Best View Stock/Chu Yong 130–1b; Walter Bibikow 104tr; Charles Bowman 103tr; Brand X Pictures/Steve Allen 45br; Alberto Campanile 296tc; Cephas Picture Library/Andy Christodolo 248–9t; Cephas Picture Library/Nigel Blythe 324clb; Comstock/Creatas 230tr; Alan Copson 318tr; Corbis 93cra, 101bc; Corbis Royalty Free 244–277sidebars, 280–325sidebars; DEA / L.Fabbri 136–7b, 269bl; DEA /N Cirani 140–1b; Design Pics Inc/Bilderbuch 90bl; Digital Vision 82–115sidebars, 118–145 sidebar; Digital Vision/Darrell Gulin 46clb; Chad Ehlers 206tl; F1 Online/Austrophoto Austrophoto 324br; Fancy 212–3t, 214tr; Berndt Fischer 182tr; Flirt Collection/ Craig Aurness 298–9t; Fresh Food Images/Graham Day 295tr; Glow Images 10–47sidebars, 92–3t, 308tr; Nick Green 36–7b; Phillip Hayson 318–9c; Hemis/Franck Guiziou 216–7t; Magnus Hjorleifsson 224bl; Hoberman Collection UK/Gerald Hoberman 308bl; Iconotec/Leroy Arthur 186–209 sidebars; imagebroker.net/dreamtours dreamtours 280–1t; imagebroker.net/Florian Kopp 172bl; imagebroker.net/Günter Flegar 143c; imagebroker.net/White Star/Spierenburg 126bl; Imagerite RF 142tr; Imagesource 212–241sidebars; Imagestate RM/Dave Houser 191tr; Imagestate RM/David South 42bl; Imagestate RM/Ethel Davies 311tc; Imagestate RM/Jose Fuste Raga 254bl; Imagestate RM/Mark Hamblin 202–3b; Imagestate RM/Mark Newman 172–3t; Imagestate RM/Mel Longhurst 297cb; Imagestate RM/Steve Vidler 102bl, 104tl, 112br, 130–1t, 131bc, 266tc, 297tl; Index Stock Imagery 186bl; Index Stock Imagery/Kindra Clineff 166cr; Index Stock Imagery/Mark Windom 181tl; Index stock Imagery/Peter Adams 50–79 sidebars; The Irish Image Collection 206clb; John Warburton-Lee Photography/Andrew Watson 294–5c; John Warburton-Lee Photography/David Bank 143tr; John Warburton-Lee Photography/Nigel Pavitt 183tr; John Warburton-Lee Photography/Susanna Wyatt 242–3; Jon Arnold RF/Gavin Hellier 158–9t, 297tr; Jon Arnold RF/Peter Adams 30tc; Jon Arnold Travel 115c; Jon Arnold Travel/Gavin Hellier 325c; Jon Arnold Travel/Jon Arnold 122tl; Jon Arnold Travel/Michele Falzone 278–9; Jon Arnold Travel/Rex Butcher 166bl; Jon Arnold Travel/Walter Bibikow 122tr, 306bl; JTB Photo 20–1t, 34–5t, 47br, 96–7t, 142tl, 166–7t, 180t, 182c, 198t, 275tr, 287cr, 293t, 296tr, 306br, 314–5c, 322clb; Juniors Bildarchiv 173cr; Warwick Kent 241tr; LOOK-foto/Bernard van Dierendonck 215tc; Mauritius/Mattes Mattes 256–7t; Mauritius/Steve Vidler 135tl; Mauritius/Vidler Vidler 138bl, 141bl; Ted Mead 150tr; David Messent 89tl, 188–9t; Nordic Photos/Frank Chmura 300–1c; Nordic Photos/Gunnar Hannesson 168–9t; Novastock Novastock 158–9b; Oxford Scientific (OSF)/Ariadne Van Zandbergen 17tl, 175tr; Oxford Scientific (OSF)/Brian Kenney 41bl; Oxford Scientific (OSF)/David B Fleetham 192bl, 193bc; Oxford Scientific (OSF)/Doug Allan 223br; Oxford Scientific (OSF)/Lucas Kane 113tl; Oxford Scientific (OSF)/Mike Powles 108tr; Oxford Scientific (OSF)/Olaf Broders 142clb; Oxford Scientific (OSF)/Scott Winer 184–5; Pacific Stock/Larry Dale Gordon 105cl; Pacific Stock/Philip Rosenberg 222bc; Pacific Stock/Ron Dahlquist 4–5, 192–3t; Panorama Media 294bl; Bruno Perousse 114br; Photodisc/Glen Allison 106–7t; Photodisc/Life File/Andrew Ward 325br; Photononstop/Anne Montfort 109tc; Photononstop/Brigitte Merle 315tr; Photononstop/Hervé Gyssels 305cr; Photononstop/J-C&D. Pratt 141bc; Photononstop/Jacques Loic 314bl; Photononstop/Jean-Paul Garcin 44tr; Photononstop/Tibor Bognar 134tr; Photononstop/Walter Bibikow 325tl; Picture Press/Fritz Poelking 326bc; Radius Images 10tr, 90br, 148–183 sidebars, 180cl, 183tl; Robert Harding Travel/Adam Woolfitt 14–5t; Robert Harding Travel/Andrew McConnell 10–1c; Robert Harding Travel/Christopher Rennie 42–3t; Robert Harding Travel/E Simanor 218br; Robert Harding Travel/Ellen Rooney 312cr, 322br; Robert Harding Travel/Gavin Hellier 116–7; Robert Harding Travel/J P De Manne 16tr; Robert Harding Travel/Lee Frost 207t, 218bl; Robert Harding Travel/Louise Murray 285cb; Robert Harding Travel/Marco Simoni 209tl, 324tr; Robert Harding Travel/Matthew Davison 312t; Robert Harding Travel/Patrick Dieudonne 203bc; Robert Harding Travel/Richard Cummins 237bc; Robert Harding Travel/Robert Francis 154bc, 236tr; Robert Harding Travel/Robert Harding 120–1t; Robert Harding Travel/Ruth Tomlinson 310tl; Robert Harding Travel/Sheila Terry 136–7t; Robert Harding Travel/Simon Harris 322tl; Robert Harding Travel/Sybil Sassoon 47tr; Robert Harding Travel/Tony Waltham 324tl; Robert Harding Travel/Travel Pix 265bc; Robert Harding Travel/Upperhall Ltd 228br; Ken Stepnell 114tr; Tips Italia /Antonello Lanzellotto 89tc; Tips Italia RF/Masino Tips 268–9b; Tips Italia/ Bildagentur RM 90–1t, 144tr; Tips Italia/Andrea Pistolesi 107br; Tips Italia/Angelo Cavalli 137bc; Tips Italia/Donata Pizzi 264bc; Tips Italia/Giuliano Colliva 264br, 269bc; Tips Italia/Guido Alberto Rossi 110–1b, 121bc, 303tl, 307bl; Tips Italia/Marcella Pedone 23tc; Tips Italia/Pasquale Sorrentino 17tr; Tips Italia/Patti McConville 288bl; Tips Italia/PH+ 264–5t; Tips Italia/Rubens Chaves 35clb; Tips Italia/Wojtek Buss 301tr, 303tr; Tips Italia/Yann Guichaoua 317tl; The Travel Library Limited 208br; View Pictures/Dennis Gilbert 134tc, 283tr; View Pictures/Inigo Bujedo Aguirre 135tr; View Stock 104tc; WaterFrame – Underwater Images/Andre Seale 161c; WaterFrame – Underwater Images/Franco Banfi 161t, 181tr; Darwin Wiggett 213bl; Yoshio Tomii Photo Studio 174tl; **Photolibrary Wales:** David Williams 65tr; **PQRS India:** Phal Girota Photo Library 92br; **Kirstin Prisk:** 237bl; **Pulsar Imagens:** 50cr, 50–1t; Palê Zuppani 151tc; **Reuters:** ARC/Dominique Favre 69bc; Shaun Best 68bc; Gopal Chitrakar 241tl; Mick Tsikas 66–7t; **Rex Features:** Alinari 96br; James D. Morgan 154br; **Robert Harding Picture Library:** Odyssey/Robert Frerck 176bl; Ursula Gahwiler 31tl; Sylvain Grandadam 43bc; Michael Jenner 27br; **Rovos Rail:** 94tr; **Saadani Safari Lodge:** 197tr; **Science Photo Library:** Simon Fraser 202–3t; L. Newman & A. Flowers 228bl; **www.skistar.com:** Jonas Kullman 215tr; **South American Pictures:** Jevan Berrange 84tl; Tony Morrison 152–3t, 153bc; Chris Sharp 155cr; **Sarah Bryce Stout:** 82–3t; **www.trekkingbritain.com:** Jamie Bassnett 239br; **VIA Rail Canada:** 94tc; **Voss Resort AS;** 214tl; **Womad.org:** York Tillyer 57bc; **Adrian Woodford:** 96bc; **Courtesy of Zach Feuer Gallery, New York:** *Material Recovery* by Danica Phelps, opening reception 271br.

JACKET IMAGES: Front: **4Corners Images:** Stefano Amantini fbr; **Alamy Images:** Jon Arnold Images Ltd t; Inge Johnsson br; **FLPA:** Minden Pictures/Cyril Ruoso bc; **Photolibrary:** age fotostock/Blaine Harrington fbl; **Pictures Colour Library**: Picture Finders bl. Back: **4Corners Images**: SIME/ Reinhard Schmid cra; SIME/Kaos3 tc; SIME/Orient br; **Alamy Images:** Blaine Harrington III tl; Mervyn Rees fbr; **Axiom Photographic Agency:** Ian Cumming tr; **Michele Falzone:** bl; **Getty Images:** The Image Bank/Eric Meola cla; Stone/Ken Fisher ftl; **Melbourne International Arts Festival:** John Sones clb; **PA Photos:** AP Photo/Ron Lewis, *Starry Bamboo Mandal* (bamboo, manila rope, hardwood dowels) 2006 Gerard Minakawa ftr; **Photolibrary:** age fotostock/Ximena Griscti fbl; Jon Arnold Travel crb; TIPS/Guido Alberto Rossi bc. Spine: **Alamy Images:** Thomas Cockrem b; **Hemispheres Images:** Franck Guiziou t. Front Flaps: **Photolibrary:** JTB Photo. Back Flaps: **Julian James** www.julianjames.com: t; **Photolibrary:** JTB Photo.

PYRAMIDS OF MEROE · GREAT PYRAMID OF CHOLULA · PYRAMIDS OF SAQQARA & DAHSHUR · BRIHADISHWARA TEMPLE · PYRAMID OF
OF MALTA · AGRIGENTO & SELINUNTE · PULA ARENA · LEPTIS MAGNA · EL DJEM · TRIER · ANFITEATRO DI MÉRIDA · ARENA DI VERONA ·
LYCIAN ROCK-CUT TOMBS · GILA CLIFF DWELLINGS · LONGMEN CAVES · BANDELIER'S ROCK-CUT PUEBLOS · CARPENTER'S CAVES · ISL
OU CAVES · TIKAL · BONAMPAK, CHIAPAS · LAMANAI ORANGE WALK DISTRICT · COPÁN · EDZNÁ, YUCATÁN · KRAK DES CHEVALIERS · P
CASTLE · TEMPLE OF SETI I · CITADELLE LAFERRIERE · SERGIYEV POSAD · PERSEPOLIS · MOUNTAIN RESORT · CUEVAS DE POMIER · ERUM
SACSAYHUAMAN · TRE CASTELLI, BELLINZONA · PAESTUM, CAMPAGNA · PANCHA RATHAS · GALLA PLACIDIA MAUSOLEUM · HATSHEPSU
NEMRUT DAGI · CHURCH OF THE TRANSFIGURATION · THIKSE MONASTERY · CHÂTEAU D'AZAY-LE-RIDEAU · VISBY · PERGAMON · SKELL
ATI-ATIHAN · OLINDA AND RECIFE CARNIVALS · TRINIDAD CARNIVAL · MAMAIA · GNAWA AND WORLD MUSIC FESTIVAL · FESTIVAL IN T
NEW YEAR, SINGAPORE · HARO WINE BATTLE · ESALA PERAHERA · ROMERIA DEL ROCIO · RATH YATRA · CIRIO DE NAZARE · MELBOURN
THE EISTEDDFOD · SYDNEY GAY & LESBIAN MARDI GRAS · HALLOWEEN PARADE, NEW YORK CITY · FANTASY FEST · GAY PRIDE, SÃO PAU
LUCIA JAZZ · GOA'S FULL MOON PARTIES · SEMANA SANTA · ASTI PALIO · NAADAM · WHITE TURF · SA SARTIGLIA · BIRDSVILLE RACES ·
CAMEL FAIR · LA FOLLE JOURNEE DE NANTES · SPLASHY FEN · CARNIVAL, BINCHE · CHRISTMAS MARKET · RUSTLER'S VALLEY FESTIVAL ·
FIESTA DE SANTO TOMAS · WINTER FESTIVAL · SAINT PAUL WINTER CARNIVAL · EASTER IN KALYMNOS · CALLE OCHO LATINO FESTIVAL
BUN BANG FAI · CHEYENNE FRONTIER DAYS · LATITUDE · BURNING MAN · GOLDEN SHEARS · MIMOSA FESTIVAL · PUNAKHA DOMCHO
GENTINA · OUD FESTIVAL · PUSHCART DERBY · VEGETARIAN FESTIVAL · TENERIFE CARNIVAL · PARRANDA · THE APOLOBAMBA TREK · CH
AL PARK · POINT REYES NATIONAL SEASHORE · GREAT OCEAN ROAD · COASTAL NORTH AFRICA · PAN-AMERICAN HIGHWAY · ANNAPURN
THE GLACIER EXPRESS · THE CANADIAN · ROVOS RAIL · INDIAN PACIFIC RAILWAY · SUNSET LIMITED · THE DEVIL'S NOSE · PILGRIMA
CANAL CRUISING · NORFOLK BROADS · LESS-TRAVELLED CHINA · GUANGZHOU · HANGZHOU · SUZHOU · CHONGQING · TIANJIN · C
NORTHWEST COAST · CINQUE TERRE IN LIGURIA · COAST OF MADEIRA · TASMAN PENINSULA · COSTA SMERALDA · KAMCHATKA PENINS
BAY BY JUNK · ANTARCTIC ICEBREAKER VOYAGE · CANAL DU MIDI · THE BLUE TRAIN · CURZON TRAIL · GIBB RIVER ROAD DRIVE · ICEF
OCEAN ROAD · CHE GUEVARA'S MOTORCYCLE ROUTE · LYCIAN COAST BY GULET · NEW YORK STATE CANALS · STEVENSON TRAIL, CÉVEN
CHIPELAGO CRUISE · TUNDRA BUGGYING FOR POLAR BEARS · KHYBER PASS STEAM SAFARI · NATCHEZ TRACE PARKWAY DRIVE · REINDE
HAUTE ROUTE · THE GOLDEN ROAD TO SAMARKAND · YANGTZE RIVER CRUISE · ZAMBEZI CANOE SAFARI · PACIFIC CREST TRAIL · SKEL
MACEDONIA · RAVENNA'S BYZANTINE CHURCHES · IMAM MOSQUE · SÜLEYMANIYE MOSQUE · TILLA KARI MADRASAH · BRITISH MUSEU
INTAN · KOUTOUBIA MINARET · GIOTTO'S BELL TOWER · QUTB MINAR · ST MARK'S CAMPANILE · CHICAGO · 9 DE JULIO · PUNING TEMP
ZOLLHOF · GUGGENHEIM BILBAO · THE GHERKIN · TURNING TORSO · CASA DA MUSICA · PONTE DELLE TORRI · SEGOVIA'S ROMAN AQU
MENT · NOTRE-DAME · D'AMIENS · STEPHANSDOM · CATEDRAL DE SANTA MARIA · KERIMAEN KIRKKO · GREAT MOSQUE OF DJENNÉ · ESP
DAILY NEWS BUILDING · PARLIAMENT HOUSE · THE SOLOMON R. GUGGENHEIM MUSEUM · REICHSTAG · FALLINGWATER · FRED AND G
TOWER · CHURCH OF ST FRANCIS · HORIZONTE · CN TOWER · AACHEN CATHEDRAL · THE MILLAU BRIDGE · NOTRE DAME DU HAUT ·
HOTEL · WIELICZKA SALT MINE · UNAM LIBRARY · BIRD'S NEST STADIUM · REGISTAN · THE KUWAIT TOWERS · KREMLIN · MUSEU OSCAR
TOWER · HALF DOME · TORRES DEL PAINE · MOUNT AUGUSTUS · PEÑA DE BERNAL · PEDRA AZUL · STONE MOUNTAIN · THE ORINOCO ·
LAKE BALATON · BAND-E AMIR LAKES · KERALA'S LAKES · BRYCE CANYON · COPPER CANYON · ZION CANYON · WAIMEA CANYON · CANYO
RUAHA NATIONAL PARK · SAMBURU NATIONAL RESERVE · LUANGWA VALLEY · LOPÉ NATIONAL PARK · MADAGASCAR · CHERRY BLOSSO
ORCHIDS IN MOYOBAMBA · SOL DE MAÑANA · TONGARIRO NATIONAL PARK · KAMCHATKA PENINSULA · BEPPU · CROATIA'S ISLANDS ·
YOSEMITE FALLS · KAIETEUR FALLS · TUGELA FALLS · MINDO-NAMBILLO CLOUD FOREST · BLUE MOUNTAINS · RAINFORESTS OF BELIZE · M
INSULA · BLUE LAGOON · BUCKSKIN GULCH · VALLE DE LA LUNA · COLCA CANYON · CURONIAN SPIT · KAA-IYA DEL GRAN CHACO NATI
GORGES DU VERDON · FINGAL'S CAVE · KODACHROME BASIN STATE PARK · GOCTA FALLS · ERG CHEBBI · NEW CALEDONIA BARRIER R
TIONAL · NORTHERN LIGHTS · LUNAR RAINBOWS · SEMENGGOH NATURE RESERVE · SHIRETOKO PENINSULA · TSINGY DE BEMARAHA
WOLONG NATURE RESERVE · ANTARCTICA · FINGER LAKES · GRACE BAY · PLAYA FLAMINGO · SHOAL BAY · SEVEN MILE BEACH · PINK SA
GORDON-FRISHMAN BEACHES · HULOPO'E · HAPUNA BEACH · KAILUA BEACH · NAPILI BAY · KE'E BEACH · TURTLE BAY · BUSUA · ISIMAN
RADHANAGAR BEACH ISLAND · GOLDEN BEACH · SANDAY · KO TARUTAO · ISLE OF HARRIS BEACHES · OCRACOKE ISLAND · WINEGLASS
D'ARGENT · ANSE LA ROCHE · ARAMBOL BEACH · BAAN MAI · BARLEYCOVE BEACH · BANGARAM BEACH · QUEEN'S BEACH · CATHEDRAL C
BEACH · MURI LAGOON · NOIRMOUTIER · KUATA ISLAND · BOSLUISBAII · PLAYA DE CABO DE GATA · DAYMER BAY · CORONADO BEACH
SPIAGGIA DEL PRINCIPE · PORTO DE GALINHAS · HANALEI BAY · JOATINGA BEACH · TAYRONA · JOST VAN DYKE ISLAND · LUKA KORCULA
MARATHON · EVEREST MARATHON · ATHENS · ICE MARATHON · TWO OCEANS · SALSA IN HAVANA · DOMINICAN REPUBLIC · SALVADOR
VIK GOLF CLUB · ANTALYA PGA SULTAN COURSE · ROYAL COUNTY DOWN · LJUNGHUSEN GOLF CLUB · CHRISTMAS ISLAND · TUFI · GULF
SKYLINE TRAIL · TREKKING IN BHUTAN · HIGH ATLAS MOUNTAINS · THE COORG · SINAI DESERT · PAPUA NEW GUINEA · TANDRAGEE
EAST · RAFTING THE KARNALI, NEPAL · DOG SLEDDING, FINLAND · SPHEREING, ROTORUA, NEW ZEALAND · SEA KAYAKING, PRINCE WIL
WALKING THE OVERLAND TRACK, AUSTRALIA · SKI-JORING, SWITZERLAND · SAILING THE ADRIATIC · CYCLING THE LOIRE, FRANCE · H
KENYA · WATCHING JAI ALAI, THE PHILIPPINES · SCRAMBLE UP TRYFAN, WALES · WATCHING THAI BOXING, THAILAND · WINDSURFING,
SHIPS, USA · HORSE-RIDING, KYRGYZSTAN · WALKING THE CHORO TRAIL, BOLIVIA · CRICKET IN THE TROBRIAND ISLANDS, PAPUA NEW
CANADA · SINGAPORE GRAND PRIX · KAYAKING THE ARDÈCHE, FRANCE · ELEPHANT POLO, NEPAL · ACROBAT DISPLAYS, BEIJING, CHINA ·
USA · LAWN BOWLS, UK · ISLAND-TO-ISLAND SWIMMING, GREECE · VOLCANO CLIMBING, GUATEMALA · MARATHON DES SABLES, MORO
STITUT DU MONDE ARABE · MUSÉE JACQUEMART- ANDRÉ · MUSÉE COGNACQ-JAY · MUSÉE NISSIM DE CAMONDO · MUSÉE NATIONAL E
HORSE · KRÖLLER-MÜLLER · ROCK ART OF THE DRAKENSBERG · JEBEL ACACUS · CRESWELL CRAGS · GOBUSTAN · CUEVA DE LA MARAVIL
LERIA BORGHESE · GALLERIA DORIA PAMPHILJ · GALLERIA NAZIONALE D'ARTE ANTICA · ETRUSCAN MUSEUM · MUSEO NAZIONALE ROM
LOWER FRANCONIA · ANDALUCIA · TICINO · BURGUNDY · THE DOURO VALLEY · PUGLIA · FESTIVAL DI SPOLETO · BREGENZER FESTIVA
LERIES · NEW MUSEUM · DEITCH PROJECTS · GALAPAGOS ART SPACE · CHELSEA'S GALLERIES · MOMENTA ART IN WILLIAMSBURG · MUSÉ
HAUS · DOMAINE DES COLLETTES · ALBA INTERNATIONAL TRUFFLE FAIR · EPIDAVROS THEATRE · CESAR MANRIQUE FOUNDATION · TH
MUSEUM · DALÍ THEATRE-MUSEUM · GUGGENHEIM FOUNDATION · CARPET MUSEUM · MUSEUM OF BAD ART · THREE CHOIRS FESTIVAL ·
MUSEUM · PERGAMONMUSEUM · ANDERSON VALLEY VINEYARDS · BIBLIOTHECA ALEXANDRINA · CARL HAMMER GALLERY · LA CHASCON
NÉE · GIARDINO DEI TAROCCHISTUDIO MUSEUM, HARLEM · THE STATE MUSEUM OF MAYAKOVSKY · CHARLES HOSMER MORSE MUSEUM ·
GHENT · ANTWERP · THE HAGUE · LESS-EXPLORED LONDON · CHINATOWN · SOUTHALL · DOCKLANDS · SMALL MUSEUMS · FREUD MU
GENT'S AND GRAND UNION CANALS · PARKLAND WALK · HIGHGATE CEMETERY, LINCOLN'S INN FIELDS · BOROUGH MARKET · CAM
HARINGEY · QUEENSWAY · ALEXANDRIA · POTOSI · LESS-EXPLORED NEW YORK · SPANISH HARLEM · ITALIAN BROOKLYN · FIFTH AVENUE ·
ROBERT F. WAGNER, JR. PARK · BROOKLYN BOTANIC GARDENS · FIRE ISLAND'S SUNKEN FOREST · GREENBELT · TODT HILL · EAST VILLA
PLACE · THE NUYORICAN POETS CAFE · UPRIGHT CITIZENS BRIGADE · CHINATOWN · KATZ'S DELICATESSEN · KOREATOWN · BROOKLYN'
THAN ROAD · HONG KONG ISLAND · CAUSEWAY BAY · MID-LEVELS · ALTFIELD GALLERY · THE RED CABINET · ABERDEEN · GOODS OF DE
TURE EXHIBITION GALLERY · MUSEUM OF COASTAL DEFENCE · FINANCIAL DISTRICT · HONG KONG WETLAND PARK · NORTHERN TERR
YUNG SHUE WAN · SOK KWU WAN · CHEUNG CHAU · HAPPY VALLEY RACECOURSE · CITY GOLF CLUB · MACAU · CENTRAL BUSINESS DIS
BURANO · TORCELLO · CHIOGGIA · ST MARK'S BASILICA · SABBIONI · SAN NICOLÒ · GIUDECCA CANAL · SAN GIORGIO MAGGIORE · PAL
VOLO · SAN FRANCESCO DEL DESERTO · THE RIALTO MARKET · CASTELLO DISTRICT · RIVA DEGLI SCHIAVONI · SAN PIETRO · SANT'ELE
HAIGHT-ASHBURY · HYDE STREET PIER · PRESIDIO · ALAMO SQUARE · SAN FRANCISCO MUSEUM OF MODERN ART · ASIAN ART MUSEU
PARK · COASTAL TRAIL · TRANSAMERICA REDWOOD PARK · CLIFF HOUSE · INA COOLBRITH PARK IN RUSSIAN HILL · MISSION DOLORES
FACTORY · SAN FRANCISCO BREWING COMPANY · FISHERMAN'S WHARF · TWIN PEAKS · BUENA VISTA PARK · TELEGRAPH HILL · BATH ·
CARNAVALET · HÔTEL DE RETZ · SAXE-BRETEUIL MARKET · PRESIDENT WILSON MARKET · CANAL ST-MARTIN · QUAI DE VALMY · PLACE STE-
DES VARIÉTÉS · PASSAGE JOUFFROY · MUSEE GREVIN · LESS-EXPLORED SYDNEY · AUSTRALIAN BUSH · THE ROCKS · SUSSEX · HUNTER VALL
PARK BEACH · DEE WHY BEACH · BUNGAN BEACH · SHARK ISLAND · QUARANTINE STATION · NORTH FORT · DEFENCE OF SYDNEY MEM
BROKEN BAY · PALM BEACH · DANK STREET FESTIVAL · CABRAMATTA'S MOON FESTIVAL · AUSTRALIA DAY · FAIR DAY · BAY STREET FERR
TOLEDO, SPAIN · QUEENSTOWN, NEW ZEALAND · SPLIT, CROATIA · GRONINGEN · TARTU, ESTONIA · SIDI IFNI, MOROCCO · SANTIAGO
SYRIA · SANTA FE, NEW MEXICO, USA · THESSALONIKI, GREECE · SIEM REAP, CAMBODIA · SHIRAZ, IRAN · SHIMLA, INDIA · SINTRA, PORT
SUCRE, BOLIVIA · SEDONA, ARIZONA, USA · GRAZ, AUSTRIA · QUEBEC CITY, CANADA · UDAIPUR, INDIA · AIX-EN-PROVENCE, FRANCE · V